RELATIONSHIPS
& IN MARRIAGE
& THE FAMILY

Third Edition

RELATIONSHIPS
&IN MARRIAGE
&THE FAMILY

Nick Stinnett
The University of Alabama

James Walters
The University of Georgia

Nancy Stinnett
The University of Alabama

Macmillan Publishing Company
NEW YORK
Collier Macmillan Canada
TORONTO

Editor: Helen McInnis
Production Supervisor: Dora Rizzuto
Production Manager: Aliza Greenblatt
Text Designer: Patrice Fodero
Photo Researcher: Chris Migdol
Photo Credits for Chapter Openers: Chapter 1, *Joel Gordon*, Chapter 2, *Joel Gordon*, Chapter 3, *Joel Gordon*, Chapter 4, *Susan Lapides/Design Conceptions*, Chapter 5, *Joel Gordon*, Chapter 6, *Joel Gordon*, Chapter 7, *Joel Gordon*, Chapter 8, *Joel Gordon*, Chapter 9, *Paul Efland*, Chapter 10, *Joel Gordon*, Chapter 11, *Joel Gordon*, Chapter 12, *Joel Gordon*, Chapter 13, *Joel Gordon*, Chapter 14, *Joel Gordon*, Chapter 15, *Joel Gordon*, Chapter 16, *Joel Gordon*, Chapter 17, *Joel Gordon*.
Illustrations: Publication Services, Inc.

Macmillan Publishing Company
866 Third Avenue, New York, New York 10022

Collier Macmillan Canada, Inc.
1200 Eglinton Avenue East
Suite 200
Don Mills, Ontario M3C 3N1

LIBRARY OF CONGRESS CATALOGING-IN-PUBLICATION DATA

Stinnett, Nick.
    Relationships in marriage & the family / Nick Stinnett, James Walters, Nancy Stinnett.—3rd ed.
        p.   cm.
    Includes bibliographical references.
    ISBN 0-02-417580-3
    1. Marriage.   2. Family.   3. Interpersonal relations.
    I. Walters, James.   II. Stinnett, Nancy M.   III. Title.   IV. Title:
    Relationships in marriage and the family.
    HQ734.S873   1991
    306.87—dc20   90-32511
                                    CIP

Printing: 1 2 3 4 5 6 7 8   Year: 1 2 3 4 5 6 7 8 9 0

PREFACE

Many of the people who marry in the 1990s will terminate their marriages long before death parts them. Many of them will remarry, and quite a few will divorce again. The reasons for this are varied. Some undertake a lifestyle that is so demanding that they cannot maintain their marriages. Others select the "wrong" partner, and still others neglect to learn about human relationships and to practice relationship skills.

No one is born a great marriage partner. Being the "right" spouse is a learned behavior that requires considerable knowledge about how relationships work. For example, one of the first lessons to be learned is how to increase our positive interactions with others. Thus, if someone begins to interact with us negatively, we need to remember that we have a *decision* to make: (a) we can decide to become angry and respond as a victim, e.g., responding aggressively and communicating our contempt and dislike, or (b) we can decide to respond in a manner that communicates our willingness to make things better, e.g., "I am sorry I offended you. I didn't mean to. How can I help?" Remember, their anger is *their* problem, and you are not required to become angry yourself. The basic decision concerning how you choose to respond affects interaction and, thus, your relationships. Chances for a great marriage are far better if the second decision is made consistently and if we indicate our desire to be helpful to others. It is not difficult to respond positively; it *is* difficult to remember that how we respond is our responsibility and not the fault of others.

This book begins where most other texts end. Most texts are a history of other people's families. They deal primarily with summaries of the research on families that are not quite like our own. They report the facts, and some are successful in interpreting what the facts mean; however, students are left to translate for themselves how they should use this information in living their own lives. For example, differences in the conflict styles of happily and unhappily married couples may be reported, but little information may be given to indicate how to handle conflict when it happens.

Gaining insight into behavior is very important but it is not enough. It is one thing to know why you are shy or why you become angry under certain circumstances, but you may not know what to do about it. In this text you will discover a wealth of suggestions on how to learn to monitor your own behavior. In this way, you can alter your behavior in order to attain your goals.

On a scale of 1 to 10, how would you rate yourself as a potential marriage partner? A 4? A 9? If you realize that with some partners you would be a 4 while with others you would be a 9, you already know the importance of making an intelligent, informed decision in choosing someone with whom to share your life. Although none of us can predict what the future will hold, each of us needs to anticipate the events that are likely to occur and to learn strategies for coping with whatever we encounter. Happiness in family life does not just happen; it requires a great deal of study, work, and planning. This course gives you an opportunity to think about and discuss those things that will affect your relationships for many years to come. This is your chance to think about "What would I do if . . . ?" This is your opportunity to examine a variety of lifestyles, to think through what kinds of relationships give worthwhile meaning to life, and to learn to understand and change your behavior so that you will become the kind of person you want to be.

Successful relationships are those in which both persons have a strong commitment for the relationship to endure even during periods in which they find each other disappointing. Mature, informed persons can realize that feelings of disappointment or discouragement usually are temporary. Terminating a relationship because of temporary feelings may not be the wisest course of action. Great marriages require people who can forgive—even the best marital partners make occasional errors.

People often indicate that having a satisfying marriage and family life is one of their top priorities. This text is your roadmap to achieving this goal. Although marriage is not for everyone, those of us who have experienced success and happiness in this adventure can tell you that it can be a part of the very best that life has to offer.

Acknowledgements

The authors wish to express their appreciation to the staff of the Office of Public Information of The University of Georgia for their assistance with photographs. The authors are especially indebted to (a) Mr. Walker Montgomery whose beautiful photographs have appeared in each of the three editions of this text; and to (b) Dr. Connor Walters of the Department of Child, Family and Consumer Sciences at The Florida State University, and to (c) Dr. Thomas Knobbe, a child clinical psychologist, for their splendid contributions to the chapter on "Relationships with Children."

The authors also wish to express their gratitude to Ms. Shea Shumake, Ms. Debi Combs, and Ms. Martha Acevedo for their many contributions to the production of the manuscript.

Nick Stinnett
James Walters
Nancy Stinnett

CONTENTS

❧

CHAPTER 1

RELATIONSHIPS AND
FAMILY STRENGTHS

Every nook and cranny of the big 747 was crowded. It took off in the middle of the night in Brazil where I'd been speaking. As it moved into the night I began to doze. I don't know how long I slept when I heard a strong voice announcing, " We have a serious emergency." Three engines had gone because of fuel contamination, and the other engine could go any second.

The steward said, "Now you must do exactly as we tell you. Pull down the curtains; in a few minutes we are going to turn off all the lights...." We felt the plane plunge and the steward barked, "Prepare for impact."

At times like that, involuntarily from deep inside us, something comes out that's never structured, planned or rehearsed. I found myself praying in a way I never thought of doing. As I buried my head in my lap and pulled my knees up, as I was convinced it was over, and as the plane was going down my last thought, my last cry was, "Oh God, my wife! My children!"

Now I should say that I did survive!! As I wandered about in the middle of the night in the airport with a knot in my stomach and cotton in my mouth, I thought, "What did I do? What did I think? What was the bottom line?"

Here's the bottom line: RELATIONSHIPS.

(Petersen, 1985, pp. 104–105)

A Potential for Happiness

"No man is an island, entire of itself" wrote John Donne many years ago. This insight expresses a truth still valid today. We are connected to other people: our parents and relatives, friends, a spouse (for over 90% of us), in-laws, our children, their children, bosses, co-workers, neighbors, and others. Furthermore, our relationships with these people are critical to life satisfaction. Thus, each of us is part of an intimate social system that has a profound effect on the way we perceive the world around us (Chesser, 1990). Important, too, is the fact that we are also part of larger systems (e.g., our community, state, and nation). Our success as individuals and as members of families is influenced by the impact of these systems on us. But we affect the systems as well. For example, one of the clear findings of research on families is that children influence their families just as parents influence their children. To understand families, it is necessary to examine the reciprocal effects that family members have on each other and how the environment in which they live serves to shape their behavior.

Berger and Berger (1983) state that close, significant relationships are vital all through life for the maintenance of identity and meaning. And for most of us, relationships in our marriages and families are the closest and most significant. The competencies we develop as family members will enable us to shape and modify our relationships and environment in ways that will contribute to our ultimate happiness and success. Many strengths are needed for individual success; in this text, however, the authors focus on those factors that contribute to family success. Although individual and family success are related, there are important differences. Many people who are highly successful professionally, for example, fail to learn those things that will contribute to a successful family life.

This book is designed to help you to achieve the kind of healthy, happy relationships you desire. It is based on the premises that you can gain greater understanding of yourself and others, that you can use information about the dynamics of relationships to improve your interactions with others, and that you can monitor your behavior in ways that will help you to attain your goals.

Understanding Self and Others

First, we cannot realistically expect to have good relationships with others until we understand ourselves and our interpersonal interactions. Why are we (and others) the way we are? One of the primary reasons is that from early childhood, we have *learned* attitudes and ways of behaving. Our parents, friends, the larger culture, and people we admire are a few of our earliest "teachers," shaping our attitudes about human interaction and ways of behaving.

Not all learning experiences prepare us for success in relationships; some of our learned behaviors must be modified if we are to reach our potential. For example, a person reared to feel ashamed about sexual feelings may have to relearn those attitudes in order to please a spouse and self. A man reared in a home in which his mother unquestioningly performed all cooking, cleaning, and household tasks may not be prepared for a wife who expects him to share in homemaking. He may find it hard to adjust long-held concepts to the reality of his own relationship. Women reared in households in which wives did not work outside the home may be challenged to balance their desire for security from their partners with their desire for independence and personal growth.

Controlling Own Behavior

It is not enough to develop insight into why people behave as they do; essential to the development

Joel Gordon

of successful relationships is a commitment to the principle that you are most apt to succeed when you concentrate on your own behavior rather than on the behavior of others. When we concentrate on the behavior of another person, we place responsibility for the direction of the relationship in the hands of that person (Chesser, 1990).

It is only when you are willing to accept responsibility for your behavior—including the willingness to modify it—that you gain control of your behavior and, consequently, take an active role in shaping the relationship. For example, Bill and Meg are having a heated argument about their budget. As the intensity of feeling builds, Meg makes a biting comment about Bill's fondness for lavishing attention on his antique car. Bill has a choice at this point. He may

react to Meg's unkind remark with criticism of her spending habits. He may reason that she has made him so angry that he is justified in hurting her as much as he can. He may do such a good job of hurting her that the relationship will be damaged. Or he may realize that he cannot control what Meg says but he can control himself. He may ignore her comment and suggest that they focus on solving their budget troubles.

Some persons will regard this approach as simplistic or unrealistic. Others will consider that it involves controlling one's own behavior in order to manipulate others. In reality, however, this approach to human interaction includes an honest and profound regard for the worth of others and a willingness to be proactive rather than reactive.

The Hoax of Romance

I have found even in my own life that the more expectations I've had of someone, the greater my disappointment. Conversely, the more I can accept a person as he or she is, the better I feel. (The other person may care less; my disappointment hurts my belly, not his!) I have discovered, since I divorced, that I like the men I was married to previously. I can afford to like them now because I see them as people; I have no expectations of them, "faults" and all. (After all, what were faults in my eyes may have been virtues to others.) When I stop expecting others to live up to my standards and satisfy my demands I feel more amiable toward them, and certainly more at peace with myself. The less I expect of anyone, the more I am apt to feel affectionate and trusting toward that person.

Source: Loudin, J. (1981). *The hoax of romance.* Englewood Cliffs, NJ: Prentice-Hall.

❧Understanding the Dynamics of Relationships

Ask yourself, "What do I want from my relationship with my partner? With my parents? With my employer? With my friends?" Although many answers could be given, a common factor probably will recur: these relationships should make us feel good about ourselves. If a boss demeans our work, or a friend insults a gesture intended to be helpful, or a parent derides a new venture, or a partner rejects an advance, we feel personal pain and inadequacy even when we may rationalize good reasons for their reactions.

Individuals who develop a productive orientation toward relationships have learned how to make others feel good about themselves. They are aware of the needs of others and are able to see the best in them. They enjoy solidly established relationships characterized by acceptance, appreciation of others, and helpfulness.

There is, however, a difference in a positive, productive orientation and an exaggerated emphasis on securing support in immature or self-defeating ways. The man who always agrees with his employer despite his own better judgment, the parent who always gives in to a child, and the spouse who never disagrees for fear of conflict are guilty of creating relationships filled with deceit.

If any relationship is to endure and be satisfying, the persons involved must recognize the inevitability of change and the need to adapt. They must be ready to face the realities of sharing their lives and must try to understand each other. Few couples approach marriage or parenthood with an accurate perception of the complexities of their future and their need for truly expert interpersonal skills.

Tom and Sue, for example, are honest, decent people who love each other deeply; they are very compatible in many ways. Even so, they do not agree on everything. Each has a few annoying habits. They will have to change some of their behaviors to please each other, but some of their behaviors are immutable and must be accepted. Knowing that relationships require accommodation will allow them to make adaptations with a spirit of developing interpersonal competence rather than feeling defeated ("My spouse has more power than I do.") or compromised.

✳ *Theories of Family Interaction*

Knowing specific details of how people behave in family relationships is helpful in developing interpersonal competence in our family relationships. Social scientists have studied family relationships for many years from several perspectives. Methods such as questionnaire and interview surveys and naturalistic and clinical observations are used to gather information about families. The data gathered provide the basis for the formulation of theories, which give a framework for organizing and interpreting data and allowing social scientists to make predictions. Several major theories are used in explaining family interaction.

Structural Functionalism

Structural functionalism is used largely in sociology and anthropology; strutural functionalists focus on the study of society rather than individuals. Central to structural functionalism is the idea that each structure (e.g., family, government, economy) has functions. For example, a government enforces order, and a family produces and socializes members of society. Areas of examination include the functions the family serves for society, functions performed by family members for its survival, and needs of individuals served by the family (Gullotta et al., 1986; Strong & DeVault, 1986).

Family itself is regarded as a system that provides companionship for adults, socialization of children, and the development of personality and social skills. Family members have functions depending on gender and age—for example, someone must earn money, and someone must care for the children (Gullotta et al., 1986; Lamanna & Riedmann, 1988).

Structural functionalism is not as popular as it was a few years ago. Critics regard it as too conservative and resistant to change. Individuals and families that deviate from tradition tend to be regarded as dysfunctional (Gullotta et al., 1986).

General Systems

According to general systems theory, society is composed of many interrelated parts. Each can act independently, but in order to have a society, the parts (or systems) must come together. The family—as a system—is made of components or units. *Boundaries* identify which parts belong to the system; they may be *open*, allowing much interaction with factors outside the system, or *closed*. Interaction takes place when a stimulus enters the family system, the family members process it, and they respond to it (Gullotta et al., 1986).

Symbolic Interactionism

Symbolic interactionists examine how persons interact by focusing on communication through symbols (e.g., words and gestures) and how we interpret them. One factor that determines how family members interact is the role each plays—for example, mother, child, student, or spouse (Gullotta et al., 1986).

Symbolic interactionism is helpful in focusing on the daily workings of the family. Critics believe, however, that it overlooks the importance of power in relationships, does not account for unconscious processes at work in human relationships, and does not place the family in the larger social context (Gullotta et al., 1986; Lamanna & Riedmann, 1988).

Social Exchange

According to social exchange theory, we form relationships on a cost-benefit basis. Relationships offering benefits (i.e., love, companionship, or

Irrational Beliefs That Get People into Trouble

Charles L. Thompson and Linda B. Rudolph summarize the work of two brilliant psychotherapists, Albert Ellis and Robert Harper, concerning the *irrational beliefs* many people have that cause them difficulty as they think about themselves and as they relate to other people:

1. It is a dire necessity for people to be loved or approved by almost everyone for virtually everything they do.
2. One should be thoroughly competent, adequate, and achieving in all possible respects.
3. Certain people are bad, wicked, or villainous, and they should be severely blamed and punished for their sins.
4. It is terrible, horrible and catastrophic when things are not going the way one would like them to go.
5. Human unhappiness is externally caused, and people have little or no ability to control their sorrows or rid themselves of their negative feelings.
6. If something is or may be dangerous or fearsome, one should be terribly occupied with and upset about it.
7. It is easier to avoid facing many life difficulties and self-responsibilities than to undertake more rewarding forms of self-discipline.
8. The past is all-important, and because something once strongly affected one's life, it should do so indefinitely.
9. People and things should be different from the way they are, and it is catastrophic if perfect solutions to the grim realities of life are not immediately found.
10. Maximum human happiness can be achieved by inertia and inaction, or by passively and uncommittedly enjoying oneself.
11. My child is delinquent/emotionally disturbed/mentally retarded; therefore he is severely handicapped and will never amount to anything.
12. I cannot give my children everything they want; therefore, I am inadequate.

Source: Ellis, A. (1983). Rational emotive therapy. In C. L. Thompson and L. B. Rudolph (Eds.), *Counseling children* (pp. 82–97). Monterey, CA: Brooks/Cole.

status) that outweigh the costs are sought. Others are terminated. Each person has resources such as intelligence, good looks, or social status that he or she uses to exchange in relationships. Generally, relationships in which the exchange is fairly equal last the longest (Gullotta et al., 1986; Lamanna & Riedmann, 1988).

Critics regard social exchange theory as difficult to assess. For example, how does one measure the value of compassion versus intelligence? Others believe the exchange process becomes complicated, unconscious, and, finally, irrelevant in complex relationships (Gullotta et al., 1986; Holman & Burr, 1980; Strong & DeVault, 1986).

Social Learning

This theory examines human development as the sum of a lifetime of learning experiences. Learning takes place through reinforcement and through modeling. *Reinforcement* occurs after the response to an event and affects the chances that the response will happen again. Positive reinforcement increases the chances; negative reinforcement decreases them. For example, a mother may praise (positive reinforcement) her son each time he cleans his room in an attempt to increase the frequency of the event. *Modeling* is imitating the behavior of others (Gullotta et al., 1986).

Social learning theory is helpful in understanding individual growth; however, critics believe it does not explain interaction adequately (Gullotta et al., 1986).

Developmental Theory

Developmental theory is an attempt to create a model to explain family relationships across the life span. Persons and families are viewed as proceeding through various stages of development (from birth to death for individuals and from courtship to death of a spouse for families). Certain tasks must be accomplished in order to proceed to the next stage. Developmentalists use concepts from the other theories discussed (e.g., family members interact according to roles, the family has boundaries and functions) (Gullotta et al., 1986).

Critics regard developmental theory as biased in terms of couples who have children and do not divorce. They believe variations on traditional family forms are neglected (Gullotta et al., 1986).

Transactional Analysis

Transactional analysis is a model for examining interactions (*transactions*). Each person operates from one of three *ego states* in every exchange with another: parent, child and adult. The *parent* in you is composed of the attitudes, rules, and values internalized from outside sources, primarily your parents. It influences your views of how you should behave. Your parent state can be helpful and nurturant or judgmental and critical.

The *child* ego state contains your natural impulses. It is the part of you that wants to have fun and avoid demanding responsibilities and painful experiences. The *adult* is the part of you that uses facts to make decisions. It acts to keep your parent and child ego states in balance. Each of us responds differently to a particular situation according to the ego state from which we are operating, as the following example illustrates.

PARENT: I'm silly and selfish to want anything so expensive.

CHILD: I don't care how much it costs. I want it!

ADULT: This is a beautiful suit and I'd like to have it, but it costs $300. I just can't afford it.

The manner in which parent, child, and adult states are expressed influences the quality of interpersonal relationships. If your parent comes across as bossy or domineering, it will offend the child in others. If, on the other hand, your parent state is nurturing, the impact on others will be positive. Your child can have a positive influence on others by being fun and loving, or it can be hurtful if it is irresponsible or inconsiderate.

Families and Culture

Another perspective is gained by studying families in various cultures. A cross-cultural examination of family relationships offers greater understanding of the universals of family life (i.e., how families are alike across cultures) as well as the rich diversity of family life around the world. Opportunities for such studies are found in other countries and in areas of the United States that have large ethnic populations.

Black Americans

Black Americans are the largest racial minority in the United States, totaling 30.3 million and representing over 12% of the total population (U.S. Bureau of the Census, 1989b). The common assumption that black marriages are wife-dominated is not true as research has indicated that most black spouses describe their marriages as "husband led" (Gray-Little, 1982).

Blacks very highly value the institution of the family. Familial status is an important predictor of satisfaction for black persons (Broman, 1988); family life is the greatest source of life satisfaction for middle-class blacks (Gary et al., 1983). Motherhood and childbearing are also very highly valued in black society (Rice, 1990).

Joel Gordon

Because there are 1.5 million fewer black men than women over age 14, there is a shortage of marriageable black men (U.S. Bureau of the Census, 1989b). This is an especially severe problem for college-educated black women because more black women than men are obtaining college degrees and because women tend not to marry men with less education than themselves. Approximately one-third of college-educated black women remain unmarried past the age of 30 (Rice, 1990).

There has been a dramatic increase in one-parent families among blacks as well as among whites. For example, in 1970, one-third of black children under age 18 were living in one-parent families, compared to 55% in 1987 (Rice, 1990). Reasons for this increase include the high divorce rate and the rapid rise in births to unmarried women. Births to unmarried black women are approximately 63% of all live births in the black population (U.S. Bureau of the Census, 1989b).

A number of important strengths of black families have been identified by various research studies (Gary et al., 1986; McAdoo, 1982; Staples, 1985). The factors that help black marriages and families to function successfully include: a love of children, a high degree of religious orientation, strong kinship bonds, a favorable attitude toward the elderly, and flexible roles.

Mexican Americans

Mexican Americans are the second largest minority group in the United States, totaling about 12.1 million (U.S. Bureau of the Census, 1989b). Traditionally, the Mexican American family was patriarchal, with the male expected to be dominant over his wife and children as a way of proving his machismo (manhood). It was acceptable for the male to prove his machismo by having extramarital affairs, but discretion was important so as not to demonstrate lack of respect for his wife. The nonsexual aspects of machismo include courage, respect for others, honor, and the proper use of authority in a fair and just manner within the family (Alvirez et al., 1981; Knox, 1988).

The more recent reports of Mexican American families indicate that male dominance is a persistent feature; he is responsible for making most decisions. The husband/father, however, exercises authority in a fair and dignified manner and shows honor and respect for other family members (Rice, 1990). The nature of the Mexican American marriage is becoming more egalitarian as more wives begin to work outside the home (Knox, 1988).

The fertility rate is high among Mexican Americans, and their families average one more child per family than do Anglo families (Rice, 1990; Staples & Mirande, 1980). Parent-child relationships are warm and nurturing; fathers tend to be playful and companionable with their children, but the mother-child relationship is primary. The relationship between Mexican American children and their parents has typically been one of respect. It is common for the younger generation to express great deference to elders (Knox, 1988).

Mexican American families are becoming more Americanized and, therefore, increasingly similar to Anglo families. For example, in a study of emotional closeness between family members in Anglo and Mexican American families, no significant differences were found (Vega et al., 1986).

The family is highly valued, and the needs of the family are emphasized above those of the individual. Individuals find their identity in the family group. The extended family is an important source of strength and help: cousins, aunts, uncles, grandparents, brothers, and sisters offer assistance as needed and may help to rear children (Rice, 1990). For example, Mexican Americans are taught to bring elderly relatives into their homes if they are unable to care for themselves (Markides et al., 1983). Approximately 75% of Mexican Americans live in intact families, and the divorce rate for this group is lower than for blacks or Caucasians (U.S. Bureau of the Census, 1989b).

Chinese Americans

The Chinese American population numbers over 860,000 (U.S. Bureau of the Census, 1989b). Chinese Americans have lower rates of divorce, fewer out-of-wedlock births, more conservative sexual values, and higher family income than the general population in the United States (McLeod, 1986).

Chinese Americans have a high degree of commitment to the family, including a sense of duty to the family and a feeling of responsibility for relatives. Children are taught that everyone needs to work for the welfare of the family. They are given a great deal of responsibility and are assigned certain chores (Rice, 1990).

Although the traditional childrearing methods were authoritarian, the more acculturized Chinese American parents have become more permissive. They give their children more freedom in decision making, use more praise, and talk and joke more with their children.

Chinese American mothers consider teaching to be an important component of their maternal role and provide regular, formal instruction to children at home. Chinese American mothers play an important role in decision making and discipline in the family (Rice, 1990).

Native Americans

Approximately 1,500,000 individuals in the United States are Native Americans (U.S. Bureau of the Census, 1989b). They have the highest birthrate and the shortest life expectancy of any group in the nation (Rice, 1990).

Native Americans have the lowest income of any group in the United States; their economic status is far below that of the total population. Approximately 25% of Native Americans live below the poverty level (U.S. Bureau of the Census, 1989b).

The suicide rate among Native Americans is much higher than the national average; suicide is the leading cause of death among Indian adolescents who are 15 to 19 years old. Crime and alcoholism are at alarmingly high rates for young males. Alcoholism is considered a major health problem of Native Americans (Strauss, 1986).

It is difficult to describe the Native American marriage and family because of the diversity among Native Americans. The major source of identity for the individual is the tribe, and the particular family structure and values vary according to tribe. Some tribes are matriarchal, while others are patriarchal. Polygamy continues to exist in some tribes (Staples & Mirande, 1980; Strauss, 1986). More than one-third of all American Indians have married non-Indians; urban Indians have a higher rate of intermarriage than do rural Indians (Hamner & Turner, 1990).

The stability of the family and the continuity of tribal traditions are provided in a central way by women. Women tend to have strong leadership roles, and there is a high proportion of female-headed households (Hamner & Turner, 1990).

The extended family is a source of strength and support for Native Americans. For many, the extended family is the basic unit for performing various family functions. For example, children often are reared by relatives living in different households. One distinctive feature of childrearing and socialization among Native Americans is the exposure of children to a wide array of adult persons with whom they can identify and from whom they can receive nurturance and love. There are important bonding patterns between children and older people; elders are perceived as having great wisdom (Hamner & Turner, 1990).

There is evidence that Indian children are prepared for independence at earlier ages than are white or black children. Adults rarely hit children, and shouting when correcting children is disapproved. Native Americans view children as tribal persons, more than merely children. They are included in social activities and are encouraged to develop a sense of community, to be responsible, and to meet their share of obligation for community living (London & Devore, 1988; Strauss, 1986).

Certain values are prominent and serve to guide marriage and family behaviors among Native Americans. Noninterference and self-determination are particularly important. For this reason, any type of intervention by government agencies or social workers is in conflict with deeply held values. Other values that are common among all tribal groups include: respect for elders, avoidance of personal glory and gain, giving and sharing with multiple generations of relatives, and a love for their land. Native Americans also value collateral relationships in which family involvement, pride, and approval are stressed as opposed to individualism (Hamner & Turner, 1990; London & Devore, 1988; Strauss, 1986).

The Search for Strong Families

During the twentieth century, the quest for self-fulfillment developed into a major thrust in American culture (Yankelovich, 1981). However, in our preoccupation with this objective, we neglected the foundation necessary to facilitate the lifelong process of self-fulfillment—that is, the development of interpersonal competence, self-confidence, self-esteem, respect of self and others, and the vision that life can be enriched. This foundation is found in a strong, healthy family.

There is considerable evidence that the quality of family life is extremely important to our emotional well-being, our happiness, and our mental health as individuals. Poor relationships within the family are closely related to many social problems, such as juvenile delinquency and domestic abuse. Therefore, strengthening family life should be a national priority.

Much of what is written about families has focused on problems and pathologies in family life.

On the newsstand we see books and magazines with articles about what is wrong with families.

Certainly we need information about the difficulties that families face, but we also need a balanced view. We need information about positive family models and what healthy families are like because we want to know how to improve family relationships. We don't learn how to do anything looking only at how it *shouldn't* be done. We learn most effectively by examining how to do something correctly and by studying a positive model.

It was with this in mind that the Family Strengths Research Project was conducted. In this project, approximately 3,000 families were questioned about their family life. Some families lived in the United States; they were from all socioeconomic levels, rural and urban areas, and from several ethnic groups. Some were single-parent families. Other families came from around the world—from Latin America, Germany, Switzerland, Austria, South Africa, and Iraq (Brigman et al., 1986; Casas et al., 1984; King, 1980; Knaub et al., 1984; Stevenson et al., 1982; Stinnett, 1983; Stinnett, 1985; Stinnett & DeFrain, 1985; Stinnett & DeFrain, 1989; Stinnett et al., 1981; Stinnett et al., 1984; Stinnett et al., 1985; Stinnett & Sauer, 1977).

When the mass of information from these families was analyzed, six qualities stood out repeatedly, even though the families presented considerable complexity and diversity. Not all six qualities appear in every family, of course. Nor is the emphasis the same in all families (Stinnett & DeFrain, 1989).

The Six Qualities of Strong Families

Appreciation

One quality of the strong families emerged from many different questions and in many unexpected ways; family members expressed a great deal of appreciation for each other, and they built each other up psychologically. Each of us likes to be with people who make us feel good about ourselves; we don't like to be with people who make us feel bad. One of the tasks of family therapists working with family members who make each other feel terrible is to get them out of that pattern of interaction and into a pattern in which they make one another feel good.

We all need to work on our ability to express appreciation. One difficulty that we have is that we fear people will think we are not sincere. This need not be a concern because we *can* be sincere. Every person has some good qualities; all we have to do is be aware of them.

For example, we all do things each day that we're "supposed" to do—fixing dinner, working at a job, driving the kids to dance lessons. These tasks take time and effort, and an expression of appreciation ("Good dinner"; "Thanks for taking the kids today") boosts the self-esteem of the receiver and creates a bond of caring between recipient and giver (Stinnett & DeFrain, 1989).

Spending Time Together

A second characteristic of strong families is that they spend a good deal of time together. They genuinely enjoy being together in many areas of life—eating meals, doing house and yard chores, and enjoying recreational activities together (Stinnett & DeFrain, 1989).

Commitment

Although many people verbalize their commitment to their "family," members of strong families support their words with action. They are deeply committed to promoting each other's welfare and happiness, and they value the family group. Family members receive top priority in terms of time and energy (Stevenson et al., 1982; Stinnett & DeFrain, 1989).

Yankelovich (1981) observed that our society is in the process of leaving behind an excessively

A Comparison: Characteristics of Strong, Healthy Families*

Pollak (1957)	Otto (1963)	Hill** (1971)	Satir (1972)	Otto (1975)
• Able to foster growth of members • Supportive • Altruism	• Able to provide for physical and emotional needs of members • Sensitivity		• Promotion of positive self-worth	• Love • Understanding • Conscious effort to develop emotional ties
• Balance of interdependence and independence • Clear generational boundaries	• Respect for individuals • Concern for family unity	• Strong kinship bonds		
• Flexibility • Compromise	• Perform family roles flexibly	• Adaptability of family roles	• Clarity as to family rules and expectations	
• Positive	• Able to use crises positively			• Seek growth experiences
	• Good community relations	• Strong work and achievement orientations	• Links to society	• Active in community
	• Effective communication		• Open communication	
	• Meet the spiritual needs of family	• Strong religious orientation		• Commitment to realizing human potential

* As identified in major research efforts.
** Research with Black families.

Sources: 1. Curran, D. (1983). *Traits of a healthy family.* Minneapolis: Winston Press. 2. Hill, R. B. (1971). *The strengths of black families.* New York: Emerson Hall. 3. Olson, D., McCubbin, H., Barnes, H., Larsen, A., Muxen, M., & Wilson, M. (1983). *Families: What makes them work?* Beverly Hills, CA: Sage. 4. Otto, H. A. (1963). Criteria for assessing family strength. *Family Process, 2,* 329–337. 5. Otto, H. A. (1975). *The use of family strength concepts and methods in family life education: A handbook.* Beverly Hills, CA: Holistic Press.

A Comparison: Characteristics of Strong, Healthy Families—cont'd

Pratt (1976)	Whitaker (1980)	Olson et al. (1983)	Curran (1983)	Stinnett & DeFrain (1985)
• Fluid organization • Shared power	• Freedom to come and go	• Family accord • Leisure activities	• Affirm and support each other • Trust • Shared leisure	• Appreciation • Time together
	• A sense of the whole; all are 'in" the family	• Children • Sexual relationship • Family pride	• Respect • Strong sense of family: rituals and traditions	• Commitment
	• Availability of all roles to all family members	• Egalitarian roles	• Balanced interaction among members • Shared responsibilities	
• Effective coping skills			• Humor • Seek help for problems	• Able to deal with crises in positive manner
• Social networks	• Open system: contacts with networks around family	• Friends	• Service to others	
		• Communication • Financial management • Conflict resolution	• Communicate and listen • Table time and conversation	• Good communication patterns
	• Members see family moving through time: family history, stories	• Religious orientation	• Shared religious core • Sense of right and wrong	• Spiritual wellness

Sources—cont'd: 6. Pollak, O. (1957). Design of a model of healthy family relationships as a basis for evaluative research. *Social Service Review, 31,* 369–376. 7. Pratt, L. (1976). *Family structure and effective health behavior: The energized family.* Boston: Houghton, Mifflin. 8. Satir, V. (1972). *Peoplemaking.* Palo Alto, CA: Science and Behavior Books. 9. Stinnett, N., and DeFrain, J. (1985). *Secrets of strong families.* Boston: Little, Brown. 10. Whitaker, C. (1980, September 5). Characteristics of a self-actualizing family: A family that grows. Workshop presentation, Minneapolis, MN.

self-centered orientation and moving toward a new "ethic of commitment" with emphasis on new rules of living that support self-fulfillment through deeper personal relationships. A significant demonstration of the commitment in strong families is that they take the initiative in structuring their lifestyle in ways that enhance the quality of their family relationships and their satisfaction.

All of us are busy, and we sometimes feel pulled in a thousand directions. The members of strong families experience the same problem. They report that when life gets too hectic, they sit down together and make a list of all their activities. Parents and children examine the list critically; inevitably

some things do not provide much happiness or are not really important. Those items are scratched off the list. This frees time for family events and relieves some of the pressure. As a result, they are happier with their lives in general and with their family situation in particular (Stinnett & DeFrain, 1989).

Good Communication Patterns

It is not surprising that strong families have good communication patterns. They spend much time talking with each other—about important things, functional things ("The bathtub drain is plugged"), and trivial things. Communication is both a use-

Joel Gordon

ful skill in dealing with the challenges of daily life and a reflection of their enjoyment of each other's company (Stinnett & DeFrain, 1989).

An important aspect of communication is that members of strong families are good listeners. Listening communicates respect. It reflects, "I respect you enough to listen to what you think. I want to know what concerns you. I want to know what thrills you."

Members of strong families are people who, in spite of their success, have arguments. They get mad at each other, but they are open about their disagreements and discuss their problems. They attack their problems more often than they attack each other. They discuss ways of dealing with their trouble and select a solution that is best for everyone. Members of strong families have learned how to deal with conflict creatively (Mace & Mace, 1980).

Spiritual Wellness

Of course, we all know individuals who are not particularly religious but who have happy marriages and good family relationships. Nevertheless, there is a positive relation between religion and marriage happiness according to the existing research (Stinnett & DeFrain, 1985).

Many members of strong families expressed their spiritual nature by participation in organized religion. Others manifested their spiritual wellness by an adherence to deeply felt values and an involvement in causes they deem worthy (Stinnett & De-Frain, 1989).

The religious quality in strong families could most appropriately be called a commitment to a spiritual lifestyle. Members of these families report that they have an awareness of God or a higher power that gives them a sense of purpose and gives their family a sense of support. The awareness of this higher power and purpose helps them to keep things in perspective, to be more patient, to be more positive, to get over anger, and to forgive more readily (Stinnett & DeFrain, 1989).

Ability to Deal with Crises

The ability to deal with crises and problems in a positive way is characteristic of strong families. They are able to deal with them constructively. They manage, even in the most difficult situations, to see positives and to focus on them. It may be, for example, that in the crisis, they realize anew how much they mean to each other.

Members of strong families use good coping skills and effective communication skills in dealing with difficult times. They are able to unite to face the crisis instead of being fragmented by it; they are supportive of each other. Also, they are more apt to seek outside help (Stinnett & DeFrain, 1989; Stinnett et al., 1981).

Crises and Relationships

In everyday life we see our relationships in a variety of circumstances. There are pleasant experiences on vacations or at celebrations; there are tense times due to work pressures or life transitions; there are inactive times when relationships may seem to stagnate.

Within family relationships one of the most critical times is during a crisis, such as a serious illness, surgery, death, marital troubles, serious conflict, or unemployment. A crisis followed by a prolonged period of readjustment brings pressure on all family members and causes major problems in interactions. Yet some families survive with individual members strengthened and wiser, while other families disintegrate. Why?

Several researchers have examined the question of how healthy families react to crisis situations (Mc-Cubbin et al., 1980; Stinnett et al., 1981). Most of these families perceived the crisis experience as having produced growth toward a valued, positive direction. Specifically, family members acted in several ways:

- They worked together (cleaning, cooking, running errands, going to the doctor or lawyer together).
- There were discussions among family members.
- There was religious involvement, including prayer.
- They gave emotional support to one another.
- They shared chores and gave practical aid. (One wife explained, "We all helped carry the burden after my husband's accident. The two children and I put up the storm windows while he told us how to do it from his bed.")

Of the strong families in one study, 77% indicated they perceived something good had developed as a result of coping with a crisis event, whereas only 18% were uncertain whether any good had developed (Stinnett et al., 1981). Positive aspects included maturity, greater appreciation of each other, greater sharing and working together, increased understanding of each other, and feelings that the family had become closer knit. They also noted they had gained a better understanding of divorce, unemployment, death, alcoholism, and the handicapped as a result of the crisis experience (McCubbin et al., 1980; Stinnett et al., 1981).

The family unit itself was a major resource in coping with crisis. The inner strength of the family appeared to develop through a process of sharing and working, which emphasized open communication. Because this sharing occurred daily, it built upon itself and developed the inner strength of individual family members, which, in turn, reinforced family unity (Stevenson et al., 1982).

Furthermore, the attitudes, expectations, and life philosophies of parents evident in family relationships are learned by children. The parents provide guidance as they move through the crisis; children watch and learn how to participate constructively in the situation. The children learn how to handle the

crises they will encounter as adults, thus building a foundation for healthy families in the future (Mace & Mace, 1980).

Dealing with Stress

Most families and individuals experience a crisis, an event requiring a major change in their lives, only infrequently. Each one of us encounters stress, however, on a daily basis; it is a common part of our lives.

Stress is the nonspecific psychological and physiological response of the body to any new demands made upon it. This can include minor illnesses, deadlines to meet, projects to be completed, waiting to hear the results of medical tests or a job interview, interruptions, noise, and overcrowding. Anything, whether unpleasant or pleasant, that interferes with the equilibrium of the body is a stressor (Schwartz, 1982).

The Stress Syndrome

What happens to our bodies when we encounter stress? The stress syndrome involves three basic reactions.

The first is the *alarm reaction*, commonly referred to as the "fight or flight" response. Adrenaline increases and blood pressure rises. Cholesterol is released into the bloodstream; respiration and heart rate increase. Chemicals that cause the blood to coagulate are released into the bloodstream to speed blood clotting time in case of an injury. All the senses become more acute, and the body is readied to fight or to flee (Schwartz, 1982).

We cannot stay in this stage very long without harmful effects to our bodies. Most importantly, neither fight nor flight responses are usually appropriate in most of our stressful situations today.

The *resistance stage* follows when the threat subsides; the body relaxes and returns to a more nearly

Social Readjustment Rating Scale

The Stress of Adjusting to Change

Events	Scale of Impact	Events	Scale of Impact
Death of spouse	100	Change in responsibilities at work	29
Divorce	73	Son or daughter leaving home	29
Marital separation	65	Trouble with in-laws	29
Jail term	63	Outstanding personal achievement	28
Death of close family member	63	Wife begins or stops work	26
Personal injury or illness	53	Begin or end school	26
Marriage	50	Change in living conditions	25
Fired at work	47	Revision of personal habits	24
Marital reconciliation	45	Trouble with boss	23
Retirement	45	Change in work hours or conditions	20
Change in health of family member	44	Change in residence	20
Pregnancy	40	Change in schools	20
Sex difficulties	39	Change in recreation	20
Gain of new family member	39	Change in church activities	19
Business readjustment	39	Change in social activities	19
Change in financial state	38	Mortgage or loan less than $10,000	17
Death of close friend	37	Change in sleeping habits	16
Change to different line of work	36	Change in number of family get-togethers	15
Change in number of arguments with spouse	35	Change in eating habits	15
Mortgage over $10,000	31	Vacation	12
Foreclosure of mortgage or loan	30	Christmas	12
		Minor violations of the law	11

Source: Holmes, T. H., & Rahe, R. H. (1967). The social readjustment rating scale. *Journal of Psychosomatic Research, 11,* 213–218.

Life change is stressful. To determine how much stress you have experienced from life changes in the last year, add up the points for each of the events listed that you have experienced in the last year. Then refer to the following chart to determine how serious your condition is. For example, if you get married, get pregnant, buy a house, take a vacation, and celebrate Christmas, your total would be 50 + 40 + 31 + 12 + 12 = 145.

Life Change Score	Chance of Illness in Next Year
0–150	37%
150–300	51
300+	80

Scores of 100 to 200 are common; 300 plus is high.

Some Symptoms of Stress Overload

1. Making decisions becomes increasingly difficult.
2. Excessive fantasizing or daydreaming about escaping or "getting away from it all."
3. Increased use of alcohol, cigarettes, tranquilizers, or uppers.
4. Excessive worrying.
5. Sudden outbursts of hostility and temper.
6. Increased mistrust and paranoid feelings.
7. Increased forgetfulness.
8. Frequent brooding and feelings of inadequacy.
9. Insomnia.
10. Fatigue.
11. Sharp changes in usual behavior.

Source: Sehnert, K. W. (1981). *Stress/unstress*. Minneapolis: Augsburg Publishing.

normal state. An individual may temporarily feel more resistant to stress, more capable, and more energized during this stage (Schwartz, 1982; Sehnert, 1981). In fact, some people enjoy the "high" of the resistance stage so much that they perpetuate it by becoming involved in one stressful situation after another (Schwartz, 1982).

The third stage of the stress syndrome is the *exhaustion stage*. This comes when overadaptation to continued stress causes the body to become susceptible to various illnesses (Schwartz, 1982).

Stress Management

Fortunately we can learn to manage stress successfully and reduce its effects on us. There are three ways to deal with stress effectively. We can (a) remove the source of stress, (b) get out of the stressful environment, and (c) employ techniques to manage stress that cannot be eliminated or avoided—that is, we can change our response to the stressor (Schwartz, 1982).

The following stress management techniques are helpful:

1. *Plan your lifestyle*. Clarify your values and determine your priorities. This helps you to focus your energies on matters that truly are important to you. Lifestyle incongruity, e.g., a marked difference between what one consumes and owns and the social class ranking of one's occupation—generates a great deal of stress. A young person whose lifestyle, as measured by material consumption and adoption of cosmopolitan behaviors, exceeds his or her social class is especially vulnerable (Dressler, 1988).

2. *Reduce fragmentation.* Many of us are involved in too many activities; we feel pulled in many directions all at once. Reducing fragmentation is one major way to decrease stress.

3. *Keep things in perspective.* Realize that stress is a normal part of life; everyone experiences it. Remind yourself that it can be managed.

4. *Develop a sense of humor.* Humor is a wonderful antidote to frustration and anger. Do not take yourself or circumstances so seriously (Chesser, 1990).

5. *Compartmentalize goals and tasks.* Trying to do everything at once can be overwhelming. Break large tasks into small, manageable segments (McLaughlin et al., 1988).

6. *Participate in an activity that relaxes you.* We all need to restore our minds, bodies, and spirits. Most of us can increase our happiness by taking time to enjoy an activity that relaxes and refreshes us (e.g., poetry, photography, reading, music, or hiking).

7. *Exercise.* Exercise helps us to release tensions and pent-up frustrations; it is one of the most powerful neutralizers of stress. Also, it is one of the best and safest tranquilizers (McLaughlin et al., 1988; Veninga & Spradley, 1981).

8. *Use relaxation techniques.* A number of muscle relaxation techniques and breathing exercises have been found to help in producing relaxation. Meditation, in which a person visualizes peaceful thoughts and images, contributes significantly to a relaxed state of mind. Also, biofeedback has been found to decrease blood pressure and pulse rate. Migraine headaches, insomnia, chronic anxiety disorders, and chronic pain have been treated satisfactorily with biofeedback (Schwartz, 1982).

9. *Develop a positive life philosophy.* How stressful an event is often depends on our perception of it. Persons who have a generally optimistic, hopeful attitude are likely to manage daily stress well. A proactive attitude ("I can change things") and the ability to see something beneficial in a bad situation are helpful.

10. *Get help.* Persons who have a network of friends and family to help tend to deal with stress and crises more effectively than those without such social resources (McLaughlin et al., 1988; Voydanoff et al., 1988).

Family Wellness

The personal wellness movement has gained momentum and popularity in recent years in the medical, educational, and business realms (Hettler, 1981). *Wellness* is defined as making a conscious decision to live our lives in ways that move us toward optimal health in the physical, emotional, intellectual, spiritual, and social dimensions (Bonaguro, 1981; Hettler, 1981). Wellness is positive and proactive; it focuses on being healthy and whole as opposed to treating disease or dysfunction.

For example, persons who are committed to wellness might plan dietary changes to reduce cholesterol and exercise on a regular basis (physical wellness). They might enhance intellectual wellness by reading a nonfiction work about the political system or by enrolling in a class. Spiritual wellness might be cultivated by practicing meditation or working to end child abuse. Emotional wellness could be aided by practicing the stress management techniques discussed earlier. And social wellness is nurtured by having healthy relationships with friends and family.

It has been suggested that a new function of families in the future will be planning and promoting a high degree of wellness for all family members—as individuals and as a family unit. Indeed, the family is a powerful force for promoting the wellness of individual members (Williams, 1988). No other support group has the concern and interest for the individual as does the family. And the combination of individual wellness and family well-being is likely; many of the factors involved in one area augment the other. For example, good communication patterns benefit family interaction and are helpful to good mental health in individuals. Appreciation creates caring bonds in families and a pleasant atmosphere in which to live; it also builds self-esteem.

Minorities and Stress

Belonging to a racial or ethnic minority may pose unique stressors as suggested by the information below.

Whites	Blacks	All Racial Minorities
Experience slightly lower than average unemployment	Experience an unemployment rate that is twice the national average	Hispanics experience an unemployment rate that is 1.5 times the national average
	More likely to be service workers and laborers	Hispanics are more likely to be service workers and laborers
Nearly 70% over age 25 have completed high school	About 50% over age 25 have completed high school	About 8% of Hispanics have graduated from college
About 18% have graduated from college	About 8% have graduated from college	Women are four times as likely to die in childbirth as white women
	Have an infant mortality rate that is twice that for whites	Native Americans are twice as likely to commit suicide as whites
	Infants are twice as likely to be of low birth weight as whites	Are more likely to die of homicide, strokes, heart disease, and cancer
		Use health care less often
		Occupy correctional institutions at a rate nine times that of whites
		Are twice as likely to have alcohol disorders as whites
		Are six times as likely to have drug difficulties as whites

Source: Adapted from Gullotta, T. P., Adams, G. R., and Alexander, S. J. (1986). *Today's marriages and families*, Monterey CA: Brooks/Cole.

Summary

- Good interpersonal relationships cannot exist unless we are willing to take control of our own behavior and adapt it in times of change.

- Several theories help us to understand the dynamics of family relationships. These models include: structural functionalism, general systems theory, symbolic interaction, social exchange theory, social learning theory, developmental theory, and transactional analysis. Although no model provides an answer in itself, each offers insight into behavior patterns and the development of interpersonal competence.

- Valuable insights may be gained by studying families within their cultures. Black Amercians, Mexican Americans, Chinese Americans, and Native Americans are important ethnic groups in the United States. Families within these groups show considerable diversity in patterns of marriage, childrearing, and kinship.

- A strong, healthy family provides the foundation for the development of self-confidence, self-esteem, respect for others, and a positive outlook—qualities that enhance our relationships with others.

- In general, strong families exhibit the following six characteristics: they appreciate one another; they enjoy spending time together; they are committed to each other and demonstrate that commitment by action; they stress open communication and the importance of listening; they are committed to a spiritual lifestyle; and they are able to deal with crises in a positive way.

- Stress, in addition to its physiological demands, can take its toll on an individual's psychological well-being—and hence on his or her interpersonal relationships. The ability to manage stress enhances our lifestyle and our relationships with others. Methods to alleviate stress include: removing the source of stress; removing yourself from the stressful environment; and employing techniques to manage stress.

- A lifestyle that promotes optimal health in all dimensions—psychological, emotional, intellectual, spiritual, and social—indicates a commitment to wellness. As the family promotes the wellness of its individual members, the well-being of the family as a unit is also strengthened.

Discussion Questions

1. Suggest ways you could manage stress better.

2. What do you think would be the reaction of your parents if you increased the level of the esteem and appreciation you show for them?

3. Think of persons you particularly enjoy? What is it that draws you to them?

4. Which of the 12 irrational beliefs listed on p. 6 give you the most difficulty in your relationships? Why?

5. Describe an important crisis your family has faced. How did your family cope? What positive and negative results emerged from this experience?

6. What are some of the ways you plan to work toward family wellness in your own family?

CHAPTER 2

CHOOSING A PARTNER

❧

Wanted: Woman from good, moral family. Preferably 18–23, small, attractive, sweet, not wealthy, who wouldn't normally answer an ad like this. Would consider lasting relationship. I am 5'11", usually weigh 178, temporarily weigh 158. Have a great sense of humor. Have GREAT 17-month-son. Am considered nice looking. Have good values; not a saint. Good job. Need to be needed. Will dedicate my being to a loving woman. No harm in talking.

❧

An Important Decision

Ninety-six percent of the persons who participated in a national survey reported that having a good family life was a very important life goal (Harris, 1981). When the editors of *Fortune* magazine asked the chief executive officers of Fortune 500 companies what they wanted for happiness and when the editors of *Playboy* asked its readers the same question, both groups responded, "marriage" (Gershenfeld, 1984). A survey of 9,000 college students revealed that 94% want to marry ("Brightest and Best," 1983). Selecting a partner is an important decision that most of us make. We choose hoping to find the "near-perfect" partner (Chesser, 1990). Yet society is filled with couples who are poorly matched and with couples who are separated or divorced, trying to understand what went wrong with their lives.

That many couples are poorly matched is not surprising. Choosing a mate is a complex process that is not completely understood. The reasons why one person is attracted to another are largely unknown. In addition, society provides few cues about making wise choices in mate selection. For example, in the fiction of novels and motion pictures, love overcomes all or at least most obstacles. Standard questions of compatibility often seem irrelevant in the face of strong attraction.

Happily, we can take steps to improve our chances in making a wise selection. One step is to understand as much as we can about ourselves and how we interact with others. Another is to learn as much as possible about the mate-selection process and the influences on mate selection.

Factors That Influence Mate Selection

We like to think that the choice of a mate or spouse is a decision we make on our own. The truth is that each society has ways of influencing that decision.

For example, in some societies certain groups of people are forbidden as marriage partners (Kalb, 1987). Society also rewards the selection of a mate from other groups by increased prestige or favor.

Many of our life experiences also affect the choice of a partner. Some of the major cultural and experiential influences on mate selection have been identified.

Propinquity

Considerable research over more than 50 years supports *propinquity*, or geographical closeness, as a major influence on mate selection (Bossard, 1932, made the classic study of propinquity). We tend to choose partners from the group of people we know, and we are most apt to know people who share a neighborhood, college campus, church, exercise club, workplace, or social organization with us.

Cultural Restrictions

Most cultures have restrictions on marriage partner selections. Sometimes these are in the form of laws; sometimes they are implied restrictions. Incest taboos are the most familiar example of certain groups of people being forbidden as potential mates. Incest taboos vary from culture to culture, being rather extensive and complicated in some societies. In the United States, parents, grandparents, siblings, children, aunts or uncles, nieces or nephews, and first cousins, generally, are regarded as too closely related to marry. Also, all states have laws that require persons to be of a certain age before they may marry without parental consent.

Cultural and Social Endogamy

Marriage within one's own race, religious group, ethnic group, or social class is an example of *endogamy*. In the United States, the laws prohibiting marriage across racial lines were declared unconstitutional in 1967 (Aldridge, 1973); however implicit norms and other factors (such as propin-

Table 2–1 Percentage of Persons Who Approve of Marriage Between Blacks and Whites

Year	Approve	Disapprove	No Opinion
1983	43%	50%	7%
1978	36	54	10
1972	29	60	11
1968	20	72	8

Source: Gallup Report. (1983, June). *Survey finds greater acceptance of interracial, interfaith marriages. Gallup Report,* no. 213, 7–13, p. 10. Adapted with permission.

Table 2–3 Percentage of Persons Who Approve of Marriage Between Jews and Non-Jews

Year	Approve	Disapprove	No Opinion
1983	77%	10%	13%
1978	69	14	17
1972	67	14	19
1968	59	21	20

Source: Gallup Report. (1983, June). *Survey finds greater acceptance of interracial, interfaith marriages. Gallup Report,* no. 213, 7–13, p. 9. Adapted with permission.

quity) still operate to limit interracial marriages. The first census data reporting the numbers of interracial marriages indicated 0.44% of all marriages in the United States in 1960 were interracial (Leslie, 1982). That number had grown to 1.5% by 1987 (U.S. Bureau of the Census, 1989b).

Marriage within one's own religious group is also encouraged by most religious sects. However, Glenn (1982) estimates that 15% to 20% of existing marriages in the United States are between spouses with differing religious preferences. His estimate does not include preferences for different Protestant denominations. In a recent survey, some 1,100 college students were asked if they would consider

Table 2–2 Percentage of Persons Who Approve of Marriage Between Catholics and Protestants

Year	Approve	Disapprove	No Opinion
1983	79%	10%	11%
1978	73	13	14
1972	72	13	15
1968	63	22	15

Source: Gallup Report. (1983, June). *Survey finds greater acceptance of interracial, interfaith marriages. Gallup Report,* no. 213, 7–13, p. 8. Adapted with permission.

marrying someone of a different religion. Approximately 57% said they would. In comparison, only 17% said they would consider marrying someone of another race (Jorgensen, 1986).

Tables 2–1, 2–2, and 2–3 provide data on the acceptance of interracial and interfaith marriages.

★Homogamy

Research by social scientists over the last several decades documents the phenomenon of "like marries like." People tend to select marriage partners who are similar to them in terms of age, intelligence, educational level, socioeconomic status, and marital status (Anderson et al., 1986; Leslie, 1982; Moss, et al., 1971; Murstein, 1980; Murstein, 1986). Some individuals even select mates who are similar to themselves in physical characteristics, such as height or attractiveness (Kalb, 1987).

The reasons why we tend to choose mates who are similar to us are easy to understand. People from the same generation who have grown up in similar economic conditions and have received the same level of education are more apt to share values, attitudes, interests, and expectations. People with common social and cultural backgrounds are more likely to share the same symbolic environment—words have the same meaning to them and are associated with similar emotions and behavior. As a

❦

Love and Marriage India-Style

Arun Bharat Ram had come home to New Delhi after graduating from the University of Michigan when his mother announced she wanted to find him a wife.

Her son was prime marriage material—27 years old, an heir to one of the largest fortunes in India, a sophisticated man who had gone to prep school with Prime Minister Rajiv Gandhi. . . .

But Bharat Ram had dated American women, and the idea of entering into an arranged marriage, though expected in India, "did not seem quite right to me." He finally agreed to see a prospective bride so his mother would stop pestering him.

Manju, the prospect, was no less reluctant. She was 22, a recent graduate of a home economics college, from a conservative, middle-class family.

She had always known that her marriage would be arranged but shuddered when she remembered how a relative had been asked to parade before her future in-laws—"like a girl being sold."

Arun and Manju met over coffee with their parents at a luxury hotel. Manju was so nervous that she dropped her cup. . . .

Arun found Manju pretty and quiet; she was impressed that he didn't boast about his background. There were four more meetings, only one with the two alone. Then it was time to decide.

Manju's parents asked their daughter, "Will you agree to marry him?"

Manju had no major objections. She liked him, and that was enough. A few days later Arun's mother came to the house. "We want her," she said. . . .

"I didn't love him," Manju recalls of the days after the engagement. "But when we talked we had a lot of things in common."

"Obviously, I wasn't in love with her," Arun remembers. "But I was quite sure we would be interesting for each other. Whenever we met, we were comfortable. According to our tradition, that would lead to love."

Today, almost 18 years and three children later, the Bharat Rams are a model of domestic contentment. They are the first to say it hasn't always been easy, but their friends marvel at how well the marriage has worked.

"I've never thought of another man since I met him." Manju says, "and I also know I would not be able to live without him."

"It wasn't something that happened overnight," Arun adds. "It grew, and became a tremendous bond. It's amazing, but in arranged marriages people actually make the effort to fall in love with each other."

Few areas separate the East more from the West than their attitudes toward love [and] marriage. . . .

In India sociologists estimate that 95% of all marriages are still arranged, including the majority of those among the educated middle class. This is changing among the urban, Westernized elite, but not entirely.

An Indian man will still come home after years of dating American girls to marry someone he hardly knows. The Sunday newspapers continue to be filled with pages of matrimonial ads.

Many Indian college women still want their parents to find husbands for them and are so sure of the wisdom of their elders that some say yes to a prospective groom after a half-hour meeting. . . .

The tradition survives in part because a new kind of arranged marriage has emerged among the growing middle class. . . .

A generation ago, even among the richest families, a bride and bridegroom rarely spoke to each other before the wedding. They had no veto power over their parents' choice, and if the marriage was miserable, so be it.

But now couples are allowed to meet several times before making a decision. . . . Some engagements last six months and more. Women can reject the choice of their parents, and many do. This is considered a breakthrough.

Since most Indian teenagers are still not allowed to date, parents think their children will be unprepared to make choices of their own. . . .

"Love is traditionally blind," says Sudhir Kakar, a New Delhi psychoanalyst. "So if you fall in love, you'll be marrying blindly."

In the Indian view, American marriages fail because of the inevitable disappointment that sets in after the first few years of romatic love wear off.

Most Indians believe true love is a more peaceful emotion, based on long-term commitment and devotion to family. . . .

But Indians also think they can "create" love between two people by arranging the right condition for it, which is a marriage of common backgrounds and interests. . . .

[I]n India love is believed to flow out of social arrangements and is actually subservient to them. In the West love must come before marriage, but in India it can only come after. . . .

Source: Bumiller, E. (1985, December 25) Love, Marriage and Sex India-Style. *The Los Angeles Times.* Reprinted by permission.

result, they have a greater likelihood of understanding and liking each other.

Parental Influence

Parents exert considerable influence, directly and indirectly, on the choice of a marriage partner (Anderson et al., 1986). Parents are a major agent of socialization for the child and thus shape values, life philosophy, likes and dislikes, and patterns of interacting with others.

Wilma grew up in a middle-income family. Neither of her parents had been able to attend college; their dream was that Wilma would complete a college education. Because her father had an unfulfilled ambition to practice medicine, he encouraged Wilma from an early age to go to medical school as well. She internalized this goal and took her education very seriously. Wilma did well in college and found her strongest friendships developed with others who also put a high priority on education. She was accepted in medical school and soon decided her favorite area of medicine was pediatrics. During her internship she married another intern. She said, "Jon and I have so much in common: our love of medicine, our goals for life, our understanding of what the other faces in terms of terrible hours and professional demands. Plus we really enjoy each other." Wilma's selection of a mate was strongly influenced by the aspirations her parents had for her.

People frequently select marriage partners who are similar to their parents. The similarity may be physical, but more often it involves values or personality traits. A person who has had a positive relationship with a parent may wish to duplicate the parent's personality characteristics in a spouse.

Parents may have a negative influence as well. If the relationship with a parent has been hostile, the individual may seek completely different personality traits in a spouse. Indeed, the very decision to marry or not to marry is affected by our perceptions of our parents' marriage. Kobrin and Waite (1984) studied 10,000 young people over a 14-year period and discovered that a decision not to marry was influenced in part by whether that person's parents had divorced.

Ideal Images

Each of us (with some help from society) constructs an image of the ideal mate (Anderson et al., 1986).

"Mr. Right" may be tall, blond, wealthy, and sensitive. "Ms. Right" may be a petite brunette with a fantastic sense of humor. Just how much the ideal-mate image biases the choice of a marriage partner depends on how accurately the ideal image reflects our true values and on how far from that ideal we are willing to vary in selecting a spouse. Then, too, some aspects of the ideal-mate image are more important than others. Physical traits (e.g., hair color or height) are less important than intelligence or personality.

Each of us also forms an image of what the right permanent relationship would be like (Nofz, 1984). For some, the ideal marriage may mean wonderful communication and sharing the outdoors; for others, it may mean a great deal of personal freedom to pursue a career and a commitment to

Susan Lapides/Design Conceptions

childlessness. As is true with the influence of the ideal-mate image, the amount of influence the ideal-relationship image has on mate selection is determined by our willingness to change the ideal image and by the accuracy of the ideal image in reflecting our true values. Similarly, some aspects of our ideal-relationship image are more important than others. Choosing whether or not to have children may be more important than sharing leisure pursuits.

Validation of Self-Image

Whether we recognize it or not, we all have an opinion of what we are like: successful, clumsy, shy, competent, and so on. The choice of a mate is strongly affected by a person's self-image. An individual usually selects a spouse who endorses that self-image. For example, the man who sees himself as successful may choose a wife who supports his efforts at work and who praises his accomplishments. In a negative sense, a person may also choose a mate who reinforces a poor self-image. For example, a woman who feels inferior may marry a man who belittles her.

Psychological Comfort

Perhaps no factor is as influential in the mate-selection process as the degree to which the couple feels comfortable with each other. We may be attracted initially to someone who makes us feel nervous, but continued interaction depends on that person responding favorably to us and reducing our tension. Generally, we like people who make us feel good about ourselves, who see the best in us, and who are supportive. We feel safer—more comfortable—with those who are nonthreatening.

Although psychological comfort results from many unknown forces, it is possible to identify some of the characteristics that promote it. These include:

Seeing things from another's viewpoint; being empathic

Having freedom from extreme guardedness; being natural

Having a helpful attitude; being supportive

Refraining from being judgmental or critical

Showing respect and consideration for others

Being genuinely interested in others

Refraining from putting on a front

Being honest and sincere

Avoiding psychological games or manipulating others

Being trustworthy and dependable

For long-term relationships, most people prefer companions with whom they are comfortable, and many of the qualities that promote comfort in a relationship also contribute to happiness in marriage. Persons marrying in haste because of sexual attraction or to escape an unhappy home may ignore the importance of psychological comfort.

Psychological Homogamy

Most of us enjoy being with people who are psychologically like us, probably because we are more apt to share a frame of reference that makes mutual understanding and communication easier. It is not surprising, therefore, that mate selection is influenced by psychological homogamy (Anderson et al., 1986).

Individuals tend to select marriage partners who have a similar degree of self-acceptance. Those with a high degree of self-acceptance are likely to select a spouse with a high degree of self-acceptance; whereas those low in self-acceptance often choose a partner who also has a low level of self-acceptance (Murstein, 1980). In a recent study, Murstein and a research associate, R. Brust, discovered that although having a high or low sense of humor does not foster or hinder romance, couples who *agree* on what is funny are more apt to like, love, or want to marry each other ("Share a Laugh," 1986). On the other hand, differentness in specific personality patterns between partners can be emotionally destructive to one or both (Kiersey & Bates, 1978).

Mate Selection: The Process

Social scientists have long tried to define the process by which one person selects another as a mate. Several theoretical frameworks have been proposed; each has support and shortcomings. It may well be that the process by which two people decide to become partners is too complex and too variable from couple to couple to be described in general terms. That does not mean that models of mate selection are without merit. They put the dynamics of selecting a mate in more concrete terms and thus clarify our understanding.

The Wheel or Clockspring Model

In 1960 Reiss proposed the wheel model of how love relationships develop. He conceptualized the growth of love as progressing from one stage to another. Although Borland (1975) suggested that the model was more like a clockspring or spiral than a wheel, both researchers described the development of a love relationship in essentially the same fashion (see Figure 2–1 for Borland's model).

In the stage of *rapport*, two people meet and get to know each other on a rather superficial basis. If they feel comfortable together and communication continues, they move on to the next stage, *self-revelation*. Earlier we considered the influence of cultural and social homogamy on mate selection. Homogamy at these stages increases the chances that the couple will share more intimate communication, values, goals, and interests and that they will continue to progress along the wheel or spring.

During the stage of *self-revelation*, the couple shares more and more of an intimate nature about themselves, including personal goals and ambitions, fears, political attitudes, religious beliefs, and feelings. As the two share more about themselves, they come to rely on each other for companionship, encouragement, and communication. Schedules are planned with the other person in mind so that they can be together. This stage is called the *development of mutual habits and dependency*.

The two stages of self-revelation and the development of mutual habits and dependency contribute to the satisfaction of the needs of the couple for intimacy, respect, understanding, support, and trust. As the couple moves through the next stage— that is, having their *personality needs met*— their

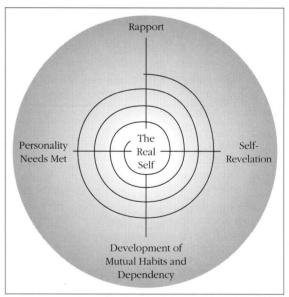

Figure 2–1 The wheel or clockspring theory of love relationships. *Source:* Borland, D. M. (1975). An alternative model of the wheel theory. *The Family Coordinator, 24,* p. 290. Copyrighted 1984 by the National Council on Family Relations, 3989 Central Ave. N. E., Suite #550, Minneapolis, MN 55421. Reprinted by permission.

Characteristics Most Valued in a Mate

One hundred undergraduate students were asked to rank the characteristics given below in order of their desirability in a potential mate. The listing gives the consensual rankings.

It is most important for a potential mate to

Be kind and understanding

Have an exciting personality

Be intelligent

Be physically attractive*

Be healthy

Be easygoing

Be creative

Want children

Be a college graduate**

Have good earning capacity**

Have good hereditary background

Be a good housekeeper

Be religious

  * More often preferred by men.
** More often preferred by women.

Source: Buss, D. M., & Barnes, M. (1986). Preferences in human mate selection. *Journal of Personality and Social Psychology*, *50*, 559–570.

comfort grows. Increased rapport leads to greater self-revelation and greater mutual dependency. This spiral continues unless a serious disagreement or threat in the relationship interrupts and reverses the process as can happen at any stage in the process.

Stimulus-Value-Role Model

Murstein (1980) proposed that couples move through a series of three stages (*stimulus, value,* and *role*) toward permanence. Murstein included aspects of exchange theory in his model of mate selection. Exchange theory states that a relationship is more likely to endure if each benefits in some way from the relationship. One factor motivating a couple to continue the mate-selection process is that each partner perceives at each stage that he or she is receiving desirable benefits from the relationship. In effect, each person evaluates the relationship in terms of costs and benefits. The evidence suggests that it is desirable for the exchange to be on an equal basis. Only persons with numerous interpersonal assets and few liabilities really "choose" each other; those with more liabilities and fewer assets more nearly "settle" for each other (Kalb, 1987; Murstein, 1980).

In the stimulus stage, two persons are attracted to each other by their physical and social qualities. If each partner regards the balance sheet as about equal concerning such qualities as good looks, attractive personality, and social skills, they are apt to be pleased with the relationship; they will likely proceed to the value stage. If the balance sheet is very uneven, the relationship usually ends.

In the value stage, the compatibility of the couple is tested in terms of values such as religious beliefs, political views, expectations of marriage, goals and dreams, and attitudes toward sex. The more similar and mutually pleasing their values are, the stronger their attraction becomes. If the exchange in the value stage is very positive and fairly equal, the couple may move into the role stage.

At the role stage the couple has an opportunity to see how values are expressed in role behavior and in real-life situations. They observe how optimistic, dependable, or selfish each one really is. The more they interact, the better idea they have of what it would be like to be married to each other. If the balance sheet of mutual benefits at this stage is positive and approximately equal, the couple may choose to marry (Leslie, 1982).

Fantasy-Testing-Assessment Model

Nofz (1984) proposed three distinct orientations that are possible when considering how one partner relates to the other. He described the first mode as *fantasy*: a time of idealistic and perhaps unrealistic images of what the other person is like. One's own nature and the relationship itself also may be fantasized. Couples in this mode are apt to feel very compatible and well suited to each other due to their ability to distort or ignore the facts.

As fantasy images are eroded by continuing real-life contact, the couple enters the testing mode. At this stage, the partners attempt to discover the true nature of each other and of the relationship. In the fantasy stage the couple said, "You must be what I expect; I must be what you expect." In the testing stage, that same couple asks, "What are you ...really; What am I...really?"

In the *assessment* stage, each partner makes a conscious evaluation of the relationship, including its costs and benefits. In this mode, the couple must answer this question: "Is what you are and how we relate worthwhile to me?" From this *assessment* stage, the couple decides whether to dissolve or continue the relationship. Note the paths shown in Figure 2–2.

If the partners opt for permanency, the ongoing nature of relationships means that they will continue to assess their relationship—hence the arrow back to *Assessment*. Partners who decide to split follow two patterns (a) the person who leaves the relationship with positive self-esteem may enter an-

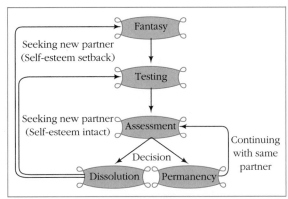

Figure 2–2 Proposed paths of FTA relationship modes. *Source*: Nofz, M. P. (1984). Fantasy-Testing-Assessment: A proposed model for the investigation of mate selection. *Family Relations, 33*, 273–28 p. 279. Copyrighted 1984 by the National Council on Family Relations, 3989 Central Ave. N. E., Suite #550, Minneapolis, MN 55421. Reprinted by permission.

other relationship with someone else in a testing mode, (b) whereas the person who feels a sense of failure or inferiority may need to retreat to fantasy.

✳Friendships and Dating: Early Relationships

Various cultures around the world have different rules for how persons acquire mates. Some seem exotic; most of us cannot imagine having our parents arrange a marriage for us, for example. Even the courtship patterns in the United States in the past seem quaint.

The approved ways of meeting potential mates generally involve friendships and dating. Contemporary dating practices usually begin rather informally with a group of men and women getting together for a movie, an outing to the beach, or an athletic event. There may not be much evidence of pairing. One person may make reservations, another may bring chips or drinks, and expenses usually are each person's responsibility. In time, the group may evolve to two or three couples and

the nature of the dating changes slightly; pairing is apparent and the process is more formalized. As relationships become more serious, couples begin to do more solo dating.

Dating begins primarily for fun and recreation and as a way to meet other people, and later it evolves into a way for a couple to get closer and to see how suitable they are. Although dating provides opportunities for mate selection, not all couples' social behavior is good preparation for a permanent relationship. Couples need chances to interact in realistic circumstances: at work as well as at play; when tired, ill, or stressed as well as when dressed up and ready to go out (McLaughlin et al., 1988; Smith et al., 1988). As shown in Table 2–4 and 2–5 the qualities sought in a date differ from those sought in a mate. We tend to choose dates who are popular or attractive and want mates who are loving and companionable.

Most couples reach a point in their relationship when they decide to stop dating others and to commit themselves to each other. Some call this "going steady" or a "pre-engagement." As the relationship develops and the couple decides to marry, an engagement period is entered. The engagement may

Table 2–4 Characteristics or Skills that Are Most/Least Important in a Date and in a Mate

	In a Date	In a Mate
Most Important	1. Interesting to be with	1. Honesty
	2. Good personality	2. Loyalty
	3. Sense of humor	3. Good personality
	4. Kindness	4. Dependability
	5. Attractiveness	5. Maturity
Least Important	1. Housekeeping skills	1. Housekeeping skills
	2. Financially sound	2. Financially sound
	3. Wants children	3. Sexy

Source: Unpublished survey of 225 University of Alabama students.

Table 2–5 Qualities Desired in Dates and Mates: A Comparison of Males' and Females' Responses

	Females	Males
Most Important in a Date	1. Interesting to be with 2. Good personality 3. Sense of humor 4. Honesty 5. Kindness	1. Interesting to be with 2. Sense of humor 3. Good personality 4. Honesty 5. Ambition
Least Important in a Date	1. Housekeeping skills 2. Financially sound 3. Wants children	1. Financially sound 2. Housekeeping skills 3. Wants children
Most Important in a Mate	1. Honesty 2. Loyalty 3. Understanding 4. Good personality 5. Maturity	1. Honesty 2. Loyalty 3. Good personality 4. Sense of humor 5. Understanding
Least Important in a Mate	1. Housekeeping skills 2. Sexy 3. Financially sound	1. Financially sound 2. Housekeeping skills 3. Ambition

Source: Unpublished survey of 225 University of Alabama students.

be informal, involving a decision to think about getting married, or it may be more formal, involving a public announcement of the impending marriage and an engagement ring.

Poor Mate-Selection Practices

Omitting Stages in the Mate-Selection Process

Many couples do not go through all the stages of mate selection discussed earlier. Their attraction for each other is so intense that they do not feel any need to go through the other stages. In their impatience to marry, they may ignore relationship difficulties or may convince themselves that they can

work out any difficulties later. Selective perception and distortion allow them to see their relationship as "just perfect." Friends and family members who see things more clearly may be puzzled by the couple's irrational behavior.

Ella and Dave met during the Vietnam conflict when both were serving in the military overseas. They were attracted immediately; both described it as "love at first sight." Their courtship was brief but intense; they spent every free moment together. Everything about the relationship seemed so perfect that they married—in spite of urgings to wait by friends— on the 1-month anniversary of their first date.

The first months of the marriage were wonderful. Their love seemed to conquer all their differences.

✻ *Engagement* ✻

When a couple reaches a certain point of intimacy and commitment and decides to marry, they typically go through a transitional period known as engagement. Engagements may be very informal, involving a decision to think seriously about getting married; either person may terminate the engagement without much fuss or trauma. Engagements may also be quite elaborate and formal, involving an announcement in the newspaper, an exchange of rings, and parties. Ending such an engagement may cause much grief and embarrassment.

The engagement period marks a passage from singlehood to married life and as such has functions and tasks. Some of these are presented briefly.

Establish couple identity to others. The formal announcement in the newspaper, the parties or showers, and the engagement ring all signal the formation of a "couple" to the world. This helps people who know or who interact with the couple to view them as a unit rather than as two individuals.

Establish couple identity to selves. It is also important for the couple to begin to see themselves as a unit—to think of "we" or "us" rather than "I." They stop dating others and may need to disengage from or modify relationships that interfere or compete with the couple relationship. This applies to very close friendships as well as romantic relationships.

Many couples spend more time together in engagement and may seek out situations that will let them learn more about each other. Greater amounts of self-disclosure and sharing may occur. This is the time to explore feelings and attitudes about money, career, children, religion, politics, life goals, and any other areas not already known. Sexual intimacy deepens for some couples.

Preparation for new roles. Closely associated with solidifying the couple relationship is the process of preparing to fill new roles—to be "husband" or "wife" rather than "sweetheart" or "lover." The couple needs to make satisfactory decisions about their future life together. Some of these may need to be modified as time goes on, and some are considerably more practical in nature than others. Wedding plans often begin the procession of decisions the couple must make. Where and how to live must also be considered. What about work? Will both work? Whose career will get preference if a choice must be made? Whether or not to have children, the choice of a birth control method, the spacing of children are decisions that must also be considered. The couple may have to settle less concrete matters such as communication patterns, decision making, division of labor, and distribution of power.

Related to preparation for new roles is the establishment of new kinship networks. They must prepare to become part of each other's family and must establish a satisfactory arrangement with regard to relatives. What kind of in-law relationships do they want? How and when will the couple spend time with each family?

Sources: 1. Jorgensen, S. R. (1986). *Marriage and the family: Development and change.* New York: Macmillan; 2. Murstein, B. (1986). *Paths to marriage.* Beverly Hills, CA: Sage; 3. Strong, B., & DeVault, C. (1986). *The marriage and family experience.* New York: West.

Both admitted that after they had been together for a while they did discover differences they had not been aware of before. But no matter; they could adapt and compromise.

After about 18 months, they were sent back to the United States and Ella's military obligations were ended. Dave decided to pursue his career in the Air Force. Both agreed with this decision. When a daughter was born, Ella reduced her job to part time. Although the marriage was rather good, both began to notice less willingness to change and compromise. Ella found that there were areas of her life and personality that she resented having to hide or pretend about just to please Dave. Dave felt the same.

Two years later a son was born. Although outwardly an apparently happy family, the relationship between Dave and Ella was changing. Their disagreements were more frequent and more serious. More and more often each retreated into silence. Sometimes weeks would pass without any real contact between them. Dave would arise early and go to work before Ella was awake. Ella worked afternoons, and Dave would come home and spend time with the children. Often he would eat an early dinner and be out bowling or with friends when Ella returned from work. She was usually absorbed in her needlework or getting the kids to bed when he came home. Dave retired early and was asleep before Ella came to bed.

The gulf separating them has widened. Their lives now are parallel rather than related. The relationship is not violent or hostile; both are devoted to the children. Neither wants to end the marriage especially, but neither reaps much satisfaction from the marriage either.

Dave and Ella are a good example of a couple who skipped some of the mate-selection stages. Their marriage took place before they had an opportunity to learn very much about each other. As a result, they discovered after the wedding that they had different ideas and tastes. Repeatedly, research indicates that length of acquaintance before marriage is positively associated with marriage success

(Leslie, 1982). Couples considering marriage need time to learn about and to resolve difficulties during the courtship period. Problems do not go away after the wedding.

Playing a False Role and Camouflaging Needs

Another frequent problem in mate selection is the hiding of real selves. It is not that we are dishonest, but we fear that we will not be liked or loved if others know what we are *really* like. Consequently, we put on fronts and assume roles that do not reveal real feelings.

Most of us are good enough at masks and camouflage to succeed in fooling others. For example, the young man who covers feelings of inferiority by a show of bravado—sports cars, drinking too much, and lying about his accomplishments—may convince others that he is confident and assured. Such behavior decreases the possibility of mutual understanding, however.

Ted acted self-confident and strong even though he felt uncertain and inferior on the inside. When Sally looked at Ted she thought, "Here is a strong and capable man who will take care of me."

Sally acted self-confident, outgoing, and talkative even though she felt uncertain and frightened on the inside. When Ted looked at Sally he thought, "Here is a strong and capable woman who will take care of me."

After marriage, each found the other was not the capable, confident person he or she imagined. Frustration, disappointment, and anger were inevitable.

A couple like Ted and Sally enter marriage with erroneous impressions and a low level of mutual understanding. Working out patterns of compatibility is much more difficult after marriage than it is before the wedding. Many people learn the hard way that marriage at any cost sometimes costs too much.

Susan Lapides/Design Conceptions

Lack of Emphasis on Being the Right Partner

The search to find a mate who is right may mask the importance of choosing one who also will benefit by the relationship (Chesser, 1990). She is right for me but will I be right for her? A one-sided relationship provides little lasting happiness for either participant.

To determine whether you are thinking only in terms of receiving, ask yourself these very important questions: Can I respond in ways that bring out the best in my prospective partner? Am I empathic (able to see things from his or her point of view)? Do I accept my partner, or do I plan to change him or her? Do I boost his or her self-esteem?

Criteria for Mate Selection

Society encourages us not to be too logical or calculating about selecting a mate. To do so seems a bit cold and inhuman. We want to believe in romance and dreams that come true. The choice of a spouse, however, is a tremendously important decision; leaving it to luck alone hardly seems wise. Therefore, it would seem beneficial to do whatever we can to increase our understanding. It will not guarantee success in mate selection, of course, but it can increase the odds in our favor.

Plenty of time and honesty are two factors that increase our chances of wise mate selection. Other criteria are helpful as well.

> ## *Shall We Go Dutch?*
>
> More than 75% of males believe that women should pay or assist in paying for a date at least occasionally. Four out of five women under age 25 do not want a man to assume responsibility for paying for the date, while older women do not feel as strongly.
>
> Women are more apt to initiate a date and/or to share expenses if they adhere to feminist beliefs. Among a group of women with feminist inclinations, 69.2% shared dating expenses as compared to 40.5% of nonfeminists.

Sources: Korman, S. K. (1983). Nontraditional date behavior: Date-initiation and date expense-sharing among feminists and non-feminists. *Family Relations, 32,* 575–581; and Simenauer, J., & Carroll, D. (1982). *Singles: The new Americans.* New York: Simon & Schuster.

Know Yourself

Knowing ourselves is not easy. We are continually in the process of understanding ourselves. Yet this is perhaps the most important step in prudent partner selection. You cannot hope to find someone who is a good psychological fit for you if you do not know what you are like.

What are your most important needs? Do you have a strong need to achieve? Do you want lots of attention and others to admire you? Do you need to have many people around, or do you prefer solitude? Do you thrive in a busy environment, or do you prefer quiet?

What type of person do you enjoy being with? Do you get along best with someone who is outgoing or reserved, casual or formal, dominant or submissive?

When you are considering marriage, it is helpful to examine your motives. Why do you wish to marry? Is it because you genuinely like the other person and want to share your lives? Is it because you have many goals and interests in common? Is it because of sexual attraction or a pregnancy? Is it a way out of an unhappy home situation or an alternative to extreme loneliness? Is it because "everyone else" is married and time is running out?

It is also wise to examine your expectations about marriage itself. What kind of marriage do you want? What do you expect for your spouse and yourself? Will you both work after marriage? Will your roles be traditional or more egalitarian? Will you have children? Will the marriage relationship be very close and important in your lives, or will it be comfortable but distant?

These questions are difficult to answer; to do so requires introspection and honesty and sometimes facing answers that are not pleasant. Thoughtful consideration of these and similar questions, however, will improve the accuracy of mate selection and give you a greater understanding of yourself.

Know the Prospective Partner

It is also important to gain considerable knowledge of your prospective mate. This seems obvious, yet many couples marry with only scanty knowledge of each other. For example, in 1990 it was estimated that 10 million Americans were AIDS carriers, and that number is growing. Consider also that in one recent study the median number of different sexual partners for 65,396 males was 16, and for 14,928 females the number of partners was 8 (Petersen, et al., 1983). Learning about the sexual history of a potential mate is relevant to one's future happiness.

What kind of person is your prospective mate? What are his or her major goals in life? What are his or her values? Do you feel comfortable together? Do you have a basic trust and respect for each other? How does he or she respond in crises or under stress?

You can learn the answers to these and other such questions by listening to your prospective mate and by observing him or her. Courtship should include some real-life situations. Some people suggest—with some seriousness—that engaged couples should be required to pass a test before marriage. They propose a variety of such tests: wall-papering a bathroom, being snowbound with a sick baby, a flat tire and no spare in the desert, or a 500-mile auto trip with small children (or teens). These are all guaranteed to teach you more about a prospective partner than a series of movie and concert dates.

Some couples think that their mate-selection process and chances for marital success can be improved by cohabitation. This belief, however, is not supported by research findings. Interview data from a national sample of 2,033 married couples revealed that cohabitation is negatively related to marital interaction (doing things together) and positively related to marital disagreement and the probability of divorce (Booth & Johnson, 1988). The cohabitation experience itself may have a negative impact on marriage if it causes either partner to feel guilty or pressured to continue a doubtful relationship. Cohabitation may modify attitudes about the permanence of marriage, or couples who cohabit may have less commitment to marriage (Booth & Johnson, 1988; DeMaris & Leslie, 1984).

Consider the Effects of the Relationship

An important way to improve mate selection is to consider the probable effects of the relationship on you and the other person. Does the relationship bring out the best in both of you? Are you happier and more optimistic as a result of being together? Can you promote each other's welfare and well-being? Can you flourish together, or will one thrive at the other's expense?

You cannot predict with perfect accuracy, but try to imagine the relationship 10 years from now. What will your relationship be like when you and your spouse are more advanced in your careers? When you are parents? Will time make it more vital and satisfying, or do you think you will grow apart?

Consider the Psychological Comfortableness Factor

One study indicated that the degree of psychological comfortableness among engaged couples was an important factor in predicting marriage success. The greater the psychological comfort of a couple, the more favorable were their chances for marital success (Haun & Stinnett, 1974).

Although comfort cannot always be assessed in concrete terms, it is possible to recognize aspects of living that make couples more or less comfortable. Some questions to consider include: Do you feel at ease with your prospective mate? Can you be yourself and act naturally? Do you confide in each other? Do you trust each other? Do you feel your intended partner is committed to you? Two basic reasons for a lack of comfort in a relationship are distrust and a feeling that commitment is lacking.

Examine the Compatibility

One factor in improving mate selection is to consider how compatible you and your prospective mate are. Are your needs similar or complementary? Are your goals and life plans oriented in the same direction? Do your personalities harmonize? When differences occur, are they ones you can reconcile? If differences cannot be resolved, can you accept and live with them?

Compatibility

Having mentioned the importance of examining compatibility as a part of smart mate selection, we want to look more closely at what compatibility is. Can two people ever be completely compatible? How would a couple assess their compatibility?

A compatibility test by Whipple and Whittle (1976) that is based on research findings, includes three facets: compatibility-one, compatibility-two, and compatibility-three.

Compatibility-One

Compatibility-one is the central part of compatibility. It involves the blending of the partners' personalities and psychological needs. There are six components of compatibility-one:

Sociability. This measure includes the need for people and the liking of people. It appears in other personality scales as extroversion versus introversion (Kiersey and Bates, 1978). *Extroverts* are defined as people who are energized by the presence of others; they go to a party and come home refreshed, for example. *Introverts* need solitude to recharge and refresh. They may have wonderful social skills, but the party that stimulates the extrovert is tiring to the introvert. If the husband must have others around, wants to attend many social events, and insists on entertaining a good deal at home but the wife prefers solitude and quiet evenings alone, they will have some adjustments to make (Kiersey & Bates, 1978).

Stability versus Instability. Persons with similar degrees of mental health have a better chance for marriage happiness (Anderson et al., 1986). People who are not stable may range from those with neuroses to those who are psychotic. The alcoholic, drug addict, compulsive gambler, and pathological liar clearly bring problems into a relationship.

Dominance versus Submission. Problems are likely to arise when both partners have a strong need to dominate. This does not mean that one partner must be a doormat or overly dependent; however, conflict is reduced when one spouse can accept a supporting role—at least part of the time. Two dominating people who are aware of their need to dominate might agree that each will take charge of certain areas of family life. Likewise, two people who do not care for a leadership role might have to divide responsibility for decision making so that each shares the unpleasant duties.

Intelligence. Major differences in intellectual ability are potential sources of trouble for couples. Different interests and ambitions as well as communication problems are possible difficulties (Anderson et al., 1986).

Sexual Need or Drive. A couple's chances of having a happy and satisfying sexual relationship are enhanced when they have similar sex drives. Sexual needs may be high, moderate, or low, but the relationship benefits when both partners express the same level of sexual need.

General Energy. Some persons have abundant energy. They undertake new projects, new jobs, and new activities. Others with lower energy levels are happy to undertake fewer projects and activities and change jobs less often. Again, partners with vast differences in energy levels are likely to experience conflicts.

A couple's personalities and needs may be considered compatible if they are similar. For example, a woman who aspires to recognition in a career must spend time and effort at work. A man who understands the desire for women to achieve would be a good choice for her. A man who disregards the desire of women to achieve might resent the time and effort she devotes to work.

A couple generally must be oriented in the same direction to be compatible. As mentioned earlier, difficulties are more frequent when there are large differences in stability, sociability, intelligence, and energy. A couple's relationship may also be harmonious if their personalities are different but complementary. Two people may choose each other on the basis of their ability to meet opposite types of needs in each other. For example, the man with a high need for dominance might be attracted to a submissive woman. Similarly, the woman who needs to be the center of attention might choose a man who admires her openly and does not compete with her for attention.

Dating and Older Persons

Dating is not confined to younger persons. Although we do not have accurate estimates of the numbers of persons over age 60 who are dating, the number is likely to increase as the numbers of persons over age 60 increase—as demographers predict will happen.

Bulcroft and O'Connor (1986) conducted an exploratory study of 35 persons over 60 who were involved in dating situations. The subjects ranged in age from 60 to 75, with the average age being 67. All participants had been married: 70% of the men and 56% of the women were widowed, 30% of the men and 44% of the women were divorced.

Most of the persons in this study lived independently and drove their own cars. Most were retired, were in generally good health, and had family living nearby. The majority dated someone who lived within two miles. (Propinquity strikes again.)

Most participants said they dated to find another mate and/or for companionship. Although not stated as a reason for dating, dating gave prestige or status to women. Because the pool of eligible men in this age group is small, the dating woman is envied as one who is "chosen." Men gained someone with whom to share feelings—a confidant.

The nature of the dating relationship is a committed, long-term relationship—similar to going steady. Most had few dating partners and tended to date one person for a period of 1 to 2 years or more. There were almost no cases of casual or noncommital dating for any length of time.

According to this study, dating partners often assume roles of confidant, friend, lover, and caregiver.

Confidant: Women most often serve as confidant. Some men report their dating partners as their sole outlet for self-disclosure.

Friend: Couples reported doing many leisure and recreational activities together. Dating partners are a buffer against loneliness.

Lover: Most of the older dating couples were sexually active. Romance or passion is viewed by most as nice but not necessary—"frosting on the cake."

Caregiver: Most care given by dating partners was in the form of advice and emotional support. Little financial, health, or home care help was exchanged.

Source: Bulcroft, K., & O'Connor, M. (1986). The importance of dating relationships on quality of life for older persons. *Family Relations*, 35, 397–401.

Social scientists have tried to resolve whether mate selection most often is based on finding someone with similar or complementary personality factors and needs. Research evidence suggests that mate selection on the basis of similar needs is more prevalent (Leslie, 1982; Murstein, 1980). Mate selection on the basis of complementary needs does occur, however. Most couples probably use a combination—being similar in some personality factors and needs and being complementary in others.

Compatibility-Two

Compatibility-two encompasses a variety of background factors, such as experiences and attitudes. Considered in compatibility-two are eight psychosocial factors that research over 40 years has shown to be important predictors of marriage success.

Premarital Pregnancy. A very high number of marriage dissolutions occur when the couples were expecting a child before they married. Studies are almost unanimous in this finding (Price-Bonham & Balswick, 1980).

Length of Courtship and Engagement. Generally, the longer the courtship the better the chances for marital success. Couples need time to get to know each other and to proceed through the stages of mate selection. Engagement is viewed by some social scientists as a time of developmental changes; these take time. Courtship and engagement periods that are filled with conflict and strife give signals of the future; marriage generally intensifies rather than eliminates strife.

Age at Marriage and Differences in Age. The average age at first marriage for men is 25.8; for women it is 23.6 years (U.S. Bureau of the Census, 1989b) Marriage at an age much younger than that may be considered more risky. For example, teenage

marriages have a very high divorce rate (Golanty & Harris, 1982). Generally, the chances of marriage success increase with age—at least to the late twenties. Also an age difference of less than 6 years is generally believed to be desirable (Leslie, 1982; Murstein, 1980).

Social Class and Residence. Generally, those from lower socioeconomic groups have a lower probability of marital success. Financial difficulties likely add to any other problems that may arise. Persons who live in the country or smaller cities have better chances of marital happiness.

Previous Divorce or Divorced Parents. There is approximately a 50% chance that a divorced person will divorce again. Also, the children of divorced parents are themselves more apt to be divorced (Greenberg & Nay, 1982).

Parental Conflict or Approval. To improve the chances of marital happiness, strive to maintain a good relationship with your own parents and select a mate who has a cordial relationship with his or her parents. It also helps when parents approve of the child's mate choice.

Religion. Persons who profess no particular religious beliefs have a divorce rate four times that of religious persons (Price-Bonham & Balswick, 1980). Mixed-faith (Catholic/Protestant or Christian/Jewish) marriages face a slightly higher probability of divorce than same-faith unions (Glenn, 1982).

Mental Health and Values. Good mental health is a positive asset in any relationship. People usually enjoy others who have similar degrees of optimism and similar values. Doesn't your personal experience confirm that your closest friendships are with people who share your values concerning such issues as religion and politics?

Value similarity is important because it helps us feel accepted by the other person. Many of our convictions are so personal and so important to us that rejection of the value is tantamount to rejection of self. Value similarity promotes a feeling of comfort between people and provides a common frame of reference for easier and more effective communication.

No two people, of course, hold identical views on everything, and it certainly is not necessary for a couple to agree always. In fact, some people regard some differences as interesting and stimulating. Value differences may enhance a relationship if great differences do not occur on issues of particular importance to one partner and if partners do not differ on too many issues.

Many marriages end because individuals ignore major value incompatibilities during courtship. It is important for couples to detect such incompatibilities before marriage and to take steps to resolve them (Markman et al., 1988). When resolution is not possible, they must decide if the discrepancies can be tolerated.

Compatibility-Three

Compatibility-three happens after marriage. It involves the willingness to give and take, to compromise, to learn to understand each other, and to nurture a mature love for one another. A commitment to the relationship and to each other seems to be a part of compatibility-three. Flexibility and determination are included too.

The idea of compatibility as ongoing has merit. Marriage is not a solidly fixed institution. Individuals will change over time, so naturally the relationship between two people will change too. Outside influences will alter the nature of marriage as well, e.g., the arrival of children, social and cultural changes. A couple cannot anticipate all the issues they will have to resolve as they go through life together. Consequently, a willingness to face those issues with honesty and kindness is a vital part of continuing compatibility (Chesser, 1990).

Much marital distress can be prevented by developing skills and clarifying values in the mate-selection process. For example, one longitudinal study of couples who were planning marriage was conducted over a 3-year period. The couples were matched for relationship satisfaction and other important variables and were randomly assigned to experimental and control groups. The couples in the experimental group were exposed to a premarital and postmarital relationship skills program throughout the 3-year period. The program emphasized issues such as communication and problem-solving skills. At the end of the 3 years, the couples in the experimental group showed higher levels of relationship satisfaction and sexual satisfaction and lower levels of problem intensity (Markman et al., 1988).

Is It Love?

Ask 100 couples why they married, and the answer you will hear most often is, "love." Love is part of the ideal relationship, and we are taught from childhood that it characterizes marriage. Certainly love is desirable, but careful attention should be given to the nature of love so that we are not misled by infatuation.

Infatuation characterizes a relationship that is based on a strong attraction to one aspect of a person to the exclusion of mutual care and companionship. Often infatuation is essentially sexual in nature. We can be physically attracted to many people with whom we would not necessarily have a sustained, loving relationship. By itself, strong physical attraction is a poor indication of love.

Infatuation is not necessarily wrong. Sometimes a relationship begins with infatuation and with time and shared experiences develops into lasting love.

One of the difficulties in discussing love is that the term is abused. People profess love for parents, pizza, the United States, button-down collars, puppies, cars, and careers. Bumper stickers proclaiming "I ♡ (love)..." are available for every love—from New York to your favorite town to a favorite pet.

Love is a favorite topic with novelists and poets. Popular music reflects some common misconceptions about love: love is a perplexing illusion or love is a game with a winner and a loser in which someone must get hurt.

The view that love is something a person "falls into" is common. Unfortunately, "falling into" suggests that love is based on some mysterious formula and is beyond our control. According to psychoanalyst Erich Fromm (1956) such ideas are largely responsible for unsuccessful relationships. Regarding love as something that one receives rather than gives results in self-centered attitudes that hinder loving relationships.

Maintaining that a great deal can be learned about love, Fromm believes that love is an art and, like any other art, must be practiced and developed. To practice the art of loving, we must become aware of the components of love: care, respect, responsibility, and knowledge. A fifth component—commitment—might be added to these.

1. *Care.* We are concerned about the persons we love. We want the best for them. We want them to experience feelings of well-being, happiness, growth and development in positive directions.

2. *Responsibility.* Normally we behave responsibly toward those we love. We do not hurt them by irresponsible acts or words. Our responsibility does not come from a sense of obligation; rather, it is a reflection of our willingness to become sensitive to the needs of others.

3. *Respect.* The Greek root of the word *respect* means "to look at." Respect involves looking at someone closely enough to be aware of his or her needs and feelings; it means seeing another person as a complex, wonderful individual and accepting him or her.

4. *Knowledge.* As we gain an awareness of the needs, values, goals, and feelings of the persons we love, understanding of the loved ones grows. On a superficial level, we can listen to a person's words. On a deeper level, however, we can increase our sensitivity to feelings as well. You may know that a friend is irritable today. On a deeper level, you may know it is the result of studying for midterms, the pressure of projects due, and having had too little sleep. Many couples who do not expend the effort to develop an understanding of each other before marriage become disillusioned by the daily marital interactions.

5. *Commitment.* Lasting love is more than a strong physical and emotional attraction. It involves a conscious decision to be dedicated to another person. Commitment is vital if trust and security are to be parts of the relationship.

Love and Changing

Persons who are likely to succeed in marriage are those who have been socialized in such a manner that they have developed the potential to love. Because being able to love is learned, those who are likely to succeed in their intimate relationships are those who consciously work to change destructive, dysfunctional ways of relating to others. We do not have to take a fatalistic attitude that we are the way we are (because of the past) and cannot change. We need not blame parents or someone else for mistreating us or teaching us incorrect ways to love. We can relearn more positive life philosophies and behaviors (Buscaglia, 1982).

Nor are we limited to loving only one person. We can respond lovingly to many people—parents, siblings, spouse, children, friends, and people in general—by mastering the major components of love.

What Is This Thing Called Love?

Love is a complex concept that challenges definition and analysis. Several classifications of love are presented here; note the similarities and differences.

* * *

Three conceptualizations of love as developed by the ancient Greeks and passed along to us are:

Eros. Erotic love; involves physical attraction, sexual desire, and sensuality.

Agape. Tender affection; involves caring, respect, commitment, and concern for another.

Philos. Brotherly love; involves concern for fellow humans and the experience of union with all persons. (Jorgensen, 1986).

* * *

Abraham Maslow (1962) classified love as follows:

D-Love. Deficiency love; loving someone because he or she gives or does something one cannot get or do alone (e.g., to alleviate loneliness or to gain approval).

B-Love. Being love; loving that is selfless, warm, nonpossessive; giving to someone.

* * *

Another way to classify kinds of love:

Self-Love. Love expressed as caring for self, assuming responsibility for own behavior, respecting those qualities that make one unique; healthy self-esteem.

Parental Love. Love expressed as nurturing and caring; protecting infants and other loved ones.

Adult Pair-Bonding Love. Love expressed by affectionate pair formation; usually involves sexual feelings.

* * *

Yet another view on kinds of love:

Passionate Love. Intense, euphoric, sexual kind of love; involves fantasy and idealization; may begin and end abruptly.

Companionate Love. Mellow, friendship kind of love; involves sharing values and goals, respect, common experiences; enduring; mature love.

* * *

Robert Sternberg of Yale University believes that love has three components—commitment, intimacy (sharing, closeness), and passion. He defines several kinds of love depending upon which components are present:

Liking. Friendship; has closeness and warmth (intimacy), but lacks passion or commitment.

Infatuation. Passion without commitment or true intimacy.

Empty Love. Commitment without passion or intimacy; exemplified by the couple who continue a dead marriage.

Romantic Love. Passion plus intimacy; the couple truly like each other but are not committed to staying together.

What Is This Thing Called Love—cont'd

Companionate Love. Intimacy and commitment but passion is lacking; quite common in long-term marriages.

Complete Love. Intimacy, commitment, and passion; an ideal.

* * *

Thomas and Marcia Lasswell (1976) have identified six styles of loving:

Best Friends. Comfortable intimacy developed over long period of sharing; rapport; companionship.

Pragmatic. Based on an assessment of the loved one's attributes; "He or she has enough good qualities to be an acceptable mate."

Game-playing. Self-centered; involves manipulation of the beloved for one's benefit; lacks commitment or fidelity.

Possessive. Intense dependency or wanting to possess another; involves much jealousy.

Unselfish. Unconditional caring, nurturing, self-sacrifice, support.

Romantic. Total involvement in the experience of love; "in love with love"; seeks total union with partner.

* * *

One final classification:

Love as emotion. Butterflies in the stomach; fireworks and bells when you touch; "head over heels"; often conditional ("I'll love you if you . . .").

Love as promise. Conscious commitment to care for someone; unconditional ("I'll love you no matter what").

Love as developmental task. Love is learned; the way we love changes over the life span; (e.g., children experience affection and friendship as prelude to empathy or a couple drawn together by passion develops mature love).

Sources: 1. Fromm, E. (1956). *The art of loving.* New York: Harper. 2. Harlow, H. (1974). *Learning to love.* New York: Jason Aronson. 3. Jorgensen, S. R. (1986). *Marriage and the family: Development and change.* New York: Macmillan. 4. Kemper, T. (1978). *A social interaction theory of emotions.* New York: John Wiley. 5. Lasswell, T., & Lasswell, M. (1976). I love you but I'm not in love with you. *Journal of Marriage and Family Counseling, 2,* 211–224. 6. Maslow, A. (1962). *Toward a psychology of being.* Princeton, NJ: D. Van Nostrand.

Will the Marriage Last?

At the time of their wedding, most couples are convinced that they do, indeed, love each other and expect to be happy together throughout life. Even in an age of high divorce rates, most people still think of their own marriages in terms of permanence.

Although it is reasonable to assume that couples usually love each other at the beginning of their marriages, it is not reasonable to assume that all marriages have the same chance of enduring. Research indicates that the probability of a marriage lasting over a period of time is dependent upon numerous factors. Many people are aware of these factors but may not attend to them when considering marriage.

Joining someone in marriage is often the result of strong emotional or social factors that tend to cloud logic and reason. Factors such as intense sexual attraction, the need to be with someone rather than alone, or the desire for security may take precedence over a rational decision to give someone up. The question, as one student put it, is not whether you can face a life together with someone, but whether you can face life without that person.

Admittedly, prediction of whose marriage is going to endure is a tenuous business, for individuals vary in their motivations to succeed, in their ability to withstand stress, and in their capacity to find happiness in their particular circumstances. But to abandon all logic and reason because of overpowering emotional attraction invites disaster. The decision to marry should be the result of thoughtful consideration.

Clearly, marriage involves a complex relationship between two people who, normally, need to be headed in the same direction (or else have considerable tolerance for differences). Marriage without love may not be desirable, but successful marriage requires more than love. Love must be supported with careful evaluation of the relationship and with planning for the process of living together (Chesser, 1990).

To Be Single

A few years ago a section on being single would not have appeared in a text about marriage and family relationships. There always have been some people who did not marry for one reason or another (e.g., economics, demands on time and energy, lack of prospective partners), but this group of never-married people has been very small in the United States; only about 5% of people are permanently single throughout life (*Information Please*, 1990). In recent years, however, more people have begun to consider singlehood as a realistic alternative. Recent changes in the roles of men and women en-

courage greater independence and have expanded our awareness of choices other than marriage and family. Naisbitt (1982) cites a trend away from an either/or mentality and toward a multiple-choice mentality as a major influence in all aspects of modern life. With the tendency to consider multiple options, people have chosen singlehood and cohabitation as lifestyle alternatives to marriage. Cohabiting couples cite one of the advantages of their lifestyle as having companionship and a close sexual relationship with someone while still remaining single ("Marriage vs. Single Life", 1982).

The rather high divorce rate of recent years has meant that considerable numbers of people find themselves single again after having been married. A number of persons also become single following the death of a spouse. Some of the divorced and widowed do not marry again and so may spend as many years single as they spent married.

The increased numbers of singles (widowed, divorced, and never married) have served to reduce the stigma of being single. Both men and women feel freer to remain single indefinitely or at least to postpone marriage. The recent increase in unmarried persons in the younger age groups can be attributed in part to the trend to marry at later ages. It is not that great numbers have decided never to marry; rather, more young people are delaying marriage in order to finish advanced education, to begin careers, or to experience a period of independence before establishing a family (Oppenheimer, 1988).

Why do single persons decide not to marry? Of course, some do not find a person whom they wish to marry. Older women, for example, have a smaller pool of eligible men from which to choose (because most men their age are married and because men tend to marry younger women). Women who are high educational and occupational achievers also have a smaller pool of eligible men from whom to choose (because women tend to marry men of equal or higher socioeconomic status).

Highly career-oriented people may prefer not to marry. The emotional and time requirements of marriage and family may deter persons who wish to devote large amounts of time and effort to a career.

Financial obligations are also a deterrent to marriage for some. Not only is the single person freer to come and go at will, but greater affluence made possible by fewer family obligations may make the freedom more fun. Two really cannot live as cheaply as one, and rearing children is expensive!

Advantages and Disadvantages

For the last several years, attention has been focused on who fares better—singles or marrieds. The studies that have addressed the issue have yielded conflicting and confusing results. Part of the confusion has been that men and women fare differently whether married or single and that never-married people fare differently than widowed or divorced persons. Generally, never-married women do as well or better than married women on a number of health, mental health, and life-satisfaction indicators. Divorced or widowed women do not do as well. Never-married men fare worse than married men (or single women) in illness, mental illness, depression, and mortality indicators (Kobrin & Hendershot, 1977; Saxton, 1990; Verbrugge, 1979).

Although society is more accepting of singles, many continue to experience an awareness of general social disapproval of persons who do not marry. Society is geared toward couples and to families.

Some members of the larger community are suspicious of singles. The assumption is that someone who has not married may be homosexual, deficient, or very selfish. Family and friends may apply continued pressure on the single person to date and to marry.

Probably the major problem facing singles is an ongoing struggle against isolation and loneliness. Lacking the automatic network of spouse and children, the single person must depend on other family members, co-workers, and friends for close relationships and companionship. Often the problem intensifies as the person ages: family members and friends die, retirement reduces contacts with others, illness and financial problems limit mobility (Keith, 1986).

Single persons enjoy some advantages, however; freedom is cited most often. Without the obligations of spouse and children, the single person has unhampered opportunities for career and/or personal growth. Change and experimentation are easier when only one person must be considered (Stein & Fingrutd, 1985).

Closely associated with greater freedom is more leisure time. Singles comprise a large part of the market for travel and vacation offers. Without the demands of laundry for four, Little League practice, violin lessons, or trips to the orthodontist, the single person has time for community college classes, entertaining, or involvement in community organizations (Stein & Fingrutd, 1985).

Stein and Fingrutd (1985) argue that the lack of marital and parental ties frees the single person to be involved in other networks. Singles may be motivated to develop friendships with diverse people. Much of the single person's social life includes activities with a relatively consistent group of friends (often other singles). The group provides companionship, emotional support, and many of the advantages of a family. Home and workplace are not as separated because co-workers may also be close friends. In contrast, marrieds may experience work as one world and family as another realm, with little or no overlap.

What about sexual freedom? Singles regard sexual freedom as both a benefit and a major difficulty (Stein & Fingrutd, 1985). Some persons believe the opportunity to have a variety of sexual partners enhances life. On the other hand, many singles do not want casual sexual relationships. More than a few find that having many partners soon destroys a sense of emotional well-being. AIDS and other sexually transmitted diseases also make multiple sexual encounters unwise.

✳ *The Singles*

1. A study of Canadian singles reveals that singles are as healthy as married people but marrieds are happier with the quality of their lives (Austrom, 1984).

2. Staples (1981) proposes that the main reason for the increase in singleness among blacks is the ongoing conflict in male-female relationships. The conflict revolves around differences in values, interests, goals, and perceived needs. The shortage of eligible men for middle-class women also contributes.

3. The rate of singlehood was high in the depression years of the 1930s; 9% of all women over age 50 had never married (probably due to economic conditions). However, by the 1950s only 4% to 5% of adults remained permanently single. The number of singles has increased a bit in recent years. Most of the increase has been in younger age groups, and it represents a delay in marriage rather than permanent singlehood. The median age at first marriage reached its lowest point this century in the mid-1950s when it was 20.1 years for women and 22.5 years for men; in 1987 the median age at first marriage was 23.6 years for women and 25.8 years for men. An estimated 10% to 12% of young adults will remain permanently single by the end of the 1980s (Jorgensen, 1986; Murstein, 1986; U.S. Bureau of the Census, 1989).

4. One dramatic figure in the marital status of men and women age 65 and over is the difference in numbers who remain single. Although 76% of men in this age group are married and only 14% are widowed, 37% of women in this age group remain married and 53% are widowed (Stein, 1978).

5. In one sample of older, unmarried women and men, about one-third never associated with neighbors or saw friends socially. Fewer were isolated from relatives, with divorced and never-married men more likely to have no face-to-face contact with relatives than were women or widowed men. More never-married men and women had contact with friends than did their divorced or widowed counterparts. Women maintained more contact with neighbors, friends, and relatives by phone than did men (Keith, 1986).

6. Singles and marrieds both face important issues of adulthood—friendships, intimacy, sexuality, career or work, living arrangements, mental health, physical well-being, whether or not to have children, life transitions, and aging. The social context within which these tasks are met, however, differs. Singles typically face these issues alone. Although friends or relatives may help, the burden of decision making and the consequences are borne by the individual (Stein, 1981).

Sources: 1. Austrom, D. (1984). *The consequences of being single.* New York: Long. 2. Jorgensen, S. R. (1986). *Marriage and the family: Development and change.* New York: Macmillan. 3. Keith, P. M. (1986). Isolation of the unmarried in later life. *Family Relations, 35,* 389–395. 4. Murstein, B. I. (1986). *Paths to marriage.* Beverly Hills, CA: Sage. 5. Staples, R. (1981). *The world of Black singles: Changing patterns of male/female relations.* Westport, CT: Greenwood. 6. Stein, P.J. (1978). Lifestyles and life changes of the never married. *Marriage and Family Review, 1,* 3–11. 7. Stein, P. J. (Ed.). (1981). *Single life: Unmarried adults in social context.* New York: St. Martin's. 8. U.S. Bureau of the Census (1989b). *Statistical abstract of the United States, 1990.* Washington, DC: U.S. Government Printing Office.

Should You Be a Single?

Such questions are impossible to answer. Remaining single offers advantages of freedom and career involvement, but loneliness is a problem.

Whether a person is single by choice or by fate also makes a difference. Widowed, divorced, and never-married persons who want to be married have a different set of circumstances than persons who choose not to marry or remarry. Widows with teenage children and few job skills have a different reality than many single-by-choice career women.

Obviously, some people choose to be single and are happy with their decision. Young, professional adults living in larger cities seem to fare best as singles. They are more apt to enjoy affluence, freedom to travel, multiple opportunities for friends and activities, and such benefits. Singles in blue-collar jobs and in smaller towns may not have money or opportunities for travel, glamorous clothes, and contacts with many other singles.

Summary

- Although people tend to choose marriage partners who are similar to them in age, intelligence, educational level, and socioeconomic status, there are other considerations that complicate the mate-selection process. Does the person meet your ideal image of a mate? Are you too willing to change that image? Do you feel comfortable with this person? Does he or she reinforce your own self-image? Do your personalities clash or are you psychologically alike?

- Mate selection is also influenced by societal forces: geographic closeness, cultural and social considerations, and parental influence.

- Researchers offer us models of the mate-selection process that help us understand how relationships develop. These models include: the wheel or clockspring model, the stimulus-value-role model, and the fantasy-testing-assessment model.

- The potential for success in mate selection can be improved by allowing plenty of time for the relationship to develop, by dealing honestly with yourself and your partner, by examining how compatible you are, and by developing commitment to the marriage that includes a recognition that many successful marriages will endure only if both partners are willing to maintain the marriage during periods in which one or both partners are unhappy.

- There are three facets to compatibility. In compatibility-one, the blending of the partners' personalities and psychological needs (e.g., sociability, intelligence, sexual drive) is evaluated. In compatibility-two, various background factors that have been shown to be important predictors of marriage success (e.g., social class, parental influence, religion) are assessed. In compatibility-three, the relationship is not tested until after marriage (e.g., willingness to nurture a mature love, commitment, flexibility, determination).

- Love is not a mysterious concept that is beyond our control. It is an art that must be practiced and developed. Love can be better understood by examining its five components: care, respect, responsibility, knowledge, and commitment. Although marriage without love is not desirable, successful marriage requires more than love.

- Remaining single is a realistic lifestyle alternative for some people.

Discussion Questions

1. What are some of the differences between a 20-year-old and a 40-year-old in terms of the criteria they might have for a marriage partner?

2. What would be your reaction if the person you wished to marry were unable to have children?

3. What would be your response to the prospect of living with someone on an isolated farm if you were from a city or town?

4. How realistic do you believe most people are in evaluating another person as a possible marriage partner?

5. How would you evaluate the importance of sexual attractiveness of another person in your list of important criteria for selecting a person with whom to share a marriage?

6. In choosing a mate, what factors should be considered that are often overlooked?

7. What are the differences between you and your parents in terms of criteria for mate selection?

8. What initially attracts you to a person you would like to date?

9. Would you consider marrying someone that your family disapproved of or did not get along with? Why or why not?

10. What is your ideal mate like?

MARRIAGE

❧

    In the summer of 1883, I met Charles in Holton, Kansas. He was a professor at the local university; I was a school teacher who returned for summer classes. We took walks and buggy rides and went on picnics. By Christmas of 1884, we decided the best thing to do would be to marry.... We wrote our families and got their consent and on the evening of January 15, 1885, we were married.

    "There were no prenuptial preparations. Charley bought a new tie and I had a fresh piece of lace for the neck of my green wool dress. I am sure that neither of us thought of a ring.

    "I do not remember that we were ever discouraged. We had no furniture or dishes. Before we were married we had bought an extra knife and fork and spoon for Charley.... We lived on less than a dollar a week each all that winter, but we had enough. Charley was getting $40 a month for teaching.

    "I am not sure that I have done the right thing on every occasion through the years, but I am certain as far as my marriage is concerned, that it was just the thing for us to do and that we did it just the right way."

    Charley and Flo Menninger spent 60 years together. Dr. Charles and their sons, Karl and Will, established the Menninger Clinic and Foundation in Topeka, Kansas, and are regarded as pioneers in the treatment of mental and physical disorders. (Menninger, 1939, pp. 210–216)

❧

Why People Marry

Marriage is among the oldest of all institutions in history. Century after century people have married. Very likely your great-grandparents, grandparents, and parents chose to marry; probably you will marry too. About 95% of the population marries at some time (Olson, 1983).

Why have 2 to 2.5 million marriages taken place each year in the United States since 1970 (*World Almanac*, 1987)? What about marriage attracts the majority of people generation after generation?

Intimacy

Most people wish to have a caring, enduring, one-to-one relationship with another person. Meier and Minirth (1985) believe that all persons suffer some degree of inferiority or feelings of insignificance. As a result, we desire to be with someone who provides emotional support by meeting our basic needs for respect, self-esteem, affection, trust, and intimacy.

Intimacy may be defined as experiencing the essence of one's self in an intense emotional, intellectual, and physical communion with another person (Kieffer, 1977). Intimacy includes the major components of interdependence, closeness, affection, warmth, and self-disclosure (Perlman & Duck, 1987). Each partner is comfortable sharing feelings, dreams, and fears because there is an expectation that the other person will comprehend and accept what is revealed and will not betray or exploit that trust. Throughout history, marriage has provided a successful way for people to satisfy their needs for intimacy (Wynne & Wynne, 1986).

Companionship

One of the primary reasons for marriage is companionship (Knox, 1988). Loneliness is the most painful and prevalent of human experiences. Several research studies indicate that lonely people do not fare well in terms of physical and mental illnesses (Saxton, 1990; Verbrugge, 1979). Yet loneliness and isolation have been the result of our society becoming industrialized, urban, and mobile. To overcome the isolation and alienation, we long for close emotional ties and companionship. In this respect, marriage has taken on a renewed importance and significance (Lacey & Jennings, 1986). It offers excellent potential for companionship—a partner to share work and burdens and a friend to share joys and leisure.

Love

Despite the difficulties of defining and understanding love, love remains the most common motivation for marriage (Saxton, 1990). This is probably because marriage, more than most other relationships except the parent-child relationship, has the potential for satisfying the basic need for mature love. We want someone who will demonstrate genuine caring, respect, and responsibility to us. We long for an opportunity to return that kind of warmth and affection in an atmosphere free of exploitation.

Happiness

Happiness is a major pursuit in all aspects of our lives: jobs, education, recreation, and personal relationships. It is not surprising, then, that many people link happiness and marriage. A Harris poll revealed that 96% of Americans consider a good family life to be one of the most important parts of life (Harris, 1981). Many research studies have indicated that married persons report considerably higher levels of personal happiness than do single persons (Glenn & Weaver, 1988). After an examination of the influence of marital happiness on general happiness, Glenn and Weaver (1981) concluded that a happy marriage is critical for a high level of overall happiness. Only rarely does marital happiness fail to outrank work satisfaction as a positive predictor of general happiness (Zollar & Williams, 1987).

Marriage Athenian Style

From decorations on vases and other household items of the fifth century B.C. archaeologists have pieced together a picture of weddings in classical Greece. The wedding was a favorite subject for paintings on objects intended to be used by women—possibly because the wedding ceremony was such an important rite of passage for women.

The wedding ceremony began with sacrifices to the gods; protection was asked for the bride as she was especially vulnerable while moving from one household to another and from childhood to adulthood. Next came elaborate and very ritualized baths for both bride and groom. The water for the baths was drawn from a specifically designated river or spring and was carried in vases designed for the occasion. Both bride and groom were then perfumed and dressed; he in a woven white cloak and crown of special plants (poppy, cress, myrtle, and mint), and she in a dress of violet or reddish, elaborate jewelry, bridal sandals, and crown.

The wedding festivities began with a sumptuous feast for families and friends. A variety of foods including roasted meats and cakes of honey and sesame were served. The feast served a legal purpose as well; since there was no written contract or license, the feast gave "proof" that the marriage had taken place. Men and women followed the custom of the time and feasted separately.

With the appearance of the evening star, the bride joined her groom to begin the procession to her new home. By torchlight and with singing and dancing, the new couple and their escorts made their way to the house of the groom. The groom's mother waited to welcome the couple into the house: dried fruits, nuts, and coins were showered on the new couple to ensure their prosperity. The groom presented gifts to the bride, and she lifted her veil.

The bride and groom then retired to the bridal chamber with its bed strewn with flowers. A friend of the groom guarded the door to prevent anyone else from entering. Friends of the bride remained outside singing to offer comfort to the bride who was alone in a strange house with a still unfamiliar husband.

In the morning the bride and groom began another day of festivities. Friends and relatives brought gifts and good wishes.

Although the wedding ceremony described took place almost 2,500 years ago, it is still very familiar to us. Many modern customs, i.e., a bridal veil, procession, and gifts, testify to the strength of the tradition.

Source: Hague, R. (1988, May/June). Marriage Athenian Style. *Archaeologist, 33,* 32–36.

Some people have the idea that marriage is a state of perpetual happiness. Indeed, many people marry thinking that a spouse will bring happiness. Problems arise when the expectation is that the other person "will make me happy" and little thought is given to promoting the happiness of the partner (Neubeck, 1982).

Sexual Satisfaction

For many people, marriage provides opportunities for sexual enjoyment and pleasure more effectively than any other relationship (Garrett, 1982; Rhyne, 1981). Marriage provides social approval, personal peace of mind, and, ideally, commitment and secu-

---

Negative Reasons for Marrying

The reasons for marrying given in the text are positive. However, some people may have other motivations for entering into marriage. These negative reasons include using marriage as a way to

Solve feelings of rejection ("on the rebound," for spite)

Obtain economic security

Escape loneliness

Have a steady, available sexual partner

Escape an unhappy situation (conflict with parents or siblings, lack of affection, poverty, crowded quarters, authoritarian parents)

Avoid having a premarital pregnancy result in an "illegitimate" child

Conform to pressure from peers or parents ("everyone else" is getting married)

---

rity with respect to sexual behavior (Saxton, 1990). Most couples regard a sexual relationship characterized by love, support, fidelity, honesty, and a lack of exploitation as more satisfying than casual sexual encounters.

What Is Right with Marriage?

One of the debates over the last several years has concerned whether marriage is a viable institution. Rising divorce rates and declining marriage rates have been cited as certain indicators that marriage is waning. Based on the growing numbers of couples who visit family therapists, it has been claimed that many marriages have serious problems.

Predictions of the demise of marriage were most common in the 1960s and 1970s when changes in the divorce rate, birth rate, and number of women entering the work force led some observers to conclude that family life was nearing an end. In reality, the birth rate has been dropping gradually since the 1820s, the divorce rate began climbing shortly af-

ter the Civil War, and the number of women in the work force has been increasing over the last 50 years. Since the mid 1970s, the pace of change has slowed: divorce and birth rates have leveled off (Cherlin & Furstenberg, 1983). The divorce rate has decreased since 1984. The marriage rate has also decreased primarily due to a growing trend to delay marriage among those in the 20 to 25 age category (National Center for Health Statistics, 1988). Figure 3–1 shows marriage and divorce rates.

Another factor that has caused some people to be pessimistic about the future of marriage has been the misinterpretation of some trends in marriage. The most obvious example has been using the number of divorces and the number of new marriages in a given year to calculate a divorce "rate." In 1988, for example, there were 1,158,000 divorces and 2,367,000 new marriages (National Center for Health Statistics, 1988). This "rate"—actually a divorce-to-new-marriage ratio—has been interpreted as meaning that one in two marriages ends in divorce. This interpretation is inaccurate because it is a comparison of the number of divorces to new marriages *only*.

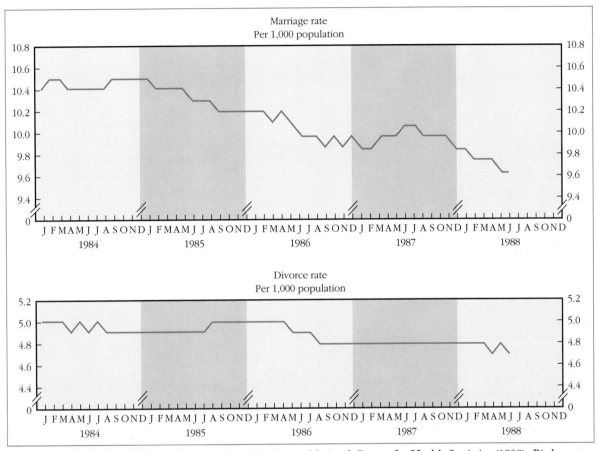

Figure 3–1 Marriage and Divorce Rates 1984–1988. *Source:* National Center for Health Statistics (1988). Births, marriages, divorces, and deaths for June 1988. *Monthly Vital Statistics Report, 37* (6). Washington D.C.: U.S. Government Printing Office.

Two other measures—the refined divorce rate and age-specific divorce rates—are more accurate. The refined divorce rate is calculated by comparing the number of divorces in a given year to the total marriage pool (*all* existing marriages that could have ended in divorce). In 1988, for example, there were 1,158,000 divorces from a pool of 52,613,000 existing marriages, yielding a refined divorce rate of 1 marriage in 45 ending in divorce (National Center for Health Statistics, 1988; U. S. Bureau of the Census, 1989a).

Age-specific divorce rates reflect differences in various age groups. In any given year, older married couples have a lower divorce rate than younger couples (Glick, 1984).

Most People Marry

In spite of criticism and predictions of decline, marriage remains one of the most durable and most valued of institutions. The marriage rate is influenced by economic conditions, wars, and social attitudes to

Table 3–1 The Marriage Rate per 1,000 Population by Year in the United States

Year	Rate
1900	9.3
1910	10.3
1920	12.0
1930	9.2
1940	12.1
1946	16.4
1947	13.9
1950	11.1
1960	8.5
1965	9.3
1970	10.6
1975	10.1
1980	10.6
1985	10.3
1988	9.7

Sources: 1. *Information please: Almanac, atlas and yearbook.* (1981). New York: Simon & Schuster, p. 804. 2. National Center for Health Statistics.(1988). Births, marriages, divorces, and deaths for June 1988. *Monthly Vital Statistics Report, 37*(6). Washington, DC: U.S. Government Printing Office. 3. *The world almanac and book of facts.* (1987). New York: Pharos, p. 770.

some degree (see Table 3–1). Current marriage rates have dropped slightly due to the tendency of young adults to postpone marriage (National Center for Health Statistics, 1988). Even so, most people marry; approximately 95% of Americans marry at some time in their adult lives (*World Almanac*, 1987).

Most Marriages Are Happy

Because we live in a problem-oriented culture, we often slip into the pattern of considering only what is wrong with marriage. Marital misery is a popular theme for movies, television, jokes, and cartoons.

In truth, most people are happy in their marriages. Research studies over the last 50 years support this conclusion:

- A classic study published in 1939 by Burgess and Cottrell showed 63% of 525 couples reported their marriages as happy or very happy. Only 29% said they were unhappy or very unhappy.

- When 408 older couples were asked in 1972 about their marriages, approximately 95% indicated they were happy or very happy. In addition, 53% believed the marriages had improved over the years (Stinnett et al., 1972).

- National studies in the late 1970s and early 1980s indicate that about 67% of married adults report being happy. Only about 3% say they are unhappy (Cherlin & Furstenberg, 1983; Leslie, 1982).

- In a 1986 national survey of 27,000 wives, 78% reported they were happily married (Greer, 1986).

These research studies provide an indication that the majority of husbands and wives find joy in their

Joel Gordon

Cancer, Marriage, and Survival

Dr. James Goodwin and his colleagues at the University of New Mexico School of Medicine used data from the New Mexico Tumor Registry to examine the relation between marital status and survival rates of cancer patients. They examined 27,779 cancer cases in New Mexico between 1969 and 1982. About one-third of their cases involved unmarried persons (divorced, widowed, never married). They identified three trends.

First, married people tended to be diagnosed at an earlier stage of the disease when cancer is more often curable. For example, 61% of married male cancer patients were diagnosed at an early stage compared to 48% of unmarried men.

Married cancer patients more often received a definitive or potentially curative program of treatment. Unmarried people were more likely to go without any treatment at all or to receive a less potentially curative treatment.

After allowing for the influence of early diagnosis and more aggressive treatment, married people still had a better survival rate. Researchers found that being married led to an increase in survival time "comparable to being 10 years younger."

Dr. Goodwin admits that they have no explanation for their findings. They theorize that marriage offers some beneficial effects: stronger emotional support, which contributes to physical well-being, and help in dealing with a crisis including greater financial resources.

Patients who were widowed or never married had better survival rates than those who were divorced.

Source: Study says marriage lengthens cancer patients' survival period. (1987, December 7). *Tuscaloosa News*, p. 21A.

---

marriages. Most couples discover the benefits and happiness worth the effort; they achieve a gratifying marital relationship.

Marriage Helps Well-Being

Although the relation between personal wellness and marital status is not clearly defined, marriage appears to promote health and longevity. Marriage is perhaps the major form of stability for individuals in our society and has consistently been found to be associated with better health and lower levels of mortality (Trovato & Lauris, 1989). This may be due to the psychological and physical support provided by the spouse and to the fact that married couples tend to live in better housing, eat better, and take better care of themselves (Trovato & Lauris, 1989). Singles tend to die younger and are more likely to commit suicide than their married counterparts (Cargan & Melko, 1981). Also, mortality and suicide rates are higher after the death of a spouse than would normally be expected (Clayton, 1979; McConnell, 1982).

How well a family functions has been used to predict physical health of family members (Blotcky & Tittler, 1982). For example, respondents who scored high on a measure of family strength also tended to score high on a personal wellness scale (Stinnett et al., 1984).

Emotional health also appears to be related to marital status. Married persons experience less loneliness and depression than do single persons (Menaghan & Lieberman, 1986; Saxton, 1990). Single men and women are more likely to show stress than their married counterparts; those who are divorced show more stress than those who are single (Cargan & Melko, 1981). After reviewing several studies of marital status and mental health, Larson (1985) concluded that psychological well-being is more often found among the married.

Myths of Marriage

As with many aspects of life, erroneous beliefs or myths exist concerning marriage. When these myths are believed, they influence both our expectations of marriage as well as our behavior. An awareness of these myths can reduce misunderstanding and conflict and can contribute to a more sensible approach to marriage.

Myth 1: Problems Galore

The problems-galore myth consists of perceiving marriage as a relationship with more problems and difficulties than anything else: marriage is synonymous with trouble. This myth is perpetuated by popular magazines, newspaper columns, cartoons, books, and movies that deal exclusively with problems and conflict in marriage. Observers are left with the impression that about the best that can be hoped for in marriage is to coexist as peacefully as possible.

Myth 2: Marriage Is a Downhill Experience

Another common myth is that marriage is *necessarily* a downhill experience, that the marital relationship naturally and inevitably becomes less and less exciting and more and more dull and empty as time passes. Movies and novels portray the young married years as the happiest time of marriage. The middle and later years have been much less discussed; attention given to these stages has usually focused on problems.

The belief that marriage satisfaction inevitably declines is not supported. Although a few research studies may be interpreted as indicative of a continued decline in marriage satisfaction over time, other studies indicate a pattern of high marital satisfaction until the birth of children. At that time marital satisfaction declines slightly and remains lowered until after the children are launched. After the chil-

dren are gone, satisfaction increases (Olson et al., 1983; Spanier & Lewis, 1980; Spanier et al., 1975).

Whether a marriage relationship deteriorates, improves, or remains about the same depends largely upon the quality of the marriage at the beginning. In a classic and well-controlled study, it was discovered that older couples whose marriage satisfaction had increased or remained the same over the years had very satisfying marriages from the beginning. On the other hand, those whose marital satisfaction had decreased over the years tended to have had unsatisfactory marriages from the beginning (Fried & Stern, 1948).

Myth 3: Marriage Is a 50–50 Proposition

This myth is based on the notion that marriage is a 50–50 proposition and that in any disagreement or difficult situation each partner should meet the other halfway. As a result, when one partner perceives that the other is not going halfway, it is easy to become frustrated and resentful because the other is not doing a proper share of the compromising (Neubeck, 1982).

In reality, human relationships—including marriage—rarely function on a 50–50 basis. Certain situations, e.g., an illness, new job, or new baby, may require one partner to give more than half. Sometimes a 60–40, 80–20, or 95–05 proposition works better than a 50–50 arrangement. In any difficult situation, one partner is often more emotionally, physically, and intellectually able than the other to go more than halfway in acceptance, understanding, and effort (Lazarus, 1985).

Patricia has just started teaching second grade. She feels the pressure of wanting to do well, and she is making numerous adjustments. As a result, she is tense and irritable. Her husband, Walt, is aware of the pressure she is experiencing temporarily. Because of his insight, he does not take offense at her crabbiness and goes the "extra mile" in conflicts. Consequently, he has kept minor problems from becoming serious quarrels. In addition, he has assumed extra household chores to give her time to prepare lesson plans. In time, Patricia will adjust to her new job and the pressure and irritability will diminish. In the meantime, Walt, by his willingness to go more than halfway, has eased the transition for both of them.

Lazarus (1985) suggests that couples should not insist on a rigid division of domestic chores on a 50–50 basis. He recommends using interests, talents, and preferences to guide the couple's division of labor. If the wife prefers laundry duty and the husband prefers to vacuum, no reason exists for each to do half the laundry and vacuuming. If her job demands early morning alertness (performing surgery or operating dangerous equipment), he could tend the baby's night feedings and diaperings during the week.

Myth 4: Male-Female Differences Are Enormous

The idea that vast emotional, intellectual, and spiritual differences exist between men and women causes problems of understanding and communication for men and women in general and husbands and wives in particular. In spite of changes in our attitudes about the roles of men and women, several false assumptions prevail. These include the beliefs that women are more loving, emotional, intuitive, and cunning than men; that men are more skillful with tools and are better at abstract thinking than women; and that men are bolder, braver, and stronger than women.

Men and women who believe these false assumptions fall into the trap of stereotyping each other and then responding to the stereotype rather than to the person. They conclude that all men are inconsiderate or that all women are scheming. By their behavior and by what they say, they pass these myths on to their children. In this way, the great-gender-difference myth passes from generation to generation, forming a real barrier to understanding between men and women.

The physical differences in men and women are most obvious; psychological differences are much more difficult to assess. Many of the differences in males and females are relative, not absolute. For example, both men and women show quite a range of physical strength. Although the average man is apt to be stronger than the average woman, some women are stronger than some men. Many personality traits attributed to women are also exhibited by men and vice versa; for example, some men are nurturant and sensitive, and some women are ambitious and logical. Many of the differences between men and women are learned rather than innate. To a large extent, culture dictates which traits are considered masculine and which are considered feminine.

Couples who can free themselves of preset notions of what men and women "must" be will be able to establish a relationship pattern that satisfies them. If both are comfortable following their preferences and talents, the wife can prepare the income tax returns while the husband bathes the baby.

Myth 5: Children Will Cure a Bad Marriage

Many people sincerely believe that a troubled marriage, particularly a childless one, will be saved by the arrival of children.

When Jack and I were having some very serious marital problems, two of my aunts advised me to have a baby. They said having a baby would stabilize us and hold us together. I took their advice, but the baby intensified our problems. In desperation, we began seeing a family therapist and only then did our marriage improve.

For couples who are happily married, the birth of a child usually brings them closer together and enhances their relationship. Although it is not impossible for a child to improve an unstable marriage, clinical and empirical evidence indicates it usually does not. Instead, the arrival of a baby tends to compound existing problems (Lazarus, 1985).

The birth of a baby is a critical point in the best of situations, bringing added responsibilities and physical and financial burdens. Conflict may escalate because both partners are tired from lack of sleep and added chores, and there are new areas for disagreement, e.g., child care responsibilities, discipline, and finances. Rather than being resolved, power struggles are apt to shift to include the child as a pawn in the couple's battle. Couple communication may become more infrequent or more indirect (via the child) and may deteriorate as a result. Attention, affection, and time must be shared by three persons instead of two.

Myth 6: Marriage Solves Problems and Unhappiness

Some individuals who experience personality problems and unhappiness believe that after they marry things will be much better, problems will disappear, and their mates will alleviate much of their unhappiness (Chesser, 1990). Unfortunately, such individuals usually are disappointed. Persons happy before marriage tend to be happy after, whereas those unhappy before tend to remain unhappy after marriage (Leigh et al., 1985).

> *Fran's family was the central part of her life. She lavished care and attention on her husband and children. When her husband died unexpectedly, and with her children grown and living elsewhere, Fran felt alone and empty. Her job had been reasonably satisfactory as a source of extra income, but it did not meet her needs. She grew unhappy with it and began to squabble with co-workers. Certain that a husband would cure her troubles, she began a relentless search for a mate. She finally found a nice gentleman of similar age and background. Soon they were engaged*

> *and she tried very hard to be thrilled. After several weeks of serious thought, Fran returned his ring. She had concluded correctly that her happiness would have to come from within her. She changed jobs until she found one she enjoyed, moved to another community with fewer memories, made new friends, and developed new interests. It took time, but eventually she achieved peace and contentment.*

Myth 7: The Successful Marriage Has No Conflict

Although it is true that an excessive amount of conflict can destroy a relationship, the idea that conflict should never be present in a successful marriage is unrealistic. Most family therapists agree that problems arise when spouses do not communicate their displeasures to each other. If couples hold disappointments within, frustration builds and resentment grows.

Individuals within marriage have different personalities, family backgrounds, metabolic rates, needs, and fatigue thresholds. Therefore, it is not surprising that they occasionally will clash. Any two people who interact in a relationship as intimate as marriage are certain to have some conflict situations. The goal is not to eliminate disagreement completely, but rather to learn to deal with such circumstances in a constructive manner (Chesser, 1990). As Mace and Mace (1980) have noted:

> *Conflict is in all marriages. The psychologists tell us now that conflict is an integral part of every close relationship. We do not tell young people that; we say, "Don't get into conflict. That's nasty!" When couples get into conflict, they get scared to death because they think something awful has happened.... That is a total misconception of conflict.... Conflict is the raw material for significant growth. Until you see conflict positively as an opportunity to grow you do not have it straight. (p. 101)*

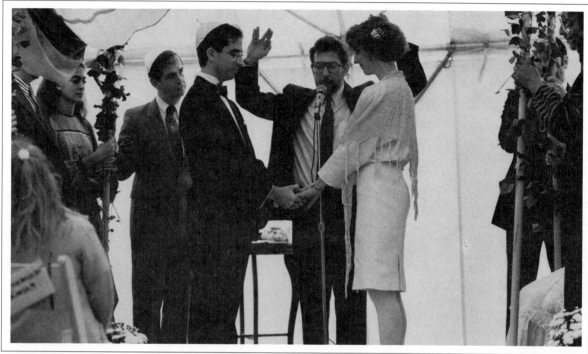

Joel Gordon

Myth 8: Marriage Benefits Women More than Men

The familiar and subtle myth that marriage is more important to women than to men is expressed by the following statements: "Monogamy is unnatural to a man" (implying monogamy is natural and needed by a woman); "When a woman gets marriage on her mind, look out!" Although such statements may be made in a joking manner, they often reflect a belief that persists. Underlying them are the convictions that bachelorhood and multiple sex partners constitute the natural state for males and that marriage is designed by women to catch men. This myth has important implications because it generates resentment and hostility between men and women.

A man who regards his marriage as a snare is certain to feel anger toward the woman who took away his freedom. Men who perceive marriage as being more beneficial to women may become bitter and resentful because they feel they have received the worst end of the deal.

Although many people have emphasized the benefits and satisfactions of marriage for women, the idea that marriage is *more* beneficial to women is not supported by research. As is often the case, research results are contradictory and fail to provide a simple answer. Several national surveys have concluded that (a) the gap in psychological well-being between married and single women is greater than that between their male counterparts and (b) marital and overall happiness are more closely related for wives (Glenn, 1975). Because married men live longer than single men while single women live longer than married women, others have theorized that marriage is a better support system for men (Bernard, 1972; Rettig & Bubolz, 1983). Marriage in some ways is particularly important to men in that they tend to have fewer close interpersonal relationships outside marriage or family than women; therefore, they are likely to depend extensively on family relationships for the satisfaction of basic emotional needs. In the majority of studies on marital happiness, men indicate greater marital satisfaction than women, e.g., Rhyne, 1981.

These observations do not necessarily reflect that marriage is more consequential to men than to women. There is no basis to conclude that marriage is more valuable to one gender than to the other. The marriage relationship is potentially beneficial, regardless of gender, because it is an intimate relationship with many opportunities for the satisfaction of fundamental emotional needs.

Myth 9: All Relationship Needs Should Be Fulfilled by Marriage

A myth responsible for much disillusionment and frustration is that marriage should fulfill all of a person's relationship needs. Many couples report that the husband-wife relationship does meet more of their relationship needs than any of their other relationships. It is, however, an error to expect marriage to meet *all* the needs we have for caring relationships. No single relationship, no matter how satisfying, can meet all of an individual's needs (Lazarus, 1985).

This myth poses a two-sided danger. First, it contributes to a selfish orientation: "My spouse will meet all my relationship needs." Or it may lead to another preoccupation: "I must satisfy all my spouse's needs." In either case, guilt, frustration, anger, and/or dependency are likely to result.

Myth 10: A Better Sexual Relationship Can Save the Marriage

This myth is based on the assumption that the quality of a marriage is dependent *only* on the quality of a couple's sexual relationship. Sexual harmony is only one of many factors that contribute to marital satisfaction. The myth ignores the fact that enhanced sexual technique will not help a couple deal with other problem areas of their relationship, e.g., personality and value conflicts, communication deficiencies, and financial or child-rearing disagreements.

A related myth is that the presence of love means that good sex inevitably results. A close, caring relationship with a solid foundation of value and personality compatibility is an excellent beginning for a gratifying relationship. Sexual skill is helpful, but the interaction between the sexual relationship and the total relationship is a complex one (Chesser, 1990). Some couples who rate their marriages as "happy" never attain a satisfying sexual relationship. For these couples, however, it is likely that there are many other aspects of the relationship that they find highly rewarding. As Lazarus (1985) has observed: "Sexual skills must be learned; love is not enough. But sexual prowess and proficiency are also not enough to promote sustained love relationships" (p. 86).

Types Of Marriage Relationships

No two marriages are exactly the same. Certain basic types of relationships, however, have been identified as a result of research and clinical observation by psychiatrists and family therapists. A very elemental classification of marriages distinguishes between *monogamy* (the joining of one man and one woman to form a family unit) and *polygamy* (the joining of one person to multiple spouses). Although it is recognized that in some churches "marriages" are performed joining persons of the same gender, these unions are not considered marriages legally; no state has yet modified its marriage laws to permit same-gender marriages. Marriage types could also be classified as *conventional* or *nonconventional*.

Nonconventional Marital Forms

Nonconventional marital forms include those with features that vary from the prevailing marriage styles. Most nonconventional marriage types appeal only to a small number of people.

Two-Step Marriage. In 1968 Margaret Mead, a well-known anthropologist, proposed a kind of marital arrangement that she called a two-step marriage. The first stage was to be a semipermanent, trial phase lasting 2 to 5 years. The couple would live together but would not have children. Divorce would be uncomplicated if the relationship was not satisfactory. The second stage would be a permanent arrangement for the couples who decided to bear children and to make a commitment to rearing them.

Although proposed during a period of interest in alternate lifestyles, Mead's two-step marriage did not receive support. No legal framework exists for the two-step marriage, but it might be argued that some cohabiting couples practice an unofficial version, i.e., living together for several years and then marrying before they have children.

Open Marriage. In 1972 O'Neill and O'Neill described a type of marriage that they termed *open*. Open marriage is characterized by a freedom for both spouses to pursue relationships with other persons for the purpose of individual growth. These other liaisons could range from temporary friendships to very serious, permanent involvements including a sexual relationship. The idea of open marriage has not been widely embraced because most marriage partners prefer to have a more ex-

clusive relationship with their spouses than is characterized by an open marriage. Also, many marriages cannot endure the strains that arise when one or both partners have sexual alliances outside the marriage.

Group Marriage. A marriage arrangement whereby several persons (at least three and possibly many more) consider themselves to be married to all others in the group is called a *group marriage*. The Oneida Colony in New York in the late 1800s was a group marriage. Group marriage was one of the alternate living styles that attracted attention in the 1970s. The few who have tried group marriage report that the relationships are intense and are complex because of the numbers of people involved. Jealousy, the delegation of daily tasks, budgeting, and social ostracism frequently are problems (Constantine & Constantine, 1973).

Swinging Marriage. In another variation, a few married couples maintain more or less traditional marriages except in the area of sexual relationships. These couples meet with other like-minded couples for the purpose of *swinging*, i.e., exchanging partners for sexual encounters. Serious emotional involvement with one's other partners is discouraged; sexual contact is kept at a superficial—almost recreational—level. The intent is to add variety and interest to the sexual aspect of the marriage without damaging the marriage.

Husbands usually are the ones who recommend this lifestyle. The vast majority who try this marital style do not remain swingers for very long.

Gay "Marriage." Some relationships between homosexual persons involve either a short- or long-term commitment and should be differentiated from purely sexual encounters. Stable couple relationships are formed by some homosexuals. The use of the term *marriage* is technically incorrect in referring to these relationships since only male-female unions are legal.

In a small number of cases, following "marriage" ceremonies—often performed by a member of the clergy—homosexual couples live together as long-term partners. Some rear children from previous heterosexual marriages, and some adopt children (Seligmann, 1990).

These gay relationships offer an alternative to short-term, unstable relationships; promiscuity; and superficiality. Lasting relationships involving mutual commitment provide physical and emotional safeguards. Gay women more frequently than gay men are successful in maintaining these relationships over a period of years. The fact that gay males seem less committed to sexual exclusivity in their primary relationships is more likely the result of having been socialized as males than of being gay. Doyle (1983) has observed that promiscuity has nothing to do with being gay, it has to do with being male.

Conventional Marital Forms

Most marriages do not take on the characteristics of the nonconventional styles described earlier. They follow more traditional patterns. Even so, variations exist in the kinds of relationships that develop. Five classic types of marital relationships are described by Cuber and Harroff (1965). Although their work is more than two decades old, it offers some of the best material available on types of marital relationships.

The Conflict-habituated Relationship. Tension and conflict dominate the conflict-habituated relationship. The husband and wife engage in nagging, quarreling, and taunting each other with the mistakes and offenses of the past. The conflict may be kept private, or it may erupt at parties and social gatherings. In its most severe form, spouses habitually ridicule and tear each other down both privately and publicly. The following case from Cuber and Harroff (1965) involves a middle-aged physician:

You know it's funny; we fought from the time we were in high school together. As I look back at it, I can't remember specific quarrels; it's more like a running guerrilla fight with intermediate periods, sometimes quite long, of pretty good fun and some damn good sex. In fact, if it hadn't been for the sex, we wouldn't have been married so quickly. Well anyway, this has been going on ever since.... It's hard to know what it is we fight about most of the time. You name it and we'll fight about it. It's sometimes something I've said that she remembers differently, sometimes a decision—like what kind of car to buy or what to give the kids for Christmas. With regard to politics, and religion, and morals—oh boy! You know, outside the welfare of the kids—and that's just abstract—we don't really agree about anything.... At different times we take opposite sides—not deliberately; it just comes out that way. Of course we don't settle any of the issues. It's sort of a matter of principle not to. No—we never have considered divorce or separation or anything else so clearcut. I realize that other people do, and that I can't say that it has never occurred to either of us, but we've never considered it seriously. (pp. 45–46)

The Devitalized Relationship. The devitalized relationship appears to be rather common. In this type of relationship, husband and wife describe themselves at an earlier time (the beginning of their marriage) as having done many things together, having had a very decent sexual relationship, and having experienced feelings of emotional closeness with each other. Their relationship during its early years was intimate, meaningful, and satisfying.

However, the marriage has deteriorated over the years. Currently, this couple spends very little time together and does not particularly seem to enjoy being with each other. Time together has become time related to duties, e.g., entertaining, participating in the children's activities at school, or taking part in civic events. Their sexual relationship is less gratifying both quantitatively and qualitatively.

Some Legal Considerations

In the rush of romance, many persons overlook the legal aspects of marriage. A collection of facts about marriage legalities follows. Consult the laws of your own state for more precise information.

Each marriage is a civil contract between the two partners and the state. The contract lasts as long as both partners live or until it is dissolved by the authority of the state. The partners cannot dissolve it by mutual consent alone.

As in any contract, both parties must show consent by signing a contractual agreement (marriage license); coercion or duress must be absent; a witness is required; and a legally accepted person (minister, justice of the peace, etc.) must officiate.

Each state has its own marriage laws; considerable variation exists from state to state.

All states require that only two persons of the opposite sex may be married at one time.

Each state sets minimum age requirements for marrying with and without parental consent. Most states allow 18-year-olds to marry without parental consent; Rhode Island insists the partners must be 21 years old. Persons as young as age 14 may marry with parental consent in several states, including Alabama, New Hampshire, Texas, and Utah.

Most states require medical tests and/or a physician's certificate to show absence of venereal disease. A small number of states now require testing for AIDS before marriage.

Incest laws prohibit marriage between close consanguineal (related by blood) relatives. A man may not marry his sister, mother, aunt, or first cousin, for example. Some states prohibit marriage between second or third cousins and between affinal (related by marriage) relatives. A woman might not be allowed to marry her stepfather, for example.

Although rarely enforced, laws exist relating to extramarital sexual intercourse (adultery) and to sexual intercourse outside of marriage (fornication).

Cohabitation is not legal in several states.

Several states allow a man and woman to gain full legal marriage status without going through a state-authorized ceremony. Usually, the pair agree to be married, live as a married couple, and present themselves as a married couple in the community (e.g., refer to themselves as Mr. and Mrs.). These are called *common-law marriages.*

Personal marriage contracts specifying the rights and obligations of each spouse have gained popularity in recent years. They have dealt with issues such as who will handle household chores, whether or not the couple will have children, who is responsible for contraception, how finances will be handled, career priorities, and where the couple will reside. The courts honor such contracts provided they are legally valid and do not conflict with existing marriage laws or public policy.

Sources: 1. Jorgensen, S. R. (1986). *Marriage and the family: Development and change.* New York: Macmillan. 2. *The world almanac and book of facts.* (1987). New York: Pharos.

There is little overt conflict. The relationship has simply become apathetic, lifeless, superficial, and void. A middle-aged woman made the following comments in a study conducted by Cuber and Harroff (1965):

> *Judging by the way it was when we were first married—say the first five years or so—things are pretty matter-of-fact now—even dull. They're dull between us, I mean. The children are a lot of fun, keep us pretty busy, and there are lots of outside things—you know, like Little League and the PTA, and the Swim Club, and even the company parties aren't so bad. But I mean where Bob and I are concerned—if you followed us around, you'd wonder why we ever got married. We take each other for granted. We laugh at the same things sometimes, but we don't really laugh together—the way we used to. Now, I don't say this to complain, not in the least. There's a cycle to life. There are things you do in high school. And different things you do in college. Then you're a young adult. And then you're middle-aged. That's where we are now.... I'll admit that I do yearn for the old days when sex was a big thing and going out was fun and I hung on to everything he said about his work and his ideas as if they were coming from a genius or something. I have the house and Bob has a tremendous burden of responsibility at the office.... You have to adjust to these things and we both try to gracefully.... Anniversaries though do sometimes remind you kind of hard..." (pp. 47–48).*

The Passive-Congenial Relationship. The passive-congenial relationship is similar to the devitalized one in that it seems apathetic and void. The husband and wife do few things together and do not seem to care deeply for each other. The major difference is that the passive-congenial relationship has been this way *from the beginning*, whereas the couple in a devitalized relationship have intense, exciting memories. In the passive-congenial marriage, spouses have had minimal personal involvement with each other from the start.

Husbands and wives establish a passive-congenial relationship in one of two ways. One way is by default; the couple drift into this lifestyle through neglect and taking each other for granted. From the beginning, however, they cherish so little about each other that a passive-congenial relationship is sufficient for them.

The second way is by deliberate intention; these are calculated arrangements by men and women whose interests and emotions center not in marriage but in other areas such as careers, homemaking, or community activities. Their emotional investments are outside the marriage relationship, and both desire this. Such husbands and wives marry for convenience or for utilitarian purposes.

An example would be the lawyer/husband married to the interior designer/wife. Both are enmeshed in their careers; both devote long hours to work. He is a good father to the children she wanted, and she enjoys his prominence in the community. Entertaining the "right" people is necessary for his professional advancement; she is the perfect hostess. Their combined incomes have allowed her to make their home a "showcase." Because her office is at home, she keeps everything running smoothly. He is proud of his beautiful and quiet home, his efficient wife, and his well-mannered children.

The Vital Relationship. In the vital relationship husband and wife are entwined psychologically and experience genuine sharing and intimacy. They find major satisfaction in their companionship.

This is not a compulsive, false type of togetherness. Husband and wife delight in being together so much that any activity is enjoyed more if it is shared. These couples may sacrifice other valued goals in order to enhance their marriages. Consider these comments by one husband, interviewed by Cuber and Harroff (1965):

⟨❦⟩

Civil Marriage Ceremonies: A Glimpse

"Ceremony in Progress" reads the sign routinely hanging outside the civil marriage room at the Los Angeles County courthouse. Each year about 70,000 marriage licenses are purchased in Los Angeles County, and about 11% of those couples opt for the civil ceremony.

Each working day, from 9 A.M. to 5 P.M. the couples line up between red ropes to wait their turn. About 30 ceremonies are performed each weekday except Friday. Fridays are higher volume with nearly 50 ceremonies being conducted. June is the most popular month; Valentine's Day the most popular day (107 ceremonies).

For those who think of marriages in terms of chapels, romantic music, flowers, and beautiful gowns, the civil ceremonies are a surprise. Some couples do come in tuxedos and gowns with flowers and friends; more come in everyday clothing or shorts and sandals. Because of the high population of foreign-born persons in Los Angeles, many come in native costumes. Many come with one friend to serve as the witness; some come alone. The hours from 11 A.M. to 2 P.M. are very busy because of the high number of couples who use lunch hours to wed (and then return to work).

The ceremony is performed in a stark green room, lighted by neon. The commissioner performing the ceremony stands behind a lectern. The couple may choose a no-ring, single-ring, or double-ring ceremony in either English or Spanish. The ceremony itself takes about two minutes. No music or photographers are allowed.

When several couples were asked why they chose a civil ceremony, most responded saying it was easy, cheap, and fast. The cost of a marriage license is $35, and the civil ceremony costs an additional $15. Some couples have receptions or parties later at home.

Not far from the line of couples waiting for licenses and/or ceremonies is another line. This line is not so happy; it is the line for filing petitions—including those for divorces.

Source: Larsen, D. (1985, September 29). Bestowing civil touch to marriage ceremonies has become a 9-to-5 job. *Los Angeles Times*, part VI, pp. 1, 10.

I cheerfully, and that's putting it mildly, passed up two good promotions because one of them would have required some traveling and the other would have taken evening and weekend time—and that's when Pat and I live. The hours with her (after twenty-two years of marriage) are what I live for. You should meet her....(p. 56)

In another interview by Cuber and Harroff (1965), a wife tells why she and her husband moved to the country:

We like this kind of life—where we can have almost all of our time together.... We've been married over twenty years and the most enjoyable thing either of us does—well, outside of the intimate things—is to sit and talk by the hour. That's why we built that imposing fireplace—and the hi-fi here in the corner. ... Now that Ed is getting older, that twenty-seven mile drive every morning and night from the office is a real burden, but he does it cheerfully so we can have our long uninterrupted hours together.... (pp. 56, 57)

In summary, husband-wife companionship is vital in this type of relationship. This does not mean that they lose their separate identities or that they never disagree. Conflict, when it occurs, is usually over matters that are important to them; they tend to settle disagreements quickly.

Total Relationship.   The total relationship is very similar to the vital relationship except that the total relationship involves even more sharing and companionship; it is more multifaceted. Cuber and Harroff (1965) described these as "relationships so total that all aspects of life were mutually shared" (p. 60).

Instead of being in competition, the various areas of the total relationship reinforce each other. An example from Cuber and Harroff's research illustrates this:

> *She keeps my files and scrapbooks up to date.... I invariably take her with me to conferences around the world. Her femininity, easy charm, and wit are invaluable assets to me. I know it's conventional to say that a man's wife is responsible for his success and I also know that it's often not true. But in my case I gladly acknowledge that it's not only true but she's indispensable to me. But she'd go along with me even if there was nothing for her to do because we enjoy each other's company—deeply. You know, the best part of a vacation is not what we do, but that we do it together. (p. 59)*

In a study of strong families begun in Oklahoma and expanded nationally, the personality characteristics of couples involved in vital and total marriages were investigated. These couples exhibited certain characteristics:

1. They enjoy doing things for each other. He brings her coffee each morning; she washes the car as a surprise for him. Each gives the other kindness, empathy, and help.

2. These couples are committed to their marriages. They make conscious efforts to keep the relationship good or to improve it.

3. Even though the marriage is of prime importance, neither spouse loses personal identity. Each remains independent and capable of making decisions; each has life goals.

4. These couples report moderately high to high sexual needs. Their sexual relationship is usually very good. (Ammons & Stinnett, 1980)

Please remember that this classification system does not represent degrees of marital happiness. Husbands and wives in any of the types may be well-adjusted, happy, and content. A major purpose of such classifications is to make it clear that marriage relationships can take varied forms depending on the people involved and their expectations of marriage.

The Circumplex Model

A recent model for classification of family types used by researchers and therapists is the circumplex model that is presented in Figure 3–2. In the model 16 types of marriage or family systems are identified that are based on two variables: adaptability and cohesion (Olson, 1986b).

Adaptability is the ability to change, to be flexible. Families that lack adaptability are termed *rigid*: roles, rules, and expectations do not change to meet circumstances. Families characterized by extreme change are termed *chaotic*: roles, rules, and expectations change so often that family members never know what to expect (Olson, 1986b; Olson et al., 1983).

Cohesion is a measure of how involved family members are in each other's lives. Families with extremely low cohesion are termed *disengaged*: family members live as individuals who share a

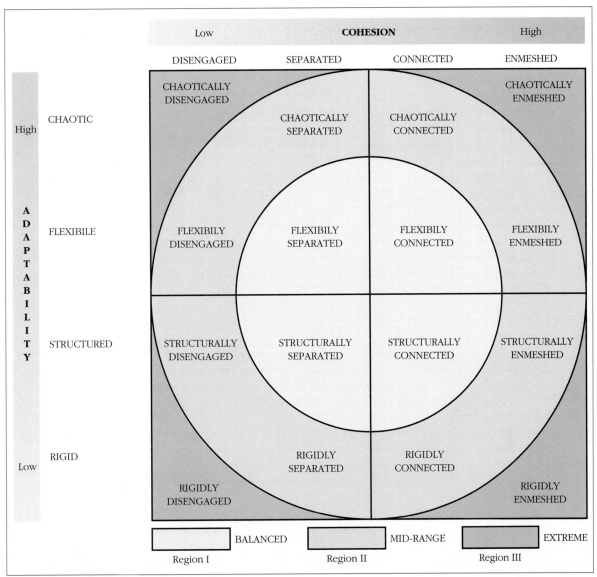

Figure 3–2 The circumplex model—sixteen types of marital and family systems. *Source:* Olson, D. H. (1986a). Circumplex model VII: Validation studies and FACES III. *Family Process, 25,* p. 339. Copyright, ©D. H. Olson, 1986. Reprinted by permission.

Arabs' Path to Altar No Walk in Park

As floodlights illuminated the scene, the richly costumed couple slowly crossed a bridge over a pool redolent of exotic flowers. Zither music and the crash of cymbals filled the moonlit night, and mustachioed men with flaming swords brought up the rear of the procession....

It was a scene repeated on a nightly basis in cities, towns, and villages throughout the Arab world... though with varying degrees of opulence. It was an enactment of the region's most hallowed institution: marriage.

Judging by the blare of motorcades, late-night celebrations, and occasional gunplay...the act of getting married has lost little of its luster in this family-oriented society. According to one study, 45% of Arab women are married by the age of 19.

...."[M]arriage is undergoing drastic changes in the Arab world," said Sari Nassar, head of the sociology department at the University of Jordan....

In the past, Arab—usually meaning Muslim—marriages were generally arranged by the family, usually involved marrying relatives, and, for men, were frequently polygamous. Under Islam, a man may have up to four wives under limited circumstances.

Now...young people will no longer tolerate arranged marriages, they tend to marry people outside their immediate families, and polygamy as an institution is rapidly dying out, although it lingers in... Kuwait and Saudi Arabia.

In addition, Arab families increasingly are grappling with the problems of divorce, and...the huge costs of paying a dowry, which...is paid by the bridegroom to the bride's family.

While the dowry can run into the thousands of dollars, the wedding itself can be a barometer of the family's social standing. The actual wedding is brief—it involves signing a marriage contract at home—but the main ceremony comes in the party that follows.

The party is also paid for by the bridegroom's family, and an average bash at an Amman hotel runs to $30,000; that does not include such other expenses as invitations, which are usually sent out to 500 relatives and close friends with an accompanying gift such as a silver plate.

In Saudi Arabia, Kuwait, and other gulf states, weddings costing between $100,000 and $500,000 are not uncommon....

Source: Wallace, C. P. (1986, November 4). Arabs' path to altar no walk in park. *Los Angeles Times*, p. 1 and 20.

house. Families with extreme cohesion are termed *enmeshed*: they are so involved that individual growth cannot occur. Families in the middle ranges on both dimensions seem to do better and have fewer serious difficulties than those in the extreme ranges (Olson, 1986b; Olson et al., 1983).

Family Life Cycle

Marriage relationships can also be analyzed using a developmental approach that gained much of its impetus from Evelyn Millis Duvall, one of the leaders in the family life movement in the United States.

Table 3–2 Family Life Cycle Stages

Family life cycle stage	Emotional process of transition: Key principles	Changes in family status required to proceed developmentally
1. Between families: The unattached young adult	Accepting parent-offspring separation	a. Differentiation of self in relation to family of origin b. Development of intimate peer relationships c. Establishment of self in work
2. The joining of families through marriage: The newly married couple	Commitment to new system	a. Formation of marital system b. Realignment of relationships with extended families and friends to include spouse
3. The family with young children	Accepting new generation of members into the system	a. Adjusting marital system to make space for child(ren) b. Taking on parental roles c. Realignment of relationships with extended family to include parenting and grandparenting roles
4. The family with adolescents	Increasing flexibility of family boundaries to include children's independence	a. Shifting of parent-child relationships to permit adolescents to move in and out of system b. Refocus on midlife marital and career issues c. Beginning shift toward concerns for older generation
5. Launching children and moving on	Accepting a multitude of exits from and entries into the family system	a. Renegotiation of marital system as a dyad b. Development of adult-to-adult relationships between grown children and their parents c. Realignment of relationships to include in-laws and grandchildren d. Dealing with disabilities and death of parents (grandparents)
6. The family in later life	Accepting the shifting of generational roles	a. Maintaining own and/or couple functioning and interests in face of physiological decline; exploration of new familial and social role options b. Support for a more central role for middle generation c. Making room in the system for the wisdom and experience of the elderly; supporting the older generation without overfunctioning for them d. Dealing with loss of spouse, siblings, and other peers, and preparation for own death; life review and integration

Source: McGoldrick, M., & Carter, E. (1982). The stages of the family life cycle. In F. Walsh (Ed.), *Normal family processes.* New York: Guilford.

From a developmental perspective, each entity (person, family, etc.) passes through a series of stages. Each stage is characterized by tasks to accomplish or challenges to meet before the entity can move successfully to the next stage. Each stage has fairly definite entry and exit points (transition periods). This concept is termed *family lifetime history, family life cycle, or family career* (Aldous, 1978; Gulotta et al., 1986; McGoldrick & Carter, 1982). The stages of the family life cycle are presented in Table 3–2.

This model emphasizes the changing nature of *each* marriage over time. John and Mary, for example, face certain challenges as a newly married couple: developing intimacy, realigning relationships with parents and friends, and learning new roles (husband, wife). When John, Jr. is born, they enter another stage and face new challenges: expanding the family to accept a new member and learning new roles (parent), for example. Years later when all their children are launched, Mary and John will encounter other tasks: renegotiation of the marital dyad, dealing with their aged parents, and learning a new role (grandparent). Because the challenges, stresses, and rewards at each stage vary, we may argue that John and Mary have a "different" marriage at each stage (Lingren et al., 1982; McGoldrick & Carter, 1982; Olson, 1986b).

Knowing the stage of the life cycle that a married couple is in helps us to understand the tasks and problems they are apt to be confronting. It also gives clues about the rewards and strengths they are likely to be experiencing (Jorgensen, 1986; Olson, 1986b). Transition periods are times of rapid change and adjustment. Understanding the stresses involved in transition periods may allow couples to view them as normal, if unpleasant, times that will pass. John and Mary, for example, can realize that they are fatigued and irritable because of the recent birth of John, Jr. and the resulting demands of role change, schedule disruption, and so forth. It does not mean that their relationship has failed, only that it is changing.

Summary

- Most people desire the enduring, monogamous relationship of marriage because it provides for intimacy, companionship, love, happiness, and sexual satisfaction. Some look to marriage, however, as an answer to other problems. These negative motivations do not make for positive relationships.

- Contrary to the predictions of its decline, marriage is still an enduring and highly valued institution. Most couples find joy in their marriage partnerships and receive benefits in the form of increased psychological well-being.

- It is important to understand the myths associated with marriage in order to alter the behavior and attitudes that result from such misconceptions. These myths state that marriage is a problem-ridden institution that grows more dull as years go by, that marriage is a 50–50 proposition with equal division of labor, that the inherent differences in the emotional and intellectual makeup of men and women cause marital problems, that marriage can solve problems, that an unhappy marriage can be cured by having children or by improving the sexual relationship, that a successful marriage has no conflict, and that a marriage will fulfill all of a person's relationship needs.

- Although each marriage is unique, research in marital relationships has led to a number of classification forms. Non-conventional forms include two-step marriages, open marriages, group marriages, swinging marriages, and gay "marriages." Conventional forms follow more traditional patterns and include the following types of relationships: conflict-habituated, passive-congenial, devitalized, vital, and total.

- Family systems and marital relationships can be classified using the circumplex model. This model identifies 16 family types based on their levels of adaptability and cohesion.

- A developmental approach to classifying marriage relationships uses the family life cycle. This model emphasizes that marriage changes over time and that with each new stage comes new challenges and new roles. The ability to understand and adapt to these changes will put less stress on the relationship.

Discussion Questions

1. What are the differences between devitalized and passive-congenial relationships?

2. Is marriage more important to men or to women? Why?

3. How important—in terms of your values—is marriage in relation to your vocational choice?

4. Why do people remain in devitalized or conflict-habituated relationships?

5. Which type of marital relationship do you prefer personally? Which of your characteristics—personality, values, lifestyle—will help you in achieving your preference? Which will hinder you?

6. If you could change one thing about the person you love, what would it be?

7. Can you think of other common marriage myths in addition to the ones identified in this chapter? Television and movies usually provide good material.

8. What would you predict to be probable areas of difficulty for couples who marry for the "wrong" reasons?

9. People marry for multiple reasons: they are compatible in many ways, they enjoy each other's company, and she is pregnant, for example. How would you advise a couple in these circumstances? Do the negatives outweigh the positives?

10. Examine Table 3–1. What general trend do you observe? Explain the lowered rates of 1930 and 1960. How do you explain the high rate in 1946?

CHAPTER 4

DEVELOPING A STRONG MARRIAGE RELATIONSHIP

❧

We celebrated our golden wedding anniversary last week. Our children collected snapshots and put together a pictorial history of our married life. The grandkids thought the clothing styles and the automobiles were hilarious, but how rich the memories: our first home, our babies (all grown now, of course), the kids' schools and birthday parties, graduations, special vacation trips, grandchildren.

We looked so young in those early years, and times were so hard because of the depression. We should have been scared to start out under those circumstances. We weren't; we didn't know any better, I guess.

All our times haven't been great. We've had financial worries, illness, grief, the stress of moving to another state, the challenge of changing jobs. But the good has outweighed the bad, and if we could turn the clock back 50 years, we'd still set out together.

❧

Defining Success

Success is difficult to measure in the interplay of human relationships. It is not how long a relationship lasts nor how intensely it is experienced; it is not who won the most points or who crossed the finish line first. And one partner cannot win while the other loses if a relationship is to succeed.

One definition of a successful marriage is one in which both partners feel they receive a high level of personal satisfaction most of the time. They believe that their physical, emotional, and psychological needs are fulfilled by their involvement in the marital relationship, and they have found the satisfaction they hoped for in the situation (Bowman & Spanier, 1978). The most satisfying and unsatisfying aspects of marriage are listed in Table 4–1.

The preceding definition illustrates one of the difficulties in defining a successful relationship—that is, the judgment is very subjective. Simply put, if husband and wife think they have a good marriage, they do.

Another difficulty is that marriage quality is a complex phenomenon, involving multiple constructs that interact and overlap (Fincham & Bradbury, 1987). Researchers and counselors have suggested criteria that should be considered in determining marital quality (Ammons & Stinnett, 1980; Bell et al., 1987; Fowers & Olson, 1986; Leigh et al., 1985; Leslie, 1982; Rao & Rao, 1986; Rowe & Meredith, 1982; Schlesinger, 1984; Stinnett & De-Frain, 1985). The list that follows represents a compilation of these criteria. Not every researcher or therapist includes all of these factors in an evaluation of marital quality. And, of course, not every happy mar-

Table 4–1 Most Satisfying and Most Unsatisfying Aspects of Marriage*

Most Satisfying	
For Men	**For Women**
Friendship	Friendship
Companionship	Personal growth
Shared interests and goals	Supportive partner
Building family together	Children
Children	Secure lifestyle
Most Unsatisfying	
For Men	**For Women**
Not sexually satisfied	Sexual relations
Money	Finances
Children too demanding	Husband's workload
Constraints on personal freedom	Children

* Survey of 129 middle-class couples in Toronto, Ontario, Canada. All couples were married more than 15 years and had at least one child.

Source: Schlesinger, B. (1984). Lasting and functioning marriages in the 1980's. In G. Rowe, J. DeFrain, H. Lingren, R. MacDonald, N. Stinnett, S. Van Zandt, & R. Williams (Eds.), *Family strengths 5: Continuity and diversity* (pp. 49–63). Newton, MA: Education Development Center.

riage includes all the factors. There is, however, evidence that marriages with the following characteristics may be termed successful or of high quality:

- Permanence; endurance
- Lack of troublesome marital differences
- Tolerance
- Mutual understanding and acceptance
- Personal comfort
- Satisfaction of emotional needs
- Friendship
- Unity or cohesion between partners
- Commitment
- Intimacy
- Interest in each other
- Facilitation of personal growth; personal space
- Integrity
- Conflict not excessive; conflict handled creatively
- Effective communication; talk
- Laughter; sense of humor
- Agreement on important matters
- Adaptability
- Marital happiness; contentment in the relationship
- Marriage meets the needs and expectations of society
- Involvement in the larger community
- Satisfactory sexual relationship
- Sharing; time together

Factors Related to Marriage Success

Even though marital success is difficult to define and measure, it remains an area of considerable interest for social science researchers and family therapists (Fincham & Bradbury, 1987; Leigh et al., 1985). As a result, many of the factors associated with marriage success have been identified.

Some of the factors related to marital success have been presented in Chapters 2 and 3. These factors are reviewed briefly in the following list:

Personal happiness. Persons who are happy are more likely to have happy, successful marriages (Leigh et al., 1985).

Parents' marriage. The children of divorced parents are themselves more apt to be divorced (Glenn & Kramer, 1987).

Parental approval. Parental approval of the marriage is important to its success.

Length of courtship. Longer courtships are associated with marital success (Whipple & Whittle, 1976).

Age at marriage. Couples who marry young have a high divorce rate and seem to have a larger share of marital difficulties (Norton & Moorman, 1987; Price-Bonham & Balswick, 1980).

Premarital pregnancy. Marriages that are begun because of a premarital pregnancy have a high rate of failure, with approximately 40% to 50% ending within 5 years (Norton & Moorman, 1987; Price-Bonham & Balswick, 1980).

Reasons for marriage. Marrying for the "wrong" reasons—to escape an unhappy home, to relieve loneliness, or to defy parents—does not necessarily doom the marriage, but it does add to the likelihood of dissatisfaction.

Mate-selection practices. Thoughtful, honest, informed mate selection does not guarantee marital success, but it does improve the chances.

Homogamy. "Opposites attract" may not be the soundest philosophy with regard to marital success. Although small differences can be stimulating, major differences in many areas more often are too challenging and stressful. For this reason, a couple similar in terms of race, ethnic group, religion, socioeconomic status, education, intelligence, sociability (introversion versus extroversion), mental health, sexual need, general energy, and values are more likely to experience marital success (Kiersey & Bates, 1978; Knox, 1988, Price-Bonham & Balswick, 1980; Whipple & Whittle, 1976).

Other factors that have not been discussed previously may also influence marital stability and success.

Personality Characteristics

Persons who possess personality traits that contribute to good interpersonal relationships in general are more likely to have happy marriage relationships. Several personality characteristics consistently have been associated with marital success (Bell, et al., 1987; Fowers & Olson, 1986; Lacey & Jennings, 1986; Rao & Rao, 1986; Schlesinger, 1984). They include the following:

Emotional maturity

Stability

Self-control

Ability to express affection

Responsibility

Loyalty

Ability to handle anger/conflict constructively

Considerateness

Kindness

Empathy

Conventionality

Honesty

Favorable self-concept

Optimism

Generosity

Flexibility

Unhappily married individuals are more apt to perceive their spouses as being impatient, unkind, blunt, aggressive, gloomy, complaining, slow to forgive, skeptical, and distrustful (Luckey, 1964). Many personality characteristics contribute to marital unhappiness. For example, extreme aggressiveness, dominance, passivity, independence, self-centeredness, feelings of superiority, or jealousy may threaten a marriage relationship. Secure individuals usually do not commit for long with the

What a Wife Wants*

What the wife wants and needs is to know by your repeated and never-failing assurances that you do enter into her thought; that you see and are not unmindful of the manner in which she strives to act well her part; that you are neither blind nor indifferent to all the nameless and assiduous attentions by which she seeks to smooth for you the way of earth and make you happy; and that the heart which you gave to her in the glad morning of your wedded life does not grow cold and careless with the passing years, but is warmer and truer still with every rolling sun.

* Written in 1872, this reflects the attitudes of the times. In 1991, husbands and wives still want these same things.
Source: Putnam, A. P. (1872). Husband, wife and child. *Monthly Religious Magazine*.

very insecure; the independent cannot long endure the very dependent (Blinder, 1985). A sense of competitiveness can also be destructive to a relationship. Some family life professionals believe that the increase in the divorce rate in recent years may have been influenced by the simultaneous increase in the number of competitive situations between spouses, e.g., jobs. Competitive situations and attitudes diminish the mutuality and unity, the shared efforts and goals that characterize successful marriages (Lazarus, 1985; Saunders & Suls, 1982).

Relationship Factors

There is evidence that marital happiness is the result of an interpersonal relationship between husband and wife in which positive psychological and emotional support are maximized. Intimacy, mutual respect, understanding, and expressions of appreciation and affection are important contributors to a good marital relationship and to happiness (Ammons & Stinnett, 1980; Stinnett & DeFrain, 1985),

Joel Gordon

as is a high degree of involvement in and commitment to the marriage by both partners. A better understanding of the types of behavior that positively affect the marriage relationship may be gained by examining the results of a study by Bell et al. (1987) who reported that a wife's marital satisfaction was related to her husband's ability to be honest and sincere, to be physically affectionate, and to act in a warm, caring, and empathic manner.

Marital-Role Expectations

We are more likely to enjoy the company of people whose expectations of us agree with our own. Friendships more often develop with such persons than with individuals whose expectations of us are in sharp contrast to our own. The same principle applies in marriage: marriage success is negatively affected by incompatibility in marital-role expectations (Blumstein & Schwartz, 1983; Fowers & Olson, 1986; Henslin, 1985; Lacey & Jennings, 1986). The more important the roles are to the individuals involved, the more important it is for the role expectations to be compatible. *Agreement* on roles appears to be more critical to marital harmony than the choice of traditional or nontraditional roles (Bokemeier & Maurer, 1987; Bowen & Orthner, 1983).

The relation between marital-role incongruence and marital adjustment is a function of the magnitude of expectation disagreement and the direction of that disagreement. The greater the discrepancy in role expectations, the greater the likelihood of conflict. When there is marital-role disagreement, the more egalitarian the orientation of the man relative to the woman, the better the marital adjustment of both (Li & Caldwell, 1987). For example, if Ward and June Cleaver, (traditional parents of the "Beaver") and Heathcliff and Clair Huxtable (egalitarian parents of the "Cosby" show) switched partners, Cliff and June would likely have fewer problems than Ward and Clair.

Communication

According to researchers, the communication patterns of happily married couples differ from those of unhappily married couples in many ways (Alberts, 1988; Bell, et al., 1987; Fowers & Olson, 1986; Jorgensen & Gaudy, 1980; Lacey & Jennings, 1986; Stinnett & DeFrain, 1985; Stinnett & DeFrain, 1989).

- They talk to each other more often.
- They more often convey the feeling that they understand what is being said to them.
- They demonstrate more sensitivity to each other's feelings.
- They keep communication channels open more effectively.
- They make greater use of nonverbal techniques of communication.

Relationships with In-Laws

One of the first critical adjustments that a newly married couple makes is the realignment of relationships with their extended families. Each must relinquish his or her primary relationship with parents so that the new spouse may be primary. The new couple is more likely to experience marital satisfaction if they can develop a network of relationships with their in-laws that is satisfying and balanced (Bader & Sinclair, 1983; Lingren et al., 1982).

Children

It is difficult to describe the effect of children on marital satisfaction, because the relation between children and satisfaction is complex. In a study of 129 Canadian couples married more than 15 years, both husbands and wives listed children as a ma-

Most Would Remarry Spouse

Only 7 percent of married women surveyed by *Ladies Home Journal* say they wouldn't marry their mate again.

[In] the poll of 608 women...88 percent [said they] would wed the same man again. The rest were undecided.

Their husband's sense of humour was cited as the reason for falling in love by 49 percent of women surveyed while 39 percent said they decided to marry him because "he shared my vision of the future."

The most common reason given for opposing the idea of remarrying the same man was that the couple had nothing in common.... This complaint was most often heard from readers ages 45 to 59.

Other problems cited as interfering with marital bliss included communication problems, a lack of emotional responsiveness and opposition to a spouse's independence.... The last complaint was most often made by women younger than 30.

A particular protest of Midwestern women who said they would not remarry their husbands was, "he's boring."

The Roper organization conducted the poll for the magazine with telephone and street interviews. The margin of error is 3 percentage points. More details are available in the June, 1988, issue of *Ladies Home Journal*.

Source: Most would remarry spouse, poll shows. (May 11, 1988). *The Tuscaloosa News*, p. 82.

jor source of satisfaction *and* as a major source of dissatisfaction (Schlesinger, 1984).

Such ambiguity is also found in a review of other research studies. When compared to childless couples, couples becoming parents reported decreased marital satisfaction and increased marital conflict (Cowan et al., 1985). When the data from several national surveys were reviewed, children were found to affect marital quality adversely (Glenn & McLanahan, 1982). Marital satisfaction has been observed to be high in the early years of marriage, to decrease slightly at the arrival of children (reaching a low point with adolescent children), and to return to a high level after children are launched

(Lasswell, 1986; Olson, 1986). (This pattern of marital satisfaction is illustrated in Figure 4–1.)

It also appears that number of children is inversely related to marital satisfaction (Bahr & Bahr, 1981). Couples with three children reported lower marital satisfaction than did couples with one child (Rowe & Meredith, 1982).

On the other hand, 43% of a sample of 30,000 parents reported feeling closer to their spouses *after* they had children (Greer, 1986). Other research indicates only a very small decline in marital happiness over the transition to parenthood (Belsky & Crouter, 1985; Power & Parke, 1984). And the presence and number of children are related to marital

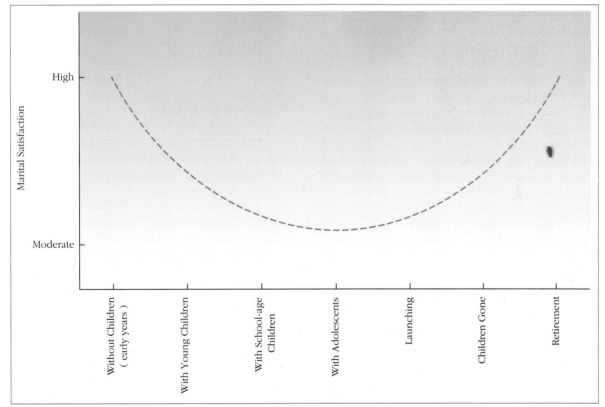

Figure 4–1 One pattern of marital satisfaction over the life span. *Source:* Adapted from Gullotta, T. P., Adams, G. R., & Alexander, S. J. (1986). *Today's marriages and families.* Monterey, CA: Brooks/Cole.

stability; couples with several children are less likely to divorce (Waite et al., 1985; White & Booth, 1985).

Other researchers believe that the effect of the birth of a child on marital satisfaction depends on the couple's adjustment prior to the birth. Happiness in marriage helps to accentuate the positive changes associated with parenting (Harriman, 1986).

Several explanations help us to understand the relation of children to marital stability and happiness. The arrival of children often brings pressures on the family: financial strain, physical demands, and relationship patterns that become more complex as more people are involved (Lasswell, 1986). For many couples, the negative changes are not compensated by the psychological satisfactions of parenting. Both individual and marital satisfaction decline. Marriages already experiencing decline for other reasons are probably more seriously affected. Increased numbers of children multiply the strain but also create more bonds between the couple.

Some couples who do not attain a high level of satisfaction stay together because of their children (see Table 4–2). Children may be one of the few sources of joy within the family, and neither spouse may be willing to lose the children through divorce. The parent-child relationship compensates for a less-than-satisfactory marriage. Also, many divorces occur in the early years of marriage before children have been born (Lasswell, 1986).

Income

Marriage stabililty is positively related to higher levels of income and to income stability. Lack of assets, income reductions, and unemployment are related to marital unhappiness (Blumstein & Schwartz, 1983; Price-Bonham & Balswick, 1980; Rao & Rao, 1986; Rowe et al., 1985). When a couple has inadequate financial resources to meet their needs, a situation conducive to conflict and hostility is created. Yet, many happy, successful marriages ex-

Table 4–2 Reasons for Having Remained Married*

Reason	Percent
Love	27
Children/family	17
Companionship	15
Commitment	14
Compatibility	12
Attributes of spouse	11
Financial security	4

* These results are from a sample of 100 couples married more than 25 years.

Source: Rowe, G. P., & Meridith, W. H. (1982). Quality in marital relationships after twenty-five years. *Family Perspective, 16,* 149–155.

ist in low-income groups. The couple's perception of satisfaction with income is more critical than absolute income levels (Leigh et al., 1985).

Based on the number of couples who cite money as a problem area, we might conclude that *financial management* is as important as income levels (Blumstein & Schwartz, 1983; Schlesinger, 1984). Disagreements arise over how money is to be spent (or not spent) even in marriages with stable, adequate incomes. (See Chapter 13 for more information about financial management.)

Occupation

In several early studies, a high proportion of stable marriages was found among professional and technical workers, managers, officials, and proprietors; a high proportion of unstable marriages was found among laborers and service workers (Cutright, 1971). Just as a satisfactory, secure income has a positive influence on marital happiness, so does high occupational prestige (Rao & Rao, 1986).

The degree of involvement in occupation also affects marriage happiness. The marriage relationship is apt to suffer when one spouse is very extensively focused on career, because time, energy, and attention are diverted from the family to the workplace. The situation is compounded when both spouses are work centered (Blumstein & Schwartz, 1983; Jorgensen, 1986). The wife of a business executive stated:

> *I feel like he is married to his job rather than to me. He spends 14 hours a day with his work. When we are together and supposed to be relaxing—even on vacation—work is what he talks about. I often feel very alone, even when he's with me.*

Employment Pattern

Traditionally wives cared for home and children, while husbands worked to earn money for the family's support. Today that pattern has changed to include several variations—the most prevalent being that many wives and mothers are employed outside the home on a part-time or full-time basis. About 52% of U.S. married couples are dual earners (Sanoff, 1988). Because research findings seem confusing and contradictory, the effect of a wife's employment on marital adjustment is difficult to evaluate and summarize. After an extensive review of research studies involving over 4,600 comparisons of marriages with employed and nonemployed wives, however, Smith (1985) concluded that the wife's "employment or nonemployment has little, if any, effect on marital adjustment" (p. 488).

Although the wife's employment alone may not have much influence on marital happiness, other factors associated with her employment do seem to affect the marriage relationship. A woman's employment has several consequences for her: increased financial power, increased equality between self and spouse, enhanced self-esteem, heightened feelings of well-being, conflict between career and wife/mother roles, less time for self, and physical and emotional overload (Berg, 1986; Hibbard & Pope, 1985; Lasswell, 1986; White et al., 1986). A wife's employment also has ramifications for her husband: the financial benefit of two paychecks, less pressure to be his wife's main source of self-esteem and self-definition, increased demands to help with child rearing and household chores, threatened perception of his role as provider, restricted career mobility, and reduced emotional support by wife (Bird et al., 1984; Rubin, 1983; Sharda & Nangle, 1981; Staines et al., 1986).

The manner in which all of these factors interact is complex and varies from couple to couple. A wife's feelings of personal achievement and satisfaction, as a result of employment, may carry over into the marriage relationship with positive results. It is also true that for some women the responsibilities of job, home, and children are too great a burden. Employed mothers with young children are especially vulnerable to being overwhelmed by demands on their time and energies (Berg, 1986; Schumm & Bugaighis, 1986). In spite of some changes, husbands of employed wives still do not assume a significantly greater share of household chores (Haas, 1982; Rachlin, 1987). As a result, many employed wives return home from salaried jobs and begin their "second jobs" of cooking, cleaning, laundry, and child care.

Men whose mothers were employed outside the home or whose wives have worked from the beginning of the marriage seem more tolerant of their wives' employment, possibly because they view it as normative (Knox, 1988). Husbands with egalitarian attitudes more easily assume household and child-rearing chores and accept their wives' financial contributions without suffering damage to self-esteem.

The effect of a wife's employment on the marital relationship depends on the circumstances of her employment, the attitudes of the couple, and their perceptions of whether the benefits of her employment outweigh the costs. The wife who pursues a career she loves with the encouragement and support of her husband is likely to experience personal and marital benefits. And so is her husband. The wife who works because of financial necessity, perhaps in a poor-paying or menial job, and whose husband feels threatened or inadequate as a result of her working is apt to suffer personal and marital discontent. If the husband leaves housekeeping and child care duties to her as well, the discontentment will be multiplied.

Religious Participation

Participation in religious activities and marriage success are related. Couples with a strong religious orientation, who attend services frequently and support their church or synagogue financially, have fewer divorces and score higher on marriage adjustment scales than nonreligious couples. The relation between religiosity and marriage success

The Smith/Appelson Wedding

When we decided to marry we knew that we wanted to develop a wedding ceremony that would respect our families' Jewish and Christian traditions and represent our own values and beliefs. Although traditional religion was no longer a daily or central part of either of our lives, it was important to our families. We designed a ceremony that drew out aspects of Christianity and Judaism that overlapped and spoke to the values that were important to us: love, hope, justice, and peace.

The ceremony took place in the Rose Garden of the State Botanical Gardens. A minister and rabbi officiated together, with each offering traditional elements of each religion, such as prayers and homilies. However, the core of the ceremony was our commitment to a lifelong partnership that was based on love, hope for the future, and also on our common values: equality between the sexes, a lifestyle nonharmful to the environment, and a peaceful world. These were reflected in readings by our family members and close friends, our music, and the minister's homily.

We spent a great deal of time on the ceremony, about 6 or 7 months, and used that time to think and talk about our individual and family differences and how to resolve them. We were very fortunate to be working closely with interested and encouraging religious officials. The minister, who was a longtime friend, saw our wedding as an opportunity to break down religious barriers and to emphasize partnerships and peace. The rabbi believed that the inclusion of Judaism in the ceremony was essential, even if our representation was not sanctioned by traditional Judaic laws. (Most rabbis refuse to marry Jewish-Christian couples unless the non-Jew agrees to convert and agrees that children will be raised as Jewish, neither of which was true for us. We located the rabbi through other interfaith couples.) Both the minister and rabbi encouraged us to use the ceremony to blend tradition and our own experiences and beliefs.

We did not resolve before we married some important family life issues that may prevent many Jewish-Christian couples from marrying. The faith of our children and the celebration of religious holidays with family members remain issues that we continue to address. Nevertheless, we are happy that we began the way we did, respecting individual differences and reaching for common meaning.

Source: Suzanna Smith and Gary Appelson.

Quality of Life

[W]hile I was working there (in the slums of London during the depression of 1930) I was simply overwhelmed by the trouble in which these people were, and after a time I began to ask some very profound questions. I watched...closely and followed up these people and I noticed something very interesting. The people who were able to cope were, for the most part, people who had come from loving, caring families, or who had for themselves established loving, caring families. The people who just folded up and collapsed and couldn't cope were very often people whose family life hadn't been very happy. So I came to the conclusion that the quality of life in any community cannot be raised to a higher level than the level of the relationships in the families that make up the community. Then, of course, I had to go one step farther and recognize that the quality of life and relationships in any family more than anything else depends on the quality of the loving, caring relationship between the two people who established the family.

Source: We open up our marriage: An interview with David and Vera Mace. (1984). *Wellness Perspectives, 1,* 21–29.

has been consistently found in numerous studies during the last 40 years (Brodbar-Nemzer, 1986; Fowers & Olson, 1986; Landis, 1960; Landis, 1975; Wilson & Filsinger, 1986).

Persons in marriages in which one or both spouses profess no religious beliefs, in general, express a lower degree of marital happiness than couples who have a religious orientation, regardless of whether their marriage is homogamous or heterogamous with respect to religion. And although marriages involving persons of different religious faiths have become more common in recent years, they are more likely to end in divorce than religiously homogamous marriages (Glenn, 1982).

Various reasons for the link between religious belief and marriage success have been suggested. Perhaps the primary reason is that the principal teachings of the major religions emphasize values that contribute to success in relationships in general. Abiding love, commitment, respect, mutual support and aid, patience, forgiveness, service, and fidelity are stressed.

Membership in a church or synagogue also aids in integrating the family into the larger community. The family gains social support, friends who value marriage and family, and assistance in times of crises. All of these help to give stability to the marriage.

Marriage Enrichment

Historically, marriage served primarily functional purposes: production of food and clothing, protection, rearing of children, care of older or infirm family members. A husband and wife who enjoyed each other and "loved" each other (and many did, of course) simply had a bonus. As many of those duties and services performed by families have come to be performed by other institutions in society, e.g., schools and hospitals, the functions of marriage have changed to the affectional realm. Companionship and emotional support are its primary purposes.

As the expectations of what a marriage should be shifted, couples who were dissatisfied either divorced or sought help. In the 1930s the fledgling field of marriage counseling was established in the United States. World War II had a devastating effect on many families; as a result, the services of marriage counselors were increasingly sought.

By the early 1960s many marriage and family counselors and educators had become alarmed by the rising rates of divorce, marital discontentment, and family violence. A few began to look for ways to prevent this marital discord. In 1962 David and Vera Mace began weekend programs for married couples. In 1964 Leon and Antoinette Smith joined the Maces in developing marriage enrichment weekends. Unknown to them, Father Gabrael Calvo had begun similar weekend retreats for couples in 1962. Father Calvo's efforts grew to become the Marriage Encounter movement. The marriage enrichment workshops designed by the Maces and the Smiths have been used by many groups (Mace, 1983).

The basic idea behind marriage enrichment is that a married couple can be active in the growth of their marriage relationship. Marriage enrichment differs from marital therapy/counseling because it emphasizes prevention of problems and promotion of growth. Couples experiencing serious difficulties require the assistance of a therapist and are encouraged not to attend marriage enrichment as a form of do-it-yourself therapy. Most family therapists and educators agree that a couple can be active in creating a marital relationship that is close, enduring, and satisfying. What are some ways of accomplishing this goal? Clinical and empirical research as well as years of observation of human behavior yield some answers.

Appreciation

Scores of modern psychologists, family therapists, and family educators agree that the need to be appreciated is one of our deepest needs. As humans, we require frequent reassurance that we are valued and regarded favorably. Without that reassurance, we feel unimportant and resentful. As one wife stated:

> *If my husband would just see my good points…if he would recognize the worthwhile things I do and let me know he is aware of what I do, it would make me feel so much better. As it is, he just criticizes and complains.*

Statements of appreciation serve to nurture relationships. Fortunately, making our admiration and approval of someone known is not difficult. A little practice is all most people need to develop the skills of perceiving laudable qualities (or accomplishments) and expressing that regard.

Commitment

Commitment is a vital ingredient for creating an emotionally meaningful, gratifying interpersonal relationship whether within or outside the family (Lindsey, 1981). When someone is consciously dedicated to the well-being of another, a powerful bond is formed, trust develops, and the dedication usually is reciprocated. Mace (1983) calls this "the internal cohesion" that sustains a relationship. In this way, commitment contributes to healthy relationships; it indicates a willingness and a promise to love. One husband reported:

> *The greatest thing about our marriage is Ruthie's devotion to me. What a feeling of security to know she is 100% for me. I can always count on her. If I'm in trouble or need help, she is going to be there at my side to help—regardless of whether I am right or wrong.*

Effort and Determination

The difference between a marital relationship that withers and one that flourishes often is determination and effort. As part of a larger study of strong families, the marriage relationship patterns of a group of couples with especially good (vital or total) marriages were examined. (See Chapter 3 for a review of vital and total marriage relationships.) These couples reported having an intense desire to build an especially good marriage and having the determination to strive for that goal (Ammons & Stinnett, 1980; Olds, 1980). Two wives who were interviewed by Olds (1980) made these comments:

Roger and I are both stubborn. We have built something over the past 19 years and we want to hang on to it. We don't believe in a throwaway society.

When a man and a woman marry, they establish something that has life in it. When they divorce, it's like putting to death a living thing. I can't see not fighting as hard for my marriage as I would fight to save my own life.

There are indications that communication, intimacy, companionship, commitment, and marital satisfaction among older couples grow through the years (Foster, 1982). Other research shows heightened commitment and companionship with length of marriage among couples married 35 to 49 years (Lingren et al., 1982).

Unconditional Positive Regard

Charles has recently been fired. In addition to the blow to his ego, he is tense about all the job interviews he is having. He is fearful about failure and finances. Depressed and irritable, Charles often snaps at his wife, Joann. Fortunately for both of them, Joann understands his fears and tension. She remains reassuring and optimistic about job prospects. She reminds Charles every day that he is very important to her and the children.

Joann's response to Charles demonstrates her unconditional positive regard; she loves and values him, as he is, not because of his job or accomplishments.

Joel Gordon

Such *noncontingent reinforcement* means that husband and wife demonstrate their esteem for each other regardless of the behavior of the spouse at the particular moment.

Often the times when we are at our worst (sick, tired, tense, scared) are the very times when we most need the support of those who love us. Knowing that being treasured does not depend on performance gives security and usually stirs a reciprocal response. Thus, the relationship is reinforced.

Development of Trust/Reduction of Threat

The trust level between a husband and wife is a key determinant of the success of their emotional and sexual relationships. When you trust someone, you feel comfortable and safe with that person; you are likely to share your feelings and dreams. When you do not trust someone, you feel self-conscious, insecure, and defensive (Patterson, 1985).

It is easy to say we should be more trusting, but there must be a reason for trusting. How can husbands and wives increase the level of trust in their relationship? Generally, trust is generated by trustworthy behavior (Millar & Millar, 1982). More specifically, we have a higher degree of trust in someone when our trust in that person has not been violated. Trustworthy behavior is honest, sincere, consistent, and dependable (Gass & Nichols, 1988; Seixas & Youcha, 1985).

Confidentiality must not be broken if trust is to develop. If you have had the experience of sharing a secret with someone and later learning the secret had been passed along, you understand the importance of guarding confidentiality.

Trustworthy behavior is further characterized by an absence of exploitation or manipulation (Seixas & Youcha, 1985). One person explained, "I trust my friend Brian because he isn't trying to impress me; he has no ax to grind, and he isn't trying to get something from me."

Most of us find it easier to trust persons who are interested in promoting our well-being; by their actions and attitudes, they indicate they are *for* us (Buller & Buller, 1987). Sometimes a husband and wife have threatened each other's self-esteem so badly that they are enmeshed in a vicious cycle of attack, defense, and attack. Because of the emphasis on retaliation, they focus on weaknesses and faults; they cannot feel good about themselves or their interaction.

Finally, persons we can trust tend to express acceptance of us; in doing so, they communicate their emotional support (Wheeless et al., 1988). One husband related:

> *For years my wife has been criticizing me for not being more successful in my work. She thinks I ought to be a manager at the car dealership instead of "just*

> *a salesman. She makes snide remarks in front of the kids and our friends.*
>
> *I guess this is the reason my involvement with Irene has become an affair. She makes me feel ten feet tall; she's always saying I'm the "best" salesman she's ever seen.*

Everyone has some characteristics he or she does not want presented to others. It is that part of ourselves we consider unattractive or unacceptable. Many marital problems are caused when husbands and wives exploit each other's limitations. In the preceding example, the wife communicated the following message:

> *You're afraid that you're not aggressive enough at work and that you are inadequate. This is true. You are a failure.*

Over a period of time, such messages about one's physical appearance, sexual response, occupational attainment, or social skills destroy a relationship. We are most attracted to individuals whose expressed evaluation of us is consistently positive; we are least attracted to those whose evaluation is negative (Tognoli & Keisner, 1972).

See Each Other as Persons

Several marriage and family therapists have observed that in the final analysis each person asks, "Who am I?" and hopes for favorable responses from others (Satir, 1967). We all seek to reinforce our positive feelings about ourselves. One challenge within the marriage relationship is to see beyond the outward appearance, beyond his or her anger, grief, or specific problem, and to see the *person*.

It is particularly necessary to discern more than the specific roles the partner plays. Husbands and wives sometimes become so accustomed to viewing each other in terms of functions, e.g., father, mother, lawyer, teacher, that they stop seeing and stop interacting with each other as persons. Instead, they interact superficially as players of roles, leaving

---

Togo

In Togo, in Africa, there is a legend that in the beginning of time God made a man and set him on earth and made a woman and set her on earth. The man and woman looked at each other—and burst out laughing. And then they went, hand in hand, to wander over the globe together.

Isn't that, after all, the way it should be? Laughing—*and* hand in hand.

Source: Chandler, S. (1985, June). Toward a perfect partnership. *50 Plus, 25,* 30.

each lonely and longing to be known more completely.

Spouses grow closer when their understanding of each other goes beyond the daily roles each assumes (Lazarus, 1985). Intimacy is enhanced when husband and wife respect each other as unique persons.

Accepting and Respecting Differences

Many people have a tendency to regard qualities, habits, and opinions of others that differ markedly from their own as inferior or wrong. This inclination causes frustration, resentment, and deterioration in a relationship.

Sandy grew up with two sisters and a brother. She and her sisters enjoyed ceramics, needlework, and painting; her brother and dad were avid fishermen—the kind who tied flies and made lures. Their home was always busy with their many projects; it was common to find pots of paint and brushes or yarn, scissors, and fabric on the kitchen table. Dad and brother usually had tackle spread out in the den.

Sandy's husband, Neal, was reared primarily by his father; Neal's mother died when he was a toddler. Neal's dad had a workshop in the garage; any projects such as painting, woodworking, or crafts were confined there. Dad's rule was that all work areas must be cleaned up every time they were used.

Sandy and Neal have encountered a problem with their differing views about keeping house. Sandy suspects Neal is compulsively neat; she resents his nagging at her to clean up her messes. On the other hand, Neal is distressed by the clutter left by his "slovenly" wife.

Both Sandy and Neal feel criticized and inferior. If they allow this pattern of interaction to continue and escalate, their negative feelings will increase. The challenge is to realize that differences are, after all, simply *differences*; they are not indicators of inferiority. Sandy is not less worthy because her attitude about clutter is casual, nor is Neal inferior because he prefers order. Sandy is not better because she is creative and relaxed, nor is Neal "right" because he is disciplined. They just disagree.

Concentrating on Our Own Responses

"It's your fault. If you hadn't nagged so much, I wouldn't have got drunk at the party."

"You drive me crazy when you start yelling like that."

"I'd stay home more if only you'd be pleasant once in a while."

We have all heard statements similar to these, and each may be more or less true. The point here,

Marital Satisfaction: The Experience of Black Couples

There are nearly 7 million black families in the United States (U.S. Bureau of the Census, 1986b). Black spouses tend to report lower levels of marital satisfaction than their white counterparts. Researchers believe this may be due to a number of factors:

Black women have a smaller pool of eligible men from which to choose a mate; consequently, their mate selection is disadvantaged (Ball & Robbins, 1986b). Black men have shorter life expectancies than their white counterparts and tend to have lower levels of education than black females. Both factors reduce the number of potential partners for black females.

The higher rates of unemployment and diminished earning capacity of black males result in chronic economic strain for many black families and in decreased satisfaction with family life (Ball & Robbins, 1986a; Schwartz, 1986).

Among black couples, both spouses are more likely to be employed than both white spouses; this is more often due to economic stresses (Knox, 1988; Landry & Jendrek, 1978).

Kinship ties have been a vital part of black family life. Many social scientists and historians regard the support of extended kin as responsible for the survival of black families in the United States. Although close ties with parents and other relatives is a valuable resource, kinship ties may sometimes take precedence over the husband-wife relationship. This seems especially true for mother-child relationships (Aschenbrenner & Carr, 1980; Knox, 1988).

Sources: 1. Aschenbrenner, J., & Carr, C. (1980). Conjugal relationships in the context of the black extended family. *Alternative Lifestyles, 3*(4), 463–484. 2. Ball, R., & Robbins, L. (1986a). Black husbands' satisfaction with their family life. *Journal of Marriage and the Family, 48,* 849–855. 3. Ball, R., & Robbins, L. (1986b). Marital status and life satisfaction among black Americans. *Journal of Marriage and the Family, 48,* 389–394. 4. Landry, B., & Jendrek, M. (1978). The employment of wives in middle-class black families. *Journal of Marriage and the Family, 40,* 787–797. 5. Knox, D. (1988). *Choices in relationships.* New York: West. 6. Schwartz, S. (1986). Earnings capacity and the trend in inequality among Black men. *Human Resources, 22,* 44–63. 7. U.S. Bureau of the Census. (1986b). *Statistical abstract of the United States, 1987,* (107th ed.). Washington, DC: U.S. Government Printing Office.

however, is that in each instance, one person is concentrating upon the behavior of a mate rather than upon his or her own responses. Each statement indicates that one partner believes that his or her responses *depend* upon the behavior of another.

Regardless of how desirable it would be for spouses to change, it is unrealistic for either to blame the other for *all* their problems. This is a destructive approach to human relationships because it focuses on the other person's inadequacies. It says in effect, "You are bad because. ..." Second, this

pattern of interaction is an evasion; "I would be good if you weren't so bad" relieves one partner of any responsibility for the condition of the relationship. Third, blaming the other person is futile. Typically, that person feels threatened and launches a counterattack.

An individual who concentrates upon the responses of a mate ignores the significant power of his or her own behavior on the relationship. When we ignore the influence we have upon a relationship, we may come to believe we have no control and may become reactors, simply responding to what others do or say (Millar & Millar, 1982).

The quality of any relationship depends upon the behavior of *both* persons. We cannot make someone respond in a certain way, but *we can control our own responses*. Logically, then, our own behavior is where we should focus our efforts.

Effective Management

Just as the individual can be more than a reactor in a relationship, the family unit can also be more than a reactor to the influences of society and life. One important lesson gleaned from the national study of strong families is that they take the initiative in managing their lives in ways that enhance their family relationships and satisfaction. Members of healthy families take the "offensive" to make life better for themselves.

Creative family management in all areas is necessary if the family is to achieve its goals and to run smoothly. Consider the logistics of one small part of family management—feeding the family. Menus must be planned; food must be purchased, perhaps in several stores—grocery, fruit stand, bakery; supplies must be stored; food must be prepared; kitchen and eating areas must be cleaned. Now consider that a budget must be taken into account when planning menus and purchasing food; work schedules must be considered for preparing and serving meals and for cleaning up. The situation is similarly complex in other areas of family life, e.g., finances, careers, hobbies, leisure and recreational activities, and household and yard chores.

Families have many resources to manage: human potential, money, time, and energy. The family that actively takes control of its destiny is more often the family that prospers (Cox, 1981).

Reshape the Marriage Environment

The term *marriage environment* refers to the immediate physical surroundings; the network of relationships one has with friends, relatives, and acquaintances; and habitual behavior patterns. The quality of the marital relationship can be either negatively or positively affected by the marriage environment. A couple having marital difficulties may analyze their situation and decide that certain aspects of their marriage environment are hurting their relationship. They may not have a comfortable, convenient place to sit and talk, for example. They can reshape the marriage environment in ways that minimize the negative elements and/or promote the positive aspects.

How much of an influence a home has on a marital relationship is not known. It is well established, however, that color, room size, and room arrangement affect the way we feel. The quality of communication within a home, for example, may be enhanced by the decor—intriguing pieces of art to stimulate conversation and the arrangement of furniture to create quiet, cozy places to talk (Galvin & Brommel, 1982). Many families use family pictures and memorabilia to decorate their homes to remind them of their commitment to each other and of good times they have shared (Stinnett & DeFrain, 1985).

Couples need to reexamine their physical environment periodically. Simple redecorating, e.g., fresh paint, houseplants, and moving the furniture, can provide a refreshing lift. Art pieces and accessories can be rearranged to renew their impact.

Reshaping Relationship Networks. The network of relationships a couple establishes with friends, relatives, and acquaintances has strong influences upon the marriage relationship. One husband related his story:

> *We were surprised when we came to our senses and realized that some of our friendships were really not enjoyable. There were three couples whom we saw on a regular basis for no reason other than because we had been doing it for years. We continued to go out with*

these couples, but we had grown in different ways and had little in common. One of the couples was cynical; they always put people and ideas and each other down. Another was very materialistic. After spending an evening with them we just didn't feel quite right. My wife and I had several discussions about this pattern of going out to have fun and coming home weary and depressed. We concluded that part of the problem was spending too much time with these three couples. The solution, we agreed, was to stop seeing them. And really there was no reason not to make a change. We phased out gradually, spending less time with them. Now we see each other once or twice a year. We can enjoy each other in small doses. We also established some new friendships, starting with a new couple who are members of our church. We have so much in common with them; we can laugh and talk for hours every time we're together. Plus we feel refreshed and optimistic afterwards.

Most couples will find it helpful, from time to time, to review their network of relationships with friends and relatives. These may need to be reordered so that the couple's associations are with people who encourage their growth as individuals, who help them to be optimistic, who are pleasant companions, who share attitudes/values about life, and who reinforce the couple's marriage.

Reshaping Habits. Consider the extent to which your life is dictated by habits—some good habits, some bad, and some that may not even be apparent, e.g., response patterns.

Again, couples occasionally need to analyze their daily routines and interpersonal response patterns for habits that may be detrimental to their marital relationship. Although changing usually is difficult, the results can be very worthwhile, as one young couple shared:

Joel Gordon

We began having some trouble a few months ago; it seemed like every day got off to a bad start. So we took a long, hard look at what was happening and discovered we had fallen into a morning routine that was the source of trouble. We had been getting up just early enough to make it to work—if we hurried and if everything went well. Naturally everything usually didn't go well; we'd have a phone call, need to iron a blouse or shirt, misplace the car keys, or get caught in heavy traffic. We'd make it to work just barely on time—maybe a minute or two late—and frazzled. More often than not we'd have an argument at home over something trivial just because we were rushing around.

Now we set the alarm clock a half hour earlier and lay out our clothes the night before. It wasn't easy giving up that little extra nap, but now we are less hurried; we have time for coffee together; we aren't late to work. The mornings are pleasant again.

Response patterns require scrutiny, too. If one spouse typically reacts to constructive criticism with sarcasm, to disagreement by becoming angry, or to gentle reminders with hostility, the response habit needs reshaping. (Chapters 6 and 8 will offer more detailed suggestions on how to do this.)

Providing Happy Experiences

Living should be a positive experience. We should feel good about ourselves and the part we play in that portion of the world we influence. Each of us has alternatives for bringing more pleasure into our daily lives. In spite of this, many couples allow their marriages to slip into a rut. Psychotherapist Herbert Otto (1969) believes we fail to realize that we can be active in improving life because we regard happy experiences as the result of luck.

One way of creating a happy life is to seek and welcome new experiences. When daily patterns become old and dull to couples, it is easy for them to feel old and dull and to feel that their marriage is old and dull, too. New experiences can help maintain excitement, adventure, and youthfulness. Try

---

Expressions of Love

Recall a time when someone demonstrated love to you.

"When I was about 3 years old, I had a teddy bear that went everywhere with me. We had been to visit relations and I left it behind. I didn't miss teddy until we had driven almost 3 hours. Dad turned around and went back for the bear."

* * *

"Last month was very hectic at work. I took work home every day and everything at home had to slide. I went home last Friday dreading a weekend of digging out my dirty house. I almost fainted when I walked in. The house was all cleaned up! My husband had hired a cleaning lady.

* * *

"We moved from Texas when I was a junior in high school. I missed all of my friends; I was miserable. Mom and Dad flew me back for homecoming. I know they couldn't really afford it!"

* * *

"My grandmother made a quilt for each of her grandchildren."

Source: Authors' files from class discussions at the University of Alabama.

shopping in a different community that is nearby, take a short vacation that involves doing something you have never done before, go on a picnic with a dozen acquaintances you would like to know better.

Satisfaction in marriage also is enhanced through more spontaneous interaction between husbands and wives. Spontaneous interplay involves a sharing of personal thoughts and ideas in which the inner self of one person reaches out to the inner self of another. The interaction is free of calculation, routine, and formality; it is a critical part of intimacy (Wynne & Wynne, 1986).

One factor that prevents couples from being more natural is that they become victims of habit in interpersonal interactions and daily routines. When this happens, behavior resists modification because it feels comfortable to stay the same even though life may be boring.

Another element that minimizes impromptu behavior is the work-ethic tendency to postpone pleasure in the present for possible gains in the future. This sometimes is necessary. A sports car buff may drive a used Honda in order to have money for college, or a couple who enjoys travel may forego several short trips to afford a month in Europe. In too many instances, however, we postpone joyful experiences without any real reason except that we have fallen into a habit of "putting off."

Husbands and wives can express love and appreciation for one another by providing pleasurable experiences for each other. This approach is simple but should not be underestimated. Some specific suggestions include the following:

- Participate in activities that bring happiness on a regular basis. Modern life is hectic and filled with demands of work, housekeeping, and child care. Unless a couple structures their schedules to allow time for special hobbies or recreation, it is not likely to happen.

- Assume the responsibility for creating a specific joyful event for a spouse. Plan and make all the arrangements for an outing, a party, or a special evening at home.

One wife whose husband enjoys surprises and ghost stories discovered that their community theater was performing "The Canterville Ghost." She made reservations and told him to keep that date open because she had a surprise planned. He enjoyed a week of wondering what the surprise could be. On the day of the performance, she told him he needed to dress to go out for dinner. Off they went to his favorite Mexican restaurant and then to the theater. He savored the suspense and was delighted when they arrived at the theater.

Some persons like to create a special day for a spouse on a regular basis. Once a month, for example, one day is designated as unique. The spouse who plans the day thinks of little surprises to add fun and excitement. Whatever especially pleases the recipient spouse is appropriate: breakfast in bed, a new cassette tape for the car, flowers delivered at work, popcorn and romantic movies on the VCR.

- Exchange love gifts. A love gift is anything one person does that gives another happiness; love gifts require more energy and thoughtfulness than money.

Many years ago I was a married graduate student at the University of Iowa. Although we had very little money, we never thought of ourselves as poor. It was impossible, however, for us to exchange the kinds of gifts that we would have liked to have given, so we began exchanging "love gifts."

I remember one Christmas my wife gave me a box of pancake flour with a note that promised she would make pancakes—a task she really disliked—for me each Sunday for a year. It was another way of saying, "I love you." My gifts included pledges to do various household tasks she disliked. With the passing of years, we continued the "love gifts" at Christmas even when our finances improved. When our children were very small, they would give a love gift that involved bringing in the milk or newspaper each morning. When my son reached the age that he loved monster movies, my love gift to him one year was to take him to all the monster movies that year.

Our love gifts are not limited to members of our family. When my son was in preschool, his gift to his godmother was to collect pinestraw and tie it in small bundles she could use to start fires in the fireplace.

As the years have passed, the love gifts have meant a great deal to the members of my family. Because they frequently involve pledges for an entire year, they remind us of our love for each other throughout the year.

Cohabitation and Marriage Success

Cohabitation is now defined for census purposes as two unrelated adults of the opposite sex living in the same quarters in which there is no other adult present (Rice, 1990). Cohabitation has increased during the last several years. There are now about 2 million cohabiting couples in the United States, representing a 47% increase since 1980 (U.S. Bureau of the Census, 1989b). Studies indicate that about 25% of college students live with a partner at some point in their college experience (Rice, 1990).

The increase in cohabitation has been influenced by major changes in our society during the last 30 years. Some of those environmental trends include:

1. The sexual revolution and the increased acceptance of premarital sexual behavior
2. The increased availability and effectiveness of contraceptives
3. The increased divorce rate and a growing number of previously married persons who cohabit for a period of time before remarriage

4. The increased tendency of young people to delay marriage to continue their education or to begin a career
5. Changes in college dormitory policies concerning curfews, coed dormitories, and off-campus living regulations; greater flexibility in student living patterns
6. Disenchantment with traditional courtship and a view of dating as superficial
7. The increased popularity of the idea that living together is an effective way to test a relationship

There is no evidence that persons who cohabit are rejecting marriage or that they are choosing singlehood as a permanent way of life. In fact, a significantly larger proportion of cohabiters than noncohabiters report that they want to get married (Tanfer, 1987). Some differences, however, do exist between individuals who cohabit and those who do not.

Cohabiters in comparison with persons who do not cohabit tend to:

1. Be less educated.
2. Be unemployed more often.
3. Be concentrated in metropolitan areas.
4. Have lower rates of church attendance and religious affiliation.
5. Have had sexual intercourse at a younger age.
6. Use contraceptives less frequently.
7. Be more unconventional (Tanfer, 1987).
8. Be much more prone to violence.
9. Be more self-disclosing (Tanfer, 1987; Yllo and Straus, 1981).

A frequently mentioned benefit of cohabitation is that it prepares a couple for marriage by allowing them to test their compatibility while actually living together. There is no evidence, however, to support this idea (Macklin, 1983). A number of studies have yielded conflicting reports, while others have shown no differences in the marriage satisfaction of couples who have cohabited and those who have not.

In a large study of 17,024 couples, Stewart and Olson ("Cohabitating Couples," 1988) found that cohabiting couples had significantly lower premarital satisfaction compared to non-cohabiting couples. Almost two-thirds of the cohabiting couples were in the low satisfaction group, while approximately two-thirds of the non-cohabiting couples fell into the very satisfied group.

One of the most comprehensive studies of cohabitation and marriage success was conducted by Booth and Johnson (1988) who obtained a national random sample of 2,033 married persons. Among those persons, 16% reported that they had cohabited with their spouse before marriage. Those persons who had cohabited with their spouse before marriage were compared with those individuals who had not cohabited on various aspects of their marriage relationships.

Booth and Johnson (1988) found that cohabitation is related to lower levels of marital interaction, higher levels of marital disagreement, and higher levels of marital instability. The probability of divorce or permanent separation by the former cohabitants was almost twice as high as it was for those persons who had not cohabited.

Booth and Johnson (1988) concluded that cohabitation does not improve mate selection or serve as good preparation for marriage. They identified the following factors as explanations for their conclusions:

1. Commitment to marriage was less among cohabiting persons.

2. Those who had cohabited reported having more doubts about the wisdom of getting married prior to their wedding.

3. Those who had cohabited indicated a greater degree of parental disapproval of the relationship from the beginning.

4. Cohabiting individuals are more likely to be poor marriage candidates because of the incidence of alcohol or drug abuse, poor money management skills, inability to hold a job, trouble with the law, and personality problems.

Summary

- Although marriage success is difficult to define, researchers have found that certain factors greatly influence a couple's chances for marital stability. These factors include: positive personality characteristics, e.g., kindness, empathy, honesty; a high degree of involvement in and commitment to the relationship; agreement on role expectations, in-law relationships, and the rearing of children; open communication; positive employment experience, e.g., income stability, occupational prestige, support of family; and religious participation.

- A married couple can actively strengthen their relationship by marriage enrichment, which emphasizes promotion of growth and prevention of problems.

- Developing a strong marital relationship requires both partners to demonstrate appreciation, commitment, trust, and unconditional positive regard for one another. A determination to succeed is also a key factor.

- A couple's ability to see the *person* beyond the role and to accept and respect each other's differences influences marital success. It is also important for each partner to examine his or her own behavior rather than to analyze a spouse in an attempt to lay blame.

- Relationships can be enhanced through active and creative family management of time, money, and energy.

- Outside influences must also be examined for their effect on the marital relationship. Our physical environment and our relationships with others may need to be restructured periodically as a way of revitalizing the marriage.

- The marital relationship is also enhanced when daily routine is altered, when couples interact spontaneously, and when new experiences and ways of expressing love are found.

- Several social trends including the sexual revolution, greater flexibility in college students' living arrangements, and readily available contraception have influenced an increase in the number of couples who cohabit. Cohabitation is more often an alternative form of courtship rather than a rejection of marriage. No evidence supports the popular idea that cohabitation improves marital success.

Discussion Questions

1. What is your personal definition of a successful marriage?

2. Select the two premarital factors that you think are most important to marriage success. Defend your choices.

3. Which three postmarital factors related to marriage success do you think are most important? Justify your selections.

4. David and Vera Mace state that it is essential to recognize that a marriage is dynamic—not static. People within a marriage change and grow over time. Can couples do anything to ensure that they will grow in mutually beneficial ways? What are some suggestions?

5. Consider the following statement: "Many stable marriages are not successful, and some marriages that are successful for a number of years eventually end in divorce." How would you respond to that statement?

6. Think about a happily married couple that you know well. What factors seem to account for the success of their marriage?

7. What family strengths are particularly important in serving to increase the probabilities of a satisfying marriage?

8. Which of your habits stand in the way of developing a great marriage?

9. How would you respond if you discovered the person you wished to marry simply did not trust you?

10. How will you balance the need for togetherness with the need for privacy in your family?

CHAPTER 5

CHANGING ROLES OF
WOMEN AND MEN

❧

What can we learn from the anthropological perspective on the male experience? One striking feature that should be apparent is that the male role in Western society in the latter part of the twentieth century is unique to our own society and its history. Other non-Western societies define the male experience in quite different ways. . . . In our contemporary society . . . it is ridiculous to hang onto the view that the male role must emphasize certain biological features that have little meaning other than to keep the sexes separate. The anthropological perspective presents us with the valuable insight that the contemporary Western male role is not universal and that change is an inevitable part of cultural features.

(Doyle, 1983, p. 86)

❧

Roles of Men and Women in Colonial America

The belief that women in America have always been subordinate to men is a myth. In an account of the American family in the past, Demos (1977) unravels the events that led to changes in the roles of women and men after the days of life in the colonies. In colonial America the partnership of women and men as reflected in the work and experiences that they shared was too strong to permit the gender stereotyping of behavior that was to follow later in this nation's history. In the eighteenth century women were very much a part of the business community, and occasionally they worked in professional careers as well. Accounts of colonial America give little reason to believe, as Demos has noted, that there was a pervasive system of deference based on sex.

An important reason for this state of affairs was functional necessity: women not only worked in the home but also engaged in field work on occasion. Women were highly valued during this era, a condition that may have been influenced by the fact that there were three men to every two women during a large portion of the colonial period. By 1750 as many as one-third of all women in some colonial communities were pregnant at the time of their marriage, a condition that hardly fits our beliefs concerning the sexual conservatism of our nation's founding mothers, and one that is remarkably similar to circumstances today.

What most of us believe to be characteristic of women's roles in early America—that women were dependent creatures who were subordinate to their husbands—did not occur until about 1890 to 1910. Social historians regard the growth of industrialization as the factor responsible for many changes in the roles of men and women. With the rise of the factory system came the physical, economic, and social separation of the home and the workplace. In the early years many women and children worked in the factories too. Gradually, as men were able to earn a wage sufficient to support their entire families, their wives and children no longer worked in the factories. In time, more and more women were relegated to the home sphere (Gerson, 1988).

At about the same time, a set of beliefs about the nature of womanhood became popular. Gordon wrote in the February 1891 issue of *Lippincott's Monthly Magazine:* "The image of an ideal woman that men had was of a beautiful creature whom they could possess but who would not possess or control them." This view was, in part, encouraged by powerful groups who endeavored to attribute deeper meaning to the family by honoring women who chose "traditional" roles of mother and wife. These are indeed honorable roles—as are the roles of father and husband—but they preclude neither education nor participation in the labor force. Ironically, this so-called reverence for womanhood led to declines in women's status. Gradually, the role of the "True Woman" became even more restricted because women were not to live for themselves but for their husbands and their children.

In time men learned to be reserved in their interaction with women—even with their wives; they became inexpressive and played a role rather than responding as they really felt. Women, too, learned to play a role. Unfortunately, neither of the roles fitted all men or all women, and this, in part, was the beginning of the conflict we still see today.

During this period women were expected to be keepers of the family and as such to be passionless and virginal. Lower-class women were lured into prostitution to serve the strong, sexual men of the era. It is likely that many wives were sexually unresponsive (or thought they should be) because the sex-is-sin myth had support from the major institutions of society (Demos, 1977).

British Marriages: 1600 to 1800

There has never been a time in recorded history when the relations between the sexes have not been highly problematic. Historians once assumed that the past was both static and uniform. Now we know better, for each new study of families and marriages seems to push back the time when variety and change were endemic features of British society. While historical demographers have identified certain features—high age at marriage, considerable remarriage, unusually high levels of celibacy—as characteristic of much of northwestern Europe in the sixteenth and seventeenth centuries, they would be the first to admit great variations both over time and between social groups. We know that the behavior of the British nobility was very different from that of any other class, with eldest sons marrying much earlier than either their noninheriting siblings or the rest of the population. The aristocracy also continued to give pride of place to kin and lineage, but treated marriage with supreme contempt. In sixteenth-century Lancashire, many lived in open adultery. They were shamed neither by their concubines nor by their bastards. When they did marry, they did so for convenience rather than affection, a principal reason why their wedlock was so frequently terminated by annulments. Lower down the social scale variety was no less evident.

By 1600 at least one-third of the population no longer had access to land or craft. Many among this burgeoning mass of migrant wage workers, squatters, expropriated peasants, and failed tradespeople were no longer subject to either church law or village custom. It was said in the mid-seventeenth century that "vagabonds be generally given to horrible uncleanness, they have not particular wives, neither do they range themselves into families, but consort together as beasts."

Marriage was a highly privileged status. At least one-tenth of the population never married, and the rates of mortality were such that the marrieds made up no more than about 30% of the population at any given time. In the early sixteenth century, all single persons in the Coventry, regardless of rank and age, were referred to as "lads" or "maids" and expected to show proper deference to the married "masters" and "dames" who were simultaneously their guardians, employers, and governors. A century later the same distinctions were still evident.

There are many societies, including our own, in which marriages are often made very informally. In the sixteenth and seventeenth centuries the very poor often established their conjugality by erecting a cabin or sleeping in the same bed. But this kind of informality was still exceptional. From the patricians down to the smallholders, three highly ritualized and successively more demanding steps constituted a proper marriage. The first was the consent of the parties, publicly announced or at least symbolized by the exchange of rings or love tokens. This was followed, where required, by the public blessing by family and close kin. And finally there was the big church wedding, preceded by banns, at which the "politics" of peers and community was played out.

Source: Adapted from Gillis, J. R. (1985). *For better, for worse: British marriage 1600 to the present.* New York: Oxford University Press. Reprinted by permission.

Why Are Gender Roles Changing?

Masculine and feminine roles have been rather rigidly defined in the more recent past. Men have been associated with such qualities as achievement, independence, physical strength, aggressiveness, competitiveness, and sexual prowess. Women have been matched with nurturance, supportiveness, understanding, passivity, dependency, and lack of competitiveness (Houseknecht, 1985). Such gender-related stereotyping begins in the early years of life (Huston & Ashmore, 1985; Pearson, 1989).

Rigidly defined gender roles have had the disadvantage of limiting males and females in achieving their complete human potential. They have been a major barrier to understanding because they force men and women to interact in terms of masculine-feminine stereotypes rather than as persons. Touching is one way to communicate, expressing a range of emotions from the hostile punch to the loving stroke. This mode of communication reveals sex differences: Men are more likely to touch others; women are more likely to be touched (Deaux, 1976).

The differences in gender roles have been due far more to cultural values and socialization processes than to biological factors. Some women are motivated to avoid success because they expect negative consequences such as feelings of being "unfeminine" or a fear of being socially rejected by men (Deaux, 1976). Several cultural changes now taking place are contributing to greater flexibility and overlapping of gender roles. Women who feel free in their lives to be both masculine and feminine, and men who are free to be both feminine and masculine, are probably happier. Fasteau (1974) has written:

> Both assertive and yielding, independent and dependent, job and people oriented, strong and gentle... the most effective and happy individuals are likely to be those who have accepted and developed both these "sides" of themselves.... Consider ... the positive "masculine" trait: the ability to organize oneself and one's actions rationally and concentratedly in pursuit of large objectives. And the central positive "feminine" trait: the ability to discern, accept, value, express, and be guided by one's feeling responses to people and situations. Our sexual stereotypes tell us that these are "opposing" abilities. But exactly the reverse is true. Each is essential to the other. (pp. 196–197)

Changing Roles of Women

In the last several decades major changes in the ways women perceive themselves and their roles in modern society have occurred. Many studies have found that, compared with men, women lack self-esteem and self-confidence (Harris, 1979). Part of the impetus for this rethinking came from the emergence of a national consensus among women that the image of woman as exclusively mother and housekeeper stifled the true feelings and needs of many women. Friedan's (1963) classic book, *The Feminine Mystique*, pinpointed the "disease which has no name" in describing the feelings of inadequacy and frustration experienced by many educated and intelligent women tied to the repetitive chores of housecleaning and child care.

As the need for changes—in attitudes, in legislation, in the workplace, and in the family—became more and more obvious, some women began efforts to bring about those changes. They have made great strides; however, the work is not finished. For example, true equality of wages and representation is lacking in American society, as reflected in the differences between women and men in terms of earned salaries. Many boys and girls still are being reared differently, with girls learning submissive, obedient roles early in life.

Resolving the Housework Dilemma

In an era when people are concerned about inequity in relationships within families, there is merit in reflecting on the lasting effects of preparing children to assume more active roles in household production. Studies currently demonstrate that mothers who are gainfully employed often assume a disproportionate share of responsibility for household maintenance in relation to the time spent by other family members. Males are often criticized for not assuming greater responsibility for the care of the home. Nevertheless, parents are responsible for rearing young boys to assume household roles. Boys who have not learned skills of household production are not likely to be well prepared for the degree of role fluidity that will be required of them as adults. Similarly, parents who are reluctant to encourage their daughters to forego learning household skills in favor of out-of-home production, may be doing their daughters a disservice.

A satisfying family life is among the goals given priority by both men and women. Therefore, it is not unreasonable to assume that household maintenance will be most efficiently achieved if the requisite skills are learned before marriage. Children who master household skills early and attain satisfaction because their efforts are appreciated can be expected to feel relatively comfortable in assuming responsibility for increasingly complex household tasks. These skills will serve them to good advantage in their family relationships in the future.

Source: Wallinga, C. R., Sweaney, A. L., & Walters, J. (1987). The development of responsibility in young children: A 25-year view. *Early Childhood Research Quarterly*, *2*, 119–131. Albex Publishing Corporation, Norwood, NJ. Used with permission.

Repercussions to the changes resulting from women's activism have been widespread. Young women find that careers previously closed to them are now open; women in their middle years discover new opportunities to complete their education or to be educated for new careers; and older women, through groups like the Older Women's League and legislation to help "displaced homemakers," have more opportunities to be independent than in the past.

Today less stigma is attached to an unmarried woman. She is recognized as a single woman who—often by choice—has preferred to remain independent and to make her own life. As women have gained economic independence, they have less often married or remained in an unhappy marriage simply for financial reasons.

The impact of the employment of women on their families is a complex issue. Research findings have been contradictory and difficult to interpret (Tiedje et al., 1990). A great deal seems to depend on how well the wife likes her job and whether she works because she wants to or because it is economically necessary. The effect of maternal employment on children is also difficult to determine. For one thing, girls appear to be influenced differently than boys by the employment of their mothers. Daughters of working mothers are more likely to want to work themselves, to have higher educational goals, to have more favorable attitudes about the employment of women, and to make fewer differentiations between household tasks deemed appropriate for men and women (Huston & Ashmore, 1985).

❧

Women's Salaries, Men's Salaries

Women earned about 60 cents for every dollar men earned from the early 1960s into the late 1970s, when the number crept up to 70 cents.

The gap in salaries is different in different fields, for different ages, and for different education levels. Quite a few women are doing considerably better than the averages would indicate.

Occupational segregation—women in low-paying jobs, men in higher-paying managerial and professional ones—accounts for 17% to 30% of the difference between the average paychecks of men and women.

In 1970, 4.5% of women employees and 14.2% of men worked as managers and administrators. By 1982, the percentage of women had risen to 7.4, while the percentage of men had gone up just slightly—to 14.7%.

Median salaries in 1985 dollars for full-time workers were as follows:

	1973	**1986**	
Men	$27,081	$24,779	minus 9%
Women	15,337	15,925	plus 4%

	Degrees Earned by Women (as a % of total degrees)	
	1975–76	**1984–85**
Business and management (Bachelor's)	20%	44%
Computer science (Bachelor's)	20	37
Dentistry	4	21
Engineering (Bachelor's)	3	15
Law	19	39
Medicine	16	30

Women accountants and auditors now earn 72 cents for every dollar their male colleagues earn; computer systems–analysts and scientists, 83 cents; those who sell business services, 79 cents.

There are signs that suggest this gap will continue to close. Take the case of business-services salespeople. The proportion of women in the field went up 6% between 1979 and 1986, while women's earnings (compared with men's) went up 21 cents on the dollar—to 79 cents. Women are not just getting jobs in the field; they are getting more of the better-paying jobs.

Women lawyers still make only 63% of what male lawyers make, but again that is an average. As relative newcomers to the field, women are bunched at the lower levels. Men are spread throughout the hierarchy and almost completely dominate the very highly paid top echelons.

Another observation is that younger women are doing better:

	Women's earnings (as a % of men's)	
Age	1975	1986
18–24	76	86
25–34	65	74
35–44	52	60
45–54	53	54
55–64	55	54

The most important reason younger women are doing better is that they are better educated and trained.

Source: Mann, J., & Hellwig, B. (1988, January). The truth about the salary gap(s). *Working Women*, p. 61.

In reaction to the more strident voices of the women's liberation efforts, many women—and men—believe that the nurturing roles of mother and homemaker have been undervalued. They believe that a women who is a homemaker is made to feel worthless and without a useful role unless she has a salaried job (Payne, 1985).

Two major problems facing women today are *role ambiguity* and *role strain*. Extreme feminists insist that women can find satisfaction only in salaried work, whereas strict traditionalists argue that only family and motherhood yield true satisfaction. Many women are confused about which choice is best and feel guilty regardless of their choice. Some women experience role strain when they try to combine career, home maintenance, and child rearing. The demands of multiple roles soon overwhelm even the most capable, energetic woman (Garrett, 1982; Gullotta et al., 1986; Payne, 1985; Pearson, 1989).

Changing Roles of Men

As role alternatives for women change, making it possible for them to enter traditionally male-dominated occupations, men must redefine their roles in order to adjust to a society in which masculine and feminine roles are less dichotomized. Many men face the dilemma of interacting with women as equal partners, while still under the influence of traditions that encourage them to take the initiative and assume a dominant role in a variety of situations.

During this transition period when the concepts of masculinity and femininity are being broadened, men are understandably confused about what masculinity is. The criteria of dominance, aggressiveness, and accomplishment in work have become less important in the definition of masculinity. Although this change is difficult for some men, it promises increased alternatives and freedom in the future. Men indicate more stress when married to an "overeducated" woman, and women indicate more stress when married to an "undereducated" man (Hornung & McCullough, 1981). As a consequence of the broadened definition of masculinity, men will feel less compulsion, as well as less anxiety, to prove their masculinity.

Another important modification in the masculine role is that men are expressing characteristics traditionally considered feminine, such as sensitivity, being understanding and considerate, and showing warmth and nurturance. It is more acceptable for men to communicate their feelings, problems, and concerns to others; they are becoming more emotionally responsive. Because expressive qualities are important in the success of interpersonal relationships, the increased internalization of such qualities will tend to improve men's skills in interpersonal relationships within as well as outside of marriage (Hiller & Philliber, 1982). A change that will significantly affect family life in the future is that men are beginning to assume greater responsibility in child rearing. As a result, children may enjoy closer relationships with their fathers than they have in the past; and both boys and girls will see the variety of parental role models and human expressions of feeling that are possible.

Factors Related to Changing Roles

In the section that follows several factors related to the changes in roles of women and men are reviewed and several trends are noted. Of the dozens of factors that have caused changes in roles or that are the result of role changes, only a sampling can be presented. They illustrate, however, how pervasive these changes have been.

Technology

The advances in technology and the way these have influenced marriage and families since the turn of the century are too numerous to list. For example, changes in laundry procedures have saved women untold numbers of hours weekly. Grandmother washed on Monday and ironed on Tuesday. Men escaped washing and ironing; much of the indoor maintenance of a household was assigned to women, whereas men were assigned to perform outdoor chores. With the advent of wash-and-wear fabrics, the total time spent in clothing maintenance has been significantly reduced. Improvements in

washers and dryers have reduced the burden of clothing care. Time saved in laundry-related activities has been time gained by women to do other things. The more hours wives are employed, the less "women's work" they do around the house (Atkinson & Huston, 1984; Huston & Ashmore, 1985).

Another example is the microwave oven. Its rapid acceptance attests to its usefulness in family meal preparation. The microwave oven saves time. Again, this represents a larger amount of time saved by women than by men because men lag behind women significantly in the amount of time spent in food preparation.

Another significant change in America's eating habits involves the acceptance and growth of fast-food outlets. More and more people each year spend greater amounts to "eat out." Establishments such as McDonald's, Kentucky Fried Chicken, Wendy's, Hardee's, Burger King, Arby's, Captain D's, Pizza Hut, Morrison's, Shoney's, Steak and Ale, Taco Bell, and Western Sizzlin'—to name a few—have had a profound effect on family eating habits and on the time women have spent in food preparation. The popularity of prepared foods available in grocery stores has also soared. Delicatessens and bakeries within grocery stores make it possible for family members to stop by and pick up a baked chicken, baked beans, salad, freshly baked rolls, a cake, cola, and after-dinner mints.

Some of these changes were in response to the needs of an increasing number of women who entered the labor force. Many have made it easier for them to do so. Successes in these areas can only lead to an expansion of others like them. The more experience this generation gains in having fast, convenient meals away from home, the more likely the pattern will persist in the future.

Voluntary Childlessness

A generation ago few women chose to remain childless forever. Having children was an expectation of marriage and an important life goal of most young people. It was believed that if a woman did not have a child either she or her husband was sterile or selfish or both. Young married couples were encouraged to get into the baby business by their parents and their friends. Few women had the courage to admit that they did not want children. Thus the desire not to have children has only recently been accepted as a viable option for couples.

Increasing numbers of women are entering occupations that are so demanding that they feel there is little time for children. A couple's lifestyle may involve so much travel that it would be difficult to have children. Some couples believe that their level of earnings simply is not sufficient enough to have children; and others do not wish to spend the time required to rear children.

It cannot be assumed, of course, that all childlessness is voluntary. From recent evidence, it appears that the number of persons who have several sexual partners has increased in the last generation, causing an increase in sexually transmitted diseases that have resulted in sterility. For example, in one study (Petersen et al., 1983) it was found that the mean number of different sexual partners for men was 16, and the mean number of different sexual partners for women was 8. Many males and females go for years without suspecting that they have a sexually transmitted disease, and although a disease may be asymptomatic, it may be rendering its victim sterile. Also, the recent popularity of delaying childbearing is responsible for some involuntary childlessness. Because fertility decreases as a woman ages, a woman who could have conceived easily in her mid-twenties may have difficulty by her mid-thirties (see Chapter 10 for more detailed information).

As in the case of technology, voluntary childlessness is both a cause and a result of changing sex roles. Removing motherhood as an inevitable event in women's lives causes us to rethink traditional ideas of femininity and womanhood. And women who do not perceive strong social pressure to bear children may devote their energies to careers (Pearson, 1989).

Remaining Single

The number of women and men who choose to remain single has been influenced by the view that marriage is not a necessary prerequisite for sexual encounters. For the majority, marriage is no longer the point in life when youth become sexually active.

Some women choose not to marry because their career goals preclude involvement in a relationship that is less than egalitarian. In fact, both men and women who are committed to careers are unlikely to make the kind of investment in their spouse that the traditional wife did in her husband. Both may be able to provide money to meet the other's needs, but neither may be able to provide the time and sensitivity that are supportive of long-term relationships (Payne, 1985).

Some couples whose career demands are great share an intimate relationship without thought of marriage or having children. Of these couples, some resolve the issues successfully and marry. Still others let the relationship run its course and then move on to a new relationship, sometimes with relief and sometimes with sadness. Whatever the benefits of remaining single, there are disappointments and periods of loneliness. Most people crave companionship and find in marriage a satisfaction that they cannot attain alone. Others, however, like being single and for them—when all advantages and disadvantages are weighed—remaining single is preferable.

The consequences of the trend toward remaining single are not entirely clear, although it is apparent that currently the onset of marriage is slightly delayed—that is, people in America are entering first marriages at slightly older ages. The fact that over 90% of people marry suggests that few persons remain single indefinitely. Even those who are divorced seldom give up on marriage entirely; most of the young and middle-aged who are divorced remarry.

Two other important trends mitigate against remaining single. Life is easier economically for those

Walker Montgomery

who marry. One house is cheaper than two; one utility bill is cheaper than two. Such factors gain special significance during periods of economic hardship. Second, concern about AIDS has caused many people to place greater value on a sexual relationship characterized by exclusivity.

Education

Forty years ago there were two male college graduates for every female who received an undergraduate degree. Today the numbers of undergraduate degrees awarded to men and women are fairly equal. Colleges of medicine, veterinary medicine, law, and business are attracting an increasing number of women.

Some of the dramatic gains in enrollments in graduate schools can be accounted for by the fact that the rate of increase in the past 20 years has been greater for women than for men. And as any administrator of graduate programs knows, the vast majority of women entering graduate programs successfully complete the requirements for their respective degrees. The barriers that once made it very difficult for women to enter educational programs that had been thought of as "men's programs" have been lowered. And equally important, women who enter occupations that were historically considered men's fields are respected.

What effects will increased education of women have on their relationships with men? Few factors have been as influential in changing women's roles as education has been. Many educated women simply refuse to be relegated to a subordinate role in relation to men in either personal or professional spheres. However, research indicates that the contributions of husbands and wives to household maintenance and child care are not equal. Even wives who are gainfully employed spend much more time in home maintenance than husbands.

Occupational Demands

The demands of an increasingly complex world require individuals with specialized skills. The attainment of these skills often entails extensive periods of education. Many women and men are willing to pursue specialization because they wish to improve the quality of their lifestyles with higher salaries and because they hope to attain satisfaction, power, recognition, and admiration from their work. Women with advanced degrees, however, continue to have lower utilization rates, higher unemployment, and lower salaries than men (National Research Council, 1983).

What are the effects of an increased emphasis on occupational specialization? Women and men strive to become occupationally successful—sometimes at the expense of their families. Studies of male corporation executives, for example, contain evidence that those who are highly successful spend large proportions of their waking hours in activities related to their occupations. At some point, the advantage to their spouses and their children may decline, and their occupational success may result in neglected relationships within the family. Although the decision that each person makes in this regard is a personal one, the costs involved are shared by the family.

When dual careers are involved, as is true in an increasing number of families, the situation is all the more difficult. The demands of two occupations may leave little time to nurture a successful marriage. Couples who do not recognize and understand this can expect happiness in marriage to decline.

Although historically wives have worked to help their husbands through school, preparation for dual careers has resulted in more situations with both spouses being in school. Income usually comes from shared part-time employment, savings, loans, and gifts from their families. This lifestyle is not easy, but most couples prefer it because they do not have to postpone marriage. Thus it is very likely that this pattern will continue.

The psychological support of husbands was of primary importance for married women returning to school. Women who experienced the least stress were those who saw their husbands as holding more liberal attitudes regarding women's roles and capabilities. One-third or more of the wives indicated that time and role demands created important problems for them. Many of them found it easier to add to their existing chores rather than to try to change the family's status quo. There was little change in the traditional division of labor (Berkove, 1979; Houseknecht & Macke, 1984).

Women in the Labor Force

If you were asked to give a realistic description of the kind of family life you would like to have in 10 years—and assuming you were typical for your age–you would probably include the following: a

Walker Montgomery

house; furniture for the house; two automobiles; one or two children; insurance (life, home, medical, and automobile); a modest savings account to help in emergencies; money for an annual vacation; and an adequate income to pay for such things as food, clothing, gasoline, utilities, medical care, entertainment, payments on the house and car, gifts, Social Security, and taxes.

Although the responsibility for providing the income for these things is shifting from "a man's responsibility," to "a responsibility shared by husband and wife," men still feel vulnerable to pressure generated by these expectations because, historically, successful men provided a "good living" for their families. Those who provide amply for their families are esteemed by themselves and others; those who fail run the risk of being considered not all that promising (Houseknecht, 1985; Payne, 1985). Many dual-career couples continue to hold traditional values: 76% of women in one sample studied believed that it was primarily the husband's duty to provide financially for the family (Scanzoni, 1980).

For a woman, the growing acceptance of "improving the quality of life" through her economic contributions has encouraged her participation in the labor force. What effects has this one decision made on her life? She may need more formal education for the work role she chooses. She may limit the number of children she bears in order to give sufficient attention to those she does have. She will need to marry someone who will share her occupational goals, just as she will need to support the occupational goals of her husband. If she is like millions of other employed women who are married, she will have limited time to do housework and will experience role strain as the result of trying to fit the roles of worker and homemaker together. She will be unable to do many of the things she would like to do in life simply because she will not have the time. Women in nontraditional occupations are more likely to experience divorce, to decline in occupational status, to change to a traditional occu-

pation, or leave the labor force (Philliber & Hiller, 1983).

Increasingly women are preparing for employment outside the "pink collar" occupations (e.g., teaching, social work, and nursing). Rather, they are pursuing a wider variety of positions. Many large corporations have more women in executive positions than a generation ago. Although differences still exist in salaries of women and men for comparable work in some areas, mechanisms have been put into motion to alleviate discriminatory practices. Also, in several fields, significant efforts have been made to recruit highly qualified women into their executive training programs. The acceptance of women in positions traditionally held by men has been accompanied by an increased acceptance of men into positions formerly the domain of women, e.g., elementary education, social work, home economics, and nursing.

Although progress has been made in the employment of women in the last generation, the rate of progress, as reflected in higher education, has been less than might have been expected. An examination of your college or university catalog will likely raise some questions. Count the number of women in key administrative positions—presidents, vice-presidents, deans, department heads, directors of research programs, service programs, or the library. Then count the number of men. Based on the ratio you find, what would be your prediction of the number of males and females in these positions in 10 years? What is the ratio of men to women in low-paid secretarial positions?

Issues pertaining to the status of women affect us all whether we are female or male. Gender discrimination is often subtle; it is invariably insidious. How many men of today's generation want their educated daughters to be denied the right to hold an administrative position because of their gender? Once an employment system is in place, however, it is not likely to be changed unless concerned people work for change.

Similarities and Differences Between Gainfully Employed and Nongainfully Employed Wives: Household Production

Gainfully Employed Wives

Slightly more frequently utilized strategies to reduce time pressures

Believe meal preparation should take as little time as possible

Spent less time on community work, leisure, and sleep

Nongainfully Employed Wives

Reported having more spare time than they needed

More often baked from scratch

More frequently checked prices—even on small items

More often prepared breakfast and lunch

More often use price-off coupons

No Differences Between Gainfully and Nongainfully Employed Wives

Whether a particular time-saving durable (e.g., microwave oven, dishwasher, freezer, dryer) was purchased

Amount spent on a time-saving durable

Use of time-saving durables to reduce pressures

Feeling guilty when serving a convenience food to their family

Shopping frequently for specials

Frequency of preparing dinner

Frequency of purchasing from a mail-order catalog

Frequency of grocery shopping

Use of frozen foods

Use of mail-order catalogs

Source: Strober, M. H. (1979). Strategies used by working and nonworking wives to reduce time pressures. *Journal of Consumer Research, 6,* 338–348. Reprinted by permission.

Two-Paycheck Marriages

A growing number of men and women marry after they have established themselves in a career or job, and they are reluctant to give up careers for a traditional pattern of married life. Even the arrival of children does not change the decision such couples make to continue with both their work lives. It may add to the complexity of planning their days and limit the time they spend as a family. But through the necessity for two salaries or the personal desire of both partners to continue to be part of the paid work force, two employed people in a marriage are becoming more and more common. Both spouses are gainfully employed in 63% of all marriages in the United States (*Statistical Abstract of the United States*, 1987).

Social scientists divide families with two workers into two categories: dual-worker families and dual-career families. Most two-paycheck families fall in the dual-worker category. In these families, one spouse pursues a career (an occupation requiring extended education or training and greater commitment), while the other is employed in a less demanding job or both have jobs rather than careers. For example, the wife teaches school and her husband does construction work, or he is a store manager and she is a waitress. In dual-career families, both spouses are committed to careers (Garrett, 1982; Pearson, 1989).

Dual-career and dual-worker families have unique stresses. A primary difficulty is overload. Today the majority of mothers with preschool children work full time in salaried positions. For these women, the pressures of combining work with home put them on a treadmill of constant activity. Most couples realize that to make such an arrangement work, they must limit themselves to the essentials in their marital and family relationships. In one study, dual-career husbands spent an average of 158 minutes more on their jobs than wives did, whereas dual-career wives spent less time in leisure activities than

Dual-Career Marriages

America has not had a sex-role revolution, but *half* a sex-role revolution. Women's roles have changed; men's have not.

I am not optimistic about quick change. Eight years ago, I surveyed my students' attitudes in a course at Cornell's ILR School. Although virtually all of the students believed in equal pay for equal work, the men and women disagreed over whether marriage partners should share equally in the housekeeping responsibilities: 99% of the women approved, 81% of them strongly so; 86% of the men approved, but only 46% did so strongly. Male support was even softer for equal sharing of child care responsibilities: 98% of the women approved, 78% strongly so; only 57% of the men approved at all, and only 29% approved strongly.

Interestingly, neither the men nor the women seemed aware of the extent of their disagreement. Most of my women students assume not only that they will proceed in their careers like the men around them, but that they will proceed with the active support and cooperation of one of those men. Given my survey results, I urge the women to administer questionnaires of their own to prospective marriage partners.

Source: Bem, D. J. (1987, Fall). A consumer's guide to dual-career marriages. *ILR Report, 25*(1). Ithaca, NY: State School of Industrial and Labor Relations, Cornell University.

husbands. Generally, however, there is little difference in the allocation of time between dual-career and dual-earner families (Chen, 1988).

Because the income of wives in dual-worker families is usually regarded as an economic necessity, some husbands may feel that they have failed to provide adequately for their families. On the other hand, wives may feel that their financial contributions have been diminished when they are viewed as just "helping out" (Pearson, 1989). Status inconsistency may be reduced by changing the relevance of the other's performance, e.g., the wife leaving the work force or entering a "traditional" occupation such as nursing, by changing the perception of the quality of the other's performance, e.g., downgrading the wife's performance or exaggerating the husband's accomplishments, or by changing the degree of closeness in the relationship, e.g., getting a divorce, or by *increasing* the degree of closeness in order to reduce the importance of the status inconsistency in their marriage (Wampler & Kingery, 1985). Wives with jobs requiring little commitment may be able to devote more attention to family but may miss opportunities for self-realization and individual achievement at work (Garrett, 1982).

On a positive note, workers who are not pursuing careers are free to choose part-time work and to drop out of the labor force when children are small. They have greater flexibility to move to allow a spouse to pursue career advancement.

Dual-worker and dual-career couples face stresses from outside the family in terms of guilt feelings over delegating much child rearing to sitters, day-care centers, or relatives. Dual-worker couples usually have lower incomes than dual-career couples and, consequently, may have to manage without day care, housekeeping, or other support services (Pearson, 1989). Some find that their social contacts are greatly reduced owing to lack of time. Grandparents may feel neglected or ignored; they may disapprove of the wife's/mother's employment (Pearson, 1989).

Dual-career couples must also make decisions regarding relocating for career advancement and pro-

motions. Difficulties arise if one partner must decide whether to accept a promotion involving a move if the career of a spouse suffers as a result. Whose career gets first priority?

Some husbands and wives may find their relationship jeopardized by a sense of competitiveness. Competitive attitudes and situations may be disruptive to unity in a marital relationship (Saunders & Suls, 1982). One longitudinal study of women in dual-worker marriages revealed that wives who had higher job attainments than their husbands were more likely to be divorced (Hiller & Philliber, 1982).

In situations in which one member of a couple finds employment in one part of the country while the other is working somewhere else, the couple may meet on weekends and days off while living separate lives during the week. This arrangement is called a *commuter marriage*.

The commuter concept is not new. But in the past it was the husband—as politician, traveling salesman, actor, baseball player—who traveled while the wife remained at home and followed a lesser career opportunity, often while caring for the children. The difference today is that it may be the wife who travels and the husband may assume primary care of the home and children (Gerstel & Gross, 1988).

The advantages of the commuter lifestyle include the freedom to work as long and as late as each partner wants, to enjoy meals and recreation in individual ways, and to come and go without the need of dovetailing into a partner's schedule. Disadvantages include feelings of guilt and resentment over such issues as whose career commitment should predominate and who is more successful. There are also increased child care and domestic responsibilities for the spouse at home with the children. Many of the couples miss the daily intimacy of marriage and the chance of marital dissolution may increase (Rindfuss & Stephen, 1990).

Friendship patterns tend to change, too. The commuter is married and, consequently, may not have much in common with singles. On the other hand, although the commuter is part of a couple, legally and emotionally, he or she is a single socially and may not fit into couples' social events (Gerstel & Gross, 1988). Couples who have been married longer, who have a spouse with an established career, and who are free of child-rearing responsibilities have found the lifestyle less stressful than those who are younger, who have been married less time, and who have children to consider (Gross, 1980).

What effects will these changes have? For one, we can expect an increase in the separation of gender and occupation. As Table 5–1 indicates, areas in which changes have been slow involve housework and child care—areas in which women still assume a disproportional share (Fox & Nickols, 1983; Pear-

son, 1989). Because of the demands of work on both men and women, many things that need to be accomplished at home simply do not get done as a result of lack of time. Thus, for example, having friends over for a home-cooked meal will give way to taking friends out to dinner.

Egalitarian Marriages

Many men and women prefer an egalitarian marriage: they appreciate equality in their relationship (Pearson, 1989). Other men and women, of course, like a role relationship in which one partner is the "head of the house." One partner may want to be the boss because it enhances his or her self-esteem; another partner may be more comfortable in a sup-

Table 5–1 Mean Time Spent Doing Housework Each Week in the Six Work-Family Role Combinations

Work-Family Role Combination	Total Hours	Wives' Hours	Wives' Proportion	Husbands' Hours	Husbands' Proportion	Others' Hours
Dual-career	25.0	16.6	.69*	5.7	.24**	6.5
Dual-earner:						
Professional/managerial husbands	31.0	19.6	.69	5.7	.19	6.3
Professional/managerial wives	34.0	21.2	.68	5.3	.23	8.1
Nonprofessional/ nonmanagerial spouses	33.0	21.8	.71	5.9	.19	6.8
Single-earner:						
Professional husbands	39.5	32.8	.82	4.3	.11	4.6
Nonprofessional/non- managerial husbands	43.7	35.0	.83	3.9	.10	5.8
TOTAL	38.4	28.9	.79	4.7	.14	5.9

* Wives' proportion of the total number of hours allocated to housework each week by family members.

** Husbands' proportion of the total number of hours allocated to housework each week by family members.

Source: Berardo, D. H., Shenan, C. L., & Leslie, G. H. (1987). A residue of tradition: Jobs, careers, and spouses' time in housework. *Journal of Marriage and the Family, 49,* 381–390. Copyrighted (1987) by the National Council on Family Relations, 3989 Central Ave. N.E., Suite #550, Minneapolis, MN 55421. Reprinted by permission.

Joel Gordon

portive role. Part of the task in building a successful relationship is finding someone whose values you share, for there is considerable likelihood that patterns of interaction developed before marriage will not change dramatically after the wedding. People can change their role orientation; however, most change is achieved slowly.

> *When I first got married more than 25 years ago, I used to think that women were born cleaning ladies. I married a professional woman; she worked full time, and I worked full time. But she did all the cooking and the cleaning and the shopping and took care of the kid; I was busy. Until one day, my wife came to me and said, "I am busy too. How would you like a divorce?" It took me five minutes to rearrange my schedule.... Now I do some of the cooking and the cleaning and the shopping, and I don't like it. I know that women don't like to clean, and men don't like to clean; even cleaning ladies don't like to clean. (Gordon, 1980, p. 246)*

Much of the acceptance of egalitarian marriages on the part of men is the result of the efforts of women. Another factor encouraging the trend toward egalitarian roles is the delay in marriage. Couples who are older when they marry tend to form a more egalitarian relationship than do persons who marry younger (Allen & Kalish, 1984).

Many contemporary parents are making very determined efforts to rear their children to be egalitarian (Pearson, 1989). Although it may be inefficient to expect equal competence of women and men in all functions, some competence in both genders leads to greater fluidity in roles. There are times when a husband may not be home to replace the spark plug in the lawn mower, and there are occasions when a wife does not have time to braid her daughter's hair in time for school. Creating helplessness in men *or* women does little to prepare them for marriage—or life.

Teaching children to become proficient in a variety of household tasks contributes to their success

Teaching Children Housework

The responsibility of maintaining a household with young children, especially for single parents or two-earner families, can be overwhelming. Families often find that time, their most valuable resource, becomes a challenge to manage.

In an effort to encourage parents to involve their children more fully in household tasks and to foster independence in young children, a 6-week project called "Homework" was initiated. The project, which involved 23 4-year-old children and their families, began by determining whether parents believed their children could perform six tasks:

1. set the table

2. vacuum

3. sort clothes

4. save energy

5. clean the bathroom after a bath

6. wake up to an alarm clock

Only 9% of parents strongly agreed that their young children could successfully complete these responsibilities.

Each week after the preschool teachers demonstrated a "Homework" task for the children in the group, they divided into smaller groups to try out the task. For instance, the teacher demonstrated how to operate several vacuum cleaners safely. Then the children selected a vacuum cleaner that looked most like the one they had at home and practiced vacuuming under the teachers' supervision. This procedure ensured that the children knew how to do the task before they were asked to do it at home.

The "Homework" tasks were well received by the children. They eagerly anticipated each new task and requested more when the project was completed. Their enthusiasm was matched, if not surpassed, by that of the parents.

After completion of the "Homework" tasks, 100% of the parents agreed that their children were capable of accomplishing the six tasks.

Helpful Suggestions

1. Limit the size of the task. If the child views the task as overwhelming, she or he will feel defeated.

2. Encourage your child's effort and be prepared to accept less than perfection. Remember your child's standards may not be the same as yours.

3. Show your child that she or he needs to prepare for the task. For example, pick up all larger items that may cause problems with vacuuming or sweeping.

4. Choose a room or an area where the success rate is likely to be high. Avoid rooms that contain your most precious possessions.

5. Remember to thank the child for her or his help with the work in the family.

Source: Adapted from Wallinga, C. R., & Sweaney, A. L. (1985). A sense of real accomplishment: Young children as productive family members. *Young Children, 40*(10), 3–8. Reprinted by permission.

Are the Roles of Men and Women Equitable?

In a review of men's work, Joseph H. Pleck addresses three perspectives that are summarized here.

The Traditional Perspective

The traditional perspective on men's family roles has been the dominant perspective. It provides a value context in which a limited role for men in family work is viewed as justifiable and appropriate. In simplest terms, this traditional perspective holds that husbands are not responsible for any substantial amount of housework and child care in the family. Rather, husbands are responsible only for providing the family's economic support through their paid employment outside the family.

The Exploitation Perspective

Starting in the early 1970s, a quite different view about men's family work began to be expressed, and its underlying theoretical basis was feminism. The feminist movement, from its very outset, identified the unequal burden of housework and child care carried by women as an important aspect of women's inferior status in society. In Walker and Woods' investigation of 1,296 upper New York State families, men's family work occupied about 1.6 hours per day, compared to 8.1 hours per day for housewives and 4.8 hours per day for employed wives.

Employed wives spent an average of 10.1 hours per day in total work (4.8 hours of family work plus 5.3 hours of paid work) whereas husbands performed an average of only 7.9 hours per day (1.6 plus 6.3 hours)—about 2.2 less hours per day. Employed wives have less free time and sleep less than their husbands. Employed wives' role overload is also associated with an increased sense of time pressure and diminished well-being.

Since the employed wife works 2.2 more hours in toto per day than her husband in these couples, it is simply not intellectually tenable to view men's limited family roles as the result of an equitable "exchange" between husband and wife resulting from their different resources.

The Changing Roles Perspective

The changing roles perspective rejects the pessimism of the exploitation perspective. The exploitation perspective is often used in a way that makes change in men's family roles seem impossible and gives little or no attention to concrete strategies that might bring change about. The exploitation perspective may provide an adequate basis for indicting men, but by itself it does not provide a basis for helping them change.

The problem today is a "psychosocial lag" between the slower rate of change in men's roles in the family compared to the relatively more rapid rate of change in women's roles in paid employment. Rather than view this discrepancy as a permanent feature of our society, it is more useful to view it as reflecting a transitional problem of adjustment. It is not intended that this perspective imply the Pollyannish optimism that we need only wait for men to transform themselves. Rather, it is implied that men can and will change if appropriate educational and social policies are implemented, requiring effort and commitment on the part of the family field.

Source: Pleck, J. H. (1979). Men's family work: Three perspectives and some new data. *The Family Coordinator, 28,* 481–488. Reprinted by permission.

as homemakers, whatever their gender. Proficiency in any enterprise is gained through practice, not as a result of some gender-specific, inherent quality. The stereotyping of family-related functions that must be performed by family members according to gender is often dysfunctional to a smooth-running operation. A daughter whose parents taught her how to change a tire will have a skill that may be really useful if at 2 A.M. she finds herself with a flat tire and a date who does not know how to repair it.

Once basic competence is attained, tasks that are divided by interest rather than gender will be performed better. If a wife prefers to work in the yard and her husband prefers to cook, isn't that the way the tasks should be assigned? Or they may prefer to do chores together while they talk. Couples who assume roles in their marriage in a way that pleases them are apt to be most satisfied (Pearson, 1989).

What are the effects of these changes on the balance of power in a family? Studies of power in marriage indicate that individuals who give far more than they receive are likely to be dissatisfied (Scanzoni & Scanzoni, 1981). Williams and Berry (1984) found that in no other area are the disagreements of husbands and wives considered more important than in the area of household responsibilities. For husbands and wives who had been married 41 years or less as a total group, it ranked first in importance. Disagreements in this area were considered more important than disagreements over the following issues: rearing children, dealing with relatives, time spent with spouse and family, financial expenditures, sharing feelings, leisure time, philosophy of life, sexual relations, friends, religious beliefs, wife's working status, and drinking/gambling. When disagreements were classified by length of marriage, wives ranked disagreements over household responsibilities first in each of four length-of-marriage categories. Husbands ranked such disagreements as only slightly less important. Clearly, disagreement about the performance of household responsibili-

ties is a major source of conflict throughout marriage. When either the wife or the husband becomes discontented, the relationship is likely to suffer; both partners eventually lose.

As Scanzoni and Scanzoni (1981) have noted, power within a family develops out of exceedingly complex processes, some of which are unconscious and some of which are conscious. An examination of the struggle for power between men and women has increasingly gained the attention of family researchers within the last three decades and has paralleled the women's movement. Clearly, women have rejected patterns of subordination. Although many men applaud their efforts, not all do, and this resistance forms the basis of the very real struggle that exists today (Scanzoni & Scanzoni, 1981).

Good relationships are most likely in those families in which the focus is on mutual support, concern, and thoughtfulness. Relationships characterized by a desire to determine who is "boss" or who can get the most while giving the least set in motion a contest that is usually disappointing and unsatisfactory.

Egalitarian marriages serve as an important model for children within the family. Children benefit from a variety of flexible role models (Pearson, 1989). Patterns of family behavior learned in families of orientation find their way into the children's families of procreation once the children establish families of their own. Couples who are sensitive to each other's needs and feelings make an important contribution to the future life of their children through their example.

Role Changes Due to Divorce

For a woman, divorce sets into motion a series of events. These include: seeking employment if she has not been employed; seeking child care if she did not already have it; trying to live on less income than she had while married; seeking a relationship with another man; developing new friendships as her former married friends "drop" her; and assuming responsibility for all aspects of family living. For many, the requirements of the new role are rewarding and worthwhile, but they are seldom easy (Price & McKenry, 1988).

Divorce is not easy for men either, but it is different. Men, more quickly than women, proceed to a new relationship. They are more aggressive in seeking companionship. They are less likely to reject sexual encounters on the basis that they are not involved affectionately with their partners. Still, men also must adjust to life without the familiar support system. And many men must face reduced contact with children they continue to love and whose presence they value (Price & McKenry, 1988).

Stress and Role Clarification

The brief illustrations presented make it clear that although life over the past few generations has become better for both women and men, it is, nonetheless, more complex. Roles that once were fairly clearly defined are now less distinct. Lack of clarity often leads to stress in interpersonal relationships. Thus, in an effort to provide greater opportunity for self-fulfillment, we have created greater opportunities for conflict.

> *A young woman is promoted into an important managerial position with a large company. She feels a great deal of pressure to perform successfully in this new position, both to further her own career plans and to prove to those who chose her that a woman can succeed at this level. She is aware of resentment from her husband and faces a period of intense stress as she begins her work.*

> *After 25 years in the same community, a family is forced to move because the company that employs both the husband and wife moves to another state. All family members react with anxiety. Friends urge them to stay, whereas work colleagues encourage them to move. Children wish to stay because of their friends; it is a stressful situation for the husband who wishes to stay but whose wife wishes to go.*

Today's changes in role expectations of women and men put great pressures on our relationships within our families and fragment our concentration on what is important. Coping with change, however, is an essential part of successful stress management.

Many families are moving through a period of role stress. Conflict in our society—the pull of the old ways against the straining waves of the new—cause apprehension and anxiety for both men and women in their daily lives. In one study it was found that specific arrangements of how husbands and wives make decisions or perform household tasks have little to do with their levels of anxiety. Shared power and shared roles are not significantly related to anxiety scores for either husbands or wives. Who does the dishes, how they decide who does them, and what follows do not directly affect the anxiety of either spouse in the marriage. How a couple *feels* about their marital solidarity, however, is important. High solidarity implies a stable and secure relationship. Low anxiety scores for both husbands and wives were significantly associated with positive evaluations by the spouse. If there were feelings of mutual approval and acceptance, anxiety in the marriage was low. Aloofness, feelings of personal threat or rejection, or feelings of apprehension about anticipated rejection by the spouse increased the anxiety level in the marriage (Lundgren et al., 1980).

Stress within interpersonal relationships can either be aggravated or lessened by the kind of communication among people. Researchers have noted that verbal exchanges often contain the basic content of messages, but it is the nonverbal communication that includes the way the message is to be interpreted. Nonverbal cues are, however, subject to error. A study by Noller (1980) indicates that the husband's ability in both sending and receiving nonverbal messages effectively seems to be crucial to the marriage relationship, inasmuch as husbands in the high marital adjustment group sent more positive nonverbal communications and made fewer errors in receiving messages than husbands in

Illustrative Findings Regarding Gender Differences in Social Interaction in Close Relationships

1. Wives disclose more personal feelings and opinions than husbands when asked to talk about both intimate and nonintimate topics (Morton, 1978).

2. Women are more likely than men to disclose their fears (Rubin, et al., 1980).

3. Women ask more questions, show greater support, and are more skilled at using "mm's" and "oh's" to indicate interest during conversation (Fishman, 1978).

4. Women in close relationships express approval through nonverbal channels during conflict more than men (Lochman & Allen, 1979).

5. Men involved in heterosexual relationships use direct (telling, asking, talking to the partner) and bilateral (bargaining and efforts at persuasion) tactics more than women in order to get their way. Women use indirect (suggestions, hints, withdrawal) tactics more than men (Falbo & Peplau, 1980).

6. Men conversing with women talk more and interrupt more (Zimmerman & West, 1975).

7. Women in close relationships are reported to cry, sulk, and criticize men for their insensitivity and lack of consideration; men are reported to show anger, to reject tears, and to call for a logical and nonemotional approach to dealing with the problem (Kelley et al., 1978).

Adapted from: Huston, T. L., & Ashmore, R. D. *Women and men in personal relationships.* (1986). In R. D. Ashmore and F. K. Del Boca (Eds.), *The social psychology of female-male relations: A critical analysis of central concepts.* (pp. 167–210). Orlando, FL: Academic Press.

Sources: 1. Falbo, T., & Peplau, L. A. (1980). Power strategies in intimate relationships. *Journal of Personality and Social Psychology, 37,* 879–896. 2. Fishman, P. N. (1978). Interaction: The work women do. *Social Problems, 25,* 397–406. 3. Kelley, H. H., Cunningham, J. D., Grisham, J. A., Lefebvre, L. M., Sink, C. R., & Yablon, G. (1978). Sex differences in comments made during conflict in close relationships. *Sex Roles, 4,* 473–491. 4. Lochman, J. E., & Allen, G. (1979). Elicited effects of approval and disapproval: An examination of parameters having implications for counseling couples in conflict. *Journal of Consulting and Clinical Psychology, 47,* 634–636. 5. Morton, T. U. (1978). Intimacy and reciprocity of exchange: A comparison of spouses and strangers. *Journal of Personality and Social Psychology, 36,* 72–81. 6. Rubin, Z., Hill, C. T., Peplav, L. A., & Dunkel-Schetter, C. (1980). Self-disclosure in dating couples: Sex roles and the ethic of openness. *Journal of Marriage and the Family, 42,* 305–317. 7. Zimmerman, D. H., & West, C. (1975). Sex roles, interruptions and silences in conversations. In B. Thorne & N. Henley (Eds.), *Language and sex: Difference and dominance.* Rowley, MA: Newbury-House.

a low marital adjustment group. Because similar relations were not found for wives, it would seem that the nonverbal communication skill of the husband is an especially important determinant of marital adjustment. Wives tend to have greater skill than husbands, particularly at receiving positive nonverbal communication correctly.

Female-male interactions are often influenced by overt impression management attempts by one or both of the partners. Men guess correctly that women want expressiveness in a man, but women often guess incorrectly that men want them to be domestic (Huston & Ashmore, 1985; Spence et al., 1985.)

Women spend more time looking directly at the other person than do men. Not only do women make more eye contact than men, but they also seem to rely more heavily on this form of communication (Deaux, 1976).

Although it is impossible for a family to escape all external stressors, much of the conflict between women and men is their own doing. The imperfect relationships that men and women create are in no small measure a reflection of their imperfect communication.

Stress also arises when men and women concentrate on the unhappiness or inequities between them. Both men and women have been manipulated and misunderstood; inequities continue. For most of us, however, happiness in interpersonal relationships is still possible and can be enhanced by acquiring understanding and skills.

Gender Differences in Beliefs about Family Life

Marriage and Family Life

Differences in the views of women and men on marriage and family life were revealed in a study by Larson (1988). The discussion that follows focuses on the gender differences in the acceptance of common marriage myths and indicates the extent to which a sample of 279 undergraduate college students believe them (see Table 5–2). A summary of the documentation that Larson presents to dispel common misconceptions is presented. It is worth noting that two issues yielded incorrect responses from nearly one-half of the 50 family science professionals (see items 1 and 18 in Table 5–2), a reflection of the fact that new research very often necessitates a change in beliefs. Larson's data provide an illustration of the dynamic nature of knowledge and demonstrate the need for a continuing examination of each of our beliefs about marriage.

1. Nearly one-half of the men believed the myth that "a husband's marital satisfaction is usually lower if his wife is employed full-time than if she is a full-time homemaker," whereas only one-fourth of the women indicated their acceptance of this myth. From recent research there is no consistent or significant evidence that the marital satisfaction of husbands is related to the employment of their wives (Fendrich, 1984; Hoffman, 1986).

2. Two-thirds of the men believed that having a child improves marital satisfaction for *both* spouses, whereas less than one-half of the women believed this was true. As Larson (1988) has noted, the majority of studies support the belief that children decrease rather than increase marital satisfaction; however, more recent evidence indicates that "the birth of a child apparently precipitates a higher degree of positive change in the lives of the parents high on marital adjustment than those low on marital adjustment" (Harriman, 1986, p. 237). Larson concludes that happiness in marriage helps to accentuate positive changes and to minimize negative changes that are likely to occur with the arrival of a child.

3. Nearly twice as many men as women believed that marital satisfaction for a wife is usually lower if she is employed full time than if she is a full-time homemaker. Current evidence fails to support this belief (Fendrich, 1984; Hoffman, 1986; Smith, 1985).

4. Nearly twice as many women as men believed their spouse should love them irrespective of their behavior. In reality, love from another is not independent of one's own behavior. Larson (1988) believes that a person usually loves his or her spouse because the spouse's behavior meets the person's needs.

5. Nearly twice as many men as women believed husbands make more lifestyle adjustments in marriage. Men are less involved in their marriages and make fewer lifestyle adjustments— men's adjustment decreases less during childbearing and child-rearing periods, and men find marriage less stressful (Bell et al., 1987; Chickering & Havighurst, 1981; Rhyne, 1981).

Table 5–2 Percent of Undergraduate College Students and Family Life Professionals Missing Each Item on the Marriage Quiz

Marriage Quiz Items	Correct Answer*	Percentage of Respondents Missing Item		
		Male Students (N = 127)	Female Students (N = 152)	Professionals (N = 50)
1. A husband's marital satisfaction is usually lower if his wife is employed full time than if she is a full-time homemaker.	F	48	27	40
**2. Today most young, single, never-married people will eventually get married.	T	45	47	8
3. In most marriages having a child improves marital satisfaction for both spouses.	F	67	47	10
4. The best single predictor of overall marital satisfaction is the quality of a couple's sex life.	F	34	25	10
**5. The divorce rate in America increased from 1960 to 1980.	T	0	4	2
**6. A greater percentage of wives are in the work force today than in 1970.	T	0	4	0
7. Marital satisfaction for a wife is usually lower if she is employed full time than if she is a full-time homemaker.	F	23	11	8
8. If my spouse loves me, he/she should instinctively know what I want and need to be happy.	F	23	24	8
9. In a marriage in which the wife is employed full time, the husband usually assumes an equal share of the housekeeping.	F	21	20	0
10. For most couples marital satisfaction gradually increases from the first year of marriage through the child-bearing years, the teen years, the empty nest period, and retirement.	F	35	50	8

Item		T/F			
11.	No matter how I behave, my spouse should love me simply because he/she *is* my spouse.	F	13	26	4
**12.	One of the most frequent marital problems is poor communication.	T	12	0	0
13.	Husbands usually make more lifestyle adjustments in marriage than wives.	F	23	10	0
14.	Couples who cohabitated before marriage usually report greater marital satisfaction than couples who did not.	F	55	50	0
15.	I can change my spouse by pointing out his/her inadequacies, errors, etc.	F	55	24	4
**16.	Couples who marry when one or both partners are under the age of 18 have more chance of eventually divorcing than those who marry when they are older.	T	23	4	0
17.	Either my spouse loves me or does not love me; nothing I do will affect the way my spouse feels about me.	F	22	4	0
18.	The more a spouse discloses positive and negative information to his/her partner, the greater the marital satisfaction of both partners.	F	89	81	42
19.	I must feel better about my partner before I can change my behavior toward him/her.	F	78	81	20
20.	Maintaining romantic love is *the key* to marital happiness over the life span for most couples.	F	45	58	14

* The explanations of why these items are true or false can be found on pages 8 and 9 of Larson's (1988) article..

** True item used as a filler to control for response style and disguise the nature of the scale.

N = Number of responses.

Source: Larson, J. H. (1988). The marriage quiz: College students' beliefs in selected myths about marriage. *Family Relations, 37,* 3–11. Used with permission. Copyrighted (1988) by the National Council on Family Relations, 3989 Central Ave. N.E., Suite #550, Minneapolis, MN, 55421.

6. Nearly twice as many men as women believed in the myth that one can change one's spouse by pointing out his or her inadequacies and errors. Evidence suggests that such "negative tracking" leads to unhappiness and dissatisfaction in the marriage and is characteristic of unhappy couples. Marriage therapists emphasize the importance of learning to switch from negative to positive tracking in order to improve the marriage (Jacobson & Margolin, 1979).

7. Five times more women than men correctly believed that a couple who marry when one or both partners are under the age of 18 have a greater chance of divorcing than those who marry when they are older.

8. Nearly five times more men than women believed that nothing they do will affect how their spouse feels about them—that their spouse loves them or does not love them. As Larson (1988) points out, "love is not an all-or-nothing phenomenon. On different days a spouse may experience different degrees of love for his/her partner. How much love and satisfaction one feels toward a spouse depends heavily upon the spouse's behavior" (p. 9).

Summary

•   Contrary to poplar belief, women have not always been subordinate to men. In fact, in colonial America a strong partnership based on shared experiences existed between men and women. It was not until the onset of industrialization and the separation of home and workplace that accompanied it that these role changes occurred.

•   Cultural values and socialization processes are more responsible for the stereotyping of masculine-feminine roles than biological factors are. Such stereotypes limit men and women from achieving their potential.

•   Although much effort has gone into achieving greater equity between men and women, change has been impeded by attitudes that reinforce "traditional" ways of thinking. Few women hold high-paying or powerful positions, and the expectation remains that women should assume a disproportionate share of home and child-care responsibilities. Great strides have been made, however, in the area of formal education. A greater proportion of women today, as compared to a generation ago, are receiving bachelor's and master's degrees, and many more are gaining acceptance in the fields that have long been considered "men's" professions.

•   As more women have entered the workplace, the demands of multiple roles—wife, mother, employee—have led to confusion and stress for even the most capable and energetic women.

•   In addition to the increased educational levels being achieved by women, the increased number of women in the labor force, and the stresses felt by dual-career and dual-worker couples, there are other factors that have influenced the roles of men and women—and hence marriage and family life. These include: technological changes; the choices made by many to remain single, to delay marriage, and to remain childless; and the differences in role beliefs between men and women.

- In an egalitarian marriage—that is, a relationship of equality rather than one of strict role definition—the focus is on mutual support, concern, and thoughtfulness. Rearing children in an egalitarian system will give them a pattern of equity to follow. Family systems that permit inequity, in any form, produce children who, as adults, tolerate and/or reinforce inequitable behavior.

- Learning to cope with changes in the roles of men and women in marital relationships and other family situations is an important part of life. The increasing number of single-parent families, the high rates of divorce and remarriage, the growing number of stepfamilies, and the great proportion of older people in American society will demand a rethinking of traditional attitudes.

Discussion Questions

1. Consider the images of men and women portrayed in television commercials and magazine advertisements. Are these image desirable? Are they realistic? How do these portrayed images influence how people feel about themselves? How do they influence the relationships between men and women?

2. Discuss some of the differences in which girls and boys are reared. For example, consider clothing, choice of toys, and choice of activities.

3. What are some strategies parents might use to avoid gender stereotyping in rearing their children? For example, would you allow your son to play with dolls or study ballet?

4. It has been observed that women have contributed to maintaining traditional family roles for women by failing to educate their sons for homemaking. Thus men are socialized to expect women to serve them as keepers of the home. To what extent is this belief correct? What are some complicating factors?

5. What are the benefits of the women's liberation movement to women? To men? To children?

6. Are men and women in conflict with each other, as Scanzoni and Scanzoni (1981) suggest?

7. Among marrieds what are the ways wives are seeking to change their husbands' role patterns?

8. What kinds of changes do men want in women that will make life better for their wives?

9. Given our present course of change, how do you believe the roles of men and women will differ in 20 years?

10. Was your mother employed outside the home when you were a child? If so, how do you think it affected you and your siblings?

11. How do you feel about men who choose to stay home and rear their children ("househusbands")?

12. Do you believe that children are necessary for a fulfilling life? Would your marriage be affected if your spouse voiced a preference to remain childless? How would your family and friends react if you and your spouse decided not to have children?

13. Do you believe that household chores and child care will ever be equally shared by husbands and wives? Why or why not?

14. For women, what are the advantages and disadvantages of both spouses being employed? For men? For children?

CHAPTER 6

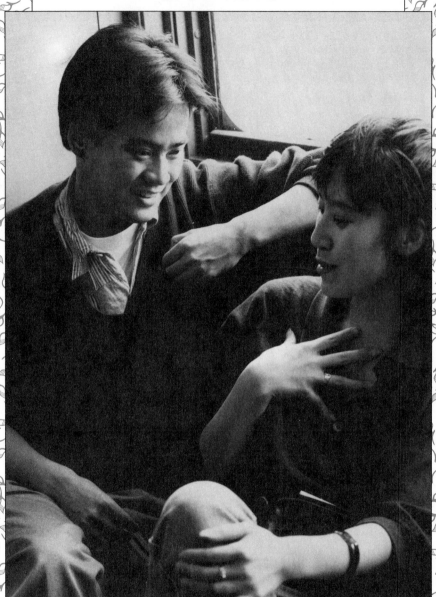

COMMUNICATION

Sue and Ed have been married almost 18 years. A few years ago, Sue finished her degree in nursing and returned to work. At about the same time, Ed enrolled in some classes in anticipation of his retirement from the military. Sue worked different shifts, and their schedules were busy with work, home, the kids, the dog, and so on.

In a short time, they noticed that it was harder and harder to talk without interruptions. But the situation was bearable. One evening Sue was clearing the dishes and remembered she needed to talk with Ed about an opportunity at the hospital: she could take additional training if she would agree to stay with the hospital for another year. She wanted the training and hoped Ed would not mind the commitment to stay.

Ed was soaking in the tub, and Sue decided that rather than waiting for him to get out and risk ringing phones and such, she would join him in the tub. They enjoyed a nice conversation without interruptions and have made a shared bath a regular part of their schedules. Their children tease them about their "baths." But they respond that at least this way they have each other's undivided attention in a relaxed atmosphere. They have plenty of time to talk, and they come out clean.

Importance of Communication

Few people could exist in a state of total isolation—not speaking or in another way exchanging ideas with another human being. Even those religious orders with a vow of silence provide human interaction through signs, expressions, and shared daily tasks.

We have a need to be understood and accepted as we are. We find happiness in sharing meaning with those with whom we feel comfortable and relaxed. We appreciate the person who gives us the benefit of the doubt and can overlook the silly or hostile things we sometimes say. As the nineteenth-century English novelist Dinah Maria Mulock Craik observed:

> *Oh, the comfort, the inexpressible comfort of feeling safe with a person, having neither to weigh thoughts nor measure words, but pouring them all right out, just as they are, chaff and grain together; certain that a faithful hand will take and sift them, keep what is worth keeping, and then with the breath of kindness, blow the rest away.*

Most of us do not live in isolation; we are fortunate to live with others who care genuinely for our welfare and who respect, appreciate, and love us. It is not enough, however, that they have those feelings; we need to have them expressed to us. Some researchers suggest that the *perception* of being loved or appreciated is as important as the communication variables that contribute to the perception (Rettig & Bubolz, 1983). Mutual expression of empathy, respect, regard, concern, and love do much to make any interpersonal relationships more meaningful and pleasant.

We spend about 80% of our waking time in communication-related activities. This amounts to about 13 hours per day of which 6 hours are spent listening, 4 hours are spent talking, 2 hours are spent reading, and 1 hour is spent writing (Millar & Millar, 1982; Swihart, 1985). Because those closest to us cannot read our minds, nor can we intuitively understand what they want or need, learning to convey likes, dislikes, hopes, dreams, goals, and desires is an essential part of a relationship with another.

When their wedding date was only a few weeks away, Tony and Beth began looking for an apartment to live in after they were married. While looking at an especially nice but tiny apartment, Beth remarked that it would be ideal until they had their first child. Then they would need more space and a yard, too. Tony was stunned; he did not want children and had assumed Beth felt the same way because she had never before talked about children. Needless to say, they postponed the wedding and spent some time comparing expectations about their life together.

Failure to share hopes, ideas, expectations, and beliefs in a clear manner can lead to marital conflict. The engagement period is an especially crucial time for a couple to learn much about each other's intentions. Many couples find it helpful to write out an informal marriage contract prior to marriage as a means of clarifying expectations about careers for both spouses, household chores, children, management of finances, and other issues.

Communication and Emotional Health

Researchers and psychiatrists have long recognized the central role communication plays in the emotional health of individuals (Satir, 1967). Many years ago, it was learned that infants deprived of physical handling and other forms of communication failed to thrive even though their physical needs were met (Spitz, 1945). We now recognize touch (a powerful form of nonverbal communication) as essential for

Axioms of Communication Theorists

1. All behavior is communicative. It is impossible not to communicate, since even silence or withdrawal indicates something about the relationship between two people.

2. Every communication has a content/report and a relationship/command aspect. The latter classifies the former and is, therefore, a metacommunication. The metacommunication is the nonverbal message about the verbal message. It is that aspect of the message that places a demand on the recipient. For example, if someone tells you that "the roads are slippery," it means that driving conditions are poor, but depending upon the tone of voice and the inflections, the person might be asking for a ride someplace, expressing concern about your ability to drive in these conditions, letting you know that he or she is not going to go someplace, and so forth.

3. Relationships are defined by the command messages and are dependent upon the punctuation of the communicational sequences between the communications. It is this command part of the message that is sometimes unclear. Misunderstanding can result when communicators are unaware of the commands they are giving, receiving, or obeying. The punctuational sequence between communicators refers to the flow of communication-response patterns. To return to the example of "the roads are slippery," if the command aspect of this message is a wish for you to drive this person someplace and you do not respond appropriately, the sender of the message may feel resentful and hurt by your lack of response, and you may feel upset because you have no idea why this person is acting hurt, since you never perceived the sender's command message—that is, the punctuational sequence has been ineffective.

4. Human beings communicate both digitally (verbally) and analogically (nonverbally). The verbal communication deals with the content/report of the message, while the nonverbal communication deals with the relationship/command aspect, which, as we noted above, is often unclear and ambiguous. Thus we are not just concerned with the meaning of the message, but also with what it says about the relationship between the communicators.

5. All communicational interchanges are either symmetrical (equal and parallel where either can lead) or complementary (where one leads and the other follows). Thus interactions are based on equality or on differences and enable us to learn about the nature of the relationship between the communicators. If the relationship is equal and symmetrical, the punctuational sequence is even and the power wielded by the demands of the metacommunication is equally distributed between the two communicators. If the relationship is complementary, one person usually dominates by demanding of the partner and by the partner's acceding to these demands. Thus, the complementary relationship pattern is of a "leader" and a "follower."

Source: Okun, B. F., & Rappaport, L. J. (1980). *Working with families: An introduction to family therapy.* (pp. 78–79). Belmont, CA: Wadsworth. Reprinted with permission.

healthy growth and development (Millar & Millar, 1982). Parents are encouraged to cuddle and snuggle their infants because it is vital to their development. Furthermore, children and adults who receive insufficient amounts of touching may develop difficulties such as allergies, eczema, and speech problems (Pearson, 1989).

A major message we all need to receive is validation of our self-worth. We require repeated reassurance that we are valued. When this message is not conveyed, particularly by significant others such as spouse and family members, an individual may experience negative psychological reactions such as loneliness and a sense of isolation (Bell & Gonzalez, 1988).

Emotional disturbances of a more serious nature also seem to be associated with communication difficulties for they interfere with the sending and receiving of clear messages and make it difficult for others to respond satisfactorily. Numerous studies have linked dysfunctional communication among parents to schizophrenic disorders in their children (Blakar, 1981). Carl Rogers (1961) has stated:

> *The whole task of psychotherapy is the task of dealing with a failure in communication. The emotionally maladjusted person, the "neurotic," is in difficulty first, because communication within himself has broken down, and second because, as a result of this, his communication with others has been damaged (p. 330).*

Communication and the Marriage Relationship

The clinical experiences of marriage and family therapists lead many to suggest that marital and family problems are primarily due to a lack of communication or to faulty communication styles. Consequently, one major objective of the therapist is to assist marriage partners in learning to communicate more effectively.

The importance of communication as a factor involved in marital success has been noted for many years (Alberts, 1988). The assumption of common-sense reasoning is that couples with a reasonable knowledge of each other's intentions, motivations, and expectations who are able to share love and respect are more likely to achieve marital happiness. A review of research over the past 20 years indicates that happy and distressed couples differ in their communication skills and styles (Anderson, 1986; Bell et al., 1987; Boland & Follingstad, 1987; Fowers & Olson, 1986; Jorgensen & Gaudy, 1980; Lacey & Jennings, 1986; Navran, 1967; Roberts & Krokoff, 1990; Stinnett & DeFrain, 1985). In contrast to distressed couples, happily married couples

- Keep communication channels open and talk more often.
- More often express greater depth and breadth of self-disclosure and are free to discuss intimate issues without restraint or embarrassment.
- More often express love, support, affection, and caring.
- Exhibit less frequency and intensity of problems and demonstrate greater conflict resolution ability.
- Use more nonverbal communication
- Express more positive nonverbal communication, e.g. pleasant voice tone, laughter, and affectionate touching of spouse.
- Demonstrate better listening skills and clarity of speech.
- More accurately interpret their partner's actions and indicate that they understand what is being said to them; they are more likely to interpret their spouse's behaviors in a positive way.
- Tend to communicate in a direct, clear manner without hidden meanings.

- More often express esteem, respect, and validation of spouse.
- Less often exchange complaints and criticism.
- Less often insist on having their own way.
- Much more often engage in positive rather than negative communication; they are less likely to escalate conflict and more likely to talk about pleasant events.

When spouses accurately understand the feelings, thoughts, and desires of each other, they are more adept at predicting how each will respond in a variety of situations and are more successful in dealing with their differences. Enhanced understanding of each other leads to positive awareness and responsiveness to each other. In this way, good communication contributes to marital happiness (Indvik & Fitzpatrick, 1982; Rice, 1990).

Kate and Eric are one of those married couples who often amaze their friends by seeming to read each other's mind. It is not uncommon when Kate begins searching for something, without saying anything, for Eric to suggest: "Your purse is in the bedroom" or "Your car keys are on the washer." He usually is correct in knowing what she is missing.

Not long ago, Eric and a friend had to conduct some business in a nearby town. They had not been gone long when they telephoned Kate: the car was stalled on the freeway, and all efforts to start it had failed. Eric said that they had pushed the car over onto the emergency lane near the Falbrook exit and he had had to cross the freeway to find a phone.

Kate set out immediately to help them. She arrived at the Falbrook exit and spotted the stalled car, but neither Eric nor his friend was with the car. She reasoned that they had walked down the exit ramp to get away from the heavy traffic on the freeway and to find a cooler place to wait. They were not on the street near the exit ramp, however. Kate recalled

that Eric had crossed the freeway to telephone, so she drove in that direction. Just across the freeway was a cluster of businesses, shops, and service stations—all with telephones. Then she remembered that she and Eric had stopped at the convenience store once several months ago. She pulled in at the convenience store and saw Eric and friend inside buying sodas. They were startled when they emerged and she was waiting for them.

Kate and Eric are not mind readers, of course. But they do know a great deal about each other and, as a result, are able to predict with considerable accuracy what the other will do under certain circumstances.

Strong families are characterized by good communication patterns. Members of strong families share many activities, e.g., household chores, cooking, yardwork, travel, camping, and sports; and they spend much time talking while they work and play. Healthy families maintain an accepting, supportive, open, and caring environment in which open and direct comunication styles can thrive (Fisher, et al., 1982; Stinnett & DeFrain, 1985, 1989).

What Is Communication?

Definition and Process

Communication is a process by which one understands others and in turn seeks to be understood by them. It is two people contacting each other; a communion; and a union of thoughts, feelings, and meaning (Swihart, 1985). This is perhaps the ultimate goal of communication within an intimate relationship, for true communication includes mutual trust, respect, understanding, and empathy. Communication in families involves sharing and companionship, every day and in many ways.

Communication includes both the verbal and nonverbal behaviors used by individuals in giving

Vietnam Veterans and Post-Traumatic Stress Disorder

I dream I am leaning over the bed to kiss a forehead goodnight, and there is a stir, and a beautiful trusting face has been transformed into the bubbled, flaking, disfigured black horror of the kid I once saw. (Ketwig, 1985, p. 295)

Vietnam ruined our lives. I keep remembering the Alan of before. He was affectionate, considerate, kind. When he returned, he had a quick temper, no patience, could not concentrate . . . right now I do not like him. (MacPherson, 1984, p. 260)

It has been estimated that 50% of the 800,000 combat veterans from the Vietnam conflict still suffer from post-traumatic stress disorder (PTSD). Post-traumatic stress disorder refers to a delayed but persistent malaise with symptoms that include depression, residual guilt or grief, nightmares, flashbacks, violent fantasies, anxiety, anger, mistrust, difficulty in relating to others, detachment, difficulty in keeping a job, suicidal feelings, feelings of worthlessness, and fear of loss of control.

Research conducted by the Veterans Administration indicates that the majority of Vietnam veterans manage to adjust and lead stable lives. Those who have made the best adjustments are those who have talked extensively about their experiences with supportive others—friends, family, or spouse.

The task of helping the veterans suffering from PTSD is complex. First, many wives do not realize that the change in their husbands is due to the trauma of combat; they may blame themselves. Others do not know how to help. Should they remain silent to avoid stirring up painful memories, or should they encourage discussion about Vietman? Finally, it is difficult to remain warm, optimistic, and loving to a husband who is aloof, abusive, or sullen.

One of the ways in which PTSD interferes with the marital relationship (and other interpersonal relationships) is by disrupting communication patterns. PTSD reduces the veteran's self-disclosure beyond the already low levels characteristic of men. Furthermore, PTSD increases the veteran's use of defensive communication. The wife's natural reaction to ongoing hostility is to develop communication apprehension and to become defensive.

Because wives of veterans are able to provide invaluable support, they need to be educated about PTSD and strategies for helping their spouses deal with it. A wife who is knowledgeable about PTSD, its symptoms, strategies for intervention, and resources (support groups for veterans and their wives, counseling programs for PTSD) will be able to do much to aid her husband's recovery. (Shehan, 1987).

Sources: 1. Ketwig, J. (1985). *And a hard rain fell: A GI's true story of the war in Vietnam.* New York: Macmillan. 2. MacPherson, M. (1984). *Long time passing: Vietnam and the haunted generation.* Garden City, NY: Doubleday. 3. Shehan, C. L. (1987). Spouse support and Vietnam veterans' adjustment to post-traumatic stress disorder. *Family Relations, 36,* 55–60.

and receiving messages. We communicate not only by the words (verbal) we speak, but also by the spirit, attitude, and intention underlying the literal content of the message being sent. Feelings are often more clearly revealed by the tone of voice with which something is said than by the verbatim content of the message. We also communicate nonverbally through facial expressions. For example, a wife may respond to her husband's invitation to join him on a business trip by clearly indicating through facial expression alone whether she wants to go or not.

Nonverbal communication has an important influence on the marriage relationship because so much of our interaction is affected by nonverbal messages. A great deal of what we exchange—feelings, ideas, information—is transmitted nonver-

bally through sight and touch. Our manner of dress, body posture, gestures, personal distance, and physical touch are other ways we send nonverbal messages.

Many feelings and thoughts are not easily conveyed in words and can more freely and adequately be expressed in nonverbal ways. Husband and wife may share "I love you" more effectively through a smile, hug, or thoughtful act than by verbalizing it. Many of us find apologies difficult so that "I'm sorry" can more readily be conveyed by a look or a touch. One may say, "I enjoy our tennis games," yet voice tone and facial expression may add, "I enjoy being with you; we're comfortable together."

Because nonverbal behavior is a vital part of communication, the ability to perceive nonverbal behaviors accurately benefits the relationship. For ex-

Susan Lapides/Design Conceptions

Nonverbal Behavior

Touch

Interpersonal touch is a nonverbal form of communication that can signal a high degree of intimacy and closeness (Anderson, 1985; Thayer, 1986). People vary considerably concerning how much they use touch in their interpersonal relationships and how comfortable they are with touching and being touched.

Numerous conditions, e.g., emotional state, marital status, and social roles, influence the amount and nature of touching deemed appropriate. Many individuals, however, are influenced by *touch avoidance*. Persons with this orientation are not comfortable with touching; they may touch when encouraged or required to do so in certain circumstances, but their touching is accompanied by negative feelings (Anderson et al., 1987).

After conducting a national study of 4,000 men and women, Anderson et al. (1987) concluded that persons with an opposite-sex touch avoidance orientation tend to be less open in their communication, less talkative, lower in self-esteem, and more apprehensive about communication. A significantly higher proportion of females evidenced opposite-sex touch avoidance. This may be due to differences in gender-role learning in which opposite-sex touching is more often discouraged and associated with negative consequences for females. The gender difference in touch avoidance may also help to explain research findings indicating that regardless of marital status men initiate considerably more sexual contact than women do (Blumstein & Schwartz, 1983).

Personal Space

Personal space is defined as the area persons maintain around themselves into which others cannot intrude without eliciting discomfort (Hayduk, 1983). The amount of space needed for comfort is influenced by degree of intimacy, circumstances, and cultural background. Although we may be comfortable "nose to nose" with a spouse or our children, we would squirm with strangers or the boss so close. Persons from Latin cultures or the Middle East typically stand closer to talk than do North Americans or Europeans. Negative emotions, anger, and stress promote a preference for more space (O'Neal et al., 1980, 1987).

The amount of space needed by persons may be categorized as intimate distance, personal distance, social distance, and public distance. *Intimate distance* extends from touch to about 18 inches and is used for showing affection, offering comfort, and giving support. *Personal distance* extends from 18 inches to about 4 feet and is used in friendly or family contexts. *Social distance* ranges from 4 to 12 feet and is used in situations that are not quite as intimate as family situations. *Public distance* exceeds 12 feet and is rarely used in family situations (Pearson, 1989).

Visual Interaction

Patterns of visual interaction, particularly initial eye glances, reflect existing status differences between two people. They also produce deference responses and immediately define the power relationship between two people in ways that influence the nature of later interaction, frequently without the awareness of either person (Dovidio et al., 1988; Rosa & Mazur, 1979).

In research conducted under laboratory conditions, women made eye contact with another person significantly more often while listening than while speaking. In contrast, men demonstrated more equivalent levels of looking at the other person both while speaking and listening. The visual pattern expressed by men is described as high visual dominance and has been associated with high social power. The visual pattern demonstrated by women has been associated with lower social power (Dovidio et al., 1988).

Sources: 1. Anderson, P. A. (1985). Nonverbal immediacy in interpersonal communication. In A. W. Siegman & S. Feldman (Eds.), *Multichannel integrations of nonverbal behavior* (pp. 1–36). Hillsdale, NJ: Lawrence Erlbaum. 2. Anderson, J. F., Anderson, P. A., & Lustig, M. W. (1987). Opposite sex touch avoidance: A national replication and extension. *Journal of Nonverbal Behavior, 11,* 89–109. 3. Blumstein, P., & Schwartz, P. (1983). *American couples.* New York: Pocket Books. 4. Dovidio, J. F., Ellyson, S. L., Keating, C. F., Heltman, K., & Brown, C. E. (1988). The relationship of social power to visual displays of dominance between men and women. *Journal of Personality and Social Psychology, 54,* 233–242. 5. Hayduk, L. A. (1983). Personal space: Where we stand. *Psychological Bulletin, 94,* 293–335. 6. O'Neal, E. C., Brunault, M. A., Carifo, M. S., Troutwine, R., & Epstein, J. (1980). Effect of insult upon personal space preference. *Journal of Nonverbal Behavior, 5,* 56–62. 7. O'Neal, E. C., Schultz, J., & Christianson, T. E. (1987). The menstrual cycle and personal space. *Journal of Nonverbal Behavior, 11,* 26–32. 8. Pearson, J. C. (1989). *Communication in the family.* New York: Harper & Row. 9. Rosa, E., & Mazur, A. (1979). Incipient status in small groups. *Social Forces, 58,* 18–37. 9. Thayer, S. (1986). Touch: Frontier of intimacy. *Journal of Nonverbal Behavior, 10,* 7–11.

ample, couples with high degrees of marital satisfaction are more adept at reading nonverbal cues than are dissatisfied couples (Boland & Follingstad, 1987; Sabatelli et al., 1982).

Couples with a high degree of marital satisfaction and families with good communication skills are likely to have a private message system that permits efficient nonverbal communication. Their private system is based on a history of agreed-upon meanings for specific nonverbal signals (Gottman & Porterfield, 1981; Stinnett & DeFrain, 1985). For example, whenever one couple we know holds hands—at the movies or watching TV—two quick, light squeezes mean "I love you." Sherrard (1980) tells of a sign she developed with her toddler. Tired of hearing herself repeating "No" to 2-year-old Andy, they devised an alternate plan as follows:

> I told him I would get his attention by calling his name. When we'd make eye contact, I would simply raise my hand, palm out, and shake my head "No!" We both loved it. It meant, for one thing, that we could communicate over some distance. If I saw him splashing water at the pool, and there was some reason for him to stop, I'd call his name, he'd look, and up would go my hand. The interruption in what he was doing, and the silent pact we had made, somehow made a change of behavior not a challenge or a reprimand, but a simple agreement between us. (p. 54)

The communication process involves the person sending the message, the person receiving the message, the message itself, and the social context within which the message is given. For example, the reactions of a wife receiving a message from her husband are influenced by the literal content of the message, the nonverbal information that accompanies it, the intention behind the message, and the manner in which her husband dispatches the message. The husband, in turn, responds to the attitude with which his wife listens and the way in which she receives his message. The meaning and intent of the husband's message as well as the wife's reaction to it are influenced by the social context that surrounds them and the message. The husband's statement, "The bill for the new stereo came today," can be a statement of fact for the wife's information. On the other hand, it can reflect hostility and resentment because he objected to the purchase; he may wish to make his wife feel guilty for her financial irresponsibility or selfishness. His voice tone, facial expression, and gestures would differ according to his intent.

Purposes of Communication

The general purpose of communication is to send and receive information. Much of the interaction in families involves the exchange of information, usually in a friendly, polite manner without any ulterior intentions. Included in this kind of communication are small talk, simple descriptions, reporting events, anecdotes, and factual information (Miller et al., 1975).

Although most communication is designed to exchange information and to contribute to the well-being of another, sometimes the intent of communication is to hurt someone or to influence a change in a person or situation. Some of the specific motivations for communication might be categorized as follows: (a) I value you, (b) I want you to value me, (c) I want to share these feelings and thoughts with

you, (d) I want to hurt you, (e) I want to control this situation.

1. *I value you.* Messages conveying affection, respect, and regard are essential for a relationship to have depth and true intimacy. Each of us requires many such messages to keep our self-esteem boosted. Judging by the number of complaints family therapists hear about lack of appreciation or being taken for granted, couples need to send more "I value you" messages.

2. *I want you to value me.* Because of the very strong human need to be valued, a great deal of communication involves a request (perhaps indirectly) for validation and approval (Bell & Gonzalez, 1988; Satir, 1967). This may take forms such as "Agree with me"; "Show me you are interested in me"; "Recognize my contributions." The plea to be valued is distorted when expressed in an immature, neurotic, or self-defeating manner.

3. *I want to share these thoughts and feelings with you.* In a broad sense, these messages indicate a desire for companionship with someone who is understanding and interested. Members of strong families report that they spend much time talking together about issues ranging from the trivial to the sublime. For them, communication is important not only to solve problems, but also as recognition that they truly enjoy each other's company (Stinnett & DeFrain, 1989).

4. *I want to hurt you.* This message may be a reflection of temporary frustration or it may be due to profound psychological and relationship problems. Commonly revealed as sarcasm, ridicule, or criticism, these behaviors are aimed at knowingly hurting another. The recipient naturally feels threatened and insecure. Prolonged use of "I want to hurt you" mes-

---

Symbolic Interaction Theory

Family researchers, educators, and therapists use many theories to explain human behavior; one of these is symbolic interaction theory. As the name implies, the two emphases in this theory are symbols and interactions. *Interactions* are the encounters and relationships we have with others; the encounters influence us and the persons with whom we interact. Through our contact with and observation of others, we develop *roles* such as husband, mother, or son; interaction consists of acting out one's roles.

The term *symbolic* refers to the idea that actions and events have meanings (symbols). Individuals have the ability to change the meanings attached to symbols or to vary the symbols for different places, people, and times. For example, a wife returns to work when the children enter school. What does this change in her role symbolize to her husband? Does it symbolize economic need (his inadequacy, perhaps) or creativity? To her children does employment mean abandonment or independence? The impact on the family will vary depending on their perceptions.

One major interest in symbolic interactionism is *self-concept*—that is, one's idea of what sort of person he or she is. Much of a child's self-concept develops in the family through interaction with parents, siblings, and other people who are important to the child. A child who is loved and hugged comes to view himself as lovable; a child who is given tasks and encouraged to do things comes to think of herself as competent. C. H. Cooley used the term *looking glass self* to describe this process of defining ourselves as we see ourselves reflected in the minds of others.

As children mature, they come in contact with more persons outside the family. Their awareness of the variety of roles they may assume grows. Interactions with many people help them to decide which roles (parent, policeman, librarian, spouse) to adopt.

Critics regard symbolic interaction theory as lacking in precision because of the implications that each family is different and that one behavior may be interpreted in several ways. Critics also contend that power and unconscious processes in relationships are ignored. In spite of shortcomings, symbolic interaction is a unique approach that has had considerable influence on family studies in recent years.

Sources: 1. Gullotta, T. P., Adams, G. R., & Alexander, S. J. (1986). *Today's marriages and families*. Monterey, CA: Brooks/Cole. 2. Lamanna, M. A., & Riedmann, A. (1988). *Marriages and families*. Belmont, CA: Wadsworth.

sages severely handicaps communication and ultimately destroys relationships.

5. *I want to control this situation.* The simple fact that we all have desires and needs motivates us to try to manage interactions with others, at least to some extent. Not all communications with this intent are necessarily counterproductive; bargaining, selling, promoting, and advocating are all attempts to influence a situation. However, when expressed excessively or in a negative or destructive manner, they are detrimental to communication and interpersonal relationships.

These motivations for communication are not exclusive categories but frequently are interrelated.

For example, an individual may send an "I want to hurt you" message to a partner because he or she has not received an "I value you" message from that partner.

Barriers to Communication

In John Steinbeck's *The Winter of Our Discontent*, Ethan ponders his relationship with his wife, Mary:

> When I am troubled, I play a game of silly so that my dear will not catch trouble from me. She hasn't found me out yet, or if she has, I'll never know it. So many things I don't know about my Mary, and among them, how much she knows about me.... (p. 48)
>
> Does anyone ever know even the outer fringe of another? What are you like in there? Mary—do you hear? Who are you in there? (p. 55)
>
> She doesn't listen to me either, and a good thing sometimes. (p. 57)

Although we think of the husband-wife relationship as being characterized by intimate communication, many couples experience meager or frustrating communication. Several factors interfere with clear interchanges in communication.

Cultural Differences

Culture is that part of ourselves that we absorb from our families, our neighborhood, our community, our schools, and the society in which we grow up. Each of us reflects the often widely varied backgrounds of our parents and grandparents. Today, with greater ease of travel, the mobility of many families, and the freedom for young people to mingle at college and work, marriages often involve two people who come from vastly different national, racial, socioeconomic, or religious backgrounds.

In the initial attraction of courtship, great understanding and tolerance between two people from different cultures may prevail. But it is important for them to face their future possibilities frankly and to discuss them openly.

Although thousands of immigrants have proved it is possible for such marriages to succeed, the problems faced by two people from dissimilar cultures are more complex. There may be vastly divergent attitudes toward sex, family life, roles of women and men, financial responsibility, or rearing of children. In some cultures, for example, birth control is a forbidden practice.

Broderick (1979) relates the situation of a young couple who sought help after their first public fight:

> After four years of struggle to get through graduate school and living in a cheap furnished apartment, this couple had found a beautiful apartment and set out to furnish it. They had no problem with furniture for the living room and study. Their tastes were very similar. Then while shopping for the bedroom, she discovered a beautiful suite that she fell in love with. She noticed that he did not share her enthusiasm. In fact, he looked grim. So she launched into a sales pitch describing all the good features of the suite and emphasizing what a great value it was because it was on sale. She concluded by adding that the twin beds should not bother him since her parents slept in twin beds and they were very happy. The fight escalated from there and included every problem they had ever had. Later he discovered that twin beds to her were a symbol of comfort and status. Struggling students might put up with a double bed, but certainly no one with a choice would. She discovered that to him the double bed was a symbol of marital unity and mutual affection. He had been very hurt by her apparent enthusiasm at leaving his bed.

Each cultural group also has its own set of rules and emphases for everyday conversations, use of words and expressions, use of praise and criticism,

Table 6–1 Factors Emphasized by Domestic Cultural Groups in Daily Conversations

Cultural Group	Factors Emphasized in Conversations
Mexican Americans	Polite behavior; relational climate (friendliness, affiliation, control)
Black Americans	Polite behavior; individuality
White Americans	Polite behavior; verbal content (supporting one's views, being relevant, staying on topic)

Source: Collier, M. J. (1988). A comparison of conversations among and between domestic cultural groups: How intra- and intercultural competencies vary. *Communication Quarterly, 36,* 122–144.

and ways of communicating (See Table 6–1). Several cultural groups deem it acceptable for discussions to be loud and animated, with a great deal of shouting and noisy exchange. In others, issues are discussed quietly, showing self-control and rational thinking. An individual reared in one style of discussion may be at a loss when a partner responds in the other style.

Differences in Gender-Role Learning

Another obstacle to communication between husbands and wives results from the different gender-role learning that takes place in childhood and adolescence. Although changes taking place in our society have resulted in gender roles becoming more similar, the traditional gender-role learning still dominates. Males traditionally are supposed to be adventurous, aggressive, active, and achieve-ment oriented. In contrast, females are expected to be passive, dependent, affectionate, and nuturant (Henslin, 1985; Oakley, 1985).

Many little boys learn what it means to be male by learning to be antifeminine or to display the opposite of female behavior (Barbeau, 1985). Under such circumstances, male children may develop perceptions such as these:

Girls are considerate and thoughtful; boys are rude.

Girls are well behaved; boys are mischievous.

Girls cry when they are hurt or sad and they hug each other; boys do not cry or hug.

As a result of men being socialized to restrain the sharing of their feelings and of women being socialized to be open and expressive, differences in communication styles are evident (Sollie & Fischer, 1985; Wheeless et al., 1988). Women provide more in-depth, intimate self-disclosure than men do; women's communication is characterized by more emotional sensitivity, sympathy, and consideration (Stephen & Harrison, 1985; Wheeless et al., 1988). Men disclose less negative information, possibly in an attempt to preserve a masculine image and use a communication style that is assertive, dominant, and aggressive (Gudykunst & Lim, 1985; Stephen & Harrison, 1985; Wheeless et al., 1988).

Although hiding true feelings is not limited to males, it is one of the problems that can arise for men who have learned that "real" men are stoic and strong. The man who masks his love, concern, hurt, or anger is likely to seem cold and indifferent to his mate. He may also be uneasy receiving warmth and tenderness from a partner (Barbeau, 1985). Misunderstandings and hostility may develop because women tend to view higher levels of expressiveness (openness and direct expression of feelings) as desirable, while men tend to view a high degree of expressiveness as "overreacting" or "too emotional" (Anderson, 1986).

Susan Lapides/Design Conceptions

Probably the greatest difficulty caused by differences in gender-role learning is that men and women come to regard each other stereotypically, as sex objects or as "housewife," "breadwinner," "father," or "mother" rather than as persons (Barbeau, 1985). The man who stereotypes his wife loses sight of her unique talents and traits. Likewise, the woman who stereotypes her mate no longer recognizes his special strengths and contributions. Stereotyping severely impairs understanding and communion with another person.

Indirect Communication

Indirect communication occurs when one person fails to let another know clearly what he or she means. Instead of expressing the intended message directly, the sender hints at the message, often leaving the receiver confused and frustrated concerning the exact meaning of the message.

For example, a wife who wishes to go to the movies may communicate this indirectly to her spouse by saying, "A good movie is playing tonight," never stating directly that she wants to see one. The husband, not realizing that she wants to go to the movies, may think she is making conversation and may respond by telling her about a movie review he has recently read. When he does not suggest, "Let's go to a movie," she may feel her request has been denied. In reality, he never realized it *was* a request. Similarly, the wish to go to the movies might be indirectly presented as someone else's desire: "Our daughter would like to go to the movies," or "You'd like to see a movie tonight, wouldn't you?"

Indirect communication can test another's feelings about something without risking rejection of the direct message in its entirety. It can be a means of avoiding embarrassment. In many instances, indirect communication serves the purpose of genuine protection and is not necessarily dysfunctional, unless it is so extreme or so frequent that others cannot understand the real meaning of an individual's messages.

Persons who use a great deal of indirect communication may do so because they established this pattern in childhood or because they have not learned more effective communication methods. Indirect communication may also be employed defensively because a mate's responses habitually are rejecting and negative.

Different Uses of Words

Another cause of misunderstandings is the assumption that "once something is said, it is understood." The sender of a message and the receiver of the same message may find themselves in trouble because they have different meanings for the same word. Heated arguments sometimes take place because one person is using a word in a particular way and the other person is using the same word in an entirely different manner.

The same word can have various overtones according to each person's frame of reference. To one person the word *school* may carry connotations of happiness, acceptance, and success. To another, *school* may mean unhappiness, rejection, and failure. Also, words can have various literal meanings. The following example from a marriage therapy session (Satir, 1972) illustrates:

HUSBAND: She never kisses or hugs me first. I always have to make the overtures.

THERAPIST: Is this the way you see yourself acting with your husband?

WIFE: Yes, I would say so. I didn't know he wanted me to make the overtures. He always said he didn't like aggressive women.

HUSBAND: I don't like *dominating* women.

WIFE: Well, I thought you would not like it if I took the initiative.

Overgeneralizations and Inaccurate Assumptions

Communication is handicapped when an individual assumes that one instance or experience is typical of all instances and experiences. Consider two generalizations as examples: "All men are mechanically minded" and "All little boys want to play football." Such assumptions can lead to responding to another person not as an individual but in terms of the overgeneralized stereotype. To continue the example, a father may insist that his son play football even though the son prefers the drama club. A wife may expect her husband to make repairs on the house and car, even though he has neither the inclination nor the skills to do so, because of her perception that all men are mechanically minded.

As adapted from the work of Satir (1967), the following are four types of inaccurate assumptions that interfere with clear communication:

1. *Assuming the other person necessarily shares feelings and attitudes.* A husband may expect his wife to enjoy playing golf because he enjoys it and may become angry when she does not share his enthusiasm. He is inaccurately assuming that everyone who tries it will love golf.

2. *Assuming that what has happened in the past or what is happening in the present cannot change.* This leads to a fatalistic attitude toward behavior and is frequently a barrier to resolving conflict. Someone may say, "I have always been that way.... I always get drunk when I am depressed. I guess I always will."

3. *Assuming that one knows the thoughts and feelings of another without checking the accuracy of these assumptions.* Misinterpretations of the feelings, desires, and motivations of another are often the result when one person projects personal emotions, tastes, and desires to a mate without attempting to discover his or her actual feelings. For example, a husband who likes practical and useful items may give his wife a vacuum cleaner as a gift. She—preferring something a bit more personal—may respond in anger, "You think I'm a drudge, your servant!" Both are guilty of *mind rape* (a term that refers to the practice of assuming you know another's thoughts without checking the accuracy of the assumptions).

4. *Assuming that another necessarily knows one's inner feelings and expectations.* Again, misunderstandings are likely when individuals do not communicate their preferences and expectations but behave toward others as if they had communicated them. For example, the newly married couple may wait anxiously, wondering why their parents do not come for a weekend visit. Meanwhile, the parents may be wondering why they have not been invited.

Wahlroos (1983) tells of a couple he counseled for communication difficulties. Their story illustrates much about inaccurate assumptions.

Dr. T was a man to be envied—a successful physician with professional recognition, respect, and wealth. He had divorced his first wife because she was very domineering, but soon he met a charming, compliant, and sweet woman who became the second Mrs. T. During their courtship she loved to surprise him with little attentions; he enjoyed it as a sign of her devotion. As a result she prided herself in knowing his tastes as well as he did.

Soon after the wedding they moved into a new home and she began redecorating without consulting him. He was not pleased, but he humored her; he

assumed her taste and his would become more similar in time. Her redecorating continued, and he grew angrier and more depressed by her little surprises. He retreated more and more often to his dark, oak-paneled study, which he had decorated himself to look somewhat like a gentlemen's club—very masculine but cozy.

Mrs. T sensed his growing depression and knew immediately what to do. Shortly afterwards, Dr. T returned home to loving kisses and an expectant look on Mrs. T's face. After a very pleasant dinner, he retired to his study to do some reading. He opened the door to discover the dark paneling covered by white wallpaper with blue flowers, the heavy, dark drapes replaced by light blue ones, and the solid tables and bookcases replaced by Danish modern versions. The shock almost ended the marriage.

She had meant so well: the new study was bright and cheerful and he had been so depressed. He had always enjoyed her surprises and she knew him so well. He was guilty of not speaking up to correct her assumptions and of believing she certainly knew how he felt.

Selective Perception

Selective perception takes place when we have a rigid manner of viewing certain aspects of human behavior and refuse to perceive them in any other way. Previously learned, subjective images persist, and rather than change in the face of evidence that clearly refutes the preconceived notions, we screen out behaviors that do not coincide with those we believe. This sometimes results in distortions of factual data in order that the established image may remain undisturbed.

A wife may have formed an image that men are interested in women only for sex and are not in the least interested in them as whole persons. Thus she may disregard her husband's behavior (consideration, affection, companionship) that does not coincide with her image. Even when he makes reasonable sexual advances, she feels and may say, "See, you aren't really interested in *me*, you're only interested in sexual gratification."

Frequently, selective perception and distortion are accompanied by behavior designed (often unconsciously) to prove the image, bringing about a self-fulfilling prophecy effect. For example, a husband with a fixed idea that all women nag may act in a manner (forgetting, failing, delaying) that prompts his wife to nag. Thus he confirms his selective perception about women.

Selective perception—in the sense of emphasizing the positive qualities of others and of life—is a desirable practice because it can nurture those positive qualities that contribute to contentment in relationships. Selective perception emphasizing negative qualities, however, constitutes a barrier to clear communication and adds to dissatisfaction in relationships.

Contradictory Communication

Confusion is added to the communication process when two or more messages sent by the same person contradict each other (Wahlroos, 1983). Contradictory messages may occur on the same or on different levels. For instance, a woman sends conflicting messages on the same level, the verbal level, when she says she would like to go shopping; then five minutes later, for no apparent reason, she says she does not want to go. Which does she mean? How does she want her family to interpret and respond? In another example, a wife may send crossed messages on different levels by remarking to her husband that she is looking forward to a camping trip with him. Yet as she speaks, she also sends a nonverbal message of boredom and disgust through her facial expression and shoulder shrugs. Which message is her husband to take seriously? And we have all heard someone say, "Nothing is wrong" in a tone of voice and with deep sighs that say, "Plenty is wrong."

In addition to being confusing, contradictory communication can have a double-bind effect on the receiver of the messages. A husband may indicate to his wife that he absolutely *does not* want her to go against his wishes in financial matters. When she complies, he complains that she lacks the spirit to stand up to him (or lacks proper financial concern for the family). This places the wife in a double-bind situation of being criticized regardless of which course of action she takes. Individuals who are subjected to long-term contradictory communication, especially with double-bind effects, may find their emotional health threatened (Satir, 1967; Wahlroos, 1983).

Contradictory communication requires an extra effort on the part of the receiver to interpret the messages that are sent. Matters usually can be clarified if the receiver feels free to question the sender. Such comments as "What did you mean by that?" or "You said you want to go camping but you look as though you don't want to go" encourage the sender to be more explicit and to eliminate the conflict.

Monologue

In the practice of monologue the assumption is made that communication is accomplished by simply *telling* another person something. This telling, or monologue, however, is an uncertain method of communication because it does not allow for exploration of the other person's feelings and ideas.

Although monologue may later give way to dialogue between individuals, the monological communicator is often so preoccupied with his or her own self and with talking about personal experiences, problems, and desires that he or she loses touch with the other person. The frustration of monologue is expressed in the following statements:

I have told my husband a thousand times, but it goes in one ear and out the other.

Many times when I come home from work I am tired and concerned about something that happened at work. My wife immediately bombards me with a tirade about her day: what the kids did and said, what mail we received, who she talked with on the phone, what she had for lunch, where she went on errands, and on and on. She doesn't even give me a chance to reply. I wish she would be sensitive to my moods sometimes.

Defensive Communication

Defensive behavior occurs when a person feels threatened by others. Partners who behave defensively expend a great deal of communicative effort in protecting themselves. Defensive feelings tend to produce defensive listening in which the individual does not hear accurately what another is saying because of concern with protecting his or her position. A marital partner's defensive listening and behavior are expressed in verbal and nonverbal cues, which in turn may increase feelings of defensiveness in the mate. Thus a cycle of defensiveness is set in motion, and the efficiency of communication is diminished.

Several specific kinds of behavior that increase defensiveness include:

1. *Evaluation behaviors.* These kinds of behaviors place blame, accuse, render judgment, or in some other way make the receiver of the message feel evaluated (usually negatively). Examples include a scolding tone of voice and messages such as, "You're a disgusting slob to leave newspapers and dirty coffee cups all over the living room."

2. *Control behaviors.* The attempt to govern another implies that the person to be controlled is somehow inadequate, immature, uninformed, or holds wrong attitudes. Control may be exercised openly or covertly (Buller & Buller, 1987). For example, Mr. Smith may tell his family, "I earn the money in this family and I'll choose where we vacation," or he may say, "Do you want to go to the mountains or the beach? Personally I prefer the beach, but you decide." If

Walker Montgomery

the family goes against his preference, he sulks and complains throughout the trip.

3. *Strategy behaviors.* A person who plays a role, feigns, or manipulates others causes feelings of resentment. Few of us enjoy being the victim of hidden motivations because we feel we have been used as an object rather than treated as a human being. (See Chapter 7 for more about stategy behaviors.)

4. *Neutrality behaviors.* Most persons want to be loved, respected, and valued by a mate. Neutral behaviors, e.g., lack of facial or voice expression and statements such as "I really don't care" convey little warmth, concern, or feeling in general and result in the receiver feeling rejected and isolated (Bell & Gonzalez, 1988).

5. *Superiority behaviors.* The person who acts superior transmits the message, "I am better than you." The receiver most often resents having his or her self-worth mininized and usually reacts negatively. An attitude of superiority may surface in a number of areas within a relationship: "My education/intellect is greater than yours"; "My salary is larger"; "My career is more noble/more important/more pres-

tigious"; "My relationship with our children is closer"; "I don't have your problem with alcohol/drugs/gambling."

6. *Certainty behaviors.* These behaviors imply an attitude of knowing all the answers and not needing information or ideas from others. Individuals who behave this way are seen as dogmatic, more interested in winning an argument than solving a problem, and intolerant of those who disagree.

Factors Contributing to Successful Communication

Positive Interpersonal Ethic for Communication

Ideally, communication in marriage is a comfortable sharing based on mutual appreciation, trust, respect, and understanding. But upon what are mutual appreciation, respect, trust, and understanding based? What makes couples try to achieve them? To a large extent such mutuality comes from a commitment—a positive interpersonal ethic—that the conditions will be created and maintained in which the potentials of both of them are best realized (Keller & Brown, 1968).

Because fulfillment of personal potential requires freedom to choose one's course of action, communication based on a commitment to achievement of personal potential must be characterized by freedom of choice. Certainty, control, and strategy behaviors (mentioned earlier with regard to defensiveness) inhibit freedom of choice. In contrast, three kinds of behaviors provide a supportive atmosphere for communication.

1. *Provisional behaviors.* In contrast to the dogmatic stance of persons using certainty behaviors, persons who are provisional are open-minded, willing to change, and willing to accept the attitudes and ideas of others. "I'm not sure about . . . . What do you think?" and "Let's examine all our options and courses of action in this matter and then we'll decide" are examples of provisional statements.

2. *Problem-orientation behaviors.* These behaviors are focused on mutual examination of issues and problem solving. Unlike situations involving control by one person, neither partner has a predetermined answer. In the example cited earlier, Mr. Smith's question of where the family would like to vacation becomes a genuine request for ideas: "The mountains will be cooler than the beach in August" or "We could stay at cousin Fred's at the beach. It would be cheaper." The focus of the discussion is to solve the issue of where to vacation, *not* to conform to Mr. Smith's wishes.

3. *Spontaneity behaviors.* A person who is sincere and who does not use strategies is viewed as someone who can be trusted with open and honest disclosures (Buller & Buller, 1987; Wheeless et al., 1988). Spontaneous behaviors do not involve maneuvers or strategies aimed at controlling another. (See Chapter 7 for more about spontaneous behavior.)

A positive interpersonal ethic for communication contributes not only to mature communication but also to a satisfying marriage relationship. Marital satisfaction is higher among couples who have communication described as relaxed, open, and attentive (Buller & Buller, 1987; Honeycutt, et al. 1982).

Mutual Regard

Positive regard for someone includes respect, trust, and acceptance. In order for the regard to be mutual, partners need to perceive each other as equals. Unless we are reasonably sure that we are valued by another and are convinced that the other is genuinely interested in our welfare, we do not feel safe in disclosing our innermost feelings and thoughts.

Handling Negative Feedback

Negative feedback comes to all of us at some time in a variety of forms; negative assessment of our abilities/accomplishments, criticism, accusations. How we interpret and handle negative feedback has a great influence on individual happiness and mental health and on our ability to care about others in productive, satisfying relationships.

A person who responds to negative or unsupportive feedback with a positive sense of self, a belief in personal efficacy, and an optimistic view of the future will be happier and more productive than the person who accepts the negative feedback as totally accurate and integrates it into his or her view of self. The ability to develop and maintain a positive self-image and optimism—even in the face of negative feedback—is a valuable human resource. Personal mental health is protected, and relationships benefit, too; persons who are positive tend to be constructive in relating to others. The ability to remain self-assured and optimistic is associated with higher motivation, more effective performance, and greater success in relationships.

Unfortunately, some couples fall into a pattern of giving each other negative feedback. They gradually accept the negative assessments as accurate, integrate them into their self-perceptions and their views about the marriage, and spiral deeper into negativism. Of course, this reduces their motivation to nurture a successful, caring relationship.

Source: Taylor, S. E., & Brown, J. D. (1988). Illusion and well-being: A social psychological perspective on mental health. *Psychological Bulletin, 103,* 193–210.

The honest expression of mutual high regard minimizes feelings of being threatened, thereby reducing guarded or defensive communication.

In contrast to evaluating or judging behaviors (which generally do not convey regard), *descriptive* behaviors are requests for information or presentations of fact or thoughts without any evaluation attached. For example, instead of saying, "You're a slob for leaving newspapers and dirty coffee cups in the living room," a person using a descriptive statement might say, "The living room would be more pleasant for me if you'd pick up the newspapers and dirty coffee cups." Table 6–2 lists behavior characteristics that promote or minimize defensive communication.

A Common Frame of Reference

There is a higher degree of happiness in marriages when the partners share similar cultural backgrounds (Kiersey & Bates, 1978; Knox, 1988; Price-Bonham & Balswick, 1980). This greater marital satisfaction and stability is due in part to better communication because they share a more common frame of reference.

A frame of reference refers to a background of experiences, ideas, and attitudes. If two people are to understand each other effectively on an intimate level, they need to share a somewhat common background of experiences, ideas, and attitudes.

One frequent cause of breakdowns in communication is that people attach widely varied mean-

Table 6–2 Behavior Characteristics that Promote or Minimize Defensiveness in Communication

Behavior that Promotes Defensiveness		Behavior that Minimizes Defensiveness
Evaluation	versus	Decription
Control	versus	Problem orientation
Strategy	versus	Spontaneity
Neutrality	versus	Empathy
Superiority	versus	Equality
Certainty	versus	Provisionalism

ings to the same event or word, primarily because of differences in past life experiences. Some couples argue endlessly as a result. When they become aware of each other's frame of reference, they often discover they are not really in disagreement. Insight can be obtained by asking, "Why do you feel this way?" "What does this particular experience/word mean to you?" and "How are you using this word?"

An example of the importance of considering another's frame of reference in communication follows:

(Jeff came in from shopping with a new slipover sport shirt that he was quite excited about.)

JEFF: How do you like my new shirt?

ANN: Oh, Jeff, it is beautiful! It makes you look so boyish.

JEFF: (in an angry voice) Boyish!!

ANN: All I meant was I think the shirt is youthful and attractive. That's what I meant by boyish.

JEFF: Oh, I see. Remember Uncle Bill? He loved to humiliate me by calling me a "boy"—even when I was a teenager and young adult. That was his ultimate insult.

Listening

She passed some cakes around to her guests and asked if they would like to try her homemade petits fours covered with arsenic. Everyone ate heartily and agreed that the icing was delicious. (Newman, 1959, p. 52)

This old story illustrates very clearly that adequately expressing thoughts and feelings—sending a message—is only one part of the communication process. Equally important is the receiving of the message, or listening.

In spite of the fact that listening is a vital part of communication, it is often neglected. One hears such statements as, "Talking to my husband is like talking to a brick wall," or "My mom and dad are so wrapped up in their lives that they never listen to me." Family members who do not listen miss a great deal about each other.

One reason why listening is so vital in communication is that listening, in and of itself, conveys a message of interest in and concern for the other person. Also implied is the significant idea that the receiver/listener values the speaker as a person and as a communicator (Bostrom & Waldhort, 1988; Cleaver, 1987).

It is just as important to "listen" to the nonverbal cues and tone of voice as it is to the literal content of the message. Nonverbal signals serve as indicators of a person's state of feeling. In interpretive listening an individual discerns meanings from another through cues given by voice tone, pitch, and changes in the rate of speaking (Bostrom & Waldhort, 1988). Ray, for example, can tell when his wife is tense because she speaks more rapidly, breathlessly, and in a higher pitch.

Learning to Listen

Alexandra Pierce, a professor of music at the University of Redlands in California, teaches listening courses. To begin, she sensitizes students to the myriad subtle sounds around; they quietly concentrate on their own breathing and then become aware of other sounds—birds outside, the hum of fans and fluorescent lights, doors closing down the hall.

Students also learn to describe sounds according to characteristics such as bend, grain, and volume. Bend refers to the line a sound makes; a singer's voice has many bends, while electric motors drone without bends. Grain describes the roughness of sounds. Metal scraping on metal is rough grained, while flute music is smooth. Analyzing sounds in this way increases awareness of bend, grain and volume in peoples' voices in everyday conversations. One result is a a heightened sensitivity to subtle tones and inflections that convey unexpected messages.

In one exercise, students take a vow of silence for a day to encourage them to listen more. In another, students list sounds they like and dislike, analyze the sounds, and examine why they respond as they do to the sounds.

Source: Dreyfuss, J. (1986, March 5). Lend an ear to this advocate of more attentive listening. *Los Angeles Times,* Part V, p. 1.

When she is tired, her voice becomes monotone and she speaks more slowly.

Checking the Meaning of Communication

In the classified ad section of a small-town newspaper, the following ad appeared on Monday:

> FOR SALE: R. D. Jones has one sewing machine for sale. Phone 958 after 7 P.M. and ask for Mrs. Kelly who lives with him cheap.
>
> On Tuesday—NOTICE: We regret having erred in R. D. Jones' ad yesterday. It should have read: One sewing machine for sale. Cheap. Phone 958 and ask for Mrs. Kelly who lives with him after 7 P.M.
>
> On Wednesday—R. D. Jones has informed us that he has received several annoying telephone calls because of the error we made in his classified ad yesterday. His ad stands corrected as follows: R. D. Jones has one sewing machine for sale. Cheap. Phone 958 after 7 P.M. and ask for Mrs. Kelly who loves with him.
>
> On Thursday—NOTICE: I, R. D. Jones, have no sewing machine for sale. I smashed it. Don't call 958 as the telephone has been taken out. I have not been carrying on with Mrs. Kelly. Until yesterday she was my housekeeper, but she quit. (Wahlroos, 1983 p. 3–4)

Inaccurate interpretations of messages happen very easily and cause needless misunderstanding and conflict. One facet of creative listening is the ability to check the meaning of messages that are not clear. Meaning can be clarified by questions or comments: "I'm not sure what you meant," or "This is my understanding of what you said," or "Let me rephrase what you said. Tell me if this is accurate." This technique is referred to as *feedback* (Wahlroos, 1983).

Empathy

Newborn babies are egocentric and require years of growth before they learn that other people have feelings, too. Maturation of the whole person involves an increasing recognition of the feelings of others. Empathy is the ability to identify with the emotional state of another—to feel with him or her.

Empathy is motivated and influenced by a genuine concern for others (Stiff et al., 1988). Consequently, individuals who are absorbed by their own interests, problems, and needs may not be empathic.

A high degree of empathy makes partners sensitive to each other: empathy helps them see beyond words to inner feelings. Because of their greater understanding, tolerance increases. Empathy inhibits aggression in interpersonal relationships and tends to minimize antisocial behavior (Miller & Eisenberg, 1988).

Acknowledging Another's Feelings

WIFE: I'm depressed. We never do anything together anymore.

HUSBAND: That's not true! Don't you remember that last Friday we went to a party and on Saturday we went to the football game? And two weekends ago we were at the beach house.

WIFE: (Silence)

HUSBAND: You still feel depressed?

WIFE: Yes, and lonely.

HUSBAND: Maybe it really doesn't matter how much we've done together lately. The important thing is that you feel sad and lonely. That's not a pleasant way to feel.

WIFE: Well, you're right. We have done quite a few things together. I guess that isn't the real reason I'm feeling bad. Maybe it will pass by tomorrow.

As this dialogue illustrates, feelings are not always logical. Sometimes what we identify as the cause of our negative moods is not the cause at all. We have a tendency to reason in this manner: "I feel bad (depressed, angry, lonely), and there must be a reason. If I examine my life, I will find it." Because our lives are not perfect, we can find something or someone to blame. In reality, negative emotions are sometimes due to hormonal/metabolic changes in the body, minor illnesses, or fatigue.

Of course, there are instances in which negative feelings are accurately based on an event or circumstances. Regardless of whether emotions are founded or not, it is therapeutic to acknowledge those feelings. In doing so, we let another know that we are aware of him or her and of what is happening in his or her life.

When parents who had experienced the death of a child to sudden infant death syndrome were interviewed about their experiences, they repeatedly mentioned that the people who had helped the most were the ones who had allowed them to grieve openly, who had cried with them, who did not chide them for being sad or regard them as crazy for grieving. Although they probably meant well, persons who said things such as, "Time heals" or "You've got to get on with your life and stop moping" inflicted pain (DeFrain et al., 1982).

Assertiveness

Communication is enhanced when it remains a way of expressing feelings and wishes without becoming a device for attack. A person who is able to state a position clearly and forcefully enough to be taken seriously and who can defend or affirm his or her opinions in a positive way is using assertive actions. In contrast, aggression involves hostile behavior—either verbal or physical—and an attack on another (Lamanna & Riedmann, 1988).

Many persons require practice to learn to express themselves assertively. Three recommendations for becoming more assertive follow:

Issues and Resolutions

Issues

Three issues are involved in communication throughout the marriage relationship: inclusion/exclusion, power, and intimacy. *Inclusion/exclusion* deals with boundaries and the question of who or what (such as in-laws, friends, career, children, pets) is involved in the marriage system and to what degree; it deals with the amount of intrusiveness that will be accepted in the relationship.

The issue of *power* is concerned with who is in charge of the relationship. Some couples struggle over who will dominate, while others struggle over who will be taken care of. Many conflicts are ignited by the question of who will tell whom what to do under what circumstances.

All couples negotiate for *intimacy* as they struggle with their need for but fear of closeness. They seek a balance between a sense of autonomy and feelings of belonging. Even when both partners are comfortable with the same level of intimacy, communication patterns must be arranged to accommodate intimacy in the relationship. Who will pursue whom, for example?

Resolutions

Couples may achieve resolution of these issues in two major ways: through symmetrical or complementary patterns. In the symmetrical pattern, spouses are in balance or competition; if one spouse adds an attribute, so does the other in an attempt to maintain equality. When each negotiates from a position comparable to the other and when each strives for equal control, they are interacting in a symmetrical pattern. Partners have equal and similar role definitions.

The symmetrical couple perceives the world through the same lens. Their strength lies in their ability to understand and harmonize with each other as well as in their capacity to push themselves and each other to fill the gaps left by their symmetry. Their weakness lies in the tendency to become overly competitive and to blame each other when things go wrong.

The complementary pattern of resolution works like a seesaw; if one partner is up, the other must be down. The more important a particular attribute is in one partner, the less important it is in the other partner. If one is knowledgeable where the other is ignorant, or if one is actively defining the relationship while the other is passively accepting, they are considered to be interacting in a complementary way.

The complementary relationship is based on differences. The strength of these couples is that each person has picked a partner who operates best in another sphere than his or her own. Complementarity operates smoothly when each acknowledges the other's competence and is willing to learn from the other. Problems occur if one always dominates and one always yields or if roles become so excessively rigid that partners are too dependent on each other.

Most couples fall somewhere in between purely symmetrical or complementary patterns. Marriages that are extremely complementary or excessively symmetrical are more rigid, more vulnerable to dysfunction, and less amenable to problem solving. Distressed couples may need to change rigid patterns of interaction in order to achieve satisfaction. For example, very competitive couples may have to learn not to keep score; a very deferent spouse may need to become more assertive.

Source: Fish, R. C., & Fish, L. S. (1986). Quid pro quo revisited: The basis of marital therapy. *American Journal of Orthopsychiatry, 56,* 371–384.

1. *Express how you feel directly. Do not avoid the issue.* Because of a fear of hurting someone's feelings, we sometimes fail to speak directly. For example, your spouse asks you to go swimming but you have promised to help a friend with an errand. Instead of trying to squeeze both into your schedule, say, "I can't swim now because I promised to help Pat, but let's go tomorrow." In another example, a woman described her quandary: her husband bought an expensive blouse for her birthday but she hated it! She did not want to wear it, but she did not want to exchange it for fear of offending her husband. She might say in an assertive mode, "I have a problem. I appreciate your gift of the blouse, but it looks terrible on me. I'd like to exchange it." If she feels strongly about his choosing clothes for her, she may also ask him to take her along on shopping trips in the future.

2. *Keep things in perspective.* Keep trivial things trivial by airing them. When problems are stored and not solved, the extent of resentment and magnitude of feelings make a reasonable resolution harder to reach (Stinnett & DeFrain, 1989).

3. *Avoid attacking.* Remember to keep the focus on discerning *what* is best, not *who* is right (Ketterman, 1985). If, for example, your spouse forgets to bring home steaks for dinner as you had asked, it does little good to comment: "You can't remember anything, you idiot!" or "You never do what I ask." The issue is what to do about dinner.

Self-Disclosure

One aspect of openness in relationships is the willingness to share feelings voluntarily and to tell things about oneself. Opening oneself to another can encourage that person to feel comfortable in openly sharing himself or herself (Buller & Buller, 1987).

Self-disclosure is fostered in an atmosphere of trust (Patterson, 1985; Wheeless et al., 1988). Trust involves both benevolence (a feeling that the partner is genuinely interested in one's well-being) and honesty (a feeling that the partner can be believed) (Gass & Nichols, 1988).

Although self-disclosure can have beneficial effects on marriage satisfaction, a word of caution is in order. The nature of the self-disclosure influences its effect on the relationship. Negative disclosures, "brutal honesty," and extreme criticism are very destructive. Satisfied couples report more self-disclosure than do unsatisfied couples; however, unhappy couples disclose more negative and unpleasant feelings than happy couples do. Moderate degrees of self-disclosure (rather than extremely high or low degrees) seem most conducive to maintaining relationships over time (Gilbert, 1976; Lazarus, 1985).

Intimacy

Each of us recalls special moments of closeness with another person—times when we have felt good about ourselves and the other person. It is fortunate when family members can experience such moments of connectedness. Although this kind of intimacy is a dream for most families, some accomplish it more successfully than others. Why?

One reason lies in the way that people communicate with each other. Intimacy has, in fact, been defined as the depth of verbal and nonverbal exchange between two individuals. It entails a true acceptance of each other and a commitment to the relationship (Galvin & Brommell, 1982; Stinnett & DeFrain, 1989). Intimacy develops in our relationships through communication patterns that are affectionate, affirming, and open.

Summary

- Communication is vital to the success of interpersonal relationships.
- Verbal and nonverbal communication play a central role in an individual's emotional well-being.
- A partner's ability to interpret a spouse's message and predict behavior or outcome as a result is a key to marital success.
- The intent of communication takes the following forms: I value you; I want you to value me; I want to share these feelings and thoughts with you; I want to hurt you; and I want to control this situation.
- Factors that interfere with clear communication include: cultural differences, differences in gender-role learning, and unsatisfactory communication styles. It is these styles, e.g., indirect communication, overgeneralization, inaccurate assumptions, selective perception, contradictory communication, monologue, and defensive communication, that leave messages open to misinterpretation and that can lead to interpersonal conflict.
- Certain behaviors diminish the efficiency of communication, e.g., acting in a judgmental, controlling, manipulative, or superior manner. Other behaviors provide a supportive atmosphere for communication, e.g., acting in an open-minded, nonjudgmental, relaxed, and spontaneous manner.
- Factors that contribute to successful communication include: the expression of mutual regard, the existence of a common frame of reference, the ability to listen, the willingness to share, and the ability to respond assertively.
- Healthy relationships are achieved by maintaining an accepting, supportive, and open environment in which direct communication styles can thrive.

Discussion Questions

1. Research has indicated that happily married and unhappily married couples differ in their communication styles. Review, in a very specific way, how these styles differ.

2. Give two examples of a negative style of marital interaction and its resulting effects.

3. Give two examples of a positive style of marital interaction and its resulting effects.

4. In what ways do you believe your own behavior is inconsistent with establishing good communication within a marriage? How can you change that behavior?

5. Discuss some ways a person you have dated has communicated with you that made you feel uncomfortable. How did you handle the situation?

6. How would you propose to change the behavior of your spouse if you believe he or she really did not listen to what you said?

7. Think of a recent disagreement you had with a dating partner, roommate, or parent. What barriers affected your communication?

8. Describe a situation in which a trivial matter triggered a large disagreement. How could the situation have been handled differently?

9. What are your strengths in communicating? What are your weaknesses?

10. Which of the factors contributing to successful communication do you think is the most important? Why?

CHAPTER 7

PSYCHOLOGICAL
GAMES

❧

Olga [Picasso's first wife] wrote [letters to Picasso] almost every day long tirades in Spanish, so that I wouldn't understand, mixed with Russian, which no one understood, and French.... Sometimes she would send a picture of Rembrandt on which she had written, "If you were like him, you would be a great artist." Pablo read these letters through to the end and was tremendously bothered by them. I suggested to him that he just put them aside but he couldn't; he had to know what she said.

(Gilot & Lake, 1964, p. 154)

❧

Games versus Intimacy

One of the challenges of modern living is developing and maintaining the truly meaningful relationships that we want and need to have with others. There are many reasons, of course, for the difficulties we experience in relationships. Contemporary life easily becomes a treadmill of work, housework, child care, social obligations, and recreation. Because of demands on time and energy, we use fixed patterns of interaction such as rituals and pastimes in many of our exchanges. The exchange of platitudes and clichés is useful and convenient, but such interaction does not allow for the development of closeness.

For some people, occupational success and social attainment are highly prized and are viewed as incompatible with close human relationships. A multitude of superficial contacts appears to be a more efficient way of achieving their goals. Or they may perceive that intimate relationships drain time and energy away from their occupational or social efforts.

Even in the relationship of marriage, the development of an honest, growing relationship sometimes is avoided (Corey, 1985). Husbands and wives play out roles and allow psychological games to become substitutes for real intimacy.

In family conflict there is frequently a great deal of psychological game playing. Unfortunately, game playing is a very nonproductive approach to conflict management; conflict may cease temporarily, but genuine resolution does not occur. Even though some people are not aware that they are game playing, their objective is to cover up motives and to trick their partners into doing what they want them to do (Galvin & Brommel, 1982).

In our search for ways to bring family members closer and to bridge the gap that often exists in relationships, it is beneficial to examine what a psychological game is and to consider some of the common games. The following definition and some examples are based largely on the work of Berne (1964) and Chapman (1968), two authors whose work on psychological games is classic.

What Is a Psychological Game?

A psychological game is defined as a pattern of interaction between two or more persons that su-

Gender, Power, and Influence Tactics in Relationships

1. Being female or relatively more feminine, having fewer structural resources than one's partner, or being more dependent than one's partner increases the use of weak tactics, e.g., dropping hints, flattering, being seductive, recalling past favors, pleading, crying, acting ill, acting helpless.

2. Being male or relatively more masculine, having relatively greater structural resources than one's partner, or being less dependent than one's partner increases the use of strong tactics, e.g., issuing threats, insults, and ridicule; exhibiting violent behavior; claiming knowledge; asserting authority.

3. Males and those who are less educated are more likely to use disengagement, e.g., sulking, making the other feel guilty, leaving the scene.

Source: Howard, J. A., Blumstein, P., & Schwartz, P. (1986). Sex, power and influence tactics in intimate relationships. *Journal of Personality and Social Psychology, 51,* 102–109.

I Don't Want to Listen

Some persons deal with conflict and reality by ignoring it. One way to do this is to refuse to listen to a spouse, parent, or child when they bring up a disagreement or unpleasant reality. Watching television, listening to loud music, cooking, and doing chores are ways to do this. Walking out of the room, changing the subject, or discussing inconsequential matters are other techniques.

Anita is the mother of two teenagers. Lately she has been tired out by work, housework, and community projects. She asks her daughters one morning, "Do you think that you could take on one or two chores each to help me out? I have too many things to get done and never seem to get enough sleep." One daughter continues to watch the morning news on television; the other studies her assignment book for school. Anita persists, "Girls, I'm afraid I'm going to be ill if I can't have some help from you. I'm not asking for much of your time—just 30 minutes a day or so." At this point, one daughter exclaims, "The bus," and they both dash off. The bus is not due for another 15 minutes.

Source: Ewy, D. (1985). *Preparation for parenthood.* New York: New American Library.

perficially appears legitimate or honest but actually has an ulterior motive. When a person plays a psychological game with someone, the interaction involves a "gimmick"; a psychological game is basically dishonest and is characterized by manipulation (Wahlroos, 1983; Saxton, 1990). For example, if someone hints for a compliment, e.g., "Do you like my new haircut?" and, after praise is given, uses it in a way that makes the giver look insincere, e.g., "Thanks, now what do you want—a loan?" or stupid, e.g., "How can you think this looks good? Anybody can see it is awful." That is a game.

Another characteristic of a psychological game is a lack of spontaneity. The person who plays the game plans the interaction to produce a desired effect, usually to manipulate and maneuver the other person into doing what the game player desires (Corey, 1985; Tedeschi et al., 1973; Wahlroos, 1983).

Psychological games *should not* be considered fun or frivolous. Some are amusing and relatively harmless, but others are vicious and destructive (Brammer & Shostrom, 1982; Coleman et al., 1980; Ma-

gran, 1981; Wahlroos, 1983). Although all of us use psychological games to some extent, the constant playing of these games may reflect an emotional disturbance. Of course, the continual use of psychological games may also *cause* emotional disturbance.

Some Common Psychological Games

Any number of psychological games are played within human relationships; however, some appear more often than others. Following is a brief discussion of some games commonly found in family situations. These games occur outside family relationships, too.

Corner

The corner game involves a process by which one person interacts with another in such a manner as

Rickey Yanaura /The University of Alabama

Why don't you ever host parties like my friends' wives do? You are the only one who doesn't. You are hurting my chances of advancing in the company because you are unfriendly.

However, if she does entertain guests, she receives this type of criticism:

Why didn't you talk more with Mrs. Anderson tonight? You should have circulated more. The flowers on the buffet table were wilted; the wine was too sweet; the food was cold.

Another example would be the mother who complains to the teen that her room is never clean. Yet, when the teen tidies her room, Mom says, "What took you so long?" or "The closet is still a mess."

Tell Me Your Problems

"Tell Me Your Problems" is a game in which one person appears to be extremely interested in the welfare of another. The apparent motive for the concern is to understand and to help; however, the real motive is to expose the person's weaknesses. The game player increases his or her feelings of self-worth by devaluing another.

For example, the wife may appear to be very concerned with her husband's situation. After listening to his enthusiastic report of a wonderful day at work, she may respond, "Yes, but tell me how you *really* feel?" With this reaction from her, he may feel that honesty requires him to reveal some troubles. She is an attentive listener and encourages him to look for difficulties by telling him that she wants to help. After learning his vulnerable areas, however, she betrays his confidence by revealing his weaknesses to neighbors or friends. She may make remarks such as these:

I am worried about Edward. He works too hard. I hate to see him getting so tired and tense because he drinks too much. He had some emotional problems a

to place him or her in a situation where anything he or she does is wrong. The game player maneuvers the other into a situation of "damned if you do and damned if you don't."

The corner game is extremely frustrating to the person who is "cornered" (Wahlroos, 1983). Clinical research suggests that much emotional disturbance is caused by an individual's having been continually cornered by a spouse or earlier in life by a parent.

For example, a husband badgers his wife to give parties for his friends at work; however, when she hosts such social gatherings, he criticizes her for the way they are handled. The wife is forced into a corner. If she does not entertain, her husband criticizes:

few years ago—a breakdown, actually. I have tried to help Edward; I don't think he could make it without me. It is such a heavy responsibility to have to "carry" someone emotionally.

In this case, the wife makes her husband appear emotionally unstable and presents herself as the strong force that supports Edward and holds him together. In doing so, she gains sympathy and admiration from others, and her ego is boosted.

We Should Do This for You

In this game, one person desires to do or have something but attempts to achieve this goal by making it seem that the *other* person needs to have or do it. For example, a wife may feel too tired to go to her in-laws' home for dinner. Instead of straightforwardly telling her husband that she does not want to go, she suggests:

> *Honey, I think we had better skip dinner with your folks tonight. Don't you think you need to stay home and study?*

Perhaps it would be best for her husband to study, but the point is that she is not revealing her true reason for not wanting to visit her in-laws. She may fear her request will be rejected if put in terms of *her* reasons for wanting to stay home; she may wish to avoid being responsible for disappointing her in-laws. As a result, she makes the request to stay home in terms of her husband's need to study.

In another example, parents sometimes insist on exclusive, expensive schools or camps for their children's benefit. In reality, the parents are satisfying their own needs for prestige or vicarious accomplishment.

Sweetheart

The "Sweetheart" game is a maneuver in which one person indirectly ridicules the other in public. The psychological "jab" is done in such a subtle manner that probably no one except the victim is aware of what is happening. The motive for this game is to make the victim feel bad about himself or herself; the game player achieves feelings of superiority at the expense of another.

For example, a husband who resents his wife's earning more money than he does may vent his hostility by using the "Sweetheart" game to accuse her of neglecting their children. At a social gathering, in the presence of several people including his wife, he tells a story about a working woman who was so wrapped up in her career that she neglected her children. He concludes the tragic tale by commenting on how unfortunate it is when parents neglect their children, after which he casually turns to his wife and asks, "Don't you agree, sweetheart?"

Because he appears to be talking about someone else and because it is an extreme case, his wife would seem unreasonable if she objects or retaliates. If she confronts him in private, he may dishonestly say, "But sweetheart, I wasn't talking about you," or "I was talking about someone else, but if you feel the story applies to you, perhaps you should do something about it."

It's Your Decision

Sometimes people who wish to escape the responsibility of making a decision place the burden of deciding on the shoulders of another with comments such as these: "It makes no difference to me," "Whatever you would like to do is fine," or "You know so much more about this than I do, you decide." Although actually very much concerned about the outcome of the particular decision, the game player insists that he or she is not and thus escapes the responsibility of facing the consequences of the decision (Wahlroos, 1983).

For example, Jack would like to go to the theater tonight, but he is quite tired and relaxing at home is appealing, too. He says, "It doesn't matter to me;

you decide" to his wife. If they stay home, he doesn't feel guilty for bypassing a good play. If they go out and the theater production is poor, he need not be angry at himself for a bad choice. In a destructive aspect of this game, he may direct his anger toward his wife and say, "You sure goofed that time. What a waste of money to see that boring play!" A really expert game player can use this game to lead into the "Corner" game.

Parents frequently play this game with each other about their children. The father, for example, may refuse to help the mother make child-rearing decisions, e.g., selecting a preschool or daycare program, choosing a music teacher, evaluating orthodontists. Then when something seems to go wrong or if one of the children gets into some kind of trouble, the father self-righteously blasts his wife with, "Are you sure you know what you are doing?"

Courtroom

Many times marriage and family therapists see husbands and wives play this game because "Courtroom" typically involves a third party (Magran, 1981). One spouse assumes the role of the plaintiff and accuses the other of wrongdoing. The partner who plays the role of defendant insists on his or her innocence, justifies his or her behavior, and counters with accusations against the partner playing the plaintiff. The third party represents the judge to whom defendant and plaintiff present their cases. Each player wants the judge to approve of his or her actions and to disapprove of the other partner.

The accuser often does not listen to the explanation of the defendant but simply continues the attack. Much of the communication of persons playing "Courtroom" is directed toward the judge rather than toward each other. This prevents them from achieving mutual understanding and a satisfactory solution to their problems. Persons playing this game often seem to be more interested in proving who is right and who is wrong than they are in solving their difficulties.

Camouflage

"Camouflage" is a technique in which one person sends a message that seems on the surface to communicate one idea but actually is intended to communicate something else. One partner hints about something rather than giving the message in a direct, clear manner. The "Camouflage" game is used to avoid confrontation or negative responses from another, thereby serving as a means of self-defense.

The unfortunate aspect of this game is that the hint may be so indirect that the person for whom it is intended never receives it. When this happens, the game player may become frustrated and resent the other person for being so "indifferent and stubborn." For example, Herb is slightly overweight. His wife wishes he would watch his weight more closely, but she will not voice her concern directly for fear that it will injure his pride or that he will retaliate in some way. Instead, she camouflages by saying, "Isn't it just unbelievable how many health problems are due to a person's being overweight?" or "Have you seen Bill lately? He's lost 20 pounds and looks really great." Herb may catch the hint, but the chances are high he will never realize her remarks are directed at him.

Martyr

"Martyr" is a game in which one person appears in some way to be mistreated or to be sacrificing a great deal in life for another. The person playing martyr talks very often about how he or she is sacrificing or about his or her unfortunate lot in life. However, it is often the case that the game player deliberately makes the sacrifices in order to play the martyr.

Lana is an insurance executive who works long hours, usually spending the evenings at her office. She misses few opportunities to remind her husband and children of how hard she works and how it hurts her health. This provides her with leverage in making family decisions, giving her the power she seeks. After all, she has given up so much for them, they would be selfish and brutish to deny her whatever she asks.

The payoff for playing martyr may be to gain admiration and sympathy. Another objective may be to make a spouse feel guilty, making it easier for the game player to get his or her way.

Why Don't You . . . Yes, But

This is a game of one-up-manship. It is illustrated by the following example:

HUSBAND: I have a problem. It's getting late and I need to get these leaves raked up before it rains tonight.

WIFE: Could the kids help?

HUSBAND: Yes, but they goof off more than they work.

WIFE: Well, could I help?

HUSBAND: Yes, but then dinner will be late and you know how I hate to eat late.

In this interaction the husband gains competitive satisfaction at his wife's expense by discrediting every suggestion she makes (Coleman et al., 1980).

Wooden Leg

"Wooden Leg" is designed to elicit sympathy and is used as an excuse for failing to become responsible or independent. In effect, the game player asks, "What do you expect of a wooden leg?" The "wooden leg" may be a personality deficiency, a physical handicap, or an unstable past (Coleman et al., 1980). For example, the parent asks, "How do you expect me to be patient with the kids? I have a short temper." Or the person who drinks too much asks, "What do you expect from someone whose parents were heavy drinkers?"

We Never Fight

Sometimes a husband and/or wife will be unwilling or afraid to face open conflict and will agree to ignore issues in order to live in false harmony. They may suppress disagreement and find alternate sources for satisfaction in their effort to present a "perfect couple" image to outsiders. How long this game works depends on their capacity for self-delusion (Rhodes & Wilson, 1981).

Look How Hard I've Tried

This is another game that marriage and family therapists often see. The payoff for the game player is relief of guilt. Although both partners state that they want to improve their relationship through therapy or improved communication, the game player is not committed to the change. He or she goes through the motions without any real dedication and then says, "Look how hard I've tried; there's nothing more I can do" (Magran, 1981). This game may be used in collusion with someone playing "Why Don't You . . . Yes, But" or "Corner" (Wahlroos, 1983).

Crazy Making

"Crazy making" refers to a variety of maneuvers used to make a partner doubt his or her sanity or to send a partner "up the wall." The crazy maker gains power over the victim (Wahlroos, 1983). Many variations of "Crazy making" are possible; several are mentioned here.

1. *Denying a feeling the partner can clearly see.* For example, the person who mopes and pouts but declares, "Nothing is wrong" or "If you don't know, what's the use in telling you?"

2. *Denying something that has been discussed and agreed upon or insisting on adherence to exact wording.* For example, "I never agreed to go out of

---

Neglected

When, for example, a woman perceives that she has been abandoned by her husband or her grown children or others, she may keep herself miserable in order to punish those who in her view are responsible for her bereft condition. If she were to make a good life for herself she would have to give up the "right" to punish. She may feel that if she were to prosper and enjoy life, she would reveal to the rejecting persons that she didn't need them so much after all, so whatever they "did" to her wasn't so bad either. That's a hard position for some "victims" to take, particularly those who derive their potency from their moral superiority. Both men and women play this game.

Source: Williams, E. F. (1976). *Notes of a feminist therapist.* New York: Prager.

town *this* weekend" or "I said you could call your sister about coming for the holidays. I didn't say you could do it right away."

3. *Building up hopes and then shattering them without an acceptable reason.* For example, the parent who agrees to take the children to an amusement park on Sunday and then asks, "Why are you dressed to go out? Where are you going? I've changed my mind and don't nag about it!"

4. *Attributing vicious motives to another.* For example, "Where did you hide my socks this time?" or "You conveniently forgot to make reservations, didn't you?"

5. *Ignoring the other person's wishes.* The person who just cannot ever be on time, the person who continues a mannerism that annoys after being asked not to do so, the child who will not pick up toys or dirty clothes are all examples.

6. *Seeing a hidden psychological significance in every action; psychoanalyzing.* For example, "People who choose cats for pets are introverted" or "Your body language tells me that you're sexually repressed."

Why Are Psychological Games Played?

The use of psychological games prevents the intimacy and understanding that most persons desire in their relationships. Game playing is not an effective way to draw close to one another or to solve conflict (Cox, 1981; Dunn, 1988a, 1988b; Galvin & Brommel, 1982; Lasswell & Lobenz, 1981; Millar & Millar, 1982). The question naturally arises, "Why would anyone resort to the subterfuge of games?"

Lack of Trust

When partners do not trust each other, it is difficult to be honest about feelings or desires (Dunn, 1988a; Rhodes & Wilson, 1981). For example, a woman who wants to spend the weekend at the beach may hesitate to suggest it directly to her partner because she does not trust him to respond favorably—possibly because of her past interactions with him.

Rickey Yanaura /The University of Alabama

She could present the idea openly, by saying:

The weather is supposed to be beautiful this weekend. I'd love to go to the beach, lie in the sun, swim, and have seafood for dinner.

Instead, she uses "We Should Do This for You" to avoid a direct confrontation. She says:

Darling, you look so very tired. I think you need a break. You know, I'll bet a weekend at the beach would do wonders for you.

Often we do not trust ourselves to achieve desired goals, and we believe we must rely upon others to achieve these goals for us. Yet, because we do

not completely trust others, we manipulate them by game playing (Dunn, 1988a; Shostrom, 1967).

Desire to Avoid Reality

For a year Tim told his wife Carrie that he was coming home later and later because of pressures at work. He was too tired for sex because he was working so much. Deep inside Carrie suspected that Tim was seeing someone else. But reality was too painful to face. Instead, she pretended that he was overworked. And Tim pretended that his extramarital relationship was not serious. The crisis came when Tim became physically ill due to the strain and told Carrie the truth. It was a hurtful time for both of them. She was angry in part because now she had to admit that they did not have an ideal, loving marriage. He had to face the fact that he had deceived her and hurt her. (LaRoe & Herrick, 1980)

As in the case of Tim and Carrie, couples may justify pretending to protect one another. And it may seem easier to continue a charade than to shed protective masks. Ultimately, however, avoiding reality requires much effort and may be very hurtful.

Honesty and self-disclosure are important in fostering intimacy in a relationship. Each, however, needs to be used judiciously. Large amounts of negative self-disclosure can affect a relationship adversely; total honesty is sometimes an excuse to be cruel. Absolute honesty all the time may not be desirable for a relationship; something left unsaid may be kinder, and large amounts of tact are often needed.

Fear of Close Relationships

Fear of close relationships is another reason for playing psychological games (Corey, 1985; Dunn, 1988b; Millar & Millar, 1982; Rhodes & Wilson, 1981). Some individuals fear intimate relationships because they have been hurt, exploited, or disappointed in the past by someone close to them. For example, a woman who has been greatly disappointed in a past love affair may be reluctant to establish another close relationship because she fears being hurt again. Also, a person who experienced miserable relationships during childhood may avoid close relationships in adulthood in order to protect himself or herself.

We may also fear close relationships because of the responsibilities involved. By avoiding involvement with others, we avoid the responsibility of being concerned about their feelings or welfare and of having to spend time with them. Whatever the reason for being reluctant to establish intimate relationships, psychological games are often used either consciously or unconsciously as a way of keeping others at a distance (Corey, 1985; Dunn, 1988a, 1988b; Millar & Millar, 1982).

The love relationships of some individuals are dominated by psychological game playing. Game-playing love is self-centered and characterized by manipulation of the partner through strategies designed to keep him or her emotionally off balance. A game player typically lacks commitment to the relationship and is reluctant to work through problems (Lasswell & Lobenz, 1981). The game player's objective is to play at love — seeming to encourage intimacy, yet holding it at a distance (Cox, 1981).

Gary and Jean had been married for 25 years when he came into therapy. Although he was an intelligent man, with a doctorate in his field, he did not know how to be loving and affectionate. Jean had reconciled herself to a cool, distant relationship, but she learned that Gary had been having an affair for 3 years. Jean demanded that he tell what had happened and why. Because Gary had been rebuffed as an adolescent when he tried to express his feelings, he refused to talk. Jean gave him a choice: talk or leave. (LaRoe & Herrick, 1980)

Unfamiliarity with Alternatives

In the case of Gary and Jean, a crisis forced Gary to seek professional help and to change. Without a crisis, many couples continue to engage in game playing because they are unaware of other ways of interacting. They may have learned psychological games as children by observing the interaction of parents and other adults or as a way of coping with their family environment (Dunn, 1988a).

Change is threatening to most of us because of our fear of the unknown. It takes courage to alter patterns of behavior and to risk trying new ways of communicating. Consequently, familiar ways of dealing with people and problems may persist even when they are less than desirable.

Getting Even: Passive-Aggressive Behavior

Passive-aggressive behavior is characterized by stubbornness, sulking, pouting, dawdling, intentional inefficiency, and procrastination. The passive-aggressive person's unannounced goal is to act aggressively without having to accept responsibility; maneuvers are calculated so that he or she can deny any aggressive intent. Passive-aggressive individuals want love, affection, and nurturance but feel unsafe and resent being vulnerable. Their uncertainty about whether to be active or passive results in their vacillating between seduction and rejection, being submissive then demanding.

Whereas overtly aggressive individuals may be insulting, combative, and assaultive and make no effort to disguise their hostility, passive-aggressive individuals give a superficial appearance of compliance and conforming. They may smile politely, be ingratiating, and complimentary while setting a trap. They attack and punish others indirectly through maneuvers that they claim are innocent.

Typical examples include "misplacing" an important document, "forgetting" homework or an appointment, creating an ambiguous communique that will lead to confusion, placing an important message on the recipient's desk in an obscure place, and mailing a check without signing it. Many thrive on stimulating jealousy, envy, and other negative emotions among colleagues; they usually are expert at spreading gossip and rumors.

Passive-aggressive behavior may develop as a coping strategy in an environment where self-expression and assertiveness are discouraged or punished. Though it may be denied or veiled, great anger and negative self-esteem are present. The passive-aggressive individual frequently develops a maladaptive strategy for building his or her self-esteem by attacking another's in the belief, "I can't feel adequate and significant; I'll see to it that no one else does either."

Passive-aggressive individuals are at their best working in organizations where people are rewarded for political manipulation rather than productivity. They function well in bureaucratic businesses and agencies where they can find security and protection in the structure of the system and can manage to avoid being held directly accountable for their destructive acts. They are often rewarded, because others wish to avoid them and will do their work for them rather than deal with them.

Source: 1. Dunn, J. R. (1988). Getting even: The dynamics of passive aggressive behavior. *The Christian Journal of Psychology and Counseling, 3*(2), 13–15.

Viewing Others as Persons to Be Used

One of the basic reasons we manipulate others is the tendency to view people as something to be used. The prevailing emphasis on economics has led to an inclination to judge a person's worth in terms of what he or she achieves or earns.

Business organizations traditionally have been interested in their employees in terms of what the employees can produce. The employee is seen as someone to be controlled for the profit of the business organization. Some salespeople and manufacturers see the potential buyer only as a customer to be manipulated into buying their product. It is not surprising, then, that many individuals, even in intimate relationships such as marriage, view a partner in terms of "What can this person do for me?"

Another factor that contributes to the practice of psychological game playing is the philosophy in our culture that "the end justifies the means." Lying and deception are perceived as acceptable behaviors if the end result is desirable or profitable (Millar & Millar, 1982).

The Roots of Psychological Games

The psychological games used in adulthood are often learned in childhood (Berne, 1972; Dunn, 1988a). Some clinical evidence suggests that game playing runs in families and that certain games appear to be passed from one generation to the next. When parents use certain psychological games with each other and with their children, the probability is high that the children will play these games themselves. Children learn the games by imitating their parents, siblings, and peers.

A person may also learn game playing during childhood through trial and error. Children notice that when they employ a particular maneuver they usually get what they want. In this way, they learn to manipulate people. They use the game over and over; it becomes a habit. Game playing within families may also reflect the fact that children, adolescents, and adults who are unable to adjust to the environments in which they are living may develop dysfunctional patterns of dealing with people in order to cope (Dunn, 1988a, 1988b).

Parent-Child Game Playing

The games that adults use between themselves to avoid confronting the realities of their relationships are often played in the parent-child context as well. For example, parents may play the "Corner" game with their children: "You didn't do your homework again. You'll never get anywhere in life" or "How did you get your homework done so quickly? Just rushed through it, I suppose." And many parents ridicule their children in public with a variation on "Sweetheart": "That child is so clumsy; he trips over his own feet. Isn't that right, son?"

Such tactics make parenting more difficult, destroy a healthy parent-child relationship, and harm the child's development (Dunn, 1988a, 1988b). A

Go-Between

The bonds most important to maintaining a family are the bonds between husband and wife. Sometimes those are weakened by conflict or neglect; sometimes they are broken by divorce. In some of those instances, the adults use a child or children as a go-between. Everyone suffers: the adults lose their relationship; the go-between often feels responsible for the relationship and guilty about its deterioration (Ewy, 1985).

Andy and Gina were divorced last month after a long and angry separation. Andy avoids all contact with Gina. When he needed to get his tools from the garage, he sent their teenage son to pick them up. He sends a child-support payment each week, but, again, it is delivered by their son. When Andy needed information to file his income tax return, he sent a note to Gina via their son. He tells his son, "Ask your mother why she did....."

Source: Ewy, D. (1985). *Preparation for parenthood.* New York: New American Library.

more positive approach recognizes the importance of a child's feelings and of understanding the child's perceptions of what is happening. Instead of game playing, parents are encouraged to talk to children in ways that preserve self-esteem and so that statements of understanding precede statements of advice or instruction. For example, if a child comes home from school looking sad, avoid the condemnatory, "What trouble did you get into today?" and instead ask, "Did something unpleasant happen today?" In this way, the child perceives understanding without condemnation or criticism and feels encouraged to talk about what happened.

A Lifestyle of Manipulation

Earlier in this chapter we described specific psychological games that families sometimes use in their interaction with each other. It is important to realize that the use of psychological games often is part of a broader style of life that might be labeled *manipulation*. Manipulation refers to a system of dealing with people that is characterized by trying to exploit, control, and use others (Brammer & Shostrom, 1982; Shostrom, 1967). The manipulator promotes his or her own interests at the expense of another (Bramson, 1981).

Manipulation is a problem not only in families but in all human relationships. It contributes to strife among nations, races, employers, and employees because it is based on dishonesty and artificiality. A person who manipulates another often maintains a false front in order to create a desired impression and often uses tricks and deceit to influence another's behavior. This dishonesty and phoniness leads to a general distrust between people. Perhaps the greatest problem of all is that manipulation contributes to people seeing each other as *things* instead of as people.

Each of us can manipulate others psychologically in a variety of ways. And we have many models from which to learn manipulation: salespersons and

Joel Gordon

television commercials that maneuver us to buy a product, people who make us feel guilty in order to control our behavior, the child who throws a temper tantrum to get a new toy, the young man who pretends he loves a young woman to convince her to have sexual intercourse, the person who feigns interest in what another is saying, the person who is always careful to say what others want to hear.

Several specific manipulative approaches to interpersonal relationships have been suggested (Brammer & Shostrom, 1982; Shostrom, 1967). When we are aware of some of the various types of manipulations, we can better understand ourselves and others.

The Dictator Type

An example of the dictator-type of manipulator is the man who dominates and controls his wife and

---

Manipulative Children

Children learn quickly that they can also manipulate and play games to accomplish their aims. Shostrom (1972) gives the following examples of how children may manipulate:

1. Whining, crying, or nagging. Finally exasperated parents concede to the child's wishes just to have some peace.

2. Threatening. "I'm going to quit school if you don't...," "I'll run away if...," or "I'll probably get sick" are examples.

3. Using love. Children may use "You don't love me (care about me, care about what I think, etc.) or you would...."

4. Comparing. This is where parents meet the elusive "everyone" and "no one" as in "Everyone at school wears Reeboks" or "No one else has a 10 P.M. curfew."

5. Playing one parent against the other. If Mom won't say yes to a request, ask Dad. If he doesn't know what she's said he might agree. Then go back to her and say, "Dad says I can."

6. Moping, depressed, melancholy. Parents attempt to cheer the sad child by doing what he or she wants.

Source: Adapted from Shostrom, E. L. (1972). *Man, the manipulator.* New York: Bantam.

---

children by ordering them around. He may dictate how every penny of the family income is to be spent on the premise that he is an authority in financial matters, for example. In relating to others, the dictator type often projects a parent or boss image and spends much time managing others for their presumed good.

The Weakling Type

An example of the weakling-type manipulator might be the wife of the dictator-type husband. She allows her husband's domination because it makes him responsible for her problems and failures in life. She entices him to dictate, control, and abuse her; then she complains about how abusive and unjust he is in an attempt to make him feel guilty. She may also elicit sympathy and solace from friends by playing the martyr. Weakling types avoid many

unpleasant and threatening demands and responsibilities by pleading "I can't ...."

The Calculator Type

The calculator-type manipulator characteristically controls others by deceiving, lying, and outwitting them. An example of this type of manipulator is the compulsive "Don Juan" who is obsessed with seducing women. Other examples are high-pressure salespersons and con artists.

The Clinging-Vine Type

The clinging-vine is similar to the weakling in that these manipulators exploit their dependency upon others. An example of this is the man who wants to be cared for and who wants his family and friends to do his work for him. This type includes persons who persist in playing the "perpetual child," the "hypochondriac," the "attention demander," and the "helpless one."

The Bully Type

The bully-type manipulator controls others through hostility and cruelty. Examples are the woman who humiliates her husband or children both publicly and privately and the man who gets his way by threats when his wife disagrees with him.

The Nice-Guy Type

The nice-guy-type manipulator exaggerates caring and love for others and uses a kind approach as a very effective way of controlling. His or her "niceness," rather than reflecting genuine caring and love, is superficial and is designed primarily as a way of managing people. An example is the person who feels others must always be pleased at all times and who always says what others want to hear.

Table 7–1 Fundamental Characteristics of Manipulators and Actualizors Contrasted

Manipulators	Actualizors
1. *Deception (phoniness, knavery).* The manipulators use tricks, techniques, and maneuvers. They put on an act, play roles to create an impression. Their expressed feelings are deliberately chosen to fit the occasion.	1. *Honesty (transparency, genuineness, authenticity).* Actualizors are able to express feelings, whatever they may be. They are characterized by candidness, expression, and genuinely being themselves.
2. *Unawareness (deadness, boredom).* Manipulators are unaware of the really important concerns of living. They have "Tunnel Vision." They see only what they wish to see and hear only what they wish to hear.	2. *Awareness (responsiveness, aliveness, interest).* Actualizors fully look and listen to themselves and others. They are fully aware of nature, art, music, and the other real dimensions of living.
3. *Control (closed, deliberate).* Manipulators play life like a game of chess. They appear to be relaxed, yet are very controlled and controlling, concealing their motives from "opponents."	3. *Freedom (spontaneity, openness).* Actualizors are spontaneous. They have the freedom to be and express their potentials. They are masters of their lives and not puppets or objects.
4. *Cynicism (distrust).* Manipulators are basically distrusting of self and others. Down deep, they don't trust human nature. They see relationships with humans as having two alternatives: to control or be controlled.	4. *Trust (faith, belief).* Actualizors have a deep trust in self and others to relate to and cope with life in the here and now.

The Judge Type

The judge-type manipulator is demonstrated by the man who attempts to dominate his wife and children by being extremely critical and by comparing them unfavorably with others. Variations of this type of manipulator, who specializes in making others feel guilty, include the "resentment collector" and the "convictor."

The Protector Type

The protector-type manipulator is overprotective and oversupportive of others in that he or she does not allow them to mature and become independent.

An example is a wife who plays "mother hen" with her husband to the extent that she makes him look like a child. Other variations of this type are the person who always suffers for others, the person who is embarrassed for others, and the martyr.

The Actualizer versus the Manipulator

Other approaches to interpersonal relationships are more satisfying than manipulation. Instead of being deceitful, phony, and controlling, each person

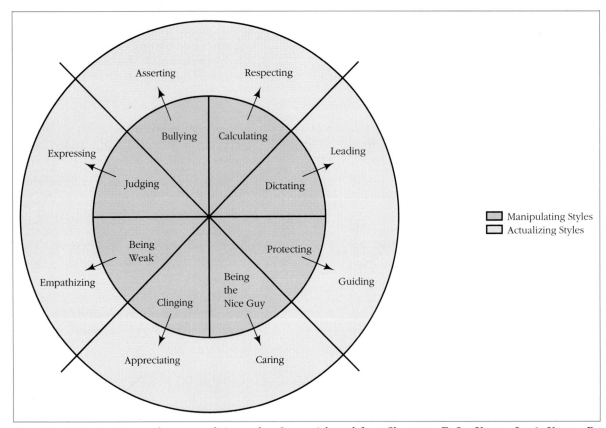

Figure 7–1 Manipulating styles to actualizing styles. *Source:* Adapted from Shostrom, E. L., Knapp, L., & Knapp, R. (1976). *Actualizing Therapy.* San Diego: EDITS. p. 142. Reprinted by permission.

has the potential to relate to others in ways that (a) reflect genuine interest in and appreciation for others, (b) acknowledge the worth and potential of others and bring out their positive qualities, and (c) promote the welfare and growth of others.

The latter type of relationship could be called the "actualizing relationship." The term *actualizing* has been made famous by Maslow's (1962) concept of the self-actualizing person. It is the thesis of Maslow that we can understand psychological health and healthy relationships by studying the characteristics of people who possess an unusually high degree of mental health and who relate to others in a very satisfying, healthy manner. Such persons have been called self-actualizing.

It is helpful to contrast some basic characteristics of the manipulator and the actualizor. As Table 7–1 indicates, the manipulator's philosophy of life is characterized by the four basic qualities of deception, unawareness, control, and cynicism. In contrast, the actualizor's philosophy of life is characterized by honesty, awareness, freedom, and trust.

Although much of human behavior is determined by personal history and forces beyond one's control, the actualizing process is based on the premises that one's future is largely undetermined and one has a wide range of *freedom to choose* (Brammer & Shostrom, 1982). Persons who recognize manipulator tendencies in themselves may wish to change to become actualizors. Many self-defeating manipulative behaviors may be naturally transformed into comparable, but honest, nondeceptive actualizing behaviors (see Figure 7–1).

Intimacy

Intimacy is a "union of personalities." It results in mutual verification of the persons involved. Intimacy requires openness, emotional responsiveness, caring, and commitment. Intimacy has many facets.

1. Emotional: sharing significant meanings and feelings; being tuned in to each other.
2. Intellectual: sharing ideas.
3. Aesthetic: closeness in experiences of beauty.
4. Creative: sharing the experience of making something, of creating.
5. Recreational: fun and playing together.
6. Work: sharing common tasks or goals.
7. Sexual: expresson of caring and enjoyment of each other.
8. Conflict: facing differences and struggling with them.
9. Crises: coping with problems and pain together.
10. Commitment: feelings of mutuality.
11. Spiritual: feeling united in sharing ultimate concerns.
12. Communication: the tool for all other kinds of intimacy.

Source: Sanborn, C., Cline, M., & Lawless, N. (1981). *Human relations: A discovery of self and others.* Lexington, MA: Ginn Custom Publishing. Copyright © 1988 by Ginn Custom Publishing. Reprinted by permission.

Logically and ideally, family relationships are the place where actualizing relationships begin. Within the family is where the child should learn how to behave in a relationship based on honesty and trust. Because the husband-wife relationship is the cornerstone for other family relationships, it sets the primary example and mood for parent-child relationships and sibling relationships that follow. There is truth in the statement, "one of the most important things a mother and father can do for their children is to establish a truly intimate, loving relationship with each other."

Summary

- The development of an honest and meaningful relationship is undermined when partners allow psychological games to become a substitute for intimacy.

- A psychological game is a dishonest type of behavior. It is a pattern of interaction that appears legitimate but actually has ulterior motives. Some games are employed as a way to avoid conflict, e.g., "We Should Do This For You," "It's Your Decision," "We Never Fight," while others are more openly confrontational, e.g., "Courtroom," "Martyr," "Crazy Making." In all cases, such dishonest behavior only heightens the conflict.

- Psychological games are played for many reasons. These include: a lack of trust in others, a desire to avoid reality, a fear of close relationships, an unfamiliarity with alternatives, and a view that others are tools to be used for the player's benefit.

- A pattern of psychological game playing can be developed by children who witness it being carried out by adults. Such behavior is harmful to a child's self-esteem and can damage the parent-child relationship.

- The manipulative behavior characteristic of psychological game playing creates an environment of deceit, exploitation, and control. This contributes to problems beyond the family. Race relations, employee relations, even international relations are affected by such a dishonest environment.

- Manipulative behavior, e.g., the weakling, the judge, the dictator, is in stark contrast to the honesty, awareness, freedom, and trust characteristic of self-actualizing behavior. Healthy relationships develop as a result of the positive approach undertaken by actualizors.

Discussion Questions

1. Describe the impact on others of a person who frequently plays the game, "It's Your Decision."

2. How do people usually respond to persons who play "Corner?" How could you respond so as to break the game?

3. What message is communicated when a person plays "Sweetheart?"

4. What is a better response to use when a person is tempted to play "Look how hard I've tried?"

5. What do persons reveal about their ability to control their lives when they play "Wooden Leg" or "Martyr?"

6. If a person plays the game, "Why don't you ... Yes, but," how should you respond?

7. Describe a situation in which you observed a couple playing one of the psychological games mentioned in this chapter. How could they have been more direct?

8. As a child, what methods did you use to manipulate your parents? How successful were you? How do you think you will handle similar situations when you are a parent?

9. Is there a particular psychological game you are likely to use? How can you avoid playing this game?

10. Which psychological game do you think is most harmful to a relationship? Why?

CHAPTER 8

DEALING WITH
MARITAL CONFLICT

History is replete with laws and customs that allowed women to be beaten, tortured, or killed by their husbands. For example, in preclassical Greece, women enjoyed relatively high status. Even so, women fell into three categories: mistresses for pleasure, concubines to attend the masters' physical needs, and wives to bear children and to be housekeepers. Marriage was the only alternative for a respectable woman; and it was arranged by her guardian without her consent.

Rome had marriage laws that spelled out the rights of husbands and the obligations of wives. Husbands were allowed to whip wives for minor offenses and to kill them for infidelity. In contrast, wives were not allowed even to reprimand their husbands for infidelity.

A sixteenth-century Russian domestic code allowed that disobedient wives should be soundly thrashed. Husbands were advised, however, not to strike on the face or ear because a blind or deaf wife would be a severe disadvantage.

(Pagelow, 1984)

Conflict Is Inevitable

A surprising number of people believe that no discordant voices are ever heard in a loving marriage; well-matched couples are protected from conflict by their deep devotion to each other. And even if other couples are unfortunate enough to fight, certainly *they* will never argue.

Always, however, there will be differences of opinion, different ideas about family life or jobs, differing aspirations, different ways of dealing with children, and different concepts of celebration or grief. No two people are alike, and their lives cannot be identical. Conflict occurs in every relationship.

> *Disagreement is really difference brought into painful encounter through coming close. But what people want to do in marriage is to come close. So when they come close many of their differences turn into disagreements because never will you find a married couple where both of them want to do exactly the same thing at the same time in the same way. (Mace & Mace, 1980, pp. 102–103)*

Although a few couples seem to thrive on disagreements characterized by loud, angry words and open hostility, most do not. When conflict comes to a relationship, we can endeavor to minimize destructive anger and to move toward a satisfactory resolution of the problem.

Mature couples accept the inevitability of conflict; they do not accept that the conflict must inevitably be harmful. They recognize that they have a choice of letting conflict become a battle, a negotiation, or a discussion. In most instances, couples in conflict have a variety of options for resolving their conflict.

One of the essentials of marriage success is for couples to learn to make creative use of conflict. Persons can learn to react and respond in ways that deal effectively with anger and conflict: disagreement can be expressed without destructive hostility,

and negotiating skills can be developed (Boland & Follingstad, 1987; Mace & Mace, 1980).

Benefits of Conflict

"Benefits of conflict" is an idea that seems contradictory to many of us; the word *conflict* is usually thought of as a signal of danger and disaster. The presence of conflict, however, does not mean that a relationship is unsatisfactory. The *presence* of conflict is less important in influencing relationship happiness than the way in which the conflict is *handled* (Hayes et al., 1981; Mace & Mace, 1980). Members of strong families report that their families experience conflict but deal with it in constructive ways (Ammons & Stinnett, 1980; Stinnett & DeFrain, 1985).

Psychiatrists and family therapists recognize that conflict may have some healthy consequences in a relationship. Bringing a long-simmering disagreement into the open may prove to be a turning point. Conflict, faced and resolved, can move a couple to new levels of intimacy (Stinnett & DeFrain, 1985).

Relief of Tension and Resentment

The expression of conflict can have therapeutic effects by releasing pent-up tension and hostility, thus lifting a burden from the individual. Keeping negative feelings locked inside and never releasing them can lead to hypertension, ulcers, and extreme nervousness (Julius, 1986).

In addition, bottled-up negative feelings eventually surface—either in a major, explosive (possibly violent) confrontation or in subtle but very destructive ways. One problem of suppressed conflict is that the anger associated with the disagreement is not resolved. Instead, the anger festers into resentment or depression, or it is vented in nonproductive ways such as abuse of alcohol or drugs, boredom, and sexual dysfunction (Broderick, 1979; Zimmer, 1988).

Tony and Martha have been married for 3 years. Martha came from a home in which her mother was the dominant family member. Martha's father preferred a passive role, so the arrangement suited them. Both her parents made frequent use of sarcasm, even though their relationship was basically happy. They regarded sarcasm as a form of witty dialogue. During their courtship, Martha minimized her inclination to take charge of things and to be sarcastic in her responses. Tony, in contrast, came from a home in which the relationship between his parents was egalitarian. Sarcasm was viewed as a degrading form of interaction. Although he had been mildly irritated by Martha's periodic sarcasm and bossiness during courtship, he had not said anything about it.

As is true of most couples, Tony and Martha were trying very hard during courtship to be pleasing to each other. After they married, Martha's tendency to dominate surfaced more frequently; the realities of daily life overcame her "courtship manners." She also used sarcasm more often. Tony, however, remained silent in spite of his growing anger and hurt. Soon after their first anniversary, he developed high blood pressure and a pattern of periodic depression. His desire for sexual relations with Martha dwindled significantly, creating another problem between them.

Finally, Tony confided in his physician about his occasional impotence, and the physician recommended that Tony and Martha see a family therapist. In time, the therapist helped them to identify the pattern of interaction that was causing their difficulties. The breakthrough came when Tony, for the first time, openly told Martha in a counseling session how much he disliked her bossiness and sarcasm. Martha was surprised; she had assumed their relationship would be similar to her parents' relationship. Once the negative feelings were aired, the resolution of the conflict was relatively easy. Martha's efforts to change were conscientious and because Tony recognized that, he was supportive of her successes. Not all of their interactional problems were completely solved—in real life they rarely are—but they achieved

a new level of happiness in their relationship. Tony's high blood pressure and depression were brought under control, and their sex life gradually improved.

Identification of Problem

Conflict often serves the useful purpose of pinpointing the exact nature of the problem in a relationship. Extraneous issues can then be discarded, and misunderstandings about the real issues can be clarified, thus allowing both partners to think clearly about the situation. The chances of resolving difficulties are increased.

Lance is a high school coach whose job is hectic and demanding. A short time ago, he began taking art lessons for relaxation. Sarah, his wife, repeatedly protested that they did not have enough money to afford art lessons. Lance continued the lessons anyway. Finally, one night, when Lance returned from art, Sarah gave full vent to her anger about the lessons. A series of quarrels followed over the next several days. It gradually became apparent that Sarah's real concern was not the cost of the art lessons. Lance was quite busy as a coach and was extensively involved in community activities. The one night that had belonged to them alone was now taken for art class. This is what really bothered Sarah. When they had identified the real problem, they appraised their lifestyle and made some changes. Lance reduced his community involvement so that he and Sarah regularly had several evenings a week to spend together. He continued his art lessons with full support from Sarah.

Increased Mutual Understanding

Conflict offers positive results if one of the end products is a deeper understanding of each other. A greater appreciation for each other's past experiences and values can be one such result. Increased understanding of each other may mean less conflict in the future.

Veronica and Ross have been married about a year and have a good relationship. Their major confrontations have been over an issue that seems as if it should be minor. Veronica has enjoyed music since early childhood, and concerts represent a source of pleasure, entertainment, and relaxation for her. She has persisted in her efforts to convert a reluctant Ross to her viewpoint. One day she came home with season tickets for the community concert series—good seats at a reasonable price and several guest artists she was anxious to hear. Ross adamantly refused to go; Veronica's frustration and disappointment resulted in an explosion. In the quarrel that followed, Ross revealed that he had been forced to take violin lessons as a child. He hated the lessons, his friends teased him about being a "sissy," and his parents pressured him to excel. Hours of practice and nagging could not make him live up to their high expectations. Not surprisingly, concerts and most music are reminders of pressure, failure, and humiliation to Ross. When Veronica became aware of his past experiences, she accepted Ross's decision and, instead, invited a friend to attend the concerts with her. Ross is happy for her to attend.

Renewed Appreciation of the Relationship

Some couples go through a period of conflict and experience a feeling of being alienated from each other. They pass through this negative stage, however, and find themselves with a renewed awareness of their positive emotional involvement with each other (Mace & Mace, 1980).

Mr. and Mrs. Scott had been married for 20 years when Mrs. Scott learned that Mr. Scott was having an extramarital relationship with another woman. They experienced a period of intense conflict for several weeks. After discussing divorce—which they both wished to avoid—they visited a family therapist. At one of the sessions, the therapist had them explore all of the things they did not like about each other and

their marriage as well as all the things they did like. They discovered that there were many positive things about their relationship. They began to focus less on the hurts and problems of their marriage and more on the positive part of their life together. They remembered vacation trips, funny times, hard times when money was tight, and projects they had worked on together. Mr. Scott ended his extramarital involvement, and they have a refreshed awareness of the loving feelings they have for each other.

Negative Aspects of Conflict

Conflict can be beneficial only if it is approached in productive ways. Improperly handled, conflict is detrimental to a relationship. Intense, unresolved conflict creates tension that can contribute to physical maladies, including loss of sexual drive and functioning (Julius, 1986; Zimmer, 1988). Conflict involving a continued attack on the self-worth of the partner can result in alienation, loneliness, and a sense of isolation (Bell & Gonzalez, 1988). Conflict is dysfunctional when it reduces interpersonal trust, results in psychological or physical injury, and fails to generate constructive changes in subsequent interaction (Feldman, 1982).

Reasons for Conflict

Conflict arises over innumerable issues (refer to Table 8–1 for some specific causes of marital conflict); however, there are several common reasons for most conflict.

Intimacy

Although it seems contradictory, one of the reasons for conflict is the intimate nature of the marriage relationship. Any close relationship will involve conflict: persons who spend much time to-

Table 8–1 Causes of Marital Conflict in Order of Frequency

Madden & Janoff-Bulman (1981) Survey Results	Jorgensen (1986) Survey Results
1. Spending money	1. Money management
2. Relations with relatives	2. Discipline of children
3. Children (rules, discipline)	3. Household jobs and duties
4. Division of housework and child care	4. In-law relationships
5. Communication, honesty	5. Too much time away from home
6. Location of residence; whether to move	6. Personalities and habits
7. Own or spouse's nonsexual attachment to another	7. Time spent as a couple
8. Husband's occupational choice; husband's income	8. Condition of house/furniture
9. Choice of recreation or vacation	9. Plans for future
10. Having children	10. Sex/affection

Sources: 1. Jorgensen, S. R. (1986). *Marriage and the family.* New York: Macmillan. 2. Madden, M. E., & Janoff-Bulman, R. (1981). Blame, control, and marital satisfaction: Wives' attributions for conflict in marriage. *Journal of Marriage and the Family, 43,* 663–673. Used with permission from The National Council on Family Relations, 3989 Central Ave. N.E., Suite #550, Minneapolis, MN 55421.

gether and who share many aspects of their lives encounter numerous opportunities for disagreement (Mace & Mace, 1980; Weingarten & Leas, 1987).

Basic Differences

Perhaps the most obvious reason for conflict between two persons is that they have basic differences. Even persons who share similar backgrounds usually have differing experiences, family cultures and traditions, attitudes, habits, goals, religious beliefs, and values. Cognitive/perceptual factors are important in understanding conflict because much marital conflict happens when couples have divergent cognitive sets—that is, a pattern of beliefs about the environment and methods by which

one typically reacts or responds to that environment. Additionally, persons often are not aware of their own or their spouse's cognitive sets and may have difficulty communicating their understanding of their cognitive/perceptual sets to their partners (Dhir & Markman, 1984).

A frequent source of discord for Robert and Elaine has been behavior at dinner. Elaine was reared in a family where dinner was an occasion for visiting and talking about whatever was of concern to the family members. A major purpose of dinner was fellowship. Robert, in contrast, came from a family that primarily ate in silence. The only purpose of dinner was to eat, after which the family members went about their business. It was not an occasion for lengthy conversations. The family customs of Robert and Elaine clashed on this issue: she was disappointed by Robert's silence at dinner; he was irritated by her insistence on talking.

Trying to Make a Partner Over

Some individuals marry with the intention of remodeling a partner's values, attitudes, likes and dislikes, interests, or certain personality characteristics. The result is usually confrontation. Each of us is likely to resist being changed by another, especially against our wishes. The act of trying to change another implies displeasure with that person. Feelings of resentment and rejection are common in the person who is the object of the attempted change.

Although constructive criticism can be beneficial, extensive and persistent attempts to change a partner almost certainly are destined to end in trouble. Gentle requests for change can evolve into nagging, which may escalate to blaming and finally to open, pointed attacks.

Power Struggles and Competition

Power involves exercising one's will to influence the present situation and decisions. Power is determined by a variety of factors: cultural authority (parents over children), gender (men over women), personal resources (money and expertise increase power), commitment (commitment equalizes power), emotional dependence (more dependent persons lose power), interpersonal manipulation, and physical violence (Jorgensen, 1986; Lamanna & Riedmann, 1988). Gender appears to be the most significant determinant of power, followed closely by money (Blumstein & Schwartz, 1983).

When each member of a couple has strong power needs, interaction can become a contest to determine who exercises the most power. Conflict erupts and, in a sense, may be regarded as necessary to resolve the power struggle. One person may enhance feelings of self-worth by dominating the other.

In American society competition is emphasized in work, school, and sports. Not surprisingly, the spirit of competition sometimes carries over into

---

Blockbusting

Sometimes persons may encounter road blocks on the way to conflict resolution. Several different blocks may prevent progress. If one partner does not understand the problem or lacks information, this is a *perceptual block*. The idea that tradition is preferable to change is a *cultural block*. Our fears may interfere with our ability to take action, or our inability to distinguish reality from fantasy may impair our understanding of the situation. If we cannot express our concerns clearly, we are facing *intellectual blocks*.

To overcome the blocks on the way to problem solving, couples may find it helpful to

1. Have a questioning attitude. Seek out details and accurate information.
2. Be flexible and ready to explore alternative solutions.
3. Set their minds free of firmly held concepts.
4. Avoid stereotyping or restrictions on their thinking.
5. Look for new connections and relationships between seemingly unrelated issues.

Source: Adams, J. L. (1976) *Conceptual blockbusting.* San Francisco: San Francisco Book Company.

marital relationships; spouses may compare themselves and compete in terms of salary, status, or community involvement.

In addition to the conflict created by a competitive attitude, marriages characterized by competition suffer the loss of emotional security (Lazarus, 1985). For example, Alice earns a promotion and salary increase. Ted perceives the promotion as his loss of accomplishment rather than Alice's gain. Instead of celebrating her achievement, he resents it or ignores it.

Tremendous Trifles

There is an adage, "It's not the great storms that destroy the oak tree, it's the little bugs." The little bugs might be compared to the tremendous trifles in marriage that can add up and damage the relationship if they are not dealt with effectively.

Slurping coffee, leaving the cap off the toothpaste tube, leaving dirty clothes on the floor, muttering, jingling coins and car keys in a pocket, and irritating verbal expressions—these are examples of tremendous trifles. Other petty irritants may be the result of language usage. The husband who addresses his wife, "Hey, woman" may do so with affection and humor, yet such an approach may anger his wife. She may recognize that on the surface his thinking involves affection and humor, but below the surface she may perceive feelings of ownership and subordination. If the wife explains why the expression irritates her, it would give the husband the opportunity to explain that he really means "I love you." If the wife still objects, he could stop. Unfortunately, many things that truly irritate us seem so petty that we are reluctant to discuss them. And, unfortunately, we sometimes disregard a partner's irritation over a matter as being too trivial to honor. One partner may reason, "Dirty clothes on the floor are no big deal; they shouldn't bother my partner. How silly!"

Petty irritations are most damaging to a relationship when they are kept inside and resentment is allowed to build. A storehouse of petty irritations over a long period of time can be quite damaging to a relationship. They do not gain undue importance when they are recognized for the trifles they are and when they are discussed as soon as they begin to be irritants. Thomas (1981) recounts the story of one couple:

Paula and Wayne worked in a bank, in responsible, demanding positions. Before their wedding, they had agreed to share equally in all household duties. But in the reality of everyday life, Paula found that Wayne did not share her standards of cleanliness and tidiness. In turn, he felt she nagged and belittled his efforts. For several months the issue simmered. Then as they drove to her mother's house for Thanksgiving, Wayne said that they would not get out of the car until they had worked things out. Isolated from outside interruptions, they talked about every aspect of the conflict during the 3-hour journey. On paper, they outlined what they expected to be done in the house, how often it should be done, and their feelings about doing it. Each then claimed the job he or she preferred to do and divided the rest between them. When they returned home, they put the new system into operation. To their surprise it worked.

Different Role Expectations

Husbands and wives bring different role expectations with them to marriage. Each has definite expectations of self, spouse, and the marriage. Sometimes their expectations contrast sharply.

Herb's mother was a full-time homemaker. He believed that it was desirable for a wife and mother not to be employed outside the home. His wife, Joan, grew up with a mother who had a career. Joan admired her mother and wanted a career herself. Herb didn't mind her working when they first married but preferred her to stop as soon as their first child was on the way.

Table 8–2 Levels of Marital Conflict Model

Level	Major Objective	Key Assumption	Emotional Climate	Negotiation Style
I. Problems to solve	Solve the problem	We can work it out	Hope	Open; direct; clear and nondistorted communication; common interests recognized
II. Disagreements	Self-protection	Compromise is necessary	Uncertainty	Cautious sharing; vague and general language; calculation beginning
III. Contest	Winning	Not enough resources to go around	Frustration and resentment	Strategic manipulation; distorted communication; personal attacks begin; no one wants to be first to change
IV. Fight/flight	Hurting the other	Partner cannot or will not change; no change necessary in self	Antagonism and alienation	Verbal/nonverbal incongruity; blame; perceptual distortions; refusal to take responsibility
V. War	Eliminating the other	Costs of withdrawal greater than costs of staying	Hopelessness and revenge	Emotional volatility; no clear understanding of issues; self-righteous; compulsive; inability to disengage

Source: Weingarten, H., and Leas, S. (1987). Levels of marital conflict model: A guide to assessment and intervention in troubled marriages. *American Journal of Orthopsychiatry, 57,* 407–417. Reprinted with permission from *The American Journal of Orthopsychiatry.* Copyrighted (1987) by The American Orthopsychiatric Association, Inc.

Many conflicts are the result of role expectations that do not match. The process of reconciling differences is tedious and requires much understanding and acceptance of each other.

Levels of Marital Conflict Model

The Levels of Marital Conflict Model (LMCM) was originated by a conflict management consultant and was adapted for application in marital therapy by a social work educator and practitioner. The LMCM identifies five levels of interpersonal conflict. Each level with associated objectives, assumptions, emotional climate, and negotiation style is given in Table 8–2.

The LMCM is used as a tool in marital therapy because it enables the therapist to focus on the dimensions of conflict interaction and to organize the confusing array of information involved in a conflict in an understandable manner. The therapist's approach will be different for a couple in level II than a couple in level V. One aim of the therapist is to de-escalate the conflict level to one in which resolutions are easier. Moving the conflict to a lower level is easier if even one partner is so inclined (Weingarten & Leas, 1987).

Marital partners may operate out of different conflict levels; a wife may be in level II while her husband is in level III, for example. Furthermore, each person's own level of conflict may vary across particular disputes and times.

Level I: Problems to Solve

Conflict at this level is not over issues that threaten the relationship; it concerns deciding between different viewpoints. Real differences exist, and tensions arise from an awareness by the partners that their goals, needs, or values are in conflict. Issues may be serious, e.g., whether or not to have children, or not so serious, e.g., where to vacation. Partners at this stage perceive they have a problem but believe it can be solved.

Level II: Disagreements

In this level, the partners perceive conflict as arising from their relationship rather than from a problem. Conflicts are motivated more by the need for self-protection than the need to solve a problem. Because trust is lowered and partners feel uncertain about each other, they may avoid confronting each other and may become defensive in communication. Third-party support from friends and family is often sought.

Level III: Contest

Conflict issues have accumulated in this level and are hard to disentangle. Hope has diminished; frustration has grown. Because they perceive resources as limited, power motives and competition are easily aroused. Marital partners have lost sight of their common interests and goals; they seek to end conflict by changing each other.

Level IV: Fight/Flight

Alienation and antagonism are characteristics of this level. The partners believe that neither can or will change, and the relationship satisifies fewer of their needs. The aim of interaction becomes hurting one another. Outsiders may be enlisted in the conflict, not in support of the marriage (as in level II), but as alternative sources of gratification. Couples who decide to end their relationship in this level are often willing parties to hostile divorce proceedings. Couples who stay together may exclude each other more and more, e.g., stop eating or talking together, forget anniversaries.

Level V: War

The conflict in this level includes not only issues but also personalities. Partners believe they cannot

Table 8–3 Behaviors for Addressing Conflict Issues

Competitive Behaviors	Cooperative Behaviors	Avoidance Behaviors
Faulting or blaming the other	Nonevaluative description of the conflict	Denial of conflict
Rejection	Qualifications	Underresponsiveness
Hostile questioning	Personal disclosure	Topic shifting; topic avoidance
Hostile joking or sarcasm	Soliciting partner disclosure	Joking
Presumptive attribution	Emphasizing support	Abstraction
Compliance seeking	Initiating problem-solving process	Ambivalence
Avoiding responsibility	Accepting responsibility	Pessimism

Sources: 1. Fitzpatrick, M. A., Fallis, S., & Vance, L. (1982). Multifunctional coding of conflict resolution strategies in marital dyads. *Family Relations, 31,* 61–70. 2. Sillars, A. (1980). *Conflict resolution strategies.* Unpublished doctoral dissertation, University of Wisconsin, Madison.

resolve differences and cannot escape the relationship except by destroying each other. Perception is distorted; irrationality is high. Violence is common as partners use compulsion and force to accomplish their aims.

Ways of Dealing With Conflict

When faced with an interpersonal conflict, an individual can avoid the conflict, focus on the conflict, or focus on the issue (see Table 8–3).

Avoidance Pattern

Some persons deal with conflict by refusing to acknowledge or be involved in it. Even though disagreement, anger, and frustration are felt, they are not expressed. The motivations for avoiding conflict vary: conflict may be regarded as cruel, vulgar, or indicative of a lack of love; engaging in conflict may represent failure of the relationship; alienating or hurting others or being hurt may be regarded as unacceptable consequences (Pearson, 1989).

The avoidance pattern of dealing with conflict is described as antisocial and is unhealthy for individuals and relationships if used routinely (Fitzpatrick et al., 1982; Sillars, 1980; Vuchinich, 1987). As mentioned earlier, unexpressed conflict tends to lead to high levels of frustration and resentment. Nondistressed couples differ from distressed couples in that they more often discuss conflict situations (Margolin et al., 1988; Stinnett & DeFrain, 1985). There is evidence that in dissatisfied marriages the husband's withdrawal or avoidance pattern contributes to the wife's increased hostility and marriage dissatisfaction (Roberts & Krokoff, 1990). Such increased hostility by the wife, in addition to reflecting frustration, may also be an effort to increase the husband's involvement.

Conflict-Centered Pattern

The conflict-centered pattern focuses on the conflict itself rather than the issue involved; it is competitive and antisocial (Fitzpatrick et al., 1982; Sillars, 1980). When this pattern is utilized, conflict becomes a game of wits where victory means the enhancing of one partner's ego by belittling

James Walters

not a competitive struggle to hurt each other (Fitz-patrick et al., 1982; Sillars, 1980).

The issue-centered pattern is described as prosocial in nature and includes several key elements (Fitzpatrick et al., 1982; Sillars, 1980), including:

- Respect for the rights of partners to disagree
- A clear identification of the problem
- Expression of each spouse's feelings about the problem
- Consideration of alternative solutions to the problem

Conflict Solutions

The types of various conflict solutions and the frequency of their use in one study are shown in Table 8–4.

Consensus

When partners can see each other's viewpoint and agree that there are several solutions, they can choose one that is good for both of them. This consensus of opinion makes them both feel in control.

the other person. This pattern usually is person-centered inasmuch as the objective is not solving the problem or gaining insight about the issue, rather it is attacking the person who takes a different viewpoint. Attacks lead to counterattacks as each mate becomes hypnotized by his or her virtues and by a mate's faults. Real issues get lost in the fray, and any true conflict resolution is prevented. Persons in levels III, IV (fight), and V of the LMCM exhibit conflict-centered patterns of behavior.

Issue-Centered Pattern

Couples in level I of the LMCM exhibit behaviors typical of the issue-centered pattern. Their focus is on solving their problem. Although they do not seek conflict, they do not avoid it either. Confrontations are a cooperative effort to handle a difficulty,

*Table 8–4 Use of Various Conflict Solutions**

Solution	Percent of Time Used
Submission (concession)	21
Compromise	14.2
Standoff (accommodation)	61
Withdrawal (avoidance)	3.8

*Based on 200 conflict episodes in videotapes of interaction at dinner of 52 families representing all socioeconomic groups.

Source: Vuchinich, S. (1987). Starting and stopping: Spontaneous family conflicts. *Journal of Marriage and the Family, 49,* 591–607. Reprinted with permission from The National Council on Family Relations, 3989 Central Ave. N.E., Suite #550, Minneapolis, MN 55421.

For example, a couple may disagree about buying a house. The wife is anxious to move out of their cramped apartment, but the husband feels that they should stay until they have more money. In a consensus solution, she will agree to postpone househunting because of financial pressures, and he will agree to help her look for a larger apartment that they can afford.

Compromise

A compromise acknowledges each partner's view. Partners meet halfway (Pearson, 1989; Vuchinich, 1987). In the example of buying a house, the wife might start a special savings fund and take on additional work to earn money for the house; the husband would contribute to the house fund while delaying the immediate move.

Concession

In concession one partner gives in to the other's suggestion and agrees to the idea (Vuchinich, 1987). For example, despite his reservations about buying a house, the husband agrees to look at houses and to discuss financing with a realtor. Or the wife may decide that having more space is not worth the financial strain, and she agrees to stay in the apartment.

Concession can be used effectively in situations in which the issue of conflict is much more important to one partner than the other. Concession will probably not be acceptable if both feel strongly about the matter.

Accommodation

Sometimes an impasse occurs where neither partner wants to concede, compromise, or reach consensus. Each partner holds his or her view about the situation, and they agree to disagree. In our example, the wife will continue to believe they should move to a house; she may continue looking at houses or may start a savings fund for a down payment. The husband remains opposed to moving out of their apartment; he does not look at houses or contribute to the savings fund. They declare a truce and put aside the issue, unable to move it in any direction.

Barriers to Dealing with Conflict Successfully

Some behaviors prevent us from dealing effectively with conflict. We can learn to recognize these behaviors and to avoid them in our interactions with others.

Refusal to Acknowledge the Existence of a Problem

Some couples have difficulty resolving marital conflict because one or both of them refuses to admit that a problem even exists. They may maintain a facade of well-being in their relationship even when the signs of trouble are obvious. Refusal to acknowledge the existence of a problem makes it almost impossible to find a satisfying solution (Fitzpatrick et al., 1982; Sillars, 1980; Vuchinich, 1987).

Avoiding Responsibility

Margaret and Gene had been married for 3 years, but their relationship had deteriorated to the point that they were considering divorce. Gene consulted a family therapist and eventually convinced Margaret to come with him to see the therapist. After a few counseling sessions, the therapist observed that Margaret's destructive interaction was part of the problem. In subtle and not so subtle ways, she made Gene feel inadequate. When she pointed this out, Margaret hotly denied it and retorted that Gene was the one who had the problem. Margaret refused to return for therapy with a therapist she described as totally incompetent.

Most of us agree intellectually that it is desirable to see the other person's point of view and to admit our wrongs. Emotionally, however, many individuals have real difficulty taking responsibility for their errors or their contribution to a conflict situation. Refusal to accept personal responsibility in a conflict creates a major barrier to successful resolution.

A serious consequence of regarding the problem as being the responsibility of one's partner is the tendency to blame the partner. The attitude becomes, "You're responsible for this problem; it is your fault. The way to solve this is for you to change." Couples in levels III and IV of the LMCM experience difficulty in resolving conflict because of these attitudes (Weingarten & Leas, 1987). Negative attributional styles (one's manner of making causal inferences about events), such as blaming problems on a partner's personal defects, are related to negative problem-solving behaviors and to marital dissatisfaction (Alberts, 1988; Boland & Follingstad, 1987; Doherty, 1982; Madden & Janoff-Bulman, 1981; Warner & Olson, 1981).

Attacking the Person

As mentioned previously, the most effective approaches to conflict resolution focus on the issue.

When the emphasis shifts to insulting, complaining, criticizing, or hurting a partner, the relationship suffers (Alberts, 1988; Boland & Follingstad, 1987; Hine, 1980). Couples in levels IV and V of the LMCM focus much of their efforts on attacking each other. Assaults on a partner may escalate beyond verbal aggression to physical aggression (Weingarten & Leas, 1987).

Collusion

Persons may actually collude in bringing about conflict situations by one provoking the other to do the very thing he or she dislikes intensely. Without their collusive action there would be much less enmity between them. Collusion usually involves self-deception or perceptual blindness to personal responsibility for the conflict (Warner & Olson, 1981).

Arthur hates it when his wife Lynn raises her voice in anger. His father was a "screamer," and Arthur cringes when he remembers yelling matches between his parents. Now when he and Lynn disagree, he re-

---

If Your Mate Does Not Cooperate

Most of us want the same things in our relationships: honesty, a sharing of feelings and thoughts, empathy, support, fun. Those of us who are not getting these qualities from our spouses might ask "Do I myself offer these same things to my mate?"

If your spouse refuses to cooperate in an effort to improve the relationship, you should begin alone. The method for doing this is very straightforward: *you* attempt to move closer to him or her; *you* take him or her into *your* confidence and share *your* thoughts and feelings. There is no guarantee that being a model of what you want will produce positive results, but the probabilities increase very dramatically.

If after two or three months of this approach little or no improvement is evident, it is time to seek professional intervention. If your spouse will not agree to this either, you should again begin alone so that you can learn to handle both the situation and your own pain.

Joel Block Ph.D., clinical psychologist

Source: Parents, April 1981, p. 68. Reprinted by permission of Joel Block.

sponds by walking away. He leaves the house and goes for a walk or drive. This frustrates Lynn because she feels he is ignoring the problem and her. She yells in a futile attempt to make him stop and listen. He feels justified in walking out. "We can't accomplish anything with you screaming," he tells Lynn. Both are ignoring their collusion: She wouldn't yell if he didn't walk away and he wouldn't leave if she didn't yell.

Focusing on Symptoms Rather than Causes

An essential part of conflict resolution is identification of the problem. One common difficulty in coping with conflict is a tendency to concentrate on superficial symptoms rather than causes. Couples may lack the analytical skills necessary to disentangle some conflicts or may be reluctant to face their real problems because of the emotional consequences. One task of marital therapists is to assist couples in diagnosing their actual problems (Weingarten & Leas, 1987).

One middle-aged couple visited a marital therapist because they were fighting over money. They described their money quarrels at length. After some time, the therapist inquired about other areas of their relationship. Both expressed concerns about the wife's health; she had undergone major surgery about a year before. As they talked about her illness and surgery, the husband confided his disappointment that their sex life had not resumed after her recovery. Deeper probing revealed that he perceived her reluctance about sex as neurotic and selfish. He had begun to hold back from her, too—with money.

Overintellectualization

Some couples approach conflict from a strictly intellectual point of view: "We will deal with the problem rationally. We will not become emotional."

To approach problems rationally and objectively is good; however, when problems are overintellectualized, a serious weakness is imposed in that important solutions may not be discussed because of the emotions that are being denied.

Purely intellectual responses are not likely to bring about lasting changes. The most effective way to deal with conflict is to come to terms with the underlying values, attitudes, and emotions that guide behavior as well as to consider the rational and objective aspects of a problem (Kieren et al., 1975). Becoming too emotional or irrational is not effective, but feelings and emotions must be considered in resolving conflict.

Lack of Communication

Lack of communication is one of the greatest barriers to dealing successfully with marital problems. Many difficulties are prevented and others resolved when husband and wife maintain good communication patterns (Margolin et al., 1988; Weingarten & Leas, 1987). Some couples share surprisingly little of their goals, expectations, joys, preferences, dissatisfactions, and limitations. A problem may exist that frustrates them; yet, they may not communicate about it. Why?

They may purposely refrain from communicating grievances to avoid conflict. They may also not mention grievances because of insecurity about their relationship, feeling they risk rejection if they communicate any dissatisfaction. Sometimes spouses have a sense of hopelessness and fatalism about a particular problem, believing nothing can change the situation (Weingarten & Leas, 1987).

It is nearly impossible to resolve a conflict when the communication channels are closed. Good communication skills are necessary to identify the problem, clarify the feelings of each spouse, and enable them to consider alternatives to solving the problem.

Inability to Accept Disageement

We may expect those close to us to agree with us on practically everything. Agreement with us is seen as support that makes us feel more secure; disagreement may be viewed as rejection. Our interpretation of the agreement or disagreement often runs far deeper than the importance the particular issue merits. An individual's sense of self-worth may be associated with agreement by the spouse. It is no surprise that such a person usually reacts to disagreement very strongly, perhaps with extreme hostility.

Fatigue, Illness, Alcohol, or Drugs

Many couples try to solve conflict situations and quarrels under less than optimal conditions. When we are fatigued or ill, we may be edgy, pessimistic, and quick-tempered. Persons under the influence of alcohol or drugs are not in the best condition for conflict resolution either; their thinking may be hazy, their perception distorted, and their emotions out of control (Hine, 1980).

> *I know this will sound funny, but when we were first married, we had most of our fights in the early evening. It finally dawned on us that we were picking the worst possible time to talk about problems. We would come home from work, tired, irritated from commuting in traffic, and hungry. We'd need to start dinner, check the mail, and walk the dog. If we tried to discuss any difficulties, we ended up in a fight. We finally agreed that unless it was an absolute emergency the time from getting home until after dinner was not a time to try to resolve conflict. And, as much as possible, we use the weekend to deal with issues that can wait.*

Extreme Anger

The expression of anger may serve useful purposes, e.g., the release of tension and clarification of feelings about the matter in dispute; however, anger used in excess becomes a negative influence and creates a barrier to effective conflict resolution. When a person feels unreasonably angry or out of control, often the best action is to withdraw to allow time to "cool off."

Basic Principles for Dealing with Conflict

Some basic rules for dealing with conflict involve principles that provide simple, specific approaches for handling conflict situations.

1. Be specific when you introduce a complaint.

2. Do not complain without asking for a reasonable change that will make the situation better.

3. Give and receive feedback of the major points to assure yourself and your partner that you understand the issue.

4. Try tolerance. Be open to your own feelings and equally open to those of your partner.

5. Consider compromise. Many conflict issues involve no clear-cut right or wrong. Your partner may have some good ideas. Do not establish a position from which you absolutely cannot move.

6. Do not allow counterdemands to enter the picture until the original demands are clearly understood and there is a definite response to them. Deal with one issue at a time.

7. Do not use mind rape. Do not tell a partner what he or she knows or feels. Never assume you know what a partner thinks. Ask.

8. Attack the issue, not each other. Refrain from name calling and sarcasm. Ban the bombs (those especially hurtful, often

secret things that a mate knows that devastate when dropped).

9. Forget the past and stay with the issue at hand. Hurts, grievances, and irritations should be brought up at the earliest convenient moment, or the partner may suspect that they have been saved as weapons.

10. Do not burden your partner with grievances. To do so can make him or her feel hopeless and suggests that you have either been hoarding complaints or do not know what really troubles you.

11. Think about your real thoughts and feelings before you speak. Listen more than you talk.

12. Show love and respect even when you cannot agree.

13. Monitor your voice tone and nonverbal behaviors, e.g., pointing a finger or turning your back.

14. Be patient. Negotiation, conflict resolution, and problem solving are all skills to be learned. As you learn, you will get better.

15. Remember that there is never a winner in an honest, intimate fight. Both either win more intimacy or lose it. (Bach & Deutsch, 1971; Hine, 1980; Stinnett & DeFrain, 1989).

Marital Violence

The studies and examples we have discussed so far have set the inevitable clashes in any relationship in a framework of rational understanding and mu-

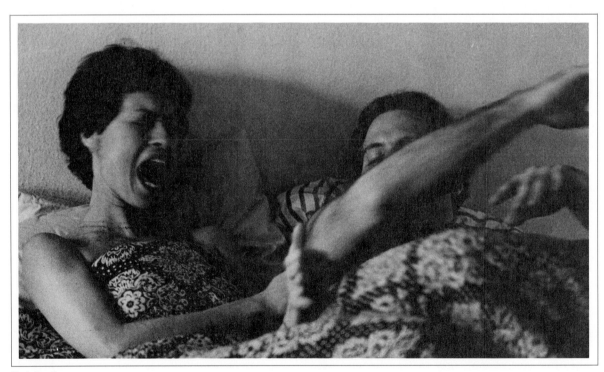

Joel Gordon

tual respect. In the past few years, however, there has been a growing awareness of physical violence between couples in conflict situations. Because women receive the brunt of violence in such relationships, much of the relatively recent recognition of violent marriages has come from the impetus of the women's movement (Pagelow, 1984). In the past, researchers, politicians, the police, and other professionals tended to ignore the reality of violence. In the *Journal of Marriage and the Family* there was no mention of the word "violence" in any article from its first issue in 1939 to 1969. O'Brien (1971) notes, "Apparently violence was either assumed to be too touchy an issue for research, or else thought to be unimportant as a feature in 'normal' families" (p. 692).

The number of couples who experience violence in their relationship is difficult to estimate. The first difficulty lies in the definition of violence. In some studies, couples have been labeled as violent if they experienced at least one act from a list ranging from slapping, pushing, and shoving to hitting with a fist to assaulting with a gun or knife. Other studies have not classified couples as violent unless severe forms of violence were repeated. The highest estimates are that about 50% to 60% of families experience some physically violent behavior between spouses, with 10% admitting regular, extreme physical abuse of a spouse (Steinmetz & Straus, 1975). In another study, 28% of couples indicated they experienced physical violence, while 21% of women in one survey (Russell, 1982) and 34% of women in another (Frieze, 1980) reported being abused. Bearing in mind problems in definitions and differing research techniques, Pagelow (1984) estimates 25% to 30% of all American women—or about 12 million women—are beaten at least once in the course of their intimate relationships. About one-third of wives who are attacked are abused five times or more (Leslie, 1982). Over 50% of abusive husbands beat their wives three or more times each year (Edelson, et al., 1985).

Violence occurs in marriages at all social levels. Problems of domestic violence appear more prevalent in lower socioeconomic groups (Lockhart, 1987; Straus et al., 1980). There seem to be no differences in domestic violence according to race when social class is controlled except that black middle-class women experience more violence than their white counterparts. This may be due to numbers of blacks with recently acquired middle-class status reacting to high stress levels or having carried over their former lower socioeconomic status norms and values (Lockhart, 1987). Military wives are more likely to be abused than are civilian wives; military wives report a desire for husbands to work late less often, drink less, and express more emotions (Griffin & Morgan, 1988).

Much of the research on spouse abuse focuses on wife abuse for a variety of reasons. Although many couples report mutual violence, researchers tend to regard husband-to-wife violence as a more prevalent and serious problem. While a few women may be extremely dangerous, many wives who become violent seem to do so in self-defense. Furthermore, they use less dangerous or injurious forms of violence and are not as apt to repeat their violence over time. Because husbands typically are larger and stronger than their wives, they may easily defend themselves; many men regard their wives' violence as mildly annoying or amusing. For example, one husband reported that his wife hit him on the arm, he laughed, and she hit again. He thought the episode was hilarious because she hurt her hand (Pagelow, 1984). Husbands also have greater resources, which allow them to leave an abusive situation (Straus et al., 1980).

Public Recognition

Historically, wives have not fared well. American law was influenced by British common law and the Napoleonic civil code. Both required wives to be legal minors throughout life. Husbands had the

Joel Gordon

Theories of Marital Violence

Marital violence is one facet of the larger area of family violence, which includes child maltreatment, elder abuse, and sibling abuse. Many theories have been proposed to try to explain violence in families; however, no single theory seems entirely adequate.

One theory that is used to explain why and how marital violence occurs is social learning theory. In general, social learning theory is based on the idea that children learn most, if not all, of their behavior by observing and imitating models, such as their parents. In addition, behavior that is reinforced or rewarded tends to be continued (Papalia & Olds, 1986). As applied to marital violence, it is theorized that children who witness aggressive acts are likely to imitate them. If aggressive acts are rewarded, they are apt to be continued. The boy who sees his mother slapped by his father is apt to try slapping a playmate to get a toy. If he gets the toy, he may hit to get another and later may slap his wife to get what he wants (Pagelow, 1984).

Social learning theory's explanation is supported by research findings that being abused as a child or observing one's parents in violent confrontation are both related to marital aggression in the next generation (Jaffe et al., 1986; McCord, 1988; Rosenbaum & O'Leary, 1981). Observing parents hitting each other is a stronger predictor of marital aggression in the next generation than is being hit by one's parents (Kalmuss, 1984). There is also a more consistent association between boys who witness or are subject to violence and later become violent men than is true for girls (McCord, 1988; Pagelow, 1984). According to social learning theory, this is due to the reinforcement that boys receive for being aggressive or violent; girls do not receive such reinforcement.

Another factor contributing to marital violence is the widespread acceptance of violence in our society. Many examples are apparent: violent sports are

right and duty to "chastise" (beat) their wives for the purpose of correction. In 1824 the Supreme Court of Mississippi upheld a husband's right to chastisement without being subject to prosecution. Not until 1871 did Alabama and Massachusetts become the first states to rescind the "privilege" of wife beating (Pagelow, 1984).

In 1971 Erin Pizzey opened a Women's Advice Centre in England and was swamped by women seeking shelter from violent husbands. Her account, *Scream Quietly or the Neighbors Will Hear*, raised awareness of the problem. Soon other women's groups joined the effort. In 1975 the National Task Force on Battered Women/Household Violence was established in the United States by the National Organization for Women. Today there are shelters and information hot lines in many areas (Pagelow, 1984).

Violence in Courtship and Cohabitation

In one study of college students, 23.5% of males and 31.1% of females reported being violent toward dating partners; 28.6% of males and 22.5% of females indicated their partners had been violent to them (DeMaris, 1987).

When freshmen and seniors at two private religious colleges and a state university were surveyed, 21% of seniors and 25% of freshmen had been involved in courtship violence (Makepeace, 1982).

In a study of students aged 15 to 19 years, 8% of males and 17% of females reported violent episodes in dating relationships (Henton et al., 1983).

In dating situations, men perceive jealousy, rejection, or being "goaded into it" as having precipitated violence; women cite anger, power struggles, and use of alcohol or drugs (Laner, 1982).

Victims and offenders share the following social profile: disrupted home and single-parent background; harsher, less close parenting; early dating; poor academic achievement; school suspension and expulsion; multiple job firings; and social isolation (Makepeace, 1987).

Men who are more traditionally masculine are more likely to have abused dating partners; women who are more traditionally feminine are less likely to have been abused in a dating relationship (Bernard et al., 1988).

Most women battered during courtship believe the violence will disappear after the wedding, but it does not (Pagelow, 1984).

When comparing the violence of singles, cohabitants, and marrieds, cohabitants were more likely to experience violence than singles or marrieds (Lane & Gwartney-Gibbs, 1985).

Cohabiting women are almost four times more apt to suffer severe violence than married women (Yllo & Straus, 1981).

Cohabitors may lack security and be unsure of each other, yet they may expect higher levels of commitment than dating partners. Jealousy may be easily aroused under those conditions. Alcohol and drug use are extensive among cohabitors (Lane & Gwartney-Gibbs, 1985).

Sources: 1. Bernard, J. L., Bernard, S. L., & Bernard, M. L. (1988). Courtship violence and sex-typing. *Family Relations, 34,* 573–576. 2. DeMaris, A. (1987). The efficacy of a spouse abuse model in accounting for courtship violence. *Journal of Family Issues, 8,* 291–305. 3. Henton, J., Cate, R., Koval, J., Lloyd, S., & Christopher, S. (1983). *Romance and violence in dating relationships.* Unpublished manuscript. 4. Lane, K. E., & Gwartney-Gibbs, P. A. (1985). Violence in the context of dating and sex. *Journal of Family Issues, 6,* 45–59. 5. Laner, M. R. (1982). *Courtship abuse and aggression: Contextual aspects.* Paper presented at the Conference on Families and Close Relationships, Lubbock, TX. 6. Makepeace, J. M. (1982). *Courtship violence on a low-risk campus.* Paper presented at the annual meeting of the Pacific Sociological Association, San Diego, CA. 7. Makepeace, J. M. (1987). Social factor and victim-offender differences in courtship violence. *Family Relations, 36,* 87–91. 8. Pagelow, M. D. (1984). *Family violence.* New York: Praeger. 9. Yllo, K., & Straus, M. A. (1981). Interpersonal violence among married and cohabiting couples. *Family Relations, 30,* 339–347.

Preventing Date/Acquaintance Rape

In a survey of 7,000 students at 35 schools, 1 out of 4 women in colleges today has been the victim of a rape or an attempted rape—and almost 90% knew their attackers. Gang rapes on college campuses are most likely to occur at parties. In a gang rape, men have the chance to show their peers how "manly" they are, according to Bernice Sandler, director of the project on the Status and Education of Women of the Association of American Colleges.

   In order to prevent rape:

1. Always have money—for a cab or to call a friend.

2. If you are dating a "stranger," either make it a date with another couple you know or meet him at a place where there will be other people.

3. Be clear about your "limits"; some men believe a woman wants a man to be "macho" or that women say "no" but mean "yes." Be firm and assertive.

4. Be considerate of how you say "no"; make it clear it is the behavior you dislike and not the person.

5. If you have doubts about his intentions, ask—you do have the right to say "no" and leave the situation.

7. Be conservative in your drinking so that you will be able to use your best judgement, no matter how the date evolves.

Source: Adapted from Preventing date/acquaintance rape. (1986). *Health Call, 4*(3), 7.

very popular; toy manufacturers make guns, missiles, swords, knives, fighter planes and ships, and play figures of combat troops; television programs and movies contain many episodes of violence; newspapers and evening news programs carry accounts of local violence; and many video games feature a "destroy-the-enemy" format. Our language includes slang expressions to express hostility and insult; many are extremely violent colloquialisms for sexual intercourse (Pagelow, 1984).

   The general acceptance of violence by society and the historical foundation of men's willingness to use force to maintain status and control over wives and children help to explain prevailing attitudes about marital violence (Stark & Flitcraft, 1981). In a series of interviews of 1,176 men and women, one-fifth approved of slapping one's spouse on "appropriate" occasions. About 25% of college-educated people approved of a husband slapping his wife; 16% of those with lesser amounts of education approved (Roy, 1977).

   Of course, many people do not become violent adults despite being exposed to violence in movies, sports, television, toys, and the evening news and despite witnessing or suffering parental violence themselves. A list of factors common to men who abuse their wives provides further insight.

1. *Low self-esteem.* Abusive husbands tend to have lower self-esteem than nonabusive husbands (Goldstein & Rosenbaum, 1985). They may be threatened when wives are successful in their careers, earn money, or return to school (Kalmuss & Straus, 1982). Physical violence may become a way of dominating their wives and regaining control (Maiuro et al., 1988).

Their own violence also acts to reduce feelings of self-worth (Koval et al., 1982).

2. *Lack of assertiveness*. Frequency and severity of battering are related to a lack of appropriate verbal assertiveness. When faced with needs, anger, or frustration, abusive men lack the skills to make their needs and emotions known in nonaggressive ways (Bagarozzi & Giddings, 1983; Guerney et al., 1987; Koval et al., 1982; Rosenbaum & O'Leary, 1981; Straus et al., 1980; Telch & Lindquist, 1984).

3. *Moodiness*. Domestically violent men have significantly higher levels of anger, hostility, fear, and depression than nonviolent men (Maiuro et al., 1988; Margolin et al., 1988). They may exhibit wide variations in mood swings (Koval et al., 1982), and they frequently have higher levels of physiological arousal (faster heartbeat, muscles tightening, body shaking, face flushed) during problem-oriented discussions (Margolin et al., 1988).

4. *Alcohol dependency*. Use of alcohol is associated with frequency and severity of battering (Bagarozzi & Giddings, 1983; Koval et al., 1982; Rosenbaum & O'Leary, 1981; Straus et al., 1980; Telch & Lindquist, 1984).

5. *Employment problems*. Unemployment, underemployment, or job dissatisfaction create financial stress, reduce self-esteem, and shift conjugal power relationships (Koval, et al., 1982; Pagelow, 1984).

6. *Social isolation*. Social relationships outside the family may be limited and shallow (Koval et al., 1982).

Dealing with Marital Violence

Professionals who help women cope with marital violence are often surprised by how long women have stayed in painful relationships. Why do they stay? The reasons are varied.

According to a study by Pagelow (1984), 47% hoped for change, 29% lacked alternatives, 15% wanted to keep the family together, and 10% stayed because of fear.

Women are socialized to view marriage as their primary source of satisfaction; to leave a marriage is tantamount to "failure." They may feel societal pressure to maintain the family unit, or they may love their husbands. A high degree of commitment to the spouse and the relationship is a major reason cited by women who remain in abusive situations (Strube & Barbour, 1983).

Wives who feel psychologically dependent on marriage may tolerate minor abuse. Wives who are economically dependent may stay in severely abusive situations because they have virtually no resources with which to make changes (Strube & Barbour, 1983). Abusive husbands prevent their wives from leaving in several ways: wives may not have transportation, wives may not be allowed to go shopping or anywhere alone, visits to and from friends or family may be forbidden or discouraged, wives may have no access to money of their own, or they may lack jobs or job skills (Pagelow, 1984). Other factors that influence a woman's decision to leave include length of marriage, prior exposure to violence in her family of origin, extensiveness of her social support system, and her emotional and physical well-being (Strube & Barbour, 1983).

Wives who respond to physical violence by fighting back or defending themselves usually discover that the level of violence escalates. Fighting back can be very dangerous (Pagelow, 1984).

Society's support systems are often not very helpful to battered wives. Calling the police may produce little or no effect; few arrests are made (Lerman, 1981). Police may counsel the couple to "kiss and make up." Men who are arrested are often home in a few hours and are inclined to retaliate (Pagelow, 1984).

Centers or shelters for battered women and their children have been most effective in providing safety and help. Shelters offer protection and provide other services: employment, psychological, and legal counseling; help in locating housing and other assistance; self-help or support groups (Pagelow, 1984).

In some areas intervention programs are available for men who are batterers. Intervention programs emphasize relationship enhancement, conflict resolution skills, assertiveness training, and communication skills (Guerney et al., 1987; Pagelow, 1984).

Summary

- Since conflict is inevitable in a marital relationship, partners must learn how to deal with it effectively.

- Conflict can be detrimental to a relationship if unresolved or improperly handled; however, it can also have healthy consequences when handled constructively. These benefits include: relief of tension, identification of the real problem, increased mutual understanding, and a renewed appreciation of the relationship.

- Most marital conflict is a result of one or more of the following: the intimate nature of the relationship, basic differences between partners, an attempt to make a partner change, competition between partners, petty irritations, and different role expectations.

- In the Levels of Marital Conflict Model (LMCM) five levels of interpersonal conflict are identified: level I, problems to solve; level II, disagreements; level III, contest; level IV, fight/flight; and level V, war. Each level is characterized by certain objectives, assumptions, emotional climates, and negotiation styles. Such a model helps therapists to categorize and de-escalate marital conflict.

- There are four strategies used to solve conflict: consensus (choosing a solution that is best for both partners), compromise (both partners meeting halfway), concession (one partner gives in to the other), and accomodation (an impasse or agreeing to disagree).

- Conflict cannot be effectively resolved when partners do not acknowledge the problem, when they avoid responsibilty for it, when a partner feels attacked, when there is a lack of communication, or when partners are ill, tired, extremely angry, or under the influence of alcohol or drugs. Recognizing such conditions exist and avoiding them in our interactions will enhance a person's ability to manage conflict.

- Violence is a learned behavior that is reinforced by societal acceptance. Women who are victimized by marital violence may feel unable to escape due to psychological or economic dependencies.

Discussion Questions

1. What are common problems that couples encounter in dealing with conflict?

2. What are the important facts to be learned from the research on spouse abuse?

3. If, indeed, much conflict occurs between husbands and wives because of differences in values concerning the use of money, what do you believe you could do to minimize conflict in this area in your own marriage?

4. Marriage and family therapists often report that the "presenting problem," or the problem a couple initially discusses with a marriage therapist, is often not the real problem the couple faces. Why is this so?

5. What are some of the factors that contribute to the physical expression of violent feelings in marriage?

6. If you found yourself in a marriage where there was constant conflict, what options would you consider?

7. How would you handle it if your spouse refused to acknowledge the existence of a problem in your relationship?

8. What steps can couples take to resolve the conflict instead of escalating it?

9. Discuss an experience in which conflict proved beneficial to your relationship.

10. What can couples do to minimize competitiveness in their relationship?

CHAPTER 9

SEXUAL ASPECTS
OF RELATIONSHIPS

◦

You want to know the secret of being an extraordinary lover?
I can tell you. The secret is loving the other person more than
yourself. That's why the sex of people who truly love each
other is usually so great: their focus on obtaining pleasure for
themselves is subordinated to their desire to please the person
they love. Sexual closeness is a reflection of their total
commitment to their relationship. Relationships are delicate
things that flourish with thoughtfulness, courtesy, kindness,
and all the other good stuff. They fade with indifference,
sarcasm, insults, and all the bad stuff. Sex is the celebration
of lovers who have enough sense to work on their total
relationship.

James Walters

◦

Sexuality

Sexuality begins at conception when maleness or femaleness is determined by the chromosome content of the fertilizing sperm cell. It involves *all* that it means to be a man or a woman, e.g., emotions, values, social relations, physical desires, and aspirations. It interrelates with every other part of life.

Sexual Happiness

Sexual Self-Acceptance

Few things contribute as much to sexual happiness as the degree of comfort one experiences with one's own sexuality and with one's sexual partner. Individuals who have been reared in an environment that is repressive sexually generally have some difficulty overcoming their shyness, awkwardness, and guilt. Fortunately, individuals can learn skills that will enable them to be more competent and comfortable sexually; they also can learn to help others to be more comfortable. An important approach to the process is to accept where you are and not become impatient if your behavior does not meet your expectations. Some couples who love each other decide to limit their affectional involvement and postpone intercourse until marriage or until they are in a committed relationship. Frequently, such couples are conservative and religious; they possess the characteristics of persons who, research has found, attain a high level of marital satisfaction. Their marriages last. In an era in which it is popular to rationalize one's behavior in order to provide "reasons" for doing what one wants to do, the advantages of a conservative lifestyle are often overlooked because such a choice means delaying gratification. Sexual conservatism has considerable merit, however, when viewed in relation to unwanted pregnancies, unwanted children, and diseases that are distressing and life threatening. Conservatism is a good fit for many people.

Managing Your Sexual Reputation

Although attitudes about sex have become more open in recent decades, most persons still regard their *own* sexual behavior as a very private matter. At the same time, many persons find the sexual activities of others to be especially interesting as a topic of discussion. As a result it is wise to forego sharing those aspects of your sexual history you do not wish to be made public.

To what extent should one disclose one's past and one's feelings to a mate in order to maximize marital satisfaction? Research on self-disclosure reveals conflicting evidence. Larson (1988) has cautioned that a limitation of several of the studies on self-disclosure is a failure to discriminate between the quality of self-disclosure, which recent research (Holman & Brock, 1986; Schumm et al., 1986) has revealed to be important. Larson (1988) concluded that a positive, linear relation between self-disclosure and marital satisfaction probably does exist *but only if the self-disclosure is positive rather than negative*—that is, individuals who reveal a great deal about themselves that violates the expectation of their spouses are likely to be less valued.

Sex as Social Interaction

Power and Satisfaction

Evidence has accumulated from research that the person who is the least invested in a relationship has the greater degree of power (Scanzoni & Scanzoni, 1981). Thus, a person who is willing to do anything in order to maintain a relationship often finds that the "cost" is too great. Those relationships in which there is a balance of power, where both persons are eager to contribute to the wellbeing of each other, are the relationships that have the greatest potential of enduring happiness. Masters et al. (1986) describe a condition of *mutuality* in sexual relationships, in which both persons are united to discover what is best for both. Neither needs to fear being harshly labeled (i.e., "prude" or "pervert") or being blamed for sexual difficulties or failures. Every relationship is different. However hard we try to put those that are similar into categories so that we can assign them a label and tell the parties involved how they *should* behave, the fact remains that each relationship is unique. If someone thinks differently than we do there is a great temptation to believe they are wrong when all that is "wrong" is that our view differs from theirs.

Communication

Clear communication is important in relationship satisfaction. Rarely are two people similar in every way, and there needs to be respect for "where the other person is at the moment." Such respect requires understanding. Difficulties occur when either partner assumes that both members of the couple think alike or that one partner knows what the other wants. Misperceptions cause difficulty, and it is worth remembering that real friends are those who, when you've made a fool of yourself, don't think you've done a permanent job.

Although it seems obvious that couples who are not ready to have children should be clear about contraception before having a sexual encounter, countless unmarried couples each year make incorrect assumptions about each other, e.g., "Surely, if she spends the night, she's on the pill," or "Surely, if he is starting this he has a condom." Unmarried couples who have not reached the level of comfort to ask, "Do you have a condom?" or "Are you on the pill?" are not ready in a practical or rational way for this level of sexual involvement. Unfortunately, the awkwardness involved in such openness is too great for some, and they must cope with the consequences.

Women interpret a variety of verbal, physical, and romantic actions in less sexual light than men do, e.g., talking about sex, playing with a date's hair, tickling or wrestling with a date, telling a date how good looking he is, and staring into the date's eyes.

To a man, these are often interpreted as signs of affection. Women are also more likely to distinguish between males and females who do such things. They feel that if a woman tells her partner he is good looking or that she loves him, her words are less indicative of sexual interest than the same message would be coming from a man (Tavris & Wade, 1984).

Respect and Empathy

Because some people find sex so personally satisfying, they are willing to expose others to unplanned, unprotected sex, without regard for their safety or the consequences. This hardly reflects the kind of respect that leads to deeply satisfying marriages. Rather, it reflects a disregard characteristic of persons who are selfish and egocentric.

The person who pressures others into sexual encounters or behaviors that they dislike reflects little empathy. The date who rapes his girlfriend believing that she will "like it" reflects concern for his own feelings; he has no empathy and is unlikely to be a caring husband. People who are sensitive sexually are those who focus on providing for their partner the most satisfying sexual relationship possible. This kind of empathy makes for deeply satisfying relationships that endure.

The Sexual Relationship

Expectations

Couples are happiest in their sexual relationships when their needs are met and when their experiences are not radically different from their expectations. Violations in expectations occur for several reasons. People vary considerably in their need for sexual activity and in the manner in which they wish to have their needs met.

Physically attractive men initiate more contact with women and rate their heterosexual contacts as more meaningful, whereas physically attractive women are less socially assertive and less trusting of men (Huston & Ashmore, 1985).

For example, if someone who has no interest in sexual activity at all chooses a partner who expects to have sexual encounters daily, these sexual dissimilarities would serve as a barrier to their happiness. Because violated expectations can result in disappointment, frustration, and hurt feelings, couples who are more homogeneous in their interest and desire for sex are more likely to be happy than those who are very different.

Sexual Evaluations

We often evaluate our own performance by comparing ourselves with our peers. Social scientists report information regarding age at first intercourse, percentage of college students who have experienced coitus, frequency of intercourse for married couples over time, and a host of other sexual concerns. Often our reaction is, "How do I measure up?" Among males, having intercourse earlier than the "average" may bring social approval. In reality, it is not the level of experience that attracts women to men, it is self-assurance. According to research if a man thinks he is sexy, he is perceived as sexy by women (Morganstern et al., 1982). Or a married couple who has intercourse 2 times a week instead of the 3.7 times that is "average" for their age group may feel deficient.

The problems with this kind of comparison are twofold: most of the statistics about human sexual behavior are reported in terms of *averages* rather than ranges and may be misleading. Second, what others are (or are not) doing may not be the best standard for you. Sexual happiness has little to do with achieving some "average"; it is the result of finding someone who thinks and feels very much as you do.

Differences in Partners

Ideally, it is desirable for persons with very similar sexual drives and interests to get together, but this does not occur always. For one thing, the peak of interest in sex occurs in the majority of males in their late teens or early twenties, whereas the peak of sexual interest among the majority of females occurs in their late thirties or early forties (Knox, 1984). Armed with this knowledge, a loving husband will understand that his wife's desire for sexual activity may be less than his and will adjust his behavior accordingly. Similarly, a sensitive wife will understand that her husband's desire for sexual activity may be greater than hers and will adjust her behavior accordingly.

Another critical difference in men and women involves the ease with which they separate sex and affection. For many men, affection is very nice but is not required for satisfying sex. Among women, sexual fulfillment is more likely within the context of a loving relationship. When, for example, a couple have quarreled, the man may initiate a sexual encounter even though the disagreement is not settled. The anger they feel does not interfere with sexual pleasure for him. She, however, may not desire such an encounter until after the anger is gone.

Many men who stop sexual activity once an orgasm has occurred fail to understand that many women wish continued, loving stimulation after an orgasm. This may require holding her in his arms and kissing her for a few minutes. Many men believe that because one orgasm is sufficient for them, that it is sufficient for their partners. Sometimes women may not wish to have an orgasm; other times, however, they may wish to have continued stimulation until several orgasms have been achieved. Couples who communicate openly about sexual concerns will more likely achieve the most satisfying encounters.

Sexual Response Cycle

The extensive research and observations of Masters and Johnson (Masters & Johnson, 1970; Masters et al., 1986) led to the conclusion that the body's

Sexual History

If our sexual ideology affects our conceptions of normality and reality in so many ways, then surely it must affect our conception of our sexual past. There is still in America a widespread belief that at sometime in our past we lived in a society in which most young people remained virginal until they married and then learned about sexuality in the marital bed and remained faithful to each other until death did part them. The Puritan period is often mentioned as one such time, yet nonvirginity was rather common during the end of the Puritan period in the eighteenth century. For example, in one church in Groton, Massachusetts, one-third of the brides confessed fornication to their minister. The nonvirginity rate was likely higher than this for it was predominantly pregnant brides who confessed fornication so that their babies might be accepted for baptism. Those nonvirgins who were not pregnant would not be under such pressure to confess. This sort of situation is not unusual historically. I have read the anthropological literature extensively in search of a culture in which males reach physical maturity (say, age 21) with the majority of them virginal. I have yet to find such a culture anywhere in the world at any time in history. Now, there may be a few such cultures that I have missed but surely they are quite rare.

Source: Reiss, I. L. (1981). Some observations on ideology and sexuality in America. *Journal of Marriage and the Family, 43,* 271–273. Copyrighted (1981) by the National Council on Family Relations, 3989 Central Ave. N. E., Suite 550, Minneapolis, MN 55421. Reprinted by permission.

physiological response to sexual stimulation is remarkably similar in all people. Although individuals show variations in how they respond, the sexual response cycle usually has four phases:

1. *Excitement phase.* The first phase can begin with any of a variety of sexual stimuli. Sexual arousal is multifaceted. Music, daydreams, or a kiss may initiate sexual arousal. This phase is characterized by increased blood pressure and heart rate. Vaginal lubrication appears in the female, and the male achieves an erection. Sexual tensions, of course, increase markedly.

2. *Plateau phase.* During the plateau phase the processes begun in the excitement phase (increased heart rate, congestion of the genital blood vessels) intensify. The plateau phase varies considerably in duration; some couples prolong it by decreasing stimulation momentarily. As a person in the plateau phase reaches the transition to the orgasmic phase, responses are less easily controlled. Many men cannot prevent ejaculation at this point.

3. *Orgasm phase.* Sexual excitement eventually reaches a peak, and sexual tensions built up during the first two phases are released in an orgasm. The orgasmic response involves contractions of the pelvic muscles and tightening of muscles in the face, feet, and hands for both men and women. Males ejaculate during orgasm; females experience involuntary vaginal contractions. Sometimes an orgasm is very intense; sometimes it is mild. It can last a few seconds or several minutes. Fictional descriptions of orgasm generally depict it as a wild, frenzied onslaught of emotional feeling. But as with every other sexual response, each indi-

vidual has a unique and personal reaction at different times. Many men can reach an orgasm within a few minutes after coitus. This is too quick for most women to achieve an orgasm, unless there has been sufficient foreplay. The majority of women, however, can achieve an orgasm within 15 minutes of foreplay and intercourse. For many men this will require careful monitoring of their own behavior.

The research of Masters and Johnson indicates that with a sufficient amount and type of stimulation a woman can experience multiple orgasms; however, fewer than 15% of all women do. This may be because their partners stop sexual stimulation too soon. Second or third orgasms generally are more intense and pleasurable than the first. Sexual therapists often recommend that couples should experiment to ascertain whether greater satisfaction is attained if the wife experiences multiple orgasms.

A few males are capable of renewed intercourse and a second orgasm after only a short time following the initial one. The period of time required to achieve a second ejaculation increases as a man grows older. Although the ability to have repeated intercourse decreases as a man ages, this is compensated by increased ability to control his orgasms. Increased control makes the sexual experience more pleasurable to both the man and the woman.

4. *Resolution phase.* After the release of sexual tension by orgasm and after the cessation of sexual stimulation, the body returns to its prearousal state. This is the resolution phase. Following orgasm, men characteristically experience a *refractory period*, during which rearousal is impossible. As a result some men prefer an abrupt end to erotic play following orgasm. However, the resolution phase is generally longer for women. Couples need to be aware of these physiological differences in males and females and need to focus on providing pleasure for the other person. The secret is in learning exactly what the other person really likes. The best

way for a couple to find out is to share this information with each other verbally.

Sexual Exclusivity

Most Americans who are in committed relationships are sexually exclusive. Our best evidence would lead to the conclusion that about two-thirds of wives and about one-half of husbands in the United States have been sexually exclusive since they have been married (Hunt, 1974; Knox, 1984), with the standard of exclusivity more readily accepted among older Americans (Brecher, 1984; DeLamater & MacCorquodale, 1979). Many people before marriage limit their lovemaking to kissing and holding each other without engaging in intercourse. A clear advantage to such activity is that it communicates one's love without exposing one's partner to an unwanted pregnancy or disease.

"A majority of young Americans do not condemn men and women who engage in premarital intercourse if they have an established relationship" (Lieberman, 1985, p. 4). In most of these relationships it is assumed that sexual exclusivity is highly valued among bonded couples. In a study of young couples who perceived themselves to be bonded, Lieberman (1985) sought to determine if there were differences in views of "cheating" among couples who were married and couples who were not yet married. Although 88% indicated that they believed that extramarital relations are wrong, nearly one-half believed that "men and women should be free to have extrapremarital relations." Although questions arise concerning the extent to which the results of a single study should be generalized, two issues should be considered given the fact that sexual exclusivity within marriage is so highly valued by the majority of persons.

1. *Is it likely that sexually nonexclusive individuals within a bonded relationship before marriage will*

be as likely to be exclusive in marriage as individuals who are exclusive before marriage?

Although the answer to this question is incomplete, there is evidence that individuals who have multiple partners before marriage are more likely to be sexually nonexclusive following their marriage (Allgeier & Allgeier, 1988). The difficulty in answering this question stems from the fact that most studies have ignored whether individuals who are dating are bonded.

2. *Can marriages withstand nonexclusive sexual relationships?* Clinical evidence indicates that many couples do withstand the strain to their marriages posed by extramarital sexual encounters. Few events pose as great a threat to the marriage as nonexclusive sex, however, and many marriages do not survive. Given that many extramarital liaisons yield only fleeting pleasure while greatly increasing the risk of contracting a sexually transmitted disease (including AIDS) and given the serious consequences of discovery, thought should be given to whether a casual encounter is worth major life disruptions.

Eight variables are related to determining the probability and cause of extramarital sexual permissiveness. The two primary variables are premarital sexual permissiveness and marital unhappiness. Secondary variables are: religiousity, gender equality, political liberality, education, gender, and age. (Reiss et al., 1981).

Sexual Guilt

Although sexual guilt is viewed as a positive force that serves as a useful sexual deterrent, its consequences can also be negative.

1. High sex guilt is negatively related to masturbatory behavior among females, yet masturbation is the best predictor of orgasms (Kinsey et al., 1953). Such guilt may play an adverse role

in female sexuality (Mosher & Vonderheide, 1985).

2. High sex-guilt youth have been found to be poor contraceptors. In fact, when high sex-guilt women become sexually active, they wait a year longer than low sex-guilt women to use a reliable contraceptive (Allgeier et al., 1977).

3. High sex-guilt youth use less effective methods of contraception (Herold & Goodwin, 1981).

4. Poor contraceptors, in turn, evidence a high rate of unintended births, and many high sex-guilt youth hold religious beliefs that preclude abortion.

Thus, high sex-guilt individuals are among those who are most affected by the impact of a premarital pregnancy and are among those who are most vulnerable to becoming pregnant. Although evidence indicates that high guilt may serve as a partial deterrent to premarital intercourse, it provides little assurance of its elimination.

Decisions

In view of the importance of sexual exclusivity within marriage—a standard most people recognize as desirable—many people who desire sexual closeness with a person other than a spouse incur feelings of guilt, particularly in situations in which their behavior has been discovered. Each of us decides, for example, whether "sex is acceptable only within marriage," or "with someone we love," or "with someone we like."

Because there are many opinions regarding what is "proper" sexual conduct, this chapter may seem too conservative for some and too liberal for others. The factors that contribute to a happy, satisfying sexual relationship and the factors that serve as barriers are presented to provoke the reader into examining his or her own ethical, moral, and religious values.

Susan Lapides/Design Conceptions

Sexual Myths: Barriers to Sexual Happiness

A variety of myths have grown up about sexuality, many of which are misleading in that they are untrue or only partially true.

Myth 1: Sex During Menstruation and Pregnancy Should Be Avoided

Some women find it somewhat painful to engage in sexual intercourse during menstruation because of reduced vaginal lubrication during this time. This problem can often be eliminated, however, by using a sterile water-soluble lubricant.

Menstrual blood is harmless to the man unless the women is a carrier of the AIDS virus. A woman's sexual desire does not usually decrease during the menstrual period. If a husband and wife desire to have sexual intercourse during menstruation, there is ordinarily no reason why they should not do so. In fact, there may be advantages for some couples: (a) intercourse that culminates in orgasm can relieve the discomfort of menstrual cramps for some women, (b) the menstrual period is a time of peak sexual desire for some women, and (c) the possibility of pregnancy is reduced during this time (it is not, however, entirely eliminated).

Usually, there is little change in most women's sexual interest during the first trimester of pregnancy. Many, however, experience a decrease in sexual desire during the last trimester of pregnancy. In some women erotic feelings are heightened during pregnancy, possibly the result of hormonal changes.

In some cases, limitations on sexual intercourse are necessary during the last month of pregnancy.

Physicians believe that strong contractions of the uterus during the orgasmic response may trigger labor contractions if the time of delivery is close. Physicians are likely to recommend abstinence if there are indications that the amniotic membrane is not intact. The leaking of watery liquid from the vagina is a signal that the amniotic membrane has ruptured. Intercourse at this time increases the danger of infection. A physician should be consulted if pain or bleeding occur during intercourse or if a couple has questions about the safety or advisability of sexual relations during pregnancy.

Myth 2: Men Are Always Confident About Sex

Many men, recognizing that great variability exists among women, are not always confident about how they should approach a specific woman. Men who have a great deal invested psychologically in a woman to whom they are attracted may feel uneasy in how they approach her because they fear rejection. Generally, they start out slowly, and the rate of progression is dependent upon their interpretation of cues provided by the woman involved. Many men who appear confident are, in reality, uncomfortable unless they get a great deal of encouragement from a partner.

As a general rule, men are more likely to push for sexual encounters earlier in the relationship than women. Men exhibit considerable variability just as women do. Although some may desire intercourse with every woman they date, others may wish to reserve sexual intercourse for someone they love or for marriage.

Myth 3: Men Are Always Ready for Sex

Most men do not regard every woman as a potential sex partner. They see little point in having an encounter with someone they do not particularly care about. Mature men are likely to consider the consequences of extramarital encounters, and many reject such encounters believing they are dishonest or immoral.

Myth 4: Women Are Not Very Interested in Sex

Affection plays a greater role among women than men in their readiness for sexual encounters. Men, to a greater extent than women, consider sex desirable in its own right, whereas many women prefer to limit their encounters to a person for whom they feel genuine affection. There are, of course, exceptions. Too, women are more cautious about sex because they run the risk of pregnancy.

Myth 5: Sexual Satisfaction Is a Necessary Condition for a Good Marriage

When most people think of a sexual relationship that extends over a significant period of time, they think of marriage. For some, marriage is the only relationship in which sex is approved. Thus, it would appear that it might be impossible to have a satisfying marriage without good sex. In their study of 75,000 young, middle-class women, Tavris and Jayarante (1976) found the majority of them believed that love, respect, and friendship were the most important factors in their marriage, and *although they rated sexual compatibility desirable, they did not consider it essential.* Thus, (a) they may feel that sex is not important, (b) they may be asexual, or (c) they may have so many positive things in their marriage that they focus on other satisfying aspects of their marriage.

Myth 6: Masturbation Should Be Avoided after Marriage

Individuals who have been socialized to avoid masturbation may wish to do so. Increasingly, however, greater acceptance of masturbation is evident. Some people who experience inhibited sexual desire are encouraged by sex therapists to masturbate in order to decrease their level of inhibition so that they can more readily relate to a spouse sexually.

Men and women who are highly sexual, for example, may masturbate in order to facilitate their accommodation to a spouse whose interest in sex is far less than theirs. Even couples who are well matched sexually may not find that their schedules or their moods make it possible for them always to share sexual activity together. Many educated persons understand the physical, psychological, and social advantages of restricting their sexual activity and may masturbate when sexual activity with their spouse is not convenient or possible. Given that nonexclusive sexual activity in marriage is one of the major reasons for divorce (Ahrons & Rodgers, 1987; Price & McKenry, 1988) and given the physical risks of multiple sex partners, masturbation would appear to be a sensible alternative during periods when married partners are away from each other.

When Brecher (1984) asked 4,246 older Americans about masturbation, two-thirds of the male respondents and nearly one-half of the female respondents who were in their fifties indicated that they masturbated, slightly over two-fifths of the men and one-third of the women in their seventies masturbated. An important reason for the persistence of the belief that masturbation should be avoided is that many adults are not completely comfortable with their sexuality.

Myth 7: A Careful Person Will Never Get Caught in an Extramarital Affair

Physicians regularly treat individuals who are "caught" by a sexually transmitted disease. Attorneys regularly appear in court representing "caught" individuals who were nonexclusive. Many people who believe that those who get caught are indiscreet, careless, irresponsible, or unknowledgable occasionally find themselves in situations they could not have imagined.

Sexual Lifestyles

As recently as when your grandparents were young adults, most people gave little thought to "lifestyle" decisions; most had limited experience with lifestyles that deviated from the mainstream. In the 1960s and 1970s, however, people became more aware of variations in sexual attitudes and practiced their option to make choices about their style of living. The increased openness with which sexual concerns are now discussed and the greater social acceptance of different lifestyles, have given people a greater number of opportunities for varied sexual expectations.

The vast majority of persons are heterosexual and prefer to confine their sexual activity to a member of the opposite gender. Although the sexual orientation of persons is traditionally classified as *heterosexual*, *homosexual*, or *bisexual*, four decades ago Kinsey and his associates (1948) discovered that some persons could not be classified as exclusively heterosexual or homosexual. For a number of persons, a range of sexual orientation is more accurate in describing their sexual preferences. For example, a male may prefer sexual contacts with females, may have a history of 95% of his contacts with females, and yet may have 5% of his contacts with males.

An important point in contemplating marriage is whether the person that is chosen has been exposed to same-gender sexual relationships and whether he or she may seek such contacts again. Just as blood examinations are required to ascertain whether syphilis has been contracted, a blood test for AIDS is appropriate if there is reason to suspect that any danger is involved.

Joel Gordon

I have never had sex with a girl and I am 21 years old. Worse still, I am not attracted to women sexually. I am very attracted to men, but I have never had sex with one. I find myself attracted to a lifestyle I cannot accept, and I don't want anyone telling me to accept a gay lifestyle for myself. I want to be married and have children. What can I do?

Can a person who is attracted to members of the same sex learn to relate heterosexually? Some sex therapists have been able to assist some clients in changing to heterosexual behavior. This does not mean that they will no longer be attracted to members of the same gender or that they will refrain from all homosexual encounters. For some persons, a change in their sexual preference is easier than it is for others. For example, a person who would be

classified as "predominantly homosexual but more than incidently heterosexual" would have less difficulty changing than someone classified as "exclusively homosexual."

Another factor influencing ease of change is one's perception of how sexual preference develops. The origins of homosexuality and heterosexuality are unknown. Some researchers believe that biological factors predispose a person's sexual preference. They base their conclusion on the existence of a nearly uniform 10% homosexual population in all societies, regardless of attitudes about homosexuality in those societies (Bell et al., 1981). No clear biological differences in homosexuals and heterosexuals have been found.

Other researchers believe that sexual preferences are learned, with experience in childhood and adult role models influencing the eventual outcome. No particular past experiences or aspects of relationships, however, have been shown to be consequential in the development of sexual preference (Bell et al., 1981).

Although attitudes toward homosexuality and bisexuality have improved over the last decade, some continue to be negative and are often characterized by value-laden terms (Masters et al., 1986). For example, children learn early by the tone of voice when someone refers to a homosexual as a "homo" that this word connotes social disapproval. Male homosexuals prefer the term "gay" and female homosexuals prefer the term "lesbian" because of the stigma attached to certain words. So important, many people believe, is gender preference that the person who chooses a lifestyle other than heterosexuality is likely to be identified in terms of his or her sexual preference.

Unsolicited Invitations

From time to time, some persons who are heterosexual, bisexual, or homosexual invite others to have sexual encounters with them. Most of them do not intend to offend the persons they invite. Sometimes, however, their judgment is faulty due to their intense desire or they may misread cues, e.g., interpreting a friendly smile incorrectly.

Persons who receive such invitations sometimes react with distress and outrage. Often they wonder what to do. Because it serves little purpose to respond with anger, many simply decline the invitation. If you wish to discourage a second invitation, it is helpful to communicate your orientation clearly.

Unexpected Consequences

One of the most unexpected and disappointing consequences of sex is an unanticipated pregnancy, particularly if the couple is young, unmarried, and has parents who disapprove of premarital sex. If they or their parents hold beliefs that preclude an abortion the situation is even more complicated.

One of the most common errors that beginners make in their sexual behavior is to assume that they will be safe if they follow the prescribed contraceptive directions. This is not always easy; investigators who applied tests of clarity and simplicity to assess the readability of instructions included in 25 brands of condoms concluded that most directions could not be understood by consumers who did not have some college education (Richwald et al., 1988). Among the common reasons for becoming pregnant when the pill is being used—aside from forgetting to take the pill—are vomiting and/or diarrhea during an illness and taking medication that may interfere with the effectiveness of the pill.

Another unexpected result of sexual encounters is contracting a sexually transmitted disease. Persons who have multiple partners or who have casual or anonymous partners are at greater risk. Most sexually transmitted diseases are easily treated *if* they are detected. Many, however, are asymptomatic and may lead to serious infections before they are detected. Herpes and AIDS currently are not curable; AIDS is fatal.

Correlates of Early Intercourse of Daughters

In a detailed review of the literature of the correlates of early intercourse of daughters, Olson (1988) found:

1. Daughters who discuss sex with their parents are more likely to engage in sexual activity at a later age (Newcomer & Udry, 1985: Rosen, et al., 1982).

2. Daughters seem to be less sexually active and there is less chance that they will become pregnant if they have received their sex education from parents as opposed to other sources (Goldfarb et al., 1977; Rosen et al., 1982; Spanier, 1977).

3. If a greater range of sexual topics is discussed, there is less sexual activity (Lewis, 1963).

4. More daughters who *frequently* discuss sex-related topics with their mothers become sexually active later (Fox & Inazu, 1980).

5. Fathers' sex education has little effect on the sexual behavior of their daughters (Rosen et al., 1982; Spanier, 1976).

6. Mothers who engage in premarital sexual activity are more likely to have daughters that also do so (Inazu & Fox, 1980; Newcomer & Udry, 1985).

7. Women whose attitudes on premarital sexual intercourse are similar to their parents' attitudes have lower rates of premarital coitus (Libby et al., 1978; Shah & Zelnick, 1981).

8. A larger proportion of adolescents living with both parents have lower premarital intercourse rates (Hogan & Kitagawa, 1985; Newcomer & Udry, 1987; Zelnick et al. 1981).

9. Conflict in the home is related to early premarital sexual activity (Lewis, 1963).

10. Daughters who had close relationships with their mothers are less likely to engage in premarital sexual activity (Lewis, 1963).

11. General unhappiness in the home is related to premarital sexual activity (Inazu & Fox, 1980; Lewis, 1963).

12. Lack of control in the home is related to premarital sexual activity (Hogan & Kitagawa, 1985).

Extramarital Sex

The publication of the original Kinsey studies (1948, 1953) provided a benchmark of the rates of sexual behavior in the United States; however, sexual patterns have changed since then. One important change is an increase in the number of married persons who engage in sexual intercourse with persons other than a spouse. Those who are most likely to remain sexually exclusive are those couples who are conservative, are religious, have children, have a history involving a very limited number of sexual partners before marriage, are happily married, maintain a residence together, are committed to marriage, and wish not to disappoint their spouse. In contrast, couples are more likely to have extramarital sex if they are unhappily married, have a history of numerous sexual contacts before marriage, are liberal, are not particularly religious, have no children, are not especially committed to their marriage, and are more likely to reject conventional standards of exclusivity. More men than women are involved in extramarital relationships.

For the majority of people, marriage carries with it the expectation of sexual exclusivity. Even husbands and wives who are not sexually exclusive themselves generally expect their spouses to be faithful to them. Among couples who become "swingers," i.e., a nonexclusive lifestyle in which both partners engage in sexual encounters with others with mutual consent, the majority become monogamous within a few years (Watson, 1981). Thus, even those who embrace a more open sexual lifestyle are likely to reject it in time.

It is difficult to state the effects an extramarital sexual relationship will have on a marriage. Many factors must be considered, such as the nature of the extramarital relationship and the condition of the marriage. Many marriages do not survive an extramarital affair, and couples who do weather one may require family therapy and much time to heal.

Sexual Changes in the Later Years

For many years we have assumed that a decrease in sexual interest and ability occurs as persons age. People who are healthy and happy with their lives, however, can usually continue to be sexually active in their later years (Brecher, 1984), although changes in their sexual behavior will occur.

Although some physical changes associated with aging have sexual implications, most of these can be remedied. Between age 50 and 70 testosterone levels in men decrease to less than one-half of that produced between the ages of 23 and 36 (Bahr, 1976). Therapists report success in renewing male sex drive with testosterone replacement. The power of suggestion may play more of a role than the hormone itself, as men who receive placebos also reported increased sex drives if they were convinced they were given testosterone (Green, 1981).

The most common sexual problem of aging men is trouble with the prostate gland. Prostate malfunctions plague about 10% of the male population at age 40 and 50% of those at age 80. If problems are treated early, however, the chances for maintenance of sexual activity are excellent (McCrary & McCrary, 1982).

Although the term "menopause" refers only to a woman's last menstrual period, many people incorrectly use this term to refer to a time more correctly called the "climacteric"—that is, the several years immediately before and after the menopause (Masters et al., 1986, p. 176). About 80% of women experience symptoms that are the result of changes in hormone levels; only a minority seek medical treatment for the relief of symptoms related to the climacteric, a transition that normally occurs between 48 and 52 years of age. The most annoying symptom is hot flashes that appear to be the result of a malfunctioning temperature control mechanism in the hypothalamus, a condition brought on by estrogen deficiency. Fortunately, estrogen replacement therapy alleviates this distress and slows the occurrence of osteoporosis, the disintegration of bones (Masters et al., 1986).

Sexual Dysfunctions

Inhibited Sexual Desire

Inhibited sexual desire may be differentiated from lack of sexual desire in that the latter normally occurs during childhood and among the very old and is associated with normal development. Some sex therapists estimate that about 40% of the problems presented to them involve inhibited sexual desire, with as many men as women having difficulties (Penner & Penner, 1988). Inhibited sexual desire may be categorized as primary or secondary. *Primary inhibition of sexual desire* may be due to a variety of factors: a homosexual orientation (but in a heterosexual relationship), the inability to be emotional, having been reared to regard sex as bad or dirty, or sexual abuse. For example, a woman who was sexually abused as a child may have very conflicting feelings about sex; she may have conditioned herself to shut off any response when she begins to feel aroused (Penner & Penner, 1988). A man who lacks self-esteem may inhibit sexual feelings because he believes no one would find him attractive. As Allgeier and Allgeier (1988) note "they turn off the sexual arousal process at its earliest stage and thus avoid the anxiety associated with sexual expression" (p. 241).

Secondary inhibited sexual desire occurs when a person who has had sexual interest loses it. For example, a woman who has enthusiasm for her sexual relationship with her husband at the beginning of their marriage but is not orgasmic may find her enthusiasm waning after a few years; she may become very frustrated and no longer experience sexual arousal. A man who is consumed by career and community activities may have no energy for or interest in sex. A person who is hurt by a spouse's extramarital relationship may find that his or her sexual desire is replaced by turmoil and anger (Penner & Penner, 1988). Treatment of inhibited desire depends on discovering the cause and treating it.

Vaginismus

Vaginismus is a painful contraction of vaginal muscles that makes intercourse exceedingly difficult and sometimes impossible. Treatment consists of the gradual dilation of the vaginal orifice, normally through the insertion of progressively larger dilators. Masters and Johnson have reported a 100%

How Common Is Sexual Dysfunction Among "Normal Couples"?

In a study of 100 well-educated, white, middle-class couples who were not involved in therapy, 83% of whom identified their marriages as "happy" or "very happy," 63% of the husbands and 40% of the wives reported having a "sexual dysfunction." In the same study, 50% of the husbands and 77% of the wives reported having "sexual difficulties."

The Wives

48% had difficulty getting excited

33% had difficulty maintaining excitement

46% had difficulty reaching an orgasm

15% were unable to have an orgasm

47% were unable to relax during sexual involvement

35% expressed a lack of interest in sex

28% were "turned off" by sex with their husbands

The Husbands

7% had difficulty getting an erection

9% had difficulty maintaining an erection

36% ejaculated too quickly

12% were unable to relax during sexual involvement

16% expressed a lack of interest in sex

10% were "turned off" by sex with their wives

Source: Abstracted from information appearing in *The New England Journal of Medicine.* Frank, E., Anderson, C., & Rubinstein, D. (1978). Frequency of sexual dysfunction in "normal" couples. *New England Journal of Medicine, 229,* 111–115.

success rate, and the correction of vaginismus is often achieved within 5 days.

Orgasmic Dysfunction

It is common to assume that nonorgasmic women are the victims of inadequate socialization or that they are suffering from anxiety. Physical bases are often discounted as causes of the inability to achieve orgasms. Yet, in a study of Hartman and Fithian (1974), approximately one-third of the women with orgasmic dysfunction were discovered to have clitoral adhesions, and when one-third of those who had clitoral adhesions had their adhesions removed they became orgasmic within a few weeks. Physical causes of orgasmic dysfunction occur with sufficient frequency that medical examinations are warranted in cases where orgasms do not occur. Smith and Meyer (1978) reported that "during... six years of evaluating and treating a wide spectrum of sexual dysfunctions, we have treated four times as many nonorgasmic women as patients with other sexual disorders" (p. 66).

Impotency

One of the most common sexual dysfunctions in males is *impotency*—that is, the inability to attain an erection. According to current evidence, the cause can be either psychological or physiological in nature—that is, diabetes, excessive use of alcohol and other recreational drugs, the use of certain pre-scribed medication, and anxiety (Penner & Penner, 1988).

Impotency frequently does not reflect a lack of sexual desire, but it may limit sexual encounters because many men who are unable to attain an erection are very embarrassed and avoid intercourse. Contrary to popular thought, aging does not bring impotence, although the changes that occur with aging, eg., concerns about career or health, may contribute to it. Some men wrongly assume they are having problems with impotency because they need more direct stimulation to achieve an erection or because their erections are not as firm. Both are normal consequences of aging and are not impotence (Penner & Penner, 1988).

Impotency occurs when in 50% of the attempts to have intercourse a man is unable to achieve an erection. Impotency is categorized as *primary* or *secondary*. *Primary impotence* describes situations in which an erection has never occurred. It is rare. Men who are concerned that they cannot attain an erection can try an easy "home" test: wrap postage stamps firmly around the penis at night before sleeping. In the morning, separated stamps indi-cated that an erection did indeed occur and that they are not a victim of primary impotency, which is much more difficult to treat than secondary im-potence. *Secondary impotence* describes situations in which a man has succeeded in intercourse previ-

ously but is unable to achieve or maintain an erec-tion at the time. Treatment of secondary impotence is highly successful. A physician or therapist can treat medical causes, such as the use of certain pre-scription drugs or hormonal imbalances.

If there is not an apparent medical reason, the wife may incorrectly perceive that it is her fault or that her husband is attracted to someone else. In many instances, however, the impotence may be a reflection of stress in the husband, e.g., fear of los-ing his job, distress he is feeling because of the way he is treated by his colleagues at work, concern about a medical condition he has developed.

Bill and Alice have been married 10 years. Bill has been highly successful in the corporation that employs him. Because of decreased product demand, however, he received a notice that his employment would be terminated within a month and that he would re-ceive 3 months severance pay. Although Bill regretted leaving his job, he decided not to share the informa-tion with Alice for he was confident he could obtain another position quickly.

Bill justified his decision not to tell Alice: she was a worrier, she was 4 months pregnant with an un-planned third child, and they had a large debt. Their mortgage was $90,000; and they were paying on two automobiles.

Following his last day at the office, he continued to leave every day to give the appearance of going to work. He approached dozens of companies and had had several interviews. Then he received his last pay-check, and he was devastated. He had sent out over 200 résumés and still did not have a job. The whole industry for which he worked was depressed.

Bill, who usually was very stable, could not sleep, and his interest in sex was virtually gone. He wanted to tell Alice everything but he had gone too far, and the realization of the situation they were in would be terribly difficult for Alice.

Alice knew that something was wrong. She could not understand Bill's lack of interest in her. At first she thought that perhaps he really did not want the baby and that he found her unattractive in her pregnancy. Later she worried that he had lost all interest in their relationship. Ultimately, she concluded that he was interested in someone else. The thought of divorce terrified her for she loved Bill very much.

Bill was embarrassed about his impotency. He would not have minded holding Alice close, but when he did she tried to stimulate him sexually and he experienced panic. He was confident that once he had a job, his problem would be resolved. In the meantime, however, he avoided close contact for he felt he could not explain why he was so upset.

As men age and need more direct stimulation to achieve an erection, they need to tell their wives what specific kinds of stimulation they would like. Wives may need to be reassured that they are still attractive and that nothing is wrong (Penner & Penner, 1987). A part of the male culture that many women may not readily understand is how sensitive men are about not being able to attain an erection. Even men who reject the "macho" concept may find it difficult to adjust to a delayed sexual response.

Masters and Johnson report that their success rate drops to 59% in treating men who experience *primary impotence*—that is, the male has *never* maintained an erection firm enough to make sexual intercourse possible. Fear and anxiety are major contributors to primary impotence. A man who experiences impotence over a prolonged period of time approaches sexual intercourse in an increasingly anxious and fearful state of mind. He may attempt to achieve erection through will power. This takes sexual interaction completely out of a pleasurable context and makes it even more difficult to achieve an erection.

When physical problems have been ruled out, successful treatment of impotence focuses upon removing the individual's fear of failure and his extreme concern with performance. Partners are encouraged to relax and enjoy sexual activities other than intercourse without any concern for perfor-

mance, ejaculation, or orgasm (Hartman & Fithian, 1984; Kaplan, 1974; Masters et al., 1986).

Premature Ejaculation

An indication of the prevalence of premature ejaculation may be seen in the fact that of 448 cases of sexually dysfunctional men treated by Masters and Johnson (1970), 186 were premature ejaculators. It is believed to be the most common of all the sexual dysfunctions in males. Approximately one-fifth of all men believe that they have climaxed too early at some time (Meyer et al., 1983). An orgasm is normally considered to be premature if it occurs within 2 to 3 minutes of intromission and if the timing is frustrating to either partner (Kaplan, 1983). In over 500 cases of premature ejaculation at the Masters and Johnson Institute, only one instance was due to an organic condition. In the vast majority of cases, the difficulty is one of socialization and/or psychological origin (Masters et al., 1986). This may be the result of early experience when males achieve an orgasm within several minutes after beginning masturbation in order to rush the pleasure. Within marriage, however, such a pattern is dysfunctional if intromission occurs early within the sexual encounter, inasmuch as a substantial number of women may require 15 minutes or more of sexual stimulation before they attain an orgasm.

Wives can play an important role in helping husbands who are premature ejaculators by employing the "squeeze" technique, a technique that involves squeezing the husband's penis just prior to ejaculation. The process involves repeated stops before the ejaculation actually occurs and applying very firm pressure to reduce the level of excitement. Considerable communication is required between the husband and wife. A man can also practice this technique for himself while masturbating. Sexual therapists have reported a great deal of success with this technique (Masters et al., 1986; Penner & Penner, 1988).

Many men can prevent premature ejaculation by using a condom; this decreases the sensitivity of the glans, hence slowing sexual excitement and orgasm. A more effective method is to apply an anesthetic ointment to the glans approximately 30 minutes before sexual intercourse. The stop-start technique is another common method. When the man perceives he is nearing orgasm, he simply stops movement, in order to relax and to permit the intensity of his excitement to subside (Kilmann, 1984). In many cases involving sexual dysfunction of women, it is recommended that the female be on top in order to control the level of stimulation; however, in cases of premature ejaculation, it is more advantageous for the male to be on top in order to stop when ejaculation is anticipated. Some men can delay ejaculation by thinking nonsexual thoughts.

By developing a method of self-monitoring, most couples can extend the period of intromission without ejaculation to accommodate the needs of both. Whatever the difficulty that one incurs in sexual encounters, there is considerable merit in developing the attitude that change can and will occur. The cases that are difficult for sexual therapists to treat are those in which the parties involved become anxious and believe they cannot change.

Retarded Ejaculation

Retarded ejaculation occurs when men simply cannot achieve an orgasm. Although not common, it occurs in most men occasionally. If a man has intercourse numerous times during a day, he readily accepts that he may not achieve an orgasm even though he is sexually excited. In cases in which the reason is not immediately evident, failure to achieve an orgasm may be puzzling. In rare instances, men can actually experience an orgasm without ejaculating, or they can have an ejaculation without experiencing an orgasm. Although these are normal occurrences, they are rare.

There are several reasons why men have difficulty with retarded ejaculation. Some men seem to have bypassed the normal process of learning about themselves as sexual beings. They may have learned to shut off erotic responses early in the sexual response cycle. Treatment involves helping these men go through the stages of self-discovery, exploration of genitals, self-stimulation, and mutual stimulation with a spouse. Treatment usually proceeds quickly (Penner & Penner, 1988). Other males have learned during adolescence to masturbate roughly; in a sexual encounter with someone they care about a great deal, these men may be hesitant to be so forceful and, as a result, fail to have an orgasm.

Still other men who have difficulty with retarded ejaculation with a partner have no difficulty in ejaculating when they masturbate. Their situation is often more complex and difficult to treat. These men may have come from a home in which the mother was very controlling and dominating or from another situation that has caused considerable ambivalence (love/hate/anger) toward women. The underlying causes must be sought and treated in these cases (Penner & Penner, 1988).

The magic of intimacy is not impaired by learning how to correct problems before they occur. People experiencing sexual dysfunction often are very uncomfortable, believing that they should be able to work out things for themselves. When they cannot, they frequently resort to blaming each other for their lack of satisfaction. Many couples do not seek professional help and put up with their lack of sexual satisfaction; others terminate the marriage.

Treatment of Sexual Dysfunctions

Much can be done to assist persons who have sexual problems. Masters and Johnson have reported approximately 80% success rates in the treatment of all kinds of unsatisfactory sexual functioning. Their success seems to be enduring. One year following treatment, the success rate is reduced by only 5%

to 6% (Masters et al., 1986). Generally, the later in the sexual response cycle that the problems occur, the easier the treatment. For example, premature ejaculation or orgasmic dysfunction are easier to alleviate than problems of inhibited sexual desire (Penner & Penner, 1988).

If professional therapy is sought for sexual dysfunction, the couple typically will see the therapist regularly and will focus at the beginning on details of a sexual history and evaluation. Often the couple will be asked to continue the discussions at home. They may be asked to abstain from all sexual activity as they begin therapy. Then they move into sexual exercises or "tasks" to be done at home.

In therapy, the husband and wife are encouraged to engage in sexual play not intended to result in sexual intercourse. Once they are able to relax and enjoy noncoital sexual play, they are usually capable of proceeding to successful sexual intercourse because the pattern of failure has been broken and a pattern of relaxing and enjoying sexual behavior has been initiated. Detailed discussions of the treatment of common sexual dysfunctions have been presented by Hartman and Fithian (1974), Kaplan (1974), and Masters et al., (1986).

In conventional therapy, only conversations take place in the therapist's office, and there is no sexual contact between patient and therapist. The goal of the therapist is to reorient sexual behavior and to help the couple unlearn negative patterns and substitute more positive ones. The American Association of Sex Educators, Counselors and Therapists can recommend approved therapists.

Destructive Aspects of Sexual Relationships

Sexually Abused Children

A summary of the literature on sexually abused children by Wishon and Eller (1984) included several major conclusions:

1. Studies on nonclinical populations show that large numbers of adults—as many as 15% to 35% of women and 5% to 15% of men—report having been sexually victimized as children, for a total of perhaps 500,000 children per year between the ages of 4 and 13 years (Fritz et al., 1981; Finkelhor, 1982). The average age of sexual abuse victims is 11 years.

2. Among reported child sexual abusers, close to 90% are men; this holds true whether the victims are boys or girls. The majority of sex crimes against children are perpetrated by persons who are known to the child—most significantly, fathers, stepfathers, and mothers' boyfriends. In the case of incest or sexual abuse by a known assailant, the victim may be trapped in a relationship for years.

3. Common injuries resulting from sexual abuse include lacerations, cuts, abrasions, fractures, and ecchymoses (escape of blood into the tissue by a ruptured blood vessel). Physical problems among the very youngest children include severe damage to the vagina and anus. Long-term consequences may include inability to bear children and an increased risk of cervical cancer.

4. LaBarbera et al. (1980) explored the hypotheses of child psychiatrists on the impact of sexual abuse and concluded that these experiences almost always cause serious psychological disorder. Although there seems to be little evidence to support the belief that an early homosexual relationship between a child and adult will dispose that child to an adult homosexual orientation (West, 1981), it is common for many child victims to grow up to lead lives of sexual promiscuousness or impotency (Summit & Kryso, 1978).

Incest includes all sexual contact with members of the same family, except that of the husband and wife. Incestuous abuse includes exploitive sexual contact or attempted contact between relatives, no matter how distant the relationships may be, before the victim is 18 years of age. Sexual encounters with children by family members can take many forms: fondling a child; having the child touch the adult's genitals; "talking dirty" to a child; exposing a child to pornography or pornographically exploiting a child; oral-genital contact; masturbating a child, forcing a child to masturbate; penetration of anus or vagina with fingers or other objects; and/or anal or vaginal intercourse (Hancock & Mains, 1987; Vander Mey & Neff, 1982). Many victims do not report incest for a variety of reasons: (a) home is the only place where their needs for survival are being met, (b) incestuous adults threaten the victims with physical punishment, (c) loyalty and love for the abuser make it hard to speak against people who are supposed to be protectors, and (d) they fear they will not be believed (Hancock & Mains, 1987).

Father-daughter incest, including a stepfather or the mother's partner, accounts for a large portion of incest (Ledray, 1984; Hancock & Mains, 1987). Sexual abuse of sons by mothers is very rare. With cases involving young children, physical evidence includes genital rashes or pain, traumatized genitalia, vaginal or anal bleeding, vaginal discharge, and venereal disease. Psychological symptoms include difficulty with friends and school, truancy, isolation from peers, depression, running away from home, suicidal gestures, delinquency, prostitution, using language or terms to describe body parts or sex acts that are not appropriate to the child's age or experience, unexplained aversion to a particular person (the abuser), and drug abuse (Hancock & Mains, 1987; Shapshay & Vines, 1982). The child most likely to be victimized is the oldest daughter in the family, although younger daughters may become subsequent victims (Herman & Hirschman, 1981).

Incest occurs irrespective of social class, rural-urban residence, religion, and ethnicity (Mayer, 1985). The Child Abuse Prevention and Treatment Act of 1975 provided for the creation of a group in each state to be responsible for receiving reports of alleged incest (Renshap, 1982). The Child Advocate Association of Chicago has estimated that only 12% of all intrafamily sexual abuse is reported to the police. If a complaint is filed against a father, the chance of the case being brought to court is very small. In a study of 250 reports of child sexual abuse in New York, for example, only 25% of those accused were brought to trial (Thorman, 1983).

Factors contributing to the onset or continuance of child sexual abuse include the father's alcohol or drug abuse, the wife being ill or not at home, father and daughter sharing sleeping quarters, overcrowded living quarters, fear of family dissolution on the victim's part, passive behavior of the victim, disbelief of the mother, an authoritarian father, a wife's rejection of sexual intercourse, and a mother's acceptance of the incest (Vander Mey & Neff, 1982). Reposa and Zuelzer (1983) suggest incest is a manifestation of severe familial dysfunction. Incestuous families are characterized as "closed"—that is, having restricted interaction with the broader community. Additionally these families suffer role confusion, poor parental communication, and parental abuse of power (Sgroi, 1985). One of the most surprising findings reported in the research is the number of mothers who know their daughters are being sexually abused by their husbands but do not acknowledge it because they feel helpless to stop it.

Although incest occurs infrequently in families, its occurrence evokes very negative psychological effects because of the guilt and ambivalence that the child/victim suffers. All persons need to know about incest in order to be more helpful to the victims.

Sibling Incest

It is believed that the most common form of incest involves brothers and sisters, with an older brother initiating a contact with a younger sister, and that most sibling incest involves exploratory play. As such it does not involve the domination, exploitation, and trauma of adult-child incest (Vander Mey & Neff, 1982).

Data from one of the major studies of sex among siblings (Finkelhor, 1980) came from a survey of students at six New England colleges and universities and two nonresidential community colleges:

1. In this survey, 15% of the females and 10% of the males reported having had a sexual encounter with a sibling: 74% were heterosexual, 10% were between sisters, 16% were between brothers.

2. Of these encounters, 40% involved siblings under 8 years old; 73% involved siblings, one of whom was older than 8; 35% occurred when one of them was older than 12. Most encounters occurred between the ages of 8 and 12. In only 23% of the cases was the difference in the ages of the siblings 5 years or more. The younger children were involved in exhibitionism; older children were involved in attempted intercourse and intercourse (13%).

3. In one-third of the cases, the encounter occurred only once, 27% of the instances occurred over a year.

4. In 30% of the cases, the sexual encounters were reported as positive, 30% reported negative experiences, and 40% did not feel strongly either way. Females (35%) reported the experiences as more unpleasant than males (22%). Males generally initiated the contacts. The greater the age difference, the more likely the experience was perceived as negative. If, however, the activity was limited to genital exhibition, it was likely to be remembered as positive.

5. Only 12% of the participants told someone about their sexual activity.

6. Women who had sibling sexual experiences that they perceived to be positive had higher sexual self-esteem in college than women who had perceived their childhood sexual experiences to be negative. Youth were at greater risk of trauma from sibling sex if their encounters had occurred when they were very young. Older children handled negative and exploitative experiences better, and their subsequent impact was minimal.

7. Sibling sexual experiences for men were unrelated to levels of current intercourse in college. Women who had experienced sexual encounters with a sibling during childhood, however, were more likely to have a higher level of intercourse in college.

Sexual Addiction

Increasingly, marriage and family therapists are being consulted by clients who report that their marriages are threatened by sexual addiction, a compulsive disorder that leads one of them to engage in sexual encounters with multiple partners. Because this behavior so violates societal norms, even understanding, compassionate spouses find it difficult to give the support they need when they discover their partner is engaging regularly in a series of extramarital affairs. The husband who believes his wife really can stop if she wants to is likely to be hurt and angered when his wife continues to "cheat" on him. Compulsive disorders are difficult to treat, and many addicts who love their spouses and who want to stop find they cannot without professional help. Gradually, with greater public education we will learn that the sexual addict, like the drug addict, is the victim of a disorder that warrants professional treatment.

Sexual Harassment

A more sexually permissive society has fostered greater informality in interaction that has been generalized to the workplace. Because sexual humor and sexual aggressiveness are parts of the social-

Sexual Addiction

A review of the literature on sexual addiction by Chapman (1990) revealed the following major conclusions:

1. Sexual addiction, compulsive sexual behavior, hypersexuality, and sexual impulsivity are all names for a pattern that refers not so much to frequency of sexual activity, exaggerated desire, number of partners, or types of activity, as to the individual's perceived lack of control over his or her sexual impulses.

2. Although the general prevalence of sexual addiction is not known, the phenomenon cuts across personality, gender, and socioeconomic divisions.

3. People who seek treatment for sexual addiction report they no longer feel in control of their sexual behavior and that their sexual behavior is often not satisfying. Engaging in activities including compulsive masturbation, multiple affairs, pornography, prostitution, homosexual behavior, exhibitionism, voyeurism, indecent liberties, child molestation, incest, and rape, addicts repeatedly make commitments to stop, only to find they cannot. Each failure is another indictment of self-control and morality, which increases negative feelings.

4. Loneliness, low self-esteem, poor interpersonal relationships, and fear of intimacy are primary anxiety-producing factors in addiction.

5. Sexual excitement plays an important role in addiction. The rush of adrenaline and the trancelike state of the waiting voyeur are mood altering qualities enhanced by the intrusive and illicit parts of the behavior. This mood alteration is compared to the experience of alcohol or drug abuse.

6. Sexually addicted persons, because of the nature of their problems, very often isolate themselves in order to keep such behavior a secret. Often their behavior becomes known through arrest, the revelation of partners, or the transmission of diseases.

Source: Adapted with permission from Chapman, S. F. (1990). *Sexual addiction.* Unpublished manuscript. The University of Georgia, Department of Child and Family Development, Athens, GA.

ization of males, many women who are gainfully employed find themselves the object of sexual remarks and other forms of sexual attention that they do not like and find difficult to handle.

Sexual harassment on the job has important effects on family life because the vast majority of victims are women who must work because of economic necessity.

Although sexual harassment is unlawful under the Civil Rights Act of 1964, many women continue to endure harassment because they believe that open defiance will reflect that they are prudish or that their advancement in their employment will be impaired. A survey reported in the *Harvard Business Review* ("Sexual Harassment", 1981) reflected that:

1. Four out of every six employees regard their supervisor's sexual harassment as more serious than that of co-workers.

2. According to 88% of the respondents, sexual behavior has no place in business.

3. The same proportion of men and women (59%) agreed or partly agreed that a smart woman should not have trouble handling an unwanted sexual approach. Thus, a very substantial minority, (41%) believed that women would have difficulty handling some sexual approaches.

4. The survey indicates that 78% disagreed with the statement: "If a woman dresses and behaves properly she will not be the target of unwanted sexual approaches at work."

Another survey ("Sexual Bureaucracies," 1983), involving persons harassed in government, reflected that:

1. Of those women who were harassed, 95% were harassed by men, 22% by women, and 2% by both.

2. Of those men who were harassed, 72% were harassed by women, 22% by men, and 6% by both.

3. The women reported that 47% of the harassment was from supervisors and 63% was from subordinates or co-workers.

Those persons who are the recipients of sexual harassment find it difficult to deal with because (a) it is difficult to define, (b) usually there is little specific, concrete evidence, and (c) in those instances when it is the supervisor who is responsible for the harassment, the employee may fear losing her job (Rowe, 1981).

Increasingly, large companies in the United States are issuing statements that reflect disapproval of sexual harassment. In the majority, top managers inform employees that harassing another could have an adverse effect on a career. Although changes are occurring gradually, the problem persists because it is difficult for some men to understand the demeaning nature of sexual harassment to a woman ("Sexual Harassment," 1981).

In employment relationships, it is in the best interest of all to divorce sex from the work setting. Maintaining warm, friendly relationships with colleagues at work is generally a desired goal, but a conservative interaction style often is best. Excessive informality may be misunderstood.

Sexually Transmitted Diseases

Because of their potential physical and psychological harm, it is helpful to be aware of the sexually transmitted diseases that are of greatest concern.

Chlamydia and Nongonoccal Urethritis

Chlamydia is the most common sexually transmitted disease in America (Judson, 1985), with 3 to 4 million Americans contracting it each year (McNair, 1988). If untreated, it can cause sterility in both females and males and infections in newborns if passed to them by their mothers during birth. Women with the disease risk miscarriage, stillbirth, and pelvic inflammatory disease (PID). Chlamydia renders approximately 11,000 women sterile each year in the United States, according to estimates of the Centers for Disease Control in Atlanta, and 3,600 suffer tubal pregnancies, which can be fatal to the mother. The damage may occur before any symptoms appear.

Many vaginal and urethral infections in women and men are caused by *Chlamydia trachomatis*, a microorganism called a T-strain mycoplasma, and require medical supervision. Chlamydia is the cause of nongonoccal urethritis (NGU) in about half the cases. Chlamydia and NGU can be effectively treated with tetracycline. Because chlamydia and gonorrhea have similar symptoms, because persons may be infected with both simultaneously, and because some clinics do not have facilities to test for chlamydia, some persons with chlamydia may be treated only for gonorrhea. Unfortunately, chlamydia is not cured by penicillin. It is recommended, therefore, that a culture be taken to check for chlamydia (Strong & DeVault, 1986).

In males, symptoms of chlamydia include a thin, whitish discharge, although 30% of males have no symptoms. The majority of females have no symptoms. In the fortunate few who have symptoms, however, mild irritation of the genitals is present as is itching and burning during urination. Cervical swelling may occur. Sexual partners should be notified immediately so they can seek treatment (Allgeier & Allgeier, 1988).

Gonorrhea

Gonorrhea is caused by bacteria that thrive in the mucous membranes such as the linings of the penis, vagina, anus, and mouth. Direct contact with an infected person is usually necessary for infection to be transmitted, as the bacteria die rather quickly outside the human body.

Women with gonorrheal infections may notice some of the following symptoms: a yellow-green, irritating vaginal discharge; persistent low backache; abdominal pain; or burning during urination. Unfortunately, the majority of women show no obvious symptoms of an early infection. Left untreated, the infection develops into PID and affects other reproductive organs such as the Fallopian tubes, which may be blocked or pulled out of shape by scar tissue, leaving many women sterile.

Gonorrhea in males may be noticed by the following symptoms: a thick discharge from the penis, often yellow-green and irritating; inflammation of the tip of the penis; burning upon urination; urine cloudy with pus and/or blood; pain in the lower abdomen or scrotum. Although people dread the

thought of such symptoms, they are clear signals that medical attention is required. Individuals who are asymptomatic can have the disease for years and not discover it until considerable damage has been done.

People who discover they have gonorrhea have a special responsibility to inform their sexual partners. Because the symptoms are not always apparent, the untreated infection poses risks to their health and fertility. An infected woman who gives birth transmits the disease to her newborn. The infant's eyes are most vulnerable. Antibiotics are used successfully in treating gonorrhea. Although penicillin is very effective on gonorrheal bacteria, some penicillin-resistant strains must be treated with tetracycline.

Syphilis

Syphilis occurs far less often than gonorrhea but has a greater potential to result in death. The microorganism that causes syphilis dies quickly without warmth and moisture, thus contact with an infected person is necessary for transmission. The symptoms of syphilis are similar for males and females. The first symptom (*primary stage*) is the appearance of a hard, crusty, painless sore called a chancre. Chancres may occur on the penis, scrotum, vaginal wall, cervix, anus, tongue, lips, or throat. Left untreated, the chancres disappear. The syphilis infection is not gone, however.

After the chancre disappears, a few months may pass before the symptoms of *secondary stage syphilis* appear. These symptoms include: a nonitching rash, reddish patches that ooze a clear liquid around the genitals, sore throat, fever, and headache. Again these symptoms disappear if left untreated. In some persons they recur and disappear several times.

Syphilis ultimately appears again as *tertiary stage syphilis* after a latent period of many years. In about 20% of the cases, ulcers develop in the lungs, eyes, liver, and digestive tract. A small percentage suffer heart and blood vessel damage that can be fatal. In some cases, damage to the brain and spinal cord causes paralysis and/or insanity.

Because chancres are painless and may occur internally, anyone discovering he or she has syphilis should inform all sex partners. Children born to women with syphilis almost always are infected. If the mother's infection is in primary or secondary stages, the infant may be blind or deaf, have deformed bones and teeth, or die soon after birth. Children whose mothers are in the tertiary stage may be born in the latent phase themselves and not show symptoms for some years. Syphilis is treated with antibiotics: penicillin, tetracycline, or erythromycin are commonly used.

Herpes

This is a viral infection caused by the virus *Herpes simplex II*. The genitals or mouth may be affected. Symptoms of a herpes infection begin with a tingling or burning sensation following by the formation of blisters. The blisters commonly develop on the vulva, clitoris, cervix, penis, scrotum, or anus. Less often they appear on the buttocks or thighs. The blisters rupture in time, and painful sores form. Eventually these heal even without treatment. The virus is still present, however, and blistering can recur. Offspring of women who have an active herpes infection during pregnancy are apt to suffer. Brain damage, blindness, and death are possible. If blisters or sores are present at the time of birth, a Caesarian section is recommended to avoid transmission to the infant.

Herpes cannot be cured; the victim carries it for life. Herpes sufferers do experience discomfort during recurrences of blisters and should avoid sexual contact during those periods. Although some people never have a recurrence, others have many. Herpes support groups help people to handle the psychological stress that occurs when they become

infected, and several treatments are available to alleviate symptoms.

Vaginitis

Any inflammation of the vagina is referred to as vaginitis. Several kinds of vaginitis are possible. Treatment depends on the organism responsible.

1. *Trichomoniasis.* This is caused by a microscopic parasite. The trichomonad can survive for several hours in a moist environment, so infection from public toilets or shared towels is possible. Symptoms of trichomonal infection are an itchy inflammation of the vagina and a frothy, white or yellow vaginal discharge. The disease is contracted by over 900,000 women. Men may also have trichomonal infections (Allgeier & Allgeier, 1988).

2. *Fungal vaginitis/moniliasis.* The organism responsible for this infection (primarily *Candida albicans*) is present on the skin of most people all the time. Under certain conditions, the number of yeast (a fungus) normally present in the vagina increases rapidly, causing the symptoms of infection. Pregnancy, diabetes, use of oral contraceptives, or use of antibiotics make women more susceptible to yeast infections. Sexual contact is *not* necessary for a woman to develop this disease. Symptoms include intense vaginal itching and a white vaginal discharge.

3. *Bacterial vaginitis.* A variety of bacterial infections of the vagina are possible. They produce symptoms similar to gonorrhea. Infection may occur without sexual contact.

Pediculosis

These are also called body lice. They are most often transmitted by close body contact, but they can be passed in bedding, towels, or clothing. The symptom of infection is itching of the head, body, or

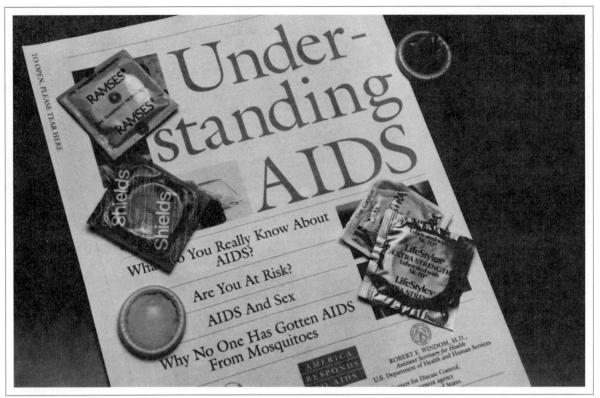

Joel Gordon

pubic area. Body lice are removed by use of an insecticidal cream or shampoo available without a prescription at drug stores. Clothing, bedding, and towels should be laundered in hot water also.

Acquired Immune Deficiency Syndrome (AIDS)

At this time there is no known cure for AIDS, and it is believed that all of those who carry the virus will eventually develop the disease. Current evidence suggests that the incubation period could be as long as 15 years.

The disease exists in many countries of the world and is spreading rapidly. Studies in the West-ern world present evidence that a disproportionate number of its victims are males who have shared same-gender sexual contacts, users of drugs who have shared needles, or hemophiliacs. Fewer of its victims are female. Transmission occurs when fluids (e.g., blood, semen) from the body of an AIDS carrier are shared with another person, e.g., unprotected sexual intercourse or blood trans-fusion. Current evidence leads to the conclusion that transmission can occur from male to female, from female to male, and between persons of the same gender. If a female tests positive for the AIDS virus, it is recommended that she not become pregnant because of the risk of infection to the fetus.

Although it is believed that the AIDS virus cannot be transmitted as a result of casual contact and that the virus in the saliva of the mouth of AIDS carriers does not exist in sufficient quantity to make transmission likely among those who share a "deep kiss," caution is advised, suggesting that present knowledge precludes a definite recommendation. Oral-genital contacts are believed to be less dangerous than genital-anal contacts, but they do not appear on the list of "safe" sex activities.

According to recent data (Painter, 1988), women are exposed to AIDS in the following ways: 30% through sex with infected men; 50% through shared needles and 20% through transfusions or other means. Men are exposed to AIDS in the following ways: 2% through sex with infected women; 68% through sex with infected men; 16% through shared needles; and 14% through transfusions or other means. In a recent survey by the American College Health Association and the Centers for Disease Control, the AIDS infection rate for the general population was determined to be 4 to 6 per 1,000 persons. In a prison population, the rate was 4 per 1,000 persons. For the college student population, the estimate was 2 infections per 1,000 persons. Although this figure for college students is lower than the infection rate for the general population, the incidence is high enough to cause concern. The effect of this concern is shown by the data in Table 9–1.

At the time of this writing, celibacy, masturbation, or a monogamous sexual relationship are strongly advised as responsible choices (Penner & Penner, 1988). Individuals who have had contacts with high-risk partners, e.g., prostitutes, persons who have had many partners, or intravenous drug users, have been encouraged to obtain an anonymous blood test to ascertain if the AIDS virus is present. Approximately 75% of persons capable of transmitting the virus are asymptomatic. Health officials recommend that persons who choose to initiate sexual contact with high-risk partners should

Table 9–1 Effect of Concern over AIDS for Unmarried College Students

Effect	Sexual Activity	
	% Not active	% Active
None	84.7	45.9
Less frequent	—	1.2
More selective	—	30.0
More selective and less frequent	—	20.0
Stopped or prevented	15.3	2.9

Source: Carroll, L. (1988). Concern with AIDS and the sexual behavior of college students. *Journal of Marriage and the Family, 50,* 405–411. Copyrighted (1988) by the National Council on Family Relations, 3989 Central Ave. N. E., Suite # 550, Minneapolis, MN 55421. Reprinted by permission.

limit their sexual activities to those that do not involve an exchange of bodily secretions, should use latex condoms consistently, and should not inject drugs or share needles (Strong & DeVault, 1986; Lamanna & Riedmann, 1988).

A disproportionate number of AIDS victims are young, the result of the fact that a greater number of sexual contacts are likely among persons who are unmarried. Because one is likely to have a sexual encounter with a person in one's age group, a higher rate of increase of victims is likely among those who are under 30 years of age. It is not likely that university health officials will be treating many AIDS patients on campuses because most students will have graduated by the time symptoms appear. It is hoped that a cure for AIDS will be discovered soon; however, since experts predict that a vaccine will not become available until the end of this century, caution must be used in sexual intimacy to avoid contracting this fatal disease.

Achieving Sexual Maturity

The majority of today's youth are sexually active before they marry; many are sexually irresponsible. Sexual responsibility involves knowledge and concern for others. Knowledgeable women and men know that women can get pregnant during their menstrual period and at the time of their first intercourse, though neither are common. Nevertheless, in 80% of the encounters involving first intercourse there was no preplanning, and many young people continue to engage in intercourse without using any form of contraception. Evidence indicates that 20% of them will become pregnant during the first month and 50% will be pregnant by the sixth month (*Teenage Pregnancy*, 1981).

Sexual irresponsibility involves a lack of commitment to the people we love. In contrast, sexual responsibility means that we will expose them to neither an unwanted pregnancy nor to a disease. The person who has a sexually transmitted disease and who has intercourse while contagious or without insisting on a condom is uncaring and irresponsible. Responsible people *are* caring. They think about the future of others and wish to protect them. They are willing to forego immediate pleasure in order to ensure the safety of others. Each of us has the responsibility to protect others even when they do not wish to be protected.

Sexual Interaction

In choosing methods of sexual interaction a couple can use the following criteria:

1. *Psychological acceptance.* An individual or couple may find certain forms of sexual interaction unacceptable because of past cultural conditioning. A couple should respond sexually in ways that are psychologically acceptable to both. One partner should not coerce another into an activity about which he or she has strong, negative feelings.

2. *Sexual pleasure.* Certain sexual activities bring more pleasure to some couples than to others. Some find erotic literature to be stimulating, whereas others find the same literature repugnant.

3. *Physical comfort.* Differing body sizes of the partners or special circumstances may make some coital positions impractical or uncomfortable. For example, the male superior position may be uncomfortable late in a pregnancy.

4. *Sexual techniques.* Many books concerned with human sexual response emphasize the importance of various techniques in sexual encounters; however, there has been some criticism of an emphasis upon focusing on technique. The criticism stems from the belief that an emphasis on sexual techniques inhibits spontaneity and results in a mechanical approach that destroys romance and pleasure. On the other hand, ignorance of sexual techniques has no special merit and may cause frustration and unhappiness. Couples may benefit from a balanced approach—learning about sexuality and sexual techniques and focusing on those things that give each other pleasure.

Sex Education

The education individuals have received as children in North America has left us with a great many personal and social problems that warrant concern. How does the sex education children in North America receive compare to the information children in other parts of the world receive?

In one study (Goldman & Goldman, 1982) a total of 838 children from Australia, England, North America, and Sweden were interviewed: 419 boys and 419 girls (approximately 18 boys and 18 girls in each of six cohorts aged 5, 7, 9, 11, 13, and 15). The major conclusions were:

1. The North American children appeared to have the least and the longest delayed sex education of all four countries.

2. Overall, the Swedish children were superior to their English-speaking peers in terms of understanding correct clinical sexual terminology.

3. There was overwhelming evidence that children wished to receive sex information, explanations, and knowledge both from their parents and teachers.

4. In Sweden, 85% of the children claimed to have some sex education in the primary school. In contrast, in the English-speaking samples less than 40% of the children at 11 years of age reported they had received any sex education in the schools up to that time. Some teenagers reported having no sex education in school at all: 30% in Australia, 27% in North America, 2% in Sweden. Nor did the evidence indicate that adequate sex education was provided in the homes.

5. Although fathers are not highly regarded as sex educators, both boys and girls reflected confidence in their mothers.

In a second study in the United States, Lewis (1973) found that when parents are the main source of sex education, their children are less likely to be promiscuous or engage in premarital intercourse.

At best the sex education of individuals has been approached somewhat haphazardly. Fortunately, sex education is a lifelong project. There is hope for individuals who have little or no sexual desire, i.e., inhibited sexual desire, and for those who have too much, i.e., the sexual addict, and for the vast majority who fall somewhere in between. If we would do as good a job in sex education as we do in math education, a great deal of unhappiness could be avoided. To do this, we will need to overcome some of the reserve that we have learned. With a trend toward greater openness, hopefully we will be able to guide the next generation more realistically to ensure their sexual happiness, which ultimately contributes to the success of marriages and families.

Summary

- Sexual relationships are most satisfying when a couple has similar sexual needs and those needs are met, when they communicate openly about sexual concerns, and when their experiences coincide with their expectations.

- Sexual happiness can be impaired by a variety of myths surrounding sexual conduct. The misinformation these myths generate leads to confusion and the formation of stereotypes that affect sexual behavior adversely.

- Choices regarding sexual lifestyles and sexual preferences are personal, but their consequences, e.g., premarital pregnancy, abortion, sexually transmitted diseases, and divorce, can be far-reaching and should be evaluated.

- Women experience sexual dysfunction primarily in the form of inhibited sexual desire, vaginismus, or orgasmic dysfunction. Men also experience inhibited sexual desire and may suffer from such sexual dysfunctions as impotency, premature ejaculation, or retarded ejaculation. Approximately 80% of those who seek treatment are successful in alleviating their sexual dysfunctions.

- Incidents that are detrimental to sexual functioning and are harmful to self-esteem include:

adult-child incest, sibling incest, sexual addiction, and sexual harassment.

- Sexually active adults should be aware of the potential for pregnancy and disease transmittal and should take responsibility for themselves and their partner.

Discussion Questions

1. Many young conservatives accept diversity in lifestyles to a far greater degree than do their parents. What factors are responsible for this change?

2. Recent evidence points to similar family backgrounds of heterosexual and homosexual men. In view of this evidence why do so many parents of homosexual children feel guilty about their children's sexual preference?

3. How might the husband or wife who discovers his or her spouse is involved in an extramarital relationship use the knowledge as an opportunity to improve the marriage?

4. What can parents, teachers, and government agencies do to prevent teenage pregnancies?

5. What kind of men make the most desirable, sensitive partners?

6. What types of women are the most sensitive to the sexual needs of men?

7. What is the best way to present sexual information to children to ensure a positive attitude?

8. Suppose you learn that the person you are dating is a carrier of the AIDS virus. In what

way would this alter your relationship with the person?

9. A number of years ago you had genital herpes. You have not had a recurrence of the disease in over a year. Would you tell your date?

10. What would be some reasons why parents might ask you whether you were having intercourse with the person you were dating? Even if you consider the question intrusive, is your relationship comfortable enough to tell the truth if you were sexually active?

11. Suppose you were being sexually harassed at work by an employer whom you like professionally but with whom you do not wish to be involved sexually. What can you say to the employer that conveys your firmness without being rude or threatening?

12. What could you say to a friend who confided in you that she had never had an orgasm and was worried about it? How could you be helpful and reassuring without making her feel embarrassed?

13. Imagine that you had a 15-year-old sibling that was sexually involved with her sweetheart. What would you do to help her so that she would not become pregnant?

14. An acquaintance dates you several times and then terminates the relationship, making fun of you to others because you are so sexually inexperienced. It hurts your feelings more than it should. If you are male, what would you do? If you are female, what would you do?

15. An acquaintance tells you that one of your friends is a lesbian. How would you respond?

16. How can we best help people to better understand the risks of having multiple sex partners?

CHAPTER 10

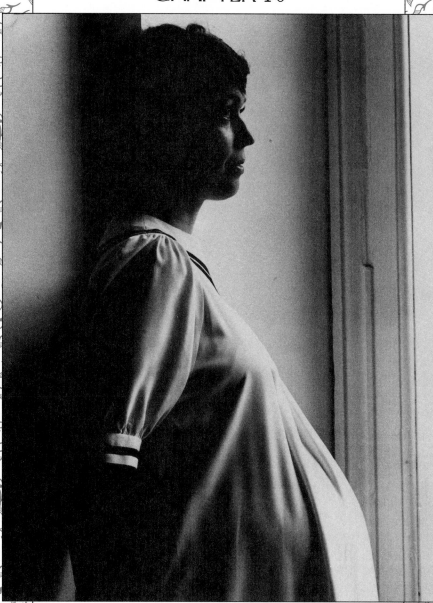

FAMILY PLANNING

❧

Children change things. Perhaps our first child, Quin, changed things most. Before he was born, we were two people struggling with a relationship, sometimes flying off with our personal demons, sometimes cleaving together, assuming a future but fearing for it, too.

Then, inadequately prepared and uninformed—which made us just like everyone else, I suppose—we created an indelible future and watched it grow, first inside me, then in the cradle next to our bed....

We took on new identities: Mom and Dad. Some days it seemed we would never be Anna and Gerry again. Some days it seemed like the hardest thing we had ever done. Most days it seemed like the best.

(Quindlen, 1988)

❧

Planning Families

When a young couple today refers to having a family, they are talking about making their own decisions about whether and when to have children. Although we readily accept such looking ahead, the freedom to choose if and when to have children has been possible only in recent decades. For many thousands of years, methods of controlling births were limited; for the most part, birth control received little attention. Because infant/childhood mortality was high and children were an economic asset, most couples were not concerned about multiple pregnancies. Women who needed to prevent pregnancy for health or economic reasons had few choices. Abstinence or withdrawal were the options open to most women.

In the early 1900s, Margaret Sanger led a movement in the United States to make birth control available. At that time it was illegal to distribute birth control devices or information. As a nurse caring for poor women in New York City, Sanger saw the suffering of the women and their families that was caused by unwanted pregnancies. She opened birth control clinics and shared the information she had; although she was arrested, she persisted until

---

"May you have 16 children and a happy life"

This common Indian greeting may not be good wishes in a country struggling to get its population problems under control. Population in India is rushing toward one billion by the year 2000 if unchecked and soon it will pass China as the most populous country in the world.

In 1951 India became one of the first developing countries to start family planning programs. Billions of dollars have been spent, yet the programs have not been entirely successful. Although 90% of the people are aware of the need for fertility control and 70% have positive attitudes about it, only 30% actually practice it.

The reasons for the difficulties are found in powerful religious and social traditions. Traditionally, a happy family in India is a very large family. Persons who agree that smaller might be better still tend to define "small" as having four or five children. Many couples are unwilling to take part in any program of family planning until they have two or more sons. Male children are highly prized; some parents do not count daughters when asked how many children they have.

In many marriages, husbands and wives do not talk with each other except in very formal circumstances. Naturally family planning is not discussed. Current government plans to improve fertility control include encouraging husbands and wives to talk about birth control.

Another government strategy is to portray the benefits of delayed childbearing and spacing of children as a health benefit for the children (including the prized sons) who are born. Past efforts to emphasize the importance of limiting pregnancies to benefit the health of mothers were not successful because the status of women is so low.

Government family planners are stressing the value of small families as economically wise; the small family is richer. The large family is being portrayed not as unhappy, but as a luxury that most can no longer afford.

Source: Tempest, R. (1986, August 17). India losing race to slow its birthrate. *Los Angeles Times*, Part I, pp. 1, 23, 24.

Table 10–1 Percentage of Wanted/Unwanted/Mistimed Pregnancies in the United States by Year and by Race

Race	Wanted		Unwanted		Mistimed	
	1973	1982	1973	1982	1973	1982
All	85.8	90.1	14.0	9.6	25.7	28.2
White	88.4	92.1	11.4	7.7	25.5	27.7
Black	68.0	77.5	31.5	21.8	27.4	32.2

Source: U.S. Bureau of the Census. (1987b). *Statistical abstract of the United States: 1988* (108th ed.). Washington, DC: U.S. Government Printing Office.

the laws were changed to allow doctors to give birth control information.

By the 1960s, the United States and several other countries including Japan, China, India, Canada, Great Britain, and Sweden had adopted government programs to support family planning. Today contraceptive services are available through private physicians and health clinics, and some birth control devices can be obtained without prescription at drug stores.

The importance of controlling fertility has been underscored in recent decades by two factors. One is a consciousness that global situations such as poverty, famine, and pollution are associated with population problems. Because the amount of living space on earth is limited, world population growth cannot go unchecked indefinitely. A second factor— on a more personal level—is the desire of couples to plan their families to suit their needs and increase their chances of happiness.

The result has been a reduction in the number of children per family. The birthrate in the United States declined from over seven children per woman in 1800 to about two children in the 1980s. Predictions for the birthrate to the year 2000 vary from two to three children per woman (Gullotta et al., 1986). Most persons now plan to have small families, and experts expect that trend to continue.

Family planning involves several important decisions: whether to have children, when to have children, how many children to have, how far apart to space the children, and what kind of contraception to use (see Table 10–1 for data on planned pregnancies). These decisions have enormous impact upon a couple's life together.

Choosing Not to Have Children

Although the idea of marriage is inextricably linked with parenthood, some persons choose to marry but not to be parents. The National Alliance for Optional Parenthood and the National Organization for Non-Parents (NON) provide support and advice for those who decide against having children. The reasons for a couple deciding not to have children are varied (see Figure 10–1).

External Concerns

A number of men and women believe that by having children they add to world population problems: more and more people are crowding this planet, using its resources, and causing pollution. By not

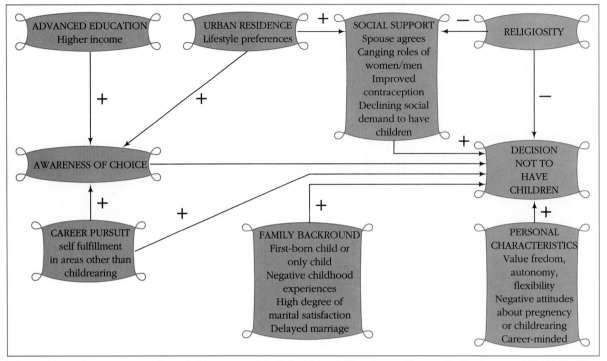

Figure 10–1 Choosing not to have children: a model of decision-making *Source*: Rogers, L. K. & Larson, J. H. (1988). Voluntary childlessness: A review of the literature and a model of the childlessness decision. *Family Perspective, 22* 43–58. Adapted with permission from the publisher.

having children, they believe they help the global situation.

Other couples think that modern life has too many uncertainties, difficulties, and confusion. One young husband stated:

> *Everyone we know is tied up in work, work, work to get more money to buy a bigger house, clothes with designer labels, and a Mercedes to replace the BMW. They have no concern for others; their lives are shallow and consumed by materialism. I just can't see bringing a child into this kind of a life.*

Personal Concerns

Others believe that they cannot cope with children because of their own temperaments, charac-

ters, interests, values, and lifestyles (Rogers & Larson, 1988). A man commented:

> *Look, what kind of life could we give a child? My wife and I both spend eight or more hours a day on the job. We bring work home in the evenings and some weekends. It's very important to us that we advance in our careers; so we have to invest this much time. I don't think we want to change much even if we had a child and that would be a lousy deal for a kid.*

Some couples enjoy their interaction with each other so much that they do not wish to make any major changes in their lifestyle. They prize freedom and mobility and do not want to lose them (Rogers & Larson, 1988). They enjoy going out or taking a trip at a moment's notice, sharing projects or long conversations, and devoting their full attention to each other (Houseknecht, 1982). Increasingly the term *childless* is replaced by *childfree* to reflect a shift in value; couples who choose not to have children are viewed as liberated (free) rather than lacking (less) (Strong & DeVault, 1988).

A few persons regard child rearing as an awesome responsibility that they do not feel adequate or willing to assume (Rogers & Larson, 1988). One wife stated:

> *When I think about bringing another human into the world and molding the way that life develops, it scares me! I have several personal problems to work out and much maturing to do before I would be ready to be someone's Mom. I may never be ready for it.*

Much of the reluctance to assume the responsibility for children may be caused by an emphasis in the mass media on the influence of parents on children and on the potential bad results parents can cause. The attention given to child abuse/neglect and incest has focused on what parents do wrong and has resulted in a reluctance by some to become parents.

Of course, there are genuine pressures, tensions, and strains in bringing up a child. It is time-consuming and physically exhausting, but there are rewards and respite. And most parents do not cause terrible damage to their children, abuse them, neglect them, or commit incest. Instead, they enjoy them.

Infertility

For most couples, infertility is not an issue, yet some 15% to 20% of married couples in the United States are involuntarily childless; they cannot conceive or carry a child to term (Berg, 1984). Approximately 10% more have fewer children than they want (Kolata, 1979).

Being unable to conceive or carry a child to term is very frustrating. Involuntarily childless cou-

ples typically feel helpless, angry, guilty, or defective (Lamanna & Riedmann, 1988; Strong & DeVault, 1988). Individuals and the relationship may suffer if the problem is not handled in an informed and caring manner.

One common misconception that causes much grief is that the infertility is "*all* her or his fault." In many instances, fertility problems arise because both partners have a small difficulty; he has a lowered sperm count and she has a hormonal imbalance resulting in irregular ovulation, for example. In about half of the cases, the woman is infertile; the man is the primary cause in 30% to 40% of the cases and a contributing cause in 10% to 20% (Brody, 1985; Culverwell, 1984). It is important for both husband and wife to see their physician. Otherwise, one may undergo expensive, uncomfortable procedures and only part of the problem will be corrected.

Another myth about infertility that hurts affected persons is that infertility is mostly emotional. Assuming that they cannot get pregnant because they are anxious about it, couples try taking a cruise, meditating, drinking alcohol to relax, and beginning adoption proceedings before they consider a medical checkup. Although worry and trying too hard are not helpful in conception, the causes of infertility are complex.

Causes of Infertility

Physical difficulties account for about 40% of the cases of female infertility, the most common being blocked or obstructed Fallopian tubes. This can be the result of scar tissue left by venereal disease, pelvic inflammatory disease (PID), repeated abortions, or abdominal surgery (Strong & DeVault, 1988).

Endometriosis, a condition in which uterine tissue grows outside the uterus on the Fallopian tubes, ovaries, or abdominal cavity, can be responsible for female infertility, too. In some cases, endometriosis results in tissue blockages of the Fallopian tubes; how it contributes to infertility in other cases is not known (Kolata, 1979).

Hormonal irregularities affect about 20% of infertile women and prevent them from ovulating. Common symptoms are absence of menstrual periods or irregular ones. There are three types of disorders: (a) production of the correct hormones but in the wrong sequence during the menstrual cycle, (b) failure to produce the hormones that cause ovulation, and (c) excessive production of the hormone prolactin, which shuts down the normal hormone production necessary for ovulation (Kolata, 1979).

In some instances, a woman's genital tract may be too acidic for sperm to survive, or, for reasons that are not completely understood, a woman may become allergic to her partner's sperm and produce antibodies against it (Strong & DeVault, 1988). Occasionally, the secretions of the cervix are heavy and mire the sperm, thus keeping them from entering the uterus. This is called *hostile mucus* (Strong et al., 1981).

Certain environmental factors may contribute to infertility in both women and men. Smoking reduces fertility in women and may result in lowered sperm counts or abnormal sperm in men (Baird & Wilcox, 1985). Sons and daughters of women who received DES (diethylstilbesterol) to prevent miscarriage often have fertility difficulties (Strong & DeVault, 1988).

Both men and women may have fertility reduced by any illness or condition that impairs healthy functioning of the body. Such conditions include poor nutrition, insufficient rest, obesity, insufficient or excessive exercise, infections, anemia, tuberculosis, and excessive use of drugs or alcohol (Bassett, 1963; "Researchers of Smoking," 1985). The recent tendency to postpone childbearing until a couple is in their thirties or forties also contributes to reduced fertility; fertility is highest when a person is in his or her mid-twenties (Lamanna & Riedmann, 1988).

Male infertility may be caused by insufficient sperm production, reduced motility (movement) of the sperm, or obstructions of the ducts through which the sperm travel. Infections or injury to the testicles, prostate disease, or hormonal insufficiencies may be the causes. *Varicoceles* are varicose veins in the scrotum that interfere with the production of sperm (Kolata, 1979; Strong et al., 1981; Strong & DeVault, 1988). Sperm production also may be reduced temporarily by exposure to high temperatures, i.e., soaking in a hot tub.

Treating Infertility

Even though couples vary considerably in the time required for them to conceive, most couples who are not using contraceptive measures and who are engaging in regular sexual intercourse achieve a pregnancy within a year (Gullotta et al., 1986). Couples who have been trying to conceive for more than a year without success should seek professional help. Many kinds of diagnostic tests are available, and the success rate for treating infertility is about 70% (Strong & DeVault, 1988).

Blocked Fallopian Tubes. The specific treatment for a particular couple will depend on the cause or causes of their infertility. The only effective treatment for blocked Fallopian tubes is surgery. This is critical because the ovum must travel through the Fallopian tubes from the ovary to the uterus. The success rate ranges from 10% to 50%, depending on the extent of the blockage (Strong et al., 1981). Similarly, sperm duct blockages may sometimes be corrected by surgery (Kolata, 1979; Strong et al., 1981).

Endometriosis. In severe cases of endometriosis, when the Fallopian tubes are closed and masses of uterine tissue are present in the abdomen or ovaries, surgery is recommended. Generally 30% to 50%

of women treated surgically are able to conceive. In less severe cases, physicians may prescribe the use of birth control pills for 6 months to shrink the uterine tissue. About 60% become pregnant after this treatment. In mild cases, no treatment may be used and some 70% of women become pregnant within 2 years anyway.

Hormone Imbalance. Female hormonal irregularities or insufficiencies may be corrected with hormone supplements. These are effective in stimulating ovulation in 50% to 90% of women. Their use is not without some risk, however, as the doses required to stimulate ovulation may result in the release of several ova and, consequently, in multiple pregnancies (Strong et al., 1981).

Identifying Ovulation. Because a woman can conceive only for a short time each month—at the time of ovulation—and because that time can be difficult to predict, some women have difficulty conceiving. Pinpointing the time of greatest fertility (just before, during, and just after ovulation) is hardest for women who have irregular menstrual cycles. Generally, women ovulate 14 to 16 days before their next menstrual period is due. Urine tests and the use of a thermometer to take a woman's temperature (it usually rises during ovulation) can be used to help couples determine the fertile period. A series of vaginal smears can be taken by a physician to identify the day ovulation begins, too. In addition, an ovulation test kit available in drug stores helps to indicate the fertile period. Makers of the test kit claim very accurate results; a 6-day test kit costs about $25. No prescription is required.

Male Infertility. The first avenues of treatment of infertility in men are an assessment of sperm quality and a sperm count. Sperm quality is determined by measuring the shape and amount of movement of sperm in a sample of ejaculate. About 80% of the sperm in a healthy semen sample have normal shapes, i.e., no double heads or tails, and excellent forward motion. Commonly accepted estimates of normal sperm counts range from 60 to 100 million sperm per milliliter of semen in an ejaculation of 3 to 5 milliliters (*Family Health*, 1980).

If, after conducting sperm count and quality testing, the physician judges these to be a factor in a couple's difficulty in conceiving, several methods of treatment are possible. Initially, the man may be asked to abstain from sexual activity for several days before his wife's fertile period is expected. By abstaining, his supply of sperm is stored and his sperm count is increased. Hormone therapy for males has been helpful in a few instances but is still largely experimental (Strong et al., 1981).

Artificial Insemination. In situations in which the sperm count is scanty, artificial insemination of the woman may be considered. In artificial insemination, semen is deposited by syringe near the cervix or in the uterus. The semen used may be collected from the husband, with several collections sometimes being used to increase the sperm count. This is termed *artificial insemination by husband (AIH)*. AIH may be used in situations in which the wife has hostile mucus or an overly acidic genital tract.

If a husband produces no sperm or has a genetically transmitted condition, a couple may use *artificial insemination by a donor (AID)* to achieve a pregnancy. In AID, the semen used for insemination is collected from a donor unknown to the couple. The success rate for artificial insemination is about 60% (Strong & DeVault, 1988).

In Vitro Fertilization. In *in vitro fertilization (IVF)*, fertilization of the ovum occurs outside the woman's body—usually in a laboratory dish—and the embryo is transplanted to a uterus (either the mother's or a surrogate's) for development and

Table 10–2 Modern Technology Helps Couples with Fertility Problems

Condition of		Fertilization			Transplant Embryo
Woman/Wife	Man/Husband	Ovum	Sperm	Procedure	
Fertile/ unable to conceive	Fertile	Wife	Husband	IVF	To wife
Fertile/ unable to carry	Fertile	Wife	Husband	IVF	To surrogate
Fertile	Infertile	Wife	Donor	AID	
Fertile/ unable to carry	Infertile	Wife	Donor	IVF	To surrogate
Infertile/ unable to carry	Fertile	Donor	Husband	IVF	To surrogate
		Donor	Husband	AIH	Ova donor is surrogate
Infertile/ able to carry	Fertile	Donor	Husband	IVF/AIH	To wife
Infertile/ able to carry	Infertile	Donor	Donor	AID/IVF	To wife
Infertile/ unable to carry	Infertile	Donor	Donor	AID/IVF	To surrogate

Sources: 1. Lamanna, M. A., & Riedman, A. (1988). *Marriages and families.* Belmont, CA: Wadsworth. 2. Strong, B., & DeVault, C. (1988). *The marriage and family experience.* St. Paul, MN: West.

birth. In vitro fertilization is helpful when the woman has blocked Fallopian tubes, and sometimes it is used when ovum or sperm donors are involved (Lamanna & Riedmann, 1988; Strong & DeVault, 1988).

Ovum or Embryo Transplant. When a woman is unable to produce viable ova, a donor for ova may be used. Depending upon circumstances, fertilization may be done by AIH, AID, or in vitro, and the embryo may be transplanted to the wife or to a surrogate (see Table 10–2).

Surrogate Mothers. In situations in which the woman is unable to carry a child to term, a substitute or surrogate mother may be used. The ovum and sperm may be from the married couple or from donor(s) and may be fertilized by AIH, AID, or in vitro. The embryo develops in the uterus of the surrogate, but after birth the baby is given to the couple who contracted for the surrogate's services.

The use of surrogate mothers is not widespread and, as Table 10–3 suggests, is not widely acceptable. The process has several complicating factors: it is expensive; it may be emotionally trying for all

Table 10–3 Acceptability of Infertility Treatments to University Students*

Procedure	Students indicating acceptability (%)
Artificial insemination of wife by husband	76
Artificial insemination of wife by a donor	20
In vitro fertilization	55
Embryo transfer	26
Using a surrogate mother	15
Adoption	86

* Based on a survey of 700 students.

Source: Dunn, P. C., Ryan, I. J., & O'Brien, K. (1988). College students' level of acceptability of the new medical science of conception and problems of infertility. *Journal of Sex Research, 24,* 282–287. Published by permission of *The Journal of Sex Research,* a publication of the Society for the Scientific Study of Sex.

parties involved; and the legal and ethical issues are complex. In 1987 Mary Beth Whitehead contracted with William and Elizabeth Stern to bear a baby by artificial insemination with Stern's sperm. Whitehead was paid $10,000 for her services, but later she returned the money and waged an unsuccessful legal battle to keep the baby. Questions arise about whether surrogacy disregards the dignity of the persons involved, whether the surrogate mother is dehumanized to a "baby-making machine" and the baby to a "product," and whether irresolvable conflicts are created. Opponents ask: Who decides what kind of prenatal care? Can the surrogate mother be forced to abort if the baby is found to be defective? What if a sickly or defective

child is born? Who is responsible for it? What if the surrogate changes her mind? If the surrogate has children of her own, are they harmed psychologically by the fear that she may give them away? (Evans, 1988).

Methods of Birth Control

Conception takes place when one of the sperm ejaculated into the vagina during sexual intercourse moves through the cervix and uterus and up into one of the Fallopian tubes where it encounters an ovum and enters it, thus fertilizing it. The fertilized ovum travels down the Fallopian tube and into the uterus where it implants. A pregnancy begins unless the process is interrupted. Methods that control the number of births do so by interrupting fertilization (contraceptive methods) or the pregnancy itself.

Most persons today expect to control the number of children they have (see Table 10–4). The only effective way to do so is to practice some form of contraception. The search for the ideal birth control method continues because the perfect method has not been found. The ideal method would be 100% effective and completely reversible, would have no

Table 10–4 Lifetime Births Expected by Wives: Percent Distribution

| Year | Number of Births Expected | | | | |
	None	One	Two	Three	Four +
1975	4.8%	10.9%	49.0%	23.2%	12.1%
1980	5.9	13.3	51.1	20.5	9.3
1988	5.4	12.4	50.1	22.9	9.1

Source: U.S. Bureau of the Census. (1989b). *Statistical abstract of the United States: 1990* (110th ed.). Washington, DC: U.S. Government Printing Office.

Table 10–5 Contraception Method or Status of Women

Contraceptive Method or Status	All Women	Age			Race	
		15–24	24–34	35–44	White	Black
Contraceptively sterile or partner is	17.8%	2.2%	19.6%	37.4%	18.3%	14.9%
Noncontraceptively sterile	7.8	0.3	6.8	19.9	7.8	7.3
Nonsurgically sterile*	1.5	0.6	1.5	2.8	1.6	1.5
Pregnant or postpartum	5.0	6.3	6.5	1.0	4.8	5.6
Seeking pregnancy	4.2	3.5	6.2	2.5	4.0	5.4
Nonuser—						
not sexually active	19.5	39.4	7.8	7.8	19.9	16.1
sexually active	7.4	9.2	6.5	6.0	6.4	13.5
Oral contraceptive	15.6	23.5	17.1	2.3	15.1	19.8
IUD	4.0	1.4	6.5	4.2	3.9	4.7
Diaphragm	4.5	3.7	6.8	2.4	5.0	1.8
Condom	6.7	5.5	7.6	7.0	7.2	3.2
Foam	1.3	0.8	1.5	1.8	1.4	1.4
Rhythm	2.2	1.2	2.8	2.6	2.2	1.6
Other (withdrawal, douche, suppository)	2.5	2.3	2.9	2.2	2.4	3.1

* Due to accident, illness, etc.

Source: U.S. Bureau of the Census. (1989b). *Statistical abstract of the United States: 1990* (110th ed.). Washington, DC: U.S. Government Printing Office.

adverse side effects, would be easy and convenient to use, would not interfere with sexual pleasure, and would be inexpensive (Golanty & Harris, 1982).

When choosing a method of contraception, persons must consider their own values, preferences, medical history, and needs. Couples may find, too, that their choice of contraception will change over their family life cycle (see Table 10–5 for a listing of contraceptive choices).

When ranked with respect to health risks, the condom and diaphragm or cervical cap are the least harmful, followed by spermicidal foams, the IUD, and the pill. The methods safest to general health are not chosen by some persons because they are judged inconvenient. And some very effective methods have undesirable side effects that are more severe in some people than in others.

The Trend Toward Delayed Parenthood

For the majority, delaying parenthood is an outgrowth of a wish to have a period free for personal development, to assure a stable marriage, and to be financially secure before taking on the responsibility of children. It may also be a prudent response to the increased probability of divorce that makes marriage today a less sure basis for parenthood. Career interests have not yet supplanted plans for motherhood, even among the most recent generation with its greater educational and occupational opportunities.

But the growing proportion of young women who expect to remain childless indicates the distress of women who are now expected to manage both career and parenthood but feel they cannot do both. Whether this conflict between work and family roles will be eased by changing work conditions, increased community child care, and other measures which enable families to combine work and parental responsibilities more easily or whether the conflict will increase and force more women to make a choice is not yet clear. The trend to delay parenthood is a temporary strategy in the face of a difficult decision. Delaying parenthood as well as the greater social acceptance of choosing to remain childless reflects a growing idea of adulthood that does not include parenting. While this new outlook is found mostly among a minority of better educated women, it clearly bears watching.

Source: Wilkie, J. R. (1981). The trend toward delayed parenthood. *Journal of Marriage and the Family, 43,* 583–591. Copyrighted (1981) by the National Council on Family Relations, 3989 Central Ave. N. E., Suite 550, Minneapolis, MN 55421. Reprinted by permission.

Sterilization

Surgical sterilization is the surest form of birth control and is relatively inexpensive. It is, in the long run, the least expensive (Shapiro, 1987). Once done, it does not need renewing or checking or remembering and so is very convenient. It also does not interfere with sexual desire or enjoyment. Over 1 million sterilizations (more frequent among females) are performed each year in the United States (Rice, 1990).

Sterilization has one disadvantage that accounts for the fact that it is not used more often. Reversal of sterilization is very difficult and uncertain. For this reason, a person considering surgical sterilization should think of it as an irreversible procedure. Individuals considering sterilization need to have completed their families and should make the decision without pressure from others.

Vasectomy. Sterilization of the man is called a *vasectomy.* Vasectomy involves an incision into the scrotum; then the vas deferens (the tube that carries seminal fluid from the testes to the urethra) is cut on each side. As a result of cutting these tubes, the sperm are prevented from being ejaculated. The operation is simple, relatively inexpensive, and involves minimal discomfort. It is performed under local anesthetic in the physician's office and takes about 30 minutes. Most men need to refrain from heavy lifting for a few days but normally do not miss any time from work (Shapiro, 1987).

A vasectomy does not interfere with sexual desire or performance. The man continues to ejaculate fluid during orgasm after the operation just as he did before. The amount of fluid produced is not noticeably changed; the only difference is that there are no sperm in the fluid after a while. Because some sperm are in the vasa deferentia when they are cut, some other form of contraception must be used for approximately 3 months following the vasectomy. A physician needs to examine a semen sample at that time to be sure that it is free of sperm (Shapiro, 1987).

Long-term side effects of a vasectomy appear to be minimal. Some studies indicate that the man's immune system may produce antibodies against the retained sperm. At this point this immune response does not seem to pose any serious health risk or to increase his likelihood of any illness (Shapiro, 1987; Strong & DeVault, 1988).

Reversal of a vasectomy is successful only about 30% of the time, with a great deal depending on the skill of the surgeon and the amount of damage done to the vasa deferentia when the vasectomy was performed (Shapiro, 1987). As a precaution against the possibility of a man changing his mind at a later time and wanting to have children, some clinics have established sperm banks in which a man may store sperm before his vasectomy. His partner could receive his sperm through artificial insemination.

Female Sterilization. The procedures for sterilizing women involve cutting or sealing the Fallopian tubes so that sperm and ova may not reach each other. In a *tubal ligation*, the abdominal cavity is opened in order to tie and cut each of the Fallopian tubes. Tubal ligation is a more serious and complicated operation than the vasectomy, and it requires hospitalization (Shapiro, 1987; Strong & DeVault, 1988).

Laparoscopy is a similar procedure that does not require overnight hospitalization because the opening of the abdominal cavity is smaller. Two small incisions of about $\frac{1}{2}$ inch are made; one near the navel and the other about 6 inches below the first. A flexible instrument called a laparoscope is inserted through the incision and into the Fallopian tubes. The instrument electrically cauterizes the interior of the tubes. In response to the cauteriza-

tion, scar tissue forms and seals the tubes. Recovery involves several days off from work to rest at home.

Compared to tubal ligation, laparoscopy is less painful, quicker, and requires less recovery time. It is also less expensive because less hospital time is needed (Shapiro, 1987; Strong & DeVault, 1988).

As is true for a vasectomy, female sterilization is very effective as a birth control method. It has no effect on a woman's sexual activity or enjoyment; neither is the production of female hormones changed in any way. There appear to be no long-term effects of sterilization. The disadvantages of female sterilization are the small but serious risk involved with any surgery and the poor success rate for reversals. Depending on the skill of the surgeon and the type of sterilization procedure used (less damaging procedures are more easily reversed), the success rate for reversals is about 60% (Shapiro, 1987). The risk of an ectopic pregnancy is somewhat increased following reversal of sterilization because of damage to the Fallopian tubes.

Oral Contraception

Oral contraceptives—the pill—have become a popular form of birth control in a relatively short period of time. More than 50 million women worldwide use them. With the exception of sterilization, this is the most effective method of birth control. When taken properly, oral contraceptives are 99.3% effective in preventing pregnancy. The effectiveness lies in giving doses of the female hormones (synthetic progesterone and estrogen) that would be present during pregnancy, thus preventing ovulation; they also thicken cervical mucus to prevent sperm entry and inhibit implantation should fertilization occur (Shapiro, 1987; Strong & DeVault, 1988).

Oral contraceptives come in packets of 20, 21, or 28 pills. The pattern for taking them is that the woman takes the first one on the fifth day following the onset of menstruation, then takes one pill each day for 20 or 21 consecutive days. The next menstrual period begins 2 to 5 days later, and the pattern is repeated. The 28-day pills are taken continuously, but 7 of them contain no hormones. Some women prefer them because it is easier to take a pill each day than to stop and start (Strong & DeVault, 1988).

The effectiveness of birth control pills depends on a steady routine of taking them. If a woman forgets to take the pill once, she should take one as soon as she remembers and then take the next at the regular time. If she forgets two, she must assume she will ovulate and use some other form of contraception until she finishes the rest of the cycle (Strong & DeVault, 1988).

The pill's potential for causing a variety of side effects is because use of it involves a woman's entire hormone balance. The hormones in the pill influence the endocrine system in a similar manner as a pregnancy does. In some ways, taking the pill simulates a perpetual state of pregnancy. It is not surprising, then, that some of the minor side effects are similar to symptoms experienced during pregnancy.

The majority of women, approximately 80%, experience only slight and temporary side effects. In fact, some women feel better physically and emotionally as a result of using the pill. However, about 20% of women experience adverse effects in such intensity that they discontinue use of the pill.

The severity of the side effects of oral contraceptives has been reduced since the dosage of hormones in the pills has been reduced; however, many women still experience nausea, breast tenderness, cramps, weight increase due to water retention, and an increased tendency to develop vaginal yeast infections. Some women suffer migraine headaches and severe emotional depression.

The pill may cause visual disorders, strokes, and sometimes can stop bone growth if taken by very young women—before physical maturity is reached. Research in Britain indicates that the pill increases the risk of heart attack and vascular disease. Risk is greater if the pills contain high doses of estrogen, if they are used more than 5 years, if the woman smokes, and if she is over 35 years old (Shapiro, 1987; Strong et al., 1981).

Women with certain conditions are not good candidates to use the pill. These are heart disease (including heart attack, angina, and blood clotting such as thrombophlebitis), liver diseases (including hepatitis, alcohol damage, and mononucleosis), kidney disease, asthma, diabetes, epilepsy, high blood pressure, and gall bladder disease (Shapiro, 1987).

Women with sickle-cell anemia are cautioned not to use the pill because it might increase the chance of developing blood disorders. About 10% of all black persons have the sickle-cell trait.

Pregnant women and nursing mothers should not use the pill. The effect of the pill on the developing fetus is not known as results of research studies are contradictory. Kricker et al. (1986) report a significantly increased risk of congenital limb deficiencies in babies of mothers who took oral contraceptives during pregnancy. And the hormones in the pill will inhibit milk production in nursing mothers (Shapiro, 1987; Strong & DeVault, 1988).

The relation of use of the pill to the development of cancer is unclear. Use of the pill for 1 year reduces the risk of endometrial cancer (as does pregnancy). Pill users have lowered rates of ovarian cancer, too—for up to 15 years after discontinuing use of the pill. The use of the pill seems associated, however, with a higher incidence of breast and cervical cancers, and users for more than 8 years have a greatly increased risk of liver cancer ("Pill Appears", 1988; Miller et al., 1986; Shapiro, 1987).

Pill users enjoy a reduced incidence of ovarian cysts, pelvic inflammatory disease (PID), trichomonal infection, and toxic shock syndrome. On the other hand, oral contraceptives cannot offer the protection against sexually transmitted disease (STD) exposure that condoms offer. The incidence of one very prevalent STD, chlamydia, has in-

Table 10–6 Relative Risk of Oral Contraceptive Use

Death Rate*	Activity
.05	Lightning
0.4	Football
0.6	Pill — nonsmoker — age 15–24
0.9	Bicycling
1.6	Pill — nonsmoker — age 25–34
2.0	Boating
2.1	Swimming
2.3	Poisoning
3.0	Pill — smoker — age 15–24
4.9	Falls
10.2	Pill — smoker — age 25–34
10.2	Homicide
19.6	Motor vehicle accident
23.0	Pill — nonsmoker — age 35–44
43.0	Hang-gliding
84.5	Pill — smoker — age 35–44

* Per 100,000 participants per year

Source: Kirkham, C., & Reid, R. L. (1987). Relative risk of oral contraceptive usage. *Fertility and Sterility, 47,* 557–558. Reproduced with permission of the publisher, The American Fertility Society.

creased dramatically among pill users (Shapiro, 1987).

The pill continues to be a popular form of contraception because it is effective, does not interfere with sexual intercourse in any way, and most women do not suffer serious side effects (see Table 10–6 for relative risk of oral contraceptives). Women who are taking these drugs should have periodic examinations at intervals set by their doctors. They should inform their physician immediately if they notice any of the following: severe headache, blurred vision, pain in the legs or abdomen, pain in the chest or an unexplained cough, shortness of breath, or irregular or missed menstrual period.

Intrauterine Devices (IUDs)

No one is quite sure how the IUD works. Centuries ago, camel drivers setting out on a long journey across the desert would insert pebbles into the uterus of a female camel to keep her from getting pregnant on the trip. The intrauterine device uses the same concept of placing a foreign element in the uterus to stop the fertilized egg from implanting itself (Strong & DeVault, 1988).

IUDs are small plastic or metal devices of different shapes and sizes. They are placed inside the woman's uterus by a medical professional and remain in place for long periods of time. One or two strings extend into the upper vagina so that she can check that the device is still in place—especially after menstrual periods because these are times when it might be expelled (Shapiro, 1987). A woman needs to do nothing else unless there are problems or she wants to conceive, in which case the IUD will be removed by a physician.

There are several different kinds of IUDs including newer, smaller IUDs that can be used by women who have not had children. The two IUDs available in the United States are the Progestasert® and the copper T 380A (Trussel et al., 1990). The copper T 380A is made of plastic with fine copper filament wrapped around it; the copper dissolves slowly, creating a mildly spermicidal environment. The Progestasert contains a slow-release progesterone that acts to prevent implantation (Klitsch, 1988b; Shapiro, 1987; Strong & DeVault, 1988).

Many people regard the IUD as a nearly perfect form of contraception because it is very effective, simple to use, inexpensive, and once successfully inserted, it may remain in place for an indefinite period of time. An exception is that the copper IUDs and the hormone-releasing IUDs must be replaced about every 2 years because their chemical component wears off over time (Strong & DeVault, 1988).

Although most women have no difficulties with the IUD, some do experience side effects such as pain upon insertion, cramping, infections, and heavier and more painful menstrual periods. The risk of PID is increased by use of an IUD. Because women who have multiple sex partners have an increased risk of contracting a sexually transmitted disease, e.g., chlamydia, which often precedes PID, the IUD is not recommended for them (Klitsch, 1988b).

Another disadvantage is that the IUD can sometimes be expelled, and this can happen without the woman being aware of it. This most often happens in younger women who have not yet given birth. For this reason, many physicians do not advise IUDs for women who have not had children (Klitsch, 1988b; Shapiro, 1987; Strong & DeVault, 1988).

Occasionally, a pregnancy will occur with the IUD in place. If the IUD cannot be removed, the risk of spontaneous abortion is greatly increased; about half of pregnancies with an IUD in place will abort spontaneously. In other situations, the pregnancy goes to term and the IUD is usually expelled in childbirth with the placenta. There is no evidence that the presence of the IUD either at conception or during the pregnancy causes any defects in the fetus (Shapiro, 1987; Strong & DeVault, 1988).

A higher proportion of pregnancies that occur with an IUD in place are ectopic pregnancies—about 1 in 20 to 30 pregnancies for IUD users compared to 1 in 200 for nonusers. This risk continues on a diminished basis even after the IUD is removed (Shapiro, 1987).

One other disadvantage of the IUD is that it sometimes pierces or perforates the uterine wall—especially at the time of insertion. Although a rare happening, this is very serious when it happens. Great care must be taken by the physician to be certain the device is properly inserted; inserting it during menstruation also reduces the possibility of perforating the uterus (Shapiro, 1987).

The IUD is not a method of birth control that all women can use. Generally, the IUD is not recommended for women who:

Have never been pregnant.

May already be pregnant.

Have pelvic infection or disease (or are at increased risk for it).

Have an abnormality of the uterus.

Have a history of very heavy or painful periods.

Have cancer of the cervix or uterus.

Have polyps or fibroid tumors of the uterus.

Have heart or kidney disease.

Have endometriosis.

Additionally, some women have ethical or moral objections to the use of the IUD. Technically, the IUD does not prevent *conception*; instead it prevents implantation of the week-old embryo. For many people this is the same as an abortion (Shapiro, 1987).

Diaphragm

The diaphragm is a flexible rubber dome about 2 inches in diameter. The specific size of the diaphragm is determined through a fitting by a physician. The diaphragm is placed in the vagina and fitted over the cervical opening to prevent semen from entering the uterus. Diaphragms are made more effective by a coating of spermicidal cream or jelly. The diaphragm may be inserted 2 to 3 hours before intercourse and must be left in for at least 6 hours afterward. If intercourse is repeated within the 6-hour period, fresh spermicide should be inserted (Strong & DeVault, 1988).

The diaphragm is a relatively effective method of birth control, with a success rate of 85% to 95%. It is more successful when a spermicide is used. Other advantages are that it is inexpensive, does not interfere with sexual desire or performance, and poses no serious health threats (Shapiro, 1987; Strong & DeVault, 1988).

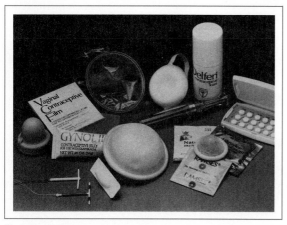

Joel Gordon

Certain disadvantages are associated with the diaphragm, however (Shapiro, 1987; Strong & DeVault, 1988). These include:

The internal anatomy of some women is not suitable for holding the diaphragm in proper place.

Diaphragms must be fitted by a physician and replaced about every year. They must be refitted following childbirth or abortion or a fluctuation in weight of 7 to 10 pounds.

Some women dislike placing any foreign object in their bodies. The woman may have difficulty learning how to insert the diaphragm and sometimes she and her partner may doubt her efficiency in this respect. Other women do not like having the total responsibility for fertility control.

A few women have allergic reactions to the rubber dome or to the spermicidal agents. Diaphragm users are somewhat more prone to develop bladder infections.

Cervical Cap

Cervical caps are dome- or thimble-shaped devices about $1\frac{1}{4}$ inches high, designed to fit snugly over the cervix. They are similar to diaphragms in appearance and in method of preventing conception. Cervical caps differ from diaphragms by being smaller.

To use the cervical cap, it is partially filled with spermicidal cream or jelly and placed in the vagina until it fits over the cervix. Suction holds it in place. The cervical cap should be left in place for at least 6 hours after intercourse; some indicate that it may be left in as long as 7 days (Klitsch, 1988a; Strong & DeVault, 1988; Powell et al., 1986). Others recommend that the cervical cap (and diaphragm) be removed after 24 hours to be cleaned and dried before reuse. They believe that toxic shock syndrome is a greater risk when barriers are left in place for long periods (Shapiro, 1987).

Problems with the cervical cap include the possibility that it may be dislodged during intercourse. It is also more difficult to fit, insert, and remove than the diaphragm (Powell et al., 1986). Cervical caps are not widely available in the United States; they received U.S. Food and Drug Administration approval for general use in 1988 (Klitsch, 1988a). The failure rates of cervical caps and other methods of birth control are listed in Table 10–7.

Contraceptive Sponge

Since 1983 a small polyurethane sponge impregnated with spermicide has been available in drug stores. It does not require fitting by a physician or a prescription. The sponge works in a manner similar to cervical caps or diaphragms: it is inserted in the vagina to block the opening of the cervix and to release spermicide. It should remain in place for 6 hours following intercourse but not longer than 24 hours at a time.

Data indicate that the sponge is 75% to 91% effective. Advantages include ready availability, ease in use, and apparent safety (Shapiro, 1987).

Disadvantages of the sponge include the possibility that it will be dislodged during intercourse and difficulty in removing it by some women. It appears

Table 10–7 Lowest Expected and Typical Failure Rates During the First Year of Use of a Contraceptive Method

Method	Percentage of women experiencing an accidental pregnancy in the first year of use	
	Lowest expected[a] (1)	Typical[b] (2)
Chance[c]	85	85
Spermicides[d]	3	21
Periodic abstinence		20
Calendar	9	
Cervical mucus method	3	
Symptothermal[e]	2	
Withdrawal	4	18
Cap[b]	6	18
Sponge		
Parous women[f]	9	28
Nulliparous women[g]	6	18
Diaphragm[b]	6	18
Condom[i]	2	12
IUD		3
Progestasert®	2.0	
Copper T 380A	0.8	
Pill		3
Combined	0.1	
Progestogen only	0.5	
Injectables	0.3	0.3
Implants	0.3	0.3
Female sterilization	0.2	0.4
Male sterilization	0.1	0.15

a. Among couples who initiate use of a method (not necessarily for the first time) and who use it *perfectly* (both consistently and correctly), the authors' best guess of the percentage expected to experience an accidental pregnancy during the first year if they do not stop use for any other reason.

b. Among *typical* couples who initiate use of a method (not necessarily for the first time), the percentage who experience an accidental pregnancy during the first year if they do not stop use for any other reason.

c. The lowest expected and typical percents are based on data from populations where contraception is not practiced and from women who cease practicing contraception in order to become pregnant. These represent our best guess of the percent who would conceive among women now relying on reversible methods of contraception if they abandoned contraception altogether.

d. Foams and vaginal suppositories.

e. Cervical mucus method supplemented by calendar in the preovulatory and basal body temperature in the postovulatory phases.

f. Women who have had children.

g. Women who have not had children.

h. With spermicidal cream or jelly.

i. Without spermicides.

Source: Trussell, J., Hatcher, R.A., Cates, W., Stewart, F.H., & Kost, K. (1990). Contraceptive failure in the United States: An update. *Studies in Family Planning, 21,* 51–54, p. 52. Used with permission.

not to be large enough to offer good protection to some women, especially those who have had children. It is recommended that it not be used during menstruation because of the risk of toxic shock syndrome (Shapiro, 1987; Strong & De-Vault, 1988).

Condom

The condom is a thin sheath made of rubber or animal membrane that fits over the erect penis. A special tip catches and retains semen when ejaculation occurs, thus preventing it from being deposited in the vagina. Condoms are available without prescription in drugstores; they are made in several colors and styles, including a hypoallergenic variety for persons who are allergic to rubber. Most are lubricated; some with spermicide.

Used properly, good quality condoms are a very effective method of contraception. The condom should be put on before any intromission takes place and should be removed (after intercourse) carefully to prevent spilling semen in the vagina. Spermicides can be used as a backup in case of condom rupture.

The condom is not acceptable to some because it disrupts the spontaneity of foreplay and reduces sensitivity in the man; however, men who have a tendency toward premature or early ejaculation may find the dulled sensation to be an advantage. Condoms have gained popularity because they offer considerable protection from transmission of Human Immunodeficiency Virus (HIV), which can lead to AIDS (Lamanna & Riedmann, 1988; Shapiro, 1987).

Oil-based lubricants such as mineral oil, baby oil, or hand lotion significantly reduce the strength of latex condoms within 1 to 5 minutes and allow leakage of the HIV virus. For contraceptive and AIDS-related safety, use only water-based lubricants (Elias, 1988).

Spermicidal Foams, Creams, Jellies, Tablets, and Suppositories

These are various forms of spermicidal chemicals. Sometimes they are used with the diaphragm, cervical cap, or condom, or they can also be used alone. The spermicidal chemicals apparently kill some disease organisms as well as sperm and, consequently, offer some protection against some STDs—especially gonorrhea, genital herpes, trichomoniasis, and moniliasis. They are available without prescription in drugstores (Lamanna & Riedmann, 1988; Shapiro, 1987).

Foams are rather like shaving cream; most come in a can with a plunger-type applicator for insertion into the vagina. Because foam spreads more evenly through the vagina, it is more effective than cream, jelly, tablets, or suppositories. A full application should be used as close to the time of intercourse as possible, and it should stay there for 6 to 8 hours. Reliability rates for spermicidal chemicals used alone vary from 75% to 96% (Shapiro, 1987).

Jellies and creams come in tubes with a plastic applicator. They, too, are inserted as near as possible to the time of intercourse and need to remain for 6 to 8 hours after intercourse. Jellies and creams tend to be somewhat more drippy or runny than foam; some couples dislike the mess.

Tablets and suppositories are products with sperm-killing chemicals in a glycerogelatin or cocoa-butter base. The tablets dissolve or the suppositories melt about 15 minutes to 1 hour after insertion deep in the vagina. They should be left in for 6 to 8 hours after intercourse.

The failure rate with tablets and suppositories is higher than with creams and jellies and much higher than with foam, presumably because the spermicide does not distribute evenly. Some persons may be allergic to the chemicals and experience vaginal or penile irritation.

Feminine hygiene products, such as deodorizing suppositories, feminine hygiene sprays, and lubricating jellies are often located on the drugstore shelves near the spermicidal chemicals. These often are advertised as a "solution to your most intimate marital problems," which mislead some into thinking that they offer contraceptive protection. This is not the case; they are intended for other purposes, such as lubrication.

Douching

Douching is a very ineffective method of contraception because it is done after sperm have been deposited in the vagina and may already be in the uterus. Douche liquid in the vagina may even push sperm into the cervix. Repeated douching may be irritating to the delicate tissues of the vagina or may upset the normal bacterial balance resulting in infection or irritation (Strong & DeVault, 1988).

Withdrawal

Withdrawal is one of the oldest methods of contraception and is practiced today by many couples. The man simply withdraws just before ejaculation so that no sperm are released into the vagina. It has the advantages of not requiring any chemicals, devices, or advance preparation.

There are several disadvantages of withdrawal; it is not very reliable because a man cannot always anticipate ejaculation and may not withdraw soon enough. Another reason for the ineffectiveness of this method is that small amounts of fluid may leak out before ejaculation; these few drops can carry thousands of sperm. This is especially likely when intercourse is prolonged.

A mistaken idea that no doubt causes failures of this method is that penetration is necessary for fertilization. Sperm are motile and occasionally those deposited near the vaginal opening find their way to the uterus (Strong & DeVault, 1988).

Withdrawal before ejaculation requires much willpower by the man and trust by his partner. It is not conducive to relaxation or pleasure for either; many couples find it very unsatisfying psychologically (Strong & DeVault, 1988).

Fertility Awareness and Periodic Abstinence

A woman's body goes through a series of changes in the course of her menstrual cycle, some of which are easily noted. Fertility awareness techniques of contraception rely on a woman's ability to learn about the changes in her body and to become attuned to her body so that she may predict with some accuracy the time of her ovulation. (Fertility awareness can be used to help women who want to conceive, too.)

Anticipating the time of ovulation is critical in fertility awareness methods because it determines the few days during each menstrual cycle when fertilization can occur. Ovulation occurs once in each menstrual cycle and ova remain viable for about 24 hours. If no sperm contact the ovum in that time, it dies and is sloughed off in the menstrual blood. Sperm remain viable for about 3 to 5 days. Allowing for the viability of both sperm and ovum, the time of fertility is about 5 to 7 days each menstrual cycle.

Fertility awareness methods require little equipment and so are inexpensive. They have no serious health consequences for users. These methods do require instruction, a very accurate keeping of records, and a good deal of couple cooperation. On a positive note, many couples enjoy the feeling of control over their fertility in "natural" ways. Many women appreciate the increased understanding of their own bodies.

Calendar or rhythm method refers to determining the time of greatest likelihood of fertility by the calendar (see Figure 10–2). After keeping accurate

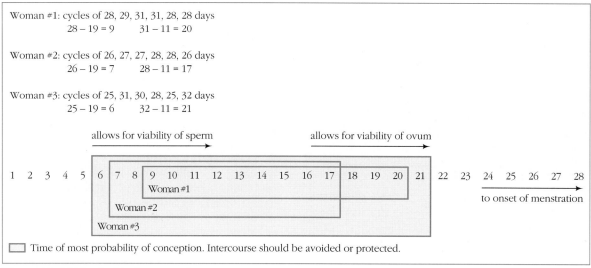

Woman #1: cycles of 28, 29, 31, 31, 28, 28 days
           28 − 19 = 9   31 − 11 = 20

Woman #2: cycles of 26, 27, 27, 28, 28, 26 days
           26 − 19 = 7   28 − 11 = 17

Woman #3: cycles of 25, 31, 30, 28, 25, 32 days
           25 − 19 = 6   32 − 11 = 21

allows for viability of sperm   allows for viability of ovum

1 2 3 4 5 6 7 8 9 10 11 12 13 14 15 16 17 18 19 20 21 22 23 24 25 26 27 28

Woman #1
Woman #2
Woman #3

to onset of menstruation

Time of most probability of conception. Intercourse should be avoided or protected.

Figure 10–2 Calendar/rhythm examples

records of the length of her menstrual cycles for a period of 6 months to 1 year, a woman can calculate a "typical" cycle. The calculations are done in the following way: Subtract 19 from the number of days in the shortest menstrual cycle to obtain the number of safe days in the first half of the cycle; then subtract 11 from the number of days in the longest menstrual cycle to get the number of safe days in the last half of the cycle. For example, Mary's records show that during 1 year, her longest menstrual cycle was 30 days and her shortest was 26 days. She calculates this way: 26 − 19 = 7, thus from day 1 of her menstrual cycle (the day menstruation begins) to day 7 is considered safe. She then calculates this way: 30 − 11 = 19; this indicates that from day 19 of her cycle until the next menstruation begins is a safe time. Conception is most likely to occur from day 7 to day 19. Sexual intercourse is avoided during this time or if intercourse is desired, another method of contraception can be employed.

Temperature method uses changes in body temperature as an indicator of when ovulation has oc-

curred. At the time of ovulation, the temperature rises from 0.5 to 1.0 degrees Fahrenheit and stays elevated until the next menstruation begins. After the rise in temperature signals that ovulation has taken place, a woman may wait 3 days (to allow the ovum to die) and then can assume that sexual intercourse is safe until the next menstruation begins.

The difficulty in the temperature method lies in anticipating when ovulation will happen because the temperature shift is after the fact (Saxton, 1990). For greatest effectiveness, women are advised not to have sexual intercourse from the first day of the menstrual cycle until 3 days after the temperature rise (Shapiro, 1987). Temperature may be affected by illness, lack of sleep, or use of aspirin, too (Strong & DeVault, 1988).

Cervical mucus method involves charting the changes that occur in secretions of the cervix as it prepares for ovulation. In the beginning of the menstrual cycle, just following menstruation, the cervix likely has a mucus plug and little secretion. The vaginal sensation is of dryness. Following this, the mucus will be thick or sticky and cloudy in color, accompanied by a wet vaginal sensation. As ovulation approaches and occurs, the mucus becomes plentiful, slippery, and clear; it is stretchy. After ovulation the mucus again becomes thick, drier, and cloudy (Shapiro, 1987).

Women using this method keep records of the condition of the cervical mucus and avoid sexual intercourse until the fourth dry day after ovulatory wetness. Sexual intercourse is allowed during the dry days at the beginning of each menstrual cycle (Shapiro, 1987).

Couples who want to use fertility awareness methods can increase their effectiveness by using a combination of methods (see Figure 10–3). Combining methods boosts reliability to 85% to 93% if followed carefully (Shapiro, 1987).

Women who have very irregular menstrual cycles may have difficulty in establishing a base of information from which to work. Because menstruation is stopped for a while after childbirth and may be very irregular when it resumes, fertility awareness methods are practically useless during the postpartum period. Emotional excitement, stress, travel, and illness can all upset menstrual cycles, too (Lamanna & Riedmann, 1988; Strong & DeVault, 1988).

Although couples use fertility awareness methods to help determine when fertile days are likely, not all will wish to abstain from sexual intercourse during so many days of each month. Couples may use methods of sexual interaction other than intercourse on those days or may use another method of birth control, such as a diaphragm or condom.

The assumption that fertility methods have no side effects has been challenged in recent years by some research indicating that conceptions occurring during use of these methods are subject to higher rates of fetal abnormality, miscarriage, and mental retardation. It is theorized that this is due to the advanced age of the ovum or the sperm since fertilization accidents would involve sperm deposited several days before ovulation or an ovum near the end of its viability. Other research fails to support this, however (Shapiro, 1987).

Abortion

The earliest record of an abortive technique is found in an Egyptian medical papyrus dated at about 1550 B.C. Throughout the years, abortion has been recognized and used as a way of terminating an unwanted or dangerous pregnancy.

In the United States the government's position on abortion was clarified in the U.S. Statute of 1873, which was aimed at both abortion and contraception. The bill forbade the mailing of all material deemed obscene and outlawed the manufacture and advertisement of any drugs, medicines, or articles for abortion or contraceptive purposes.

As these laws were enforced and arrests were made, abortions were slowly driven out of sight. Illegal abortions developed into a secret business, enriching many unscrupulous persons and causing death and disease to thousands of women. At one time almost half of the deaths related to childbearing in New York City were attributed to abortion.

In 1973 the U.S. Supreme Court granted women the right to have legal medical abortions during the first 6 months of pregnancy. Since that time the death and disease rate from abortions has dropped dramatically; prior to 1973, illegal abortions were the direct cause of 20% of all pregnancy-related deaths. Today very few deaths are related to abortions ("Researchers Confirm," 1982).

Abortion is not regarded as an appropriate choice for routine fertility control even by those who favor easy access to legal abortions. Some women seeking abortions have been using some form of contraception and have experienced a failure in their contraception efforts; an abortion is sought as a last resort. The large numbers of abortions each year, however, suggest that this is not the case for many who seek abortions (see Table 10–8).

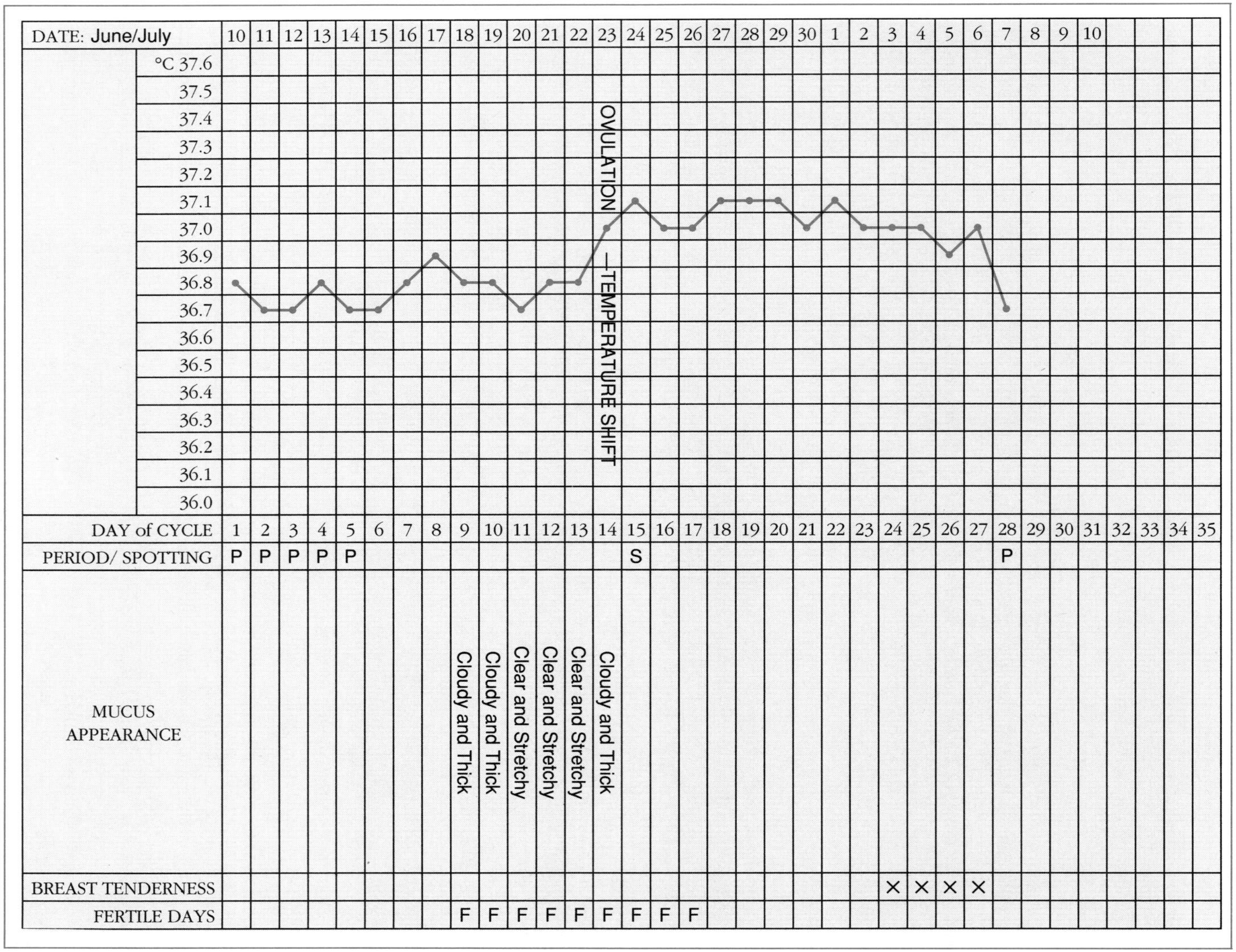
DATE: June/July
10 11 12 13 14 15 16 17 18 19 20 21 22 23 24 25 26 27 28 29 30 1 2 3 4 5 6 7 8 9 10
°C 37.6
37.5
37.4
37.3
37.2
37.1
37.0
36.9
36.8
36.7
36.6
36.5
36.4
36.3
36.2
36.1
36.0
OVULATION —TEMPERATURE SHIFT
DAY of CYCLE
1 2 3 4 5 6 7 8 9 10 11 12 13 14 15 16 17 18 19 20 21 22 23 24 25 26 27 28 29 30 31 32 33 34 35
PERIOD/ SPOTTING
P P P P P S P
MUCUS APPEARANCE
Cloudy and Thick
Cloudy and Thick
Clear and Stretchy
Clear and Stretchy
Clear and Stretchy
Cloudy and Thick
BREAST TENDERNESS
X X X X
FERTILE DAYS
F F F F F F F F F

Figure 10–3 Charting the Temperature Method and the Cervical Mucus Method *Source:* Adapted from Shapiro, R. (1987). *Contraception: A practical and political guide*. London: Virago Press.

Table 10–8 Number of Abortions in the United States

Year	Total Number Women (Age 15–44)	Abortions	Ratio per 1,000 Live Births
1972	44,588,000	586,800	184
1977	49,814,000	1,316,700	400
1980	53,048,000	1,553,900	428
1983	55,340,000	1,575,000	436
1985	56,754,000	1,588,000	425

Source: U.S. Bureau of the Census. (1989b). *Statistical abstract of the United States: 1990* (110th ed.). Washington, DC: U.S. Government Printing Office.

Abortion is a very emotionally charged issue because it involves the termination of a pregnancy (rather than the prevention of conception). Most people have strong feelings about it—whether they favor legal abortions, oppose them, or favor abortion only under certain circumstances.

There are five basic methods of abortion. Each is described below.

Vacuum Aspiration. The majority of abortions in the United States and Canada are performed by this method. The suction method is done under local anesthetic injected around the cervix. A vacurette, or sterile tube, is then inserted through the vagina into the uterus until it touches the amniotic sac, at which point the fetus and tissues are sucked away from the uterine wall into the tube.

The suction method may be used up to 12 weeks after conception. It is usually performed on an outpatient basis. The procedure takes only a matter of a few minutes and recovery is fast. Women experience some bleeding for several days after and are advised to refrain from sexual intercourse, douching, or the use of tampons for about 3 weeks (Shapiro, 1987; Strong & DeVault, 1988).

D and C Method. Dilation and curettage is used during the first trimester of pregnancy and involves the dilation of the cervix and the use of a curette (a spoon-shaped instrument) to scrape the uterine lining and fetal material. More danger of perforation of the uterine wall and of hemorrhage exists with D and C than with vacuum aspiration.

As with vacuum aspiration, a local anesthetic is used. The procedure takes only a few minutes, and recovery is fast. Some physicians recommend an overnight hospital stay.

Saline- or Prostaglandin-Injection Method. Both of these methods involve the injection of a substance—either saline (salt) or the hormone prostaglandin—into the amniotic sac. The saline solution poisons the fetus. Labor usually begins within 24 to 36 hours, and the fetus is expelled. Prostaglandins are present in the body, normally increasing at the end of a full-term pregnancy and triggering the onset of labor. Injected into the amniotic sac, they do the same, usually within 12 to 24 hours.

The injection methods are used for pregnancies advanced beyond 12 weeks, usually for those beyond

Abortions Alarm Soviet Authorities

Soviet medical officials are alarmed about the large number of abortions—about 10 million—performed in their country each year. It is not unusual for a Soviet woman to have 4 or 5 abortions, with some having had as many as 20. The lack of effective contraceptives—pharmacies are able to meet only about one-fourth of the demand—is one factor in the high number of abortions. For most couples, abortion is, of necessity, the primary method of birth control.

Although discouraged by government policy, abortions are legal and available from clinics for a cost of 5 rubles (about $6.50). Physicians charge up to 50 rubles ($65) for private abortions, with anesthetic that is not used otherwise.

Another factor contributing to the large number of abortions is the strong desire of most Soviet couples to limit their family size. Nearly all adults must work, and childbearing is regarded by many to be a burden.

In many parts of the Soviet Union the birthrate has fallen below the replacement rate, and officials are concerned about population losses. Demographers calculate that 2.6 children per married couple are needed to keep the population stable. Currently, the birthrate is about 2.3—except in urban areas where it is below 2.0.

Abortions are costly to obstetrical and gynecological hospitals and clinics, which may spend half of their budgeted funds to perform abortions. Abortions are regarded as a major factor in determining the incidence of gynecological conditions, infant mortality, miscarriages, infertility, and child morbidity.

Source: Eaton, W. J. (1986, January 13). Health effect of abortions alarms Soviet authorities. *Los Angeles Times*, Part I, pp. 1, 8.

16 weeks. Both require the woman to undergo labor and delivery of the fetus. In some instances, when the fetus is 20 weeks or more in development, it may be delivered alive and die within a few minutes. Recovery is similar to recovery after childbirth.

D and E Method. Dilation and evacuation is used for pregnancies from 13 to 20 weeks. It is similar to D and C or vacuum aspiration except that the fetus and accompanying tissues are larger, making it necessary to use a combination of vacuum aspiration and curette to remove it all. D and E is thought to be safer than saline or prostaglandin injection (Strong & DeVault, 1988).

Hysterotomy. A hysterotomy is actually a Caesarian section abortion and is major surgery. An incision is made in the lower abdomen and uterine wall, after which the fetus and placenta are removed. A hysterotomy is the most dangerous of the methods of abortion that have been discussed; it requires a hospital stay of several days. Recovery is longer, and it is more expensive.

New Contraceptive Methods

Researchers are always working on new ideas for safer, easier, and more reliable methods of birth control. Some contraceptive methods are available in other countries but not in the United States. Because of rigorous testing of products before they can be used in the United States, some are introduced in other parts of the world first. Additionally,

The Artificial Control of Gender

Genetic research and technology have presented couples with many options in family planning. Recent technology adds selecting a child's gender to that list of options.

By using various substances as filters, sperm can be sorted so that very high proportions of X-bearing or Y-bearing sperm are selected. When artificially inseminated with X-bearing sperm, the chances of conceiving a female child are increased; use of Y-bearing sperm increases the chances of conceiving a male. The likelihood of giving birth to an infant of the desired gender is about 80%.

Questions about human and family relationships naturally arise. Will babies become commodities? Is the value of marriage lessened? How much control should humans exercise over genetic destiny? Will this be the beginning of selective "breeding" for desired traits?

Source: Uzzell, O. (1985). Family planning: The artificial control of gender. *Family Perspective, 19,* 279–282.

some products or devices are removed from the U.S. market because they do not meet safety standards.

Two long-term injectable contraceptives are available outside the United States. Both are forms of synthetic hormones that are injected deep in a muscle; injections must be renewed every 8 to 12 weeks. Their action in preventing pregnancy is similar to that of oral contraceptives (Shapiro, 1987).

Many of the advantages and disadvantages are also the same as for oral contraceptives. Women report very irregular menstrual cycles on the injectables, and fertility may not return for several months after the injectable is gone. Women who experience undesirable side effects have little recourse except to endure them until the injectable wears away (Shapiro, 1987).

Contraceptive implants are small capsules containing synthetic hormones that are placed under the skin. They release the hormone for 5 years but can be removed at any time. Their action, advantages, and disadvantages are similar to those of oral contraceptives (Shapiro, 1987).

Vaginal rings are small, plasticlike rings impregnated with synthetic hormones. They are worn in the vagina more or less continuously, although they can be removed for intercourse. Some users complain of increased vaginal discharge and a foul odor (Shapiro, 1987).

One long-sought birth control remedy is a "morning-after pill," a pill or treatment that can be taken *after* coitus. Such a treatment is available in some European countries; it consists of a 2-day regimen of hormones in pill form. The hormones do not prevent conception; they alter the lining of the uterus so that implantation cannot take place (Shapiro, 1987).

Currently being tested is a drug called RU-486, labeled a contragestive agent by its manufacturers. RU-486 prevents the cells of the uterine wall from getting progesterone, thus making implantation impossible to sustain because the uterine lining sloughs off in menstruation. Manufacturers claim it can be used as a once-a-month birth control pill or as a postcoital pill. It does not contain hormones or have their side effects. Much testing must be done before it will be available, and it will not be acceptable to some couples because it is a form of early chemically induced abortion (Goodman, 1986).

Research focuses on new methods of male contraception as well. Current investigation includes testing of the substance gossypol, a pigment from cotton plants, as an antifertility drug. Gossypol was discovered to be an accidental cause of male infertility in many rural communes in China in the 1950s. Preliminary testing seems to indicate that it is effective with no adverse effects on sexual desire; however, it does reduce serum potassium levels (Liu et al., 1987).

Another possibility for both men and women is the development of a reversible tubal ligation or vasectomy. The use of flexible latex plugs to block the Fallopian tubes or vasa deferentia is one suggestion. These could be removed when the person wished to have fertility restored.

Summary

- Couples today have many decisions to make regarding childbearing: whether or not to have children, how long to delay childbearing, and how many children to have. More couples are postponing having children and are having smaller families.

- For many couples, childbearing decisions are complicated by infertility. Both partners should be evaluated for an early diagnosis, as various treatments are available. In addition to surgical procedures and drug therapies, couples who are involuntarily childless may need to consider options such as artificial insemination, in vitro fertilization, embryo transplantation, or surrogacy.

- A variety of contraceptive methods are available, and couples may select the method or combination of methods that provides the reliability, convenience, and safety they want. It is desirable for couples to share the decisions and responsibility for fertility control.

- Abortion is not regarded as an appropriate choice for routine fertility control; however, there are large numbers of abortions performed each year in the United States. The personal nature of this decision and the fact that it involves termination of a pregnancy (rather than the prevention of conception) make this a very emotional and volatile issue.

Discussion Questions

1. Discuss the relative merits of different forms of birth control.

2. Evidence continues to accumulate that knowledgeable couples frequently have one or more children than they planned. Why does this happen?

3. A doctor has just performed a saline-injection abortion and delivered a struggling but live infant. The pregnancy apparently was more advanced than the doctor and mother had estimated. With immediate attention the infant might survive. What should the doctor do? The mother is aware of the situation. What should she do?

4. How do you think your marriage would be affected if one of you had fertility problems? How far would you go to conceive a child?

5. Discuss the factors you would consider in deciding whether to use artificial insemination, in vitro fertilization, or embryo transplant. Would you use a surrogate mother?

6. What factors should a man consider before undergoing sterilization? What factors should a woman consider?

7. Some persons believe the IUDs are equivalent to abortions because IUDs prevent the fertilized egg from implanting itself. Discuss both sides of this issue.

CHAPTER 11

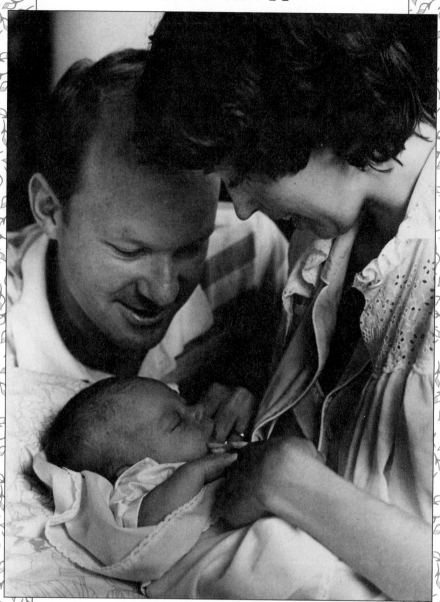

PREGNANCY

Andy was born a robust 8 pounds, 10 ounces, 21 inches long.... After a few hours' recuperation following a long, confusing labor and smooth delivery, the nurse brought my first child to me. I held the little stranger in my arms.... I stared at him with awestruck concentration and a kind of disbelief.... The overwhelming experience of pregnancy and birth was over. I was now a *mother*. Unexpected tears rolled gently down my cheeks. I was indeed a mother, but I didn't feel like one.

About the third day I began to fall in love with my little stranger, Andy, my son. I began to recognize his gusty cry as he was brought down the long hospital hall to my room. After nursing he would tuck himself against my soft tummy and I could feel his sleepy, full self sink heavily into the outside of my body as if delighting in these brief moments of transition from a cozy womb to a big airy world. He seemed more and more my boy. The puzzling strangeness, the disappointing distance of those first days were slowly, unmistakably turning into affinity, warmth, and love. With great relief, I began to feel like a mother and to like the feeling very, very much.

(Sherrard, 1980, p. 29)

Making the Decision

Before the advent of safe, reliable contraception, women expected to have several children and often were worn out by repeated, closely spaced pregnancies. The availability and acceptance of birth control methods today allows couples more choice in childbearing decisions. Although there are still "accidents," inasmuch as no contraceptive method is 100% reliable and human beings are occasionally irresponsible, most persons who have children make a positive and deliberate decision to do so.

Just as the amount of choice involved in having children has changed, attitudes concerning pregnancy, birth, and parenthood have changed with social swings. In the 1950s parenthood and family togetherness were idealized; happy families were romanticized by the media. Then in the 1960s a more negative approach came into vogue and the "hard facts" about parenting were spelled out—with the emphasis on the unpleasant realities.

In the 1980s a more balanced approach developed. Would-be parents seemed more aware that having a baby is both a joy and a tremendous responsibility (Leslie, 1982). Many invested time and effort in learning about parenthood and the impact of parenthood on marriage. The 1990s promise to be a continuation of an intelligent approach to parenthood. Children are highly valued, though a significant minority plan not to have children (a disproportionate number of whom are among the highly educated).

Why Have Children?

Deciding whether or not to have children is a difficult decision for many people, and the reasons behind their decisions are varied. Some reasons are positive and sound, while some are negative or reflect immaturity. Among the common reasons are the following:

1. *To love, nurture, and guide another human being to adulthood.*

2. *To have someone who will love the parent.*

3. *To have someone who will be dependent on the parent.* As a result of this dependency, the parent is important to the child. Each of us has the strong psychological need to feel important to someone; parenthood fulfills this need for many.

4. *To satisfy the expectations of society.* There have been in the past, and still are today, such intense pressures for married couples to have children that few question whether they will have children or not. For many couples the real decision is not whether to have children but *when* to have children. Because of such societal expectations, couples who do not want children and others who are not emotionally suited for parenthood drift into it anyway.

5. *To prove virility or femininity.* For some people having children is a manifestation of their sexuality. Parenthood is a symbol of prestige as a "real" man or woman.

6. *To provide grandchildren for the couple's parents.* Some couples believe they owe it to their parents to have children so that they may enjoy being grandparents. Even in the absence of overt pressure, couples may perceive that their parents desire grandchildren and may feel guilty about remaining childless.

7. *To carry on the family.* Some people want to have children so that their family will not end with their death. They may feel an obligation not to "fail" their family by letting it end. Others derive a sense of immortality by continuing to live through the lives of their children.

8. *To provide a playmate and companion for an only child or for themselves.*

9. *To compensate for an unhappy marriage.* Some individuals have a baby in order to fill an

empty marriage, believing that the baby will provide the affection, love, and companionship that is lacking in the marriage relationship. Others have a child hoping that the child will cure an ailing marriage by bringing husband and wife closer together. Although a few troubled marriages have been helped this way, the advent of a child more often only complicates a poor marriage situation.

10. *To create a human life.* Having a baby is one way that some individuals fulfill their need to be creative; the miracle of pregnancy and birth is a most satisfying form of creation.

Table 11–1 lists the various aspects of parenting that provide satisfying experiences.

The Best Time to Have a Child

Certain conditions increase the probability that the childbearing experience will be positive:

1. *When the child is wanted by both husband and wife.* It can be tragic for both the child and the parents when a child is unwanted. A child who is wanted has a much greater chance of receiving the love, care, and attention that every child needs. Also, when the child is wanted, the parents are much more likely to be happy and well-adjusted.

2. *When the mother is between the ages of 20 and 35.* Maternal age is related to some birth de-

*Table 11–1 Sources of Satisfaction as Parents**

Most Important	Least Important
Watching children grow and develop	Reliving childhood
Love for children	Feel more adult
Pride in children's achievements	Security for old age
Sharing	Doing what is expected of me
A growth experience	Less boredom in my life
Passing on values	Passing on family name
Fun to do things with	Relationship with own parents is closer
General enjoyment	Meeting new friends through children
Feeling of being part of a family	More things to talk to spouse about
Self-fulfillment	Pleasure for grandparents

*Based on responses of 702 parents.

Source: Meredith, W. H., Stinnett, N., & Cacioppo, B. F. (1985). Parent satisfactions: Implications for strengthening families. In R. Williams, H. Lingren, G. Rowe, S. Van Zandt, P. Lee, & N. Stinnett (Eds.), *Family strengths 6: Enhancement of interaction* (pp. 143–150). Lincoln, NE: Department of Human Development and the Family, University of Nebraska. Reprinted by permission.

fects and mental retardation in the child. Generally, very young women (under age 20) and older women (over age 40) have greater chances of bearing children with physical difficulties or mental retardation (Mansfield & Cohn, 1986; Schiamberg, 1988; Strong & DeVault, 1988).

3. *When there are few or no genetic problems in the family histories of both husband and wife.* This reduces the risk of genetic defects—birth defects—for the child (Schiamberg, 1988).

4. *When the health of both father and mother is good.* Good physical health helps to ensure that the parents have the necessary strength, endurance, and energy to bear and rear a child.

5. *When both husband and wife are prepared emotionally, financially, and intellectually for the child.* A couple with adequate financial resources and occupational stability will likely find the situation of having a child easier. Periods of great emotional stress are not the best times for pregnancy and can adversely affect the unborn child (Mansfield & Cohn, 1986; Schiamberg, 1988).

Spacing of Children

Couples who make the decision to have one child must also decide if they will have additional children, and, if so, how many and how they will be spaced. Many couples believe that it is best to have children within a 1- to 2-year period of each other; others favor a wider spacing of children. While there are no absolutely right or wrong ways to space children, there are certain advantages and disadvantages to consider.

Many persons who favor having children within a 1- or 2-year period of each other believe that the children have greater companionship and do more things together as they grow up because they are closer in age. Another perceived advantage is that the parents complete their child-rearing roles in a shorter period of time.

On the other hand, there are some major disadvantages of close spacing of children, including higher rates of infant mortality and prematurity. Medical reports indicate that it takes a woman approximately two years to recover fully after the birth of a child. If a second pregnancy occurs within this time, it may place a strain on the mother's physical health. In addition, a pregnant woman's health may be taxed by having to lift, bathe, chase, and carry a toddler.

Cherie's first child, Angela, was born in December. One year and 2 weeks later, her second, Jeffrey, was born. Cherie estimates that she didn't get a complete night's rest until Angela was almost 18 months old. Angela had sleeping problems until then and would awaken two or three times each night needing to be held and comforted. She still is bothered by nightmares on occasion. Jeffrey had problems with colic and was 3 months old before he began to settle into a routine.

Close spacing also has some disadvantages for the children. Although they have the advantage of being playmates, the chances of sibling rivalry are greater. Close spacing makes it more difficult for each child to receive all the attention he or she desires.

Spacing children very far apart has possible disadvantages, too. When children are spaced as far apart as 8 years, they miss much sibling companionship; the older often assumes an almost parental role. Parents who have children spaced far apart have noted that their situation is as if they have reared two separate families or as if they have reared two "only" children.

Although it is impossible to state the optimal time between children, many family-life specialists believe that an interval of approximately 3 years seems to be most advantageous. The children are still close enough in age to be able to enjoy doing things together. And sibling rivalry is reduced in that the older child is better able to understand and accept a new family member. Also the age differences may mean fewer demands on the time and resources of parents. For example, a 2-year-old and an infant would *both* be in diapers and would later *both* be needing help with college tuition at the same time.

Symptoms of Pregnancy

When a woman conceives, it is important that she know as early as possible that she is pregnant. When a woman knows or suspects she is pregnant, she should always inform any physician treating her for any illness, because it may influence the kind of treatment she receives. For example, certain antibiotics should not be used during pregnancy and dental or chest X-rays can damage the fetus.

There are several signs of pregnancy, usually classified as either presumptive or positive symptoms. *Presumptive symptoms* are exhibited by the mother; consequently, they are not definite indications of pregnancy because other conditions may cause the same symptoms. Usually, however, a combination of presumptive symptoms represents a strong indication of pregnancy. *Positive symptoms* are exhibited by the baby and represent definite evidence of pregnancy.

Presumptive Symptoms

Missing a Menstrual Period. Failure to menstruate is often the first indication of a pregnancy. A woman who is usually regular in her menstrual cycles may consider a delay of 10 or more days to be rather strong evidence that she is pregnant. It must be remembered, however, that delays in the onset of menstruation can also be caused by such things as emotional upsets, severe stress, illness, thyroid disturbances, anemia, or malnutrition. Some women may menstruate after conception, although the flow is usually much less than normal.

Changes in the Breasts. Pregnancy may be indicated by certain changes in the breasts, such as enlargement of the breasts, increased size of the nipples, increased tenderness, and a tingling sensation, primarily around the nipples. The increased blood supply to the mammary glands may make the veins more visible. The areola—the pigmented area around the nipple—becomes darker (Birch, 1981).

Nausea. Approximately one-half of pregnant women experience some nausea, many by the time their first menstrual period is missed. The nausea is due to the biochemical changes in the body that accompany pregnancy. Because many women experience the nausea in the mornings, it is often called *morning sickness*. In reality, it can happen any time of day. Many women have observed that it tends to be worse when they are too hungry or overly tired. Usually the nausea disappears in approximately 4 months (Birch, 1981). Avoiding spicy, greasy, or hard-to-digest foods and resting after meals helps in many cases. Medication is available for severe nausea.

Fatigue and Need for Extra Sleep. Because of the many physical changes taking place, some women are very fatigued and need extra sleep or rest during pregnancy.

Increased Frequency of Urination. This presumptive sign occurs somewhat later in a pregnancy as the enlarging uterus presses on the bladder and produces the sensation of needing to urinate more often (Birch, 1981).

Increased Size of Abdomen. One of the more obvious signs of pregnancy is an increase in the size of the abdomen. The expanding uterus causes a slight bulge in the lower portion of the abdomen, which is noticeable late in the third month or early in the fourth.

Increase in Basal Body Temperature. The body temperature of a person upon waking in the morning is referred to as *basal body temperature*. Because basal body temperature increases during pregnancy, a temperature level of 98.8 to 99.9 degrees that is maintained for more than 16 days is highly indicative of pregnancy.

Changes in the Vagina and Cervix. Vaginal secretions increase, and the vaginal lining becomes congested and bluish in color in pregnancy. The cervix, which is firm in the nonpregnant state, softens during pregnancy.

Positive Symptoms

Movement of the Fetus. Fetal movements usually become noticeable to the mother during the fourth or fifth month of pregnancy. They are a positive and dramatic sign of pregnancy.

Fetal Heartbeat. The fetal heartbeat can be detected as early as the tenth to twelfth week after the last menstrual period. The heartbeat of the fetus varies from 120 to 160 beats per minute, which is approximately twice the mother's normal heart rate.

Seeing the Fetus by Ultrasound. Ultrasound involves bouncing high-frequency sound waves at the uterine area in order to produce an image of

---

Developmental Tasks of Pregnancy

Pregnancy is a time of such obvious physical change that the psychological changes are easily overlooked. Pregnancy presents several developmental tasks that must be mastered. For a woman, the four tasks are to

1. Develop an emotional attachment to the fetus as characterized by concern for the health of the fetus and a desire to take care of self to protect the fetus.
2. Differentiate self from the fetus. This occurs later in the pregnancy with the selection of names and acquisition of nursery furniture and clothes.
3. Accept and resolve the relationship with her own mother. Pregnancy seems to change perceptions of motherhood and one's own mother.
4. Resolve the dependency issues, such as greater physical and emotional dependencies due to the number and magnitude of changes caused by pregnancy.

For a man, the four developmental tasks are to

1. Accept the pregnancy and attach to the fetus as characterized by attending childbirth classes with wife or purchasing items for the baby.
2. Evaluate practical issues such as financial responsibilities, providing a larger home, insurance.
3. Accept and resolve relationship with his own father. To be a father means giving up some of being a son.
4. Resolve dependency issues. Some men feel abandoned or neglected as their wives are involved with their pregnancies.

Source: Adapted from Valentine, D. P. (1982). The experience of pregnancy: A developmental process. *Family Relations, 31,* 243–248.

the fetus on a small TV-like screen. The image can be photographed for a permanent record. The ultrasound image provides vital information, such as fetal size, stage of development, and some structural details. Ultrasound exams are helpful in the diagnosis of multiple births. Most physicians believe ultrasound exams are safe as a diagnostic tool in pregnancy; they are painless and take only a few minutes.

Feeling the Shape of the Fetus. The shape of the fetus can be felt through the abdominal wall by a physician at about the fifth month.

Pregnancy Tests

Chemical tests to determine whether a pregnancy has begun are based on the detection of human chorionic gonadotropin (HCG), a hormone produced by the developing placenta. HCG is detectable in the pregnant woman's blood and urine. Blood tests can be used as early as 10 days after conception and results are available within a day (Wolfe & Goldsmith, 1980). Urine tests require about two hours to perform and are 95% to 98% accurate when performed two weeks or more after the missed menstrual period should have begun (Cox, 1981; Wolfe & Goldsmith, 1980).

Several home pregnancy tests are available. These can be done as early as one day after a missed period should have begun. They take from 5 to 30 minutes and cost approximately $12 in most drugstores. Home pregnancy tests provide privacy and a quick confirmation for women who need to know if they are pregnant. Accurate test results depend on following the test instructions very carefully. About 20% of the time the home pregnancy tests indicate the woman is not pregnant when she actually is pregnant (Rice, 1990). Consequently, a second test is recommended a week later to confirm the initial diagnosis, and a physician should be consulted before pregnancy is definitely determined (Birch, 1981).

Stages of Prenatal Development

The 9-month period of time required for the fertilized egg cell to develop can be divided into distinct stages. As can be seen in Figure 11–1, each stage changes the body both internally and externally.

The Fertilization-Implantation Period

The fertilization-implantation period begins with conception and extends through the second week of life when the fertilized egg is implanted in the wall of the uterus (Schiamberg, 1988). Conception happens when a sperm cell of the man unites with the ovum or egg cell of the woman, usually in one of the Fallopian tubes. At the time of ovulation, the mature ovum travels to the uterus through the Fallopian tube. For most women, ovulation occurs 14 to 16 days before their next menstrual period is due. The sperm that unites with the ovum is one of approximately 500 million contributed by the father. Conception must occur within approximately 24 hours of ovulation (Saxton, 1990).

After fertilization, the ovum—now called a *zygote*—begins to grow by cell division (Schiamberg, 1988). The zygote continues down the Fallopian tube to the uterus. It is about the size of a pinhead by the time it arrives.

The zygote is unattached and moves freely for about a week. On about the tenth day after fertilization, the zygote attaches itself to the wall of the uterus; this is called *implantation*. By attaching itself in this manner, the developing zygote obtains nourishment from the mother through the blood vessels in the uterine wall.

For various reasons that are not completely understood, the zygote occasionally implants in an area outside the uterus—usually in the Fallopian tube. Approximately 4 in 1,000 pregnancies are tubal or ectopic pregnancies. As the zygote grows,

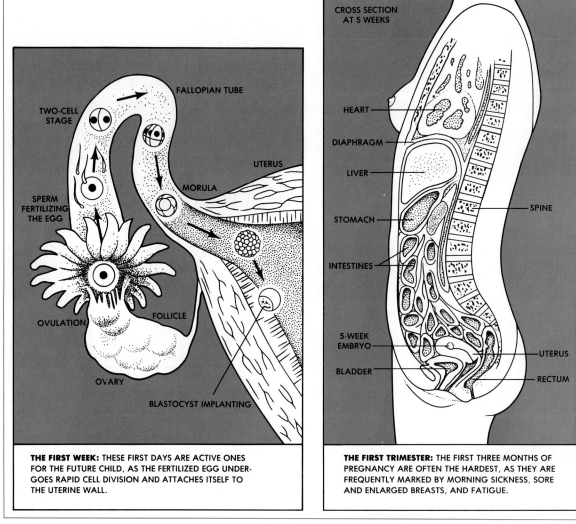

Figure 11–1 How pregnancy changes your body. *Source:* Bierer, L. How Pregnancy Changes Your Body. *Parents,* December 1980, pp. 58–59.

the Fallopian tube ruptures and the resulting internal bleeding may cause maternal shock and death. Treatment of a tubal pregnancy usually involves surgical removal of the damaged Fallopian tube (Strong et al., 1981).

The Embryo Period

The embryo period extends from the end of the second week to the end of the second month. The embryo, as the unborn baby is called during this

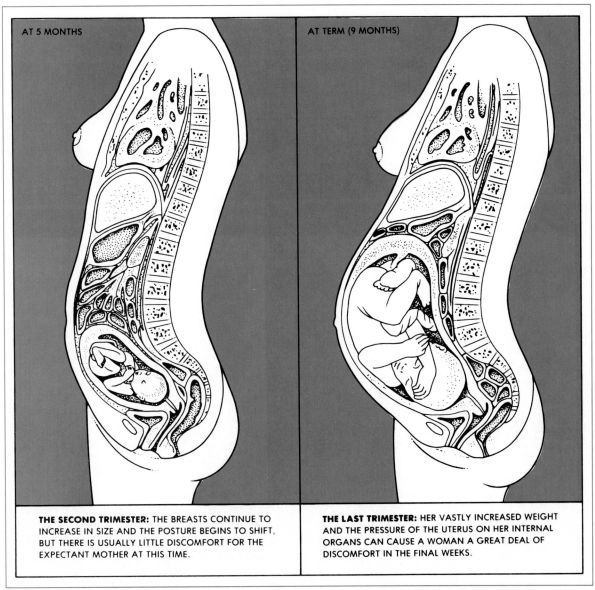

AT 5 MONTHS

AT TERM (9 MONTHS)

THE SECOND TRIMESTER: THE BREASTS CONTINUE TO INCREASE IN SIZE AND THE POSTURE BEGINS TO SHIFT, BUT THERE IS USUALLY LITTLE DISCOMFORT FOR THE EXPECTANT MOTHER AT THIS TIME.

THE LAST TRIMESTER: HER VASTLY INCREASED WEIGHT AND THE PRESSURE OF THE UTERUS ON HER INTERNAL ORGANS CAN CAUSE A WOMAN A GREAT DEAL OF DISCOMFORT IN THE FINAL WEEKS.

Figure 11–1 (Cont'd) How pregnancy changes your body. *Source:* Bierer, L. How Pregnancy Changes Your Body. *Parents,* December 1980, pp. 58–59.

period, undergoes extremely rapid development and growth. Although the body of the embryo is only about 1.5 inches long and weighs only about 0.03 ounces by the end of the embryo period, about 95% of the important internal and external features of a human being are formed by the end of the embryo stage. For example, facial features such as eyes, ears, lips, and tongue are present; fingers and toes are well formed, and the heart is functioning (Schiamberg, 1988).

Because virtually all body systems begin their development during this period and because the beginning of development is an especially critical time, the unborn child is extremely vulnerable to disruptions of normal growth during the embryo stage. Exposure to chemicals or radiation and maternal illness are examples of the kinds of factors that may disrupt the course of prenatal development (Schiamberg, 1988).

In addition to the embryo itself, special structures that protect and nourish the baby until it is born also develop during the embryo stage. These include the placenta, the umbilical cord, and the amniotic sac.

The placenta develops from the mass of thread-like structures the zygote sent into the uterine wall during implantation. The placenta is the organ that transports nutrients from the mother to the embryo and wastes from the embryo to the mother. It also serves as an endocrine gland, producing the hormones such as progesterone and estrogen that are essential to the maintenance of the pregnancy. The placenta reduces its production of progesterone and estrogen just before delivery and thus plays a role in initiating labor (Katchadourian & Lunde, 1972; Papalia & Olds, 1989).

The umbilical cord is the connecting link between the placenta and the embryo; it attaches to the placenta at one end and to the embryo's abdominal wall at the other. The cord eventually grows to a length of 10 to 20 inches, thus making fetal movement and activity possible.

The amniotic sac is a water jacket or bag within which the embryo develops. In addition to containing the embryo, the amniotic sac contains a watery fluid called amniotic fluid. It also serves the important function of protecting the embryo from injury.

The Fetal Period

The fetal period is the longest of the three prenatal stages, lasting from the end of the second month to birth. Much growth occurs during this time, but it is primarily a refinement or an extension of what has already begun; few new features appear. At the end of the third month the fetus is about 3.0 inches long and weighs about 1.0 ounce; by the fourth month it reaches 6.0 inches and is large enough that the mother feels its movements. The fetus reaches the age of viability by about 28 to 30 weeks of gestation, which means that it has a chance of surviving if born at this time (Schiamberg, 1988).

Prenatal Influences on Development

In the United States nine of every ten babies are born perfectly healthy; only 7% suffer some kind of birth defect. Most prospective parents, however, want to do all they can to safeguard their baby (March of Dimes Birth Defects Foundation, 1983; Papalia & Olds, 1989).

Parents can help to ensure successful prenatal development by providing the best possible environment in which the child lives before birth. *Early* diagnosis of pregnancy and prenatal care by a physician are very important. The woman who does not realize she is pregnant for several weeks or who delays prenatal care for "just a few more weeks" may jeopardize her child's well-being; recall that the first 8 weeks of gestation are especially critical. Certain factors have been identified as influencing prenatal development.

Joel Gordon

Genetic Disorders

Our genes are, so far at least, unchangeable. Geneticists, however, are able to tell us much about the transmission of about 250 genetic disorders. Some common genetic disorders are listed briefly.

Huntington's Chorea. In Huntington's chorea normal production of hemoglobin is prevented. Poor appetite, listlessness, and increased susceptibility to infections are symptoms (Sills & Henry, 1980).

Tay-Sachs Disease. Tay-Sachs disease is caused by an enzyme deficiency and a resulting inability to metabolize fats in the nervous system. Toxins accumulate in the brain causing retardation, deafness, and death by about age five. Tay-Sachs is most common in Jews of Russian and Polish descent (Cowley, 1990; Schiamberg, 1988; Sills & Henry, 1980).

Cystic Fibrosis. Lung infections and digestive disorders characterize cystic fibrosis. About 10 million Americans carry the gene responsible for cystic fibrosis. Because the inheritance of cystic fibrosis is recessive, persons may have an affected gene and not exhibit the disorder itself.

Sickle-cell Anemia. Sickle-cell anemia is caused by a malformation of the red blood cells. It occurs most frequently among blacks; about 7% carry the mutated gene and 1 in 500 has the condition (Cowley, 1990; Schiamberg, 1988).

Phenylketonuria (PKU). Phenylketonuria is another enzyme deficiency responsible for the in-

---

Pregnancy Risks High Among Blacks

For most white American women, the fear that they will not survive childbirth belonged to their grand-mother's generation. For black American women the risk is very much in the present. According to data gathered in a study done by researchers from the University of Michigan, black women die in childbirth at three times the rate of white women.

In 1983 the national maternal mortality rate was 8.0 per 100,000 live births. For white women the rate was 5.9; for black women the rate was 18.3. Most of these deaths are partially due to poverty, discrimination, and lack of opportunity; many are caused by hypertension, hemorrhage, infection, and other problems that need not be fatal if properly diagnosed and treated.

Source: Mall, J. (1986, August 17). Pregnancy risks high among blacks. *Los Angeles Times*, Part VI, p. 10.

ability to metabolize a specific amino acid. If not treated, retardation may result. PKU symptoms can be alleviated by diet and medication. Most states require that screening tests be administered immediately following birth (Schiamberg, 1988; Papalia & Olds, 1989).

Trisomy-21 or Down's Syndrome. Down's syndrome is the most common genetic disorder. It is caused by the inheritance of three of the number 21 chromosomes, instead of the usual two chromosomes. Approximately one in every 800 babies is born with Down's syndrome. Older parents have a higher risk of bearing a child with Down's syndrome. Babies with Down's syndrome have a variety of physical complications including slanting eyes, shortened bodies, and increased susceptibility to infections. Mental retardation also is characteristic (Schiamberg, 1988; Papalia & Olds, 1989).

Hemophilia. Blood does not clot properly in persons with hemophilia. A blood test can identify carriers with great accuracy (Sills & Henry, 1980).

Genetic counseling is advisable for any person who has a genetic disorder personally or within his or her family. Detailed family histories, chromosomal analyses of the parents, or blood tests help to determine whether prospective parents are carriers of genetic disorders. If a disorder is suspected, a procedure known as *amniocentesis* may be used to ascertain the status of the fetus (Cowley, 1990; Saxton, 1990; Strong & DeVault, 1988).

In amniocentesis, a needle is inserted through the mother's abdominal wall and into the amniotic sac. A small amount of the fluid surrounding the fetus is withdrawn. Because the amniotic fluid contains cells sloughed off by the fetus, it can be examined microscopically and chemically to detect a variety of disorders (Franke, 1982; Sills & Henry, 1980; Strong et al., 1981). Amniocentesis is usually performed at 14 to 16 weeks of pregnancy and results require 2 to 3 weeks.

Many physicians consider amniocentesis a must for women over age 35 because of the increased risk of Down's syndrome. It is also indicated if the couple already have a child with a genetic disorder or if either parent is a carrier of a genetic disorder. Amniocentesis is not recommended as a routine procedure or to satisfy parental curiosity about the gender of the fetus. It does involve small risks to the fetus and the mother and occasionally triggers a spontaneous abortion (miscarriage).

A relatively new procedure called *chorionic villus sampling* involves removal through the cervix of tiny pieces of the membrane surrounding the fetus. Microscopic and chemical analyses of the tissue provide information about the status of the fetus as in amniocentesis. Chorionic villus sampling may be performed at 8 to 12 weeks, but it is not as widely available as amniocentesis and is associated with spontaneous abortions in 1.5% of cases as compared to 0.5% with amniocentesis (Strong & DeVault, 1988).

X-Ray Exposure

The expectant mother should avoid exposure to X-rays early in the pregnancy because the effects on the fetus are likely to be severe. The most common adverse effects include *microcephaly* (a form of mental retardation characterized by a small, pointed head), malformations, stillbirth, miscarriage, and decrease in birth weight.

Maternal Emotions

The emotional state of the mother during pregnancy can influence the developing baby in various ways. Although a pregnant woman cannot escape all stress, severe and prolonged emotional states are associated with pregnancy and birth complications. When the mother experiences such strong emotions as anger or anxiety, her nervous system sends certain chemicals into her bloodstream, which in turn produce changes in the fetal bloodstream and in the fetal activity level. For example, the production of epinephrine in the mother as a function of stress may cause a reduction in the supply of oxygen for the fetus (Stechler & Halton, 1982; Schiamberg, 1988). Emotional disturbances in the mother are associated with increased fetal activity, which is associated with lower birth weight and with greater than average postnatal adjustment difficulties.

Mothers having severe emotional stress during pregnancy from sources such as marriage conflict or the death of a loved one are more likely to have children with Down's syndrome, mental retardation, cleft palate and lip, and infant stomach disorder (Schiamberg, 1988).

Nutrition

Nourishment for the unborn child must come from the maternal bloodstream; therefore, it is essential that the mother's diet contain the necessary nutritional elements. Ideally, a woman should be in good nutritional condition before she becomes pregnant. A lifetime of poor nutrition cannot be remedied overnight, and nutritional deficiencies are difficult to correct during pregnancy as the nutritional demands on the woman's body are increased due to the pregnancy.

What are some of the effects of inadequate nutrition during pregnancy? Malnutrition during pregnancy is associated with premature births, stillbirths, miscarriages, congenital defects, illness during infancy, and small size. It can also result in the child's developing physical problems such as rickets, general physical weakness, cerebral palsy, epilepsy, and extreme nervousness (Schiamberg, 1988). One of the most common causes of fetal death is prolonged maternal malnutrition.

Researchers have also found that the stress of malnutrition during pregnancy disrupts the mother-child relationship because both mother and infant may lack the energy to stimulate each other. As a result the infant may be deprived of interactions that support social and cognitive development (Barrett et al., 1982). Other older studies have demonstrated the association between maternal malnutrition and reduction in intelligence of the child. For example, mothers who had protein or B-vitamin deficiencies during pregnancy had children who had lower IQ test scores and who were having difficulty in school (Churchill, 1968; Hurlock, 1972).

The probability of inadequate nutrition during pregnancy is high among adolescent mothers. The reason is that teenage girls tend to have poor diet habits because of their desire to be slim and the popularity of snack foods.

Many women are concerned about weight gain during pregnancy. The typical pattern of weight gain during pregnancy is shown in Figure 11–2.

The average optimal gain of 22 to 26 pounds can be analyzed in the following way:

Average baby	7 pounds
Placenta	1 pound
Amniotic fluid	2 pounds
Increased weight of uterus	2 pounds
Increased breast tissue	2 pounds
Excess water	6 pounds
Increased blood volume	3 pounds
	23 pounds

Much depends upon the weight of the woman before pregnancy. Thin women and younger women tend to gain more, whereas heavier women tend to gain less in pregnancy. This is certainly not a time for women to try to lose weight, as extreme restriction of calories can be harmful to the baby and the mother.

A well-balanced diet should include protein from lean meats or fish; milk, cheese, and eggs; whole grains or cereals; fresh fruits and vegetables. Women who are concerned about weight gain may select lower-calorie protein sources such as fish and poultry, use skim milk, and substitute fresh fruits for high-calorie desserts and snacks. Most physicians prescribe iron and/or calcium supplements.

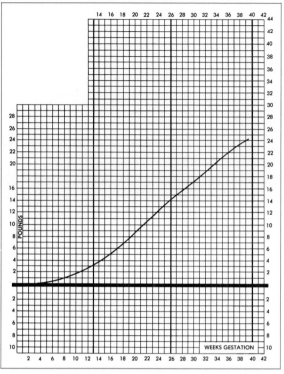

Figure 11–2 Prenatal weight gain. The pattern of weight gain shown on the grid is for a woman of normal weight. Individuals will vary from this pattern somewhat. *Source*: Birch, W. G. (1981). *A doctor discusses pregnancy.* Chicago: Budlong Press, p. 142. Used with permission.

Infectious Diseases

Infectious diseases such as rubella (German or 3-day measles), syphilis, gonorrhea, herpes, or AIDS if contracted during the early months of pregnancy are particularly damaging to the fetus. These diseases can cause mental deficiency, still-births, miscarriages, blindness, deafness, or death (Schiamberg, 1988).

A viral disease called *cytomegalovirus disease* is generally not extremely serious in adults, but it may cause severe consequences if it occurs during pregnancy. If the mother contracts cytomegalovirus disease during the first trimester of pregnancy, fetal death is likely. If contracted later in the preg-

nancy, abnormalities of the brain and eyes are likely (Moore, 1983). Newborns infected before birth may develop pneumonia or severe blood disorders (*Family Health*, 1980). (Infant mortality rates in selected countries are given in Table 11–2. Disease, nutrition, and prenatal care are factors that influence the variation in infant mortality around the world.)

Rh Blood Incompatibility

Incompatibility between the Rh blood types of the mother and baby is responsible for some fetal difficulties. The difficulty arises when the mother's

Table 11–2 Infant Mortality Rates for Selected Countries

Country	Infant Mortality per 1,000 live births
Argentina	35.3
Australia	8.1
Bangladesh	120.0
Canada	8.0
China	33.0
France	8.2
Greece	12.2
Guatemala	66.0
India	96.0
Iraq	63.3
Israel	11.2
Kenya	83.0
Korea (South)	25.0
Mexico	42.0
Norway	7.8
Philippines	56.0
South Africa	
Africans	94.0
Whites	14.9
USSR	25.2
United Kingdom	9.1
United States	10.0

Source: The world almanac and book of facts. (1990). New York: World Almanac.

blood is Rh negative and the baby's blood is Rh positive. The small amounts of the fetal blood that naturally pass through the placenta to the mother's bloodstream cause the mother to produce antibodies in response to the Rh factor. The mother's antibodies then pass back through the placenta to the fetus. These antibodies destroy Rh positive red blood cells in the fetus. This results in anemia, miscarriage, or stillbirth. First babies usually have little or no problems because time and exposure to fe-

tal blood are required for the mother to build a sufficient level of antibodies to damage the fetus.

Couples in which the wife has an Rh negative and the husband an Rh positive blood type are the only couples for whom the Rh blood incompatibility is a potential problem. The Rh blood factor is genetically controlled by one pair of genes, with Rh positive being a dominant trait and Rh negative being recessive. Proper prenatal care requires blood typing for the mother and would detect Rh negative blood type. If the mother is Rh negative, the father's blood type must also be determined to ascertain the probability of Rh blood incompatibility between mother and baby. This combination of an Rh negative woman and Rh positive man occurs in about 12% of American marriages; approximately 18% of children (26,000) born in these marriages have some form of Rh complication (Schiamberg, 1988).

Medical science has greatly reduced the consequences of Rh blood incompatibility. Following the birth of an Rh positive baby, it is possible to give the mother an injection of a special gamma globulin that prevents her from developing her own permanent antibodies. This reduces the risk of damage to future babies. This injection must be given after the birth of every Rh incompatible baby (or miscarriage) and is *not* effective for mothers who have already developed antibodies in a previous pregnancy. Physicians also monitor the antibody level in the mother's bloodstream during pregnancy. If the antibody level begins to get high late in the pregnancy, labor may be induced to prevent or minimize damage to the unborn child. Babies suffering from Rh difficulties can also be protected by intrauterine transfusions and complete blood exchange at birth.

Drugs

The Committee on Drugs of the American Academy of Pediatrics has noted that *no* drug, whether prescription or over-the-counter remedy, has been proven to be safe for the unborn child when used by the mother. For example, a popular drug for acne, Accutane, may severely damage the fetus if used during pregnancy (Oakley, 1988). Many physicians urge pregnant women to avoid the use of all medications unless necessary to treat a serious illness that threatens either mother or child. The use of medications to treat every minor discomfort or complaint is discouraged.

Women who even suspect they are pregnant should tell any physician or dentist treating them for any condition. Many drugs used routinely are not advisable in pregnancy. For example, tetracycline, an antibiotic, damages teeth and bones of the fetus resulting in permanently discolored teeth and stunted growth. Pregnant women are also very susceptible to tetracycline-induced liver damage (Strong et al., 1981).

Extensive use of barbiturates during pregnancy may interfere with the oxygen supply to the fetal brain and result in brain damage and asphyxiation. Thalidomide, a tranquilizer used to treat morning sickness, caused thousands of tragic birth defects in England, Germany, Scandinavia, and Canada in the 1960s (Carlson, 1984). It produced malformations of arms and legs.

Mothers who use heroin, morphine, codeine, or opium (the opiate drugs) on a regular basis have babies who are addicted at birth. Babies of drug-addicted mothers who have drugs withdrawn from them shortly before or at birth are, themselves, soon in withdrawal and may vomit, cry, become hyperactive, tremble, and have rapid respiration (Householder et al., 1982; Papalia & Olds, 1989). Most babies recover from their withdrawal symptoms in about 3 days; however, some die.

Other drugs such as cocaine, PCP, and marijuana should also be avoided in pregnancy. There is increasing research evidence of an association between heavy marijuana use and birth defects (Hingson et al., 1982; Papalia & Olds, 1989). Mothers who used cocaine or alkaloidal cocaine ("crack") during pregnancy had significantly higher rates of preterm delivery, more babies of low birth weight, and more babies with small head circumference (Cherukuri et al., 1988; Chouteau et al., 1988). Babies whose mothers consume cocaine during pregnancy often develop chromosomal problems resulting in congenital abnormalities such as eyes set too far apart. It is thought that these children have been subjected to a number of small strokes prior to birth because of abrupt changes in their mothers' blood pressure with drug use. The use of cocaine is affecting an alarmingly high number of babies. For example, of all babies born in inner-city hospitals in 1989, 25% were born addicted to cocaine (Brazelton, 1989).

The babies of PCP users display muscle-tone difficulties similar to children with cerebral palsy and defective motor ability. One pediatrician noted that the babies of PCP users still cannot get their tongues to coordinate by age 20 to 24 months and try to learn how to walk but appear not to know where their legs are. The lethargy, irritability, and motor difficulties present at birth do not seem to improve (Roark, 1985).

Smoking

Although researchers do not agree on the exact way in which it happens, they do agree that cigarette smoking by pregnant women deprives their fetuses of oxygen (Lindblad et al., 1988; Schiamberg, 1988). The lack of oxygen in the developing fetus has serious consequences including increased risk of spontaneous abortion, premature birth, congenital heart disease, cleft lip and palate, fetal death, or neonatal death (Birch, 1981; Dwyer, 1984). Pregnant women who smoke more than 10 cigarettes a day are more than twice as likely to have babies of low birth weight than mothers who do not smoke (U.S. Department of Health, 1985). Babies born to mothers who smoke are an average of 7.0 ounces lighter than babies of nonsmokers (Dwyer, 1984). The lower-weight babies generally catch up in terms of weight, but there are long-term effects;

7-year-old children of mothers who smoked during pregnancy were shorter in height, tended to have retarded reading ability, and had lower social adjustment than children of nonsmoking mothers (American Cancer Society, 1982).

Alcohol

The impact of maternal alcohol consumption is considerable for both the infants and mothers who are moderate or heavy drinkers (Schiamberg, 1988). Approximately 40% to 50% of children born to mothers who drank excessively in pregnancy have a recognizable set of physical and mental difficulties called *fetal alcohol syndrome* (*FAS*). Infants with FAS tend to be small physically and do not catch up to normal growth; they also show varying degrees of mental deficiency. Many have heart defects, facial abnormalities, poor coordination, and behavioral problems (Brody, 1986; Foster, 1986; March of Dimes, 1980). Furthermore, infants of women addicted to alcohol are also addicted and go through withdrawal symptoms after birth.

The use of even moderate amounts of alcohol by pregnant women is discouraged as well. The children of moderate or social drinkers have problems such as lower levels of infant arousal, increased time spent in a nonalert state, deficits in sucking responses, and learning and behavior difficulties (Brody, 1986; Streissguth et al., 1983). The National Institute on Alcohol Abuse and Alcoholism considers more than two drinks per day to be a significant risk. Two drinks are defined as two mixed drinks (1.5 ounces of hard liquor in each), two glasses of wine, or 24 ounces of beer (Birch, 1981). And as little as two drinks per *week* may do damage (Brody, 1986).

Maternal Age

Today a growing number of women are having babies later in life, after they have established themselves in a career and feel ready to take some time to concentrate on motherhood. But women are affected by biological constraints. The optimum age for pregnancy seems to be between the ages of 20 and 35 (Schiamberg, 1988). Fertility is greatest in a woman's twenties. There is a higher frequency of birth defects, miscarriages, stillbirths, and premature deaths among mothers below the age of 20 and over the age of 35. Before the age of 20, a woman's reproductive system is not fully matured and the production of hormones has not reached optimum levels. Women over 35 are more likely to experience endocrine disorders and declining reproductive systems. A woman's ova are all in place at her birth; she produces no new ova. Consequently, the ova of older women have been subjected to years of stress from pollution, chemicals, medications, and/or radiation. As a result, they are more likely to have chromosomal or other defects. The highest proportion of children with Down's syndrome are born to mothers over 40 (see Table 11–3). Older mothers have somewhat higher rates of Caesarian section delivery and infant mortality (Friede et al., 1988; Mansfield & Cohn, 1986).

Table 11–3 Rate of Down's Syndrome and Maternal Age

Mother's Age	Rate
20	1 per 1,923
25	1 per 1,299
30	1 per 885
35	1 per 365
40	1 per 109
43	1 per 53
45	1 per 32
47	1 per 20
49	1 per 12

Source: Excerpted from Goodman, R. M. (1986). *Planning for a healthy baby.* New York: Oxford. Used with permission.

Labor and Birth

Pregnancy and the prenatal development of the child culminate with birth approximately 266 days after conception. Certain changes take place for the mother a few weeks before birth in preparation for delivery. One of these changes is that the fetus drops to a position lower in the mother's abdomen approximately 3 or 4 weeks before delivery. Another change that prepares the mother for delivery is a softening of her cervix. Just before labor begins, there is often a small, slightly bloody discharge caused by the expelling of the plug of mucus that has been blocking the opening of the cervix. The amniotic membranes enclosing the fetus break during labor in order to make the delivery possible. In about 10% of pregnant women these membranes rupture before labor begins; this is signaled by a flow of amniotic fluid from the vagina. Labor usually starts within 24 hours after these membranes have broken. If labor does not begin during this time, there is a risk of infection and the mother needs to be hospitalized for observation.

Stages of Labor

The work the mother does in giving birth to the child is called *labor*. True labor is indicated by regular uterine contractions that get closer together and become more intense. The process of labor may be divided into three stages.

First Stage of Labor. The first stage of labor is the longest and involves the opening of the cervix until it is wide enough for the baby to pass through. The cervix is a thick, narrow band of muscle and fibrous tissue that forms the opening of the uterus. During the first stage of labor the cervix thins and widens from less than 2.0 centimeters to about 10.0 centimeters (Schiamberg, 1988). Because the cervix is made of muscle, it is potentially quite elastic and capable of stretching. In situations in which the mother is fearful or tense, however, the muscles

may tend to tighten and cause her discomfort to increase.

Because the first stage of labor takes the longest, it is helpful to divide it into three substages.

1. *Early labor.* During this time the cervix dilates to about 3.0 centimeters. Contractions are mild and may be 5 to 20 minutes apart. The amniotic membranes may rupture if they have not already done so. Most women remain at home or at work during this phase. Resting or continuing light activities is recommended. Toward the end of this phase, the couple go to the hospital.

2. *Active labor.* As the cervix dilates from 3.0 to 7.0 centimeters, contractions become stronger and closer together. Specific relaxation techniques as are taught in prepared childbirth classes are helpful. Medication can be given to ease discomfort.

3. *Transition phase.* Dilation is completed as contractions become more intense and closer together. This phase is the most uncomfortable for most women. Relaxation techniques and breathing exercises are helpful.

Second Stage of Labor. The second stage continues from the time of complete dilation of the cervix until the baby is delivered. This stage may last a few hours or a few minutes: the average length of time for first births is 1.5 hours, with second births taking only half as long.

Rhythmic contractions of the uterus during the second stage of labor gradually bring the baby out, a push at a time. The mother can assist by gently bearing down and pushing with her diaphragm and abdominal muscles, thereby reinforcing the uterine contractions. This type of cooperation speeds the delivery. The baby emerges head first in most cases. Following delivery, mucus and fluids are cleared from the baby's mouth and nose, and he or she begins to breathe—usually with a protesting cry. The umbilical cord is clamped and cut, and the baby is wrapped or placed in a warming crib and identified (Birch, 1981).

Third Stage of Labor. The third stage of labor takes place after the baby has been delivered and is called the *afterbirth*. This stage involves the necessary expelling of the placenta and membranes. It usually occurs 5 to 15 minutes after the baby is delivered and takes only a few minutes.

At this time the physician repairs any tears of the perineum (the skin and deeper tissues between the

vaginal and anal orifices) that may have occurred during delivery. In order to prevent such tears of the perineum, an episiotomy is performed by many physicians. An *episiotomy* is a surgical incision of the perineum made to facilitate the passage of the infant's head. If an episiotomy has been performed, the physician sews up the incision during this stage. For several days following delivery, these stitches cause discomfort and itching; however, episiotomy incisions usually heal more quickly and with fewer complications than do tears of the perineum (Birch, 1981).

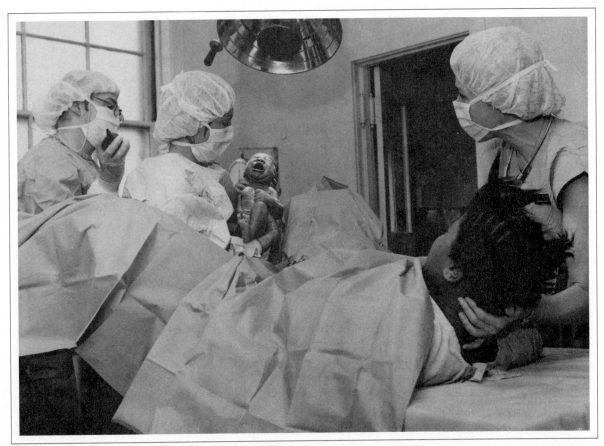

March of Dimes

Caesarian Section Births

Under certain conditions a vaginal delivery may not be advisable; these include an extremely narrow pelvis in the mother, a placenta placed very low in the uterus near the cervix (placenta previa), the placenta detaching itself from the uterine wall, abnormal positioning of the baby, toxemia or herpes in the mother, or indications during labor that the baby is in distress. In these situations, a Caesarian section delivery is used.

The rate of Caesarian deliveries has risen from 5.5 per 100 deliveries in 1970 to 20.3 per 100 deliveries in 1983 (U.S. Department of Commerce, 1985). The surgery itself for a Caesarian delivery is not complicated; the uterus and abdomen are opened, and the baby is removed. Today it is possible for the mother to discuss with her physician if she wants a spinal rather than a general anesthetic so she can be awake for the birth. And in some cases, fathers may stay with the mother during the birth. Caesarian section deliveries are only slightly riskier than normal births (Schiamberg, 1988).

Prepared Childbirth

If you have never skied before, you may be able to put on a pair of skis and somehow make it down a hill. But you'll avoid a lot of pain and anxiety if you prepare yourself beforehand by learning how to move and hold the poles. The same holds true for childbirth. (Sills & Henry, 1980)

Beginning in the 1960s, women became educated to the realities of childbirth and began to want control over events involving their bodies. Women and physicians began to be aware of the dangers of heavy medication during birth for mothers and infants, and more women began to ask for options in birthing. Prior to the 1960s, the extensive use of medications and anesthesia in childbirth had been routine.

Responsible physicians recognize the dangers of medication during the birth process: sedative and pain-relieving drugs used in labor transfer to the baby. Their effects upon newborns include respiratory distress, depressed heart rate, poor muscle tone, and decreased sucking response.

Although the term *natural childbirth* has been used to describe childbirth with minimal medication, the term misleads some women into feeling that they have failed if they do not have fast, easy deliveries without medication. Birth *is* a natural process; however, it is also challenging, and some women do require medication to ease their pain. Being informed as to how certain drugs may affect her and her unborn child help a woman to make wiser choices in the event she needs medication.

Prepared childbirth is a better description of what most women and physicians hope to achieve. Dr. Grantly Dick-Read was a pioneer in promoting techniques that women could learn to make birth less painful, healthier, and a more positive experience. Dick-Read (1955) surmised, "The best way of avoiding unnecessary pain is to understand what occurs during labor and how to meet the changes" (p. 15). He recommended exercises and breathing techniques to learn relaxation and control for labor.

Dr. Fernand Lamaze's concept was to condition women for labor by teaching them to respond to contractions with specific sets of breathing patterns. The woman's concentration on her breathing would focus her attention away from her discomfort and would allow her to be in control of the process.

More recently, Dr. Frederick Leboyer has added to the idea of making birth a more pleasant experience by emphasizing the need to make it less harsh for the infant. He stresses welcoming the infant into the world with a quiet, dark room; placing the baby on the mother's abdomen after birth; not cutting the umbilical cord until the baby is breathing readily on its own; bathing the infant in warm water soon after birth; and stroking the baby gently (Wolfe & Goldsmith, 1980).

Prepared childbirth classes have become very popular and are offered by most hospitals. Although the specific formats may vary, most include:

1. Education about the birth process, often with films, photographs, and models.
2. Techniques for breathing and relaxation to be used during labor.
3. Exercises to keep the body in good physical condition for the demands of labor.

The fathers of the babies or friends of the mothers-to-be attend classes with them. They serve as coaches during labor, helping the mothers with breathing, relaxation, and comfort. The coach may rub the mother's back, help her to change positions, remind her about breathing techniques, and offer encouragement and support.

Birthing Arrangements

In recent years, the usual arrangement for childbirth has been to use a hospital labor room for labor and to move to a delivery room for the actual birth. Many hospitals now offer birthing rooms. These are furnished to look more like a bedroom in a home than a hospital room. Mother and father are in one room for labor and delivery. They may choose relaxing music and soft lighting; occasionally grandparents and older children may be present for labor and/or delivery. In some cases, the physician may allow the father to assist in the delivery.

Many hospitals have adopted suggestions from Leboyer and from other cultures. Newborns are no longer whisked off to the nursery; many are offered to their mothers to be cuddled or nursed for a while. Some hospitals offer rooming-in arrange-

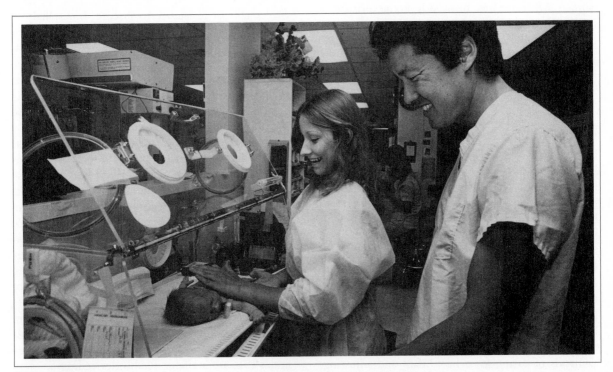

Walker Montgomery

ments in which the baby and mother stay in the same room. Delivery tables have been replaced in some hospitals by birthing chairs or modified delivery tables/beds that allow a variety of positions for the mother (i.e., reclining, sitting, squatting).

Home Births. Although 98% to 99% of American babies are born in hospitals (Strong & DeVault, 1986), birthing at home is attractive to some women because it offers privacy and lower cost. Very importantly, however, it is not recommended for women who have *any* risk factors in their pregnancies. Most physicians are reluctant to attend births at home because they are apprehensive about unanticipated difficulties.

Midwives. The use of a midwife to deliver a baby is another alternative that is attractive to some women. Midwives may be used in home births and in some hospital births. Some midwives are trained by other midwives and are referred to as *lay midwives*; others are trained as registered nurses, with additional training in obstetrical techniques and are called *certified nurse-midwives* (Strong & DeVault, 1988).

Many couples feel that the use of a midwife makes the birth process seem more natural and less of a medical "problem." Couples considering the use of a midwife need to be sure that no risk factors are involved in the pregnancy. Check the credentials of the midwife and determine what types of backup services are available in the event of an emergency (Levinson, 1980).

Care after Birth. In the past women rested in bed for more than a week following delivery, but the emphasis now is on early activity. New mothers are encouraged to get out of bed soon after giving birth and often go home within 24 hours, though the average hospital stay is 2 to 5 days. Because the demands of caring for a new infant and adjusting to new roles are challenging, most couples bene-

fit from some assistance at home for a few days or weeks. This usually comes from friends or family members.

Feeding the Baby

Whether to breast-feed or bottle-feed the new baby is a question of concern to most American mothers. About half (58%) choose to breast-feed (Wootan, 1985). Those who choose to bottle-feed may do so because of physical constraints limiting their ability to breast-feed, because of the need to leave the baby to return to work, or because of personal reasons.

Breast-feeding has several advantages for both infants and mothers. Babies who are breast-fed are more resistant and immune to disease. Even before delivery, the breasts produce *colostrum*, a yellowish liquid high in antibodies that give the baby the benefit of resistance to disease. Breast-fed babies tend to exhibit very positive patterns of weight gain, physiological reactions, and body composition. Mother's milk is more easily digested, so breast-fed infants have fewer intestinal disturbances such as colic and constipation (Birch, 1981; Strong et al., 1981). Additionally, the baby benefits by close physical contact with the mother.

Breast-feeding has advantages for the mother as well. The mother who nurses her baby returns more quickly to her prepregnant state because nursing stimulates the uterus to contract to its nonpregnant size. Several months of nursing seem to improve the firmness and shape of breasts of women whose breasts tend to have much fatty tissue. Close physical contact with their infants coupled with the affirmation of their ability to nurture and nourish another gives many women a sense of well-being.

Regardless of which method is chosen, women may feel comfortable: babies thrive with both. Because of our technological sophistication, the formulas that are available for bottle-feeding are very similar to human milk. And women who bottle-

Fathers Feel Pregnant, Too

Some fathers-to-be gain weight while their partners are pregnant; others admit to being jealous and feeling left out. Others have nausea, vomiting, abdominal cramps or bloating, backaches, colds, or other symptoms that cannot be explained objectively. Some 11% to 65% of men with pregnant partners experience "sympathetic" symptoms of pregnancy (Clinton, 1987; Lipkin & Lamb, 1982; White & Bulloch, 1980).

Because of their increased involvement in pregnancy and delivery—attending childbirth classes and serving as childbirth coaches, for example—American males may be experiencing a syndrome called *couvade*, after the French word meaning to hatch or to brood. Couvade is not unique to American males; it occurs around the world. In certain groups in South America and the Philippines and among the Hopi, men follow work restrictions, prohibitions against killing animals, rest patterns, or dietary practices while their partners are pregnant (Strong & DeVault, 1988).

Sources: 1. Clinton, J. F. (1987). Physical and emotional responses of expectant fathers throughout pregnancy and the early postpartum period. *International Journal of Nursing Studies, 24,* 59–68. 2. Lipkin, M., & Lamb, G. (1982). The couvade syndrome: An epidemiologic study. *Annals of Internal Medicine, 96,* 509–511. 3. Strong, B., & DeVault, C. (1988). *The marriage and family experience.* St. Paul: West. 4. White, K. L., & Bulloch, P. (1980). *Health of populations.* New York: Rockefeller.

feed reap the psychological benefits by holding and cuddling their babies during feeding (Birch, 1981).

Fathers

In most cases, the mother-to-be is part of a couple. The father-to-be has a role to play in the prenatal development of his child, too. His primary job is the care and support of his partner through pregnancy. Results of one study indicated that women locked in stormy marriages run a higher risk of bearing a psychologically damaged child (Verny & Kelly, 1982). Research also indicates that the quality of the marriage relationship is a major influence on postpartum adjustment; the more positive the relationship, the more positive the postpartum period (Valentine, 1982).

A husband may help his wife and child by attending childbirth classes, by coaching her through labor, and by being present for the delivery. Fathers who are present during delivery report childbirth as an important experience for them (May & Perrin, 1985).

Some new fathers may feel overwhelmed at their new responsibilities and role demands. They may not be prepared for parenting roles, increased financial burdens, or changes in their marital relationship. Strong & DeVault (1988) suggest that fathers who are involved in the care, cuddling, bathing, dressing, and feeding of their infants "experience family from within rather than as a burdened provider" from without.

Adjustments to Birth of a Child

Pregnancy is a lengthy, gradual process of preparation for the arrival of a child. Once the baby is born, however, the husband and wife find them-

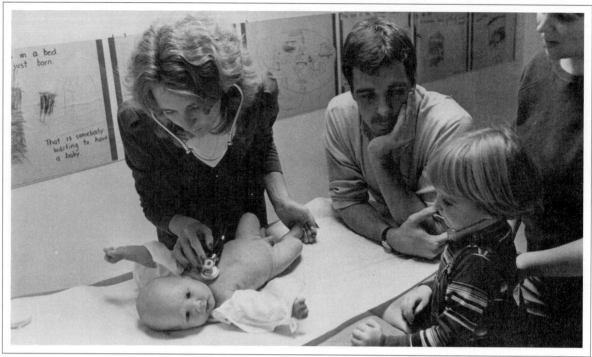

Joel Gordon

selves abruptly assuming the role of parents. This new role is a 24-hour endeavor from which there is little respite. The transition to parenthood brings alterations in the lives of the new parents, and couples do not always anticipate the nature of these changes.

Relationships

The birth of a child changes the marriage relationship simply because a third person is introduced into the family. Before the advent of a child, husband and wife normally give full attention to each other, considering themselves, their desires, and their needs in everyday life. With the birth of a baby, the couple no longer enjoy each other's *undivided* attention. A child's needs and interests often conflict with those of the parents, and parents must spend long hours in tending to a baby's needs.

Physical Demands

The basic physical care of a newborn is demanding: feeding, washing, changing diapers, rocking, and cleaning seem to go on in a continual flow. One new mother wrote:

> *The first big shock was how weak and tired I was after delivery (never having been ill before). I was physically unable to do what I wanted to. I had a lot of help after I got home. (Sollie & Miller, 1980, p. 158)*

A father asked to comment on the first few days noted he was, "Too tired for any meaningful statements." Another mother noted:

> *Because an infant is so demanding there are days when one wishes the baby did not exist. Knowing*

that these things are normal, however, makes coping with the day-to-day routine possible. (Sollie & Miller, 1980, p. 158)

Most parents are very tired by the daily round of caring for a baby, especially in the early months. Exhaustion and loss of sleep are widespread problems of new mothers. Newborns often need to eat every 3 to 4 hours around the clock, and housekeeping and laundry chores are increased by the arrival of a baby.

Disruption of Daily Routines

General disruption of the couple's daily routine occurs with the coming of a baby. Babies sleep and eat when they feel like it, and adults must adjust *their* schedules. One mother noted:

I love to sleep late—until 8 A.M. or so, but since we've had the baby I've had to change. He wakes up hungry and howling at 6 A.M. And I don't know how he seems to know just when we're ready to sit down to dinner. I wonder some days if I'll recognize hot food whenever I have some again!

Curtailment of Social Life

Although most parents enjoy their infants and want to be with them as much as possible, parents need some time apart from the baby. Some parents encounter difficulty in arranging time to be apart from their child. Babysitters may be hard to find and are expensive, and extra effort in planning to go out is required. One father said that having a baby "decreases freedom to go at will." And one mother wrote:

My husband continues to go on about his routine and plans his evenings for activities as he has always done—only now instead of going with him as I had previously done or making plans of my own—I stay at home to take care of the baby. I feel resentment a lot of times, but I have always seemed to be able to

cope with my feelings so far. (Sollie & Miller, 1980, p. 159)

Another mother of three commented:

Because we had neither grandparents nor close friends nearby, I seldom left my baby for the first few months. I just did not trust a teenage sitter. This was unfortunate as I resented being tied down. New mothers need to find someone experienced with young ones and to get out as early as four weeks after the baby arrives. It does the mother a world of good and is ultimately better for the baby and their relationship.

Career Changes

The most negative aspect of having a baby for me has been giving up my career of teaching. I enjoyed my job tremendously, and I miss it. At this point I do not feel fulfilled in my role as a mother. At times I feel frustrated and slightly depressed, but I know that I couldn't do a good job of handling the many responsibilities that go along with being a full-time teacher as well as being a good mother and homemaker. (Sollie & Miller, 1980, p. 163)

For many women who have been employed before a baby arrives, the loss of a career or job is a major adjustment. They miss the world of work and adult conversations; life at home with a small child can be very isolating. The strains caused by the loss of income when the wife stops working may lead to conflict. Fathers in one study were more likely to comment on this than mothers. One man reported that the birth of his child had caused "some financial concerns," and another commented, "Our income was cut in half" (Sollie & Miller, 1980).

In situations in which the wife is earning more than her husband, it may be financially better if he takes on the major role of child care while she remains in her job. Many women enjoy part-time employment as a compromise between returning to full-time work or full-time staying home.

Positive Changes

Although many parents feel the transition to parenthood is uncomfortable in many respects, most feel that having a child is well worth the adjustments, and most *do* adjust.

Shortly after the birth of his child one father said:

> *He has given me some moments of extreme happiness, like when he smiled at me for the first time. He does grow more enjoyable each week, and I appreciate him more as he develops. (Sollie & Miller, 1980, p. 151)*

Another father said:

> *I can't fully express the fullness of joy I have with him. It is a magnificent blessing, increasing the love I give and feel that I receive. (Sollie & Miller, 1980, p. 151)*

And although a mother spoke of the responsibilities of parenthood, she noted:

> *The rewards for all the efforts and hard work are well worth the trouble. The look in a child's eyes as he or she looks at you makes a warm feeling go through you. Love flows through those eyes and hands that reach out for Mama or Daddy. A child can make a drab working day into an enjoyable evening with just a look, a smile, and hurried crawling toward Mama. (Sollie & Miller, 1980, p. 150)*

Summary

- Deciding whether or not to have children, when to have them, how many to have, and how far apart to space them are all very personal choices made for very different reasons.

- Optimal conditions for the childbearing experience occur when (a) the child is wanted by both partners, (b) the mother is between 20 and 35, (c) there are no family histories of genetic problems, (d) both partners are in good health, and (e) both partners are prepared emotionally, financially, and intellectually for a child. Although many single parents manage beautifully, rearing children is easier if there are two parents.

- Early diagnosis of pregnancy and initiation of prenatal care will help to ensure successful prenatal development by providing the best environment for the baby before birth.

- Prenatal development occurs in three stages: the fertilization-implantation period, the embryo period, and the fetal period. Factors that influence development during these stages include: genetic disorders, X-ray exposure, maternal emotions, maternal nutrition, infectious diseases, Rh blood incompatibility, drugs and alcohol, smoking, and maternal age.

- Choices regarding childbirth techniques stress education of and involvement by both partners. These choices include the Lamaze and Leboyer techniques, birthing rooms, home births, and midwives. A couple must also choose between bottle-feeding and breast-feeding for their baby.

- When a new baby arrives, a family must make many adjustments; there are relationship changes, physical demands, disruption of daily routine and social life, and changes in career status for some. Although this transition may be difficult, most people feel the benefits of parenthood are well worth the adjustments.

Discussion Questions

1. If you were permitted to have your husband with you at the time of the birth of your baby, would you want him with you? If you were permitted to be with your wife at the time of the birth of your baby, would you want to be with her?

2. Evidence indicates that the period during a marriage when a husband is most likely to engage in an extramarital sexual encounter is during the last trimester of his wife's pregnancy. Because this causes so much pain in the relationship, how can this best be prevented?

3. What are some of the positive aspects of pregnancy? Some of the negative aspects?

4. A young woman who is unable to have children is in love with a man 10 years older than she, who very much wishes to be married and have children. Should she tell him the truth?

5. The era of test-tube babies and surrogate mothers is here. What do you see as the advantage and the problems of these pregnancy developments?

6. What options would you want to consider if amniocentesis revealed the likelihood of a genetic disorder?

7. What do you consider the most important reasons for having children?

8. How were children in your family spaced? What advantages and disadvantages did you experience because of the spacing?

9. Examine the infant mortality rates given in Table 11–2. What factors account for the wide variation in the rates?

10. What changes can our society make to reduce the rate of infant mortality in this country?

CHAPTER 12

RELATIONSHIPS WITH CHILDREN

Nothing—not politics, religion, science, or art—would be the same if men spent more of their lives in the infants' and toddlers' world. One cannot help but wonder how differently some of our political leaders might act if they had ever spent time caring for children ... cleaning, feeding, dressing, and loving them. Instead men are cut off from children, both by personal fears and by our culture's mores. We lose touch with life's beginnings, and our own. It requires almost an act of rebellion for men to discover and to admit that an infant can reveal to a full grown man a new level of loving, something I have been able to share with him that I hadn't been allowed with anyone else.

(Gerzon, 1982, p. 208).

The Challenge of Parenthood

The great majority of married couples in the United States will eventually become parents. The consequences of this fact are serious and far-reaching and at the time of marriage are not considered by most couples. Many people assume that they will learn parenting skills easily *after* they become parents. Yet parenthood involves some of the most important challenges that most people ever experience.

In the past, research in the area of parent-child relationships was almost exclusively focused on the way parents influenced their children. Such a view was simplistic, for we now know that many people in addition to parents serve to shape the behavior of children in significant ways. Equally impor-

tant, the child's own unique personality affects his or her parents in ways that can make the difference in the total realm of family relationships and even in whether a marriage endures or not. Thus, the family is a unit of interacting personalities—not only do adults contribute to the development of children, but children influence the ease with which one can be an effective parent.

The Myths of Parenthood

Myth 1. Rearing Children Contributes Much to Marital Satisfaction. Marital happiness declines with the birth of children, continues to remain lower throughout child rearing, and then increases to near prechildbearing levels during the postparental phases of the life cycle. Research has

Susan Lapides/Design Conceptions

consistently demonstrated that the presence of children produces role strain that has a negative effect upon a couple's marital relationship (Cole, 1984). This does not mean, however, that marriages suffer terribly or that parents do not value their children. Most find that children contribute richly to their satisfaction in life, for they serve to maintain family legacies and provide hope that better things can come about in future generations.

Myth 2. Children Will Turn Out Well If the Parent-Child Relationship Is Good.

Parents who believe that if they do the "right" things, they will have happy, productive children underestimate the number of factors that influence the development of children. A child's temperament, peers, grandparents, teachers, television, religious institutions, and school systems significantly affect children. Thus, child guidance involves more than managing the parent-child relationship: it involves childhood management, or the supervision of all of the influences to which children are exposed. The complexity of this process can be seen in the example of a child who has a wonderful teacher yet who is in a school system that stimulates anxiety and fear. Too, a teacher who is a good fit with one child in the family may be a poor fit with another child. Managing parent-child relationships is only one part of the process of parenting, and managing a childhood can be achieved with only partial success because every child grows up in a cultural system over which parents have limited control. Thus, not all children who have good parents turn out well; conversely, children from families in which the parenting skills are far from ideal may grow into adulthood happy and productive (Pocs, 1989).

Myth 3. Everyone Can Adjust to Parenthood.

The belief that families can learn to adjust to *any* eventuality is not supported in the literature. For example, parents of developmentally delayed children have divorce rates three times greater than parents of normal children, they experience high desertion rates, and they have suicide rates double the national average. Of those couples who remain together, many (a) diminish their circle of acquaintances and contacts with close relatives, (b) change their friends, (c) terminate joint leisure activities, (d) belong to fewer organizations, (e) attend church less often, (f) visit less with neighbors, friends, and relatives, and (g) have poor sexual adjustments. This does not mean that parents with developmentally delayed children cannot achieve happiness; rather it means that new skills are required. Many people who have been subjected to stress overcome adversity and are strong, happy people. Even with very normal children, people are different in their ability to cope, to be patient, and to be loving. Some couples believe that parenthood is too demanding for them (Price-Bonham & Addison, 1978).

Myth 4. Advances in Modern Medicine and Knowledge about Child Development Have Made Child Rearing Easier.

There are direct benefits today from advances in the medical care of children; diphtheria, polio, smallpox, and other childhood ailments that used to cause the death of young children have been eliminated. Mothers, too, have benefited from advances in the areas of prenatal care and women's health. Yet because of family mobility, parents today receive less help from their extended families in bringing up their children than in the past and face new problems as the result of more complex societal expectations.

Myth 5. There Is One Correct Way to Rear Children.

Parents often experience anxiety over whether they are guiding their children well. Although there is evidence that certain child rearing styles are associated with more positive social and emotional adjustment in children than others, it should be remembered that such findings apply to the groups of people that have been studied and may not apply to a specific parent and child and

Attitudes Toward Children Throughout History

1. In ancient Babylonia, a child was considered the property of his father and could be sold, exchanged, or killed by him.

2. Under the Hebrew Code, a father had the right to kill his children. Ancient Hebrews were not tolerant of disrespectful children, and it was understood that children who cursed their fathers or mothers were to be put to death.

3. In the early history of Greece, parents were permitted to kill their children. Daughters were considered an inconvenience. During the second century in one locality in Greece, only 1% of 600 families raised more than one daughter.

4. Under Roman doctrine, a father was permitted to sell, mutilate, or kill his children.

5. The practice of killing infants did not end with the fall of the ancient civilizations. During the Middle Ages, for example, ratios of men to women—an indication of the use of infanticide—were reported to be 1.56 to 1 and 1.72 to 1 in different localities.

6. The burial of children in the foundations of buildings continued from the Middle Ages until 1843 in Germany. Dead infants were still a common sight in London during the 1890's.

7. In the early days of England, a father was permitted to sell his son into slavery.

8. Fathers were permitted, in both the English and early American law, to labor their children. In England, in the early 1800's, some children worked 16 hours a day. Some were chained with irons to prevent their running away. The system of apprenticeship, which bound children to masters for 7 years, was used in both England and the United States.

9. Unquestioned obedience was expected of children. Martin Luther noted that it was the highest duty of parents to "break the will" of their children in order to make room for God's will. Luther wrote, "I would rather have a dead son than a disobedient one." It was the emphasis on obedience that provided the justification for the beatings to which children were subjected prior to the twentieth century.

10. How could such abuse of children be tolerated by the law? There were formerly two lines of authority in the United States by which the law limited parental beatings of children. In some jurisdictions, parents could not be criminally liable for beating their children unless permanent injury resulted or malice, hatred, passion, or anger were proven. It was irrelevant whether the punishment was unreasonably or excessively severe. The other standard limiting parental liability required that the beating inflicted upon the child be shown to be unreasonable.

11. Quoting the *Massachusetts Stubborn Child Law:* "If a man have a stubborn or rebellious son of sufficient years of understanding, viz., which will not obey the voice of his father or the voice of his mother … such a son shall be put to death." An updated version of the Massachusetts law was still being enforced in 1971 with the maximum punishment reduced to 6 months imprisonment and a $200 fine. In 1973 the law was finally repealed.

12. A review of the child-rearing literature by de Mause revealed that a very large percentage of the children born prior to the 18th century were what today would be termed battered children.

13. Today, *all* corporal punishment is banned in Sweden whereas only seven of the United States by 1985 had banned corporal punishment in the public schools. Local prosecutors in the U.S. are generally quite reluctant to file charges for child maltreatment unless the abuse is unusually severe.

14. Over ninety percent of American adults in 1970 had been subjected to corporal punishment as children, and approximately the same percentage of today's children face the same treatment.

Source: Herman, Dean M. (1985). A statutory proposal to prohibit the infliction of violence upon children. *Family Law Quarterly, 19*(1), 1–52. Adapted with permission.

Resilient Children

Even in the most terrible homes, some children develop healthy personalities and display a remarkable degree of resilience, i.e., the ability to recover from or adjust easily to misfortune or sustained life stress.

Resilient Children Have Four Characteristics in Common:

1. An active, evocative approach toward solving life's problems, enabling them to negotiate successfully an abundance of emotionally hazardous experiences.
2. A tendency to perceive their experiences constructively, even if they involved pain or suffering.
3. The ability, from infancy on, to gain other people's positive attention. They find a great deal of emotional support outside their family.
4. A strong ability to use faith in order to maintain a positive vision of a meaningful life.

Ways to Encourage the Development of Resiliency:

1. Accept children's idiosyncrasies and allow them some experiences that challenge, but do not overwhelm, their coping abilities.
2. Convey to children a sense of responsibility and caring. Reward them for helpfulness and cooperation.
3. Encourage children to engage in activities that contribute to their self-esteem.
4. Model a belief that life makes sense despite the difficulties that everyone encounters.
5. Encourage children to develop a network of significant others—relatives and friends—that will help to make their lives meaningful.

Source: Adapted from 1. O'Connell-Higgins, R. (1983). Psychological resilience and the capacity for intimacy. Qualifying paper, Harvard Graduate School of Education. 2. Warner, E. E. (1984). Resilient children. *Young Children, 40* (1), 68–72.

their special circumstances. A permissive method that is successful with one parent and child may not be successful with another, for example.

Myth 6. Parents Should Be Able to Control Their Children so that Their Children Will Do What Is Right. Parents whose primary focus in rearing children is to get them to do the things that they consider "right," rather than on developing a loving relationship that is characterized by warm, supportive guidance, are likely to incur difficulty. Children are guided by their own goals, motivations, and aspirations. Each child has a unique inheritance and may behave in a manner that is different than parents wish. Parents whose motives are to produce "stars" may find that they have failed in having a child who has learned to be happy. Couples who have not had experience with children may be frustrated because of unrealistic expectations—especially with a first child. As they become more experienced, they generally become more sensitive in allowing their children greater freedom. Parenting practices that support development of an *internal locus of control*, i.e., behavior that is guided by the child's motivation rather than by an *external locus of control*, i.e., behavior that is guided by the motivations of parents and others, require that the parent sometimes "lose the battle in order to win the war." This means that if parents wish to rear children to be independent and to think for themselves, they cannot expect their children always to give in to their parents' wishes. Parents who remember that one of the greatest gifts they can give their children is to enjoy them soon develop confidence because of the way children respond to warm, loving, caring attention.

Myth 7. If Parents Make Mistakes in Their Parenting Responsibilities, there Will Be Residual Effects that Will Cause Difficulties in Their Children Later. Some children are easier to rear than others because they are placid and compliant. Resistant children may shake the confidence of anyone, even though most parents are reasonably successful. In looking back, however, all parents can pinpoint things they would have done differently. Yet most children are resilient, and many who have been treated badly profit from their parents' mistakes when they become parents. Occasional mistakes, if they occur in a loving, accepting relationship, will not have lasting effects. Children remember the "big" picture, the overall tone of their family life—not specific lapses in parental competence. Children who are abused either physically or psychologically over a prolonged period of time, however, may develop problems that will negatively affect their future.

Love Is Not Enough

As Bettleheim (1950) described in *Love Is Not Enough* four decades ago, child rearing involves considerably more than loving children. Some people who love their children abuse them physically and psychologically in an effort to control their behavior. If a child has the courage to retaliate, parents may rebound with increased amounts of pressure with the explanation that if they did not love them, they would not resort to such strong measures. The child may be left either physically or psychologically "whipped" and convinced that he or she cannot cope with the world without defeat. Serious emotional problems are not generally produced by occasional mistakes that occur within a healthy parent-child relationship, but serious psychological problems can result from destructive, unhealthy relationships over a period of time.

A balanced, relaxed, and positive approach is most helpful as parents face the task of child rearing. Although methods of child rearing that work for some persons may not be effective for others, children who are wanted, respected, and appreciated may be expected to develop reasonably well (Cox, 1981; Pocs, 1989).

Criteria for the Selection of Child Care

Whether by choice or necessity, more women than ever before are participating in the labor force. Slightly over 61% of all women with children under the age of 18 and 48 % of all women with children under 6 are now employed outside the home (Alexander, 1984), and their numbers are increasing. One important task for these mothers is to find a satisfactory child-care arrangement. This may take the form of a relative or friend who cares for the child while the mother works; a babysitter or "nanny" who comes into the home; home-based day care, in which an individual's home becomes the setting in which the children of others are cared for; center-based day care; or institutionally based day care, in which a large business such as a hospital or other corporation provides day care for the children of its workers.

The quality of day care is of tremendous importance. How well a child responds to day care psy-

My Brother

As a child, I witnessed the agonizing day-to-day torment of my older brother as we were raised by two unhappy parents. The psychological suffering he endured was by far the most damaging.

He tried to fight back in various ways: I saw him stand up to his so-called father when he was 9 years old, only to be mocked, laughed at, beaten down, and humiliated. I saw him beat up the local school bully. I was impressed by his above-average grades. It was a valiant effort, but he faced it alone. As the oldest child he had no one to look up to, no one to tell him he was worth something.

There was one moment when he was 15 years old that I'll never forget. On a hot quiet summer night I woke with a start. In his bed on the other side of the room my brother was crying. It was the most despairing, forlorn sound I've ever heard. It came from the bottom of his soul. It frightened me. Now I understand the meaning of that dreadful sound. It was his death cry. He literally gave up. He turned from a fighter to a vegetable. He is 35 years old now: he shuns friends and social activities; he is emotionally indifferent; except for odd jobs, he is a total recluse.

Competent child-raising is the most important force behind an enlightened and happy society. I fully support any efforts to make parents and would-be parents aware of society's resolve that the rights of children be respected. I support any and all programs that would motivate or pressure parents to do a more effective job.

Unsigned
Ohio

Source: The Futurist, February 1979, p. 73, published by the World Future Society, 4916 St. Elmo Avenue, Washington, DC 20014. Used with permission.

chologically and intellectually and how it affects the child's relationship with his or her parents is greatly determined by the *quality* of care provided (Belsky, 1984a; Gamble & Zigler, 1986). In addition, a working mother's job satisfaction has been related to her satisfaction with her child-care arrangements (Bradbard & Endsley, 1986). What makes up high-quality day care? Research has been devoted to the effects of group size, caregiver-child ratio, caregiver training and experience, and licensure/regulation (Belsky, 1984a). Most important, however, is the relationship between the caregiver and the child. The same growth-facilitating care that characterizes a healthy home environment for children (e.g., positive affection, verbal interaction, inductive discipline, firm control, high maturity demands) also characterizes quality day care (Belsky, 1984a). Couples are more likely to choose high-quality day care when the husband is highly educated, when there is dissatisfaction with previous day care arrangements, and when the husband and wife make the decision together. When there are three or more children in the family and the decision is influenced more by convenience factors, lower-quality day care is more likely to be chosen (Endsley et al., 1984).

Examples of items that were found to discriminate above-average from below-average quality child-care centers in the research by Endsley and Bradbard (1978) are found in Table 12–1. The plus items reflect those items that best differentiated the two kinds of programs and thus are most important, and the minus items were those that were of

Table 12–1 Characteristics Differentiating Above-Average-Quality from Below-Average-Quality Child-Care Centers

1. Health and Safety
   + Floors are carpeted or have a non-skid covering.
   + The children's eating area is clean and attractive (for example, no leftover food or evidence of bugs).
   − The center displays a day-care license (Georgia Department of Human Resources).
   − *At least* one adult (in the center at all times) has knowledge of first aid procedures.

2. Adult-Child-Peer Interactions
   + Enough adults are available so that children can be given individual attention (for example, children can be held, talked to, played with) if they need it.
   + Male adults are employed by the center.
   − Adults appear warm and affectionate toward children (for example, children are hugged, smiled at, cuddled, spoken pleasantly to by adults).
   − Adults are not observed spanking, pinching, shaking or otherwise physically abusing the children.

3. Home-Center Coordination
   + Lunch and snacktime menus are posted (so that mothers will not duplicate meals at home and to show that balanced meals are being served).
   + The center posts a sign encouraging parents or those involved in child care at home to visit the day-care center at any time during the day.
   − The center posts a schedule of the daily program (for example, indoor and outdoor times, routines, activity periods, snack and mealtimes).
   − The center director is willing to answer questions or talk about the program.

4. Materials, Equipment, and Program Activities
   + Attractive and well-written story and picture books are available for the children.
   + Both children and adults are involved in the process of cleaning up after activities (for example, children help adults set up tables for meal and snacktimes, wipe up spills, fold the laundry, set up materials for play activities).
   − Adults encourage children to do some or all or the following:

Get a drink of water alone	Button and snap their clothing
Wash their hands	Put on their shoes and socks
Hang up their clothing	Zip their jackets
Put away their personal possessions	

   − Adults ask some questions of children that require more than "yes" or "no" answers.

5. Physical Characteristics of the Center
   + The outdoor play area is well drained and covered with both a *soft surface* (for example, sand, bark, or grass) as well as a *hard surface* for riding toys.
   + Windows are low enough for children to see outside.
   − Some of the children's art work (pictures, projects, etc.) is observed in the center.
   − The toileting fixtures are child-size or platforms are available so that adult fixtures can be used by children.

Source: Endsley, R.C., & Bradbard, M. R. (1978). Helping parents select quality day care through the use of a guide. *The Family Coordinator*, 27, 167–172. Copyright (1978) by the National Council on Family Relations, 3989 Central Ave. N.E. Suite #550, Minneapolis, MN 55421. Reprinted with permission.

little importance. The assumption that the most expensive care is necessarily the best is unwarranted; there are many moderate cost centers that provide excellent programs for young children.

Learning the Basics of Child Development

An important part of preparing for parenthood is learning the basic concepts and principles of child growth and development. This can be done in a number of ways: by enrolling in child and family courses, by participating in community study groups, by reading and studying on one's own, and by talking with parents and others who have child-care expertise. Through such experiences, individuals will learn that children have a distinctive mental perspective that is qualitatively different from that of adults in their approach to reality, in their view of the world, and in their understanding and use of language.

For example, children younger than 7 or 8 are characterized by *egocentric thinking*, and cannot easily distinguish personal points of view from those of others, e.g., the toddler who hits another toddler and is astonished when he or she burst into tears; the child who exclaims, "I didn't do it" when he hears his father cursing the foul weather or the child who turns off the TV during a cartoon and expects it to pick up where she left off when she returns to the TV an hour later. Young children often believe that others have the same thoughts and feelings as themselves. They often reflect a lack of empathy for another's position or feelings. Therefore, forcing a child to

Joel Gordon

"share" is to a large extent, developmentally inappropriate for very young children.

Animism, another characteristic of young children, is observed when children attribute human characteristics to inanimate objects, e.g., the father stubs his toe on a chair, and the child spanks the chair saying, "Bad chair: you hurt daddy," the little boy who looks into the night sky and says, "Look mommy! The stars are winking at me!" Young children believe that objects such as footballs, clouds, or pumpkins have thoughts, feelings, and motivations.

Young children are also incapable of *reversible mental thought*—that is they cannot mentally combine and take apart an object or sequence of ideas or think through an act and then think it undone. Suppose, for example, a parent comes into a child's room and seeing scattered toys demands, "Now you put all these things back just the way they were!" Such a statement may be quite incomprehensible to the child who cannot think back through the acts and procedures used to arrange the room as it was just a short time before. Another common characteristic, *impulsivity*, is reflected when the child responds to stimuli upon first impulse without thinking through the possible consequences of those actions.

Even adolescents are limited in certain aspects of thought by lingering egocentricity. Young teenagers are frequently overly concerned with their appearance and behavior; this extreme self-consciousness leads to reacting to an *imaginary audience*—the adolescent believes he or she is center stage for all to see and is the continual focus of attention. If his parents are whispering in the next room, he may believe it is about him. If her friends are laughing across the hallway at school, she may believe they are laughing at her.

The adolescent's belief in his or her own uniqueness of thought and feeling is known as the *personal fable*. No one else has or can experience things as he does. No one has loved, no one has dreams or aspirations as she does. Also part of this fable is

the false assumption that he or she is mythically protected from the rules or natural consequences that affect others. The teenage girl thinks that only other girls get pregnant, or the boy believes that getting hooked on drugs only happens to other, less intelligent, people. Some youth believe that the odds shift in their favor every time they lose. If for example, you are stopped for speeding and ticketed, you are "safe" from the police for awhile.

These are just a few illustrations of how children and youth think and feel differently than intellectually mature adults. An understanding of children's cognitive, emotional, and physical capacities and limitations helps in the parenting process. As a result of an informed understanding of what children are like, parents form more realistic expectations and can approach discipline humbly, realizing that children's motivations—though irrational or ridiculous in terms of adult logic—are quite reasonable and justifiable from their point of view. Knowing that some males are not ready neurologically to be toilet trained until they are $3\frac{1}{2}$ years old and some are not ready to read until they are 7 years old will help parents to be realistic about the expectations of their children's behavior.

Needs of Children

Through a knowledge of child development, we understand that children have important emotional needs: security, trust, love, acceptance, self-esteem, freedom, and limits (Erikson, 1963).

Security. Basic to the emotional health of children is the need to see the world as reliable, safe, and nonthreatening. When parental behavior is unjust and inconsistent, the child becomes anxious and believes the world is unsafe and unreliable. An important factor in the development of a sense of security is that children perceive themselves as having the inner resources to deal successfully with the world. Adequate amounts of loving attention and physical affection as well as opportunities for intellectual and physical stimulation are important.

It is well to remember that children within the same family may need very different amounts of physical and psychological strokes, and, for all practical purposes, they have very different family environments because of differences in their perceptions of their individual worlds. Parents should pick up an infant every time he or she cries to build security and trust. We often attribute adult motivations such as manipulation or control to infants who do not yet have the cognitive capacity to scheme. Studies show that babies who are responded to quickly and consistently cry *less* than babies allowed to cry themselves to sleep or responded to arbitrarily.

Trust. When their physical and emotional needs are satisfied, children learn a sense of trust, perceiving the world as good and reliable. If these needs are not satisfied, however, they are more likely to develop mistrust, believing that the world is hostile and unreliable. When they consistently receive support from all of their caregivers, they are more likely to develop trust in their relationships with others.

Gene Brody

Love. Each of us thrives better when we feel we are loved. Affectionate relationships are important at all ages. Parents normally provide children the first experiences that help them to feel that they are loved. Children who receive a great deal of affection and who know that adults truly care for them learn to see themselves as persons of worth and as lovable. Children who are genuinely loved for themselves *without any conditions attached* are likely to develop strong, positive self-concepts and are better able to love others. The failure to receive love from others is a basic factor in the development of emotional maladjustment.

Acceptance. Another factor contributing to emotional health and to the development of a healthy self-concept is being accepted. Children who are accepted unconditionally are likely to develop a sense of belonging, stability, and security. On the other hand, children who are not accepted are likely to feel rejected and undesirable; they may develop negative self-concepts and fear intimate relationships with others because of the possibility of being rejected. Such persons find it difficult to accept others because they perceive they have not been accepted.

Self-esteem. Most parents want their children to value themselves and their contributions and to feel that they are worthwhile. To achieve this, we strive to help children to respect their potential, worth, and achievement. Self-esteem during childhood is largely dependent upon the recognition, attention, and appreciation received from others. When children's needs for self-esteem are unfulfilled, they often experience feelings of inferiority, inadequacy, and helplessness, which, in turn, lead to an array of behaviors that are uncomfortable both to themselves and to their families. Fulfillment of the need for self-esteem contributes to feelings of worth, usefulness, competence, and self-confidence. Also, persons who hold themselves in high esteem are

Cultural Differences

We often assume that ethnic groups are homogeneous within the group; they are not. For example, Hispanic families may be from any number of subcultures: Mexican, Puerto Rican, Cuban or Central American.

Some of the differences in child rearing attributed to ethnic differences may instead be due to social class differences. For example, Mexican-American mothers were observed to use more directive statements, "Do it this way!" whereas Anglo mothers used more praise and carefully directed questions. When the mothers were matched for educational level, however, the apparent ethnic differences disappeared.

Many carefully controlled studies have revealed ethnic differences in child-rearing practices. Some examples follow:

1. Hispanic families place a greater emphasis on traditional values, such as respect for authority, than do other ethnic groups.

2. Black families place a higher value on achievement in both sports and school than do white families.

3. There are lower levels of interaction between parents and children in black families compared with white families.

4. Black children spent more time watching television than white children did.

5. Black families are more likely to use physical punishment than white families.

Sources: 1. Laosa, L. M. (1982). School, occupation, culture and family: The impact of parental schooling on the parent-child relationship. *Journal of Educational Psychology, 74*, 791–827. 2. Medrich, E. A., Roizen, J., & Rubin, V. (1982). *The serious business of growing up.* Berkeley, CA: University of California Press. 3. Schiamberg, L. B. (1988). *Child and adolescent development.* New York: Macmillan. 4. Zill, N. (in press). *Happy, healthy, and insecure: A portrait of middle childhood in the United States.* New York: Cambridge University Press.

better able to respond to the worth and potential of others.

Freedom for Exploration.   Children have a desire for freedom within reasonable limits—to explore, to be independent, to make decisions, and to learn. When their freedom is restricted or when their interests are ignored and someone else's interests are continually pushed upon them, they cannot develop independence easily. Children who are forced to remain dependent upon caregivers are likely to find their development of independence and the ability to make decisions impaired. Important characteris-

tics of satisfying human relationships are the mutual granting of freedom to be one's self and to be different.

Limits.   The establishment of limits and boundaries is important to the sense of security of children. The problem behavior of children who have never been told "no" is often a signal for someone to set limits and to indicate they care enough to provide guidance. But parents can misunderstand this concept and believe they are being good parents when, in reality, they are unduly restrictive. There is an important difference between restrictiveness and guidance. The role of guidance is to enable the child to become completely self-directive. In order to experience the most positive and rewarding interpersonal relationships during childhood and later in adulthood, children need to learn to respect the rights and feelings of others. The setting of limits requires a sensible balance. Limitations that are severe or unfair contribute to the child becoming passive and dependent or aggressive or both. Limits should always be stated with *the reason behind the limit*. This is part of the process that helps children develop the ability to reason and make intelligent decisions.

Knowledge of these needs is not enough to ensure effective parenting. But guided by this knowledge, parents can learn skills that will help them to meet their children's needs. One of the secrets of great parenting is to learn to become skillful in reading cues of children's behavior to anticipate when guidance is needed to avoid harm. Just as it is important to anticipate a child's behavior when he or she starts to run into the street, it is important to anticipate when guidance is needed when children start to embark on a course of action that is potentially psychologically harmful.

Communicating with Children

Communication is a part of all of our relationships. The quality of the relationships parents have with children is largely determined by the messages that are communicated and *how* they are communicated. Most parents are genuinely interested in learning how to communicate effectively with children. But it is also important that children learn to communicate with their parents and others in a positive manner as well. Because children learn many of their communication patterns from their parents, it is especially important for parents to serve as good models.

Here are some guidelines for communicating with children:

1. *Treat children and youth as persons.* Recognize *their* feelings and needs. For example, when some parents turn from conversation with another adult and begin talking to their children, their manner changes completely. Their voice tone becomes condescending; they speak more loudly and crisply. Some communication with children is so artificial that the child easily senses it is not genuine—for example, the parent who pretends interest or excitement about something the child is doing in a manner that even children recognize is superficial.

2. *Be an active listener.* Many older children and adolescents fail to communicate effectively with adults because their parents rarely listened to them or encouraged child-to-parent communication when they were younger. Perhaps nothing establishes good communication patterns with children more effectively than being a good listener.

Active listening involves listening not only to the words the child says but also to the child's feelings. When we talk about something that concerns us, it is usually the feelings we have about the issue that matter most to us; words are merely a way of trying to share those feelings. Active listening, thus, includes the process in which the parent attentively listens both to the content and the feeling of the child's communication. The goal of active listening is to *understand* the child—not to instruct, or to demand, or to reprimand.

Active listening also requires time to give attention to *what* children say and *the way that they say it*. Active listening requires empathy and the ability to think and feel from the point of view of the child. Children normally respond positively when parents provide acceptance, empathy, interest, and attention. Such thoughtful behavior provides a model that assists children in clarifying their feelings and in encouraging them to share their feelings and concerns.

An important part of active listening—in addition to listening to understand the child's message—is the practice of reflecting back to the child what you think the child meant. This type of feedback helps children clarify their feelings and encourages them to communicate their feelings in a more specific way. This feedback process is so important it is worth reviewing:

a. The child sends a verbal and/or a nonverbal message.

b. You listen for the purpose of understanding the message content *and* the feeling or emotion being expressed. You may respond, "Let me see if I understand. . . ." You paraphrase the meaning of the child's communication, using different words or phrases to restate what the child has said.

c. In this last step you wait for the child to respond and then confirm what you have understood. Then you allow the child to clarify or expand upon the original message if the message has been misunderstood.

Giving feedback minimizes the possibility of misunderstanding. It provides a method of verifying whether the message you received is the message the child intended. As with all ways of responding, feedback is more effective if it is not overused. Be careful when phrasing lead-in statements so the feedback does not sound artificial or insincere.

3. *Owning feelings*. Assuming ownership of feelings is another helpful communication technique. To own feelings, you identify and express how you personally feel about a situation. And, as in active listening, you refrain from blaming, accusing, and from interpreting the child's motivations. This technique involves a three-step process:

a. First, evaluate what feelings you are experiencing. Identifying the specific emotion in yourself such as anger or embarrassment is not as easy as it may seem.

b. Next, acknowledge that *your* feeling is *your* responsibility and is under your control. You need not be a mere reactor to the behavior of the child.

c. Use "I" statements to express your feelings(s). "I feel annoyed. . . ." "I am hurt. . . ." "I want you to. . . ." Do not blame and accuse the child by using "You" statements. "You make me so mad. . . ." "You always. . . ." "You should. . . ." "You don't care." These phrases tend to make the child defensive. Examine these contrasting examples.

"You Statement": "*You* are so irresponsible! You leave everything until the last minute and expect me to bail you out. *You* really are thoughtless."

"I Statement": "Very honestly, *I* don't like the pressure of having to be responsible for your problems at the last minute because of poor planning. *I* don't think it is fair."

"You Statement": "*You* only think of yourself. *You* don't care how much you inconvenience the rest of us as long as you are taken care of."

"I Statement": "*I* am really disappointed in getting started so late. *I* feel hurt when I am under pressure."

Some people believe there may be little distinction in some cases between an "I" and a "You" response. But the key is to identify the personal feeling and express it rather than blaming or ridiculing the child.

4. *Minimize put-down messages*. It is easy to get into a pattern of sending put-down messages to children: "You're dumb," "You never get anything right," or "Why did I have children like you." Put-down messages include ridicule, sarcasm, and criticism and have the effect of decreasing self-esteem. Depreciating children as persons and emphasizing their inadequacies may have consequences that conflict with the goals of self-reliance

Single Parenting

About 9 million parents today are rearing children without the presence of a spouse. About 8 million are mothers; 1 million are fathers. Most are separated, divorced, or widowed, but about 25% are never-married mothers (Hanson & Sporakowski, 1986).

Single parents face all the same challenges and concerns of other parents, but those problems take on greater magnitude when there is no partner to share the burden. There are some specific problems of particular significance to single parents.

1. *Finances.* For single mothers, finances are often a problem. Women who have been deserted usually receive no financial assistance from their children's fathers. Divorced mothers may receive sporadic or insufficient child support payments. Most single mothers must seek employment.

2. *Role Conflict and Strain.* Single parents frequently experience overload and strain. The demands of work, parenting, and care of a home can be exhausting.

3. *Isolation and Loneliness.* Single parents need adult companionship and connections. They may have difficulty explaining their involvement with other adults to their children or may not have time or energy for a social life. Also, children may disapprove of Mom dating.

When the situations of single mothers and single fathers are compared, single fathers fare better in two areas: (a) they usually make more money, and, (b) they are more often regarded as heroic figures for caring for their young. Most single fathers are confident in their abilities as single parents but report having much to learn about child rearing and housework. Both mothers and fathers report loneliness, overload, and a vague fear that all is not as good as it could be for their children (DeFrain, et al., 1987).

A review of the research on single-parent homes and children's adjustment and development does not lend support to the idea that this is a hazardous context for rearing children. In general, when the parent is doing well, the children do well, too (DeFrain, et al., 1987).

Sources: 1. DeFrain, J., Fricke, J., & Elmen, J. (1987). *On our own: A single parent's survival guide.* Lexington, MA: Lexington Books. 2. Hanson, S. H., & Sporakowski, M. J. (1986). Single-parent families. *Family Relations, 35,* 3–8.

that parents have for them. One of the most severe put-down messages is to deny children attention and interest. Such a message may be interpreted as, "My parent doesn't really love me." It makes children feel badly about themselves and their ability to have a loving relationship with the parent.

It is difficult to avoid sending put-down messages to children completely. Parents get busy with the problems in meeting their own needs, and sometimes it is difficult to pay attention to children when their problems seem so very unimportant. Most of us, however, could reduce the number of put-down messages we send to children with little real effort if we stopped to think of the consequences that those messages have.

Guiding Children

Many people think of discipline as a punishment for undesirable behavior and a reward for desirable behavior. They believe that responses will increase in frequency and intensity when they are rewarded and that those responses that are punished will become extinguished. If the process were this simple, rearing children might very well be considerably easier.

In reality, the impact of the discipline parents provide is dependent upon the relationship between parents and children. Children who dislike their parents may persist in responding in ways that parents punish because of the satisfaction derived in defying parents. The rewards they receive from seeing their parents distressed at being unable to regulate their behavior is often greater than the distress they experience as a result of being punished.

Many children would rather receive punishment from their parents than be ignored. When parents fail to show their children that they are important, children often behave in ways that parents consider displeasing in order to establish that they are persons with whom to be reckoned. Not infrequently, these children later pose problems as adults when they continue to attain recognition by being destructive.

Discipline may be thought of as a way in which parents attempt to control the behavior of children. It is difficult for anyone to control the behavior of another, however, over a prolonged period of time; attempting to do so is conducive to conflict. Discipline may be best defined in terms of parental behaviors that assist children to

1. Control their own behavior and develop self-direction.

2. Accept responsibility for the consequences of their own behavior.

3. Become sensitive to and respect the needs and feeling of others.

Discipline is a necessary part of the role of all caregivers of children, including family members, teachers, and friends. Society demands that children learn and accept social requirements. If children do not learn self-discipline from their caregivers, they are likely to learn it later, often at a higher cost, from others in society.

The question of discipline is actually a matter of type and degree. What type of discipline should be used? Where should the line be drawn between arbitrary discipline by the parents and free experimentation by the child? Philosophies on discipline move in both directions. The extremes are represented by the overdisciplined child who lacks security and spontaneity and the child who has never been told "no." Some parents are reluctant to discipline their children, fearing that they will lose their child's love or that they will damage the child psychologically.

Control Behaviors and Support Behaviors

Research has shown that there are two major types of parental behaviors that influence the socialization of children: *control behaviors* and *support behaviors* (Rollins & Thomas, 1979). Parental control involves attempts to direct the behavior of the child in a manner considered desirable by parents. Parental support can be defined using various labels; however, in general, it is related to the degree of nurturance, warmth, and acceptance shown by parents. Support behaviors help the child feel comfortable and loved.

There are three basic types of control behaviors used by parents: coercion, love withdrawal, and induction.

1. *Coercion* is any attempt to force the child through the use or threat of physical punishment; verbal assaults such as sarcasm, ridicule, or yelling; or the withholding of resources.

2. *Love withdrawal* is composed of behaviors that reflect disapproval of the child's behavior. The child receives the message that love and approval will not be restored until the offending behavior is changed. Love withdrawal is accomplished through the use of psychological detachment from the child by ignoring, showing indifference, or giving the child "a cold shoulder" treatment. One can also physically withdraw from the child and avoid any contact or proximity to the child.

3. *Induction* reflects an attempt to get children to comply by using reason, explaining consequences, and/or providing acceptable alternatives. The intent of this form of guidance is to maintain the respect and rights of both adults and children. Induction provides a child with information about what to do instead of focusing on what *not* to do.

Results of the Three Control Styles

Now what are the results of the use of each of these three control styles? It should be noted that coercion is often initially used because the parent does not have to spend time and energy with explanations or logical reasons. Parental authority is maintained at a high level, at least while the child is young. Parents are reinforced for using coercion because of the immediate results they get, even though the unwanted behavior may stop only for the moment.

Coercion. What are some of the negative consequences if coercion is used consistently as the preferred method of guidance? Its uses have been shown to be related to lower self-esteem in the child, lack of self-control, and less empathy for others. Its use is also negatively related to cognitive development, creativity, and conformity. It will also increase the antisocial aggression of children and is related to other behavior problems, such as drug use. The use of coercion also tends to cause the child to avoid the punishing agent (Patterson, 1982). The parent-child relationship is damaged, and the parent has less influence in future control attempts. The consistent use of punishment usually does not suppress the behavior on a long-term basis and has the additional disadvantage of failing to show acceptable alternatives to the child.

Although coercion is considered a successful method by parents who are concerned with immediate conformity rather than long-range consequences, in its more extreme degree it tends to have negative effects on children. It is usually reflected in discipline that is punitive, either psychologically or physically, and is often coupled with the attitude of "do this because I say so and if you don't, I will punish you," and with very little effort to explain to children the reasons for the request. When children are told they are "bad," there is always the danger that they will eventually believe they *are* bad and then act out the life script their parents have provided for them. "Bad people" learn (a) if they can "get away" with a certain act they will do it, (b) not to consider their behavior in terms of its effects upon others, and (c) not to be concerned, personally, if a behavior is immoral. These are the correlates of the "bad people" role assigned to children by their parents and other caregivers.

The evidence suggests that when power is exercised entirely by parents, children lose their sense of control—that is, their belief that their signals and responses make a difference in the way they are treated by their parents (Maccoby, 1980). In contrast, when the power is shared by parents *and* children, and high demand for mature behavior is placed on the children, children experience responsibility as being within themselves and also tend to be more active, sociable, cheerful, and responsive to the needs of others (Maccoby, 1980). Extreme authoritarian parenting frequently results in passivity or hyperaggression on the part of the child (Maccoby, 1980). There is also evidence that mothers who use physical punishment rarely reason with

Characteristics of Nurturing Families

Charles Thompson and Virginia Rudolph summarize the work of Virginia Satir, the noted psychotherapist-theorist, concerning the values of nurturing families:

1. People are listened to by others and are interested in listening to others.

2. People are not afraid to take risks because the family understands mistakes are bound to happen when risking.

3. People's bodies are graceful, and their facial expressions are relaxed.

4. People look at one another and not through one another or at the floor.

5. The children are friendly and open, and the rest of the family treats them as people.

6. People seem comfortable about touching one another and showing their affection.

7. People show love by talking and listening with concern and by being straight and real with one another.

8. Members feel free to tell one another how they feel.

9. Anything can be discussed—fears, anger, hurt, criticism, joys, achievements, and so on.

10. Members plan, but if something does not work out, they can adjust.

11. Human life and feelings are more important than anything else.

12. Parents see themselves as leaders and not as bosses. They acknowledge to their children their poor as well as their good judgment; their hurt, anger, or disappointment as well as their joy. Their behavior matches their teaching.

13. When nurturing parents need to correct their children, they rely on listening, touching, understanding, and careful timing, being aware of children's feelings and their natural wish to learn.

14. Nurturing parents understand that children can only learn when they are valued, so they do not respond in a way to make the child feel devalued.

Source: Thompson, C. L., & Rudolph, L. B. (1983). *Counseling children.* Monterey, CA: Brooks/Cole. Used with permission.

their children and tend to have children who do not achieve well in school (Barton et al., 1974).

Withdrawal of Love. This method of controlling a child's behavior is used most frequently among middle-class parents. The evidence is not conclu-sive, but psychiatrists maintain that the excessive use of withdrawing love can have deleterious effects. This manner of discipline puts love on a conditional basis and stimulates insecurity in the child, often creating a situation far more harmful than the behavior that led to the discipline. The child may not even know what he or she has done to cause this treatment or what can be done to regain the love and approval of the parents.

Induction. Unlike coercion, induction methods of discipline are related to high self-esteem, increased self-control, prosocial orientation, and intellectual achievement (Belsky, et al., 1984). This form of discipline is not hurtful to the child and reflects respect for the child by providing reasons, pointing out possible consequences, and by providing choices of "correct" behaviors.

This method is characterized by warmth and acceptance and involves providing children with a reasonable degree of freedom. They are helped to see the consequences of behavior for themselves and other people. Children from these homes are found to be cooperative, self-reliant, and well-adjusted in social situations. They assume responsibilities well and demonstrate perseverance (Maccoby, 1980). Such qualities provide a good foundation for satisfying adult relationships later in life.

Permissive-Indulgent Behavior

This method is characterized by a "hands-off" policy. Few, if any, limits or boundaries are set for children. A child reared this way may be impulsive, aggressive, overly independent, or irresponsible (Maccoby & Martin, 1983). Such children may respond to discipline and to parental denial of their own requests with impatience, temper tantrums, or physical-verbal assaults. Children reared in a permissive-indulgent atmosphere very often lack social responsibility and personal independence, which jeopardizes their potential for healthy development (Maccoby, 1980).

Another adverse effect of an indulgent atmosphere on children is that parents do not encourage the development of habits involving regularity or fastidiousness. Low habit regularity and low fastidiousness are predictive of later psychiatric disorders among children (Graham et al., 1973).

Fostering a Favorable Family Climate

One of the most important factors in promoting favorable development of children is a family climate characterized by parental supportiveness, warmth, and acceptance (Maccoby, 1980). There is evidence, for example, that children who are rejected by their parents are likely to express such problems as emotional instability, quarrelsomeness, resentment of authority, and restlessness. In contrast, children who perceive themselves to be accepted by their parents tend to be more considerate of others, high in self-esteem, altruistic, and friendly (Maccoby, 1980).

The importance of parental support and warmth to the development of the child is illustrated in a classic study by Baumrind (1967) that compared parents of preschool children who exhibited positive behavior with parents of children

Joel Gordon

Latchkey Children

Latchkey Children and Their Families

The term "latchkey" (or child self-care) describes children who care for themselves for extended periods and denotes the housekey they carry to let themselves in and out of their houses. A U.S. Department of Labor (1982) report has estimated there are approximately seven million children age 13 and under (13%) who care for themselves when not in school.

Latchkey children report more nightmares and higher levels of fear than children supervised by adults; they also have significant personality adjustment and academic achievement problems.

In contrast, it has been suggested that the early responsibilities imposed upon latchkey children make them more independent and resourceful. Latchkey children interviewed were found to be better informed regarding self-care and emergencies than children supervised by adults.

Studies of children living in relatively safe urban and rural communities have failed to find differences in the emotional adjustment or academic achievement of latchkey children and their adult-supervised peers. These findings suggest the environment in which latchkey children live may determine whether they suffer or benefit from their self-care status.

It is unclear what influence child self-care has on parent-child relations. Parents have expressed concern and uncertainty as well as satisfaction and pride in their children's self-care status. Some adults who were latchkey children have reported their self-care status made them feel their parents trusted them, while others have reported anger with their parents for their "insensitivity" toward them.

A variety of school and community programs for school-aged children are being developed. These include extended day care in public schools, neighborhood "block mothers," after-school phone-in services, and cooperative efforts between community agencies in operating before and after school centers (Coleman et al., 1984).

Latchkey Children: Guides for Self-Care

The following guidelines represent minimum requirements that parents may use to evaluate the readiness of their child for self-care:

Physical. A child should be able to

1. Manipulate locks and doors so that he or she will not be locked in or out.
2. Operate safely any equipment to which he or she will have access while alone. This might include stove, blender, or vacuum cleaner. If it is not safe to operate, he or she should not have access to it.

Emotional. The child should

1. Be able to tolerate separations from adults for the length of time required without undue loneliness or fear.
2. Not exhibit a pattern of withdrawn, hostile, or self-destructive behavior.
3. Be able to handle usual and unexpected situations without excessive fear or upset.
4. Be able to follow important rules without always "testing the limits."

Cognitive. The child should

1. Be able to understand and remember verbal and written instructions.
2. Solve problems without relying on irrational solutions.
3. Be able to read and write well enough to take telephone and other messages.

Social. The child should

1. Be able to solicit help from friends, neighbors, and designated helpers when appropriate.
2. Understand the role of police, fire fighters, rescue squads, and other community resources.
3. Be willing and able to call in those resources when needed.
4. Be able to maintain friendships with other children and adults.

It is not only the child or children in the family who must be assessed to determine suitability for self-care. Parents or guardians should be able to

1. Maintain some level of communication and supervision of their children, even if they are not physically present.
2. Be available for emergencies or designate several other adults who will be.
3. Be stable enough to provide emotional security for their children.
4. Provide training for their children in the special issues that may arise in self-care.

Source: Adapted with permission from 1. Cole, C., & Rodman, H. (1987). When school-age children care for themselves: Issues for family life educators and parents. *Family Relations, 36,* 92–96. 2. Coleman, T. M., Robinson, B. E., & Rowland, B. H. (1984). Latchkey children and their families. *Dimensions, 13* (1), 23–24. 3. U.S. Dept. of Labor, Women's Bureau (1982). *Employers and child care: Establishing services through the workplace.* Pamphlet No. 23. Washington, DC: U.S. Government Printing Office.

who were discontented, distrustful, withdrawing, and who had little self-control or self-reliance. The parents of the preschool children exhibiting positive behaviors were markedly more supportive and loving toward their children. Parents of the children expressing more negative behaviors were much less supportive and used withdrawal of love and ridicule as incentives for their children.

Parental support is positively related to such child outcomes as high self-esteem, increased cognitive development, and self-control. Its use is negatively associated with aggression and behavior problems such as drug abuse. It appears that if parents will provide a great deal of support and love, children

will have a better chance to grow up emotionally healthy, secure, and happy.

The Use of Specific Techniques to Achieve Goals

Punishment

Although punishment is one form of coercive control that has already been discussed, it so permeates the thinking of parents as a method of guiding children that its use as a specific technique warrants special attention. *Punishment* may be defined as an unpleasant event following a behavior that tends to decrease the occurrence of that behavior. Many parents use threats and verbal and physical punishment in guiding children even though the advisibility of the use of these techniques is questioned. Punishment may result in a child learning not to perform certain acts in front of parents, but it serves little use in terms of directing the child to use more desirable forms of behavior. As noted earlier, it often leads to decreased feelings of self-esteem, resentment, and rebellion.

Rather than using punishment to alter a toddler's behavior, parents will be more successful if they redirect their children's behavior, divert their children's behavior or distract their children creatively and positively. For example, 18-month-old Tommy is intent on taking a toy car away from his same-age cousin. Instead of slapping his hand or telling him to share, his mom quickly offers him another similar toy car.

Parents of preschoolers are more likely to achieve success in altering their children's behavior if they focus on stating clear limits and provide reasons that are appropriate to the development of the child, rather than using punishment. Redirecting undesirable behavior to more acceptable activity that meets the needs of the child frequently works. For example, you can say "Billy, if you'll give Davey a turn on the tricycle, you can help me open the package from grandma. Then we'll all go out for lunch, and you guys can play at the park."

Altering the behavior of older children will be more likely if the parents view the behavior from the child's viewpoint by (a) identifying the real problem that has led to the behavior, (b) thinking through possible solutions to the problem, (c) reviewing solutions that are agreeable to both the child and his or her parents, (d) helping the child to achieve the solution, and (e) checking the success of the solution. If the solution is not successful, begin the process again.

Obviously, success at parenting varies. Children vary in their temperament: some are "difficult" from infancy onward, while others are "easy." There are children who, due to attentional, intellectual, or emotional factors, experience extreme difficulties in learning to control their behavior. Not all parents have the expertise to guide more difficult children. Some will seek the counsel of a qualified child psychologist who can guide them in learning those parenting skills that are required when the more traditional approaches fail. The misbehavior of hyperactive children, for example, often cannot easily be redirected or ignored because they are so inattentive and noncompliant and their behavior is so impulsive.

Modifying Behavior

Behavior of children may be modified by parents serving as a model or a standard for children to copy and by parents reinforcing desirable behavior. Behavior modification involves the use of social reinforcement, e.g., reward, recognition, and praise, to help children develop desirable and positive forms of behavior (Martin & Pear, 1988).

Most of us tend to continue behavior for which we are rewarded. Parents sometimes unintentionally reward their children for problem behavior by giving more attention to their children when they are engaged in problem behavior than at any other time. For example, a child may persist in hitting her brother because she has found that when she hits him, her parents scold her but focus complete attention upon her.

One way of modifying behavior to achieve a desired result is for parents to praise and recognize the child for responding positively so that greater attention is obtained for manifesting nonproblem behavior. For example, big sister is complimented for playing nicely with little brother; if she hits, he receives attention but she gets only a brief reprimand. Giving the child positive attention for positive behavior tends to eliminate the child's motivation to respond negatively, especially if the parents work hard to stop reinforcing negative behavior (Martin & Pear, 1988).

Behavior modification may include the use of material rewards. For example, parents who have difficulty getting their son to pick up his toys from the sidewalk in front of the house might use a contract system in which he earns a few points every time he does pick up his toys. After he earns a certain number of points he is given a tangible reward. He may receive five points every day that he picks up the toys. After he accumulates 25 points, he is permitted to decide the kind of dessert the family will have for dinner. One criticism of behavior modification is that it encourages development of an external locus of control—that is, behaving to please others or to get something instead of responding to a set of internal values.

The following strategies can be employed to modify behavior:

1. *Identify specifically the desired behavior change.* Parents should pinpoint these in terms like "my son whines to get his way" or "my daughter throws her clothes on the floor." A good approach is to count the behaviors and keep a record of them. Parents should be able to observe small changes in the child's behavior and reinforce those efforts. If there is no change, they will also be able to see this and alter their behavior change programs so that they are more effective.

2. *Be consistent.* Many problems with children's behavior are the result of parental inconsistency. Many inappropriate behaviors are made worse by parents' inconsistent attempts either to punish misbehavior or reward good behavior. Consistency is essential until new patterns of behavior are established.

3. *Be contingent.* When children behave in the way that parents desire, it is important to reward them as quickly as possible. Conversely, behaviors that parents want to eliminate should receive contingent consequences that make those

behaviors less likely to occur again. The difficulty that most parents have is not really following these obvious rules. It is fine for parents to show children attention and affection noncontingently, but parents who have children who are especially difficult may wish to be careful not to reward inappropriate behavior. Also, it is desirable to save the most powerful rewards for those behaviors that parents most want to encourage.

4. *Provide immediate rewards.* Providing immediate rewards is most important in the earliest stages of helping a child learn a new behavior. Whenever possible, reinforcement should be given immediately after the behavior. The simple statement, "that's right"

Walker Montgomery

is a reinforcer and takes little time to say. Waiting several minutes before rewarding the child reduces its effectiveness.

5. *Break down the desired behavior that the child is to learn into small steps and initially reward each small step.* Gradually require larger amounts of appropriate behavior before giving the reward. For example, in helping children learn to pick up their room, parents may start with rewards for each item they pick up, then reward them only after they have picked up all of their room, and finally the parents can require a week of neat rooms before the reward is given. In this case, it is desirable to mark down the points for a clean room daily. The reward for a week of cleaning needs to be larger than that for picking up one item; so parents should start with small rewards. If the child stops the desired behavior, parents must either change the reward, go back to smaller steps required for the reward, or both.

6. *With older children, these programs go more smoothly if parents set them up on a contractual basis.* If a contract system is used, parents and children should discuss what behaviors it is reasonable to change and the reinforcers to be used. Desired reinforcers are more effective than those that are only slightly interesting. When a contract system is used, children can see the similarity between behaviors required of them and the rewards they receive and the requirements of adults' jobs and their salaries.

For most children, the techniques used in behavior modification should not be used rigidly. It is well to remember that life should be satisfying for both children and parents. The idea behind behavior modification is to help children to learn to gain control of their behavior so that they will be happier in their social relationships and not be handicapped by their inability to handle their own actions constructively.

Admittedly, however, there are children whose behavior is so extreme that for them to function in society within the law they need the guidance of psychologists who are more skillful than parents in developing modification strategies that work. The goal, all agree, is not just to make children mind their parents, but to guide them in ways that will lead to increasing self-direction. Wise parents will seek the counsel of appropriate specialists when they encounter problems they cannot handle.

Child Maltreatment

While some cultures rarely resort to physical punishment as a method of discipline, our society often encourages it. "Spare the rod and spoil the child" is a proverb universally recognized in our culture. The U.S. Supreme Court (in *Baker v. Owen*, 1975 and *Ingraham v. Wright*, 1977) endorsed the use of corporal punishment in America when it ruled that public schools may use it to control disobedient children. The boundaries for what constitutes child maltreatment are to a great extent defined by culture, and it is only when the cultural expectations and boundaries for discipline or general treatment of the child are exceeded that the behavior is called *abuse.*

A problem facing child abuse researchers is determining the extent to which child abuse actually occurs. For example, the injuries (physical and emotional) may not be obvious. Parents who are chronic abusers may shift hospitals or doctors to avoid detection, and responsible professionals may fail to report a maltreatment case. Neighbors may feel reluctant to report another parent's treatment of a child. Several researchers have estimated that between 340,000 to 500,000 children, or about 1 in every 40 children suffers from abuse or neglect annually (Watkins & Bradbard, 1982).

The effects of abuse upon these children goes beyond the immediate injuries they suffer, including irreparable neurological damage and handicapping conditions. It may also delay or impair language development or have serious social-psychological consequences. George and Main (1979) found in a study of abused and nonabused toddlers aged 1 to 3 years that the abused children more frequently physically assaulted other children in day care settings. Unlike the toddlers with whom they were observed, the abused children verbally and physically assaulted their caregivers. In another study, it was found that children from abusive households displayed almost 50% more negative behaviors than their unabused peers (Burgess & Conger, 1978). Children who have been abused have been found to be unique in their response to friendly overtures from caregivers: when a friendly overture was made to an abused toddler, the child either avoided the caregiver entirely or exhibited approach-avoidance behavior, such as approaching from the side or rear or even by turning around and walking backwards toward the caregiver. Because abused children often display aggression and the tendency to avoid social interaction, they may be labeled "difficult" children (George & Main, 1979).

There are serious "sleeper" effects as a result of child abuse. Several researchers have reported a relation between maltreatment and later delinquency. The lack of warm, caring parenting may result in the child's failure to develop empathy, which may contribute to his or her own potential to abuse others later in life (Belsky, 1980).

While most abusing parents were themselves victims of child abuse, not all victims of abuse will become abusive. Most research into the causes of child abuse arrive at similar conclusions: Many abusing parents are under high levels of stress, but not all highly stressed parents abuse their children. Most abusing parents are from lower-class families, but not all lower-class families abuse their children. Even though some groups may be more vulnerable to abuse than others, maltreatment occurs at all economic levels and without respect to religion or race. As a result, research has tended to describe abusive families rather than to predict what kinds of families are most likely to become abusive.

Most research in the past has approached child abuse from three perspectives. The psychological approach first attempted to deal with maltreatment as the result of mental illness in the parent. This approach has given way to a search for personality traits and demographic data that characterize these parents and how they handle stress within the family. Research has failed to produce an agreed-upon set of such characteristics (Watkins & Bradbard, 1982).

A second approach has been an inquiry into the social interaction within abusing families. Factors examined from this perspective include the patterns of interaction between parents and children, between the parents themselves, and also among the siblings (Burgess & Conger, 1978; Schmitt & Kempe, 1983). Another factor is the child's characteristics. The child who is somehow "different" or who exhibits characteristics such as irritability, responsiveness (or lack of it), and physical unattractiveness may be singled out for abusive treatment (Belsky, 1980).

A third area of investigation has involved an examination of factors outside the home that exert an influence on the individuals and processes within the family. Unemployment, for example, has been frequently associated with incidence of abuse (Gil, 1971). Similarly, job dissatisfaction, social isolation, lack of community support systems, and cultural values that endorse violence and aggressive behavior, corporal punishment of children, and the devaluation of children all contribute to the general problem of child maltreatment (Parke & Lewis, 1981).

Because there is such diversity in the contributors to the maltreatment of children, several researchers have employed Bronfenbrenner's (1977, 1979) ecological model. This model holds that the development of the family takes place in an environment with its own peculiar ecology, which can be divided into three systems: (1) *the microsystem*, which includes what takes place within the immediate household; (2) *the exosystem*, which includes the social context in which the family is embedded, e.g., parents' jobs, the schools, networks of relatives and friends; and (3) *the macrosystem*, which includes the cultural values that influence what happens in the exosystem and the microsystem. Belsky (1980) broadens this model to include the individual traits the parents bring with them into the family that

cause them to behave in an abusive or neglectful way, labeling these factors the *ontogenic development level*. These four levels form an ecology—a "balance"—in which the factors at one level exert influence over factors in the others. Child maltreatment, from this point of view, must be understood in terms of multiple causation by forces at each level of the ecology. Thus, any attempts at prediction, prevention, or treatment of abusive families must take into account the total ecology, rather than focusing on one or two obvious problems.

Summary

- Understanding the stages of child development will help parents to form more realistic expectations of their children and to approach discipline from a rational perspective.

- Security, trust, love, acceptance, self-esteem, freedom, and limits are important emotional needs of children. Parents who recognize these needs and develop skills to help their children's needs be met are likely to create a healthy, positive enviornment for their family.

- Communication is vital to successful parent-child relationships. Parents who actively and respectfully listen to their children and respond positively to them provide role models from which children will learn important communication skills.

- Discipline can be an area of struggle for many families, but it can have positive results if done in the context of a warm, loving, and supportive atmosphere.

- Four of the techniques parents use to modify their children's behavior are coercion, love withdrawal, induction, and permissiveness. Of these four, induction, i.e., using reason, explaining consequences, and providing alternatives, is the technique that holds the most promise for a child's positive emotional growth.

- Both parents and children thrive when they learn to value each other for their strengths, are thankful for the help they receive from each other, and develop an appreciation for the happiness they bring one another. Parents who serve as models of strength, appreciation, and happiness are often rewarded with children who reflect these same characteristics.

- The goal in parenting that is most important is to keep one's focus on those aspects of life that are significant and discount those events that may cause momentary stress yet in the course of a lifetime warrant little concern.

Discussion Questions

1. Describe the specific ways in which your parents contributed to your feelings of self-esteem.

2. Why should children know the reasons for the limits that parents impose on their behavior?

3. What are the different ways parental acceptance can be communicated to infants, to school-aged children, and to adolescents?

4. What are some of the long-range consequences of not learning to trust others?

5. If a school-aged child makes a parent very angry, what are several positive ways of responding?

6. What are the effects of parental ridicule, sarcasm, and criticism?

7. Give an example of the three types of control behaviors, and indicate the kinds of effects that each of these behaviors is likely to have on children.

8. Sleeper effects are those effects that are not immediately identifiable but show up sometime later in a child's life. Discuss the long-range effect that psychological neglect of a father may have on a son once the son is grown and has a son of his own.

9. What are some of the best ways to teach children self-discipline?

10. What are some of the characteristics of resilient children?

11. How do you explain the fact that some children who appear to be advantaged become unproductive and unhappy adults?

12. How should couples who wish to create families that are characterized by supportiveness, warmth, and acceptance achieve these goals?

13. How can an unfortunate childhood event serve you to good advantage when you are an adult?

14. What are the things that occur in school that serve to decrease self-esteem in children? How can parents offset negative out-of-family influences?

15. What are the things that have contributed most to your happiness in life? Your unhappiness? How important are families in helping children to maximize opportunities for happiness?

16. Evidence indicates that among older middle-class parents many of their relationships with their adult children are not particularly close, although they love them. Why is it that family members become so separated from each other psychologically?

17. Describe the kind of family that you believe contributes most effectively to rearing children.

18. What can be done to educate persons better for parenthood?

19. Identify the strengths in your family system that have contributed to your success as a future parent.

20. Describe an example of a guidance situation in which the parent does not support the negative behavior of a child but communicates unconditional regard.

CHAPTER 13

FAMILY FINANCIAL MANAGEMENT

Some people have the good sense to make nearly every dollar they get do the work of two. They're not necessarily smarter than other people, but they live better. The truth is having money may not bring happiness but it rarely does you much harm, and sometimes it's very convenient. Only a small number of people become wealthy by winning the Publishers Clearinghouse Sweepstakes. A surer way of acquiring wealth is by planning rather than hoping. The first step is to make a decision to acquire it. The second is to find out how to do it well. The third step involves how to use it wisely. Even the richest men in the world wait to purchase a stock when it is cheap. When you consider the number of dumb people who have money, you know it has to be easier than many people suspect. It does, however, require learning and doing, and if you have a knack for wasting money, you're very likely always to be poor.

James Walters

Americans and Their Money

In a national study of Americans and their money, Lieberman Research Corporation surveyed 2,250 adults to ascertain how economic patterns had changed. The study was the fifth survey over a 5-year period (*Americans and Their Money*, 1987). Some of the major findings were as follows:

1. Although savings and investments had increased from the previous year, 10% reported they have no savings or investments. Of those earning less than $15,000, 25% reported no savings or investments.

2. Following several years in which consumer debt increased, debt was observed to decline. Consumer loans and the use of credit cards were both down from the previous year.

3. The sample was divided in terms of being content with their personal financial situation, that is, 59% were comfortable, 41% were uncomfortable–a response that was about the same as the previous year.

4. The average amount in savings and investments, excluding real estate, increased from $39,900 to $44,200.

5. Two out of three people reported they went on spending sprees, more often when they were in a good mood rather than in a bad mood. Twice as many women as men went on shopping sprees when they felt depressed.

6. Things that the majority believe are overpriced include cars, car insurance, lawyers' fees, and interest charges on credit cards.

Money and Conflict

One-half of all married couples argued during the last year about money. The three most important issues were: deciding what to spend money on (29%), spending beyond budget limits (26%), and the price to spend on things (21%). Higher-income couples, (with annual incomes $50,000 and over), more than lower income couples (with annual incomes more than $15,000), argued more about how much to save for retirement and investments (*Americans and Their Money*, 1987).

For over a half of a century, family investigators have reported that one of the most frequent sources of conflict in American families has been the use of money. Family therapists commonly report that conflict over money serves as a shield for underlying problems such as who has the power in the family. A wife who earns more than her husband may resent his telling her she spent too much for a dress. The same wife may resent her husband purchasing a car without her approval when she believes that the car payments will take a good bit of their discretionary income. Men who come from families in which the father made the economic decisions and who are married to women from families in which the mother made the major economic decisions are likely to encounter *greater* conflict. Couples from families where there was greater equity between the mother and father in economic decision making are likely to be happier.

Although many couples are able to resolve conflicts involving economic decisions, many must go through a learning period that is not easy. As in most conflict resolution efforts, it is important to recognize that even though your partner and you do not agree, you can learn to appreciate the viewpoint of the other person. Few couples will agree always, but they can practice being respectful of each other, and they can accommodate differences in viewpoints: "I'll accept your irrationality about clothes if you accept my irrationality about investing in the stock market."

At times, however, stalemates occur. In many instances, family therapists can be of real value in helping couples to examine their differences. In

James Walters

Economic Changes

In recent years recession and inflation have had a profound impact on American family life. Families are worried because of their lack of economic progress and look back to the the 1950s and 1960s when the future looked promising because of the significant increases in family income. The trend in the economic well-being of families is clearly seen in Table 13–1. Between 1950 and 1970, dramatic increases were evident in incomes of families in the United States. Over the last two decades, however, little progress has been made in median income. Today, there is little doubt that how we manage our resources as a nation and as family members greatly affects the quality of our family life and the happiness we obtain.

matters involving financial decisions regarding insurance, taxes, and wills, certified financial planners are very helpful. For guidance regarding investment, real estate, and tax shelters, chartered financial consultants can guide couples so that they will make sound financial decisions that are based upon their particular circumstances (Garman & Forgue, 1988). Just as it is often wise to seek the guidance of a specialist in construction before purchasing a house, seeking the guidance of a financial consultant makes good sense in planning ways to establish estates, in considering insurance alternatives, in determining ways to take advantage of tax-deferred annuities, and in selecting a savings plan. Because of the complexities of laws, few families can solve all of the problems that life presents without the guidance of an array of competent specialists. Wise guidance from a professional who understands your needs can save your family thousands of dollars over a lifetime. Be sure your advisor is qualified to provide you with the guidance you seek, and choose someone whom you trust and with whom you can interact comfortably.

Table 13–1 Changes in Median Family Income in Constant Dollars Over the Last Generation

	Median 1983 Current Dollars	Median 1983 Constant Dollars	% Change Constant Dollars
1950	$ 3,319	$13,736	
1960	$ 5,600	$18,907	37.6
1970	$ 9,867	$25,317	33.9
1980	$21,023	$25,418	0.4
1981	$22,388	$24,525	-3.5
1982	$23,433	$24,187	-1.4
1983	$24,580	$24,580	1.6

Source: U.S. Bureau of the Census. (1985c). "Money income of families—Median family income in current and constant (1983) dollars, by race and Spanish origin of householder: 1950 to 1983." *Statistical abstract of the United States: 1985*, 105th ed. Table 743, p. 446, Washington, DC: U.S. Government Printing Office.

Because we are a people who have been socialized to expect increasing affluence, many of us have not learned to save, to shop wisely, to use credit carefully, or to conserve the materials we have. We have operated on the philosophy that if we want it we should have it. The economic indicators suggest, however, that we need to be less wasteful, to be better shoppers and managers, and to be satisfied with living within our income. We have grown up with the expectation that our economic situation should get better each year. Increasingly, families assume that to a large extent, their future well-being is determined not by their own actions but by what happens to the nation. As noted in Figure 13–1, there is an upward trend in median family income, and, as

of 1990, unemployment rates in the United States are low. Unfortunately, however, many young people entering the labor market are finding that pay for beginners is low and that child care for young people with children is often difficult to find and is expensive.

Managing Finances

Because, as individuals, we often are able to do little to affect public policy or the state of our national economy, it is far more effective for us to change what we can—the management of our personal finances—in order to increase our enjoyment of life. Money management is an important

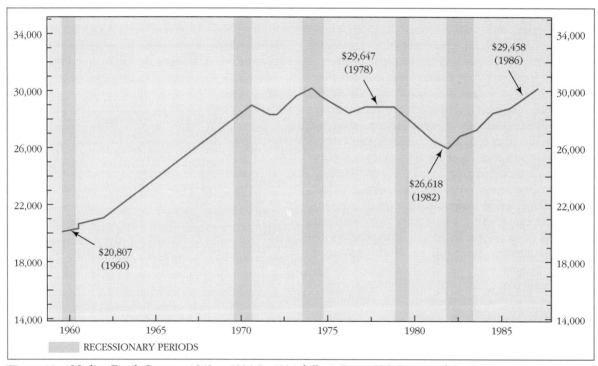

Figure 13–1 Median Family Income: 1960 to 1986 (in 1986 dollars) *Source*: U.S. Bureau of the Census (1986a). "Money income of households, families and persons in the United States." *Current population reports.* Series P-60, No. 159, p. 2. Washington, DC: U.S. Government Printing Office.

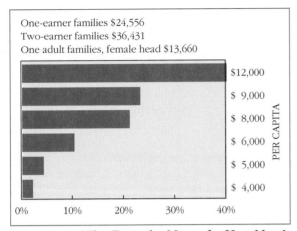

One-earner families $24,556
Two-earner families $36,431
One adult families, female head $13,660

PER CAPITA

$12,000

$ 9,000

$ 8,000

$ 6,000

$ 5,000

$ 4,000

0%   10%   20%   30%   40%

Figure 13–2 Who Earns the Money for How Many? *Source*: U.S. Bureau of the Census. (1985b). "Money income of families—Aggregate mean, and per capita income, by family characteristics. *Statistical abstract of the United States: 1985*, 105th ed. Table 746, p. 448. Washington, DC.

aspect of marriage and can assist a couple in reducing stress within their relationship and in achieving many of their goals. Although the accumulation of money itself is rarely cited as a goal in life, the realization of many goals depends on money. Because money is closely tied to security and the achievement of goals, lack of skill in handling money or disagreement on how to handle it is often a source of conflict.

Many families have to forego luxuries in order to maintain economic stability within the family. This is readily understood by a review of Figure 13–2 in which data are presented that in the United States the per capita annual income for approximately 10% of the population is approximately $6,000, and that slightly over 20% have only $8,000. With the average family with one person employed earning only $24,556, it is often necessary for both the husband and wife to be employed in order to achieve the standard of living they wish to attain. Two difficult tasks for most families are (a) recognizing what they need compared to what they want and (b) set-

ting realistic financial goals. For example, a second car may be essential for a family without access to public transportation, but it may be a luxury for a family living in an area with buses and trains providing adequate services. Also, the intensity of economic pressures within a family depends on the presence or absence of children. Each stage of the family life cycle, from marriage through old age, has economic needs specific to it. How these needs are met affects later phases of the life of the family and its individual members (Mullis & Schnittgrund, 1982).

Because few families have enough money to buy everything they want, it is important to establish priorities about what things and what experiences are most important (Garman & Forgue, 1988). No one can tell you what to purchase or what experiences to save for because family and individual goals vary tremendously. In considering a purchase, it is important to ask, "Can I live without it?" Such a question tends to inhibit impulse buying, one of the chief causes of wrecked budgets.

One important principle to remember in setting and adhering to priorities is that errors not only cost money, but peace of mind as well. The most common errors in financial management include using savings too freely to meet expenses, purchasing things one cannot afford, waiting too long to have cars repaired, and using savings for luxuries. By eliminating errors in spending, families can save more money, lower their stress level, and achieve greater satisfaction. All of us have grown up as consumers and have learned dozens of sound principles, such as, "the least expensive article is not always the best value." It is important to review these principles periodically to keep ourselves from making decisions based on momentary impulses.

Devising a Spending Plan

Few activities are dreaded more than developing a spending plan. Some people believe it is impossible and reject the concept, believing that they can do as well without one. Others find the structure of a plan for their earnings and spending helpful. Planning how money will be used, however, can lead a couple to communicate their values about the use of their resources more realistically and to define their priorities more clearly. Gitman and Joehnk (1987) describe a typical strategy:

1. Develop a statement of your financial goals.
2. Plan strategies to put your goals in action.
3. Implement your plan.
4. Assess your progress periodically.
5. Evaluate your results and make corrections in your plan.
6. Revise your goals when they are achieved or changed.

Marriage often heightens the sensitivity people feel regarding their personal use of money. It is unrealistic for husbands and wives to assume that this area of living together will be conflict-free. Nevertheless, openness and careful resolution of many differences of opinion will make it easier to enjoy using money together. Staying within the budget in order to reach goals, such as purchasing a home, is an important factor that can contribute to happiness. Families who budget are better able to control their spending, to avoid financial problems, to attain goals, to increase wealth, and to improve their life (Schnittgrund & Baker, 1983).

A spending plan is a specific plan for using the family's income over a time period of a few months or a year; it is a method of financial planning that is designed to assist families in utilizing financial resources in such a way that their goals and needs are best fulfilled with the income available. A couple should consider the following in making a budget:

1. *The major family goals.* Each family has its own goals that vary with income, number of children,

interests of family members, and stage of the family life cycle. An important step in effective financial planning is to identify what the goals of family members are. Unity in family objectives and the ability to place family needs and objectives above individual goals were identified by Maddux (1988) as factors important in a family's ability to withstand economic crises. Couples need to ask themselves, "What is most important to us in life?" Long-range as well as short-term goals need to be pinpointed so that couples will have a better idea how financial resources can best be used. Long-term goals may include the purchase of a home or a college education for the children. Short-range goals may include a vacation or a new car. If a budget is to assist in the attainment of family goals, it must be realistically based on level of income, it must be checked periodically, and it must be adjusted to meet changing conditions.

2. *Estimated expenditures.* It is important for the family to estimate approximately how much money will be spent each month. An efficient way of doing this is first to establish expense categories: (a) money set aside for long-term goals and an emergency fund, (b) fixed or regular expenses, such as car payments, insurance premiums, rent or house payments, and (c) variable or irregular expenses, such as clothing expenditures, automobile upkeep, food, and recreation. Then a record of monthly expenditures can be made in order to develop a realistic budget (Stribling, 1987). This is a time-consuming procedure, but it can help to give you an accurate idea of where your money is going. The kind of information you should collect is shown in Table 13–2.

On-going budgeting, however, does not need this daily collecting of every detail. If you always spend 75 cents for bus fare to work, you can budget that over a week or month. Everyone who uses a budget goes through a period of trial and error. Because events and situations change, no one system will be perfect. Budgets should be flexible to allow for fluctuations in various areas of spending. For example, $40.00 a month for gifts may be adequate except during the Christmas season. That variation should be included in the budget. The ideal budget should help you to make the best use of your financial resources; it should not enslave the budget-keepers.

Some expenses remain fairly constant throughout the year, such as house payments or rent, automobile payments, and insurance premiums that are monthly. These can be budgeted with a good deal of accuracy. Other items vary slightly, such as food and clothing. For example, September clothing expenses may be high if children must be outfitted for school. Some expenditures may come once or twice a year, such as an automobile insurance premium. Big items may be spaced throughout the year as follows:

January: His life insurance payment

February: Her dues to a professional society

March: Income protection policy payment

April: College fund for children

May: Car tune-up and car emergency fund

June: Vacation

July: His life insurance payment

August: House taxes

September: Clothes for school for children

October: Her life insurance payment

November: Christmas or Hanukkah gifts

December: Entertainment for holidays

When predictable payments are examined over a year, ways of structuring them at different times become apparent. For example, in this case the husband's insurance payments are made semiannually and are scheduled at times when other expenses are less. Some families contribute to charities, to local organizations, synagogues, or churches on an annual basis; others choose to give amounts each month or week.

It is necessary as well to plan for financial emergencies. Few families get through any given year without unexpected expenses. A reserve fund is certainly helpful in meeting unforeseen expenditures; otherwise, families must use credit or savings if income is not sufficient to absorb the extra expense. If the family is fortunate enough to have a full emergency fund at year's end, it can always be transferred to savings. Extra money is rarely a problem.

3. *Balance between income and expenses.* Families occasionally spend more than their income. One purpose of a budget is to help avoid overspending so that they may live within their income. Examining past expenditures helps to determine where current expenses can be reduced, thus aiding the task of making income and expenses balance. Often it can be helpful to calculate what percentage of your earnings you are spending on the essentials such as food, shelter, and travel to work. Generally, you can spend about 25% of your salary on shelter without getting into financial difficulties. Of course, if you can afford it, you may wish to plan 35% for shelter.

4. *Commitment to a spending plan.* Before making a decision to follow a particular form of planning, both partners should ask themselves some practical questions about putting it into operation: Is the plan realistic? Does it meet the needs of family members reasonably well? Does it provide for major long-range and short-range family goals? Does the budget allow for the possibility of emergencies? Does it permit the family to live within its income?

Budgets and the Single-parent Family

In a study focusing on the nation's families from 1985 to 2000, several changes are clearly apparent. One of these affecting family finances is that the

Table 13–2 Record of Your Expenses

Date	Item (or Service) Bought	Food and Beverages	Household Operation and Maintenance	Furnishings and Equipment	Clothing
		$	$	$	$
Total		$_____	$_____	$_____	$_____

Source: Reprinted from "A guide to budgeting for the family." (1972). *Home and Garden Bulletin No.* 108. Washington, DC: U.S. Department of Agriculture.

number of single women rearing children is increasing. In 1978 a total of 14.4% of all families were headed by a woman (Masnick & Bane, 1980b).

By 1985 there were 19.7 million more households, and 2.3 million more single or previously married women with children at home. This means that the traditional pattern of the husband working to support his wife and children is changing. More and more women, both single and married, are gainfully employed outside the home. In 1979, 42.4% of the civilian labor force was made up of women, up from 38.2% in 1970. It is estimated that 51.1% of women aged 16 and over are now employed (Masnick & Bane, 1980b). As a group, single-parent families face different financial concerns than other families. For these families, financial knowledge and careful planning for using their resources are critical to their survival.

Sarah is 31, divorced, and rearing her 5-year-old daughter. Initially, she felt very uneasy that she had to make financial plans and prepare for the future on her own. She decided to go back to law school to prepare for a well-paying legal job to support herself and her daughter. She obtained a loan to help meet her educational and personal expenses for the 3 years in law school, and with a monthly income of $760 she budgeted as follows:

Income

Child support	*$250*
Loan & part-time jobs	*510*
Total	*$760*

Expenses

Rent	*$250*
Utilities	*55*
Telephone	*30*

Personal	Transportation	Medical Care	Recreation and Education	Gifts and Contributions
$	$	$	$	$
$_____	$_____	$_____	$_____	$_____

Food	*170*
Clothing	*50*
Car insurance, maintenance	*100*
Cleaning, personal, medical	*65*
Misc.	*40*
Total	*$760*

Sarah realized that the tight budget she was forced to live within was temporary. As soon as she finished her studies, she found a position as a law clerk to a judge at a salary of $18,000. She was able to begin putting some money aside for savings, to take out life and disability insurance, and to repay the school loan.

In one study of couples following divorce, the men experienced a 42% improvement in their level of living, whereas the women experienced a 73% decline in theirs (Lenore J. Weitzman, cited in Weinstein, 1986). Such a study not only illustrates the inequity that often follows a divorce, it emphasizes how carefully women should plan so they will not be disadvantaged should a divorce occur. The more money a woman earns, the greater the likelihood that she'll get divorced. For those who earn over $50,000 a year, the divorce rate is four times the average (Weinstein, 1986). In any event, women can no longer afford to be excluded or to exclude themselves from the financial management of their households (National Center for Health Statistics, 1982).

Coping with Inflation

In the development of a balanced spending plan, all families must cope with inflation, especially when increases in their income do not keep up with the increase in the cost of goods and services. Although inflation may be low in one year, in another year it may be high (see Table 13-3). Families have re-

Table 13–3 Cost of Items in Relation to a Hypothetical 6% Rate of Inflation

Item	1990 Cost	2000 (6% inflation)
Sports jacket	80.00	145.00
Belt	14.00	25.00
Blouse	40.00	72.00
Blue plate special	5.00	9.00
Shirt	25.00	45.00
Shoes	42.00	75.00
Coat	290.00	520.00
House	150,000.00	270,000.00
House	56,000.00	101,000.00
Tuition (semester)	630.00	1,125.00
Tuition (semester)	1,200.00	2,150.00

sponded to inflation by reducing expenditures in practical ways:

1. *Eliminate purchases or expenses that are not absolutely necessary.* A family may decide they do not have to maintain two cars, so one car payment can be eliminated. Or they can decide to repair their present automobile instead of purchasing a new one.

2. *Acquire services and commodities through some means other than money.* In some communities families make extensive use of exchange or barter. Each contributes special skills or service in exchange for needed service or goods. For example, a friend might help you paint the interior of your house in exchange for your helping to put insulation in his attic or in exchange for child care.

3. *Increase shopping skills.* Small reductions in a number of expenses significantly reduce the to-

tal amount being spent. Because food costs are a fairly large part of each budget, some tactics to cope with food expenditures are listed.

a. Use unit pricing (how much an item costs per pound or per ounce) to decide on the best buy. Without a calculator, it can be difficult to tell whether 18 ounces of peanut butter for $1.98 is a better buy than 16 ounces for $1.85. However, many supermarkets do provide unit prices.

b. Larger sizes often are less expensive per ounce or per serving. Check unit prices to be sure. They are not economical, however, if your family does not use them. If only one family member likes grapefruit, it is wiser to buy 2 or 3 at 50 cents each than to buy a 20-pound bag and have most of them rot.

c. Bakery products are cheaper when they are a day old.

d. House brands or generic goods are usually cheaper than highly advertised name brands.

e. Look for seasonal specials like apples in the fall or strawberries in early summer.

Rickey Yanaura / The University of Alabama

---

10 Ways to Save Money on Energy Sources

1. *Set your thermostat at conservative levels.* Try 78 degrees in the summer and 68 degrees in the winter. Each degree increased in the summer and each degree reduced in the winter can save 3% to 5%.

2. *Use fluorescent lighting as much as possible.* A standard light bulb uses at least three times as much energy to produce the same amount of light as a fluorescent bulb.

3. *Use cold or warm water to wash your clothes whenever possible.* A water heater is one of the largest energy users in the home.

4. *Set your water heater at no more than 140 degrees.* This temperature is adequate even if you have a dishwasher.

5. *Watch how long you preheat your oven.* When you use the oven for broiling or roasting, preheating is normally not required. When preheating the oven for baking, avoid preheating longer than necessary.

6. *Plan menus so that more than one dish can be prepared in the oven at once.* Small, on-the-counter ovens are great energy savers as are microwave ovens.

7. *Carefully insulate your home.* Insulation can pay for itself within a few years and is an excellent investment.

8. *Wrap heating/air conditioning ducts under the house with insulation materials as well as pipes from the water heater.*

9. *Consider the use of storm windows.* Often they save on both heat and air-conditioning bills.

10. *Use an attic fan.* An attic fan can serve to reduce the temperature markedly in an attic during hot summer months, thus reducing air-conditioning costs.

---

f. Meat is one of the most expensive food items. Experiment with vegetarian dishes or try casseroles that use small amounts of meat.

g. Plan menus for a week at a time. Make a shopping list and follow it. Resist the urge to pick up extra items. If you find you cannot do it, limit yourself to two unplanned items. Do not shop when hungry.

h. Read grocery ads in the newspapers, and plan menus around specials. Clip and redeem coupons for items that you usually buy. In some communities grocers allow double the value of the coupon on certain days of the week. As a result some families can easily save several hundred dollars each year.

i. Be aware of marketing techniques that make economy shopping difficult. Often higher-priced items are placed on shelves at eye level, whereas less expensive items are on the bottom shelves or much higher. The hasty shopper may never see the better buys. Cereals are often located at child level on the assumption that children will see them and pressure parents to buy them.

Clothing, linen, or furniture outlet stores offer name-brand goods at reduced prices. Compare costs not only of the item but also of credit, especially when purchasing a car, furniture, or a house.

Finally, the wise consumer resists impulse buying (Gitman & Joehnk, 1987). One of the best ways to curb impulse spending is to allow a cooling-off period before buying an item. The buyer's perspective often changes in a day or two.

Overspending and Misuse of Credit

One of the dangers of borrowing is overspending, especially because it is so easy to do. Normally, it is considered improper (routinely, at least) to use credit (a) to meet basic living expenses, (b) to make expensive impulse purchases, and (c) to purchase nondurable goods, except those purchased for convenience, such as gasoline (Gitman & Joehnk, 1987).

Everyone has heard, "You get what you pay for." We sometimes use this rationalization to justify what we want but believe we cannot afford. We give ourselves permission to spend too much even when we believe we should be prudent economically. Occasionally, an opportunity to purchase at a price we "can't afford to pass up" comes along. Like a child selecting food in a cafeteria line, however, the credit consumer can be tempted to overconsume. Usually, we can justify all sorts of purchases, even though we may regret them later.

On the other hand, inferior merchandise may give less than adequate performance. The performance, of course, depends on what we expect of it. Shoes worn only a few times to formal occasions do not require the quality construction of shoes worn daily to school. Children who live in jeans may not need expensive clothing. In contrast, working parents may need a more extensive wardrobe. Wise consumer behavior calls for a good fit between the needs we have and the quality of the products we purchase and a credit reserve to be able to take advantage of unusual opportunities when they present themselves.

The temptation to buy more than we need, or better quality than our needs dictate, coupled with the ease of consumer credit make overspending quite seductive. It is clear that the misuse of credit leads families into financial difficulty and has led many people into bankruptcy. Personal bankruptcies in the United States have dramatically increased in the last decade.

Few things facilitate misuse of credit faster than the indiscriminate use of credit cards. Through overuse of their bank cards, many families quickly find themselves in debt. What can they do to remedy the situation? Perhaps the most important first step is to review fixed expenses and obligations to obtain a realistic picture of how much money is left after these expenses are met. The family may then decide that some expenses can be eliminated or reduced.

In using credit cards to charge purchases, it is wise to use the minimum payment option only during temporary financial emergencies. When more than 6 months is needed to repay a credit balance, it is better to obtain a cash loan. One of the primary advantages of credit cards, however, is that they preclude the necessity for carrying a large amount of cash and they are more readily accepted than personal checks. The fact that you are provided with a monthly bill helps you to monitor how you have spent your money (Lang, 1988).

Another helpful step in reducing debt is to contract no new debt until a significant reduction has been achieved in the debt level. Some families may need to turn to a family service agency or a nonprofit consumer credit counseling service for guidance.

If the family owes several different creditors, it may be desirable to take out a new loan for the purpose of consolidating the debts. The advantages of this are that the family then owes only one creditor and gains needed time to repay the money. It may also reduce the monthly payments to a level the couple can handle. When a consolidation loan is considered, care should be exercised in the selection of a loan agency. All the costs of credit must be examined and compared. Usually, the consolidation loan increases the cost of credit because the repayment is extended over a longer period of time.

Some people trying to consolidate their debts have fallen prey to unethical debt-consolidation agencies. In many states commercial debt adjusters are not permitted to provide services. The Legal Aid Society, some professional unions, credit unions, and other organizations offer assistance to people with large debts. The National Foundation for Consumer Credit has been instrumental in the establishment of consumer credit counseling services in many states and in Canada.

Families that are overextended financially will probably have to commit themselves to a lower level of living until a significant reduction in the debt level has been achieved. This adjustment is easier if they recognize that this sacrifice is temporary and that they are making progress toward the goal of solvency (Rosefsky, 1989). There are three ways to adjust to financial problems: change the level of consumption, increase the efficiency of resource use, and expand income (Hogan, 1980).

Cost of Credit

Few people realized how much they were paying for credit until the U. S. Congress passed the Consumer Credit Protection Act, which made it mandatory for the lender to indicate to the borrower the finance charge and the annual percentage rate of the loan. The finance charge is the cost the customer pays to obtain the credit, which on many cards is about 18% annually or 1.5% each month. One advantage of the Consumer Credit Protection Act is that it clarifies how much consumers are paying for credit and enables them to weigh alternatives. Often the amount saved by buying an item on sale does not compensate for the interest on the loan over an extended period. There is merit in adding the cost of the interest to the purchase price of an article as a matter of routine to determine its true cost. An

$8,000 used car, for example, may end up costing well over $9,000 if the payments are extended over a period of years.

Past financial advice has always been to avoid credit and pay cash. But today, it is recognized that in some instances it is wise to buy on credit. For example it is normally a good idea to

1. *Use credit to avoid price increases.* If you are reasonably certain that an item is going to increase in price, it is often better to get reasonable credit to finance the purchase than to delay making the purchase. This is particularly true if major items can be purchased on sale.

2. *Use credit when it is interest free.* Generally credit payments come due after a certain period of time. If you buy something on October 4 on a credit card for which billing is October 5, the charge will not show up on your bill until the November statement.

3. *Use credit when you know you will be reimbursed for the bills.* For example, if you have a hospital bill, use your credit card to pay for it. By the time the charge clears the credit card company and comes back to you, you probably will have received reimbursement from your insurance company.

4. *Keep a record of all credit purchases.* Keep receipts as a record, or have a sheet of paper to record the running total so that you know how much you owe at one time. Set a ceiling for your credit debt—for example, 15% of your take-home pay. This should include all credit debts except your mortgage payment.

5. *Keep credit limits to a minimum.* This may help you to avoid the temptation to overspend. Avoid using them except for large items.

There are hazards in getting involved in credit agreements. Do not accept verbal warranties or pledges of salespersons; always get agreements in writing. Do not be in a hurry to sign any installment contract or agreement, especially if you are

Consumer Protection: It's the Law

The Federal government has enacted a number of laws to protect your consumer rights.

Truth-In-Lending Act. Requires lenders to inform prospective borrowers of the terms of loan agreements, including the finance charge, the annual percentage rate, and how these are computed. Provides the form for such disclosures and establishes limits and conditions for creditor liability.

Equal Credit Opportunity Act. Prohibits credit discrimination based on age, sex, marital status, race, color, religion, national origin, place of residence, income from public assistance or alimony, or because you have made a good faith exercise of any of your rights under the federal consumer credit laws. If credit is denied, notification must be in writing, and consumers have the right to request and receive the reason for the denial.

Credit Card Authorization. Prohibits the issuance of unsolicited cards. Limits cardholder liability to $50 for unauthorized use if reported promptly.

Fair Credit Billing Act. Establishes procedures for consumer resolution of billing errors while protecting consumer's credit rating. Sets rules for length of billing period, crediting of payments and return of goods.

Fair Credit Reporting Act. Restricts the use of consumer credit reports, and requires deletion of obsolete information and sending of corrections. Mandates notifications and availability of report to consumers. Sets up procedures for investigating disputed information and making corrections.

Real Estate Settlement Procedures Act. States that consumers must receive complete disclosure of settlement costs in advance of closing. Establishes procedures for escrow accounts, and prohibits kickbacks and "hidden" closing costs.

Electronic Fund Transfers Act. Establishes rules for operation of electronic banking systems. Requires documentation of transfers and disclosure of terms and conditions. Sets up error resolution procedures, and limits consumer liability for unauthorized transfers.

Others. There are a number of other consumer protection laws that cover a variety of issues: consumer leasing, advertising, debt collection practices, garnishment of wages, data on home loans, and community reinvestment. To learn more about consumer laws relating to the financial services industry, contact any of the following in Washington, D.C.: Federal Reserve Bank, Federal Home Loan Bank Board, or The National Credit Union Administration.

Source: Consumer protection: It's the law. (1987). *Citicorp Consumer Views,* *18*(3), 104. Published with permission by Citicorp, 330 Madison Avenue, New York, NY 10017.

not sure you want it and have not consulted your spouse. Do not sign any loan contract with blank spaces that could be filled in to your disadvantage. Take time to read and understand the terms of any contract or agreement you sign. Do not allow salespersons to pressure or rush you.

Intelligent consumers know that the cost of credit varies with the lending agency, and they "shop" for credit. Life insurance loans—for those who have owned life insurance for several years and have built up significant loan values—are normally one of the better values with their low interest rates.

Also, persons who are members of credit unions should explore the cost of credit there as well as at other lending agencies.

Borrowing Money

Of course, unanticipated needs and opportunities occur that require borrowing money. Normally, one obtains information from several lending sources in the community. One couple, however, who found their request denied by their bank found another source from which to borrow.

Nick and Nancy planned to move from California to Alabama where Nick had obtained a new position on the faculty of the University of Alabama. There was one problem, however; Nick had secured an estimate of the cost of moving his furniture and learned that he was going to have to come up with approximately $6,000.00. This was no problem, he believed, because he had an excellent credit rating. When he went to his bank, however, he learned that he was ineligible for the loan because he was moving out of state. Obviously, he had to find another solution. He remembered that his life insurance policy had a loan provision that would enable him to borrow the money he needed, so he called his insurance agent who provided him with the forms he needed to apply for the loan. What he hadn't expected, however, was the very

low rate of interest he had to pay. He vowed that he would repay the loan promptly so that in the future when he needed money, he would always have the opportunity to take advantage of this valuable resource.

Savings and Debt

Savings should be a part of every family's plan if at all possible. A savings account that grows over the years provides a sense of security, and it can help families avoid paying interest when they want a new television or have an opportunity to purchase a car at a good price. The financial success of many families is based upon their determination to continue to set aside money even when they are acquiring new debt (Heffernan, 1982).

The advantage in saving money is fairly apparent to most people; the difficulty is in knowing how. The old adage, "A penny saved is a penny earned," has little value. Suppose, however, a young family could save a dollar a day—every day—over a period of years. Many families can save a dollar every day without significantly affecting their level of living and with interest compounded over a period of time, such a savings plan can provide a financial "buffer" in emergencies (see Table 13-4).

Keep in mind that the people with the most limited resources must utilize resources most effectively. Poor people cannot afford to make mistakes,

Table 13–4 How Much Can You Save Each Month?

How Savings Grow*	$5 Monthly	$10 Monthly	$15 Monthly	$20 Monthly	$30 Monthly	$50 Monthly
1 year	62.63	125.26	187.89	250.52	375.78	626.30
5 years	369.22	738.44	1,107.66	1,476.88	2,215.32	3,692.20
10 years	917.87	1,835.73	2,753.60	3,671.46	5,507.19	9,178.65
20 years	2,944.55	5,889.10	8,833.65	11,778.20	17,667.30	29,445.50

* Based on 8% interest compounded quarterly.
Source: First National Lincoln, Lincoln, NE.

because they usually have the least amount in reserve to carry them over when emergencies arise. Remember that emergencies arise for everyone, and those who suffer the least are those who are best prepared. Savings are a good way to keep financial difficulties to a minimum (Stribling, 1987).

There are several different ways of saving. Banks today are offering new ways of saving in an effort to encourage people to put more money into savings accounts. Check with your local banks and see what they offer before deciding which bank provides you with the greatest rewards.

In recent years in the United States there has been little change in the proportion of income that individuals have saved, yet debt has risen. The danger of such a trend lies in the fact that should a

Joel Gordon

family encounter a difficult financial period, they might not have sufficient funds to pay their bills. Many families do not have savings equal to the 2 months of earnings that is generally recommended by family economists. With employment disability insurance, some protection is afforded, but savings are needed for emergencies that you do not expect, such as paying a large amount to the Internal Revenue Service.

Why do families incur large amounts of debt and so little savings? It is far easier to adjust a lifestyle upward than to do without, and it is easy to rationalize large expenditures, e.g., "It makes much better sense to trade cars for only $3,000.00 and get a car that is one year newer than to pay for an upcoming repair bill, especially when the amount I pay each month in car payments is just the same."

Homeowners, for example, believe that if they can handle the additional cost of a larger house and the increase in taxes and homeowners insurance, they will have no other house-related expenses; but they have not considered that the new, larger house costs more to heat. Most families believe that the furniture they have presently will "fit" their new house very well. In reality, a change in houses very often requires changes in furnishings. It is surprisingly easy to spend $5,000.00 on just a few things, as families have discovered when they find that new curtains and draperies and a new furnace are required. Becoming overextended financially can cause real stress that leads to arguments and unhappiness.

Insurance

Life insurance, most families believe, is necessary. The need for life insurance varies with the number and ages of family members. Studies have shown that—considering the amount of income lost when wives leave employment to have children—it costs, on the average, approximately $200,000 to support a middle-class child from conception through college.

Obviously, if a spouse dies when the children are very young, the remaining adult faces an economic burden that may be difficult to carry alone. Many families that are mindful of the costs of child rearing seek to provide protection during the years when demands for protection from economic disaster are greatest. After considering various alternatives, many couples decide on term insurance.

Term insurance provides protection for a specified period and is less expensive than ordinary life insurance; however, if death does not occur within the specified term, the holder receives neither the money paid into the plan nor interest on money paid (Rosefsky, 1989). The purchase of life insurance should be made after consideration of many factors. Family financial counselors and reputable life insurance agents can provide information to assist in making decisions. It is wise to discuss needs with several representatives to be sure that the facts are understood correctly. If resources are limited, planning must be executed even more carefully. Many young couples, relatively inexperienced in long-term financial planning, are unaware of the many factors to be considered.

Because of competition among companies, their success in management, their willingness to insure high risks, and numerous other factors, considerable variation exists in the amount each individual pays for insurance. One cannot assume that everyone pays about the same amount, regardless of the company.

In order to encourage sales, a variety of plans have been developed by companies, and the options should be considered individually. For example, some term insurance policies can be converted to ordinary life insurance within a specific period without proving insurability. The conversion requires higher premiums, but it is an extremely attractive feature if, for example, one develops a permanent disability that would prevent obtaining life insurance.

Over the years the cost of term insurance increases because the probability that death will occur in a given year increases with age. In most families, income increases during the early years of marriage. On the average, couples have a greater income at 35 than they do at 25. As soon as they can afford it, some couples wish to obtain *ordinary life insurance* that provides protection throughout the entire life of an individual. Most people do live past middle age and will need life insurance—although normally not so much—after their children become economically independent.

Another type of insurance policy is called *permanent life insurance*. The amount of money a person pays in premiums with this type of policy, in contrast to term insurance, does not increase throughout life. The amount of premiums the individual pays on the policy depends upon the age at which the policy is purchased. The younger the person is at the time, the less the death risk (Rosefsky, 1989). The person pays more for permanent life insurance premiums than is actually required for protection during the younger years in order to maintain lower premiums during the later years.

An *endowment policy* is essentially life insurance that is paid in full within a specified period of time. Money paid into the policy accrues interest, and all the money, including interest, can be withdrawn at the end of the specified period (Garman & Forgue, 1988). Therefore, this type of plan is often used by parents to provide educational funds for their children. It is also frequently used for retirement benefits. A $25,000 endowment policy that is designed to mature when a child is 18 provides money for college in the amount of $25,000 when the child reaches that age. If the parent dies before the child reaches 18, he or she collects $25,000 as a beneficiary.

The quality of family life can be secured if families protect themselves from financial disaster through adequate insurance protection. For this reason it is important that families have medical and hospitalization insurance; major medical insurance for serious, extended illnesses; and disability income protection insurance to ensure that income

Protection from Losses

Insurance is a financial tool that allows you to protect your family against risks you face in everyday life. These risks include premature death, disability, large medical expenses, loss of property, liability to others, and unemployment.

Premature Death

A major financial objective is to protect dependents from financial consequences of death. Needs vary from family to family, but the following categories apply to most families.

1. Final lump sum expenses (last illness and burial expenses, cost of settlement and administration of the deceased's estate, and any federal estate and/or state death taxes that may be due).
2. Income for family.
3. Income for spouse after children are self-supporting.
4. Special needs (paying off mortgage or educating children).

Planning devices to cover losses due to premature death are

1. Life insurance
   a. Individual life insurance
   b. Group life insurance
      • through insured's employer or business
      • through association group plan, through professional or fraternal association
      • Credit life insurance payable to a creditor to pay off a debt
2. Social Security survivor's benefits
3. Death benefits
   a. Private pension plans
   b. Profit-sharing plans
   c. Tax sheltered annuities, Keogh, IRA
4. Other income or investments

Disability

The total and permanent disability of a family breadwinner can be more catastrophic economically than premature death. Your family still has their normal living expenses, plus the increased costs due to the disability.

Some planning devices to protect against disability income loss include the following:

1. Health insurance
   a. Individual disability income insurance

b. Group disability income insurance
- through employer or business
- through association group plan

c. Credit disability income insurance payable to a creditor.

2. Disability benefits under life insurance policies
3. Social Security disability benefits
4. Workmen's compensation disability benefits
5. Disability benefits under private pension and profit-sharing plans
6. Employer sick-pay plans
7. Other income and investments

Medical Care

With the high cost of medical care, families need to protect themselves against medical care costs. Major sources for coverage of medical care costs include the following:

1. Health insurance
    a. employer-provided medical expense coverage
    b. individual medical expense insurance
2. Medical payments coverage under liability insurance policies and "no-fault" automobile coverage
3. Social Security benefits (Medicare)
4. Workmen's compensation medical benefits
5. Other income and investments

Property and Liability

Most families are exposed to risk of loss or damage to their real and/or personal property. Types of property owned by families that are subject to loss include:

1. Home (including vacation home and investment real estate)
2. Furniture, clothing, and other personal property
3. Cars
4. Credit cards, cash

Liability losses can result from negligent acts. Examples of liability exposures that might result in claims are

1. Ownership of property (residence, vacation home, rental property)
2. Ownership, rental, or use of automobiles or boats.
3. Professional and business activities

Source: Maddux, E. (1988). *Family planning basics.* Athens, Ga: Cooperative Extension Service. Reprinted by permission.

will be available in the event of a disabling illness. Although income protection insurance that provides benefits beginning with the onset of illness is quite expensive, there are programs that begin payment after an extended period, such as 90 days of illness, and these policies are fairly reasonable. Although many families can endure 3 months without income, few could endure indefinitely without some support. Such programs are essential for families who find it difficult to borrow from financial institutions, who do not have a large savings account, or who cannot rely on family or friends during extended periods of illness without income.

Some financial advisors regard disability income insurance as important as life insurance. Most insurance specialists agree on the following considerations with regard to disability insurance:

1. The policy should provide income for a period of at least 5 years for sickness or accident.

2. The policy should pay benefits if you cannot practice your regular occupation. Many fail to pay if you can perform any kind of work.

3. Look for a recurrent disability clause so that benefits will begin anew if you are disabled, recover, and are disabled by the same condition again. Some policies simply pick up where they left off, thus eligible time of coverage is reduced.

4. Make sure the policy is noncancelable and guaranteed renewable. Some policies are cancelable at any time; if renewable, premiums may be increased (Garman & Forgue, 1988; Gitman & Joehnk, 1987; Rosefsky, 1989).

When shopping for disability insurance, request price quotations from several agents; the savings can be considerable. Because each policy defines disability differently, be sure you know what the provisions are in the policy you purchase. Concentrate on those policies that have a reasonably liberal definition of disability; the premium may be slightly higher, but it is worth it. A long waiting period following a disability may impose minor hardships, but it lowers the cost of your premium and so enables you to purchase extended benefits for a long-term disability (Lang, 1988). Fortunately, many employers provide disability insurance for their employees. You should understand the provision of the policy thoroughly so you will not be unaware of its limitations and its advantages.

A young couple with extremely limited resources may put off the purchase of such protection until they are better able to afford it. Often, however, they drive relatively new cars, own stereos and televisions, and go on vacations. One of the reasons that we do not always anticipate financial reality accurately is because we assume that neither spouse will be disabled or die and that our income will remain stable for many, many years.

Insurance programs designed to protect individuals and families make good economic sense. Families not covered by such programs frequently face economic problems that cannot be readily solved and regret that they failed to plan for such emergencies.

Children

The cost of rearing children is rising steadily. According to figures of the U. S. Department of Agriculture, the total cost of rearing a child at a moderate cost level from infancy to the age of 17 is now in excess of $100,000 ("Updated Estimates," 1988). When indirect costs such as the value of time or personal services performed by family members, the value of earnings foregone in time spent rearing children, or the impact on career opportunities due to time out of the labor force are considered, the costs of rearing children are much higher. These estimates also do not include expenses involved in having a baby, such as prenatal care, maternity clothes, or nursery furnishings.

Walker Montgomery

An important aspect of the cost of rearing children for parents involves the cost of education beyond high school. It is a major expense for most families. The costs for tuition, room and board, and fees for public and private universities have increased each year for decades. There is little doubt that this is the most expensive period for parents. In response to economic problems caused by inflation, more young people remain at home longer. Thus, many parents support their children well into young adulthood, and are faced with a shorter period for financial recovery between launching the children and retirement.

Buying a Car

Purchasing a car involves far more than agreeing on a price. There are other questions and expenses to be considered: Is service readily available? Are parts easily obtained? Will the car be satisfactory as family needs change? Is it comfortable for daily use? Is it fuel efficient? How much is the insurance? Just as with homeowner's insurance, the larger the deductible, the smaller your premimum.

If you own more than one automobile, it is usually less expensive if you insure all of your automobiles with the same agent. It is highly desirable to have an agent that you can rely on completely to give you excellent service in terms of an accident or theft. In the long run, the policy that is the least expensive may not be the best buy.

One of the most common errors that is made in purchasing a car is that the owner is likely to purchase insufficient liability insurance simply because it costs less. If you are involved in an accident and are sued because of an injury to another party, you may be faced with paying $100,000 in damages only to learn that your liability insurance will pay only the first $50,000.

Prospective buyers can obtain an indication of repair costs for most automobiles by reading *Consumer Reports*. Each year the editors poll its readers to obtain repair ratings of the major makes of automobiles. Of course, such ratings can only serve as a guide and may not necessarily apply to a particular car. Personnel in lending institutions can also provide useful information concerning costs of different makes of automobiles in the current market.

An experienced mechanic is another valuable resource. A car may look good on the outside but may actually belong in a junk yard. It is frequently assumed that used cars are cheaper to own than new cars. This may not necessarily be true. Because of maintenance costs and gas consumption, some older automobiles are actually more costly to own. If a seller is reluctant to have a used automobile inspected by a mechanic of your choice, it is best to go elsewhere.

Buying a House

Home ownership is a goal of many people. Achieving this goal often necessitates saving money for a down payment that can range up to 30% or more of the purchase price of the house. The higher your original down payment, the lower your monthly mortgage expense will be. As a general rule, the purchase price of a home should not exceed $2\frac{1}{2}$ times the buyer's annual income. A monthly house payment that does not exceed 25% of one's income is considered safe (Maddux, 1988).

The financial commitment to buy a house is one of the major events in a family's life. Often it is the most expensive investment ever undertaken, involving long-kept savings and long-held dreams. The difficult part about buying a house is separating the realities of the financial facts from the fantasies of life. The first house you purchase is not likely to have all the amenities you would like.

In deciding whether or not to buy a particular house, it is helpful to ask yourself some of the following questions.

Costs

1. Is the price reasonable compared to the prices of similar houses?
2. What are the taxes on the property?
3. Can the owner's mortgage be assumed?
4. What is the interest rate on the mortgage?
5. What is the down payment?
6. How much will monthly payments be?
7. What are the total closing costs (e.g., title search, legal fees)?
8. What are the upkeep costs (e.g., insurance, painting, repairs)?
9. What is the cost of electricity, gas, and water per month? Per year?
10. Are these costs in keeping with your personal budget for housing?

Changes Needed

1. Is the outside of the house in good condition, or will repainting or repairs be necessary?
2. Will interior decorating and painting be necessary?
3. Will major structural changes be needed to make the house acceptable?
4. Is there adequate storage?

5. Does the pattern of rooms fit the family's lifestyle?

6. Does the particular attraction of outstanding features, e.g., huge windows overlooking garden, fancy lighting, lead you to ignore some major disadvantages?

7. Is the house safe for children?

8. Are the appliances in good condition?

9. Do the windows have working storm-screen combinations?

10. Is the electrical wiring in good condition and adequate for modern appliances? Are plumbing and water pipes in good condition?

Personal Considerations

Often realtors make assumptions about what families are looking for when buying a house and show properties that are quite unsuitable although attractive. Keep in mind that the house you buy must be right for your particular family's needs. If you dream of a vegetable garden, then an overgrown patch of undeveloped yard will be far more attractive than a smooth green lawn with no room for growing anything. And if you or your partner is talented in painting, papering, and fixing up, a run-down house in less than perfect condition may be the ideal house for you to consider, particularly when it will cost less than houses in better shape.

Make a list of the most important features you need to have in your own home, and keep it with you as you go through houses. Often it helps to draw a simple floor plan as you look to remind you of particular layouts. Try to visualize realistically how your family will fit into the space available. Many families fail to estimate accurately their need for storage.

It is also a good idea to read about buying a house and about home ownership. Go to your public library and review at least 10 books on housing. Make sure you have the house appraised by a reputable appraiser before you buy. If you do not know where to find one, go to your bank or a savings and loan association for recommendations.

Mortgage and Other Options

A *mortgage* on a home is a debt to the bank that you are expected to pay back at monthly intervals. Paying the mortgage is no different from paying rent; if you fail to make your payment, you may be evicted from your home. It may be better to take over the present owner's mortgage rather than to obtain a new loan because it may be at a lower interest rate than the one presently being offered by banks. If the present owner's interest is 10% on a $40,000 mortgage, compared to 12%, for example, the saving would be $100.00 a month, or $1,200.00 a year. Another option is for you to obtain a second mortgage, if the house has appreciated in value considerably and the owner is anxious to sell.

In the house-buying situation, it is advisable to consult with an experienced and trustworthy lawyer if you are unsure of any of the steps to take. The actual sale will also be completed by lawyers from both sides. Because of today's high interest rates, many savings and loan associations and other mortgage-lending institutions are offering new types of loans that can be carefully tailored to meet a family's financial circumstances. These include graduated payment mortgages, which include a flexible loan insurance program; home ownership made easier mortgages; the rollover mortgage; and the variable rate mortgage.

Because these are more complex financing arrangements, it is important to check them out thoroughly with local mortgage authorities to see which types of loans are available in each area.

In the past few years inflation has inspired new ways of buying and selling houses as prices have continued to increase. In some states you can buy a house in a partnership arrangement in which an investor who provides most of the down payment and a home buyer who pays the mortgage and lives in the house buy the place together.

New Housing Markets

Families have traditionally moved from renting apartments to buying houses, but there are several new trends. Many families have decided to invest in a condominium, which enables them to live in a more expensive neighborhood for less money and offers the same tax advantages as buying a house. Another alternative is the cooperative apartment, where the entire building is jointly owned by the tenants who collectively make decisions on running it. Before selecting one of these options, it is recommended that you consult a realtor or a lawyer with some experience with condominiums or cooperatives.

The Total Cost of Housing

When considering buying a house it is necessary to get as many of the facts as possible to make an intelligent decision. Many young couples who ask the question, "What is the down payment on this house?" actually mean, "How much money do we need to get into the house?"

Assume you live in a small town where houses are relatively inexpensive and your first house costs a total of $60,000. You make a down payment of $10,000, which includes all of the *closing costs*—that is, all of the fees that are normally associated with obtaining the loan (title examination and insurance costs, survey and appraisal fees, credit report cost, and attorney's fees). You are able to secure a 9% interest rate on the remaining $50,000 that you owe. Your monthly payment would be approximately $400.00 for a 30-year loan. In addition, you might wish to pay your taxes and your homeowners' insurance, which the lending institution will require you to have, along with your house payment. Assume these costs total an additional $75.00 a month. Your

total cost now reaches $475.00. "Not bad," you conclude, "But it will take a long time to save $10,000 for the down payment."

There are several important things to remember in considering the cost of housing. The most important is that considerable variability exists in the cost of housing from community to community. The cost of a house in a suburb of Los Angeles or New York could easily cost twice the amount that the same house would cost in a small community in Kansas or Oklahoma. The extra $5,000 that you may earn in a large city may seem like a great deal, but you may be better off, from a financial viewpoint, to accept the position that pays less if it is

Table 13–5 Characteristics of New Housing, 1987

Type of Financing	
FHA-insured	15%
VA-guaranteed	6%
Conventional	59%
Farmers Home Administration	2%
Cash	18%

Sales Price of Houses, 1987*	
Under $60,000	9%
$60,000–$69,999	8%
$70,000–$79,999	10%
$80,000–$99,999	21%
$100,000–$119,999	13%
$120,000–$149,999	15%
$150,000–$199,999	13%
$200,000 and over	13%

* Only 21% of houses sold in 1987 included closing costs in the sales price.

Source: U.S. Bureau of the Census. (1988). *Current Construction Reports-Series C25 Characteristics of New Housing: 1987.* Washington, DC: U.S. Government Printing Office.

in a community where living costs are low. Individuals moving from rural Georgia or North Dakota, for example, to a large city in the northeast may be surprised at the difference in the cost of living. It is always wise in undertaking any change in lifestyle to consider the financial aspects of the change to be certain that you understand all of the advantages and disadvantages of each decision you make.

Housing gets mixed up with people's dreams, and it is easy to become part of an adventure that you basically cannot afford (see housing prices for 1987 in Table 13–5). Remember to allow about 25% of the cost of your house for furnishings; on an $80,000 house you can expect to spend another $20,000 for furniture, draperies, and accessories, although many young couples are inventive and build some of their own furniture, receive gifts from family members, and shop at garage sales and auctions.

Renting a House

The cost of renting a house versus owning one can be estimated, although accurate estimates are difficult because of such unknown factors as cost of required repairs. Furthermore, home ownership has great emotional value to some families.

Most people believe that because they can deduct interest payments on federal income tax, ownership of a home actually means big savings. Comparisons of the actual amount paid for rent and the actual amount paid for ownership, however, reflect a smaller difference than many consumers think. If the house is owned for only a few years, renting is usually less expensive.

Awareness of Available Resources

Within the last several decades there have been so many financial options developed for so many things that it is difficult for consumers to be certain that the choices they make are the wisest. Indeed, it is far easier to make a mistake than you might suspect. Assuming that it is true that buyers want the most for their money, there are two obvious alternatives: they must obtain the facts themselves so they will have a clear understanding of the alternatives available or they must seek the advice of financial specialists who are highly trained and who will represent their interests. In purchasing large-cost items, such as houses, automobiles, and insurance programs, it is wise not to trust your own judgment unless you are a specialist in the area in which you intend to make a purchase.

In most larger communities, there are certified financial planners, tax attorneys, and investment managers whose guidance it would be wise to seek. Some financial specialists believe that if you have an annual income of $35,000 or more, you should consider relying on the expertise of a professional financial planner (Garman & Forgue, 1988). A certified financial planner (CFP) is a specialist in securities, insurance, taxes, and wills who has passed a rigorous examination. Another financial planner you may wish to rely on is a chartered financial consultant (ChFC) who can guide you in your investment, real estate, and tax shelters. Before consulting anyone for the first time, you may want to get a referral from a bank or other lending institution that is greatly respected in your community. Before you seek advice, ask what their charges are: most charge by the hour and they normally are willing to give you some idea of how long it will take. In seeking advice from any professional who charges by the hour, it is a good idea to write out your questions before you see them so that you will not waste their time or your money.

With the number of decisions to be made, many public libraries are a great source of information. Reading *Consumer Reports* of automobile purchase costs and repair performance records, for example, can provide you with valuable information about what is good and inexpensive; equally important, it

Renting With a Lease

Advantages of a Written Lease

It includes the rights and responsibilities of both the *tenant* and the *landlord*. It lists all rules. It indicates how much monthly *rent* is, when you have to pay, and what happens if you do not pay. It usually stops the landlord from raising your rent during the lease term or it states when a raise is allowed.

Disadvantages of a Lease

It commits you to pay rent for the whole term of the lease. You may pay once a month, but you owe for the whole time. So if you want to move out 6 months after you sign a 1-year lease, you still owe 6 more months' rent. The landlord may free you of this obligation, but he or she does not have to.

Your Rights with a Lease

If you follow the written rules, you have the right to live without interference from the landlord. Even if you break the rules and the landlord wants you out, he or she must tell you so, in writing, 30 days ahead of time. You have the right to maintenance services stated in the lease, such as electricity, gas, and water.

Your Responsibilities with a Lease

You must obey the rules you agreed to. You cannot make major physical changes in your housing. For any change not permitted by the lease, you will need permission from the landlord. You, *not* the owner, are responsible for accidents caused by your own carelessness.

The Landlord's Rights with a Lease

The landlord can use the courts to evict you if you break the rules or do not pay your rent. You will be expected to take reasonable care of the property.

The Landlord's Responsibilities with a Lease

The landlord must do the repairs and provide the services agreed to. Your privacy must be respected: the landlord cannot enter your home without permission, except in an emergency. The landlord must provide a "habitable" place to live. The landlord must keep halls, laundry rooms, and other public areas in good and safe condition.

Source: deSlosser, H. (n.d.). *Renter's guide*. Ithaca, NY: Cooperative Extension, New York State College of Human Ecology.

Renting Without a Written Lease

Advantages of Renting without a Lease

You can move out more quickly if you wish, because the rental term is usually short.

Disadvantages of Renting without a Lease

You and the landlord may forget what you each agreed to when you rented the property. Arguments may result and both of you will be unhappy. The monthly rent can be increased easily.

Your Rights without a Lease

You still have the right to live free of interference by the landlord, as long as you live by the spoken promises you agreed to. You have the right to a 30-day notice if the landlord wants you out.

Your Responsibilities without a Lease

You must tell the landlord 30 days before you leave. If you do not leave when you promise, the landlord may increase the rent. You are responsible for accidents that occur because of your carelessness.

The Landlord's Rights and Responsibilities if you Rent without a Lease

After the landlord gives you a 30-day warning, he or she may use the courts to evict you.

Should you Sign or not Sign a Lease?

If you plan to stay a year or more, you will probably be better off with a lease. The lease will spell out what you and the landlord must do. You will be protected legally as long as you follow the agreement. If the landlord breaks the agreement, you have rights in court.

Source: deSlosser, H. (n.d.) *Renter's guide*. Ithaca, NY: Cooperative Extension, New York State College of Human Ecology.

will stimulate your thinking in formulating questions to ask that you would otherwise have neglected. Libraries can also provide you with information about low-risk (and high-risk) investments sources.

Inasmuch as the quality of married life is affected by the skill of the partners in managing their money, and by their ability to discuss financial issues openly, it is highly important for families to take advantage of the available resources to understand and improve their finances.

Poverty in the United States

In spite of the economic achievements of the past generation, and despite the fact that most young people today will achieve a higher level of affluence

Benchmarks of Poverty

1. Black children under 6 experienced a 51.1% poverty rate in 1984—the highest since the Census Bureau began recording such data. Among all black youth under age 18, nearly one-half were living in poverty in 1984, compared with 39.6% in 1969.

2. About 13.8 million (22%) of all Americans under 18 live in poverty, up from 14.3% in 1969.

3. Female-headed households account for almost one-half of all poor American families; in 1984 there were about 3.5 million female-headed families living in poverty.

4. Two-thirds of black children in female-headed households are poor, and nearly three-fourths of children of Spanish origin in similar circumstances are poor.

5. By 1994 some 87% of black youth and 46% of white youth will have lived in one-parent situations at some point during their childhood.

6. Among "persistently poor" children—those who have remained poor for at least 10 years—90% are black and 61% lack a father at home.

Source: The Washington COFO memo. (1985, December 15). Malvern, PA: Coalition of Family Organizations.

than their parents, there is also a growing level of poverty in our country. The increase in the number of female-headed households, largely the result of the dissolution of hundreds of thousands of marriages, means that more children will grow up poor. Growing up poor, as your grandparents who lived through the Great Depression will tell you, involves more than not having things you need. It often involves psychological feelings of unworthiness because of the lack of opportunities, including advanced education. Among the things that all of us need to work for to improve our economic future are: (a) increased stability in marriage, (b) equity in the pay of women and men, (c) increased personal responsibility in supporting ourselves and our children, (d) delaying having children until after marriage, and (e) the election of leaders who will support balanced county, state, and federal budgets. Although we can do much within our families to develop the discipline to live within our incomes, we must also support the development of a national climate that contributes to the elimination of poverty and contributes to the development of opportunities for every person to succeed.

Summary

- Because money is closely tied to security and goal achievement, it is one of the most frequent sources of conflict for American families.

- Two keys to financial management are (a) recognizing needs versus wants and (b) setting realistic financial goals. Devising a spending plan or budget forces couples to make decisions regarding these two key factors—that is, it forces them to communicate their values about the use of their resources and to define their priorities more clearly.

- Careful financial planning is most crucial for the growing number of single-parent families in this country.

- Families must carefully monitor and evaluate their use of credit cards to avoid overspending.

- Protection from economic or personal disaster can be obtained through insurance purchases. Wise consumers educate themselves regarding the various types of insurance available and make purchases to provide for their family's future.

- The high cost of rearing children makes financial planning a necessity.

- The purchase of a home is often more than a monetary investment; however, the economic commitment a family undertakes through such a purchase warrants that the decision be made after much evaluation. Buyers must be aware of the costs beyond their loan amount when making a purchase decision; taxes, insurance, closing costs, realtor's fees, and furniture must all be considered.

Discussions Questions

1. If in the future there is little progress in the median income of families, how will families be able to improve their quality of life?

2. What are some of the common errors that families make in spending? What are some of the ways that errors can be eliminated?

3. How can young families keep their installment debt within reasonable limits yet manage to have money for the things they want?

4. In an inexpensive furniture store that sells a lot of junk furniture there are likely to be several items of real value at a bargain price. Even though you may be relatively inexperienced at identifying real values, what do you think should be some of the criteria that you could use in making wise selections?

5. What are some simple ways to keep yourself from writing a check that is greater than your bank balance?

6. Sometimes people who begin recording their expenses for the first time are surprised how quickly they could have paid for a VCR, for example, if they had limited their purchase of beverages. What are other advantages of recording your expenses?

7. Obviously, if both husband and wife are gainfully employed, there are going to be some work-related expenses that would not be incurred if either the husband or the wife remained at home to care for the children and the home. In some cases, the costs are greater than the net income of one of the earners. What are some of the more obvious work-related expenses?

8. A young couple was offered several credit cards through the mail. Within 2 years they had charged the limit on five credit cards. They were able to pay only the minimum amount each month, and the total amount of inter-

est they were paying was staggering. What are some of the specific dangers in incurring this level of debt? What is a reasonable limit?

9. Suppose you are in the market to purchase a house. You have read several books from your local library. You have gone through about 30 houses in the community and have a general idea of the cost of housing in your area. You have found a house you really like. How can you find out if the house is well built and what its potential problems are?

10. Anna and Keith put aside $50 each month for a vacation each summer. Keith's brother lost his job, and he and his family are out of money. His brother asks for a loan of $500. The only extra money Anna and Keith have is $450 they have in their vacation fund. If you were Anna or Keith what are the factors you would discuss with each other in arriving at a decision?

11. When Susan and Chris were going to have their first baby, Susan wanted to obtain a 6-month leave of absence from her job to care for the baby. Susan's employer agreed. It took every penny of both of their incomes to meet their expenses. Suppose you were one of the members of this couple, what are some things that might be done to reduce expenses?

12. Jim forgot to record a fairly large check—a check he had cashed when he was with a group of business associates in another city. He paid a large bill for the entire crowd for drinks and dinner at an expensive restaurant. They all wanted to flip a coin to see who would pay for the bill, but Jim was reluctant to admit he could not afford to take the chance so he ended up with the bill. He fully intended to tell Lynda about it, but when he thought about it, it was never the "right" time. The bank called Lynda to inform her that they

were overdrawn in their account. She went to the bank and discovered that Jim had written a check for over $200. He had done this once before. How would you go about seeking a solution to this problem?

13. Connor received a telephone call and learned she had won a fabulous prize—a free weekend for two in a highly desirable resort. All she had to do to claim her prize was send in a check for $9.99 for some vitamins. Although it really sounded too good to be true, she decided to take the chance because the person on the telephone sounded very sincere. She never received the vitamins or the prize. What should she do?

14. Americans, in relation to citizens of some other highly industrialized nations, save very little money. Why is this? What are some of the real advantages of having savings beyond handling emergencies that require money?

15. What kinds of liability insurance do most families carry? Why do most states require that automobile drivers carry liability insurance? If you have a car, how much do you pay for your liability insurance? What is the maximum claim your liability insurance will pay?

16. Why do you believe many people do not consider the cost of children in planning their families?

17. How much comparative shopping do you do? Do you regularly shop sales? Discount stores? What are some of the unusual places you go to look for good buys? Have you ever been to a pawn shop? What are some of the things that are sold in pawn shops?

18. What are the current interest rates on home mortgages? Where can you find out? What does it mean when you assume the mortgage loan another person owns?

19. How much do your parents pay annually for taxes on their home? How much do your parents pay annually for interest on their home?

20. Many people find a house that is inexpensive that is in disrepair but has lots of possibilities. If you wanted to take on such a project but realized that you would have to do a lot of the work yourself, how would you go about finding someone who would teach you how to paint and to hang wallpaper? Why is it better if both wives and husbands share such work rather than expecting the other person to do it alone?

CHAPTER 14

RELATIONSHIPS WITH RELATIVES

∝

Call it a clan, call it a network, call it a tribe, call it a family. Whatever you call it, whoever you are, you need one. You need one because you are human. You didn't come from nowhere. Before you, around you, and presumably after you, too, there are others. Some of these others... must matter a lot to you and, if you are very lucky, to one another. Their welfare must be nearly as important to you as your own....

For most of human history, looking for a tribe was the least of anyone's worries. Our tribes and clans were right in plain sight, like our kneecaps. We were born into tribes, or married into them, or they enslaved us, and that was that. Our tribe kept the howling wolves at bay, and shielded us from savage aliens. It made our decisions for us. It named us, bred us, fed us, taught us how to earn a living, found us our mates, and willed us its property. It told us who we were, what we stood for, and what we might hope to become. After we died, it honored our memory....

A couple of anachronistic tribes of this sort still survive today, but most such august and enveloping clans have long since evolved into families.

(Howard, 1980, pp. 277–278)

∝

A Network of Kin

Family extends far beyond spouse and children to parents and in-laws, siblings, aunts, uncles, stepparents, grandparents, and cousins of all kinds. Interaction with our relatives is an important part of our relationship experience. Relatives provide a sense of belonging, an opportunity for emotional support, occasional financial help, and periodic assistance with child care or household chores—roots and security in the midst of a hectic and fragmenting world (Davies, 1988). But there is another side. Because relatives are linked to us by ties of blood and family that we did not choose, there can also be conflicts and incompatibility.

Kinship networks have been expanded in recent years by two developments: (a) the increasing number of divorces and remarriages, which create very complex relationship patterns, and (b) a growing awareness of the role close friends play in our need for support and relationships with other adults. If links between family members weaken, those between friends from school, from the neighborhood, and from work may be strengthened. A network of friends with whom the family (or the individual) celebrates joys and endures sorrows is now as accepted as closely knit family relationships. A model of social networks is presented in Figure 14–1. For example, in terms of maintaining morale in older persons, it is of relatively greater importance to have a range of friends for companionship than to be in touch with grandchildren and family. The interaction of older persons with relatives is not always pleasant and gratifying. Old (and young) persons need relationships with others who appreciate them and share their interests. Because friendship rests on mutual choice, mutual need, and a voluntary association between equals, it may sustain a person's sense of usefulness and self-esteem more effectively than family relationships (Glenn & McLanahan, 1981).

Geographic Closeness to Kin

Most people live reasonably close to their relatives. Studies over the last 25 to 30 years yield consistent results: many persons (50% to 68%) live in the same community with their parents or in-laws. Of those who do not live in the same community, a large number live within 100 miles of parents or other relatives. Only a small number (about 7%) live more than 2 hours by car from parents or relatives (Adams, 1968; Komarovsky, 1964; Maynard, 1980).

The traditional kinship structure in our society stressed the need for kinship proximity or common households and face-to-face contact with relatives. Modern technology has permitted communication and the transmission of many important services over geographic and social distance (Litwak & Kulis, 1987).

Common indicators of the strength of kinship ties include: (a) geographic closeness, (b) face-to-face visits, (c) telephone calls, (d) providing a variety of services to aid in day-to-day life, and (e) emotional support. One very important indicator of the strength of kinship ties is the providing of services. People who have low incomes have a much greater need of kin services because they cannot afford to use formal organizations. For example, a low-income individual who needs a babysitter may not be able to hire one but will depend on friends or kin to help (Litwak & Kulis, 1987).

Kin are the major source of help for older persons, too (Dail, 1986; Kendig, 1983; O'Bryant, 1988). The type of kin service provided to the older person varies greatly according to the distance away the helping kin live. For example, when the older individual and the helping kin live in the same household, 77% of the older persons receive light housekeeping help. Interestingly, only 26% of older persons who live only a small distance away (from one to five blocks) and 8% of those who live

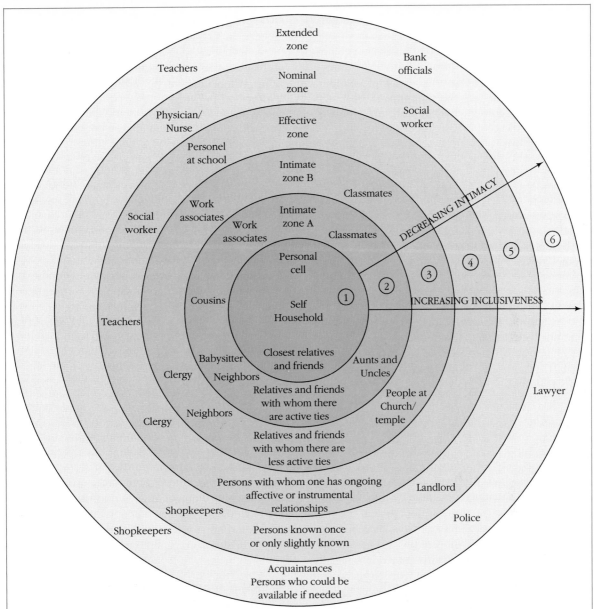

Membership in the zones is dynamic. There is considerable movement across boundries. For a relatively well-functioning person, zones one through four may include well over one hundred people. Most people have their strongest emotional ties to members of their primary sector— usually zones one through four. Persons in other zones, however, have an effect on personal life. Chronic psychiatric patients and other marginal members of society may have their most significant, frequent, and reliable contacts with members of the secondary sectors of their networks—zones five and six.

Figure 14–1 A model of social networks. *Source:* Kliman, J., & Trimble, D. W. (1983). Network therapy. In B. P. Wolman & G. Stricker (Eds.), *Handbook of family and marital therapy* (pp. 277–314). New York: Plenum.

more than 30 minutes away receive light house-keeping help. In contrast, the service of providing emotional support is much less influenced by distance. It was reported that 87% of the older persons who live in the same household as the helper receive emotional support. This compares with 83% of older persons living one to five blocks away and 73% living more than 30 minutes away from the helping kin (Litwak, 1985; Litwak & Kulis, 1987).

Amount of Contact with Relatives

Couples spend more time with relatives than is usually presumed. Residence in rural or urban areas does not seem to affect the frequency of interaction with relatives. Studies over the last two decades indicate that married couples tend to see at least one relative each week (Blood, 1969; Leslie, 1982).

Individuals are likely to have considerable interaction with close relatives such as parents, adult children, or siblings and far less interaction with distant relatives such as cousins (Leigh, 1982). Most of the visits between relatives are between parents and adult children. Although some visits are done from a sense of obligation, most contact is voluntary.

Parents tend to expect visits from their married children. If both sets of parents are equally accessible, an equal amount of contact is normally expected. If one set of parents lives close by and the other set lives far away, a couple may balance frequent weekend visits to the close parents with longer vacation visits to the more distant parents. Visits with parents may not always be equal, however. The couple may be more compatible with one set of parents, or extreme distance may interfere with visiting. In some circumstances, one parent (or set of parents) may need more contact, such as when one is widowed or seriously ill.

As might be expected, geographical distance has a negative effect on the amount of interaction—especially face-to-face contact—with relatives. Substantial interaction, however, does occur despite geographical distance (Leigh, 1982). Individuals who live large distances apart keep in touch by telephone, by writing letters, and by exchanging audio or video tapes. Vacations and holidays provide opportunities for family reunions—often the only time of year some family members see each other. Some families have several get-togethers during a year: a Labor Day barbecue, Christmas Eve dinner, and Easter egg hunt, for example.

Differences have been observed in middle-class and working-class individuals concerning which relatives are most closely associated to each other. Middle-class persons are more oriented toward parents or adult children. Working-class individuals, in contrast, tend to be more oriented toward siblings and same-generation relatives, live closer to their relatives, and interact with them more frequently than do middle-class persons (Kliman & Trimble, 1983). Close-knit kinship networks play an important role in influencing marital behavior among working-class couples (Hill, 1988).

Research on strong families indicates that for some ethnic or racial groups the extended family plays a prominent role in contributing to family strengths. This was true for Russian immigrant and black families (Lingren et al., 1982; Lonnborg, 1980; Peters, 1981).

Interaction with Kin

In order to understand the nature of interaction within kinship networks, the factors of social class, race, ethnicity, and gender must be considered. These influence the way households are organized as well as our expectations of kin, social institutions, church, and friends. The kinship interactions of an urban poor black woman are not the same as

---

Family Reunion

Many persons enjoy an opportunity to get together with the "whole" family—aunts, uncles, cousins, and on and on. It gives a time to renew relationships, to see the new babies born into the larger family, and to mourn the passing of family members who have died. Persons who have had family reunions offer some suggestions for planning one:

1. Select a location as convenient for as many family members as possible. Using the same location year after year has some advantages: continuity and fewer decisions to make. On the other hand, if families are scattered, it may help some to attend if the location is closer part of the time. And one family (or group of families) does not always have host duty. Consider a community center or church fellowship hall to relieve the pressure of finding someone's home that is large enough.

2. Pick easy activities: a band for listening and dancing or a variety of music on tapes; a play corner for children; badminton, croquet, horseshoes for the yard; chairs for sitting and talking; cards, dominoes, checkers.

3. Keep the decorations simple. Use homemade tablecloths and disposable plates and flatware. Flowers from the garden or roadside make casual bouquets. Plain white candles and greenery are nice, too. Decorate the walls with pictures of former reunions and/or big events in the family.

4. Make the meals potluck. Have everyone bring a favorite dish or two (and the recipe) and a cooler of drinks.

5. Hire local teenagers to help with setting up chairs and tables, cleaning up, and entertaining the younger children.

6. Appoint some family members to take photographs or videotapes. (Every family has one or two shutterbugs.) Tape record oral history from older family members. Update address books and mailing lists.

---

those of a middle-class suburban Jewish man, for example (Kliman & Trimble, 1983).

Gender influences the interaction in kinship networks across economic and ethnic lines. Women are reared to be involved with family, to bind a family together, and to plan social activities within the family (Rosenthal, 1985). Consequently, women tend to initiate and watch over family and kin interaction (Kliman & Trimble, 1983). For example, women generally have more contact with their relatives, know more relatives, are more involved in obligations and activities with kinfolk, and fre-

quently assume responsibility for relaying to their husbands what goes on with relatives (Ambert, 1988). In many situations, aging parents facing a crisis are more likely to look to a daughter for help.

The economic situation of households also affects the nature of kin relationships. Kin relationships play a particularly important and useful role among working-class families by providing mutual services. Native American families have similar network patterns (Staples & Mirande, 1980). For example, the grandmother often is a major influence in the socialization of children, as she may assume the

Joel Gordon

role of parent to the grandchildren and take care of household tasks while the children's parent(s) work (Lamanna & Riedmann, 1988; Stack, 1980).

In addition, there is much cooperation between adult siblings who may share the same dwelling or live near one another. Often the responsibility for providing clothing, shelter, food, transportation, child care, and other family needs is shared by several households (Kliman & Trimble, 1983; Lamanna & Riedmann, 1988; Stack, 1980).

Such a network arrangement is adaptive and ensures basic survival for people who might not be able to do so independently. It has disadvantages for those who want to break out of poverty; the individual cannot accumulate resources because ev-

erything is shared. To "get ahead" it is necessary to leave the network (Kliman & Trimble, 1983), as the following example illustrates:

Magnolia's uncle died in Mississippi and left an unexpected inheritance of $1,500 to Magnolia and Calvin. It was the first time they had ever had a cash reserve. Their first hope was to use the money as a down payment on a little home. Three days after they received the check, news of it had spread through their domestic network, and a niece borrowed $25 so her phone would not be turned off. When another uncle became ill, Magnolia and her sister were called to help. Magnolia bought train tickets for them and her three youngest children. Winter was cold and Mag-

Family Stories

Human lives—and family lives—are full of stories about work, characters, and historical events. Stories tell about events, family members, and family relationships; sometimes themes and ideas recur.

Recently 56 families were asked about their storytelling. Their responses follow:

Who tells the stories?
mothers (34%), fathers (22%), parents (9%), self (8%), grandmothers (6%), grandfathers (4%), aunts and uncles (5%), cousins (1%).

Who are the main characters in the stories?
grandfathers (22.5%), grandmothers (19%), uncles (18%), aunts (15%), great-grandfathers (7.5%), mothers (4%), fathers (3%), siblings (3%).

What are the themes in the stories?
Personality description (crazy Uncle Freddie with 100 cuckoo clocks, for example) (23%), work (22%), family (16%), death and dying (13%), activities (11%), caregiving (5%), health (3%), education (2%), religion (2%), adventures (1%).

Many stories recall very personal events and bits of family history; others contain references to historical events such as the Civil War, the Great Depression, World Wars I and II, Vietnam, emigration, a ride in a trolley car or plane, purchase of a Model T car, a gold rush. Another favorite type of story is a recounting of a relationship with a famous person.

A typical family story follows:

Whenever we all gathered at my grandmother's the conversation would—without fail—turn to two of the family's infamous. One was a great-great-grandfather who went off to fight in the war with Mexico over Texas. He never came back, and rumor had it that he set up housekeeping with some woman out west. The other was a horse thief; Grandma denied he was actually part of the family. According to her he was a drifter, hanged for horse stealing. Our family took pity and allowed him to be buried in the family plot. She was a little embarrassed about the horse thief. And of course, all the kids loved it!

Source: Martin, P., Hagestad, G. O., Diedrick, P. (1988). Family stories: Events (temporarily) remembered. *Journal of Marriage and the Family, 50,* 533–541.

nolia's children and grandchildren were missing school because they needed coats. Magnolia and Calvin decided to buy coats, hats, and shoes for all the children (at least 15). In 6 weeks, all the money was gone. (Stack, 1974, pp. 105–106)

One prominent quality of strong families is their powerful kinship bonds; when they seek "outside" assistance for help with problems, it is usually from relatives (Gary et al., 1986). In contrast, families of the middle-class are more apt to turn to institutions or paid service providers—babysitters, nurses, car rentals, or maid service (Kliman & Trimble, 1983).

Within the middle class, the sharing of economic resources typically is restricted to immediate relatives and takes the form of gifts or loans. This kind of kinship network gives greater privacy and rewards self-reliance (Kliman & Trimble, 1983).

Mutual aid is most often between parents and children. In situations in which three generations are involved, assistance usually flows from the middle generation to the other two. The family members in the middle, sometimes termed the *sandwich generation*, are usually middle aged and well established in their jobs. Thus they have the economic and physical resources to aid their elderly parents and can still help their young, adult children who may be getting established in a new home and job.

Although kin relationships in the urban, white middle-class have not involved mutual service and sharing to the degree evidenced in some other groups, as more middle-class families have two wage earners and as more are headed by single parents, the network patterns may change. There may be need for more kin support (Lamanna & Riedmann, 1988; Stack, 1980).

The nature of kinship networks among the very wealthy is thought to be similar to that of the middle class. The wealthy value privacy, however, and are able to maintain it (Kliman & Trimble, 1983).

Many people who regard themselves as independent turn to relatives during times of crisis or disaster. The aid they receive may include economic assistance, advice, or emotional support.

Kinship Patterns Among the Remarried

With the growing numbers of divorced couples and the corresponding increase in remarried couples, the kinship patterns of persons who are remarried need to be examined. Three major patterns of kinship connection for remarried families have been suggested.

The Expanded Kinship Network

This pattern involves the most flexibility and the greatest frequency of interaction between the remarried family and relatives, including in-laws. The quality of these relationships is more positive and less characterized by unresolved conflict. This pattern is the most inclusive and is considered the most beneficial to those families who are able to accomplish it (Whiteside, 1989).

One of the reasons that the expanded kinship network pattern is considered beneficial is because children who see both stepparents and biological parents as family members have a good relationship with both the nonresident parent and with their stepparents, perceive a lack of hostility between the adults, and are able to move back and forth among households. Children who perceive only the biological parent with whom they live as family are the most emotionally upset and dissatisfied with life (Gross, 1986). The expanded kinship network provides the child with a larger sense of family identity and therefore with a large network of primary relationships.

There are two different levels of inclusion within the expanded kinship network pattern. One level is termed the *perfect pals* group. At this level both adults and children define former in-laws as family, and traditions and important occasions are more likely to be celebrated with former in-laws (Ahrons & Rodgers, 1987). The second level is called the *cooperative colleagues*. At this level adults are less close to former spouses and in-laws. Cooperative colleagues, like perfect pals, maintain contact with former in-laws, and major life events are planned jointly between the remarried family and the household of the child's biological parents. The cooperative colleagues, however, typically have a lower degree of inclusion and maintain a more distinct boundary between households as well as a more formal, explicit negotiating of plans (Ahrons & Rodgers, 1987).

The Contracted Kinship Network

In this pattern, major portions of the potential kinship connections are cut off and not considered to be a part of the family. There are three levels within this kinship network pattern. In one level, the *angry associates*, much negative emotional energy is invested in the denial of the relationships and the boundaries between families are rigid. Major life events and traditions are celebrated in an uncoordinated, rigidly separate, parallel manner. For example, a child's birthday is celebrated separately by the custodial parent's household and by the noncustodial parent's household. Naturally, occasions such as holidays, birthdays, and graduation become very stressful.

One 16-year-old girl whose parents refused to speak directly to one another and both of whom have remarried reported, "My father will not allow me to speak of anything which goes on in my mother's house since she remarried. How can he care about me if 90% of what is important in my life cannot be shared?" (Whiteside, 1989). In situations in which the boundaries between households are very rigid, the child's frequency of contact with the noncustodial parent tends to decrease over time (Ahrons & Rodgers, 1987).

A second level of the contracted kinship network is called the *fiery foes*. At this level major celebrations in children's lives, such as holidays and birthdays lose much of their special joy because so much energy is expended by the adults in the struggle for control and/or in trying to exclude each other. The conflict between former spouses intrudes into the remarried families' lives and disrupts special ceremonial occasions that might provide opportunities for positive connections with the noncustodial parent and former in-laws (Ahrons & Rodgers, 1987). Unfortunately, for families who fall into the fiery foes group, occasions that should be happy often deteriorate into reflections of bitterness and blaming each other for the child's problems and finding fault with each other.

An example of the fiery foes level of interaction is described:

> One family...consisted of father, stepmother, the father's 10-year-old daughter and 13-year-old son. When the children came to their father's house on holidays and vacation times, their father and stepmother made efforts for the children to be included in special celebrations. On Thanksgiving their dinner was interrupted repeatedly by phone calls from the children's mother. When a call would come the father would angrily answer the phone, refuse to allow her to speak to the children, and hang up. As tension rose, the children became more and more sullen, upset, and unresponsive to their stepmother's overtures. (Whiteside, 1989, p. 38)

A third level of the contracted kinship network pattern is one which is more of a totally dissolved relationship. This level is called the *dissolved duos*. In this level of interaction, the couples have virtually no contact or exchange of information from household to household (Whiteside, 1989).

It may be easier for children to feel part of an expanded family network following a divorce and remarriage than it is for adults. For example, in a study by Furstenberg and Spanier (1984), some 85% of the custodial parents reported that their children considered their noncustodial parent's family as their relatives, while only 32% of the parents regarded their former in-laws as relatives.

The Substitution Pattern

The substitution pattern of kinship occurs where a vacuum exists because of a decision to cut off all contacts with a former spouse and the former in-laws. This vacuum necessitates the drawing in of stepkin as a substitute for biological relatives. For example, if the biological parent (usually the mother) and the child have lived as a true single-parent household before remarriage and the other biological parent is not present (and his family is defined by the mother and child as *not* being part of their family), then when the mother remarries, the task of the stepfamily becomes the integration of the new husband's family with the mother's family. For those families that successfully substitute stepkin for the nonresident biological parent's kin, family rituals and kinship patterns more closely resemble patterns of nuclear families undisrupted by divorce (Whiteside, 1989).

Importance of In-law Relations

In-law relationships have so long been a theme for jokes that many couples enter marriage expecting problems with their in-laws. This is unfortunate when it sets the stage for trouble with in-laws. Why are good relationships with one's in-laws important?

> *There is an old saying among psychotherapists that when a couple gets into bed there are really six people present: the woman and her mother and father, and the man and his mother and father.... [I]n other aspects of marriage as well as sex the relationship each partner has had with his or her parents is relevant as well. (Deutsch, 1979, p. 24)*

The kind of person you are is a result of the genes you inherited from your parents and of the variety of influences you have experienced as you matured. Throughout life those influences will continue to affect you and, similarly, your partner. The style of life you have chosen; the foods you eat; the books you read; your religious attitudes; your views on sex, marriage, friendship, and how men and women treat each other are all influenced by your parents. It can be very helpful to meet your partner's parents and other relatives to understand how he or she became the person you know. In some cases,

it can help you realize why there has been rejection of parental teachings; in others, it can bring you closer to appreciating the style of life of a parental generation.

A man married for 15 years stated:

> *I have a very close relationship with Jill's parents. One reason we get along so well is that I have always realized how important they are to her. I didn't expect her to stop seeing them just because we got married. Financial problems forced us to live with them in our third year of marriage. It gave me an opportunity to know them on an everyday basis. And I realized that so many of the good qualities I love in Jill came from her parents. Her marvelous wit is from her father; her optimism and enthusiasm from her mother.*

Those who work in the area of relationships have long recognized the influences of the early parent-child relationships in human development. The mother-son dyad is a crucial element in the development of the male personality in general, and especially his relations with women. If a boy has a relationship with his mother that is nurturing but that allows him to test his own abilities, if she strikes a balance between caring and letting go, then he can relate to women in a healthy way.

The relationships between mothers and daughters are equally important. Early in life a daughter needs to receive support from her mother to develop a strong sense of selfhood and individuality. She will then be able to relate to her husband as an adult and not see her mother as a threat to that relationship.

Patterns of In-law Relations

Establishing New Boundaries

One major course of conflict in relations with in-laws centers around the expectation in our soci-

---

Building Successful Extended Families

The following are some practical suggestions for developing satisfying relations with in-laws and other relatives acquired by marriage:

1. Be realistic but optimistic. Many adult children and their parents and in-laws and other kin have very satisfactory relationships.

2. Deal with problems that arise before they grow. Use your best human relationship and communication skills. Stay calm. Resist the urge to be defensive.

3. Expand your concept of family. Expect to regard your in-laws and other "new" kin as family. Allow time for comfort and affection to grow between you. Visit, spend time together, learn about each other.

4. Mind your manners; treat all adults as adults. Do not offer advice or be critical or competitive. Do not expect grandparents to babysit anytime, all the time, or without notice; and do not redecorate your daughter-in-law's home or pry into your son-in-law's finances, for example.

5. Respect the good in each other; accept differences. Avoid conflict over the trivial or what cannot be changed.

---

ety that children eventually become independent of their parents. Unlike many cultures in the world where children—even as adults—are under the domain of aging parents until the older generation dies, we emphasize autonomy in children.

At the time of marriage, the new husband and wife face a series of difficult tasks. Each must redefine the relationship with his or her own parents; the child role of earlier times must be left behind. Loyalties and priorities must be shifted, too, from parents and siblings to spouse. Each also faces the task of building a relationship with his or her new in-laws, and learning to respect the partner's family values, rituals, and traditions (Lasswell, 1986; Lingren et al., 1982; Strong & DeVault, 1988).

Achieving independence causes troubles for both the new couple and their parents. The new couple has difficulty because true independence takes years of maturing. First attempts at independence may be

severe to the point of rebellion. Young adults' reactions to real or presumed threats to their independence may be inappropriate or alienating. It may not be easy to learn to balance loyalty to a spouse and loyalty to one's parents.

In a classic study of in-law relations, Duvall (1954) noted that the most frequent complaints against children-in-law were that they were indifferent, distant, thoughtless, inconsiderate, and too busy to be interested in the parents' lives. Many of these may be reflections of extreme or unskilled attempts to assert their autonomy. Kelly (1988) provides the following list of problems that are apt to occur during visits with in-laws: parents giving unsolicited advice on anything, behavior of the grandchildren, what to watch on television and who decides, what time everyone goes to bed, what time everyone gets up, comments about how the household is run, grown children "too

Joel Gordon

busy" to spend time with parents, housework, political arguments, and trying to mend old family wounds.

At the time of a marriage, the parents of the new couple face a series of challenging tasks as well. They, too, must build new relationships—with their own child and with a new son- or daughter-in-law. Relinquishing the parental role may be very hard; it is a role most have had for over 20 years, and habits are hard to change. To parents, children do not cease to be children just because they marry. And opening themselves to strangers who have be-

come official family members through a marriage ceremony is quite stressful to many (McGoldrick, 1989).

It is not surprising that married couples consistently report that the problems with their mothers- and fathers-in-law include being meddlesome, nagging, criticizing, being possessive, being aloof, and being thoughtless (Duvall, 1954). Many of these may be the result of an inability to drop the parental role (meddling, nagging) or the result of an unskilled attempt to give the new couple autonomy (being aloof).

Perspective

[O]ur expectations are that things should always go smoothly and easily, and that something is very wrong if we run into problems. This is the worst view a family can have of each other and it makes for nothing but unhappiness, if not outright disaster. Because, you see, a family doesn't prove itself by always having a good time together; everybody—your worst enemy—is willing to have a good time with you. For that you don't need family.

We need our family when things are rough and tough. Then we need a family because no stranger will come to our rescue.

Source: Bettelheim, B. (1982). Difficulties between parents and children: Their causes and how to prevent them. In N. Stinnett, J. DeFrain, K. King, H. Lingren, G. Rowe, S. Van Zandt, and R. Williams (Eds.), *Family strengths 4: Positive support systems* (pp. 5–14). Lincoln: University of Nebraska Press.

Younger couples are likely to have more problems with in-laws than are older couples. Persons who marry very young often have the complicating factors of a premarital pregnancy or of parental disapproval of the marriage. Parents are more apt to disapprove because schooling may not be completed, the young couple may not have steady employment, or parents may not judge them to be mature enough for marriage. Any of these conditions makes a harmonious relationship between the generations difficult (Strong & DeVault, 1988). Persons who are older before they marry tend to have settled the issue of independence from their parents *before* the marriage.

Role Comparisons

Most conflict with in-laws involves the women in the family, specifically the mother-in-law and daughter-in-law dyad (Duvall, 1954; Marotz-Baden & Cowan, 1987), followed by sisters-in-law.

One reason for the amount of conflict between mother-in-law and daughter-in-law is that their roles are similar. Despite employment outside the home, most women retain the major responsibility for care of the home, cooking, and child care. In these areas, the mother-in-law is apt to identify her daughter-in-law's role with her own and may compare their performance (Strong & DeVault, 1988). Furthermore, most of these roles are openly and consistently available for inspection and comparison. An event as simple as a cookout, for example, provides many opportunities to note: "Is the house/yard tidy?" "Do the children mind their manners?" "Does my son look healthy or too tired?" "Did she plan a nice meal?" "Too much, too little salt?"

And although wife and mother-in-law perform many of the same roles, they may have learned to do them very differently. Personal immaturity can contribute to these differences becoming sources of conflict if, for example, different methods/preferences are considered inferior just because they are different or if constructive suggestions are interpreted as meddling.

In contrast, fewer male roles are openly available for inspection and comparison. The father-in-law and son-in-law are not apt to be employed in the same profession or to work together if they are. How each fulfills his occupational niche is usually not easily observed by the other.

Some changes in the amount and intensity of conflict between in-laws have been observed in recent years: in-law relations may be becoming quieter and more cordial (Marotz-Baden & Cowan, 1987; Maynard, 1980). This is attributed to changes in the lives of women. Many women in both generations are employed outside the home and are less available to in-law interference. Women are apt to be involved in resuming their studies or volunteer work, too. Although a decrease in friction is desirable, lack of involvement in someone's life cannot be equated with peaceful relations with that person.

Positive Relations

Because much of the discussion on relationships with in-laws has focused on conflict, it would be easy to assume that all persons have trouble with their in-laws. This is not the case. In one survey, women reported that their relationship with their in-laws was no different than their relationship with their own parents (Maynard, 1980). In another study, 72% of daughters-in-law said they were satisfied with their mothers-in-law's respect for their privacy and only 30% reported disagreements on important goals and values. Nor was the relationship as problematic as had been expected (Marotz-Baden & Cowan, 1987).

Many married couples enjoy cordial relationships with both his and her parents. They manage to work out visiting and helping arrangements that are fair to both sets of parents. Many parents are helpful to their children and children-in-law. They may loan money for a down payment on a home, assist when grandchildren are born, or help during a move or during an illness.

Remarriage and Relationships

The in-law and kin network that emerges from a remarriage is complex and often confusing. The network includes people and relationships from the family prior to divorce and those added as a result of remarriage: blood kin, in-laws, former in-laws, and stepkin (see Figure 14–2). These may be organized as follows:

- The first level of family membership is that of the household of the remarried couple and their biological and adopted children.

- The second level of family membership is that of the binuclear family, which includes the households of both of a child's biological parents. The binuclear family becomes very complex if both parents have remarried and/or if the stepparents have been married before and have children.

- The third level of family membership involves the extended families surrounding the binuclear households, including former in-laws, step-in-laws, grandparents, stepgrandparents, uncles, aunts, and other relatives (Ahrons & Rodgers, 1987; Whiteside, 1989).

The complex nature of the kinship system of the remarried family can create considerable stress simply due to the many options and obligations that are present. This is true when the relationships are cordial; the situation is even more complicated when hostile feelings are involved. Where does a college student go over semester break—to visit her mother and stepfather or to visit her biological father? Which grandparents does she see at Thanksgiving? What obligation do her stepgrandparents have when she graduates? Unfortunately, there are few guidelines available to help people make such decisions. The mother of a teenager said:

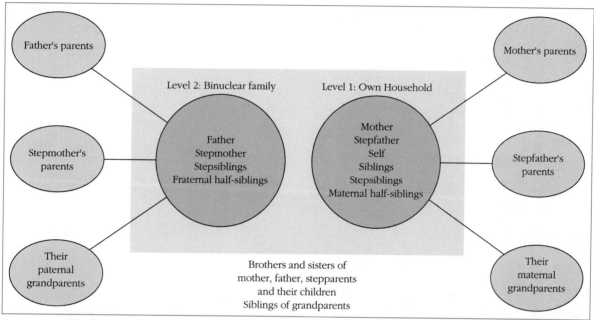

Figure 14–2 Kinship system of the remarried family from the perspective of a child living with mother and stepfather. *Sources:* Based on Ahrons, C. R. & Rodgers, R. H. (1987). *Divorced families: A multidisciplinary developmental view.* New York: W. W. Norton. Whiteside, M. F. (1989). Family rituals as a key to kinship connections in remarried families. *Family Relations, 38,* 34–39.

As I tell my daughter, she has the best of both worlds. She can stay at home with me and be the "whole hog," or she can go to her father's and be a "piece of the pie" with her stepmother, stepbrother, and half-brother and sister. (DeFrain et al., 1987, p. 246)

Stepgrandparents and Stepgrandchildren

The probability of a child having a living grandparent is higher today than at any time in history. There are about 48 grandparents per 100 parents now, as compared to 14 per 100 at the turn of the century (Serow, 1981). Because about 10% of children in the United States live with a stepparent, the chance of them having stepgrandparents is good. Remarriage of both biological parents can add as many as four stepgrandparents to the family network (Sanders & Trygstad, 1989).

The role of stepgrandparents is ambiguous. Stepgrandparents differ from grandparents in that they have no biological tie to the young person and they have had a shorter history of relationship with the young person. Also the child may not live with the son or daughter of the stepgrandparents, thus changing the nature of the stepgrandparent-stepgrandchild relationship. Additionally, the attitude of the stepgrandparents and stepgrandchildren about the remarriage—whether they favor or disapprove of it—can influence the way they feel about each other (Sanders & Trygstad, 1989).

Walker Montgomery

Sanders and Trygstad (1989) noted differences in the perceptions of children concerning their relationship with grandparents and stepgrandparents as follows:

- Contact with stepgrandparents was less than with grandparents.
- Stepgrandchildren were less likely than grandchildren to rate the stepgrandparent relationship as important.
- Stepgrandchildren were more likely to rate the strength of the relationship with their stepgrandparent lower than did grandchildren with a grandparent.

One explanation for these differences is that many children acquire stepgrandparents at a later age and often have had a much shorter period of time to develop a relationship with them. This is supported by research findings that very young children who acquired stepgrandparents were more apt to regard that relationship as more important (Trygstad & Sanders, 1989).

Grandparents Deserve Visiting Rights

"It took us fourteen hard, long and painful months to get to see our grandson after the divorce. We couldn't even stand to go into stores and look at children's clothes. It just hurt too much. Why should the grandchildren and grandparents pay for the mistakes the parents make?" asks a Lansing, Michigan grandmother.

In 1982 the United States Select Committee on Aging's subcommittee on human services held hearings on "Grandparents—the other victims of divorce and marital dissolution." For the first time the pain and anguish of grandparents was exposed, showing how they lost the chance to enjoy their grandchildren, to help in their development and to provide support after a divorce or separation.

A national organization, Grandparents'–Grandchildren's Rights, Inc., is fighting for visitation rights for grandparents in cases of divorce or separation. Without visitation privileges, . . . many grandparents feel that they are deprived of one of the most important relationships. Some state laws are in effect at present, and the National Conference of Commissioners on Uniform State Laws is examining them.

Source: The Record/Washington Post News Service, December 27, 1982. Hackensack, NJ. Used with permission.

The fact that grandparents seem to play a more important role in the lives of children than do stepgrandparents does not mean that stepgrandparents are unimportant. Indeed, the stepgrandparent can play a valuable role in the family and in the development of the stepgrandchild. Viewed positively, stepgrandparents offer potential for support for the child and positive intergenerational connections (Furstenberg & Spanier, 1984). And research indicates that 48% of children view the relationship with a stepgrandparent as important or very important. About 63% would like to have more contact with stepgrandparents (Sanders & Trygstad, 1989).

Friendships

Modern times make it imperative for persons to have a network of friends (Howard, 1980). Often blood kin live long distances away and may not be accessible to us on a daily basis. And we do not select our blood relatives; we get them by the chance of birth. Consequently, we may not always get along with them.

Closeness and support come from friendship networks at work, in the neighborhood, at church or synagogue. In many ways it is easy to exchange experiences with a friend who is in the same situation. One woman commented:

I get to feeling depressed and mean, so I call my friend and she and I talk. She tells me that she had such a big phone bill and electric bill that she can't pay both so she has had to shuffle money all around, and I feel better about my bills. And I complain about how my husband is insensitive, and she tells me some stunt that hers has done and I feel better. And we laugh about the crazy things our kids have done. And somehow we reassure each other that things will be okay.

Many couples are isolated from extended kin (or do not have many extended kin due to smaller family size) and, as a result, receive support services from friends instead. For example, some marriage enrichment programs have resulted in the formation of support groups composed of the couples from the marriage enrichment program. The support groups have continued for years after the marriage enrichment program had been completed, and a variety of services have been exchanged including: babysitting; carry-in meals for new babies, illness, or emergencies; transportation; assistance in finding a job (Dyer & Dyer, 1982).

From our friends we gain intimacy, someone to care about us, people to respect us as competent humans and bolster our self-esteem, assistance, and relief from isolation and loneliness. We also have an opportunity to give through our friendships and gain by nurturing and supporting someone else (Strong & DeVault, 1988). As one man observed:

A good friend visited us last weekend. She is having a rough time right now with her teenage daughter. The daughter is very rebellious and has a rough group of friends. Her mom—our friend—is afraid for her daughter. She knows they have wild parties with liquor and drugs and dangerous driving. She has tried to keep the daughter home, but she sneaks out. The daughter's friends have suggested that mom may have to be beat up to get her to leave them alone. Naturally, our friend is very upset. We had talked with her by phone and invited her to come for a visit to get away from it all. We didn't do anything special; we did go to a very nice new exhibit at the art museum. We listened when she wanted to talk about her difficulty. And mostly we talked about other things—funny things we have done together and ideas and plans and politics. When she got home she sent a note that said, "Thanks! I really needed that!"

Sometimes friends become so close that they become as family to us. Persons who are incorporated into a family exchange network and who gain the status of a relative are referred to as *fictive kin*. It is true that relatives sometimes are friends. Many persons, when asked to list their friends, name family members. Women tend to mention their mothers and sisters as confidantes; men mention their brothers.

Summary

- Our relationships with relatives offer us a source of emotional, physical, and financial support.

- Geographic closeness is an indicator of kinship ties because it allows for more face-to-face visits, provision of services, and emotional support.

- The interaction within kinship networks is affected by social class, race, ethnicity, and gender.

- As the number of divorced and remarried couples grows, the network of relationships with relatives changes. Three patterns have emerged: the expanded kinship network, the contracted kinship network, and the substitution pattern.

- When a child marries, parents are forced to recognize their child's autonomy, which is difficult for some parents to accept and equally difficult for some children to assert. As a result, relationships with in-laws have the potential for conflict. In-law relationships may also be complicated by the role similarities of mothers-in-law and daughters-in-law.

- Closeness and support from strong friendship networks may substitute for strong kinship relationships when relatives live far away or when interactions with relatives are not positive.

Discussion Questions

1. What specific things can young people do to ensure positive relationships with their in-laws?

2. Why is a young woman's relationship with her father-in-law likely to have less conflict than her relationship with her mother-in-law?

3. Why is it unrealistic to assume that there will be little contact with one's in-laws following marriage?

4. Suppose you moved to Florida and your spouse's retired, widowed parent decided it would be nice to spend 3 months each win-

ter with you. How would you feel about this? If you did not favor an extended visit of this length, how would you handle the situation so that feelings would not be hurt?

5. Which is more important in forming a close relationship with someone—blood relationship or how you feel about the person? Discuss the concepts of "relatives as friends" and "friends as family."

6. Discuss your relationship with your siblings now that you are adults. Has it changed since childhood and, if so, how?

7. How can grandparents help or hinder children in adjusting to divorce and remarriage?

8. A newly married couple is having difficulty agreeing on whose parents to visit during the upcoming holidays. The distance involved does not make visiting both families a possibility. What solutions or compromises would you suggest?

CHAPTER 15

THE MIDDLE AND LATER YEARS

❧

As I look back on my six decades of life, I have tried to think of the most important thing I have learned about family life that has contributed the most to my happiness. It is this: a great deal of the unhappiness that occurs in marriage and parenthood is the result of discrepancies that occur between one's expectations and one's realities. Whenever reality fails to meet my expectations, I frequently choose to accept my reality by adjusting my expectations. This does not keep me from working to change the situation or influencing others. But becoming angry, to me, is illogical. Many times, I find that the best solution is to change my perception of the problem: I accept life's realities and myself. Flexibility became possible when I acknowledged the fact that I am not always right and that some of the greatest blessings in life come disguised as disappointments. Adversity *can* contribute to our strength by providing us with important lessons that we can use to good advantage in the future. Not everyone thinks as I do, and somewhere in my twenties, I no longer expected them to.

James Walters

❧

The Changing Context of Lives: Contrasting Two Cohorts

In a fascinating comparison representing yesterday's and tomorrow's young-old, Hagestad (1987) compared two groups or *cohorts*: (a) individuals who were over 85 and (b) the early baby boomers, the first of whom are now turning 45. The comparison is an important one because it illustrates clearly how demographic and social changes reshape the context of lives and relationships.

When those over 85 were born, life expectancy was 49. Death was a part of life for all age groups. By age 15, the majority had lost a sibling or a parent. There was always the fear of diseases; many were potential killers.

Fewer than one-third completed high school, and less than 10% graduated from college. Approximately one-half of the men were still employed in their late sixties. Although data about this group are limited, it is reasonable to assume that approximately 70% have at least one living child, the average age of whom is about 59. About three-fourths are grandparents and greatgrandparents (Hagestad, 1987).

In contrast to the 2 million who are over 85 in the United States, by the time the first cohorts of baby boomers reach 85, there will be about 10 million of them. As they approach their 45th birthday, most will have both parents living. By the time they are in their late sixties, nearly one-third of the women will have at least one parent surviving. At birth their life expectancy was 67, yet by the time they reached 20 they could expect 53 more years of life. More than 80% graduated from high school, and 20% graduated from college. It is estimated that less than 10% of the men in this cohort will be employed when they reach their late sixties (Hagestad, 1987).

Between these two remarkably different cohorts are today's young-old (ages 65–75). They expect to live nearly 20 more years. Constituting approximately 60% of the old, people 65 to 74 overwhelmingly function without limitations due to their health; fewer than 10% require assistance with their daily living. Changes in mortality, work, and education present whole new potentials for new life careers and family life (Hagestad, 1987).

This comparison lends support to a fact that is highly important in understanding persons who are "old": It is not so much a person's age that is responsible for differences among generations, rather it is the varying cultures in which different attitudes, knowledge, and beliefs were learned. Thus, the person that you will become at 40 is likely to be different from the kind of person your mother or father was at 40. An understanding of cohort effects is highly important in gaining a perspective and an appreciation of persons of different generations. Members of generations change over the years to be sure, but there are residual effects that influence their values and their relationships with other people throughout their lives.

Compassionate people develop an appreciation of these differences and understand that each of us reflects a unique life experience. To be appreciative of the differences among cohorts will require an interest in learning more about the things that are distinctive to each age and to each era in which each age group was socialized. If we accept or tolerate the roles of our own group only, we run the risk of failing to take advantage of many intergenerational relationships that can contribute significantly to our happiness in life and to the happiness of others.

If we stereotype older people, we run the risk of becoming a victim of a self-fulfilling prophesy. If we learn to focus on the variability that exists among people at every age in order to avoid the traditional notions that older persons are all alike, however, we can join the activists for change and become the kinds of people we *wish* to become as we age. And in a very significant way we can help our parents become the kind of people they would like to become as well.

Older Persons: Their Number Is Growing

By the time persons in their early twenties today reach their sixties, the number of older persons in the United States will have doubled. Some of the changes we can expect in the future will include the following:

1. Our older generation will continue to get older and the number of four- and five-generation families will increase in many nations throughout the world (Beck, 1990). Every day approximately 5,000 U.S. citizens reach their sixty-fifth birthday, and each day about 3,600 persons aged 65 and over reach the end of their lives (Pagels, 1981). Thus, each day there is a net gain of about 1,400 older persons. This group currently makes up about 12% of the population. Over 9 million of the elderly are 75 or older. By the year 2000, the number will have grown to 12 million. The largest percentage increase, however, will be those 85 years of age and older (Piscopo, 1985).

The number of persons 65 and over increased from 17% to 18.9% between 1965 and 1985, and is projected to increase from 18.95% to 38.9% (more than double) between 1985 and 2060. In 1940 there were 11 older persons for every 100 young persons. This proportion is estimated to grow to 21 older persons in the year 2000 and to 30 persons in the year 2020 (Chen, 1987).

To show you how vast these changes are, assume we decided to determine when people could retire based upon the number of years they had worked in relation to total life expectancy. If we used 1940 as the year to begin the calculations, a retirement age in 1985 that would be equivalent to a retirement age of 65 in 1940 would be 69 years and 2 months; the equivalent age in the year 2000 would be 70 years and 7 months; and by the year 2060 the equivalent age would be 73 years and 1 month (Chen, 1987). Thus, a child born in 1987 might be expected to work until age 73 before he or she could retire.

Walker Montgomery

One of the assumptions that is made in the examination of population trends is that the elderly persons of the future will represent a crushing burden on the working population. Such a view considers the elderly as liabilities (Chen, 1987). Many elderly are, however, economic assets, and with increasing education many more in the future will be as well.

These trends will affect you for the rest of your life—your taxes, the amount you will contribute to Social Security, and the age at which you will be able to retire. It is likely *you* will not be eligible for Social Security retirement benefits until you are well past 65 (Quinn, 1990). The most important consequence, however, is that the probability of *your* living past the age of 80 has increased markedly. By the year 2000 a sharp increase is expected in the number of those reaching 65. This group is comprised of those who were born just following the Great Depression. Not surprisingly, many persons of your generation will live even longer. This will mean that people will work longer—but not necessarily in the job they had during their middle years. Less demanding work for the elderly may become commonplace.

2. Many more women than men will spend their last years without a spouse. Sixty years ago, the proportion of older women and men in the United

States was about equal. Fifty years later, however, there were only 69 men for every 100 women past 65. By the year 2000 the difference in the numbers of women and men is expected to increase (Markson, 1985).

Upon the death of a spouse, men are much more likely to remarry than women, and when they remarry they often marry younger women. Because of the way in which the present generation of older women were socialized, they are far less likely than men to assume the leadership in initiating opposite-sex contacts, and many are dependent upon others in terms of their feelings of self-worth. Without the intimacy of a loving relationship that marriage frequently provides, many could become isolated and lonely unless they are encouraged by their children and their peers to seek nonfamily friendships. Although the majority have grown children and grandchildren who provide opportunities for satisfying relationships, the mobility of families often makes contact with family members difficult. Direct face-to-face support from family members will be infrequent for some; however, others will continue to have a close association with their children.

As seen in Figure 15–1, approximately one-half of the women aged 65 to 74 in the United States are living with husbands. By age 75 less than one-fourth are living with a husband. In contrast, well over three-fourths of the men in the same age group are living with a wife, and over two-thirds of those over 65 have a wife.

Very few older persons live alone: many live with nonrelatives—a pattern that is more common for women than men. The older persons who live with relatives are likely to be women over 75. Although the vast majority have children, once their children reach adulthood, they rarely live in the same household with their parents. It should be noted, however, that the vast majority of older persons prefer not to live with their adult children.

3. Because men reach the end of their lives sooner than women, they experience fewer lingering illnesses and fewer severe disabilities during the last stage of their lives. The medical patterns of women and men are quite different. Many are not a function of a gender per se, but rather are due to the fact that women live longer. Women who assume occupational roles that are similar to men reflect medical histories that are more similar to those of men. Cancer and hypertension, for example, have been found to be related to the level of stress incurred in life (Eysenck, 1988). As women enter high-stress occupations, they are becoming more vulnerable to disabling conditions.

4. Many older women of the present generation will experience poverty in the latter stages of their lives because many are dependent upon their husbands for their primary source of their incomes. The majority of older people have adequate incomes; however, it will become increasingly difficult to live on a retirement income that has not kept up with inflation. Too, the increases in the costs of medical care have far exceeded the anticipations of older persons. Substantial improvements have been made in recent years in medical insurance that have benefited older Americans, yet gaps in the coverage pose a serious threat to many families.

The complexity of modern living makes it clear that young women who depend on their husbands financially are placing their futures at considerable risk. Far less risk is involved if both men and women are prepared for employment.

5. A greater proportion of women than men will sustain significant memory losses related to organic changes because so many live past 80 when memory loss is likely to become a problem. Women are, in fact, twice as likely as men to be diagnosed as having severe memory loss that is related to organic changes associated with aging. Because there is apparently relatively little memory loss among the young-old, the higher incidence of memory loss among women in old age may be an artifact of their longer life expectancy (Markson, 1985). Young people can better relate to members of their family if

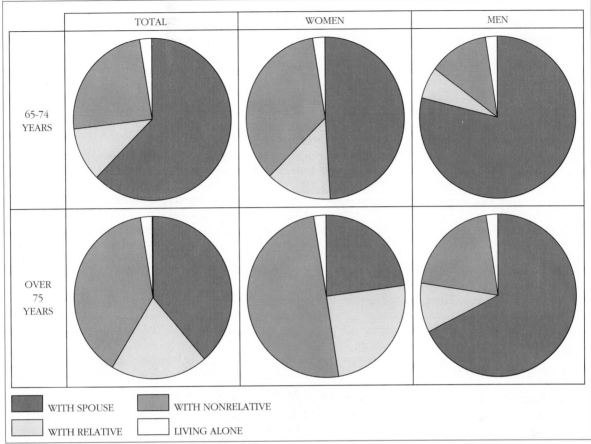

Figure 15–1 Noninstitutional Living Arrangements of the Elderly: 1985 *Source*: U. S. Bureau of the Census. (1985a, March). Marital status & living arrangments. *Current Population Reports*, Series P-20, No. 410. Washington, DC: U.S. Government Printing Office.

they understand and accept the changes that come with age. If your grandparents fail to remember to send their good wishes on your birthday, it may very well reflect the fact that they have forgotten and not that you are less loved.

6. Each group of persons approaching 60 years of age will be different from the previous cohort. Medical science has provided each new generation with benefits that were unavailable to the previous generation. There is a growing awareness of how to maintain one's health and a greater number of health professionals to assist the elderly when health crises occur. With the rapid expansion of health education and science, you will very likely retain many youthful physical and psychological qualities longer than your parents. Persons of your generation upon reaching the age of 65 will no longer be considered "old."

7. Because each cohort of people reaching the later years has had more formal education, their knowledge of how to achieve a satisfying life will be

Gender Differences in Medical Characteristics in Later Life

The very different circumstances under which men and women have lived and have grown old mean that they have very different characteristics. Some of these differences, summarized in a review by Rusin (1989) are manifested in the types of medical conditions that are likely to be present.

Osteoporosis. This leading cause of disabling and life-threatening fractures occurs at a much higher rate for women than for men. Every postmenopausal woman is at risk. Women appear to lose bone mass at a rate that is two to three times as great as the bone mass lost by men (Kaplan, 1985).

Cancer. The incidence of cancer of the reproductive organs peaks during the sixties. Women entering later life are also entering the period of peak risk for sickness and disability from other forms of cancer (Mann, 1985).

Alzheimer's disease. Women are more frequently affected with this disease than men (Kosick & Growdon, 1982). However, because the risk for the expression of the disease is linked to chronological age, it is likely that more women than men have the disease because women, on the average, outlive men (Powell, 1985).

Cardiovascular disease risk factors. Although both men and women suffer from hypertension, it does not occur as frequently in women as in men, and the effects are not as devastating on the average. For example, hypertensive women are less likely than hypertensive men to suffer from strokes and heart attacks (Krakoff, 1985). Elevated serum cholesterol levels are a second risk factor. Before menopause, women typically have lower cholesterol levels than men, but this advantage seems to disappear after menopause. Older women need to be advised of necessary alteration in their diet to take this change into account (Rice et al., 1984). Psychological factors, including reaction to stress, stressful life events, and an overall coping style have been associated with cardiac disease and complications (Herd, 1984). Whether women demonstrate higher incidences of cardiac disease and death from cardiac-related causes as they enter professions and take on lifestyles more similar to men's remains to be seen.

Late effects of polio. More women than men are now reporting symptoms of the late effects of polio. It is not clear yet whether women are more vulnerable to late effects than men are or whether we are simply observing women's tendency to report more health problems to physicians (Laurie et al., 1984).

Chronic health problems. On the average, older women have more chronic health problems than do older men. The incidence of arthritis, diabetes, anemia, migraine, sciatica, varicose veins, digestive and urinary problems, allergies, and orthopedic problems is higher for women than for men. On the other hand, older men are more likely to suffer from medical conditions that are more deadly, such as cardiovascular conditions, arteriosclerosis, emphysema, and asthma. Thus, when men have a medical condition, they are more likely to die from it. Women's success at survival comes at a cost: they are more likely to sustain and suffer from chronic medical conditions. They experience more limitations in their functional abilities and mobility than their male peers do; almost one of every five women over the age of 65 experiences significant problems in independent ambulation (Verbrugge, 1985).

Sources: 1. Herd, J. A. (1984). Cardiovascular disease and hypertension. In W. D. Gentry (Ed.), *Handbook of behavioral medicine* (pp. 221–281). New York: Guilford. 2. Kaplan, F. S. (1985). Osteoporosis. *Women and Health, 10,* 95–114. 3. Kosick, K., & Growdon, J. H. (1982). Aging, memory loss and dementia. *Psychosomatics, 23,* 746. 4. Krakoff, L. R. (1985). Hypertension in women: Progress and unsolved problems. *Women and Health, 10,* 75–83. 5. Laurie, G., Maynard, F. M., Fischer, D. A., & Raymond, J. (Eds.) (1984). *Handbook on the late effects of poliomyelitis for physicians and survivors.* St. Louis: Gazette International Networking Institute. 6. Mann, W. J. (1985). Reproductive cancer. *Women and Health, 10,* 63–73. 7. Powell, L. S. (1985). Alzheimer's disease: A practical, psychological approach. *Women and Health, 10,* 53–62. 8. Rice, D. P., Hing, E., Kovar, M. G., & Prager, K. (1984). Sex differences in disease risk. In E. B. Gold (Ed.), *The changing risk of disease in women: A epidemiological approach* (pp. 1–24). Lexington, MA: D.C. Heath. 9. Verbrugge, L. M. (1985). An epidemiological profile of older women. In M. R. Haug, A. B. Ford, & M. Sheafor (Eds.), *The physical and mental health of aged women* (pp. 41–64). New York: Springer.

Adapted with permission: Rusin, M. J. (1988). Clinical rehabilitation issues. In J. Walters (Ed.), *Women with disabilities: Through the doors of full employment* (pp. 39–59). Athens GA: Georgia Center for Continuing Education. Used with permission.

Joel Gordon

better. Fifty years ago only one woman completed college for every two men. Today more women receive bachelor's degrees than men, and the proportion who have received master's degrees, compared to a generation ago, has increased dramatically. A better educated generation is likely to attain the resources that make life more pleasant.

8. Couples will have more time together. When couples think of the things they would like to do together, one of the restrictions they face is lack of time. In retirement there is greater time to follow mutual interests than at any other period in life. Until they leave the work force, however, many older people find it difficult to do many of the things they like (Sporakowski & Hughston, 1978).

9. Individuals will have greater freedom to do what they wish. Because your generation will live longer, there will be time to pursue individual as well as mutual interests in the later years. Many of the things you wished to do but did not find time for will be possible. When individuals are asked about the things they enjoy most about retirement, they frequently mention the freedom they have in charting their own course in life and their surprise at how much they enjoy being able to work as little as they wish.

Those who believe that retirement must be bad because it leads inevitably to death are surprised to learn that the studies from the 1950s onward indicate that retirement increases neither deterioration in health nor risk of death (Ekerdt, 1987).

10. High morale will exist for many—but not all—in the later years because of the opportunity to focus on the marital dyad. Gilford (1984) found that over the early stages of the later years (55 to 62), a period during which the last of the children leave home, couples experienced an increase in marital happiness. Time exists not only to attend to one's own needs but to focus on doing thoughtful things for one's partner and to engage in activities that had been put off in order to meet the demands of children. In a study of families over a 40-year period, it was found that people who are psychologically and emotionally stable at 30 will most likely remain that way into their seventies. Young adults who are depressed, fearful, or rigid often remain troubled in their later years. Thus, psychological problems that are incurred during youth clearly should be resolved (Eichorn et al., 1981).

Attitudes Toward Aging

The emphasis in our culture on aging as a primarily biological process is not characteristic of other cultures around the world. In other societies, aging is viewed as both a cultural and a spiritual process. Growing older represents a continuing opportunity to gain knowledge, experience, wisdom, prestige, and authority. The difference in emphasis makes a good deal of difference in attitudes about aging.

The lives of the elderly are influenced by the attitudes of society toward them. When professionals view the elderly as "naturally" forgetful, weak, confused, anorexic, or incurable, very treatable conditions may be neglected (Goldstein, 1981).

Ageism that surfaced in our national addiction to youth in advertising is giving way to more accurate portrayals of older persons. Ads are no longer just

The Later Years: Myths and Facts

The Myths

There are many stereotypes surrounding older people that have influenced social attitudes and social policy, including beliefs that older people are:

1. Physically slow in movement and thinking.
2. Not creative.
3. Rigid and inflexible.
4. Unable to learn new concepts and ways of behaving.
5. Distrustful of change.
6. Traditional and conservative.
7. Prone to live in the past.
8. Egocentric and demanding.
9. Irritable and cantankerous.
10. Given to reminiscing and being garrulous.
11. Failing, both mentally and physically.
12. Often ill and unable to work.
13. Feeble, uninteresting, and awaiting death.
14. A burden to society, to family, and to self.

The Facts

In a comprehensive review of the literature, Anastasi (1974) reported on the state of our knowledge as related to the psychology of aging:

1. Individual differences within any one age level are much greater than age differences between age levels.

2. When considering the performance of older and younger persons, it is important to differentiate between age differences and age changes. Age differences may reflect educational or other cultural differences between the generations rather than physiological or psychological effects of aging.

3. The activities in which one has engaged over time have influences on whether abilities increase, decrease, or remain stable. Educational and vocational activities are two examples that influence the selective improvement of some abilities and the decline of others. What emerges as important is what one has been doing during the life span, not how long he or she has lived.

Source: 1. Anastasi, A. (1974), Individual differences in aging. In W. C. Bier (Ed.), *Aging* (pp. 84–95). New York: Fordham University Press. 2. Mowsesian, R. (1986). *Golden goals, rusted realities: Work and aging in America.* Far Hills, NJ: New Horizons Press.

aimed at youth; they also depict older people as fun, intelligent, energetic, and sexy. Television no longer perpetuates the notion of the conservative, cranky, "boring" older adult. Many elderly are no longer guilty of believing the negative stereotypes of old age themselves. Increasingly, we are coming to accept the fact that at every age people can be attractive. Members of your generation will be less concerned about growing older because important discoveries in nearly every area of human endeavor will assure that the life ahead for you as you grow older will be a great one.

Myths of the Later Years

Like other periods of life, the later years remain associated with myths that perpetuate stereotypical thinking among some persons. By concentrating upon the negative aspects of old age, its positive, rewarding aspects may be ignored. Understanding the myths of the later years can be valuable once we understand that there is very little evidence to support them.

Myth 1. Older persons are unhappy and dissatisfied. Such a belief has the effect of serving as a barrier to great relationships: "Who wants friends who aren't vibrant and fun?" As reflected in Figure 15–2, however, enjoyment of life does not decline with advanced age. Over three-fourths of both women and men rate enjoyment of their lives to be high. The dread that some people have of the later years does not appear warranted based on the evidence obtained by Brecher (1984).

In a national study of psychological well-being composed of 9,928 subjects aged 25 to 74 years, no significant age, birth cohort, or time differences were found in any of the analyses. Thus, contrary to the belief that as people reach their later years they are more likely to suffer psychological ill-effects, there is strong evidence of the stability of mean levels of psychological well-being throughout adult-

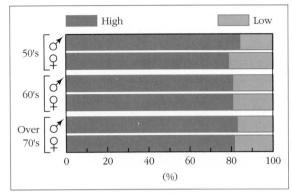

Figure 15–2 Age and Life Enjoyment *Source*: Brecher, E. M. (1984). *Love, sex and aging*. Boston: Little, Brown & Co.

hood. Too, the evidence points to the fact that personality dispositions and processes of adaptation do not decline among the young-old (Costa et al., 1987).

On the basis of this study, one wonders whether the focus of investigators on the "decline" in morale and life satisfaction as one grows older is warranted. Reports that happiness declines with age and that old age is a time of depression and dejection is clearly a myth. Inasmuch as there is increasing illness in old age, how is it possible that the level of well-being remains stable well into old age? Because changes in health are expected, illness does not apparently lead to increased worry or concern for most people (Costa et al., 1987).

These findings do not mean, however, that there is little variability among groups of people. In a second study of women and men from young adulthood to the old-old, there was greater acceptance of death by the old-old, suggesting that these individuals are prepared to face death. Women at all ages viewed life as more under control than men did. Having a sense of control was a strong predictor of psychological and physical well-being, especially for the young-old and the old-old (Reker et al., 1987).

Although the majority of the evidence supports the notion of continued well-being throughout adulthood to age 75, there are, however, periods along the way when circumstances affect satisfaction. For example, in a study comparing male retirees, males who had been retired 13 to 18 months had lower levels of overall life satisfaction. Greater optimism was more evident among those recently retired, suggesting a "honeymoon" effect that is characterized by great enthusiasm followed by a letdown during the second year of retirement (Ekerdt, et al., 1985). Thus, there are ups and downs, but the overwhelming evidence points to happiness in the later years.

Myth 2. Marriage satisfaction declines during the later years. Another prevalent myth is that marriage satisfaction declines during the later years of life. Researchers have found that most experience high levels of satisfaction (Brecher, 1984). Communication, intimacy, companionship, commitment, and marital satisfaction grow through the years and are better than ever in the later years of life (Foster, 1982; Lingren et al., 1982).

In an investigation to assess the importance of life cycle stage in terms of marital satisfaction, Rollins and Cannon (1974) found that the stage of the life cycle that one was in accounted for only 8% of the variance of marital satisfaction. This means that 92% of the satisfaction attained was dependent upon other factors such as levels of income, health, and social support from family and friends. Not all of the evidence, however, is so comforting. A decrease in marital happiness among those aged 70 to 90 was noted in a study by Gilford (1984), and a decrease in satisfaction in life was reported by Swensen et al., (1981). Such findings are not unexpected because of the variability of the ages of respondents in the studies as well as other differences.

Women are far more likely to be alone as the result of the death of a spouse. Also, many men and women past 70 are faced with chronic health problems, low incomes, high inflation, and death of peers and a spouse. Also, the rapid pace of cultural change serves to keep the generations apart because of differences in interests. This is something we may wish to change—especially among members of our own families.

Myth 3. Older persons can no longer function sexually. Another common misconception is that older persons have little sexual interest and cannot function adequately. On the contrary, many older persons remain sexually active. One of the most important factors associated with the continuation of sexual behavior in the later years is the opportunity for regular sexual expression. Older men and women who had active sexual lives throughout adulthood tend to continue this active pattern during the later years (Walters, 1987).

Many of the causes of the decline in sexual activity during the later years are social and psychological rather than physiological in nature. Fatigue, fear of failure, boredom with a partner, and preoccupation with work, for example, seem to be more important in contributing to a decline in sexual activity than aging in and of itself. An important fact to remember is that once sexual activity ceases, it is difficult psychologically for some couples to resume sexual activity.

Myth 4. Most older persons suffer from too much leisure time. Many people believe that older persons are unhappy because they have too much leisure time and can find nothing to do. The fact is, however, that many older persons are quite happy being at the stage of life when they have the opportunity to pursue interests, hobbies, travel, and other activities they never had time for before. Whereas a minority have difficulties adjusting to their change in status, many go back to school, start a second career, volunteer in community activities, and are extremely happy with their freedom from the responsibility of employment. Young adults would do well to remember to begin activities they wish to do in their later years long before they retire.

Myth 5. Older persons can no longer do acceptable work.   Our system of mandatory retirement reinforces the idea that the ability to do good work deteriorates during the later years. Many older persons are able to do high-quality work, however, as is reflected in the performance of the members of the Supreme Court of the United States and in the U.S. Senate and House of Representatives. Increasingly, society is making effective use of the skills and knowledge that older persons have acquired over a period of 40 or 50 years. We can expect a dramatic increase in the number of workers past 65 among persons of your generation (Beck, 1990).

Although physical strength declines during the later years and the capacity for heavy labor is less than it was at the age of 40, older persons often perform as well or better than young people in jobs that are not physically demanding. The quality of work done declines very slowly after the age of 45. Also, the age at which individuals do their best work does not coincide with the period at which they reach their peak physically. Many famous scientists, artisans, musicians, diplomats, writers, and philosophers, for example, have made their most significant contributions when they were past 60 years old. Many changes that occur with an increase in age are not in the direction of decline or deterioration. For example, speed in learning decreases during the later years; however, level of general intelligence is maintained; vocabulary, information capacity, and the ability to think and reason *increase*, given good health and continued use of these facilities. Young adults have an important role to play in the socialization of persons of their parents' and grandparents' generations in providing encouragement and support for older people to remain active.

Myth 6. The elderly are poor.   Approximately 70% of the net worth of all American households is controlled by people over 50, and they are earning more and spending more than ever before. Although in 1985 households with heads aged 65 or older comprised only 8% of the $25,000-and-over income bracket, the number is expected to increase to 16% by 1995, 29% by 2005, and 34% by 2015. The net worth of elderly households in the United States is over $60,000. One-fourth of elderly households are estimated to have a net worth of $100,000 to $250,000. There are, however, large segments of elderly minorities who live in poverty—36% of blacks and 23% of Hispanics (Gordon, 1988). As we increase the educational opportunities for minorities, however, we can expect to see significant reductions in their poverty.

Myth 7. Social Security benefits provide the largest portion of the income of the elderly.   Social Security benefits provide approximately 40% of the income of senior citizens in the United States. The major portion of income is generated from assets, as opposed to earnings. In 1980, 75% of the elderly owned their own homes, 80% of which were completely paid for. Clearly, the majority of the present cohort of the elderly were products of the Great Depression and were savers. Although there is substantial encouragement within society to spend as you go, there is some evidence that more people in the United States are increasing savings.

Social Security benefits provide an important source of income in retirement to the vast majority of workers in the United States. For individuals retiring in 1990 who were earning $20,990 annually and were 65 years of age, their approximate annual benefits would be $7,600. Workers earning $49,200 annually in 1990 would receive approximately $10,300 per year (Porter, 1987). Persons who pay in less receive a somewhat smaller benefit. Persons who retire before age 65 receive a slightly smaller amount. The point to remember is that most lower- and middle-class people cannot live on Social Security benefits alone. Some cannot live on their Social Security and the retirement they receive from their place of employment. Many people must augment their income during retirement by working at a later-life job—which, hopefully, will be less demanding—or from income derived from investments they have obtained during the years of their employment before retirement (Quinn, 1990).

Myth 8. The majority of the older generation live in the sunbelt states. Although the sunbelt states such as Florida, Arizona, and California have attracted a large number of older people, the majority are concentrated in the central regions. Less than 10% of retired persons move more than 200 miles from where they lived prior to their retirement. The vast majority live in their own homes. Although 5% live in nursing facilities, it is anticipated that approximately 25% will eventually require long-term care (Gordon, 1988), most of whom will be women. Given the fact that one out of every five middle-aged women is single, whether by choice, widowhood, or divorce, the problems involved in providing care for aging females becomes especially acute in a nation in which independent living is so valued. This problem may decrease, however, as women who have been gainfully employed throughout their lives reach retirement age with healthy retirement resources.

Myth 9. Because of the advances in medical science, only a very few people in their later years have disabilities. Although this is true for the young-old, over 50% of those 75 years of age and older have significant limitations due to chronic conditions, (Poon, 1988), and 40% of those over the age of 80 need help in daily living. For many, their physical disabilities make living alone impossible (Beck, 1990; Rusin, 1988).

Of the 3 million persons 85 and over, approximately 32% require some kind of personal assistance. Although family members provide much of the assistance that is needed, many require outside help. Close to 46% of all Medicare users of home health care have to purchase additional services beyond those that Medicare and unpaid caregivers offer, most of which is for unskilled assistance. In 1982 only 25% of the disabled elderly were receiving skilled (nursing) care (Kane, 1989).

Myth 10. Older people are unaccepting of the behavior of young people. The assumption of the present generation is that older people hold highly restrictive views about the sexual behavior of youth. Although youth today are less conservative than their parents, many are not *very* different. Persons of different generations do, however, misperceive each other. Excellent examples can be found during the period of adolescence when many youth believe that parents could not possibly understand how important it is to be included in the group, to have a new dress for a formal dance, or how they feel after the first car wreck. Not only can parents readily identify with such feelings, grandparents can identify as well. Thinking how much alike members of different generations are, rather than how different they are, serves to bring persons of different generations closer together. In many situations, however, it is youth who will have to take the first step, because many older people believe that youth reject them because of their age.

Marriage Satisfaction

For many, the marriage relationship is important to psychological and emotional well-being. In certain respects, marriage may be of greater consequence to some persons in the later years of life than in the younger years. The older person often depends more upon a spouse than anyone else to fulfill critical emotional needs, such as the needs for affection, respect, and meaning in life. An older married person may increasingly rely upon a mate for the satisfaction of basic emotional needs, largely because interaction with institutions in society and with children declines in the later years. Older individuals gradually withdraw from the demands of work and child rearing and find themselves spending more time with their marriage partner.

Jane Carroll

How Happy Are Older Marriages?

Marriage relationships during the later years have the potential for being very satisfying. Older spouses have more time to be with each other and to engage in activities they both enjoy. Very often they are unencumbered by career pressures. In a sense, they have a freedom to enjoy life they did not have when they were younger. Knowing each other for a long time provides couples the opportunity to achieve understanding and empathy for one another and the chance to develop communication patterns that are deeply satisfying. The evidence indicates that older couples are as happy *if not happier* than when they were younger (Foster, 1982).

Although many factors contribute to a happy marriage, it appears that physical attraction is important in a long-term married couple's relationship, especially for the male spouse. As unbelievable as it may seem, in one study older men were more concerned than older women about their physical appearance. The aging husband's satisfac-tion with his appearance was found to enhance the wife's satisfaction with the relationship (Peterson & Miller, 1980). A large proportion of the respondents in Brecher's (1984) study who were married rated their life enjoyment as being high as shown in Figure 15–3.

Retirement

One of the most significant changes in the last century is the increase in the length of the last stage of marriage. This stage—the retirement years—is now the longest stage of the family life cycle (Olson et al., 1983). Early retirement options and a longer life span mean it will not be uncommon to spend one-fourth of one's lifetime in retirement. Career roles that have occupied a large portion of life are left behind or modified. There are many significant changes that accompany retirement that many persons find deeply satisfying.

Financial Planning

Retirement programs and pension plans are offered through most places of employment. All individuals should become familiar with the specific provisions in the programs available through employers.

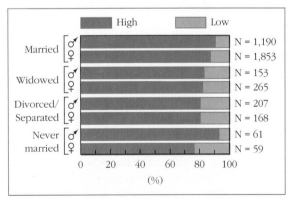

Figure 15–3 Marital status and life enjoyment *Source*: Brecher, E. M. (1984). *Love, sex and aging*. Boston: Little, Brown & Co.

Why Are Americans Retiring Early?

There is little understanding why American workers are retiring early beyond the fact that generous incomes and poor health are two factors that affect early retirement. Important differences were found in a recent study in retirement patterns across occupations and industries. Blue-collar workers retired earlier than white-collar workers, with service workers falling in between. Employees in service and trade tended to delay retirement, whereas those in manufacturing, transportation, and construction retired earlier.

Three factors are commonly believed to be related to early retirement: job dissatisfaction, workplace injury or illness, and declining productivity on the job.

1. It has been found that white-collar workers are more satisfied with their work than blue-collar workers. Professional and technical employees, managers, officials, and proprietors report the most job satisfaction; operatives and laborers were least satisfied.

2. Blue-collar workers experience more poor health than white-collar workers do. Older workers in heavy industry and construction are absent from their employment more often than younger workers, although age is not significant in clerical and light manufacturing jobs.

3. Different productivity profiles do explain why workers in some sectors retire earlier.

In reality, not all of the factors that lead workers to retire are fully understood, but the fact that many *are* retiring early leads to the conclusion that many people look forward to their years ahead without their current work responsibilities with some enthusiasm and relief.

Source: Adapted from Mitchell, O. S., Levine, P. B., & Pozzebon, S. (1988). Retirement differences by industry and occupation. *The Gerontologist, 28,* 545–551.

It can be an important consideration before accepting a job, because benefits in programs vary tremendously. Although most people beginning a career do not remain in the same position until they retire, it is desirable to learn about retirement benefits of the firm that employs you as a basis for future comparisons.

When one considers that many persons live 15 years after retiring, it is obvious that having planned for adequate retirement benefits can significantly affect their quality of life over an extended period of time. Most people will have income from Social Security and from some form of pension plan. This income will not, however, be sufficient to maintain the lifestyle to which they are accustomed. Because Social Security benefits usually provide only a small portion of the total income required in the later years for middle-class people, there is merit in planning to supplement income from other sources during retirement (Quinn, 1990). Examples of such additional sources of income include:

1. Regular saving accounts, tax-sheltered annuities, or individual retirement accounts. Such savings should ideally be started by age 40.

2. Investments such as stocks, bonds, and mutual funds.

3. Other investments such as rental property or sale of real estate.

4. Part-time or full-time work. A retired person prior to age 70 can only earn a certain amount

of money without losing a portion of his or her Social Security benefits. In contrast, income from annuities, rent, pensions, dividends, and interest, or any other form of "passive" income, does not preclude receiving full Social Security benefits.

Lifestyles

Retirement tends to reduce the differences between the roles of husband and wife. Husbands and wives become more alike in their activities when they retire. Many focus on the psychological and emotional aspects of the marriage relationship, such as providing love, understanding, affection, and companionship for each other. Retired husbands and wives see companionship and understanding as the most important benefits a couple can give each other.

In general, people remain much the same throughout life, yet there is evidence of some personality shifts that begin in the middle years and extend through the later years. Men tend to become more sensitive, more reflective, more familial, and less aggressive. Women become more aggressive, assertive, dominant, and oriented away from

Walker Montgomery

the family. Women tend to gain power, and the relationship becomes more egalitarian (Hess & Markson, 1980; Zube, 1982).

Men generally show greater reluctance in relinquishing their preretirement role pattern than women, because male identity is more exclusively associated with an occupational role. Women with a career are more likely to derive identity from their home and family-related roles as well as occupational roles. Retirement tends to benefit marriage because

1. It contributes to the egalitarian nature of the relationship by promoting cooperation in many of the same roles. This is important because older couples who are happily married are characterized by greater equality between partners than is true of unhappily married older couples (Zube, 1982).

2. It encourages a common identity that results from sharing many of the same roles.

3. It encourages the couple to dwell upon the psychological and emotional aspects of the marriage relationship rather than upon the traditional instrumental, preretirement role patterns. Husbands and wives who approach retirement focusing upon the expressive aspects of their relationship have a better chance of experiencing a satisfying relationship in retirement than those who emphasize traditional roles.

December Marriages

Today an increasing number of senior citizens are marrying.

Ella, age 70, had devoted her life to teaching school and had never married. She entered a retirement community but made few friends. One gentleman, a widower, persisted in joining her in the dining hall for meals. Soon they were taking walks in the evening and had joined a bridge group. In a few months they married. Both say they are happier than they have been in years.

A desire for companionship is the most frequently given reason for marriages that take place in later life (Garrett, 1982; Troll et al., 1979). Many persons, prior to their marriages, report experiencing feelings of uselessness, of being isolated, and of missing out on experiences that had formerly constituted a large part of their lives.

> *I had nothing or no one to fill my days. I ate alone; I went for days without a good conversation with someone. I finally decided that I had to find someone or else I'd die. Life is just too empty otherwise.*

Disadvantages of the Later Years

1. *Reduced level of living because of inflation.* Suppose you determine that because your home is completely paid for you will need, in addition to income from Social Security, approximately $15,000 a year to live on. In order to maintain your level of living, you will need to have $19,000 at the end of 5 years, provided we have only a 5% inflation rate.

If, however, we have a 9% inflation rate, you will need $23,000 at the end of five years and $55,000 at the end of 15 years to maintain the same level of living. You may assume correctly that the increases you will receive each year from Social Security and pensions will help to offset the higher incomes needed as a result of inflation, but they will not completely solve your need for additional income. Suppose you start out at retirement with $35,000 annual income and experience a 9% inflation rate. Within 15 years you would need an annual income of $127,000 in order to maintain the living that you had just 15 years earlier with an income

of $35,000. The small increases in Social Security and retirement pensions will not provide you with the additional resources you will need. What will you do?

You can do without a great many things you enjoyed in your earlier life or you will need to generate sufficient income during retirement to make up the difference. It is no secret that to implement a plan that will generate such an amount requires long-range planning and financial discipline. Dual-income couples whose combined income is less than $40,000 a year, for example, can each contribute $2,000 a year to an individual retirement account (IRA) and have the taxes on this account deferred until retirement. A person at 40 who begins such a plan will accumulate over $50,000 by the age of 65 from which he could earn income throughout life. Some people are eligible to save for their retirement is by purchasing tax-deferred annuities. The advantage of deferring taxes on money saved while they are young is that they are able to earn interest until retirement on the money that would have otherwise been paid in taxes to the government. Over a period of many years—because of compound interest—the benefits are very substantial (Quinn 1990).

Some economists believe this is very important because current projections of your length of life may be underestimated. Instead of living to be 80, you may very well live to be 90. If you are 20 now and you retire at 65, you may live as long after you retire as you now have already lived. Consequently, you will need to develop a long-range financial plan. By age 30 some type of savings should be in place for long-range goals, (e.g., buying a house, establishing a fund for your children's college education). By 40 a portion of your earnings, in addition to your contributions to Social Security and the retirement plan you have, should be invested to help you manage the inflation of the later years. One goal to strive for is to have your house paid for by the time you retire.

2. *Isolation through the death of a spouse and peers.* From research on family crises, it is clear that one of life's greatest stressful events is the loss of a spouse. For the majority, this occurs during the later years. Men are more likely to precede their wives in death; however, if they outlive their spouse, they are far more likely to remarry than women are. Because men are likely to marry women who are younger, a disproportionate number of women find themselves alone. Although many older women find happiness in the companionship of their friends and children, many miss the intimacy that is associated with marriage. Since 1970 a significant change has been observed in the pattern of single men who live alone: the median age of men living alone has dropped from over 50 years of age to under 40 years of age. With increasing divorce rates, men tend to live alone. In contrast, women live with their children and often with their parents (see Figure 15–4).

A good way to provide yourself with a buffer against loneliness throughout life is to develop a strong network of friends.

Mary Simpson is a retired professional widow with a large number of friends. Several nights a week she has different friends to her home for dinner. If they ask her if they can bring something, she'll suggest something that is easy to prepare, inexpensive, and very good. Sometimes she'll ask "Would you like to bring a salad or a dessert?" She may have one or two or three friends. About once a month she'll have a larger group. All of these people, in turn, invite Mary to their homes and out to dinner as well. It is rare that Mary eats dinner alone. She has a great time preparing food and thoroughly enjoys the company. After reading a magazine or a book she has purchased, she will share it with one of her friends and they do the same for her. When she goes on a trip, she'll purchase a dozen small gifts to share with her friends. Her friends do the same. She receives a dozen calls a day and calls a dozen friends. She sends people home with cookies and flowers from her yard, and they do the same for her. She has a lifestyle that would be the envy of most 20-year-olds. If she's lonely at 11P.M. at night, she'll call friends to come over for a goodnight drink and she'll serve hot popcorn. She's extraordinarily sensitive to the needs of her friends, and when someone calls her she says "Let's get together and do something fun!"

3. *Involuntary retirement.* That many people choose to retire early is reflected in the fact that many retire at 62 — as soon as they are eligible for partial Social Security benefits. Indeed, for each year that workers are willing to work beyond the age of 65, they receive an additional benefit — currently 3% more — until the age of 70. Thus, in spite of the economic advantage to stay on the job from 62 to 70, few workers elect this option; they would prefer to have less income for the privilege of retiring early. By 1992, however, workers will not be eligible to receive Social Security benefits until 65.

There are, however, some people who face involuntary retirement and find the changes required difficult. Among those are not only individuals whose income is insufficient to maintain their lifestyle, but individuals who have learned to do little else but

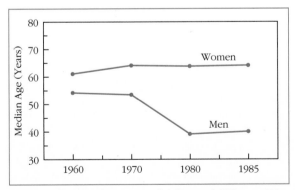

Figure 15–4 Median Age of Men and Women Living Alone. *Source*: U.S. Bureau of the Census. (1985a, March). *Marital status & living arrangements:*, Series P-20, No. 410. Washington DC: U.S. Government.

work. There are many people whose sense of identity and whose feelings of adequacy are linked with their employment. A part of this feeling undoubtedly can be traced to the way society values certain occupations. The physician, for example, who feels his or her acceptance by others is linked to the importance of the profession may contemplate being valued less during retirement. There is little doubt that feelings of status are, for many, related to their work.

Well-educated people, for the most part, find retirement satisfying, particularly if they are economically comfortable. Specialists who write the books on retirement stress the need for planning for retirement thoughtfully. One suggestion that is most frequently made is to begin the activities you wish to do after retirement before the time arrives.

4. *A decline in physical activity.* The decline in physical activity associated with advancing age is, in part, due to the fact that a variety of illnesses and ailments in the old-old make activity difficult. Exercise during the later years, however, contributes to physical well-being. Increasingly, older persons are learning how planned physical exercise can contribute to a sense of wellness and can help to contribute to maintaining physical attractiveness as one grows older. In many larger communities where there are organized programs for older persons, physical exercise plays an important role in scheduled activities.

5. *Physical ailments.* The longer a person lives, the greater the probability that he or she will have chronic health problems (Kuypers & Bengtson, 1983).

6. *Shifts in parent-child relationships.* Because of the mobility of families, there are fewer extended families today to provide a network of psychological and social support. Although many parents keep in touch with their children by telephone calls, letters, and infrequent visits after they marry and have children of their own, many see their children and grandchildren only during holiday visits. Most of these relationships are highly important and meaningful, yet they fail to provide the close, day-to-day intimate support that many would like. Studies of these relationships indicate that the major social networks of many older persons are made up of friends and not relatives. This does not mean that many families do not care for each other, but simply that because of the distances between family members there is little opportunity for frequent visits.

7. *Sexual problems.* With the onset of menopause there is likely to be a change in the tissue of the vaginal walls, which can make intercourse painful for women who have not had estrogen replacement therapy. As men age, many experience problems of impotence, which leads to a reduction in frequency of sexual intercourse. Problems also occur when differences exist between the levels of sexual interest of a husband and his wife and when one has no partner with which to share sexual activity. Most members of the current older generation had relatively limited sexual experience outside of marriage and will forgo sexual activity with another because it violates their moral standards. As the length of time between sexual encounters increases, a person becomes more adjusted to a life of sexual inactivity. Many older people are able, however, to maintain a warm, loving relationship that is intimate without sex. Many others maintain a loving sexual relationship without sexual intercourse (Murphy et al., 1980; Walters, 1987).

Some older husbands and wives do not talk about sex a great deal because they find it difficult to discuss their sexual needs openly. As impotence increases with advancing age, many older men cope by decreasing the number of sexual encounters with their wives. Relatively few men who were born before World War II will seek to have penile implants because it was not an ordinary, accepted part of their generation. Those born after World War II, in contrast, are likely to consider the procedure "no big deal" and will accept the idea just as they may have adjusted to having a vasectomy earlier in life.

8. *Discrepancy in spousal expectations regarding household chores.* There is a growing belief among American families that relationships between women and men should reflect greater equity. This trend extends to household chores. Before World War II very real differences in role expectations existed between men and women. As women have entered the labor force, expectations regarding roles have changed substantially. Expectations of women have changed more than those of men. Men are gradually making more household contributions than in the past, and evening meals increasingly are eaten outside the home. Women are demanding a greater level of sharing, and husbands are following their wives' lead, sometimes ineptly and often reluctantly (Keith & Brubaker, 1979).

9. *Less privacy for the wife.* One of the disadvantages that wives have had to face with the retirement of their husbands is that they have less opportunity to be alone, to be with friends, or to pursue their interests. Some find that having husbands at home is a great deal of trouble. Because many couples facing retirement today have both been gainfully employed, for the first time they have the opportunity to spend large amounts of time together. Some find it a mixed blessing. Generally, however, most couples whose marriages have endured to the point of retirement find satisfaction in the opportunity to undertake projects and vacations that they never had time for before (Keating & Cole, 1980).

Each couple must discover the level of "togetherness" that they can enjoy most. For some couples, the choice will be to spend nearly all of their time together; for others, the choice will be to develop new patterns that will serve to keep them apart. By trial and error, it is a journey that is quite different for each couple. Some wives will never like fishing or football games, and some husbands will never like shopping. Whatever the pattern that is developed, the focus of both partners should be to choose a lifestyle that will provide the greatest happiness.

Facing Death in the Family

Many years ago I read a book by the late Dale Carnegie entitled, How to Stop Worrying and Start Living. *It recommended that individuals could prepare for severe stress by anticipating those events in life of which they were most afraid and then, in advance, plan step by step what they would do should the event occur. Because my mother was elderly and in poor health, one of the things I dreaded most in life was knowing that someday her life would end. Initially, I avoided thinking of it because the thought was too painful. Eventually, however, I thought I would function better when the time came if I developed a plan. The first question I asked myself was "What would my mother want me to do?" I imagined that if she anticipated her death she would want to see me and, however difficult it might be, I knew I would wish to go to be with her. I started to imagine how the events would unfold. First, because I lived in a different city, I imagined someone would call me. I concluded that wherever I was, I would pick up the phone and call the airport and say, "There is an emergency in my family. I must get home. When is the next plane to Topeka?" Once I had made the first decision, I planned each step. After I arrived in Topeka, I imagined I'd call a cab and go to my mother's home or to the hospital—wherever she was.*

I pictured myself at home, talking to my mother, telling her how glad I was to see her. I knew that I would be helpful in any way I could. If the dishes needed to be washed, I'd wash them. If calls needed to be made, I'd make them.

Years later my sister called just as I arrived home from spending the day at the beach with my wife and children. She told me that our mother was to have surgery in the morning and was not expected to live. I remembered my plan. I looked up the number of the airline. As I talked to the reservation clerk I repeated the words I had remembered to say. The reservation clerk asked if I could get to the airport in 45 minutes.

The Stages of Grief

Although persons respond to death differently because of their circumstances, common stages are as follows:

Shock. "I can't believe it. This isn't really happening to me," is a typical reaction. Friends provide the support needed in the initial stages of grief.

Recoil. "I can't go on" is a feeling many persons experience. It is frequently coupled with feelings of abandonment, anger, and self-destruction. After the initial period of shock when friends are helpful, friends are uncomfortable in discussing the loss. In the case of a loss of a spouse, loneliness results as married friends gradually pull away and leave the bereaved to handle feelings themselves.

Recovery. "I will make it. I must!" are feelings that mean much to the bereaved. Such feelings can be encouraged by friends who remind the bereaved that they are loved and that life is not over, but that a new life is just beginning. The determination to endure and to be happy reflects the beginning of the recovery period.

Source: Adapted from Walters, J. (1980). Widowhood: The clapping of one hand. In J. E. Montgomery (Ed.), *Handbook on aging* (pp. 59–67). Washington, DC: American Home Economics Association.

I said I could. When I hung up the phone, I said to my wife, "My mother is having surgery tomorrow. I am leaving in 30 minutes. Please help me pack." It was just 4:00 P.M. My wife and children helped me find things. I explained I would call and arrange a later flight for them. By midnight I was in Topeka, and was told I could see my mother in the morning at the hospital. I was so relieved I had made it. However terrified I was, I was grateful I was there and that I could see her once again.

Miraculously, she survived the operation and lived until her death several years later at the age of 92. I could never remember wanting to see my mother so much in my life as I did that day I received the call. The flight I had taken was the last flight until the following morning. I had responded quickly because I had already developed a plan.

Many of the things in life we dread the most, I concluded, can be faced if we plan ahead in a step-by-step fashion and develop mental images of ourselves carrying out the plan.

The death of a loved one is one of the most difficult things we face in life. However badly one might wish to deny death, life necessitates that we accommodate to its reality. At such a time, a plan can be helpful. One of the things many people find helpful in times of stress is to assume a caretaker role: simply focus on taking care of others. In the old western movies of the 1930s, when the physician came to the house to deliver the baby, he often asked the husband to boil some water. Very little boiling water is required to deliver babies, but it did provide the husband with a task to do. In times of stress, assigning tasks can alleviate anxiety because it helps people know what they should do next, and it helps them feel useful.

When a Spouse Dies, How Are Lifestyles Changed?

Economics. As many persons become widowed, particularly women who have been full-time home-

Death Customs: An Alternative Viewpoint

Funerals and wakes are designed to provide an acknowledgment that death has occurred. The purpose is not so much to honor the dead; they are for the living. They are not designed to hurt the living, but they often do. They reflect an acknowledgment of death when no acknowledgment is needed and require problem-solving efforts involving numerous people and situations at a time when it is difficult to think of adequate solutions. They require a demonstration of strength at a time when little strength exists.

The death of a spouse leaves one vulnerable. Requiring the remaining spouse to cope with the grief of others in addition to their own is, for some, too much to expect. Grief involves a depth of feeling that rarely can be shared with self-control. Memories of failures to cope adequately during periods of grief often haunt even those who have learned to think of themselves with kindness.

Why present this alternative viewpoint? Because most people have been led to believe that funerals and wakes and burials are good for practically everyone. Yet for some widows and widowers, the funeral prevents the acknowledgment and expression of grief. It does not promote healing; it may only deepen the wound in the heart of the living spouse. Although not having a funeral or a memorial service is rare, it is possible, and it is an alternative that some persons can choose.

James Walters

makers, they face the reality that they cannot live on their existing financial resources. Inflation, in recent years, has made it especially difficult for widows who were full-time homemakers and have no pension benefits. Many have to find employment.

Fortunately, employment opportunities are increasing for the elderly. There is a slight positive relation between industrial productivity and worker age, and older workers have a better absenteeism record than younger workers. Also, they have fewer injuries. In certain occupations, however, older workers, very young workers, and minority groups face discrimination in our society. There may always be employers who discriminate against workers on the basis of age, sex, racial origin, and religious background. Increasingly, however, reasonable people are realizing the limitations of such thinking.

Environment. In spite of the fact that approximately 15% of older Americans live with their children, most older persons would prefer not to live with their adult children. Most children also prefer that their parents not live with them. It is not that parents and children dislike each other; it is that members of different generations have somewhat different lifestyles, particularly if there are adolescents remaining in the home. Frequently, the children of older persons do not wish their parents to know all of the details of their family life, and it is difficult to conceal details of everyday interaction when older persons share their home. Older people who have spent a lifetime collecting things that have meaning for their lives do not wish to dispose of them, and rarely is there room for all of their things in their children's home.

Economic adjustments that are necessary when the income of older persons is reduced involve mov-

---

Children Are a Comfort in Old Age: Or Are They?

The data provide no substantial support for the view that in American society having children has contributed, on the average, to happiness and satisfaction in late middle age and beyond. The only evidence for positive effects is for relatively unimportant dimensions of satisfaction rather than for global happiness; and, in the case of black men and highly educated white men, the evidence is predominantly negative even on the dimensions of satisfaction. The best evidence now available indicates that the present young adults should not decide to have children on the basis of expectations that parenthood will lead to psychological rewards in the later stages of life. The prospects for such rewards seem rather dim, at best.

Source: Adapted from Glenn, N. D. & McLanahan, S. (1981). The effects of offspring on the psychological well-being of older adults. *Journal of Marriage and the Family, 45,* 409–421.

ing into a smaller house or apartment. Leaving an environment identified with memories of the lost loved one often makes the adjustment easier. Yet the decision to move should be made carefully. It may be a good idea to delay moving to a time when there are not many other major changes.

Shared Housing. One of the practices that is gaining renewed interest involves shared housing. Sharing a house has always been common for two sisters who find themselves alone or for an aging widower who has his unmarried or widowed sister move in so she can take care of him; however, there is a trend emerging in which housing is shared by unrelated persons. In some cities it has met a real need, enabling older persons who have been caught in a period of rapid inflation to keep their home rather than to move into less expensive quarters. Also, it helps the older person who may need support in maintaining the house and lawn or who needs someone with a car to run errands in exchange for living in a portion of his or her house.

Sexuality. One of the most significant changes in widowhood involves the loss of a partner with whom one has enjoyed a sexual relationship. Personal and societal situations make it difficult for many older adults to have a satisfying sexual relationship with another person. Examples of these include: (a) strong feelings against sexual encounters outside of marriage; (b) the tendency for older men who become widowed to marry younger women, thus leaving a disproportionate number of older women without potential partners; (c) declines in sexual drive due to long delays in sexual functioning; and (d) feelings of being embarrassed and uncomfortable in beginning anew with someone else after having been sexually exclusive for many years.

Family Strengths in the Later Years: A Reflective View

Have you ever thought about being old? Have you thought what you would look like? Have you thought what you would be like? Have you thought about what marriage will be like when you are old?

There are several reasons to think about aging as you consider marriage and family living. One is that marriages and other intimate relationships last a lifetime whether the relationship is broken or not. Likewise, we have our families for a lifetime. And, it is possible to have some control over what we will become.

Shared Housing

Shared housing is actually a modernized version of a historic living arrangement, earlier thought of as boarding and lodging in private homes. In nineteenth-century Boston, for example, more than one-quarter of all households, usually older couples or widows, took in unrelated persons to supplement household income (Hareven, 1974).

In the late 1980s, affordable housing for the financially marginal single person was elusive. For the elderly person with a limited informal network, the housing problem was compounded by the cost and nonavailability of support services provided on a one-to-one basis. The shared housing of today, which is attracting a great deal of attention, grew out of these issues. A shared elderly household is defined as a facility housing at least two unrelated people, where at least one is over 60 years of age.

Home-sharers consist of two groups, home providers and tenants. The provider is one who has extra living space and is in need of a service or additional income. The tenant is in need of affordable housing and will provide a service in exchange for no rent or reduced rent. Many organizations that have realized the need for matching services have initiated shared housing programs.

The major benefit that shared housing offers providers is the opportunity to remain in their homes and increase their social and economic resources. Since about two-thirds of the personal wealth of the elderly is in the form of physical assets such as real estate, increasing the income of the elderly while homeowners can remain in their homes is a significant benefit. Otherwise, the providers would be forced to seek alternatives such as moving, selling, taking out a conventional mortgage, or making a philanthropic donation with the stipulation of living in the home until death (Fuchs, 1983).

Adapted with permission: Redeker, D. A., & Sweaney, A. L. (1988). Shared housing as an alternative living arrangement for the older adult. *University System Advances in Gerontology and Geriatrics: Creative Energies for Now and Tomorrow*, Volume II, Poster Abstracts, Technical Report 88-02, Athens, GA.

Sources: 1. Fuchs, V. R. (1983). *How we live*. Cambridge, MA: Harvard University Press. 2. Hareven, T. K. (1974). The family as process: A historical study of the family life cycle. *Journal of Social History, 7*, 322–329. 3. Leibowitz, B. (1978). Implications of community housing for planning and policy. *The Gerontologist, 18*, 138–144. 4. Murray, P. (1979) *Shared housing: A housing option for older people*. Washington, D.C.: International Center for Social Gerontology. 5. Streib, G. F., Folts, E., & Hilker, M. A. (1984). *Old homes—new families: Shared living for the elderly*. New York: Columbia University Press.

As persons get older, they change some, but, also, many of their characteristics become more pronounced. It is possible to identify those characteristics and behaviors that we do not like and quit practicing them. Everytime we engage in a behavior or express an attitude, it becomes more ingrained in our repertoire of behaviors and attitudes. Thus, it seems reasonable to practice those attitudes and behaviors that will promote lasting and deeply satisfying relationships, including those attitudes and behaviors that we want to be known for when we are old.

We begin to grow old gracefully while we are still young. Alertness in old age is partially a function of the mental discipline we exercise during youth and throughout the adult years. Being interesting in old age is the outcome of having interests and being interesting when we are young.

If you want to know what you will be like when you are old, take a good look at yourself today and remember that what we practice in the routine process of living will have a great influence on what we will become. Older people often report that they do not feel old and different; they feel like the person they have always been.

Those years we refer to as the later years of life in many respects feel very much like the earlier years of life because we do not perceive ourselves to have changed a great deal. Just as you will become more of what you are today, so do others. Just as you will wish to be treated in accordance with the way you feel and not like just any old person, so do others. Thus, these thoughts on how we age serve both as a guide to our own aging process and a guide to working with others who are also in the process of aging.

Summary

- Stereotyping older people has two important residual effects: (a) we may become the victims of our own beliefs, and (b) we may fail to understand the potential of other older perons. Both beliefs have important implications for future generations.

- The number of older persons in the United States will continue to grow as life expectancies lengthen. There are disadvantages to such long life expectancies (spending your last years without a spouse, memory losses, financial and medical problems), but there are advantages as well (greater freedom to pursue mutual interests and more emphasis on healthy lifestyles will lead to satisfaction in later years.)

- The lives of the elderly are greatly affected by the attitudes of society toward them. Negative myths that perpetuate stereotypical thinking regarding older persons leave the positive aspects of aging ignored.

- Retirement can be a very fulfilling time if a couple makes the necessary emotional adjustments and has followed a financial plan.

- The death of a spouse changes the lifestyle of the widowed partner. He or she will have to make emotional, physical, and financial adjustments to survive the loss.

Discussion Questions

1. Obviously, many of the facts concerning people past 70 do not conform with attitudes we have about the aged. Why are so many of our attitudes out of date?

2. What are your attitudes toward marriage of your family members when they are past 60? Do you believe that 20-year-olds or 40-year-olds are more in favor of older persons

marrying? Why do you believe this difference exists?

3. Evidence indicates that many older couples reflect greater satisfaction with their marriages than younger couples. Explain this phenomenon.

4. Couples in the 60-year-old group are having intercourse twice as frequently today as persons of the same age a generation ago. How could you account for such a change?

5. Studies of the bereaved indicate that older women adjust to the death of a spouse better than younger women even though the probabilities of a remarriage are less. Why?

6. Studies of the bereaved indicate that men are more adversely affected by the death of a spouse than are women. Why?

7. At what age will you consider yourself "old"? Why?

8. How can society's attitudes about aging be changed? Discuss the impact of TV shows such as "Golden Girls" and movies such as *Cocoon*.

9. What is your relationship with your grandparents? What kind of relationship do you want to have with your grandchildren?

CHAPTER 16

DIVORCE AND
REMARRIAGE

◈

❧

My wife, Nancy, said she wanted to talk with me about something. I yawned and ambled into the living room, assuming it was about the bills or Saturday's bridge club. She said the marriage had died for her and that she wanted me out of the house as soon as possible. I couldn't believe it! The next few days I alternated between being a zombie and a bundle of raging emotion. I also felt like someone had emblazoned some words on my forehead that everyone could read: "This man is a failure. His family dumped him." Everyone seemed to be pointing fingers at me and whispering, "Shame, how disgusting."

(Sprenkle & Cyrus, 1982, p. 53)

❧

High Divorce Rate

The divorce rate in the United States is one of the highest in the world (Price & McKenry, 1988; United Nations, 1985). Divorce is accepted by an increasing number of persons as a regrettable alternative for couples facing marital problems that they find impossible to resolve. Although divorce is often associated with regret, the period following a divorce has for many provided new hope, and some find this time a stimulating one filled with exciting challenges (Kaslow, 1984). In many cases, the dissolution of the marriage is the choice of both partners, and they are eager to get on with their lives. As Ahrons and Rodgers (1987) have noted, "there is little evidence that the rise in divorce indicates a disillusionment with marriage. The remarriage statistics indicate that a more accurate interpretation would be that divorce represents dissatisfaction with a specific marriage, not "marriage in general" (p. 2). For some people divorce is a very positive life event (Price & McKenry, 1988).

The high divorce rate may not necessarily mean that there are more unhappy marriages today. Sometimes those in unhappy marriages choose to remain there. The divorce rate does, however, reflect that men and women are demanding more from their marriages. If they do not find what they want, they are prepared to end a relationship.

Among the reasons for the changing divorce statistics are the following:

1. Divorce judges and the courts have become more accepting of the realities of marital breakdown, and the grounds for divorce have been expanded to include "no-fault" divorce.

2. Public attitudes have changed over the years so that today there is far less stigma attached to divorce than a generation ago (Jorgensen & Johnson, 1980). Although it is often viewed with regret, it is usually viewed with understanding.

3. Industrialization and urbanization have provided a situation in which most Americans live among thousands in a city environment. This has weakened the community ties of a smaller neighborhood, while at the same time offering freedom of restraints from family and neighbors. Studies show that in urban areas with high migration rates divorce rates are high.

4. Women today are better able to support themselves financially so they do not have as many pressures to stay married for economic reasons.

5. As living standards rise and education increases, more people recognize the availability of divorce options and are able to afford the expense of legal termination.

6. One factor that has been suggested is the American belief in "making things right" and the consequent refusal to tolerate discomfort. This philosophy leads to a readiness to choose divorce because it enables individuals in an unsatisfactory marriage to search for a partner who is a better fit.

7. Marriage success now makes demands very different from those early in the century. The more pragmatic demands of the past focused on economic support, mutual commitment for life, cooperation in rearing children, and financial support. Today, compatibility, personal satisfaction, and individual happiness are expected within marriage.

There are a variety of reasons why marriages fail. One is that one or both spouses engage in negative behaviors, such as drinking too much, drug abuse, being unfaithful, being domineering, or being overly involved in work (Kitson & Sussman, 1982). In situations in which couples lack conflict resolution skills or the motivation to change, much dissatisfaction is likely. Sometimes, too, persons change radically. An accident resulting in paralysis or a major lifestyle change, such as switching careers, may result in spouses becoming strangers.

Factors Related to Divorce

After reviewing the research on divorce from the last decade, Price and McKenry (1988) noted the following factors that are related to divorce:

1. *Age*. Persons who marry at a younger age are more likely to divorce. Many teenage marriages are due to a premarital pregnancy, and many couples subsequently change during adulthood so that they are no longer compatible.

2. *Premarital pregnancy*. Higher marital dissolution rates are consistently associated with premarital pregnancy. Not only do many of the premarital pregnancies occur among the young, but having children early creates stress with which many youth are unable to cope.

3. *Parental divorce*. Persons whose parents were divorced are more susceptible to divorce themselves. Recent evidence adds support to the idea that persons whose parents were divorced tend to have more permissive attitudes toward divorce as an alternative to an unhappy marital situation.

4. *Religion*. Interfaith marriages (Jewish-Gentile, Catholic-Protestant) more frequently dissolve than homogamous marriages. Persons with no religious preference have the highest divorce rate; Catholics, Mormons, and Jews have the lowest.

5. *Education*. The divorce rate among men and women with less than a high school education is approximately twice as great as that of college-educated men and women. Among women who move on to graduate work, however, a greater portion are divorced when compared to those who complete only a four-year degree. Highly educated black women are even more likely to be divorced than their white counterparts ("The Graduate School Divorce Itch," 1980).

6. *Race*. Although interracial marriages are less stable than same-race marriages, racial differences in the rates of divorce and desertion disappear when factors such as income level are controlled.

7. *Previous marriage*. A greater percentage of second marriages end in divorce than first marriages, and a greater percentage of third marriages end in divorce than second marriages (Brody et al., 1988).

8. *Children*. Having children may no longer serve as the barrier to divorce as it once did, yet having a baby does serve to delay divorce for approximately 2 years (Waite et al., 1985).

Divorce Theory

One of the reasons why an engagement is such a happy experience is the anticipation of entering into a close, intimate union with another person. The adventure of building and sharing one's life with the person who has been selected over all others is exciting. Conversely, one reason why divorce is so unpleasant and depressing is the realization that it involves taking steps to separate from the person with whom one eagerly anticipated establishing a pleasant, satisfying union.

According to the *social exchange theory of divorce*, if personal benefit from a marriage is unrewarding, the lack of rewards decreases the chances that the relationship will endure. Thus, if the costs involved in the interaction are greater than the rewards, the relationship is likely to end in divorce. Similarly, in the *economic theory of divorce*, individuals compare

---

The Personal and Social Meaning of Divorce

If divorce is looked upon as the voiding of a social contract rather than as an act which pronounces the previous relationship as a failure, it would be possible to view divorce as a judgment regarding future prospects of the relationship rather than as judgment regarding past quality of interaction.

Few people consider divorce as a sign of mental emotional health. Yet, for some, divorce is exactly that. Today there are many who are divorcing in order to "save" themselves, i.e., in order to preserve their identity, to ward off further exploitation, emotional dependency, loss of self-esteem, and dehumanization. For many of these persons, divorce is an act of courage and great risk. For others, it is a matter of self-affirmation and self-assertion equal to no other act of their adult life. For these people, the magnitude of the raging internal conflict is such that they are literally fighting for their lives.

Some divorces are a sign of psycho-emotional health, of personal growth, and of the ongoing struggle for personal fulfillment. To some extent this has always been so. Even in past-time, divorce was not always a sign of failure. Today, however, there is a change in the social milieu wherein many persons are less reluctant to remain in a non-productive, non-rewarding relationship. No one can ascertain what percentage of the total annual divorce rate represents this quest for psycho-emotional health and/or growth and self-fulfillment. However, a logical premise is that a significantly greater number of people, especially women, are divorcing today because they are no longer socially stigmatized and/or locked into a destructive relationship as in past-time.

Source: Crosby, J. F. (1980). A critique of divorce statistics and their interpretation. *Family Relations, 29,* 51–68. Copyrighted (1980) by the National Council on Family Relations, 3989 Central Ave. N.E., Suite # 550, Minneapolis, MN 55421. Reprinted by permission.

the costs and benefits of the current marriage versus alternatives to determine whether the degree of profit they receive, e.g., psychological satisfaction, by remaining in the marriage is greater in contrast to the satisfaction they would receive if they were divorced and able to pursue another relationship. If individuals perceive their marriage to be less than they expected it to be, then they are likely to terminate the relationship (Price & McKenry, 1988).

Separation

For many couples the first step in the divorce process is a separation. One study (Kitson, 1985) found that of those who were still married, 10% had separated at least once. Of those seeking divorce, 40% had separated at least twice before making their decision.

The separation may be the most painful and upsetting part of the breakup of the marriage. Men and women suffer from "separation distress," and few events in a person's life cause as much change, upheaval, and physical and psychological stress. One separated man commented: "What do you do with your own pain, the ache you have inside for the person you lost or couldn't keep? When word gets out that you've broken up, it's as if you have a disease and none of your friends wants to catch it."

Phases of Divorce

Divorcing oneself from a spouse is complex and difficult because at least six different types of experiences occur simultaneously:

1. The emotional divorce, which centers around the emotional problems of the deteriorating marriage relationship.

2. The legal divorce, which is concerned with the grounds for divorce.

3. The economic divorce, which focuses upon finances and property settlement.

4. The coparental divorce, which is concerned with child custody, single-parent home, and visitation.

5. The community divorce, which centers around the change of community and friendship patterns associated with most divorces.

6. The psychic divorce, which involves the problem of regaining individual autonomy (Bohannan, 1970).

A better understanding of each of these types of separation experiences gives us greater insight and empathy concerning divorce.

The Emotional Divorce

A marriage relationship necessarily involves the emotional interaction and interdependence of the partners to some degree. At least at the time the couple married, their emotional feelings about one another were positive and supportive. At the time of divorce, however, the couple's emotional feelings tend to concentrate upon the shortcomings of each other's personalities and upon the weak points of the relationship. In short, the couple finds the emotional relationship with each other is no longer satisfactory. One or both partners then gradually sep arate emotionally from each other as much as possible.

Divorce is one of the most severe crises, in terms of emotional stress involved, that anyone experiences in life. Much evidence suggests that the experience of divorce poses a threat to the well-being of a large proportion of persons whose marriages are disrupted (Spanier & Furstenberg, 1982). If the spouse that is lost is loved, the emotional divorce often results in feelings almost as intense as the death of a mate. Grief and disorientation are natural reactions to such a loss. In some instances, grief occurs even if the "loved" one is hated. It is natural to mourn the loss of any intimate relationship in which there was a high degree of involvement and a backlog of happy memories. The amount of mourning that one experiences depends upon the

Joel Gordon

Decisions

Before or during the period of separation, whether it leads to reconciliation or divorce, there are many decisions that a couple must make. Some of these include:

1. Where is each spouse going to live? Who stays in the original domicile, and where does the other spouse live? Who takes care of the original domicile?

2. How are the costs of such items as utilities, food, clothing, maintenance, transportation, medical/dental care, and insurance to be paid?

3. If the couple has only one car, is a second car needed? Who selects it? Who cares for it? How is it to be paid for?

4. What is the family's financial situation? If one spouse is unemployed, does this spouse seek employment? Should the standard of living be reduced for one spouse or for both spouses?

5. How and when are children, extended family, and friends to be told about the separation?

6. Where do the children live? Why?

7. What are both parents' rights and responsibilities in relation to the children?

8. Do children have any say (and if so, how much) as to whom they are going to live with or the amount of contact they are to have with parents?

9. Who makes decisions for children on a daily basis?

10. Who makes major decisions about children?

11. How is it to be handled if parents and/or children disapprove or disagree with plans for children?

12. When and under what circumstances should spouses contact each other?

13. What are the guidelines for the sexual/social lives of spouses while still legally married?

14. How will spouses handle conflict?

Source: Price, S. J., & McKenry, P. (1988). *Divorce: A major life transition.* Beverly Hills: Sage. Reprinted by permission of Sage Publications, Inc.

degree of emotional involvement in the relationship. Mourning over the emotional divorce may last for months or years. Not all couples, of course, experience grief, but few can divorce without feeling disoriented.

The emotional divorce is particularly difficult because it entails deliberate rejection of one person by another. This emotional frustration is often borne alone. The distress over the emotional divorce is somewhat eased after divorced persons make new arrangements for living and establish new daily routines.

The Legal Divorce

Couples who decide to dissolve their relationship generally obtain a legal divorce. Couples should have a checklist of specific questions ready beforehand when they consult with an attorney. The cost for a half-hour averages about $50. It may, however, cost much more. There is no obligation to use the lawyer for any of the legal proceedings. In fact, it is possible to consult with more than one lawyer to gather information and to discuss financial questions.

It is important for the two partners to talk to each other about the best way they can terminate the marriage and divide their possessions. For one partner to tell a lawyer simply to send the legal papers to the other partner often provokes bitter retaliation.

Other options available today include the use of a mediator, who uses techniques of arbitration and discussion to see if an agreement can be reached. Lawyers or family service agencies may recommend them. And there are "do-it-yourself" books and advice leaflets for those who do not want to involve a lawyer in the family situation and feel they can handle the stress alone (Krantzler, 1981).

Whatever the emotional problems and conflict the couple have experienced in living together, whatever the reason they feel they can no longer live together with each other, these real situations as revealed to their lawyers must be taken by the lawyers and translated into language that the law recognizes. When the divorce action goes into court, it must be written in a way the court can legally accept.

No-fault divorce. Historically, the legal system required specific grounds for divorce and required that one partner be "guilty" of adultery or cruelty, for example. Fortunately, the concept of no-fault dissolution of marriage has been well accepted as a means of legally terminating marriage.

Under the no-fault system, a person may file for dissolution of the marriage without making accusations against the spouse. The grounds in this instance are irreconcilable differences or an irretrievably broken marriage. All of the states but one now

---

Conciliation Courts

The Conciliation Court of Santa Clara, California, is representative of those courts that refer child custody and visitation cases to counselors for decision making. Referred couples complete an intake form providing the counselor with needed background information about the family. Attorneys for both sides are then interviewed, issues are presented, and the role of the counselor is explained. The spouses are seen together, often with their children. The goal of this process is to assist the parents in negotiating an agreement that they can accept as both functional and consistent with their children's needs and best interests. Most couples adopt a reasonable, cooperative stance, as indicated by the fact that fewer than 10% of the cases fail to reach an agreement.

Following the decision-making process, the attorneys, clients, and counselor meet. At this time, the counselor recites his or her understanding of the terms of the agreement. A draft is then prepared, and the parties return to court for approval of the agreement by the judge, which then takes the form of a court order. When the parties cannot agree on the solution, the counselor makes independent recommendations to the court.

Source: Price, S. J., & McKenry, P. C. (1988). *Divorce: A major life transition.* Beverly Hills: Sage. Reprinted by permission of Sage Publications, Inc.

No-Fault Divorce

No-fault legislation has changed four major components of traditional divorce law.

1. It has eliminated the idea of fault-based grounds for divorce. No one is accused or judged guilty of any offense. The marriage is merely declared unworkable due to undescribed irreconcilable differences and then is dissolved. The individual is empowered to decide when a divorce is justified; one spouse can obtain a divorce without the consent of the other.

2. It has eliminated the adversary process. It assumes that the adversarial legal process generates hostility and trauma by forcing husbands and wives to be antagonists.

3. It has based division of financial assets on equity, equality, and economic need rather than fault or gender-role assignments. Financial rewards are not tied to innocence, and it is not assumed that women need to be supported by men. Community property is equally divided under the assumption that both partners have contributed equally, if differently, to the marital partnership. Child custody is based on the gender-neutral principle of the "best interests of the child" rather than maternal preference.

4. It has redefined the traditional responsibilities of husbands and wives by instituting a new norm of equality between the sexes. The husband and wife are regarded as equal partners, equally responsible for the support of the household and care of the children. Provision of alimony is based on the assumption that the wife will be employed.

Source: Price, S. J., & McKenry, P. C. (1988). *Divorce: A major life transition.* Beverly Hills: Sage. Reprinted by permission of Sage Publications, Inc.

have a no-fault provision; some have retained fault-based provisions so that fault may be claimed and used to base maintenance and alimony payments.

The Economic Divorce

The economic aspects of divorce are often underestimated by divorcing couples. They include legal fees, court costs, division of property, alimony, and child support.

Legal fees and court costs. Many persons are surprised to learn the price of legal fees and think they are being overcharged by lawyers. Many lawyers, however, regard the fees set by the court as too low. Such lawyers may make additional charges

for the other services they perform for their clients. Most divorce lawyers work on an hourly rate and adjust the rate to the particular income level of clients.

Ownership of property. Laws differ by state as to ownership of property. In some states individuals keep whatever property is in their name; if the house is registered in the husband's name only, he will keep the house. In other states "equal distribution" applies, which means that all property acquired since marriage will be divided equally, no matter in whose name it may be registered. This does not apply to property acquired before marriage. There is also a court procedure of "equitable distribution," which does not mean equal distribution. It does mean that if a couple cannot reach a decision about the division of property, the judge will decide what is fair in each particular situation.

Money. If a couple has joint checking and savings accounts, the court may rule on distribution of funds in these accounts according to the distribution of property. However, since the atmosphere before the divorce may be unpleasant, it is usually better for partners to put their money in separate accounts to forestall one partner's taking all the funds.

In terms of debts for credit cards or joint charge accounts, both partners are held responsible, even if only one purchased an expensive stereo set or new furniture. These commitments continue even after the divorce. It is best to write to credit card companies informing them of marital changes and to decline to take responsibility for charges made after a certain date.

Alimony. Alimony or maintenance is the payment of money during and after divorce, usually but not exclusively, by the ex-husband to the ex-wife. Payment of alimony is based upon the expectation that a husband takes on the duty of supporting his wife at the time of marriage. In some states alimony is viewed as a form of punishment of the husband for mistreating his wife. In such states if the wife is the "guilty" party in the divorce, she is not entitled to alimony.

Generally, the amount of alimony depends upon

1. The "moral" or "immoral" conduct of the wife that comes to the attention of the court. An innocent wife is awarded more than a wife who is judged guilty of immoral conduct.
2. Need of the wife. The greater the economic need of the wife, the higher the alimony payments are set. In determining the need of the wife, such factors as her level of education or

training, health, age, and number of children may be taken into consideration.

3. Ability of the husband to pay. The greater the husband's ability to pay, the higher the alimony payments awarded.

The court may be petitioned by either spouse to adjust the alimony payments as the result of a change in either the former wife's need or the former husband's ability to pay. Usually, all alimony stops at the time of the former wife's remarriage.

Child support. The responsibility for child support usually lies with the father as long as he is physically and financially able to provide or until the child reaches the age of majority. The father makes child-support payments regardless of whether his former wife remarries or not. In setting child-support payments, the court considers the father's ability to pay, his health, and the needs of the child. The average amount awarded for child support in both 1978 and 1981 was 13% of the father's income (Weitzman, 1985). Child-support payments can, however, constitute up to one-half of the father's monthly income if several children are involved. The average child support paid and the proportion of income that it represents have declined approximately 25% since 1978. Child support payments account for about 15% of the income of women who receive them (Select Committee on Children, 1989). In the few situations in which fathers are granted custody of the children, the mothers may be required to make child-support payments.

When her parents divorced, Adrienne, age 23, chose to stay with her mother. Her father was angered and refused to continue to pay her college tuition. She was dismissed from the university after her junior year because she owed $6,700. Adrienne took her father to court, claiming that she had been harmed by his failure to honor his promise to send her to college.

A state appeals court agreed and ordered the father to continue to pay her college fees ("Split Decisions," 1982).

Tax concerns. Alimony payments are deducted from the taxable income of the spouse who makes the payment. Child support, however, is not a deductible expense for the person paying. Consequently, many men prefer to give ex-wives alimony, and benefit from the tax deduction, rather than pay child-support specifically.

Women and the economics of divorce. An analysis of the economic effects of divorce reveals that many American children will spend some part of their youth in single-parent families headed by their mothers and that these families often suffer economic deprivation. Generally, wives are left worse off financially than their former husbands after a divorce. Most earned less than their husbands when married, and, because the woman usually gets primary custody of the children, she must assume primary responsibility for their care—on about half as much money (Weitzman, 1985). In fact, 18% of all divorced women with children are living at the poverty level (Select Committee on Children, 1989), and 50% of all poor, female-headed families are headed by women who are divorced or separated (U.S. Bureau of the Census, 1987a). One study of divorced couples revealed that 5 years after the breakup, one-third of the women were enmeshed in a daily struggle for economic survival. One-half were able to maintain a modest standard of living but worried about large, unexpected expenses. Only one-fifth of the women were financially secure, either because of remarriage, regular and generous child-support payments, or because of their personal earning power (Wallerstein & Kelly, 1980).

As well as coping with custody of the children, women routinely face impediments in the labor market with lower pay and inadequate employment opportunities. Wallerstein and Kelly (1980) reported that about 75% of the divorced women in their study were employed. Many were dissatisfied, however, with their pay. Many were constantly looking for better-paying jobs. Investments in education, job training, and health care can significantly help improve economic circumstances of women following divorce.

Other financial problems result from the fact that many men do not comply with their financial obligations of child support. Wallerstein and Kelly (1980) reported that 68% of fathers made their child-support payments regularly; 19% paid some support irregularly; and 13% were completely delinquent. Others report that up to 50% of divorced mothers received no money from their children's father (Rice, 1990). Wives often do not take them to court about their failure. An International Women's Year survey showed that over one-third of the divorced and separated women whose ex-husbands were not in compliance with the law had not initiated any action against them. Most women

The University of Georgia

How Much Is Enough?

Recommendations of the *Family Law Section* of the American Bar Association:

1. Where there are no dependent children
   a. The nonworking dependent spouse (who has no outside income) shall receive 25% to 40% of supporting spouse's spendable income.
   b. The working and/or income-receiving dependent spouse shall receive 0% to 20% of the difference between supporting spouse's income and dependent spouse's income.

2. Where there are dependent children
   a. Where custody is awarded to the nonworking dependent spouse (with no outside income) that spouse shall receive from the supporting spouse:

Number of Children	% of Supporting Spouse's Spendable Income
1	30 to 40
2	35 to 50
3+	45 to 60

   b. Where custody is awarded to the spouse who is working and/or who has monthly spendable income
      i. If the custodial spouse's monthly spendable income is equal to or less than the noncustodial spouse's monthly spendable income, then the custodial spouse shall receive from the noncustodial spouse:

Number of Children	% of Noncustodial's Spendable Income
1	15
2	20 to 30
3+	25 to 35*

   * Plus 0 to 20% of the difference between spendable income of custodial and noncustodial spouses.

      ii. If the custodial spouse's monthly spendable income exceeds the noncustodial spouse's monthly spendable income, then the custodial spouse shall receive from the noncustodial spouse:

Number of Children	% of Supporting Spouse's Spendable Income
1	0 to 20
2	0 to 30
3+	0 to 40

Source: Bair, E. S. (1979). How much temporary support is enough? Guidelines for judges and lawyers. *Family Advocate,* *1,* 36–41, 48. Reprinted by permission.

cannot afford to wage an unsuccessful battle for child-support payments.

The federal government has a parent locator service that is available to parents of children whose fathers fail to pay child support mandated by the court. Such a law permits access to various government record-keeping systems. Thus, fathers who fail to pay child support can be traced and made to pay (Weitzman, 1985).

The Coparental Divorce

In a marriage in which there are children, there are additional difficulties, i.e., explaining to the children what has happened and making decisions about their future care. Quite possibly the most enduringly painful aspect of divorce is the coparental divorce. Coparental divorce simply refers to the fact that a child's parents are not living with each other. Even when both parents share joint legal custody, the child usually lives with one parent and visits the other occasionally.

Custody of the child is usually given to the mother. The form of over 80% of postdivorce families is that of a custodial mother with whom the children reside and a father with visitation rights (Wallerstein & Kelly, 1980). Generally, the father does not get custody of the child unless the court is convinced that the moral character, economic situation, or emotional instability of the mother will

Why Don't Fathers Seek Primary Custody?

Some authors argue that more fathers could have primary custody. This argument is based on the fact that when fathers do seek custody, they obtain custody in about 50% of the cases. Some of the reasons put forth to account for fathers not seeking primary custody include the following:

1. Fathers fear a bitter court battle and the subsequent possibility of having a poor relationship with their children and former spouses.

2. Fathers see it as unchivalrous, if not unmanly, to attack the character of their wives and to seek to carry out what society has defined largely as a female role, i.e., child rearing.

3. Many fathers merely do not want what they perceive as the burdensome responsibility of having primary responsibility for child rearing.

4. Many mothers fervently seek primary custody to enhance their general financial settlement and/or to avoid social stigma when, in fact, they might be very satisfied with their former husband's having primary custody.

5. The Equal Rights for Fathers Organization contends there is a "quiet conspiracy" among judges, probation departments, conciliation courts, and even fathers' attorneys to dissuade divorced men from seeking custody.

6. Courts still base custody decisions to some extent on fault, and it is easier to prove the father at fault and thus a less-able parent than the mother.

Source: Price, S. J., & McKenry, P. C. (1988). *Divorce: A major life transition.* Beverly Hills: Sage. Reprinted by permission of Sage Publications, Inc.

have a deleterious effect on the child. The court usually awards custody of all children to one parent so that brothers and sisters will not be separated. Custody decrees are temporary and may be challenged at any time by the parent without custody. In recent years, however, more and more single fathers are rearing their children.

A noncustodial parent may have difficulty relinquishing the influence he or she had on the children and may miss daily contact with them.

In the first weeks after my divorce, I was in shock— angry at my ex-wife and her new boyfriend and deeply hurt. But the real mourning I did was for the loss of my son. I can only see him every other weekend.

The custodial parent is faced with the challenge of coping with a single-parent household. He or she must make most of the decisions concerning the child's life, such as general lifestyle, education, recreation, and social and cultural activities.

Joint custody. One innovation growing in popularity is the concept of joint custody of children—

that is, shared legal responsibility for and shared physical custody of children. Joint physical custody can take a variety of forms to fit the needs of parents and children. Children may spend several days weekly with each parent or may alternate weeks or months (Wallerstein & Kelly, 1980). Some couples have their children spend school days with their mother and occasional weekends with their father. In more complex situations where, for example, the mother lives in New York and the father in California, they may solve the problem by having a daughter live with her mother during the school year. Vacation months may be spent with her father. Additionally, the father can maintain contact with his daughter with weekly letters and phone calls. Advocates of joint custody stress that the crucial factor is that the children realize they still have two caring and committed parents.

There are criticisms of the concept of joint custody. It is important for the child to know that one adult will continue to have the same amount of responsibility and authority for his or her daily care in one place. Movement between two houses may be confusing and unsettling to children.

The Community Divorce

When a couple is divorced, it is not uncommon for at least one of them to move to another community. In some cases, the moves are due to financial necessity. The move to a new community requires adjustments—new friendships, a new social life, moving into a new home, and becoming established in another location. This helps many persons, providing them with a sense of starting a new life. Moving may be disruptive for children, however, placing on them additional burdens of loss of friends and adjustment to a new school. Some children fear that they will move again farther away from their noncustodial parent (Wallerstein & Kelly, 1980).

Walker Montgomery

Even when divorced persons remain in the same community, friendships are likely to change. Some previous friends may have "taken sides" during the divorce. The divorced person may feel "out of place" interacting with the couples with whom he or she and a former marriage partner had socialized. Many who are divorced associate more and more with unmarried persons and join organizations for single persons, such as Parents Without Partners. Regardless of whether the divorced person moves to a new community or not, the community life as he or she knew it is changed.

The Psychic Divorce

People identify with the personality and influence of their marriage partners. They depend in varying degrees upon their spouses psychologically. Most think of themselves as a couple. When a divorce is finalized, most individuals then become aware of their psychic divorce.

The psychic divorce challenges the divorced person to become an autonomous individual again. Learning to live without a partner means coping with daily problems and challenges alone. It is a trying process for many and a time during which many divorced persons need the help of friends and relatives, and some need the assistance of a marriage and family therapist. On the positive side, the psychic divorce offers opportunities to achieve increased self-understanding and to find personal autonomy.

Effects of Divorce on the Marital Partners

The effects of divorce are not easy to determine because they are influenced by several factors, including the quality of the marriage, the degree to which the partners were emotionally involved with each other, whether the divorce was desired by one or both of the partners, the personality characteristics of the partners, and the couple's views concerning the sacredness and permanence of marriage.

Rediscovering Feelings of Self Worth

It is not uncommon for some married persons to interact with each other in such a destructive manner that they damage each other's self-esteem. After years of destructive interaction, divorce can be an escape from devastating interaction and an opportunity to establish new relationships. A 25-year-old divorcee illustrates this:

My ex-husband continually belittled me and not just in private either. When we went out, he would put me down in front of others. He often turned me away sexually, which made me feel totally undesirable. About a year before we were divorced, we were separated due to a temporary job I had in another town. That separation was like a whole new world. I found that people liked me and treated me as though I was worth something. I was a more attractive, happy person. I was more interested in people. When I returned, a friend remarked about the change in me. She had never seen me so enthusiastic and confident before. I fully realized how poor our marriage was, and I decided on a divorce.

The divorce has been hard in many ways, but I have few regrets. My social life has expanded. I have established new friendships with people who have a high regard for me. I date a variety of men who consider me attractive. This has done wonders for me.

The divorce wasn't all my husband's fault. I think we were not a good team. I made him feel insecure. I failed to reassure him. This was a big reason why he felt compelled to put me down. An interesting thing is that since we have been divorced, he has seemed to become a much more considerate and secure person.

We have both prospered by getting away from each other.

A Sense of Failure in the Marriage Relationship

Many divorced persons feel guilty, believing that the divorce is a result of their own failure. If only they been more considerate, more appreciative, more understanding, more loving, or more determined, they could have made the marriage work. Some have serious doubts about their ability to maintain another intimate relationship. Others, however, view the divorce not so much as a personal failure, but more as an unwise selection of a mate.

Developing a Fear of Intimate Relationships

Some divorced persons are reluctant to commit themselves to another marriage. Although they may become physically intimate with another within a relatively short period of time, many are reluctant to become psychologically committed and dependent upon others. They adopt an if-you-stay-uninvolved-you-don't-get-hurt attitude. And some retain a cynical attitude about marriage.

Depression and Alienation

The depression and alienation that many persons suffer as a result of divorce are reflected in the high suicide rate among the divorced. Divorced men and women commit suicide at a rate of three to four times more often than do married persons. Such persons believe that their way of life has ended, and they no longer have anyone to whom they belong. The severity of their feelings depends on several factors, including their emotional stability and the presence of supportive friends and relatives. Research concerning adjustment to divorce has iden-

tified various conditions related to the degree of distress that women experience with divorce (Price & McKenry, 1988).

1. *Length of marriage.* Persons who have had long-term marriages generally experience more difficulty adjusting to divorce because of the greater commitment to the marriage relationship.

2. *Age.* Older women experience more adjustment problems. The possibilities for establishing a satisfying new life may be more limited for the older woman. Also, she may have difficulty reentering the job market.

3. *Number of children.* The presence of two or more children is associated with more difficulty in adjusting to divorce. The responsibility and concerns of rearing a number of children, especially small children, are often perceived as a very substantial burden. There is also a tendency to worry about the effects of divorce upon children.

4. *Who suggested the divorce.* The greatest amount of distress generally is suffered by the person who did not suggest or who did not want the divorce. Many persons are disturbed by being "the rejected partner."

5. *Decisiveness about the divorce.* Lack of confidence about whether the decision to divorce is a good one is associated with greater difficulty in adjustment. Indecision about the divorce, or the "on again, off again" approach, creates a strain and contributes to anxiety and insecurity.

Changes in Lifestyles

Some of the changes in lifestyle following divorce are illustrated in the following example:

One of things that was the hardest to adjust to was the change in daily habits. I always took my little boy to the park on Saturday morning. Now I can't because Virginia has custody of him and has moved away. After 2 years I am still not accustomed to this new father-son relationship.

Virginia used to fix a big breakfast for me every morning. Now I fix it myself. That is a very minor thing, but I can tell you, it took me a while to get accustomed to it. Also, I found it hard to reorganize my social life. I gradually was excluded from going out with most of the couples we used to see regularly. I feel awkward about it.

I developed new hobbies and participated more in group activities to combat the loneliness. It was very unpleasant to accept the fact that I no longer had a regular sex life. I had taken sex for granted.

The most difficult times since the divorce have been at Christmas. We had always bought presents together and decorated the tree. Then I found myself spending Christmas alone, and I was not going through those rituals anymore. I literally hurt with depression.

Divorce inevitably forces the people involved to make changes in their daily routines, social patterns, and general lifestyles. The longer the couple has been married, the greater the shock associated with a forced change in lifestyle.

Adjustment to Divorce

A variety of factors relate to adjustment following a divorce. Persons who did not want a divorce and persons who experienced sudden, unexpected separations have greater adjustment problems. Being able to make a "clean break"—to sever affective ties to a former spouse—aids adjustment (Pocs, 1989). Having young children or several children contributes to greater depression in the postdivorce period. Custodial parents experience stress from added parental obligations; noncustodial parents are stressed by not being with their children as much as they wish (Price & McKenry, 1988).

Having the support (money, child care, companionship) of family and friends aids in postdivorce adjustment. Divorced persons who have active career and social lives have fewer difficulties (Price & McKenry, 1988). Involvement in clubs, community organizations, church or synagogue, and dating are helpful forms of social involvement (Daniels-Mohring & Berger, 1984).

Men and women face some different kinds of problems after a divorce. Although women are more likely to receive custody of their children, they often face added financial difficulties and role strain. The divorced mother may have little time for her own social life. Too, women who are traditionally oriented do not fare as well in adjustment as nontraditional, career-oriented women. Divorced fathers with custody of their children experience role strain and lack of personal time. Additionally, divorce may have an impact on a man's occupational success. Being unmarried is negatively related to occupational success (Price & McKenry, 1988).

On a positive note, most individuals experience an increased sense of well-being 3 to 4 years after their final separation regardless of whether they remarry or not. One longitudinal study of divorce and remarriage, however, concluded that remarriage after divorce was not associated with enhanced well-being (Spanier & Furstenberg, 1982).

The following characteristics are associated with positive adjustment following divorce (Thomas, 1982): assertiveness, self-assurance, intelligence, creativity, social boldness, liberalism, self-sufficiency, ego strength, tranquility, and egalitarian sex-role attitudes.

The Continuous Nature of the Relationship after Divorce

A contradictory aftermath of divorce is that the relationship between the couple tends to continue. A divorce generally is never quite final. Many persons

⤝

Patterns of Relationships with Ex-Spouses

Perfect Pals: 12%. These continue involvement in each other's lives. They often do not remarry someone else.

Cooperative Colleagues: 38%. These have moderate contact. They minimize conflict and get along because it is in the best interest of the children.

Angry Associates: 25%. These have moderate conflict-filled contact. They have difficulty separating parent and spouse roles.

Fiery Foes: 25%. These have little contact but it is hostile.

Source: Stark, E. (1986, May). Friends through it all. *Psychology Today*, pp. 54–60.

divorce with the expectation that they will completely cut off the relationship with their former spouse, only to find, in reality, that although the relationship is greatly altered and their contact with each other is markedly reduced, the relationship persists in various ways (Price & McKenry, 1988).

A few divorced persons see each other regularly. The form of this ongoing relationship varies. Some couples may have dinner or lunch together on a regular basis.

When there are children, of course, the parent-child bond promotes the continuation of the relationship between the former spouses. Noncustodial parents nearly always have visitation rights; as the parent visits the children, the couple can hardly avoid interacting with each other. The child is a bond between the couple, and the divorced parents most probably will talk with each other about the child's future plans, school progress, success, health and problems.

Not infrequently one of the divorced partners has established a close relationship with the parents of the former spouse. This relationship may be so loving that the person maintains contact with the in-laws after the divorce. Again, where there are children, contact with grandparents usually means a continued relationship with one's former in-laws. Contact with the parents of the former partner results in a continuation of the relationship with that partner in subtle ways. Mention would naturally be made concerning the former spouse's health, plans, accomplishments, and problems, as well as of memories of happy and special events the couple had shared in the past.

In rare cases, divorced persons continue to be friends after the divorce. They may attend social functions together, exchange Christmas and birthday presents, and help each other in solving various problems. A very small percentage of divorced couples find this supportive friendship so meaningful that they eventually remarry each other.

Effects of Divorce on Children

Even when parents are responsible in their actions leading to a divorce, children are deeply affected by the breakup of a marriage. In a rare study of both mothers' and children's perceptions of divorce, the children's views differed markedly from their mothers' on several issues. For example, 86% of the mothers believed the atmosphere in the home had improved, whereas only 46% of the children thought it was better. While 63% of the children said they were sad and upset following the divorce, their mothers perceived that only 43% were upset. Only 63% of the children thought divorce was the right thing, compared with 86% of the mothers. The most important difference was in the children's comments about their fathers; 72% wished they spent more time with their father, and 50% said the worst thing about divorce was that they missed their father. Although 82% of the children rated their relationship with their fathers as good or excellent, only 44% were considered to have good or excellent relationships by the mothers (Hingst, 1981).

Wallerstein and Kelly (1980) also note the discrepancy in adults' and children's perceptions about divorce. They found that many marriages that had been unhappy for the adults had been reasonably comfortable and gratifying for the children. Five years after the divorce, most adults (80%) approved of the decision to divorce. Over one-half of the children, however, still did not regard the divorced family as an improvement over their predivorce family situation.

Unlike adults, who improved in psychological adjustment following a divorce, children did not show improvement in their psychological adjustment. Only children who were separated by divorce from a rejecting, demeaning, or psychiatrically disturbed parent showed improvement (Wallerstein & Kelly, 1980).

In a continuation of this research a rare, 10-year follow-up was completed with these same children and their mothers. The major results reported by Wallerstein and Blakeslee (1989) include the following:

- 50% saw one of their parents get a second divorce in the 10-year period following the first divorce.

- 50% grew up in families where the parents continued to be angry at each other during the 10-year period.

- 25% experienced a severe and enduring decrease in their standard of living and observed a major and lasting discrepancy between the economic conditions in their mothers' and fathers' homes. Very few were assisted financially with their college educations, even though they continued to visit their fathers regularly.

- 60% felt rejected by at least one parent, feeling as though they were psychological or economic baggage left over from a regretted journey.

- Almost 50% of the children entered adulthood as worried, self-deprecating, underachieving, and sometimes angry young women and men. Some felt used in the battle between their parents, and many others felt deprived of parenting, encouragement, and family protection or security.

- 68% of the children had engaged in mild to serious illegal activities during adolescence or young adulthood.

- Approximately 66% of the children indicated that their childhood and adolescence had been significantly burdened by the divorce.

The predominent mood associated with their looking back over the last 10 years was one of sadness and regret.

- Most of the children expressed a strong desire to avoid their parents' mistakes and have a lasting marriage.

- Approximately 30% of the young women reported being worried about their potential marriage relationships and fearful of being rejected.

- 25% of the young women had experienced abortions.

- Many of the children felt they had benefited by having to assume more responsibility as a result of the divorce, i.e., contributing to the care of the household, taking care of younger children, and assuming responsibility for themselves at a very young age. Many also felt that the price had been too high; they felt they had been pushed to grow up too early and that a significant amount of school and play time had been sacrificed.

- Those children who were older (age 9 or older) at the time of their parents' divorce experienced more severe effects than did those children who were younger at the time of divorce.

More than 1 million children per year see their parents get divorced (Select Committee on Children, 1989). While children are still much more likely to live with their mothers after a divorce, the number living with divorced fathers has almost quadrupled since 1970. Many adjustments are required, and there is no doubt that children experience major problems as a result of their parents' divorce (Price & McKenry, 1988).

A study by Hetherington, Cox and Cox (1985) revealed that adjustment to divorce was more difficult for males than females in mother-custody, one parent households, and for children who were less intelligent, or preadolescents or early adolescents. Divorce for children who were temperamentally "difficult" was much harder than for "temperamentally" easy children.

Wallerstein and Kelly (1980) reported that preschool and kindergarten children (3 to 5 years old) responded to their parents' divorce with fear of being abandoned, regression in toilet training or behavior, bewilderment at what had happened, guilt, and increased aggression. Young school-age children (6 to 8 years old) experienced grief, fear, feelings of deprivation, yearning for the departed parent, anger at parents, fantasies of reconciliation, and conflicts in loyalty. Older school-age children (9 to 12 years old) expressed anger and a shaken sense of identity. Children of this age group seemed especially vulnerable to aligning with one parent against the other. Adolescents (12 to 18 years old) felt hurried into adulthood and anxious about their own sexuality. They also experienced anger, mourning, and loyalty conflicts. For all the children in their study, the time of the parents' divorce was a sad and frightening time—often having taken up a significant amount (one-half or more) of their childhood or adolescent years.

Researchers have sought to answer the question of whether an intact, unhappy home situation or a divorce is better for the children. Wallerstein and Kelly (1980) concluded that neither an unhappy home nor divorce is good for children. Each has its own stresses.

Seven potentially traumatic situations that may exist for the child of divorcing parents are:

1. Having to adjust to the knowledge that divorce will probably take place.

2. Having to adjust to the fact of divorce.

3. Being "used" by one or both parents as a weapon against the other.

4. Having to redefine relationships with the parents.

5. Having to make readjustments with the peer group.

6. Recognizing the implications of their parents' failure in marriage.

7. Adjusting to stepparents if the parents remarry.

Whether or not children of divorce sustain less negative effects than children of unhappy, conflict-ridden, unbroken homes, it is certain that children of divorce do experience problems, particularly when the child loves both parents and

Joel Gordon

experiences a feeling of divided loyalty. Many children also feel that they were somehow responsible for the divorce.

The effects of divorce upon the child depend upon many factors, including the age of the child, the quality of the child's relationship with both parents, whether the parent the child is living with remarries and the quality of the child's relationship with the stepparent, the personality and emotional stability of the child and the parent, the availability of parent substitutes for the child, and the financial situation of the one-parent family.

Remarriage

The majority of both men and women who divorce eventually remarry, and they tend to marry another divorced person. Remarriages make up about one-third of all marriages in the United States (Price & McKenry, 1988). Marriage rates for persons who have been divorced are higher than for single persons of the same age and gender. Approximately 90% of those who divorce before the age of 40 remarry. There is a tendency to remarry rather soon after the divorce, with the average time between the divorce and remarriage being approximately 3 years (Eshleman, 1985).

Characteristics of the Remarriage

Remarriages are different from first marriages in that they are much less likely to involve presents, bridal showers, a reception, or a honeymoon. Remarriages in which one or both partners have been divorced receive less enthusiastic support and celebration from family and friends than do first marriages. There is less optimism among family and friends concerning the remarriage. This pattern holds true regardless of how accepting the attitudes of friends and families are toward divorce (Brody et al., 1988).

Remarriage of divorced persons is much more likely to be opposed by family members. If one partner has not been married before, his or her family may express concern about the success of the marriage. "Why did the other person's marriage fail?" "Does that person possess characteristics that make failure of the present marriage likely?" Such suspicions are not uncommon among family members. Both partners in the remarriage must learn to cope with these doubts.

The divorced person's family is likely to compare a new marriage partner with the previous one. The new marriage partner naturally senses the comparisons and may have some difficulty in accepting them.

Many remarriages involve children from previous marriages, making remarriage vastly different from the first marriage. An individual may not experience immediate acceptance by the children. Rapport, trust, and love must be developed in relationships with the children, and this takes time. Some individuals also find it difficult to adjust to the fact that the spouse's former marriage partner has visitation rights with the children. The couple may also experience financial pressure if the husband has to pay alimony and child support in addition to supporting his present family.

Facets of Remarriage

Goetting (1982) suggests that persons who remarry must undo some of the adaptations they have made to divorce. She suggests six "facets" of remarriage that parallel the six phases of divorce mentioned earlier.

Emotional remarriage. Emotional remarriage is the slow, sometimes painful, process by which the divorced person reestablishes a bond of attraction, commitment, and trust with someone. Divorced persons may find the establishment of a new marital-type relationship difficult because they fear failing again and because they have been hurt and disappointed.

Psychic remarriage. Psychic remarriage involves relinquishing the autonomy and personal freedom brought about by the psychic divorce. The remarried person once again is one component of a partnership.

Community remarriage. Reentrance into the "couples" world takes place in community remarriage. Unmarried friends typically are lost owing to lack of common interests. New friendships among other couples develop. Because some friendships are lost, persons find community remarriage to be difficult.

Parental remarriage. For persons with children, the parental remarriage may be the most difficult part of remarriage. Children represent a tie to the previous marriage and as such are a potential source of marital disruption if they make a new spouse feel like an outsider. Also, because a new marital relationship and new parental relationships must be assumed simultaneously, the remarried couple may feel cheated of the opportunity to establish a primary couple bond without the intrusion of children. Marital and parental problems compound each other. Finally, stepparents are often confused about the exact nature of their role. They frequently share parenting roles with natural parents without benefit of any social guidelines for this joint parenting. Confusion, resentment, and frustration are common.

Economic remarriage. Economic remarriage entails the establishment of a household. Typically, the economic situation of remarried couples improves owing to pooled resources. Many families, however, are unsure about how much money they will have each month. Child-support payments may not arrive regularly. Equitable division of resources is also a difficult area. If his son is given music lessons, is her son entitled to join Scouts?

Legal remarriage. The legal ramifications of remarriage are just beginning to be explored. The remarriage has special legal considerations because of relationships from the former marriage—his or her former spouses; his, her, and their children. Questions arise such as which wife should receive life insurance and retirement benefits: Should it be his ex-wife, who has custody and responsibility for his children, or his current wife? Inheritance laws typically favor the current spouse and natural children. Consequently, anyone wishing to provide benefits to stepchildren or to a former spouse needs a clearly defined will.

Remarriage Success

How successful and happy are the remarriages of the divorced? From research it appears that the increased divorce rate in recent years has not been accompanied by any major decline in the "happiness rating" of remarried divorced men and women compared with those who have never been divorced. Three national surveys support the idea that remarried men and women tend to be as satisfied with their marriages as people in their first marriages. Remarried persons usually consider the new marriage more satisfactory than the one that ended in divorce. In one study, 88% of the remarried persons stated that their present marriages were "much better" than their former marriages had been (Albrecht, 1979).

Unfortunately, not all remarried persons experience satisfaction in their second marriages. Research studies indicate that the remarriages of divorced persons are more likely to result in divorce than first marriages. One-third of first marriages will end in divorce, whereas close to one-half of remarriages will do so. Remarriages between two persons who have both been divorced once are about twice as likely as first marriages to end in divorce. The probability of divorce increases with each subsequent remarriage of a divorced person. For example, approximately eight out of ten remarriages between partners who have been divorced two or more times result in divorce (Brody et al., 1988). "The tendency for remarriages to be less stable than first marriages may be due largely to a greater prevalence in first marriages of persons, who, for religious reasons, or because they perceive no preferable alternatives, will not terminate unsatisfactory marriages" (Glenn & Weaver, 1977).

These findings also suggest that for many persons, the problems that contributed to the termination of their first marriage are perpetuated in their second and third marriages. Perhaps the trouble does not lie so much in their choice of a marriage partner as it does in their manner of interacting and responding in interpersonal relationships. This suggests the need for making human-relationships education and remarriage education available to divorced persons.

Remarriage and Children

Many of those who remarry bring children with them from their earlier marriage. Of the marriages that end in divorce, about 50% involve children, and about 80% of the parents will remarry and create stepfamily relationships. One in every five adults will become a stepparent. This growing number of parents and children face a range of new situations, new emotional experiences, and unexpected challenges within the family.

In a study of older children by Hetherington (1989), stepsons were found to be more disengaged from their families than were sons from nondivorced families. During the early stages of remarriage neither mothers nor stepfathers were successful in controlling and monitoring their children's behavior in stepfamilies. In the first two years following remarriage, conflict between mothers and daughters was high. Daughters exhibited more demandingness, hostility, and coercion, and less warmth toward both parents than did girls in divorced or nondivorced families.

Although mothers and stepfathers initially viewed sons as extrememly difficult, the sons' behavior improved over time. This improvement was found only when the remarriage occurred before adolescence. Stepsons, but not stepdaughters, in longer remarried families, reported being close to their stepfathers, enjoying their company, and seeking their advice and support. Among the remarried families closeness in the marital relationship and active involvement in parenting by the stepfather were associated with high levels of conflict between the child and both the mother and stepfather.

Stepparents must usually share the parental role with the previous parent. The child may idealize the biological parent, particularly the father, from whom he or she is separated. At the same time, the stepparent may be expected to replace the biological parent from whom the child is separated. The stepparent can easily become disillusioned and frustrated when this expectation is not realized, thus adding tension to the relationship with the stepchild.

Some children have little trouble in adjusting and achieve very positive relationships with their stepparents. There are others, however, who experience considerable difficulties. Age of the child is an important factor in the child's adjustment. Younger children have a closer and more affectionate relationship with stepparents than do older children. Very young children and adult children accept a stepparent much more readily than do adolescents. Children adapt more easily to stepparents when the previous marriage was ended by divorce rather than death.

Other interesting findings concerning the relationship between children and stepparents are as follows:

1. Stepchildren more often express a preference for one parent or the other (either the stepparent or their biological parent) than do children who live with both biological parents.

2. Children perceive that their stepparents discriminate against them more often than their biological parents and that stepparents of the opposite sex discriminate against them the most. Children feel that the stepmother discriminates against them more often than the stepfather.

3. Female children involved in remarriages express feelings of being rejected by parents more often than do male children.

4. Both male and female children involved in remarriages more often desire to emulate their biological parent rather than a stepparent.

Another situation that can strain relations between stepparents and stepchildren occurs when each parent brings children into a remarriage. Competition and rivalry may arise among the children. There is often a tendency for each parent to favor his or her own children.

Other factors that can create problems between children and stepparents include:

1. An expectation that there will automatically be instant love and an instant family feeling between stepparents and children.

2. Hypersensitivity by the stepparent to various events and responses from the child as proof that he or she is not regarded by the child as a "parent."

3. A tendency for the stepparent, particularly the stepmother, to interpret any behavior or emotional difficulties of the stepchild as being due to her personal shortcomings as a parent.

4. An attitude that there should only be positive feelings between stepparents and stepchildren.

5. An expectation that if the stepparent or stepchild were the biological parent or child, the relationship would be more loving and positive.

6. An expectation that the stepparent, particularly the stepmother, will be unloving toward the children.

7. A tendency for both stepchild and stepparent to misinterpret certain actions of each other as representing rejection and lack of love.

Many problems between stepparents and children, as can be seen from the previous list, are caused by unrealistic and negative expectations as well as by a tendency to misinterpret various responses as representing rejection. Problems can be minimized and more positive relationships between stepparents and stepchildren may be developed if stepparents are ready to remember the realities of the situation and to allow time for relationships to develop.

Summary

- The high rate of divorce in this country is a reflection of the change in attitudes regarding marriage and family as well as a result of unhappy marriages. Men and women today have very high expectations for marriage, and if these expectations are not met, divorce becomes a viable and accepted alternative for many.

- The following factors have implications for the likelihood of divorce: age, premarital pregnancy, parental divorce, religion, education, race, and previous marriage.

- There are six dimensions to the divorce process, all of which add to the complexity of the situation. These dimensions include: the emotional, legal, and economic issues, the child-rearing implications, the changes in social life patterns, and the problems of regaining individual autonomy.

- Although a divorce is intended to terminate a relationship, other factors make a complete termination unlikely. Monetary obligations; visitation rights of the noncustodial parent; favorable relationships with in-laws; and shared relationships with co-workers, neighbors, and friends make it difficult for a couple to put an end to their relationship. Couples may be able to terminate the marriage, but terminating the relationship is often not easy.

- Most people who divorce eventually remarry, but the duration of second marriages is even more uncertain than the probability of success in the first marriage. The dimension of stepparenting for remarried couples creates unique problems that can be overcome if stepparents and stepchildren do not have negative or unrealistic expectations of one another.

Discussion Questions

1. Women with less than two years high school education and women with graduate study have higher divorce rates than women with college educations. How do you account for that?

2. Should a wife who sacrifices career or education to benefit her husband receive payment in the event of a divorce?

3. What do you think is the most difficult adjustment that marital partners must make to a divorce? What is the most difficult adjustment for children?

4. It seems that neither an unhappy home nor a divorce is easy for children. With this in mind, what recommendations would you make to a husband and wife with two children involved

in a very unhappy marriage? What might the parents do to help their children if (a) they do not divorce or (b) they do divorce?

5. How do you think the courtship of formerly married persons would differ from the courtship of never-married persons? How would it be similar?

6. What are the advantages and disadvantages of joint custody for both parents and children?

7. Many men fail to pay child support. Why?

8. What can divorced persons planning to remarry do to minimize their chances of divorce in the new marriage?

9. What can divorced persons planning to remarry do to help their stepchildren adjust to remarriage and life in a stepfamily?

10. If two divorced parents marry and bring with them their adolescents, they are likely to have considerable difficulty within their family. Why?

11. Why do so many remarriages fail?

12. A large number of couples who have been married previously are living together before marrying. Are there disadvantages to this?

13. When couples divorce, do children frequently miss the absent parent?

14. Is it realistic to expect to develop the same kind of a relationship with a stepmother as it is your natural mother?

15. What should be the role of younger family members when their grandmother decides to remarry at 70?

CHAPTER 17

FAMILIES AND HOMES OF THE FUTURE

Many people do not fully understand the effects that home environments have on them. They know what they like or dislike but are unable to differentiate the specific effects that subtle changes in their environment can have. As research in the area grows and is translated into construction, families in the future will be able to enjoy a superior level of living.

In the Xanadu House, one of the innovative houses of the future, a sensorium will hold an array of computer-linked audio and video equipment that is capable of producing an environment that can change by command or in response to human body signals picked up by biofeedback sensors. Not only can it help in the alleviation of stress, it can provide physical therapy and promote self-awareness of normally automatic body functions through biofeedback. It can produce states of heightened awareness and healthy excitement.

(Manson, 1983)

Predicting the Future

It is hard to foretell what families will be like in 50 or 100 years. Our society has been subject to great changes in the last 50 years; history shows that other nations also have weathered years of great change. The comments and predictions in this chapter are based on current trends and on suggestions from experts in a variety of areas. The following four methods are commonly used to predict the future:

1. Charting recent trends and extending those trends. This assumes those trends will continue.
2. Assuming that all trends are cyclical. With this method past cycles are examined and used as a basis for making predictions.
3. Considering current trends and those factors that appear to be affecting the trends.
4. Identifying the underlying causes of trends and factors that may counterbalance the trends makes it easier to recognize those situations when a simple extension of a trend might not be appropriate (Walters & Walters, 1982).

Society rarely moves ahead on a predictable course. Unexpected developments, new discoveries, changes in political and social patterns, and swings against currently accepted practices can all affect the way men and women think and behave. Yet there is merit in anticipating events that are ahead in order to evaluate their consequences for families.

Projections of Population

The census projections on populations through the year 2000 are based on the assumptions that (a) each family will—on the average—have about two children, (b) there will be little change in life expectancy, (c) there will be a constant rate of immigration from outside, and (d) there will be no new medical cures of chronic diseases. Using these criteria, the total population for the year 2000 is expected to be slightly above 260 million. Several important medical breakthroughs, however, are expected in the near future, so this prediction may reflect an underestimate of the growth in population. In the years ahead there will be substantial growth in the proportion of older persons and a decline in the number of young adults. This change has been anticipated for several years, and innovations are in process to provide greater security to older citizens.

Changes in the Family

More Overlapping of Gender Roles

In the past, men were associated with such qualities as achievement, independence, physical strength, aggressiveness, competitiveness, and sexual prowess; women were characterized as nurturant, supportive, understanding, passive, dependent, and lacking aggressiveness and competitiveness. Such gender-related stereotyping begins in the earliest years of life, but as discussed in Chapter 5, gender-role stereotyping is decreasing.

Rigidly defined roles have the disadvantage of limiting males and females in fulfilling their human potential and have often been a major barrier to understanding between men and women because they interact in terms of masculine-feminine stereotypes rather than as persons. It is commonly believed that the differences in gender roles have been due far more to the influences of cultural values and socialization processes than to biological factors. Several cultural changes now taking place are contributing to greater flexibility and overlapping of gender roles.

Transfer of Major Functions from the Family

Major functions the family performed in the past, such as economic production, protection, recre-

Projections of the Population: 1990 to 2010

1. The following projections have been predicted in the United States: 249,891,000 in 1990; 267,747,000 in 2000; and 282,053,000 in 2010.

2. California is projected to remain the most populous state for the next 25 years. New York will remain in second place until after 1990 when Texas will push it to third place. Florida will continue to be the fourth most populated state.

3. In 1990 Wyoming heads the list of the least populated states, followed by Vermont and Alaska. In 2000 Wyoming and Vermont will remain the least populated states, but North Dakota is expected to lose population and move to third place, pushing Alaska to the fourth position.

4. During the last decade of this century, the numbers of children under age 5 are projected to decline by 1.5 million, while the numbers of school-age children will increase by over 3 million. The maturing of the baby boom generation is reflected in the growth in the population aged 45 to 64 between 1990 and 2000 for all four regions of the country. By 2000 the Northeast will still have the oldest age distribution, while the West will continue to have the youngest. Between 2000 and 2010, the number of children under age 5 is projected to remain constant in the United States.

5. During the next 25 years, for all four regions, the dependency ratio, i.e., how many young and elderly there will be for every 100 people of working age, is projected to decline.

6. By 1990 the median age in the United States is projected to rise to 33.0 years, an increase of 1.3 years since July 1, 1986.

7. Between 1980 and 2010 the black population is projected to increase at a rate more than twice as fast as the white population. During this time period, the black population will increase by 45%, compared with the 17% for the white population. By the year 2010 blacks will constitute almost 14% of the total population. By the year 2010 the nation's black population is projected to number almost 39 million, an increase of over 12 million since 1980. The white population will be almost 229 million.

Source: U.S. Bureau of the Census, (1981). *Projections of the population of states by age, sex, and race: 1988–2010. Current Population Reports,* Series P-25, No. 1017, Washington, DC: U.S. Government Printing Office.

ation, and education, have been largely transferred to other institutions. The family of the past was held together by these functions, which represented tangible, utilitarian, and materialistic bonds. Now the family is held together by less tangible, psychological qualities of love, happiness, and the fulfillment of basic emotional needs of individual members.

More Fragmented Family Life

Our technological and industrialized society has made life fast-paced and complex, resulting in a family life that is somewhat fragmented. People are pressured to be involved in occupational matters and in various civic activities. These demands often leave little time for family life, interaction with spouse and children, or performance of family roles.

Less Extended Family Contact

As our society has become more industrialized and urbanized, we have experienced greater geographical and social mobility. Approximately 50 million people in America move each year. The average American moves 14 times in a lifetime (Golanty & Harris, 1982). Such mobility has resulted in fewer close interpersonal relationships with extended family members, and as a consequence, the influence of aunts, uncles, cousins, and grandparents is not as great as it was in the past.

Although face-to-face personal contact may decrease, there will be growth in electronic contact. The long-distance rate for telephone calls has been steadily reduced, and phone calls halfway around the world are not unusual. Mail and other written communication media are also developing faster and more efficient services. In the past it could take weeks for news of a major event to reach the bulk of the population; today, families thousands of miles apart are informed of national and international events within minutes.

Decreased Family Size

The size of families in the United States has steadily decreased. The average number of persons per family was 5.8 in 1790, yet is only about 3.2 today. This change is due in part to the move away from the extended family system and also to the fact that the number of children per family has decreased from an average of 3.43 in 1800 to approximately 3.19 presently (U.S. Census, 1988). With more couples choosing to have fewer children or choosing to remain childless, and with the growing number of single-parent families, family size is likely to remain small.

Marriage at Later Age

Age at marriage in the United States has increased during the last few decades. In 1950 the median age at marriage was approximately 23 for males and 20 for females; today it has increased to approximately 25 for males and 22 for females. The trend toward later age at marriage is due to more people choosing to continue their education and/or to work for a time before getting married. It is also affected by the increased incidence of cohabitation, the increased acceptance of goals other than marriage for women, and more people choosing to remain single.

Increased Divorce

Although the divorce rate has grown considerably during this century, it does not necessarily mean that there is more marital unhappiness today, but rather that divorce is easier to obtain legally and is more socially acceptable now than it was in the past. Also the general affluence of the United States has increased over the last 100 years, and there is a relation between divorce rates and economic prosperity. In times of prosperity couples can more easily afford to divorce.

One picture of contemporary family life in America that may be drawn from these major changes is that the family is more focused upon the fulfillment of emotional needs, more emphasis is placed on individuals, and family life has become more fragmented and less stable than in the past.

Changes in Child Rearing

In major surveys of American families, sponsored by General Mills (1978, 1982), the majority of parents are described as *traditionalists* (57%) who continue to support the basic values by which they were reared. They are stricter disciplinarians and more demanding of their children than are *new breed* parents. But they are also influenced by new values and try to reconcile newer concepts with older theories and beliefs.

New breed parents (43% of all fathers and mothers of children under 13 years of age) tend to reject many of the traditional values by which they were reared: marriage as an institution, the importance of religion, saving and thrift, patriotism, and work for its own sake. They tend to be better educated and more affluent, and question the idea of sacrificing in order to give their children the best of everything. They are firm believers in equal rights of children and parents. They regard children not as a social obligation but as an option that they have freely chosen. These changes in attributes and attitudes of parents have changed the way child rearing takes place in several important ways.

Parents in America, particularly in the middle and upper classes, are relinquishing authoritarian child-rearing methods and are increasingly emphasizing democratic parent-child relationships. Parents are less rigidly demanding and are guiding children to make their own decisions. Democratic methods used include appealing to the child's reason, explaining rules, and providing a reasonable degree of freedom in which the child can express desires and feelings.

Children today are encouraged to develop a high degree of autonomy and independence from parents. In a sense, separatism from adults, including parents, is emphasized. As a result, peer groups have assumed a very influential role for children, particularly during adolescence (Hammer & Turner, 1990).

In the future more children will be reared at least part of their lives in one-parent families. This change will be largely due to the high number of divorces, single-parent adoptions, and unmarried women who choose to have babies. In recent studies, investigators have shown that there are few differences in school performance, attitudes toward school, peer relationships, self-concept, and mother-child relationships between children in two-parent families and those in single-parent families. In analyzing the effect of the father's presence on the family, one researcher found that the father's level of participation in the family was so low when he was present that his absence was not very significant. Children of more interactive fathers had higher self-esteem and school performance than those with more passive fathers (Feldman, 1979). The long-term effects of being reared in a single-parent family may not be as dramatic in the families of the future as one might believe.

Many social scientists predict that parents will share a larger part of the socialization and education of children with child-development specialists. Children will spend more time in nursery schools and day-care centers; this will be largely the result of the growing number of women employed outside the home. The proportion of parents' lives devoted to childbearing and child rearing will decrease as (a) the life span increases, (b) the number of children in the family decreases, and (c) the number of parents who work outside the home increases.

Biological Changes

Many discoveries of recent years may revolutionize our lifestyles and bring about major changes in marriage and family relationships. Ideas that only a few years ago were topics for science fiction have become real possibilities because of recent advances in research. The following possibilities in the biological revolution are all feasible based on what we now know.

Genetic Designing

Recent breakthroughs in biological knowledge make it increasingly possible to manipulate human genes and thus control human heredity (Cowley, 1990). For example, the ability to control the gender of the unborn child is well within the range of possibility. We can easily determine the gender of

Joel Gordon

the unborn child, and many scientists believe that controlling gender is only a step away. In fact, one fertility expert in California, Ronald J. Erickson, has patented a method of gender selection (”Preselection of Sex,” 1983). One of the advantages of gender control is that it would enable us to eliminate gender-linked disease. A danger in controlling the gender of the child is, of course, that too many parents might prefer one gender over the other. This could result in a large imbalance of men to women or of women to men, thus creating problems for society.

Genetic designing offers the real possibility of controlling IQ and physical characteristics of children. Two decades ago, Alvin Toffler (1970) in *Future Shock* observed that through genetic manipulation we would be able to breed children with superior musical or artistic ability, superior vision, hearing, or muscular abilities. This new knowledge would also enable us to preselect inferior qualities. Various writers and scientists question whether we would eventually produce a ruling class and a slave class similar to that described in Aldous Huxley's (1953) *Brave New World*.

When we have the ability to determine mental, physical, and emotional characteristics, we immediately face ethical questions, such as how many people with extremely high IQs does society need? Already the problem of "underemployment" has surfaced. A study of working conditions for the Department of Labor over a decade ago, revealed that 35% of all workers believed they were overqualified for their jobs ("Underemployment in America," 1976). How many doctors and lawyers, how many laborers and white-collar workers do we need? Who decides what characteristics a person will have and the type of life each will have in the future? The dilemma becomes even greater because the time is near when couples may choose genetic screening to determine whether a child will have any of some 250 genetic defects plus a *tendency* to develop certain conditions. They must then decide if they would abort to avoid having a child with Down's syndrome or cystic fibrosis or obesity or stuttering—all are traceable to genetic markers (Cowley, 1990).

Cloning

Cloning is one of the most fantastic possibilities suggested by the biological revolution. *Cloning* is a process by which offspring are produced without the use of sperm or egg cells. Cloning would involve taking a cell from a particular person, making the genetic data in that cell accessible, and from the nucleus of this cell growing a new organism. The new organism would, in a sense, be a human copy and would have the same genetic characteristics of the person who contributed the cell.

Cloning has been done successfully with frogs, rabbits, and other animals. The success of these experiments is proof that the genetic information necessary to produce an organism is coded in the nucleus of each cell in the organism.

Organ Technology

Organ technology (organ transplants and production of artificial organs) is an area in which tremendous progress has been made in recent years and which promises to have far-reaching implications for life in the future. Successful heart, kidney, liver, pancreas, and ovary transplants have been reported.

The limited availability of organs for transplants has motivated production of artificial ones. Artificial replacements for tissues and organs are likely to become common. Cardiac patients wear "pacemaker" devices that send electrical pulses to activate and regulate the heartbeat. Other persons have artificial joints; some have implanted hearing aids. The length of life may be extended and the quality of life improved significantly as a result of continued discoveries in this area.

Effects of the Biological Changes

The possibilities we have discussed—genetic designing, embryo technology (in Chapter 10), cloning, organ technology—can have profound influences upon human relationships, values, and the family. The following are only a few possible influences:

1. Our concept of parenthood and family may change. As childbearing is separated from its traditional biological base (a life conceived by a man and woman united in a sexual relationship who then become the parents of the child), alternative types of parenthood and families will emerge (Feligmann, 1990).
2. Our values concerning human life may change. As storage banks become common and people are able to buy organ replacements, we are required to make decisions about who will receive an organ transplant and who will not. This forces us to decide who is worthy to live and who is not. The biological revolution can quickly place us in the position of having to make serious philosophical decisions.
3. Future generations may consist of persons with superior intellectual, physical, and personality traits. Far fewer people may be born with birth defects.

4. The life span will be lengthened, and the quality of life may be enhanced. The physical aspects of aging could be slowed.

The Future of Marriage and Families

What will marriage and the family be like in the future? Major predictions concerning family life in the future follow:

1. Families will become stronger in the future despite a high divorce rate (Walters & Walters, 1982). Our tolerance for poor marital relationships will continue to decline.
2. As our society becomes more decentralized and the energy deficits and economic problems remain prominent, family members will become more dependent upon each other to meet physical needs (Walters & Walters, 1982). Indeed, there is growing resistance to too much governmental control.
3. Educators, government officials, and practitioners will become increasingly aware that strengthening family life is essential to the prevention of many of our social problems (Stinnett & Defrain, 1989).
4. The suburban commuter family will become less prevalent as energy costs force more people to live and work in the same area.
5. Legal, monogamous marriage will remain the prevalent form of a man-woman relationship. Most people will continue to have a high level of commitment with one person of the opposite sex (Price & McKenry, 1988).
6. Couples will marry at later ages and marriages will last longer (Ahrons & Rodgers, 1987). There is some basis for making the optimistic prediction that marriage relationships will become closer and more intimate

in the future. The growing desire in our society to improve the quality of human relationships is illustrated by the growth in recent years of marriage and family enrichment groups and in the rapid development of marriage and family therapy. Marriage and family enrichment groups emphasize the development of constructive, intimate relationships. They have been successful in improving marital relationships by encouraging less artificiality; less psychological game playing; less stereotyping; more sensitivity to needs; and greater ability to communicate inner feelings among husbands, wives, and children.

7. Within marriage, fulfillment of both partners will take precedence over traditional family concepts and values. There is growing evidence of the desirability of equity in relationships. Although change has been slow, both men and women are accepting the fact that a superordinate-subordinate partner relationship often leads to dissatisfaction in the marriage.

8. More couples will choose to have one or no children so that they can have greater freedom to pursue individual goals and interests (Melville, 1980; Wiseman, 1981).

9. There will be a redefining of the life cycle, with role responsibilities being less rigidly connected to one's age (Melville, 1980).

10. There will continue to be a trend toward relationships being more person centered rather than gender-role stereotyped.

11. Marriage will be viewed less frequently as a relationship in which the wife is dependent financially on her husband.

12. Although motherhood will continue to be important to women, there will be less emphasis upon motherhood as the only role for women.

13. The roles of husbands and wives will become increasingly similar, particularly concerning homemaking, parenting, careers, and

Joel Gordon

decisions influencing family life (Delora et al., 1980; Footlick, 1990).

14. Men will increasingly gain custody in divorce cases (Price & McKenry, 1988).

15. Androgynous roles that permit women and men to engage in a variety of kinds of work and activities regardless of their gender will be more generally accepted (Balswick & Peak, 1982).

16. Serial marriage will become more common with a projected slight increase in the divorce rate (Brody et al., 1988). Divorce will simply become a more frequently accepted aspect of

Families of the Future

Jacqueline P. Wiseman, a distinguished family researcher and theorist, predicts the following in the years ahead.

1. Alternative lifestyles will be less self-indulgent, based less upon a flouting of sexual, political, and drug-use mores, and more upon an outgrowth of economic necessity and emotional needs. Thus, there will be a rise in the number of affiliative families of single persons of mixed ages living together because of housing shortages and high costs. Childless couples will increase. At the same time, there will be greater awareness of the needs of single-parent families, particularly female-headed households. There will also be greater acceptance of single fathers and gay parents. Communes of the elderly may also emerge.

2. The current housing crunch has already resulted in the beginning of a resurgence of the one-household extended family. From all signs (including the projected aging population), this economically-instigated phenomenon can be expected to expand and eventually result in a large number of "new consanguine families." The result should be new patterns of interaction between generations, a drop in the isolation of the elderly, and a reduction in age-graded neighborhoods.

3. As the energy crunch forces people to live and work in the same area, the suburban commuter family, as a form, will also decline. This movement back to cities and small towns with their own identity and industry will result in family-actuated urban renewal. The number of families interested in their communities will increase. On a more personal level, a decline in the number of commuting fathers (with a concomitant increase in the number of working mothers), will aid androgyny and result in fathers spending more time with their children.

4. The grown-up products of a generation of middle-class parents who have taken the currently popular parenting skills courses will start to be ready for research and evaluation.

5. If history repeats itself cyclically, the children of hippie parents or parents who cohabited without getting married, will be very traditional in their own approach to sex and marriage. Thus, we may have a situation opposite to that of the sixties—embarrassed children trying to decide how to explain their parents' lifestyle to their friends.

6. The continuing economic independence of women will increase the divorce rate, but general economic pressures and emotional needs will counter this trend with a high remarriage rate. Therefore, step parenting will increase to the point where it will get the research attention it deserves.

7. The forecast for sexual activity is mixed. It will continue to occur both in and out of marriage with less guilt and more enjoyment. However, there are already signs that the generation of free and/or open sex adherents are becoming jaded and disappointed with easy-going sex without commitment.

8. Exploratory sex-role research, per se, will be about exhausted. Researchers will start looking at the types of continued value differences between men and women. They will begin "mapping," so to speak, the areas of androgyny and traditional sex-role maintenance, and the situations under which each mode is dominant.

Source: Wiseman, J.P. (1981). The family and its researchers in the eighties: Retrenching, renewing, and revitalizing. *Journal of Marraige and the Family, 43,* 263–266. Copyrighted (1981) by the National Council on Family Relations, 3989 Central Ave. N.E., Suite #550, Minneapolis, MN 55421. Reprinted by permission.

marriage, with the majority of divorced persons remarrying as they do today.

17. Based on statistical trends, many social scientists believe that premarital sexual behavior will follow present trends and remain permissive. This is because of a tendency to dissociate sex and parenthood, improved methods of birth control, and a weakening of the religious and moral sanctions restricting sexual behavior (Walters & Walters, 1982).

18. As the impact of AIDS becomes greater in the early 1990s, greater exclusivity in sexual behavior is likely.

19. It is projected that the number of youth in our population will *not* expand, but a new cycle of expansion of the middle aged and elderly groups will begin (Beck, 1990). This population shift will reverse the trends in rates of marital failure; conservative and traditional attitudes will be evident (Delora et al., 1980).

20. More people will choose to remain single for longer periods of time in the future. The singles lifestyle will become very acceptable but will by no means replace marriage (Simenauer & Carroll, 1982).

21. Greater diversity in lifestyles will be accepted. Many social scientists predict that more persons will choose cohabitation, extramarital relationships, homosexual marriage, and single-parent families (Seligmann, 1990).

22. One-half of those born in 1980 will live part of their lives with a single parent (Simenauer & Carroll, 1982).

23. When a divorced man and a divorced woman enter into a relationship, they are especially likely to live together before entering a second or third marriage; however, marriage will be the preferred lifestyle for the majority (Simenauer & Carroll, 1982).

24. The emphasis on companionship in marriage will be extended to the parent-child relationship as well. Parents will establish more of a person-to-person relationship with their children. Parental authoritarianism will give way to more democratic relationships. Several recent studies show changes in the traditional stereotypical behavior of men and women as parents, and provide support for this prediction. In one study, fathers were as competent as mothers in providing affection, stimulation, and care for newborn infants; most fathers joined in play with their children of both sexes more than mothers did (Smith & Daglish, 1977). In another study, women were willing to press men for changes in roles and the men appeared more amenable to change than they were 10 years ago (Pleck & Land, 1978).

25. There will be an increase in the development of family encounter groups in which parents learn about themselves and their children from their children and children learn about themselves and their parents from their parents. A major goal of family encounter groups is to build authentic person-to-person relationships between parents and children. Another indication of the trend toward improved relationships between parents and children is the emergence of a type of parent education in which respect for the parent as a person with rights and feelings is emphasized as well as respect for the child (Brubaker & Sneden, 1978; Hamner & Turner, 1990).

26. The responsibility of children for home care will be recognized, and more adolescents will become involved in household maintenance. This development will be the result of an increasing number of mothers pursuing careers and jobs outside the home (Brubaker & Sneden, 1978).

Joel Gordon

27. The forms of day care will change as more and more young mothers go to work.

28. Greater flexibility in work schedules may make it easier for families to work out parental care schedules or to share in cooperative arrangements with other families (Hofferth, 1979).

29. Many elderly family members will be considered an essential economic resource and will work for pay well past 65 years of age (Chen, 1987; Quinn, 1990). Thus, for many older persons, a pattern of multiple careers will be the norm. For a significant portion, this will mean retraining to meet work force demands. With a focus on productivity, age discrimina-

tion should give way to productivity discrimination—workers who are unproductive simply will not be tolerated (Mowsesian, 1986).

30. Housing and energy costs will make it desirable for many older people to live with friends who can share household duties and expenses.

31. As the need for services to the old-old, i.e., 75 and over increases, a greater number of the young-old will assume a role in providing for their care (Chen, 1987).

32. If predictions about the home of the future are correct, men and women will be freed from some of our current homemaking chores and will have expanded leisure time. For example,

The Future of Older Persons in the Labor Force

Due to personnel shortages, several industries, e.g., merchandising, banks, financial services, are increasing their efforts to attract older employees. Instead of becoming a period of disengagement from employment, the later years are likely to become a period of reengagement. Projections reflect that over the next several decades the proportion of workers between 20 to 65 will decline in relation to those under 18 and over 65. As a result, many positions will be assumed by older persons. This makes good sense for, as a group, older people today are far better educated and healthier than their parents. Also, their expectations are greater than ever before. They are important consumers who will stimulate the demand for goods that will enable the economy to remain strong. Thus, the traditional view of old age as a period of inactivity and quiet reflection will increasingly be reserved for those persons 75 years and older. Larger numbers of the aged will be involved in new activity that will contribute significantly to American life.

Source: Adapted from Morris, R. M. (1989). Challenges of aging in tomorrow's world: Will gerontology grow, stagnate, or change? *The Gerontologist, 29*, 494–501.

housecleaning will be reduced because sonic cleaning devices and air-filtering systems will eliminate much of the dirt that finds its way indoors, thereby eliminating the need for frequent dusting and vacuuming. Some houses already have such air systems (Horn & East, 1982).

33. The revolution in food preparation will continue. It is suggested that in the future food preparation in the home may be programmed and computerized; we will decide before going to bed at night what we will have for breakfast and dinner the next day. The next day, meals will be cooked and waiting to be placed on the table. The meals will already be planned and balanced nutritionally so that individuals will not have to worry about making choices for good nutrition (Horn & East, 1982).

34. Clothes of the future will need little care inasmuch as they will be easily cleaned, soil resistant, wrinkle resistant, or disposable. As more clothing becomes disposable, clothing fashions will change much faster than they do today (Horn & East, 1982).

35. There will be an increase in factory-made and prefabricated homes. Home buyers will purchase modular units or rooms from a factory, with each room coming completely wired and equipped with all the necessary plumbing and appliances. A couple may start with a modular kitchen, bedroom, bathroom, and living room, and then add other rooms as their housing needs change. The modular units will allow homeowners to rearrange the floor plan of their homes as often as they wish. The home of the future may be purchased equipped as a unit, including the furniture.

36. Increased mobility of the family in the future may make owning and transferring one's own furniture obsolete (Horn & East, 1982).

37. There will be a decrease in single-family dwellings and an increase in multifamily dwellings, particularly in urban areas. It has been predicted that by the year 2000, single-family dwellings will constitute only half of all new housing, whereas the other half will be comprised of multifamily dwellings, such as

Medical Care Trends

According to the U.S. Census Bureau, an aging population should mean an increase in the need for health care, which among other things should translate into an increase in hospital occupancy rates and possibly length of stay. Rising medical costs are causing concern for business, governments, insurers, and consumers and are influencing the way the health care industry is viewed and used.

Hospital occupancy rates are actually declining, as is the length of hospital stays. At the same time the number of beds declined, the average length of stay decreased from 7.2 days in 1979 to 6.6 in 1984.

Since it appears that the demand for services traditionally provided by a hospital is not decreasing, the demand must be shifting elsewhere. One possibility is nursing homes. Another is the new emergency care centers or outpatient treatment centers that are appearing in shopping centers and local communities with increasing frequency. Data are sketchy in this area, but industry experts say that it does not appear that all of the demand is shifting to these establishments.

Some industry analysts think that there is a growing home health care industry. Home health care providers include those who furnish management of medical care in a home setting in accordance with a medical order. In some instances, this means preventative care; in other instances, it is follow-up care that allows patients to go home from the hospital sooner. According to the *1986 Industrial Outlook*, a patient requiring three weeks of antibiotic therapy in the Washington, D.C. metropolitan area could save $5,640 by being treated at home rather than in a hospital.

The traditional doctor's office also is changing. At one time a doctor's office was just that, an office and a waiting room with a receptionist/nurse. Today a doctor's office takes on many different configurations. Some are only slightly more sophisticated than the traditional office; while others have several doctors, computerized patient information, and the latest diagnostic and treatment facilities available in the same office. All of these decrease the need to send patients elsewhere for tests and treatment.

In 1984 there were about two doctors for every 1,000 people. By the year 2000, there will be three doctors for every 1,000 people—some people believe this represents a surplus. This alleged surplus along with the improved productivity should increase the competition for patients, causing more specialization, advertising, and if we are lucky—some doctors may even start to make house calls again. The idea of doctors making house calls would fit with the increasing shift to home health care.

Americans' attitudes toward self-reliance and personal improvement are also contributing to changing the way health care is viewed. To avoid the high cost of health care, more people are trying to take preventative measures, such as monitoring their diets and getting more exercise. This move is not only affecting the health care industry, but it is also creating demand for other industries, such as health clubs and health foods.

Source: Powell-Hill, P., & Buckley, P. (1985). *Service sector in the next 10–15 years: Jobs, lifestyles, and data needs.* Washington, DC: Bureau of the Census.

apartments, townhouses, and duplexes. This trend may accelerate quite rapidly if land becomes extremely expensive. Strict laws limiting single-family housing are already common in Europe.

38. There will be spectacular entertainment innovations in the home. As more and better entertainment and education are brought into the home by electronic devices, there may be less demand for outside activities such as movies and concerts.

39. Labor-saving devices in the home along with the probability of shorter workweeks give us greater opportunity for more family interaction and greater participation in community life, art, and education. The future will challenge us to learn to use leisure time in pleasant, growth-facilitating ways.

Houses of the Future

Representative of the innovations in the housing industry in the future are the Apple House, NEST Housing, the Smart House, and the Xanadu House.

The Apple House

The features of the Apple House can be incorporated into houses that have already been completed. The addition involves a computer, software, and some attachments. According to Blankenship (1984), several of the features include:

Voice request. This module permits you to talk to the computer using a microphone instead of typing in commands.

Phone control. This serves as an intelligent answering machine. You are able to call your home and request information about your house.

Security management. This module permits detection of movement outside the home and notifies a neighbor or the police to alert them.

Event timing. Each entry is an action to be taken and the time for it to occur, e.g., turning on lights at a certain time of day.

Internal movement. This permits you to keep track of where people are in the house, an ideal feature to alert you to a burglar.

NEST Housing

An area of technology that has resulted in a broad range of types of houses is the New Expanded Shelter Technology—NEST houses—a factory-produced type of housing that uses standardized modules. One of its primary features is that of flexibility. Depending on the number of modules that are used, the houses can be small or large. Careful design has made it possible to eliminate much of the wasted space found in conventional homes. For example, rotating closet systems like those found in drycleaning establishments reduce the space normally required for closets. Beds fold into wall storage units to increase floor space during the day. The degree of privacy that is desired can be determined by expanding or contracting accordionlike connector spaces. The connectors include a foyer, vestibule, or solarium library. A guest-study module connects the rest of the house via an outdoor central deck ("Floor Plan," 1989).

The Smart House

The Smart House is actually a wiring system that involves whole-house automation for energy distribution, communication, and control systems. Involving a single cable design, it consolidates the TV, telephone, audio, security, doorbell, thermostat, and power. Its use of especially designed receptacles means that the homeowner can plug stereo

Protecting Your Home in the Future

Most people give little thought to the fact that their home may be burglarized. Moreover, a recent study by the U.S. Justice Department indicated that three-fifths of all rapes and one-third of all assaults that occur are committed during burglaries. Sales of alarm systems are up 150% in the last five years. According to the Federal Bureau of Investigation, one in three homes will be burglarized this year.

Home insurers give a 2% to 15% decrease on home insurance to those families that have alarm systems. A variety of systems exist. Some alert security personnel; others involve the use of a loud bell, a siren, or a strobe light that alerts neighbors, passers-by, and police. Studies have reported that homes without alarms are approximately six times more likely to be broken into as those that have them.

The cost can vary from $250 to $1,500 or more. An excellent source for reputable firms is your police department. By 1992 the number of homes with security systems will increase to 17 million. Window locks, watch dogs, alarm decals, and Neighbor Watch Programs are a few other ways to make a burglary more difficult.

Sources: 1. Burdick, G. S. (1987). Protect your home with an alarm system. *Consumer Research, 70*(8), 22–25. 2. Erlanger, D. W. (1988, January). Home security: Peace of mind starts at $800 or less. *Money,* pp. 145–146. 3. Schaeffer, C. (1989, January). Burglarproofing your home. *Changing Times,* pp. 69–72. 4. Thayer, W. (1988, April). Home alarms like those the pros put in. *Business Week,* p. 112. Reprinted by permission.
Adapted with permission: Blackistone, A. (1989). *Protecting your home in the future.* Unpublished manuscript. The University of Georgia, Department of Housing and Consumer Economics, Athens, Georgia.

speakers into centers located any place in the home and receive music from an entertainment center that is in some other room. Each convenience center will accept a telephone, TV, VCR, video camera, or any other Smart House product ("An Introduction to *Smart House,*" 1988).

It is anticipated that by the year 2000, the Smart House will be appearing throughout the United States. For example, the Smart House will permit the display of a message on the TV screen when the washing machine has completed washing the clothes. The stereo could be set automatically to lower the volume when the phone rings. The heating and air conditioning system will lend itself to energy-efficient zoned control. The system enables electric and gas outlets to be de-energized until a valid request for energy is made, thus reducing gas-related and electrical hazards. A switch next to the bed can control the bedroom light or every light in the house in order to deter an intruder. The system can include sensors that monitor humidity, air quality, smoke, sound, light, energy consumption, and motion. Such a system offers special advantages to senior citizens, the disabled, and those who are ill. It will be easy to protect children from a stove or a potentially dangerous power tool (Smith, 1988).

The Smart House has a unique feature that differentiates it from the Apple House: it has a universal outlet that will make 120V and 240V outlets a thing of the past. The separate electrical and communications systems in the home, including electrical service, telephone, cable TV, security systems, and the wiring for doorbells, thermostats, and audio will be combined into a single system. Gas appliances may also be attached to these outlets (Smith, 1988).

The Xanadu House

This house has several features that differentiate it from other intelligent homes. The most notable is its construction—geodesic domes made out of polyurethane insulation sprayed 5 to 7 inches thick on the inside of a large inflatable balloon. The balloon is peeled away to reveal the rounded structure. The construction of the shell is about 20% less in cost than the construction of most homes (Manson, 1983).

Photoelectric solar sensors on the roof, inside the outside walls, and near the door and window openings convert sunlight directly into electricity. The House Brain takes advantage of the solar cells and a small wind turbine to produce electricity when conditions are favorable, and it stores solar-heated water (Manson, 1983).

An electronic hearth includes a large TV screen, a VCR, a compact disc player, and a video game console. It also gathers and processes information. It does this by use of several media: two-way cable TV, a modem connected by telephone lines to other computers, signals beamed directly from satellite to dish antenna, selectively scanned regular TV broadcasts, and from data personally entered and stored by household members. Entertainment and educational possibilities are excellent, and it will permit more people to have an office in the home (Manson, 1983).

Furniture and Accessories of the Future

With more families moving across the nation and facing high moving costs, families will have to give attention to weight of furniture and ease of transporting it. Although ready-to-assemble furniture began being shipped to the United States over 30 years ago, only in recent years has it attracted a great deal of attention. Much of the furniture tends to be of a proportionally smaller scale and is easy to assemble and disassemble. It is comfortable and comes in a variety of styles and colors. Modular units for kitchens are available as well and can be moved from house to house. Counters can be adjusted up or down, and shelves and doors can be interchanged.

Because it is lightweight, such furniture is inexpensive to ship from distant lands and inexpensive to move from state to state. Families who rent trucks to move their furniture find it packs well because it can be disassembled for moving.

Telephones

One of the innovations that will be helpful to families in the future is the computer telephone, which will permit families to keep track of their telephone calls. Families that have a specific amount of income allocated for the telephone will be better able to monitor their spending. In addition, answering machines will permit a husband to call the home answering machine and leave a message for his wife. The wife who at her place of business finds that she cannot reach her husband will be able to pick up her phone, push in their code, and receive the message. Such a system could be very useful in cases of emergency. Telephones permit the caller to send a signal by phone that automatically notifies medical personnel, the police, and fire department. Such a system helps protect the family from an intruder or fire and helps obtain medical attention quickly—a valuable aid to those who must leave children or elderly persons home alone.

Computers

As home computers become much more common, the home will tend to become a primary communication center for entertainment, education, and work (Horn & East, 1982). Families will be able to select an endless variety of computerized programs.

Today it is already possible for businesses to locate their offices in one town and have their records

Computers: The Future

Prodigy

The impact of computers on families in the future is clearly illustrated in the development of *Prodigy*,® an interactive videotex services software package that was developed by Trintak, a subsidiary of IBM Corporation. It is used to provide entertainment, information, home shopping, and banking services. Costing less than a cable TV service, a 10 million subscriber base has been predicted over the next decade.

After a subscriber signs up for the service, Trintax completes a profile of the subscriber, and then advertisements are tailored to the specific characteristics of the subscriber. When a customer desires more information, he or she will request more detail. To have advertisements run, the advertisers will pay from $25,000 to $85,000. Three of the nation's leading merchants, Sears, K-Mart, and J.C. Penney have already signed up. In addition, through the Prodigy system a trip can be planned, e.g., airline, hotel, and car rental reservations can be made, and other financial transactions can be made, e.g., ordering groceries. Product reviews can be obtained from *Consumer Reports* (Markowitz, 1988a & b).

Because the Prodigy service requires a personal computer with at least 512K bytes of memory and a 1,200 bit-per-second modem for communication over the telephone lines to the computer at Trintex in White Plains, New York, it will not be available for everyone (Barrstow, 1987; "Prodigal Spenders," 1988). But as home computer systems advance—and surely they will—such a system is likely to meet with success.

Prodigy is a registered trademark of Trintak, a subsidiary of International Business Machines.

Sources: 1. Barrstow, J. (1987, November 10). Sears and IBM give Videotex a try. *PC Week*, p. 10. 2. Markowitz, A. (1988a, July 18). Prodigy to give big apple a taste of PC shopping. *Discount Store News*, p. 118. 3. Markowitz, A. (1988b, August 22). K-Mart joins Prodigy service: Looks to gain upscale market. *Discount Store News*, p. 58. 4. Prodigal spenders. (1988, September 26). *PC Week*, p. 145. Reprinted by permission.

and other materials available at a computer center thousands of miles away. Computerized wholesale houses can dispatch goods from a warehouse far removed from the main business offices. And individual salespersons or workers can stay at home and keep in touch with their offices by using a home computer and "hooking into" other computer systems. It will be possible to use a screen and communications computer link-up to receive the newspaper, to order food and other consumer goods, to make reservations for travel, and even to vote. Home computers will be connected to central meal-planning terminals that provide menus, complete with recipes and shopping lists. The home computer will be capable of selecting and ordering supplies and food and delivering electronically prepared meals to the table (Horn & East, 1982).

Financial transactions will increasingly be planned and controlled by computer. It will prove far easier and less expensive for a worker to be given a computer at home than to spend time and energy traveling in and out of a central city area each day. The home will once again become the economic focus of the family's life, a place for both work and play, for entertainment, and for communication with the outside world.

Because of the widespread use of home computers in the future, formal education will be more accessible to both children and adults in the home. More adult education will be accomplished through the home computer; many job skills that adults need to develop will be learned in the home.

We will become much more dependent on computers for education. One contributing factor to this development will be cost. Schools will simply not have the resources to teach (by traditional means) all the subjects that are demanded.

Work and Family

Except for very wealthy families—less than 5% of the population whose work, or marriage, or ancestors have made them wealthy—a great majority of the families in the future who will attain a high level of material success will be dual-career families (The State of Working America, 1988) whose efforts to improve the level of living for their families often result in role strain and dissatisfaction with the demands of work. One of the great challenges of the future will be to find ways to make their lives function more smoothly while meeting the requirements of their employment.

Although most of the future trends that have been reviewed are positive for families, there may be merit in remembering that regardless of how much families may be willing to work to obtain more things, the relationships that exist within families must be nurtured if they are to be successful.

Summary

- Although predictions of family life in the future are difficult to make, we know from past experience that change is inevitable. Our ability to adapt to it is necessary for our future happiness.

- Changes that will affect family life include: more equitable gender roles, more fragmented family life, less contact with extended family, decreased family size, later marriage age, increased divorce rates, and changes in child rearing.

- Advances in genetic design may also change our attitudes toward parenting, our values concerning human life, and our life span potential.

- The trend toward convenience will affect the meals we eat, the homes we live in, the furniture we buy, and the rituals we undertake.

Discussion Questions

1. What are some of the predictions of the future you have read or heard about that are not discussed in this chapter?

2. Fifty years ago few women in the western world were enrolled in colleges of medicine or colleges of law; few men majored in the area

of home economics. Now majors of both genders in these areas are common. What other changes in education do you believe will occur in the future? What impact will these changes have on the families of the future?

3. Greater geographic mobility may be expected as we have more dual-career families. How do you believe families will adjust to an increasing number of husbands and wives working in different cities and different states? In what ways, for example, do you believe this will influence decisions to have children?

4. Age at first marriage has increased for both men and women in the last generation. What do you believe the trend will be in 50 years, just as you are retiring?

5. Do you believe that the impact of divorces in the future will be more adverse for husbands or wives or children? Why?

6. What are some changes you would like to see in family life in the future?

7. In what ways has your life been better than the lives of your parents and grandparents? In what ways do you anticipate that the lives of your children will be better in the future than yours is today?

8. What are some of the disadvantages and the advantages of having the human life span lengthened in the future as the result of scientific research?

9. Are there ways in which you believe that members of your generation are smarter than the members of your parents' and grandparents' generations? In what ways do you believe persons of your children's generation will be smarter than members of your generation?

10. It has been estimated that by 1995 one out of every two automobiles produced will be leased. Do you believe that such a marked change in automobile ownership will occur within such a brief period? What are the reasons to suspect that it will happen?

11. Innovations in housing construction are highly desirable in terms of convenience, safety, and beauty. What features that are described in the chapter have you actually seen? What features would you like to incorporate into your house if you were to build one?

12. Fifty years ago when a couple obtained a set of china or silverware at the time of marriage they anticipated keeping it forever, yet later discovered that over the years their preferences changed and they wanted something different. Given this fact, do you believe in the future that there will be a greater recognition that the choices made today will not last? What influence will this have on the things that you will choose to purchase?

13. What are some of the specific ways that marriage and family life will improve in the future?

14. Do you believe that in the future we will be better able to monitor and modify our perceptions and attitudes in order to control the negative feelings we experience? How successful are you in modifying your behavior to avoid feelings of stress and depression?

15. With increasing emphasis being placed on attaining excellence and prestige in life, is there danger in the future of placing too little emphasis on pleasure and fun? Are families who are able to acquire lots of things happier than families whose lifestyle might best be described as "moderate"?

REFERENCES

Adams, B. N. (1968). *Kinship in an urban setting.* Chicago: Markham.

Adams, J. L. (1976). *Conceptual blockbusting.* San Francisco: San Francisco Book.

Ahrons, C. R., & Rodgers, R. H. (1987). *Divorced families: A multidisciplinary developmental view.* New York: W. W. Norton.

Alberts, J. K. (1988). An analysis of couples' conversational complaints. *Communication Monographs, 55,* 184–197.

Albrecht, S. L. (1979). Correlates of marital happiness among the remarried. *Journal of Marriage and the Family, 41,* 857–867.

Aldous, J. (1978). *Family careers.* New York: John Wiley.

Aldridge, D. P. (1973). The changing nature of interracial marriage in Georgia: A research note. *Journal of Marriage and the Family, 35,* 641–642.

Alexander, L. (1984, November). Employer supported child care programs are good for business. In *Women & work.* Washington, DC: U.S. Department of Labor.

Allen, S. M., & Kalish, R. A. (1984). Professional women and marriage. *Journal of Marriage and the Family, 47,* 375–382.

Allgeier, A. R., & Allgeier, E. R. (1988). *Sexual interactions* (2nd ed.). Lexington, MA: D. C. Heath.

Allgeier, E. R., Przybyla, D. P., & Thompson, M. E. (1977). Planned sin: Sin, guilt and contraception. *Bulletin of the Psychometric Society, 10,* 253.

Alvirez, D., Bean, F. D., & Williams, D. (1981). The Mexican American family. In C. H. Mindel & R. W. Habenstein (Eds.), *Ethnic families in America* (3rd ed.), (pp. 269–292.) New York: Elsevir.

Americans and their money. (1987). New York: Money.

Ambert, A. (1988). Relationships with former in-laws after divorce: A research note. *Journal of Marriage and the Family, 50,* 679–686.

American Cancer Society. (1982). *Why start life under a cloud?* New York: Author.

Ammons, P., & Stinnett, N. (1980). The vital marriage: A closer look. *Family Relations, 29,* 37–42.

Anastasi, A. (1974). Individual differences in aging. In W. C. Bier (Ed.), *Aging* (pp. 84–95). New York: Fordham University Press.

Anderson, J. F., Anderson, P. A., & Lustig, M. W. (1987). Opposite sex touch avoidance: A national replication and extension. *Journal of Nonverbal Behavior, 11,* 89–109.

Anderson, P. A. (1985). Nonverbal immediacy in interpersonal communication. In A. W. Siegman & S. Feldman (Eds.), *Multichannel integrations of nonverbal behavior* (pp. 1–36). Hillsdale, NJ: Lawrence Erlbaum.

Anderson, S. A. (1986). Cohesion, adaptability and communication: A test of an Olson circumplex model hypothesis. *Family Relations, 35,* 289–293.

Anderson, S. A., Bagarozzi, D. A., & Giddings, C. W. (1986). Images: Preliminary scale construction. *The American Journal of Family Therapy, 14,* 357–363.

Aschenbrenner, J., & Carr, C. H. (1980). Conjugal relationships in the context of the black extended family. *Alternative Lifestyles, 3*(4), 463–484.

Atkinson, J., & Huston, T. L. (1984). Sex role orientation and division of labor early in marriage. *Journal of Personality and Social Psychology, 46,* 330–345.

Austrom, D. (1984). *The consequences of being single.* New York: Long.

Bach, G. R., & Deutsch, R. M. (1971). *Pairing.* New York: Avon Books.

Bader, E., & Sinclair, C. (1983). The critical first year of marriage. In D. Mace (Ed.), *Prevention in family services* (pp. 77–86). Beverly Hills, CA: Sage.

Bagarozzi, D. A., & Giddings, C. W. (1983). Conjugal violence: A critical review of current research and clinical practices. *American Journal of Family Therapy, 11,* 3–14.

Bahr, R. (1976). *The virility factor*. New York: G. P. Putnam.

Bahr, S. J., & Bahr, H. M. (1981). Work, friends and marital satisfaction. *Family Perspective, 15,* 55–62.

Bair, E. S. (1979). How much temporary support is enough? Guidelines for judges and lawyers. *Family Advocate, 1,* 36–41, 48.

Baird, D., & Wilcox, A. (1985). Cigarette smoking associated with delayed conception. *Journal of the American Medical Association, 253,* 2979–2983.

Baker v. Owen, 395 F. Supp. 294 (M.D.N.C.), *affirmed without opinion,* 423 U.S. 907, 96 S.Ct. 2.210, 46 L. Ed. 2d 137 (1975).

Ball, R. E., & Robbins, L. (1986a). Black husbands' satisfaction with their family life. *Journal of Marriage and the Family, 48,* 849–855.

Ball, R. E., & Robbins, L. (1986b). Marital status and life satisfaction among black Americans. *Journal of Marriage and the Family, 48,* 389–394.

Balswick, J. O., & Peak, C. W. (1982). The inexpressive male: A tragedy of American society. In R. H. Walsh & O. Pocs (Eds.), *Marriage and family 81/82: Annual edition.* Guilford, CT: Dushkin.

Barbeau, C. (1985). The man-woman crisis. In J. M. Henslin (Ed.), *Marriage and family in a changing society* (pp. 164–170). New York: Free Press.

Barrett, D. E., Radke-Yarrow, M., & Klein, R. E. (1982). Chronic malnutrition and child behavior: Effects of early caloric supplementation on social and emotional functioning at school age. *Developmental Psychology, 18,* 542–556.

Barrstow, J. (1987, November 10). Sears and IBM give videotek a try. *PC Week,* p. 10.

Barton, K., Dielman, T. E., & Cottell, R. B. (1974). Child rearing practices and achievement in school. *Journal of Genetic Psychology, 124,* 155–165.

Bassett, W. T. (1963). *Counseling the childless couple.* Englewood Cliffs, NJ: Prentice-Hall.

Baumrind, D. (1967). Childcare practices anteceding three patterns of preschool behavior. *Genetic Psychology Monographs, 75,* 345–388.

Beck, M. (1990, Winter/Spring). The geezer boom. *Newsweek,* Special edition, pp. 63–68.

Bell, A. P., Weinberg, M. S., & Hammersmith, S. K. (1981). *Sexual preference: Its development in men and women.* Bloomington, IN: University of Indiana Press.

Bell, R. A., Daly, J. A., & Gonzalez, M. C. (1987). Affinity-maintenance in marriage and its relationship to women's marital satisfaction. *Journal of Marriage and the Family, 49,* 445–454.

Bell, R. A., & Gonzalez, M. C. (1988). Loneliness, negative life events and the provisions of social relationships. *Communication Quarterly, 36,* 1–15.

Belsky, J. (1980). Child maltreatment: An ecological integration. *American Psychologist, 35,* 320–335.

Belsky, J. (1984). Two waves of day care research: Developmental effects and conditions of quality. In R. Ainslie (Ed.), *The child and the day care setting: Qualitative variations and development.* New York: Praeger Scientific.

Belsky, J., & Crouter, A. (1985). The work-family interface and marital change across the transition to parenthood. *Journal of Family Issues, 6,* 205–220.

Belsky, J., Lerner, R. M., & Spanier, G. B. (1984). *The child in the family.* Reading, MA: Addison-Wesley.

Bem, D. J. (1987, Fall). A consumer's guide to dual-career marriages. *ILR Report, 25* (1). Ithaca, NY: State School of Industrial and Labor Relations, Cornell University.

Benchmarks of poverty. (1985, December). *The Washington COFO memo.* Malvern, PA: Coalition of Family Organizations.

Berardo, D. H., Shehan, C. L., & Leslie, G. H. (1987). A residue of tradition: Jobs, careers, and spouses' time in housework. *Journal of Marriage and the Family, 49,* 381–390.

Berg, B. (1984, May). Early signs of infertility. *Ms,* p. 68.

Berg, B. (1986). *The crisis of the working mother.* New York: Summit Books.

Berger, B., & Berger, P. L. (1983). *The war over the family: Capturing the middle ground.* Garden City, NY: Anchor Press/Doubleday.

Berkove, G. F. (1979). Perceptions of husband support by returning women students. *The Family Coordinator, 28,* 451–457.

Bernard, J. (1972). *The future of marriage.* New York: World.

Bernard, J. L., Bernard, S. L., & Bernard, M. L. (1988). Courtship violence and sex-typing. *Family Relations, 34,* 573–576.

Berne, E. (1964). *Games people play.* New York: Grove.

Berne, E. (1972). *What do you say after you say hello?* New York: Grove.

Bettelheim, B. (1950). *Love is not enough.* New York: Free Press.

Bettelheim, B. (1982). Difficulties between parents and children: Their causes and how to prevent them. In N. Stinnett, J. Defrain, K. King, H. Lingren, G. Rowe, S. Van Zandt, & R. Williams (Eds.), *Family strengths 4: Positive support systems* (pp. 5–14). Lincoln, NE: University of Nebraska Press.

Bierer, L. (1980, December). How pregnancy changes your body. *Parents.*

Birch, W. G. (1981). *A doctor discusses pregnancy.* Chicago: Budlong Press.

Bird, G. W., Bird, G. A., & Scruggs, M. (1984). Determinants of family task sharing: A study of husbands and wives. *Journal of Marriage and the Family, 46,* 345–355.

Birth defects: The tragedy and the hope. (1975). White Plains, NY: The National Foundation/March of Dimes.

Blackistone, A. (1989). *Protecting your home in the future.* Unpublished manuscript, The University of Georgia, Department of Housing and Consumer Economics, Athens.

Blakar, R. M. (1981). Schizophrenia and familial communication: A brief note on follow-up studies and replication. *Family Process, 20,* 109–112.

Blankenship, J. (1984). *The Apple house.* Englewood Cliffs, NJ: Prentice-Hall.

Blinder, M. (1985). The domestic homicide. *Family Therapy, 12,* 1–24.

Block, J. (1981, April). *Parents,* p. 68.

Blood, R. O. (1969). *Marriage.* New York: Free Press.

Blotcky, A., & Tittler, B. (1982). Psychological predictors of physical health: Toward a wholistic model of health. *Preventive Medicine, 11,* 602–611.

Blumstein, P., & Schwartz, P. W. (1983). *American couples: Money, work, sex.* New York: Morrow.

Bohannan, P. (1970). *Divorce and after.* New York: Doubleday.

Bokemeier, J., & Maurer, R. (1987). Marital quality and conjugal labor involvement of rural couples. *Family Relations, 36,* 417–424.

Boland, J. P., & Follingstad, D. R. (1987). Relationship between communication and marital satisfaction: A review. *Journal of Sex and Marital Therapy, 13,* 286–313.

Bonaguro, J. A. (1981). PRECEDE for wellness. *Journal of School Health, 51,* 501–506.

Booth, A., & Johnson, D. (1988). Premarital cohabitation and marital success. *Journal of Family Issues, 9,* 255–272.

Borland, D. M. (1975). An alternative model of the wheel theory. *The Family Coordinator, 24,* 289–292.

Bossard, J. H. S. (1932). Residential propinquity as a factor in marriage selection. *American Journal of Sociology, 38,* 219–224.

Bostrom, R. N., & Waldhort, E. S. (1988). Memory, models, and the measurement of listening. *Communication Education, 37,* 1–13.

Bowen, G. B., & Orthner, D. K. (1983). Sex-role congruency and marital quality. *Journal of Marriage and the Family, 45,* 223–230.

Bowman, H. A., & Spanier, G. B. (1978). *Modern marriage.* New York: McGraw-Hill.

Bradbard, M., & Endsley, R. (1986). Sources of variance in young working mothers' satisfaction with child care: A transitional model and new research directions. *Advances in Early Education and Day Care, 4,* 181–207.

Brammer, L. M., & Shostrom, E. L. (1982). *Therapeutic psychology: Fundamentals of counseling and psychotherapy.* (4th ed.). Englewood Cliffs, NJ: Prentice-Hall.

Bramson, R. M. (1981). *Coping with difficult people.* New York: Ballantine.

Brazelton, T. B. (1989, March 14). Interview on Bill Moyer's "World of Ideas."

Brecher, E. M. (1984). *Love, sex and aging.* Boston: Little, Brown.

Brightest and best: What do they want? (1983, February 6). *Parade Magazine.*

Brigman, K., Schons, J., & Stinnett, N. (1986). Strengths of families in a society under stress: A study of strong families in Iraq. *Family Perspective, 20*, 61–73.

Brodbar-Nemzer, J. Y. (1986). Divorce and group commitment: The case of the Jews. *Journal of Marriage and the Family, 48*, 329–340.

Broderick, C. (1979). *Couples*. New York: Simon & Schuster.

Brody, G. H., Neubaum, E., & Forehand, R. (1988). Serial marriage: A heuristic analysis of an emerging family form. *Psychological Bulletin, 103*, 211–222.

Brody, J. (1985, March 20). Infertility: Not uncommon male problem but often treatable. *The New York Times*, p. 21.

Brody, J. (1986, February 23). Any drink during pregnancy may be one too many: Latest research on FAS. *Minneapolis Star and Tribune*, p. 13F.

Broman, C. (1988). Satisfaction among blacks: The significance of marriage and parenthood. *Journal of Marriage and the Family, 50*, 45–51.

Bronfenbrenner, U. (1977). Toward an experimental ecology of human development. *American Psychologist, 32*, 513–531.

Bronfenbrenner, U. (1979). *The ecology of human development*. Cambridge, MA: Harvard University Press.

Brubaker, T. H., & Sneden, L. E. (1978). Aging in a changing family context: Special issue. *The Family Coordinator, 27*, 297–504.

Bulcroft, K., & O'Connor, M. (1986). The importance of dating relationships in quality of life for older persons. *Family Relations, 35*, 397–401.

Buller, M. K., & Buller, D. B. (1987). Physicians' communication style and patient satisfaction. *Journal of Health and Social Behaviors, 28*, 375–388.

Bumiller, E. (1985, December 25). Love, marriage, and sex India-style. *Los Angeles Times*, p. 31.

Burdick, G. S. (1987). Protect your home with an alarm system. *Consumer Research, 70*(8), 22–25.

Burgess, E., & Cottrell, L. (1939). *Predicting success and failure in marriage*. Englewood Cliffs, NJ: Prentice-Hall.

Burgess, R. L., & Conger, R. D. (1978). Family interaction in abusive, neglectful, and normal families. *Child Development, 49*, 1163–1173.

Buscaglia, L. (1982). *Living, loving, and learning*. New York: Holt.

Buss, D. M., & Barnes, M. (1986). Preferences in human mate selection. *Journal of Personality and Social Psychology, 50*, 559–570.

Cargan, J. F., & Melko, M. (1981). Is marriage good for your health? *Family Perspective, 15*, 107–114.

Carlson, E. A. (1984). *Human genetics*. Lexington, MA: D. C. Heath.

Carnes, P. (1983). *The sexual addiction*. Minneapolis, MN: CompCare.

Carroll, L. (1988). Concern with AIDS and the sexual behavior of college students. *Journal of Marriage and the Family, 50*, 405–411.

Casas, C., Stinnett, N., DeFrain, J., Williams, R., & Lee, P. (1984). Latin American family strengths. *Family Perspective, 18*, 11–17.

Chandler, S. (1985, June). Toward a perfect partnership. *50 Plus, 25*, 30.

Chapman, A. H. (1968). *Put-offs and come-ons*. New York: Bantam.

Chapman, S. F. (1990). *Sexual addiction*. Unpublished manuscript. The University of Georgia, Department of Child and Family Development, Athens.

Chen, L. (1988). *Time allocation between husbands and wives among dual-career and dual-earner households*. Unpublished master's thesis, The University of Georgia, Athens.

Chen, Y. P. (1987). Making assets out of tomorrow's elderly. *The Gerontologist, 27*, 410–416.

Cherlin, A. J. (1981). *Marriage, divorce, remarriage*. Cambridge, MA: Harvard University Press.

Cherlin, A., & Furstenberg, F. (1983). The American family in the year 2000. *The Futurist, 17*, 7–14.

Cherukuri, R., Minkoff, H., Feldman, J., Parekh, A., & Glass, L. (1988). A cohort study of alkaloidal cocaine ("crack") in pregnancy. *Obstetrics and Gynecology, 72*, 147–151.

Chesser, B. R. (1990). *21 myths that can wreck your marriage*. Waco, TX: Word.

Chickering, A. W., & Havighurst, R. J. (1981). The life cycle. In A. W. Chickering and associates (Eds.), *The modern American college* (pp. 16–50). San Francisco: Josey-Bass.

Chouteau, M., Namerow, P. B., & Leppert, P. (1988). The effect of cocaine abuse on birth weight and gestational age. *Obstetrics and Gynecology, 72,* 351–354.

Churchill, J. (1968, July 28). It really may be food for thought. *The New York Times,* p. 10E.

Clayton, P. J. (1979). The sequalae and nonsequalae of conjugal bereavement. *American Journal of Psychiatry, 136,* 1530–1534.

Cleaver, G. (1987). Marriage enrichment by means of a structured communication programme. *Family Relations, 36,* 49–54.

Clinton, J. F. (1987). Physical and emotional responses of expectant fathers throughout pregnancy and the early postpartum period. *International Journal of Nursing Studies, 24,* 59–68.

Cohabiting couples have lower premarital satisfaction. (1988, Fall). *PREPARE/ENRICH Newsletter,* Minneapolis, MN, p. 1.

Cole, C. L. (1984). Marital quality in later life. In W. H. Quinn & G. H. Hughston (Eds.), *Independent aging* (pp. 72–90). Rockville, MD: Aspen Systems.

Cole, C., & Rodman, H. (1987). When school-age children care for themselves: Issues for family life educators and parents. *Family Relations, 36,* 92–96.

Coleman, J., Butcher, J., & Carson, R. (1980). Psychological therapies: Transactional analysis. In J. Coleman, J. Butcher, & R. Carson (Eds.), *Abnormal psychology and modern life* (6th ed.). Glenview, IL: Scott, Foresman.

Coleman, T. M., Robinson, B. E., & Rowland, B. H. (1984). Latchkey children and their families. *Dimensions, 13*(1), 23–24.

Collier, M. J. (1988). A comparison of conversations among and between domestic culture groups: How intra- and intercultural competencies vary. *Communication Quarterly, 36,* 122–144.

Comfort, A. (1967). *The anxiety makers.* Nashville, TN: Thomas Nelson.

Constantine, L. L., & Constantine, J. M. (1973). *Group marriage.* New York: Macmillan.

Consumer protection: It's the law. (1987). *Citicorp Consumer Views, 18*(3).

Corey, G. (1985). Transactional analysis. In G. Corey (Ed.), *Theory and practice of group counseling* (2nd ed.) (pp. 311–336). Monterey, CA: Brooks/Cole.

Costa, P. T., Jr., Zonderman, A. B., McCrae, R. R., Cornoni-Huntley, J., Locke, B. Z., & Barbano, H. E. (1987). Longitudinal analyses of psychological well-being in a national sample: Stability of mean levels. *Journal of Gerontology, 42,* 50–55.

Cowan, C. P., Cowan, P. A., Heming, G., Garrett, E., Coysh, W. S., Curtis-Boles, H., & Boles, A. J. (1985). Transitions to parenthood: His, hers, and theirs. *Journal of Family Issues, 6,* 451–482.

Cowley, G. (1990, Winter/Spring). Made to order babies. *Newsweek,* Special edition, pp. 94–100.

Cox, F. D. (1981). *Human intimacy: Marriage, the family and its meaning* (2nd ed.). St. Paul, MN: West.

Cuber, J. F., & Harroff, P. B. (1965). *The significant Americans.* New York: Appleton.

Culverwell, M. (1984, January/February). New hope for infertile couples. *Mother Earth News, 85,* pp. 142–143.

Curran, D. (1983). *Traits of a healthy family.* Minneapolis, MN: Winston.

Cutright, P. (1971). Income and family events: Marital stability. *Journal of Marriage and the Family, 33,* 291–306.

Dail, P. W. (1986). Stronger intergenerational family relationships. In S. Van Zandt, H. Lingren, G. Rowe, P. Zeece, L. Kimmons, P. Lee, D. Shell, & N. Stinnett (Eds.), *Family strengths 7: Vital connections* (pp. 127–139). Lincoln, NE: Center for Family Strengths, Department of Human Development and the Family, University of Nebraska.

Daniels-Mohring, D., & Berger, M. (1984). Social network changes and the adjustment to divorce. *Journal of Divorce, 8,* 17–32.

Davies, J. C. (1988). The effects of kinship ties on parental attitudes toward early childhood dependency. *Family Perspective, 22,* 61–72.

Deaux, K. (1976). *The behavior of women and men.* Belmont, CA: Brooks/Cole.

DeFrain, J., Fricke, J., & Elmen, J. (1987). *On our own: A single parent's survival guide.* Lexington, MA: Lexington Books.

DeFrain, J., Taylor, J., & Ernst, L. (1982). *Coping with sudden infant death syndrome*. Lexington, MA: Lexington Books.

DeLamater, J. D., & MacCorquodale, P. (1979). *Premarital sexuality: Attitudes, relationships, behavior*. Madison, WI: University of Wisconsin Press.

Delora, J. S., Warren, C. A., & Ellison, C. R. (1980). *Understanding sexual interaction*. Boston: Houghton.

DeMaris, A. (1987). The efficacy of a spouse abuse model in accounting for courtship violence. *Journal of Family Issues, 8*, 291–305.

DeMaris, A., & Leslie, G. (1984). Cohabitation with the future spouse: Its influence upon marital satisfaction and communication. *Journal of Marriage and the Family, 46*, 77–84.

Demos, J. (1977). The American family in past time. In A. S. Skolnick & J. H. Skolnick (Eds.), *Family in transition* (2nd ed.) (pp. 59–77). Boston: Little, Brown.

deSlosser, H. (n.d.). *Renter's guide*. Ithaca, NY: Cooperative Extension Service, New York State College of Human Ecology.

Deutsch, C. (1979, November). Do your parents haunt your marriage? *Parents*, p. 24.

Dhir, K. S., & Markman, H. J. (1984). Application of social judgment theory to understanding and treating marital conflict. *Journal of Marriage and the Family, 46*, 597–610.

Dick-Read, G. (1955). *The natural childbirth primer*. New York: Harper & Row.

Doherty, W. J. (1982). Attributional style and negative problem solving in marriage. *Family Relations, 31*, 201–205.

Donahue, W. (1971). Psychological aspects in the management of the geriatric patient. In E. V. Cowdry & F. U. Steinberg (Eds.), *The care of the geriatric patient*. St Louis: C.V. Mosby.

Dovidio, J. F., Ellyson, S. L., Keating, C. F., Heltman, K., & Brown, C. E. (1988). The relationship of social power to visual displays of dominance between men and women. *Journal of Personality and Social Psychology, 54*, 233–242.

Doyle, J. A. (1983). *The male experience*. Dubuque, IA: William C. Brown.

Dressler, W. W. (1988). Social consistency and psychological distress. *Journal of Health and Social Behavior, 29*, 79–91.

Dreyfuss, J. (1986, March 5). Lend an ear to this advocate of more attentive listening. *Los Angeles Times*, Part V, p. 1.

Dunn, J. R. (1988a). Getting even: The dynamics of passive aggressive behavior, part one. *The Christian Journal of Psychology and Counseling, 3*(2), 13–15.

Dunn, J. R. (1988b). Getting even: The dynamics of passive aggressive behavior, part two. *The Christian Journal of Psychology and Counseling, 3*(3), 7–9.

Dunn, P. C., Ryan, I. J., & O'Brien, K. (1988). College students' level of acceptability of the new medical science of conception and problems of infertility. *Journal of Sex Research, 24*, 282–287.

Duvall, E. (1954). *In-laws: Pro and con*. New York: Association Press.

Dwyer, J. (1984, August). Impact of maternal nutrition on infant health. *Resident and Staff Physician, 30*, 19–28.

Dyer, P. M., & Dyer, G. H. (1982). Intimate networks of families: A serendipitous result of marriage enrichment. In N. Stinnett, J. DeFrain, K. King, H. Lingren, G. Rowe, S. Van Zandt, & R. Williams (Eds.), *Family strengths 4: Positive support systems* (pp. 153–170). Lincoln, NE: University of Nebraska Press.

Eaton, W. J. (1986, January 13). Health effect of abortions alarms Soviet authorities. *Los Angeles Times*, Part I, pp. 1,8.

Edelson, J. L., Eisikovits, Z., & Guttmann, E. (1985). Men who batter women. *Journal of Family Issues, 6*, 229–247.

Eichorn, D. H., Clausen, J. A., Haan, N., Honzik, M. P., & Mussen. P. H. (Eds.). (1981). *Present and past in middle life*. New York: Academic Press.

Ekerdt, D. J. (1987). Why the notion persists that retirement harms health. *The Gerontologist, 27*, 454–457.

Ekerdt, D. J., Bosse, R., & Levkoff, S. (1985). An empirical test for phases of retirement: Findings from the normative aging study. *Journal of Gerontology, 40*, 95–101.

Elias, M. (1988, November 14). Oil lubricants can damage condoms. *USA Today*, p. 1.

Ellis, A. (1983). Rational emotive therapy. In C. L. Thompson & L. B. Rudolph (Eds.), *Counseling children* (pp. 82–97). Monterey, CA: Brooks/Cole.

Endsley, R. C., & Bradbard, M. R. (1978). Helping parents select quality day care through the use of a guide. *The Family Coordinator, 27,* 167–172.

Endsley, R. C., Bradbard, M. R., & Readdick, C. (1984). High-quality proprietary day care: Predictors of parents' choices. *Journal of Family Issues, 5,* 131–152.

Erikson, E. H. (1963). *Childhood and society* (2nd ed.). New York: Norton.

Erlanger, D. W. (1988, January). Home security: Peace of mind starts at $800 or less, *Money,* pp. 145–146.

Eshleman, J. R. (1985). *The family: An introduction.* Boston: Allyn & Bacon.

Evans, A. R. (1988). Surrogate mothers: The new bondswomen. In G. P. Regier (Ed.), *Values and policy* (pp. 25–44). Washington, DC: Family Research Council of America.

Ewy, D. (1985). *Preparation for parenthood.* New York: New American Library.

Eysenck, H. J. (1988). Health's character. *Psychology Today, 27*(12), 28–32, 34–35.

Falbo, T., & Peplau, L. A. (1980). Power strategies in intimate relationships. *Journal of Personality and Social Psychology, 37,* 879–896.

Family health and medical guide. (1980). New York: Hearst Books.

Fasteau, M. F. (1974). *The male machine.* New York: McGraw-Hill.

Feldman, H. (1979). Family life by the year 2000. *Journal of Marriage and the Family, 41,* 453–455.

Feldman, L. B. (1982). Dysfunctional marital conflict: An integrative interpersonal-intrapsychic model. *Journal of Marital and Family Therapy, 8,* 417–428.

Fendrich, M. (1984). Wives' employment and husbands' distress: A meta-analysis and a replication. *Journal of Marriage and the Family, 46,* 871–880.

Fincham, F. D., & Bradbury, T. N. (1987). The impact of attributions in marriage: A longitudinal analysis. *Journal of Personality and Social Psychology, 53,* 510–517.

Finkelhor, D. (1980). Sex among siblings: A survey on prevalence, variety and effects. *Archives of Sexual Behavior, 9,* 171–194.

Finkelhor, D. (1982). Sexual abuse: A sociological perspective. *Child Abuse and Neglect, 6,* 95–102.

Fish, R. C., & Fish, L. S. (1986). Quid pro quo revisited: The basis of marital therapy. *American Journal of Orthopsychiatry, 56,* 371–384.

Fisher, B. L., Giblin, P. R., & Hoopes, M. H. (1982). Healthy family functioning: What therapists say and what families want. *Journal of Marital and Family Therapy, 8,* 273–284.

Fishman, P. N. (1978). Interaction: The work women do. *Social Problems, 25,* 397–406.

Fitzpatrick, M. A., Fallis, S., & Vance, L. (1982). Multifunctional coding of conflict resolution strategies in marital dyads. *Family Relations, 31,* 61–70.

Floor plan combines private spaces with family gathering areas, (1989, February). *Professional Builder.* Footlick, J. K. (1990, Winter/Spring). What happened to the family? *Newsweek,* Special edition, pp. 15–20.

Footlick, J. K. (1990, Winter/Spring). What happened to the family? *Newsweek,* Special Edition, pp. 15–20.

Foster, B. G. (1982). Self-disclosure and intimacy in long-term marriages: Case studies. In N. Stinnett, J. DeFrain, K. King, H. Lingren, G. Rowe, S. Van Zandt, & R. Williams (Eds.), *Family strengths 4: Positive support systems* (pp. 351–366). Lincoln, NE: University of Nebraska Press.

Foster, J. W. (1986). Possible auto-immune component in the etiology of the fetal alcohol syndrome. *Development Medicine and Child Neurology, 28,* 654–656.

Fowers, B. J., & Olson, D. H. (1986). Predicting marital success with PREPARE: A predictive validity study. *Journal of Marital and Family Therapy, 12,* 403–413.

Fox, G. L., & Inazu, J. K. (1980). Patterns and outcomes of mother-daughter communication about sexuality. *Journal of Social Issues, 36,* 7–29.

Fox, J. D., & Nickols, S. Y. (1983). The time crunch. *Journal of Family Issues, 4*(1), 61–82.

Frank, E., Anderson, C., & Rubinstein, D. (1978). Frequency of sexual dysfunction in "normal" couples. *New England Journal of Medicine, 299,* 111–115.

Franke, L. B. (1982). *The ambivalence of abortion.* New York: Random.

Fried, E. G., & Stern, K. (1948). The situation of the aged within the family. *American Journal of Orthopsychiatry, 18*, 31–54.

Friedan, B. (1963). *The feminine mystique.* New York: Norton.

Friede, A., Baldwin, W., Rhodes, P. H., Bueler, J., & Strauss, W. (1988). Older maternal age and infant mortality in the United States. *Obstetrics and Gynecology, 72*, 152–162.

Frieze, I. H. (1980). *Causes and consequences of marital rape.* Paper presented at the annual meeting of the American Psychological Association, Montreal, Canada.

Fritz, G., Stoll, K., & Wagner, N. (1981). A comparison of males and females who were sexually molested as children. *Journal of Sex and Marital Therapy, 1*, 54–59.

Fromm, E. (1956). *The art of loving.* New York: Harper.

Fuchs, V. R. (1983). *How we live.* Cambridge, MA: Harvard University Press.

Furstenberg, F. F., & Spanier, G. B. (1984). *Recycling the family: Remarriage after divorce.* Beverly Hills, CA: Sage.

Galvin, K. M., & Brommel, B. J. (1982). *Family communication: Cohesion and change.* Glenview, IL: Scott, Foresman.

Gamble, T., & Zigler, E. (1986). Effects of infant day care: Another look at the evidence. *American Journal of Orthopsychiatry, 56*(1), 26–42.

Garman, E. T., & Forgue, R. E. (1988). *Personal finance* (2nd ed.). Boston: Houghton Mifflin.

Garrett, W. R. (1982). *Seasons of marriage and family life.* New York: Holt.

Gary, L. E., Beatty, L. A., & Berry, G. L. (1986). Strong black families: Models of program development for black families. In S. Van Zandt, H. Lingren, G. Rowe, P. Zeece, L. Kimmons, P. Lee, D. Shell, & N. Stinnett (Eds.), *Family strengths 7: Vital connections* (pp. 453–468). Lincoln, NE: Center for Family Strengths, Department of Human Development and the Family, University of Nebraska.

Gary, L. E., Beatty, L. A., Berry, G. L., & Price, M. (1983). *Stable black families: Final report.* Institute for Urban Affairs and Research. Washington, DC: Howard University.

Gass, G. Z., & Nichols, W. C. (1988). Gaslighting: A marital syndrome. *Contemporary Family Therapy, 10*, 3–16.

The General Mills American family report 1976–77: Raising children in changing society. (1978). Minneapolis, MN: General Mills.

The General Mills American family report 1980–81: Strengths and strains—families at work. (1982). Minneapolis, MN: General Mills.

George, C., & Main, M. (1979). Social interactions of young abused children: Approach, avoidance, and aggression. *Child Development, 50*, 306–318.

Gershenfeld, M. (1984). Changing family concerns for the 1980s. In G. Rowe, J. DeFrain, H. Lingren, R. MacDonald, N. Stinnett, S. Van Zandt, & R. Williams (Eds.), *Family strengths 5: Continuity and diversity.* Newton, MA: Educational Development Center.

Gerson, K. (1988). Women's work and family decisions. In N. D. Glenn & M. T. Coleman (Eds.), *Family relations: A reader* (pp. 210–229). Chicago: Dorsey.

Gerstel, N., & Gross, H. (1988). The commuter as a social isolate: Friends, kin, and lovers. In N. D. Glenn & M. T. Coleman (Eds.), *Family relations: A reader* (pp. 257–275). Chicago: Dorsey.

Gerzon, M. (1982). *A choice of heroes: The changing faces of American manhood.* Boston: Houghton Mifflin.

Gil, D. G. (1971). Violence against children: Physical child abuse in the United States. Cambridge, MA: Harvard University Press.

Gilbert, S. (1976). Self disclosure, intimacy, and communication in families. *The Family Coordinator, 25*, 221–229.

Gilford, R. (1984). Contrasts in marital satisfaction throughout old age: An exchange theory analysis. *Journal of Gerontology, 39*, 325–333.

Gillis, J. R. (1985). For better, for worse: British marriages 1600 to present. New York: Oxford University Press.

Gilot, F., & Lake, C. (1964). *Life with Picasso.* New York: McGraw-Hill.

Gitman, L. J., & Joehnk, M. D. (1987). *Personal financial planning* (4th ed.). Chicago: Dryden.

Glenn, N. D. (1975). The contribution of marriage to the psychological well-being of males and females. *Journal of Marriage and the Family, 37*, 594–600.

Glenn, N. D. (1982). Interreligious marriage in the United States: Patterns and recent trends. *Journal of Marriage and the Family, 44*, 555–566.

Glenn, N. D., & Kramer, K. B. (1987). The marriages and divorces of the children of divorce. *Journal of Marriage and the Family, 49*, 811–825.

Glenn, N. D., & McLanahan, S. (1981). The effects of offspring on the psychological well-being of older adults. *Journal of Marriage and the Family, 43*, 402–421.

Glenn, N. D., & McLanahan, S. (1982). Children and marital happiness: A further specification of the relationship. *Journal of Marriage and the Family, 44*, 63–72.

Glenn, N. D., & Weaver, C. N. (1977). The marital happiness of remarried divorced persons. *Journal of Marriage and the Family, 39*, 331–337.

Glenn, N. D., & Weaver, C. N. (1981). The contribution of marital happiness to global happiness. *Journal of Marriage and the Family, 43*, 161–168.

Glenn, N. D., & Weaver, C. N. (1988). The changing relationship of marital status to reported happiness. *Journal of Marriage and the Family, 50*, 317–324.

Glick, P. C. (1984). Marriage, divorce, and living arrangements: Prospective changes. *Journal of Family Issues, 5*, 7–26.

Glick, P. C., & Spanier, G. B. (1980). Married and unmarried cohabitation in the United States. *Journal of Marriage and the Family, 42*, 19–30.

Goetting, A. (1982). The six stations of remarriage: Developmental tasks of remarriage after divorce. *Family Relations, 31*, 213–222.

Golanty, E., & Harris, B. B. (1982). *Marriage and family life*. Boston: Houghton Mifflin.

Goldfarb, J. L., Mumford, D. M., Schum, D. A., Smith, P. B., Flowers, C., & Schum, C. (1977). An attempt to detect "pregnancy susceptibility" in indigent girls. *Journal of Youth and Adolescence, 6*, 127–144.

Goldman, R., & Goldman, J. (1982). *Children's sexual thinking: A comparative study of children aged 5 to 15 years in Australia, North America, Britain, and Sweden*. London: Routledge & Kegan Paul.

Goldstein, D., & Rosenbaum, A. (1985). An evaluation of the self-esteem of maritally violent men. *Family Relations, 34*, 425–428.

Goldstein, R. K. (1981). Inextricable interaction: Social, psychologic, and biologic stresses facing the elderly. *American Journal of Orthopsychiatry, 51*, 219–229.

Goodman, E. (1986, March 3). Drug could make moot whole abortion furor. *Los Angeles Times*, Part II, p. 5.

Goodman, R. M. (1986). *Planning for a healthy baby*. New York: Oxford.

Gordon, J. (1891, February). Men's women. *Lippincott's Monthly Magazine*.

Gordon, P. A. (1988). *Developing retirement facilities*. New York: John Wiley.

Gordon, S. (1980). Sexual concerns of adolescents: Implications for sex education. In N. Stinnett, B. Chesser, J. DeFrain, & P. Knaub (Eds.), *Family strengths: Positive models for family life* (pp. 237–251). Lincoln, NE: University of Nebraska Press.

Gottman, J. M., & Porterfield, A. L. (1981). Communication competence in the nonverbal behavior of married couples. *Journal of Marriage and the Family, 43*, 817–824.

The graduate school divorce itch. (1980, October). *Psychology Today*, p. 20.

Graham, P., Rutter, M., & George, S. (1973). Temperamental characteristics as predictors of behavior disorders in children. *American Journal of Orthopsychiatry, 43*, 328–339.

Grandparents deserve visiting rights. (1982, December 27). *The Record/Washington Post News Service*.

Gray-Little, B. G. (1982). Marital quality and power processes among black couples. *Journal of Marriage and the Family, 44*, 633–646.

Green, R. (1981). Endocrine therapy of erectile failure. In G. Wagner & R. Green (Eds.), *Impotence: Physiological, psychological, surgical diagnosis and treatment*. New York: Plenum.

Greenberg, E. F., & Nay, W. R. (1982). The intergenerational transmission of marital instability reconsidered. *Journal of Marriage and the Family, 44*, 335–347.

Greer, K. (1986, October). Today's parents. How well are they doing? *Better Homes and Gardens*, pp. 36–46.

Griffin, W. A., & Morgan, A. R. (1988). Conflict in maritally distressed military couples. *American Journal of Family Therapy, 16*, 14–22.

Gross, H. E. (1980). Dual-career couples who live apart: Two types. *Journal of Marriage and the Family, 42,* 567–576.

Gross, P. (1986). Defining post-divorce remarriage families: A typology based on the subjective perceptions of children. *Journal of Divorce, 10,* 205–217.

Gudykunst, W. B., & Lim, T. S. (1985). Ethnicity, sex, and self perception of communicator style. *Communication Research Reports, 2,* 68–75.

Guerney, B. Jr., Waldo, M., & Firestone, L. (1987). Wife-battering: A theoretical construct and case report. *American Journal of Family Therapy, 15,* 34–43.

A guide to budgeting for the family. (1972). *Home and Garden Bulletin, no. 108.* Washington, DC: U.S. Department of Agriculture.

Gullotta, T. P., Adams, G. R., & Alexander, S. J. (1986). *Today's marriages and families.* Monterey, CA: Brooks/Cole.

Haas, L. (1982). Determinants of role-sharing behavior: A study of egalitarian couples. *Sex Roles, 8,* 747–760.

Hagan, J. M. (1980). Family adjustments in financial management. *Family Economics Review,* 8–12.

Hagestad, G. O. (1987). Able elderly in the family context: Changes, chances, and challenges. *The Gerontologist, 27,* 417–422.

Hague, R. (1988, May/June). Marriage Athenian style. *Archaeologist, 33,* 32–36.

Hamner, T. J., & Turner, P. (1990) *Parenting in contemporary society* (2nd ed.). Englewood Cliffs, NJ: Prentice-Hall.

Hancock, M., & Mains, K. B. (1987). *Child sexual abuse: A hope for healing.* Wheaton, IL: Harold Shaw.

Hanson, S. H., & Sporakowski, M. J. (1986). Single-parent families. *Family Relations, 35,* 3–8.

Hareven, T. K. (1974). The family as process: A historical study of the family life cycle. *Journal of Social History,* 322–329.

Harlow, H. (1974). *Learning to love.* New York: Jason Aronson.

Harriman, L. C. (1986). Marital adjustment as related to personal and marital changes accompanying parenthood. *Family Relations, 35,* 233–239.

Harris, L. (1981, January). Factors considered important in life. *Louis Harris Survey Release.*

Hartman, W. E., & Fithian, M. A. (1974). *Treatment of sexual dysfunction.* New York: Jason Aronson.

Hartman, W. E., & Fithian, M. A. (1984). *Any man can.* New York: St. Martin's.

Haun, D. L., & Stinnett, N. (1974). Does psychological comfortableness between engaged couples affect their probability of successful marriage adjustment? *Family Perspective, 9,* 11–18.

Hayduk, L. A. (1983). Personal space: Where we stand. *Psychological Bulletin, 94,* 293–335.

Hayes, M. P., Stinnett, N., & DeFrain, J. (1981). Learning about marriage from the divorced. *Journal of Divorce, 4,* 23–29.

Heaton, T. B., Albrecht, S. L., & Martin, T. K. (1985). The timing of divorce. *Journal of Marriage and the Family, 47,* 631–639.

Heffernan, C. (1982). Determinants and patterns of family savings. *Home Economics Research Journal, 11*(1), 47–55.

Henslin, J. M. (1985). Why so much divorce? In J. M. Henslin (Ed.), *Marriage and family in a changing society* (2nd ed.) (pp. 424–428). New York: Free Press.

Henton, J., Cate, R., Koval. J., Lloyd, S., & Christopher, S. (1983). Romance and violence in dating relationships. Unpublished manuscript.

Herman, D. M. (1985). A statutory proposal to prohibit the infliction of violence upon children. *Family Law Quarterly, 19*(1), 1–52.

Herman, J., & Hirschman, L. (1981). Families at risk for father-daughter incest. *The American Journal of Psychiatry, 138,* 967.

Herold, E. S, & Goodwin, M. S. (1981). Premarital sexual guilt. *Canadian Journal of Behavior Science, 13,* 65–75.

Hess, B. B., & Markson, E. (1980). *Aging and old age.* New York: Macmillan.

Hettler, W. (1981). Family wellness—your choice. In N. Stinnett, J. DeFrain, K. King, P. Knaub, & G. Rowe (Eds.), *Family strengths 3: Roots of well-being* (pp. 165–176). Lincoln, NE: University of Nebraska Press.

Hibbard, J. H., & Pope, C. R. (1985). Employment status, employment characteristics, and women's health. *Women and Health, 10,* 59–78.

Hill, M. D. (1988). Class, kinship density, and conjugal role segregation. *Journal of Marriage and the Family, 50,* 731–741.

Hill, R. B. (1971). *The strengths of black families.* New York: Emerson Hall.

Hiller, D. V., & Philliber, W. W. (1982). Predicting marital and career success among dual-worker couples. *Journal of Marriage and the Family, 44,* 53–62.

Hine, J. R. (1980). *What comes after you say "I love you"?* Palo Alto, CA: Pacific.

Hingson, R., Alpert, J. J., Day, N., Dooling, E., Kayne, H., Morelock, S., Oppenheimer, E., & Zuckerman, B. (1982). Effects of maternal drinking and marijuana use on fetal growth and development. *Pediatrics, 70,* 539–546.

Hingst, A. G. (1981). Children and divorce: The child's view. *Journal of Clinical Child Psychology, 10,* 161–164.

Hofferth, S. L. (1979). Day care in the next decade: 1980–1990. *Journal of Marriage and the Family, 41,* 649–658.

Hoffman, L. W. (1986). Work, family and the child. In M. S. Pellak & R. O. Perloff (Eds.), *Psychology and work: Productivity, change and employment* (pp. 173–220). Washington, DC: American Psychological Association.

Hogan, D. P., & Kitagawa, E. W. (1985). The impact of social status, family structure, and neighborhood on the fertility of black adolescents. *American Journal of Sociology, 90,* 825–855.

Holman, T. B., & Brock, G. W. (1986). Implications for therapy in the study of communication and marital quality. *Family Perspective, 20,* 85–94.

Holman, T. B., & Burr, W. R. (1980). Beyond the beyond: The growth of family theories in the 1970s. *Journal of Marriage and the Family, 42,* 729–740.

Holmes, T. H., & Rahe, R. H. (1967). The social readjustment rating scale. *Journal of Psychosomatic Research, 11,* 213–218.

Honeycutt, J. M., Wilson, C., & Parker, C. (1982). Effects of sex and degrees of happiness on perceived styles of communication in and out of the marital relationship. *Journal of Marriage and the Family, 44,* 395–406.

Horn, M. J., & East, M. (1982). Hindsight and foresight: Basics for choice. *Journal of Home Economics, 74,* 10–17.

Hornung, C. A., & McCullough, B. C. (1981). Status relationships in dual-employment marriages: Consequences for psychological well-being. *Journal of Marriage and the Family, 43,* 125–141.

Householder, J., Hatcher, R., Burns, W., & Chasnoff, I. (1982). Infants born to narcotic-addicted mothers. *Psychological Bulletin, 92,* 453–468.

Houseknecht, S. (1982). Voluntary childlessness: Toward a theoretical integration. *Journal of Family Issues, 3,* 459–471.

Houseknecht, S. K. (1985). Achievement of women outside the home is the phantom factor in marital breakdown. In H. Feldman & M. Feldman (Eds.), *Current controversies in marriage and family* (pp. 117–130). Beverly Hills, CA: Sage.

Houseknecht, S. K., & Macke, A. S. (1984). Marital disruption among professional women: The timing of career and family events. *Social Problems, 31,* 273–284.

Howard, J. (1980). *Families.* New York: Berkeley.

Howard, J. A., Blumstein, P., & Schwartz, P. (1986). Sex, power and influence tactics in intimate relationships. *Journal of Personality and Social Psychology, 51,* 102–109.

Hunt, M. (1974). *Sexual behavior in the seventies.* Chicago: Playboy.

Hurlock, E. B. (1972). *Child development.* New York: McGraw-Hill.

Huston, T. L., & Ashmore, R. D. (1985). Women and men in personal relationships. In R. D. Ashmore & F. K. Del Boca (Eds.), *The social psychology of female-male relations: A critical analysis of central concepts.* Orlando, FL: Academic Press.

Huxley, A. (1953). *Brave new world.* New York: Bantam.

Inazu, J. K., & Fox, G. L. (1980). Maternal influence on the sexual behavior of teenage daughters: Direct and indirect sources. *Journal of Family Issues, 1*(1), 81–102.

Indvik, J., & Fitzpatrick, M. A. (1982). If you could read my mind love... Understanding and misunderstanding in the marital dyad. *Family Relations, 31*, 43–57.

Ingraham v. Wright, 430 U.S. 651 (1977).

Information please: Almanac, altas and yearbook. (1981). New York: Simon and Schuster, p. 804.

Information please almanac. (1985). Boston: Houghton Mifflin.

An introduction to *Smart House.* (1988, December). *Smart House* L.P., 400 Prince George's Boulevard, Upper Marlboro, MD 20772–8731.

Jacobson, N. S., & Margolin, G. (1979). *Marital therapy.* New York: Brunner/Mazel.

Jaffe, P., Wolfe, D., Wilson, S., & Zak, L. (1986). Similarities in behavioral and social maladjustment among child victims and witnesses to family violence. *American Journal of Orthopsychiatry, 56*, 142–146.

Jorgensen, S. R. (1986). *Marriage and the family: Development and change.* New York: Macmillan.

Jorgensen, S. R., & Gaudy, J. C. (1980). Self-disclosure and satisfaction in marriage: The relation examined. *Family Relations, 29*, 281–287.

Jorgensen, S. R., & Johnson, A. C. (1980). Correlates of divorce liberality. *Journal of Marriage and the Family, 42*, 617–626.

Judson, F. N. (1985). Assessing the number of genital chlamydial infections in the United States. *The Journal of Reproductive Medicine, 30* (Suppl.), 269–272.

Julius, M. (1986). Marital stress and suppressed anger linked to death of spouses. *Marriage and Divorce Today, 11*, 1–2.

Kalb, M. (1987). Meditations on the hunt: A reexamination of the issue of choice in the process of mate selection and its implications for psychotherapy. *Psychotherapy, 24*, 809–815.

Kalmuss, D. (1984). The intergenerational transmission of marital aggression. *Journal of Marriage and the Family, 46*, 11–19.

Kalmuss, D., & Straus, M. A. (1982). Wife's marital dependency and wife abuse. *Journal of Marriage and the Family, 44*, 277–286.

Kane, N. M. (1989). The home care crisis of the nineties. *The Gerontologist, 29*, 24–31.

Kaplan, F. S. (1985). Osteoporosis. *Women and Health, 10*, 95–114.

Kaplan, H. S. (1974). *The new sex therapy.* New York: Brunner/Mazel.

Kaplan, H. S. (1983). *The evaluation of sexual disorders: Psychological and medical aspects.* New York: Brunner/Mazel.

Kaslow, F. (1984). Divorce: An evolutionary process of change in the family system. *Journal of Divorce, 7*, 21–39.

Katchadourian, H. A., & Lunde, D. T. (1972). *Fundamentals of human sexuality.* New York: Holt.

Keating, N. C., & Cole P. (1980). What do I do with him 24 hours a day: Changes in the housewife role after retirement. *The Gerontologist, 20*, 84.

Keith, P. E., & Brubaker, T. (1979). Household roles in later life: A look at masculinity and marital adjustment. *The Family Coordinator, 28*, 497–502.

Keith, P. E. (1986). Isolation of the unmarried in later life. *Family Relations, 35*, 389–395.

Keller, P. W., & Brown, C. T. (1968). Interpersonal ethic for communication. *The Journal of Communication, 16*, 73–81.

Kelley, H. H., Cunningham, J. D., Grisham, J. A., Lefebvre, L. M., Sink, C. R., & Yablon, G. (1978). Sex differences in comments made during conflict in close relationships. *Sex Roles, 4*, 473–491.

Kelly, D. (1988, November 14). Don't turn visiting in-laws into outlaws. *USA Today*, p. 4D.

Kemper, T. (1978). *A social interaction theory of emotions.* New York: John Wiley.

Kendig, H. (1983). Blood ties and gender roles: Adult children who care for aged parents. In *Proceedings of the Australian Family Research Conference (Vol. 5): Family Support Networks.* Melbourne, Australia: Institute of Family Studies.

Kern, S. (1974). Explosive intimacy: Psychodynamics of the Victorian family. *History of Childhood Quarterly: The Journal of Psychohistory, 3*, 452–454.

Ketterman, G. H. (1985). Good family communication. In G. Rekers (Ed.), *Family building* (pp. 107–120). Ventura, CA: Regal Books.

Ketwig, J. (1985). *And a hard rain fell: A GI's true story of the war in Vietnam.* New York: Macmillan.

Kieffer, C. (1977). New depths in intimacy. In R. W. Libby & R. N. Whitehurst (Eds.), *Marriage and alternatives: Exploring intimate relationships* (pp. 267–293). Glenview, IL: Scott, Foresman.

Kieren, D., Henton, J., & Marotz, R. (1975). *Hers and his: A problem solving approach to marriage.* New York: Holt.

Kiersey, D., & Bates, M. (1978). *Please understand me: An essay on temperament styles.* Upland, CA: Prometheus Nemesis.

Kilmann, P. R. (1984). *Human sexuality in contemporary life.* Boston: Allyn & Bacon.

King, J. (1980). The strengths of black families. Unpublished doctoral dissertation. University of Nebraska, Lincoln.

Kinsey, A., Pomeroy, W. B., & Martin, C. E. (1948). *Sexual behavior in the human male.* Philadelphia: W. B. Saunders.

Kinsey, A., Pomeroy, W. B., Martin, C. E., & Gebhard, P. (1953). *Sexual behavior in the human female.* Philadelphia: W. B. Saunders.

Kirkham, C., & Reid, R. L. (1987). Relative risk of oral contraceptive usage. *Fertility and Sterility, 47,* 557–558.

Kitson, G. C. (1985). Marital discord and marital separation: A county survey. *Journal of Marriage and the Family, 47,* 693–700.

Kitson, G. C., & Sussman, M. B. (1982). Marital complaints, demographic characteristics, and symptoms of mental distress in divorce. *Journal of Marriage and the Family, 44,* 87–101.

Kliman, J., & Trimble, D. W. (1983). Network therapy. In B. J. Wolman & G. Stricker (Eds.), *Handbook of family and marital therapy* (pp. 277–314). New York: Plenum.

Klitsch, M. (1988a). FDA approval ends cervical cap's marathon. *Family Planning Perspectives, 20,* 137–138.

Klitsch, M. (1988b). The return of the IUD. *Family Planning Perspectives, 20,* 19, 40.

Knaub, P., Hanna, S., & Stinnett, N. (1984). Strengths of remarried families. *Journal of Divorce, 7,* 41–55.

Knox, D. (1984). *Human sexuality: The search for understanding.* St. Paul, MN: West.

Knox, D. (1988). *Choices in relationships.* St. Paul, MN: West.

Kobrin, F. E., & Hendershot, G. E. (1977). Do family ties reduce mortality? Evidence from the United States, 1966–1968. *Journal of Marriage and the Family, 39,* 737–745.

Kobrin, F. E., & Waite, L. J. (1984). Effects of childhood family structure on the transition of marriage. *Journal of Marriage and the Family, 46,* 807–816.

Kolata, G. B. (1979, June). Early warnings and latest cures for infertility. *Ms,* p. 85–87.

Komarovksy, M. (1964). *Blue-collar marriage.* New York: Random.

Korman, S. K. (1983). Nontraditional dating behavior: Date-initiation and date expense-sharing among feminists and non-feminists. *Family Relations, 32,* 575–581.

Kosick, K., & Growdon, J. H. (1982). Aging, memory loss and dementia. *Psychosomatics, 23,* 746.

Koval, J. E., Ponzetti, J. J., Jr., & Cate, R. M. (1982). Programmatic intervention for men involved in conjugal violence. *Family Therapy, 9,* 147–154.

Krakoff, L. R. (1985). Hypertension in women: Progress and unsolved problems. *Women and Health, 10,* 75–83.

Krantzler, M. (1981). *Creative marriage.* New York: McGraw-Hill.

Kricker, A., Elliott, J. W., Forrest, J. M., & McCredie, J. (1986). Congenital limb reduction deformities and use of oral contraceptives. *American Journal of Obstetrics and Gynecology, 155,* 1072–1078.

Kuypers, J. A., & Bengtson, V. L. (1983). Toward competence in the older family. In T. H. Brubaker (Ed.), *Family relationships in later life* (pp. 221–228). Beverly Hills, CA: Sage.

LaBarbera, J. D., Martin, J. E., & Dozier, J. E. (1980). Child psychiatrists' view of father-daughter incest. *Child Abuse and Neglect, 4,* 147–151.

Lacey, D., & Jennings, G. (1986). Couples with diverse personalities and strong marriages. In S. Van Zandt, H. Lingren, G. Rowe, P. Zeece, L. Kimmons, P. Lee, D. Shell, & N. Stinnett (Eds.), *Family strengths 7: Vital connections* (pp. 13–24). Lincoln, NE: Center for Family Strengths, University of Nebraska.

Lamanna, M. A., & Riedmann, A. (1988). *Marriages and families: Making choices and facing change.* Belmont, CA: Wadsworth.

Landis, J. T. (1960). Religiousness, family relationships and family values in Protestant, Catholic and Jewish families. *Marriage and Family Living, 22,* 241–247.

Landis, P. (1975). *Making the most of marriage.* Englewood Cliffs, NJ: Prentice-Hall.

Landry, B., & Jendrek, M. P. (1978). The employment of wives in middle-class black families. *Journal of Marriage and the Family, 40,* 787–797.

Lane, K. E., & Gwartney-Gibbs, P. A. (1985). Violence in the context of dating and sex. *Journal of Family Issues, 6,* 45–59.

Laner, M. R. (1982). Courtship abuse and aggression: Contextual aspects. Paper presented at the Conference on Families and Close Relationships, Lubbock, TX.

Lang, L. R. (1988). *Strategy for personal finance* (4th ed.). New York: McGraw-Hill.

Laosa, L. M. (1982). School, occupation, culture and family: The impact of parental schooling on the parent-child relationship. *Journal of Educational Psychology, 74,* 791–827.

LaRoe, M. S., & Herrick, L. (1980). *How not to ruin a perfectly good marriage.* New York: Bantam.

Larsen, D. (1985, September 29). Bestowing civil touch to marriage ceremonies has become a 9-to-5 job. *Los Angeles Times,* Part vi, pp. 1, 10.

Larson, D. B. (1985). Marital status: Its association with personal well-being, economic status and psychiatric status. In G. Rekers (Ed.), *Family building* (pp. 237–258). Ventura, CA: Regal.

Larson, J. H. (1988). The marriage quiz: College students' beliefs in selected myths about marriage. *Family Relations, 37,* 3–11.

Lasswell, M. (1986). Turbulent periods in marriage. In S. Van Zandt, H. Lingren, G. Rowe, P. Zeece, L. Kimmons, P. Lee, D. Shell, & N. Stinnett (Eds.), *Family strengths 7: Vital connections* (pp. 315–329). Lincoln, NE: Center for Family Strengths, Department of Human Development and the Family, University of Nebraska.

Lasswell, M. E., & Lobenz, N. M. (1981). *Styles of loving.* New York: Ballantine.

Lasswell, T., & Lasswell, M. (1976). I love you but I'm not in love with you. *Journal of Marriage and Family Counseling, 2,* 211–224.

Laurie, G., Maynard, F. M., Fischer, S. A., & Raymond, J. (Eds.). (1984). *Handbook on the late effects of poliomyelitis for physicians and survivors.* St. Louis: Gazette International Networking Institute.

Lazarus, A. A. (1985). *Marital myths.* San Luis Obispo, CA: Impact.

Ledray, L. (1984). Victims of incest. *American Journal of Nursing, 84,* 1010.

Leibowitz, B. (1978). Implications of community housing for planning and policy. *The Gerontologist, 18,* 138–144.

Leigh, G. F. (1982). Kinship interaction over the family life span. *Journal of Marriage and the Family, 44,* 197–208.

Leigh, G., Ladehoff, G., Howie, A., & Christians, D. (1985). Correlates of marital satisfaction among men and women in intact first marriage and remarriage. *Family Perspective, 19,* 139–150.

Lerman, L. G. (1981). Criminal prosecution of the wife beaters. *Response, 4,* 1–19.

Leslie, G. (1982). *The family in social context* (5th ed.). New York: Oxford.

Levinson, A. (1980, Fall). Home birth: Joy or jeopardy? *Medical self care,* 42–46.

Lewis, R. A. (1963). Parents and peers: Socialization agents in the coital behavior of young adults. *Journal of Sex Research, 9,* 156–170.

Li, J., & Caldwell, R. (1987). Magnitude and directional effects of marital sex-role incongruence on marital adjustment. *Journal of Family Issues, 8,* 97–110.

Libby, R. W., Gray, L., & White, M. (1978). A test and reformulation of reference group and role correlates of premarital sexual permissiveness theory. *Journal of Marriage and the Family, 40,* 79–92.

Lieberman, B. (1985). *Extrapremarital intercourse.* Unpublished manuscript, University of Pittsburg, Department of Sociology, Pittsburgh, PA.

Lindblad, M., Marsal, K., & Anderson, K. (1988). Effect of nicotine on human fetal blood flow. *Obstetrics and Gynecology, 72,* 371–382.

Lindsey, K. (1981). *Friends as family.* Boston: Beacon.

Lingren, H., Van Zandt, S., Stinnett, N., & Rowe, G. (1982). Enhancing marriage and family competencies throughout adult life development. In N. Stinnett, J. DeFrain, K. King, H. Lingren, G. Rowe, S. Van Zandt, & R. Williams (Eds.), *Family strengths 4: Positive support systems* (pp. 385–406). Lincoln, NE: University of Nebraska Press.

Lipkin, M., & Lamb, G. (1982). The couvade syndrome: An epidemiologic study. *Annals of Internal Medicine, 96,* 509–511.

Litwak, E. (1985). *Helping the elderly: The complementary roles of informal networks and formal systems.* New York: Guilford Press.

Litwak, E., & Kulis, S. (1987). Technology, proximity, and measures of kin support. *Journal of Marriage and the Family, 49,* 649–661.

Liu, G., Lyle, K. C., & Coo, J. (1987). Clinical trial of gossypol as a male contraceptive drug. *Fertility and Sterility, 48,* 459–461.

Lochman, J. E., & Allen, G. (1979). Elicited effects of approval and disapproval: An examination of parameters having implications for counseling couples in conflict. *Journal of Counsuling and Clinical Psychology, 47,* 634–636.

Lockhart, L. L. (1987). A reexamination of the effects of race and social class on the incidence of marital violence: A search for reliable differences. *Journal of Marriage and the Family, 49,* 603–610.

London, H., & Devore, W. (1988). Layers of understanding: Counseling ethnic minority families. *Family Relations, 37,* 310–314.

Lonnborg, B. (1980, December 22). New studies emphasize the strength of the black family. *Chicago Tribune,* Section 2, p. 1.

Loudin, J. (1981). *The hoax of romance.* Englewood Cliffs, NJ: Prentice-Hall.

Luckey, E. B. (1964). Marital satisfaction and personality correlates of spouse. *Journal of Marriage and the Family, 26,* 217–220.

Lundgren, D., Jergens, V., & Gibson, J. (1980). Marital relationships, evaluations of self and spouse, and anxiety. *Journal of Psychology, 106,* 227–240.

Maccoby, E. E. (1980). *Social development: Psychological growth and the parent-child relationship.* New York: Harcourt Brace Jovanovich.

Maccoby, E. E., & Martin, J. A. (1983). Socialization in the context of the family: Parent-child interaction. In E. M. Hetherington & P. H. Mussen (Eds.), *Handbook of child psychology: Socialization, personality, and social development* (Vol. 4) (pp. 1–102). New York: Wiley.

Mace, D. (Ed). (1983). *Prevention in family services: Approaches to family wellness.* Beverly Hills, CA: Sage.

Mace, D., & Mace, V. (1980). Enriching marriages: The foundationstone of family strength. In N. Stinnett, B. Chesser, J. DeFrain, & P. Knaub (Eds.), *Family strengths: Positive models for family life* (pp. 89–110). Lincoln, NE: University of Nebraska Press.

Macklin, E. D. (1983). Nonmarital heterosexual cohabitation: An overview. In E. D. Macklin & R. H. Rubin (Eds.), *Contemporary families and alternate lifestyles: Handbook on research and theory* (pp. 49–73). Beverly Hills, CA: Sage.

MacPherson, M. (1984). *Long time passing: Vietnam and the haunted generation.* Garden City, NY: Doubleday.

Madden, M. E., & Janoff-Bulman, R. (1981). Blame, control, and marital satisfaction: Wives' attributions for conflict in marriage. *Journal of Marriage and the Family, 43,* 663–673.

Maddux, E. (1988). *Family planning basics.* Athens, GA: Cooperative Extension Service, The University of Georgia.

Magran, B. (1981). Transactional analysis in marital therapy. In G. P. Sholevar (Ed.), *The handbook of marriage and marital therapy*. (pp. 335–345). Jamaica, NY: Spectrum.

Maiuro, R. D., Cahn, T. S., Vitaliano, P. P., Wagner, B. C., & Zegree, J. B. (1988). Anger, hostility and depression in domestically violent versus generally assaultive men and nonviolent control subjects. *Journal of Consulting and Clinical Psychology, 56*, 17–23.

Makepeace, J. M. (1982). Courtship violence on a low-risk campus. Paper presented at the annual meeting of the Pacific Sociological Association, San Diego, CA.

Makepeace, J. M. (1987). Social factors and victim-offender differences in courtship violence. *Family Relations, 36*, 87–91.

Mall, J. (1986, August 17). Pregnancy risks high among blacks. *Los Angeles Times*, Part VI, p. 10.

Mann, J., & Hellwig, B. (1988, January). The truth about the salary gap(s). *Working Women*, p. 61.

Mann, W. J. (1985). Reproductive cancer. *Women and Health, 10*, 63–73.

Mansfield, P. K., & Cohn, M. D. (1986). Stress and later-life childbearing: Important implications for nursing. *Maternal-Child Nursing Journal, 15*, 139–151.

Manson, R. (1983). *Xanadu*. Washington, DC: Acropolis Books.

March of Dimes. (1980). *Pregnant? Before you drink, think*. White Plains, NY: Author.

March of Dimes. (1983). *Genetic counseling*. White Plains, NY: Author.

Margolin, G., John, R. S., & Gleberman, L. (1988). Affective responses to conflictual discussions in violent and nonviolent couples. *Journal of Consulting and Clinical Psychology, 56*, 24–33.

Markides, K. S., Hoppe, S. V., Martin, H. W., & Timbers, D. M. (1983). Sample representativeness in a three-generation study of Mexican Americans. *Journal of Marriage and the Family, 45*, 911–916.

Markman, H. J., Floyd, F. J., Stanley, S. M., & Storaasli, R. D. (1988). Prevention of marital distress: A longitudinal investigation. *Journal of Consulting and Clinical Psychology, 56*, 210–217.

Markowitz, A. (1988a, July 18). Prodigy to give Big Apple a taste of PC shopping. *Discount Store News*, p. 118.

Markowitz, A. (1988b, August 22). K-Mart joins prodigy service: Looks to gain upscale market. *Discount Store News*, p. 58.

Markowski, E. M., Croake, J. W., & Keller, J. F. (1978). Sexual history and present sexual behavior of cohabiting and married couples. *The Journal of Sex Research, 14*, 27–39.

Markson, E. W. (1985). Gender roles and memory loss in old age: An exploration of linkages. In B. B. Hess & E. W. Markson (Eds.), *Growing old in America* (3rd ed.) (pp. 265–274). New Brunswick, NJ: Transaction Books.

Marotz-Baden, R., & Cowan, D. (1987). Mothers-in-law and daughters-in-law: The effects of proximity on conflict and stress. *Family Relations, 36*, 385–390.

Marriage vs. single life: Has the rising divorce rate caused Americans to become more wary of marriage? (1982, Autumn). *Institute for Social Research Newsletter*, University of Michigan.

Martin, G., & Pear, J. (1988). *Behavior modification* (3rd ed.). Englewood Cliffs, NJ: Prentice-Hall.

Martin, M. J., & Walters, J. (1990). Familial correlates of selected types of child abuse and neglect. Unpublished paper, Department of Human and Family Resources, Northern Illinois University, Dekalb.

Martin, P., Hagestad, G. O., & Diedrick, P. (1988). Family stories: Events (temporarily) remembered. *Journal of Marriage and the Family, 50*, 533–541.

Maslow, A. H. (1962). *Toward a psychology of being*. New York: Van Nostrand.

Masnick, G., & Bane, M. J. (1980a). *The nation's families: 1960–1990*. Boston: Auburn House.

Masnick, G., & Bane, M. J. (1980b). *Types of households, 1975 and 1990*. Dover, MA: Auburn House.

Masters, W. H., & Johnson, V. E. (1970). *Human sexual inadequacy*. Boston: Little, Brown.

Masters, W. H., Johnson, V. E., & Kolodny, R. C. (1986). *Masters and Johnson on sex and human loving*. Boston: Little, Brown.

May, K. A., & Perrin, S. P. (1985). Prelude: Pregnancy and birth. In S. M. H. Hanson & F. W. Bozett (Eds.), *Dimensions of fatherhood*. Beverly Hills, CA: Sage.

Mayer, A. (1985). *Sexual abuse*. Holmes Beach, FL: Learning Publications.

Maynard, J. (1980, June). The other man in your marriage: Your father-in-law. *Redbook*, pp. 25, 58–60.

McAdoo, H. P. (1982). Stress absorbing systems in black families. *Family Relations, 31*, 479–488.

McConnell, K. (1982). The aged widower. *Social Work, 27*, 188–189.

McCord, J. (1988). Parental behavior in the cycle of aggression. *Psychiatry, 51*, 14–23.

McCrary, J. L., & McCrary, S. P. (1982). *McCrary's human sexuality* (4th ed.). Belmont, CA: Wadsworth.

McCubbin, H., Joy, C., Cauble, A., Patterson, J., & Needle, R. (1980). Family stress and coping: A decade review. *Journal of Marriage and the Family, 42*, 855–871.

McGoldrick, M. (1989). The joining of families through marriage: The new couple. In B. Carter & M. McGoldrick (Eds.), *The changing family life cycle* (pp. 209–233). Boston: Allyn & Bacon.

McGoldrick, M., & Carter, E. (1982). The stages of the family life cycle. In F. Walsh (Ed.), *Normal family processes*. New York: Guilford.

McLaughlin, M., Cormier, L. S., & Cormier, W. H. (1988). Relation between coping strategies and distress, stress, and marital adjustment of multiple-role women. *Journal of Counseling Psychology, 35*, 187–193.

McLeod, B. (1986). The oriental express. *Psychology Today, 20*, 48–52.

McNair, N. (1988). Chlamydia is not a flower. *Health Call, 4*(2), 3.

Mead, M. (1968). A continuing dialogue on marriage—Why just living together won't work. *Redbook, 130*, 50.

Medrich, E. A., Roizen, J., & Rubin, V. (1982). *The serious business of growing up*. Berkeley, CA: University of California Press.

Meier, P. D., & Minirth, F. B. (1985). Spending time together. In G. Rekers (Ed.), *Family building* (pp. 67–86). Ventura, CA: Regal.

Melville, K. (1980). Trends and forecasts: The future isn't what it used to be. In K. Melville (Ed.), *Marriage and family today* (2nd ed.). New York: Random House.

Menaghan, E. G., & Lieberman, M. A. (1986). Changes in depression following divorce: A panel study. *Journal of Marriage and the Family, 48*, 319–328.

Menninger, F. V. (1939). *Days of my life*. New York: Richard R. Smith.

Meredith, W. H., Stinnett, N., & Cacioppo, B. F. (1985). Parent satisfactions: Implications for strengthening families. In R. Williams, H. Lingren, G. Rowe, S. Van Zandt, P. Lee, & N. Stinnett (Eds.), *Family strengths 6: Enhancement of interaction* (pp. 143–150). Lincoln, NE: Department of Human Development and the Family, University of Nebraska.

Meyer, J. K., Schmidt, L. M., & Wise, T. N. (1983). *Clinical management of social disorders*. Baltimore: William & Wilkins.

Millar, D. P., & Millar, F. E. (1982). *Messages and myths: Understanding interpersonal communication*. Palo Alto, CA: Mayfield.

Miller, D. R., Rosenberg, L., Kaufman, D. W., Schottenfeld, D., Stolley, P. D., & Shapiro, S. (1986). Breast cancer risk in relation to early oral contraceptive use. *Obstetrics and Gynecology, 68*, 863–868.

Miller, P. A., & Eisenberg, N. (1988). The relation of empathy to aggressive and externalizing/antisocial behavior. *Psychological Bulletin, 103*, 324–344.

Miller, S., Nunnally, E. W., & Wackman, D. B. (1975). *Alive and aware*. Minneapolis, MN: Interpersonal Communication Programs.

Mitchell, O. S., Levine, P. B., & Pozzebon, S. (1988). Retirement by industry and occupation. *The Gerontologist, 28*, 545–551.

Moore, K. L. (1983). *Before we are born* (2nd ed.). Philadelphia: W. B. Saunders.

Morganstern, M., Naitch, S. W., & Smith, G. W. (1982). *How to make love to a woman*. New York: C. N. Potter.

Morris, R. M. (1988). Challenges of aging in tomorrow's world: Will gerontology grow, stagnate, or change? *The Gerontologist, 29*, 494–501.

Morton, T. U. (1978). Intimacy and reciprocity of exchange: A comparison of spouses and strangers. *Journal of Personality and Social Psychology, 36*, 72–81.

Mosher, D. L., & Vonderheide, S. G. (1985). Contributions of sex guilt and masturbation guilt to women's contraceptive attitudes and use. *Journal of Sex Research*, *21*, 24–39.

Moss, J. J., Apolonio, F., & Jensen, M. (1971). The premarital dyad during the sixties. *Journal of Marriage and the Family*, *33*, 50–59.

Most would remarry spouse, poll shows. (1988, May 11). *Tuscaloosa News*, p. 42.

Mowsesian, R. (1986). *Golden goals, rusted realities: Work and aging in America*. Far Hills, NJ: New Horizons Press.

Mullis, R. J., & Schnittgrund, K. P. (1982). Budget behavior: Variance over the life cycle of low-income families. *Journal of Consumer Studies and Home Economics*, *6*, 113–120.

Murphy, G. R., Hudson, W. W., & Cheung, P. P. L. (1980). Marital and sexual discord among older couples. *Social Work Research and Abstracts*, *16*, 11–16.

Murray, P. (1979). *Shared homes: A housing option for older people*. Washington, DC: International Center for Social Gerontology.

Murstein, B. I. (1980). Mate selection in the seventies. *Journal of Marriage and the Family*, *42*, 777–792.

Murstein, B. I. (1986). *Paths to marriage*. Beverly Hills, CA: Sage.

"My brother." (1979, April, p. 23). *The Futurist*. Washington, DC: The World Future Society.

Naisbitt, J. (1982). *Megatrends*. New York: Warner.

National Center for Health Statistics. (1983). *Health, United States, 1982*. Washington, DC: U.S. Government Printing Office.

National Center for Health Statistics. (1988). Births, marriages, divorces, and deaths for June 1988. *Monthly Vital Statistics Report*, *37*(6). Washington, DC: U.S. Government Printing Office.

National Research Council (1983). *Climbing the ladder: An update on the status of doctoral women scientists and engineers*. Washington, DC: National Academy Press.

Navran, L. (1967). Communication and adjustment in marriage. *Family Process*, *6*, 173–184.

Neubeck, G. (1982). Impossibilities and possibilities: Expectations in the marriage relationship. In N. Stinnett, J. DeFrain, K. King, H. Lingren, G. Rowe, S. Van Zandt, & R. Williams (Eds.), *Family strengths 4: Positive support systems* (pp. 133–140). Lincoln, NE: University of Nebraska Press.

Neugarten, B. L. (1982). Older people: A profile. In B. L. Neugarten (Ed.), *Age or need: Public policies for older people*. Beverly Hills, CA: Sage.

Newcomer, S. F., & Udry, J. R. (1985). Parent-child communication and adolescent sexual behavior. *Family Planning Perspectives*, *17*, 169–174.

Newman, J. E. (1959). Communication: A dyadic postulation. *The Journal of Communication*, *9*, 51–58.

Nofz, M. P. (1984). Fantasy-testing-assessment: A proposed model for the investigation of mate selection. *Family Relations*, *33*, 273–281.

Noller, P. (1980). Misunderstandings in marital communication: A study of couples' nonverbal communication. *Journal of Personality and Social Psychology*, *39*, 1135–1148.

Norton, A. J., & Moorman, J. E. (1987). Current trends in marriage and divorce among American women. *Journal of Marriage and the Family*, *49*, 3–14.

Nuta, (1986). Emotional aspects of child support enforcements. *Family Relations*, *35*, 177–181.

Oakley, A. (1985). Childhood lessons. In J. M. Henslin (Ed.), *Marriage and family in a changing society* (2nd ed.) (pp. 152–163). New York: Free Press.

Oakley, G. (1988). *Memorandum, Division of Birth Defects and Developmental Disabilities*. Atlanta, GA: U.S. Centers for Disease Control.

O'Brien, J. E. (1971). Violence in divorce-prone families. *Journal of Marriage and the Family*, *33*, 692–698.

O'Bryant, S. L. (1988). Sibling support and older widows' well-being. *Journal of Marriage and the Family*, *50*, 173–183.

O'Connell-Higgins, R. (1983). *Psychological resilience and the capacity for intimacy*. Qualifying paper, Harvard Graduate School of Education.

Okun, B. F., & Rappaport, L. J. (1980). *Working with families: An introduction to family therapy*. Monterey, CA: Brooks/Cole.

Olds, S. W. (1980, October). Do you have what it takes to make a good marriage? *Ladies' Home Journal*, p. 78.

Olsen, S. F. (1988). *Parental influences on daughters' premarital sexual activity.* Unpublished paper, Home Economics Department, Dixie College, St. George, UT.

Olson, D. H. (1983). How effective is marriage preparation? In D. Mace (Ed.), *Prevention in family services* (pp. 65–75). Beverly Hills, CA: Sage.

Olson, D. H. (1986a). Circumplex model VII: Validation studies and FACES III. *Family Process, 25,* 337–351.

Olson, D. H. (1986b). What makes families work? In S. Van Zandt, H. Lingren, G. Rowe, P. Zeece, L. Kimmons, P. Lee, D. Shell, & N. Stinnett (Eds.), *Family strengths 7: Vital connections* (pp. 3–12). Lincoln, NE: Center for Family Strengths, University of Nebraska.

Olson, D. H., McCubbin, H. I., Barnes, H., Larsen, A., Muxen, M., & Wilson, M. (1983). *Families: What makes them work?* Beverly Hills, CA: Sage.

O'Neal, E. C., Brunault, M. A., Carifo, M. S., Troutwine, R., & Epstein, J. (1980). Effect of insult upon personal space preference. *Journal of Nonverbal Behavior, 5,* 56–62.

O'Neal, E. C., Schultz, J., & Christianson, T. E. (1987). The menstrual cycle and personal space. *Journal of Nonverbal Behavior, 11,* 26–32.

O'Neill, G., & O'Neill, N. (1972). *Open marriage.* New York: Evans.

Oppenheimer, V. K. (1988). A theory of marriage timing. *American Journal of Sociology, 94,* 563–591.

Otto, H. A. (1963). Criteria for assessing family strength. *Family Process, 2,* 329–337.

Otto, H. A. (1969). *More joy in your marriage.* New York: Hawthorn.

Otto, H. A. (1975). *The use of family strength concepts and methods in family life education: A handbook.* Beverly Hills, CA: Holistic Press.

Pagelow, M. D. (1984). *Family violence.* New York: Praeger.

Pagels, C. E. (1981). *Healthcare and the elderly.* Rockville, MD: Aspen.

Painter, K. (1988, November 7). Women's risk of AIDS on upswing. *USA Today*, Section D, p. 1.

Papalia, D. E., & Olds, S. W. (1989). *Human development.* (4th ed.). New York: McGraw-Hill.

Parke, R. D., & Lewis, N. G. (1981). The family in context: A multilevel interactional analysis of child abuse. In M. R. Bradbard (Ed.), *Parent-child interaction: Theory, research, and prospectsi.* Orlando, FL: Academic Press.

Patterson, C. H. (1985). *The therapeutic relationship: Foundations for an eclectic psychotherapy.* Monterey, CA: Brooks/Cole.

Patterson, G. (1982). *Coercive family process.* Eugene, OR: Castalia Press.

Payne, J. M. (1985). The traditional family with the woman as homemaker and the man as breadwinner is best for most families and for society. In H. Feldman & M. Feldman (Eds.), *Current controversies in marriage and family* (pp. 101–116). Beverly Hills, CA: Sage.

Pearson, J. C. (1989). *Communication in the family.* New York: Harper & Row.

Penner, C., & Penner, J. (1988a). Diagnosis and treatment of sexual dysfunction—Part I. *The Christian Journal of Psychology and Counseling, 2,* 1–4.

Penner, C., & Penner, J. (1988b). Diagnosis and treatment of sexual dysfunction—Part II. *The Christian Journal of Psychology and Counseling, 3,* 12–14.

Perlman, D., & Duck, S. (Eds.). (1987). *Intimate relationships.* Newbury Park, CA: Sage.

Peters, M. F. (1981). "Making it" black family style: Building on the strengths of black families. In N. Stinnett, J. DeFrain, K. King, P. Knaub, & G. Rowe (Eds.), *Family strengths 3: Roots of well-being* (pp. 73–92). Lincoln, NE: University of Nebraska Press.

Petersen, J. A. (1985). Expressing appreciation. In G. Rekers (Ed.), *Family building* (pp. 87–106). Ventura, CA: Regal.

Petersen, J. R., Kretchmer, A., Nellis, B., Lever, J., & Hertz, R. (1983, January). The *Playboy* readers' sex survey. *Playboy*, p. 108.

Peterson, J. L., & Miller, C. (1980). Physical attractiveness and marriage adjustment in older American couples. *The Journal of Psychology, 105,* 247–252.

Philliber, W. W., & Hiller, D. V. (1983). Relative occupational attainments of spouses and later changes in marriage and wife's work experience. *Journal of Marriage and the Family, 45,* 161–169.

Pill appears to provide long-term protection against endometrial cancer and ovarian cancer. (1988). *Family Planning Perspectives, 19,* 126–127.

Piscopo, J. (1985). Physical health and wellness of older adults. In T. Tedrick (Ed.), *Aging: Issues and policies for the 1980s.* New York: Praeger.

Pizzey, E. (1974). *Scream quietly or the neighbors will hear.* London: Penguin Books.

Pleck, J. (1979). Men's family work: Three perspectives and some new data. *The Family Coordinator, 28,* 481–488.

Pleck, J., & Land, L. (1978). *Man's family role: Its nature and consequence.* Wellesley, MA: Wellesley College Center for Research on Women.

Pocs, O. (1989). *Our intimate relationships: Marriage and the family.* New York: Harper & Row.

Pollak, O. (1957). Design of a model of healthy family relationships as a basis for evaluative research. *Social Service Review, 31,* 369–376.

Poon, L. W. (1988). Aging and rehabilitation: A psychosocial perspective. In J. Walters (Ed.), *Women with disabilities: Through the doors of full employment* (pp. 39–59). Athens GA: Georgia Center for Continuing Education.

Porter, S. (1987). *Your financial security.* New York: William Morrow.

Powell, L. S. (1985). Alzheimer's disease: A practical, psychological approach. *Women and Health, 10,* 53–62.

Powell, M. G., Mears, B. J., Deber, R. B., & Ferguson, D. (1986). Contraception with the cervical cap: Effectiveness, safety, continuity of use, and user satisfaction. *Contraception, 33,* 215–232.

Powell-Hill, P., & Buckley, P. (1985). *Service sector in the next 10–15 years: Jobs, lifestyles and data needs.* Washington, DC: U.S. Government Printing Office.

Power, T., & Parke, R. (1984). Social network factors and the transition to parenthood. *Sex Roles, 10,* 949–972.

Pratt, L. (1976). *Family structure and effective health behavior: The energized family.* Boston: Houghton Mifflin.

Preselection of sex can have its benefits. (1983, February 11). *Lincoln Journal,* Lincoln, NE.

Preventing date/acquaintance rape. (1986). *Health Call, 4*(3), 7.

Price, S. J., & McKenry, P. (1988). *Divorce: A major life transition.* Beverly Hills, CA: Sage.

Price-Bonham, S., & Addison, S. (1978). Families and mentally retarded children: Emphasis on the father. *The Family Coordinator, 27,* 221–230.

Price-Bonham, S., & Balswick, J. (1980). The noninstitutions: Divorce, desertion, and remarriage. *Journal of Marriage and the Family, 42,* 959–972.

Prodigal spenders. (1988, September 26). *PC Week,* p. 145.

Putnam, A. P. (1872). Husband, wife and child. *Monthly Religious Magazine.*

Quindlen, A. (1988, December 6). Maria's beginning means an end to column. *Tuscaloosa News,* p. 19.

Quinn, J. B. (1979). *Everyone's money book.* New York: Delta.

Quinn, J. B. (1990, Winter/Spring). Growing old frugally. *Newsweek,* Special edition, pp. 102–105.

Rachlin, V. (1987). Fair vs. equal role relations in dual-career and dual-earner families: Implications for family intervention. *Family Relations, 36,* 187–192.

Rao, V. V. P., & Rao, N. (1986). Correlates of marital happiness: A longitudinal analysis. *Free Inquiry in Creative Sociology, 14,* 3–8.

Redeker, D. A. (1987). *Shared housing.* Unpublished manuscript, The University of Georgia, Department of Housing and Consumer Economics, Athens.

Reiss, I. L. (1960). Toward a sociology of the heterosexual love relationship. *Marriage and Family Living, 22,* 139–145.

Reiss, I. L. (1981). Some observations on ideology and sexuality in America. *Journal of Marriage and the Family, 3,* 271–273.

Reiss, I. L., Anderson, R. E., & Sponaugle, G. C. (1980). A multivariate model of the determinants of extramarital sexual permissiveness. *Journal of Marriage and the Family, 42,* 395–411.

Reker, G. T., Peacock, E. J., & Wong, T. P. (1987). Meaning and purpose in life and well-being: A life-span perspective. *Journal of Gerontology, 42,* 44–49.

Renshap, D. C. (1982). *Incest.* Boston: Little, Brown.

Reposa, R. E., & Zuelzer, M. B. (1983). Family therapy with incest. *International Journal of Family Therapy, 5,* 111–126.

Researchers confirm induced abortion to be safer for women than childbirth; refute claims of critics. (1982). *Family Planning Perspectives, 14,* 271–272.

Researchers of smoking report risk of senility and female infertility. (1985, May 24). *Omaha World-Herald.*

Rettig, K. D., & Bubolz, M. M. (1983). Interpersonal resource exchanges as indicators of quality of marriage. *Journal of Marriage and the Family, 45,* 497–509.

Rhodes, S., & Wilson, J. (1981). Hazardous relationship styles. In S. Rhodes & J. Wilson (Eds.), *Surviving family life.* New York: Putnam.

Rhyne, D. (1981). Bases of marital satisfaction among men and women. *Journal of Marriage and the Family, 43,* 941–955.

Rice, D. P., Hing, E., Kovar, M. G., & Prager, K. (1984). Sex differences in disease risk. In E. B. Gold (Ed.), *The changing risk of disease in women: An epidemiologic approach* (pp. 1–24). Lexington, MA: D.C. Heath.

Rice, F. P. (1990). *Intimate relationships, marriages, and families.* Mountain View, CA: Mayfield.

Richwald, G. A., Wamsley, M. S., Coulson, A. H., Morisky, D. E. (1988). Are condom instructions readable? Results of a readability study. *Public Health Reports, 103,* 355–359.

Rindfuss, R. R., & Stephen, E. H. (1990). Martial noncohabitation: Separation does not make the heart grow fonder. *Journal of Marriage and the Family, 52,* 259–270.

Roark, A. C. (1985, December 5). Effects of PCP, cocaine on unborn: A tragic picture. *Los Angeles Times,* Part II, pp. 1–3.

Roberts, L. J., & Krokoff, L. J. (1990). A time-series analysis of withdrawl, hostility, and displeasure in satisfied and dissatisfied marriages. *Journal of Marriage and the Family, 52,* 95–105.

Rogers, C. (1961). *On becoming a person: A therapists' view of psychotherapy.* Boston: Houghton Mifflin.

Rogers, L. K., & Larson, J. H. (1988). Voluntary childlessness: A review of the literature and a model of the childlessness decision. *Family Perspective, 22,* 43–58.

Rollins, B. C., & Cannon, K. L. (1974). Marital satisfaction over the family life cycle: A re-evaluation. *Journal of Marriage and the Family, 36,* 271–282.

Rollins, B. C., & Thomas, D. L. (1979). Parental support, power, aid and control techniques in the socialization of children. In W. R. Burr, R. Hill, F. I. Nye, & I. L. Reiss (Eds.), *Contemporary theories about the family* (Vol. 1). New York: Free Press.

Rosa, E., & Mazur, A. (1979). Incipient status in small groups. *Social Forces, 58,* 18–37.

Rosefsky, R. S. (1989). *Personal finance* (4th ed.). New York: John Wiley.

Rosen, R. H., Herskovitz, L., & Stack, J. M. (1982). Timing of the transition to nonvirginity among unmarried adolescent women. *Population Research and Policy Review, 1,* 153–170.

Rosenbaum, A., & O'Leary, R. D. (1981). Marital violence: Characteristics of abusive couples. *Journal of Consulting and Clinical Psychology, 49,* 63–71.

Rosenthal, C. (1985). Kinkeeping in the familial division of labor. *Journal of Marriage and the Family, 47,* 965–974.

Rowe, G. P., & Meredith, W. H. (1982). Quality in marital relationships after twenty-five years. *Family Perspective, 16,* 149–155.

Rowe, G., Williams, R., Lee, P., & Johnson, S. (1985). The impact of economic stressors on rural and urban family relationships. In R. Williams, H. Lingren, G. Rowe, S. Van Zandt, P. Lee, & N. Stinnett (Eds.), *Family strengths 6: Enhancement of interaction* (pp. 341–354). Lincoln, NE: Department of Human Development and the Family, University of Nebraska.

Rowe, M. (1981, May–June). Dealing with sexual harassment. *Harvard Business Review,* 42–46.

Roy, M. (1977). *Battered women: A psychosociological study of domestic violence.* New York: Van Nostrand Reinhold.

Rubin, Z. (1983, May). Are working wives hazardous to their husbands' mental health? *Psychology Today*, pp. 70–72.

Rubin, Z., Hill, C. T., Peplau, L. A., & Dunkel-Schetter, C. (1980). Self-disclosure in dating couples: Sex roles and the ethic of openness. *Journal of Marriage and the Family, 42*, 305–317.

Rusin, M. J. (1989). Clinical rehabilitation issues. In J. Walters (Ed.), *Women with disabilities: Through the doors of full employment* (pp. 39–59). Athens GA: The University of Georgia, Georgia Center for Continuing Education.

Russell, D. E. H. (1982). *Rape in marriage.* New York: Macmillan.

Sabatelli, R. M., Buck, R., & Dreyer, A. (1982). Nonverbal communication accuracy in married couples: Relationship with marital complaints. *Journal of Personal Social Psychology, 43*, 1088–1097.

Sanders, G. F., & Trygstad, D. W. (1989). Stepgrandparents and grandparents: The view from young adults. *Family Relations, 38*, 71–75.

Sanoff, A. P. (1988). Marriage: It's back in style. In J. G. Wells (Ed.), *Current issues in marriage and the family*, (4th ed.) (pp. 31–38). New York: Macmillan.

Satir, V. (1967). *Conjoint family therapy.* Palo Alto, CA: Science & Behavior Books.

Satir, V. (1972). *Peoplemaking.* Palo Alto, CA: Science & Behavior Books.

Saunders, G. S., & Suls, J. (1982). Social comparison, competition and marriage. *Journal of Marriage and the Family, 44*, 721–730.

Saxton, L. (1990). *The individual, marriage, and the family.* Belmont, CA: Wadsworth.

Scanzoni, J. (1980). *Sex roles, women's work, and marital conflict.* Lexington, MA: D. C. Heath.

Scanzoni, L. D., & Scanzoni, J. (1981). *Men, women, and change* (2nd ed.). New York: McGraw-Hill.

Schaeffer, C. (1989, January). Burglarproofing your home. *Changing Times*, pp. 69–72.

Schiamberg, L. B. (1988). *Child and adolescent development.* New York: Macmillan.

Schlesinger, B. (1984). Lasting and functioning marriages in the 1980's. In G. Rowe, J. DeFrain, H. Lingren, R. MacDonald, N. Stinnett, S. Van Zandt, & R. Williams (Eds.), *Family strengths 5: Continuity and diversity* (pp. 49–63). Newton, MA: Education Development Center.

Schmitt, B. D., & Kempe, C. H. (1983). Abusing neglected children. In R. E. Behrman & V. C. Vaughn (Eds.), *Nelson textbook of pediatrics* (pp. 99–105) (12th ed.). Philadelphia: W. B. Saunders.

Schnittgrund, K. P., & Baker, G. (1983). Financial management of low-income urban families. *Journal of Consumer Studies and Home Economics, 7*, 261–270.

Schumm, W. R., Barnes, H. L., Bollman, S. R., Jurich, A. P., & Bugaighis, M. A. (1986). Self-disclosure and marital satisfaction revisited. *Family Relations, 35*, 241–248.

Schumm, W. R., & Bugaighis, M. A. (1986). Marital quality over the marital career: Alternative explanations. *Journal of Marriage and the Family, 48*, 165–168.

Schwartz, J. (1982). *Letting go of stress.* New York: Pinnacle.

Schwartz, S. (1986). Earnings capacity and the trend in inequality among black men. *Human Resources, 22*, 44–63.

Second marriages are better with childless husbands. (1982, March). *Psychology Today*, p. 18.

Sehnert, K. W. (1981). *Stress/unstress.* Minneapolis, MN: Augsburg.

Seixas, J. S., & Youcha, G. (1985). *Children of alcoholism.* New York: Harper & Row.

Select Committee on Children, Youth, and Families. (1989). *U.S. children and their families: Current conditions and recent trends.* Washington, DC: U.S. Government Printing Office.

Seligmann, J. (1990, Winter/Spring). Variations on a theme. *Newsweek*, Special edition, pp. 38–46.

Serow, W. J. (1981). Population and other policy responses to an era of sustained low fertility. *Social Science Quarterly, 62*, 323–332.

Sexual bureaucracies. (1983, May). *Psychology Today*, p. 6.

Sexual harassment: Some see it . . . some won't. (1981, March–April). *Harvard Business Review*, 77–94.

Sgroi, S. M. (1985). Family treatment. In S. M. Sgroi (Ed.), *Handbook of clinical intervention in child sexual abuse* (pp. 221–268). Lexington, MA: Lexington Books.

Shah, F., & Zelnick, M. (1981). Parent and peer influence on sexual behavior, contraceptive use, and pregnancy experience of young women. *Journal of Marriage and the Family, 43*, 339–348.

Shapiro, R. (1987). *Contraception: A practical and political guide.* London: Virago.

Shapshay, R., & Vines, D. W. (1982). Father-daughter incest: Detection of cases. *Journal of Psychosexual Nursing and Mental Health Services, 20*, 23–26.

Sharda, B. D., & Nangle, B. (1981). Marital effects on occupational attainment. *Journal of Family Issues, 2*(1), 148–163.

Share a laugh? Share a life. (1986, July 22). *News Chronicle*, Thousand Oaks, CA.

Shaw, G. B. (1931). *Man and superman.* New York: Dodd Mead.

Shehan, C. L. (1987). Spouse support and Vietnam veterans' adjustment to post-traumatic stress disorder. *Family Relations, 36*, 55–60.

Sherrard, J. (1980). *Mother/warrior/pilgrim: A personal chronicle.* New York: Andrews & McMeel.

Shostrom, E. L. (1967). *Man, the manipulator.* Nashville, TN: Abingdon.

Shostrom, E. L., Knapp, L., & Knapp, R. (1976). *Actualizing therapy.* San Diego: EDITS.

Sillars, A. (1980). *Conflict resolution strategies.* Unpublished doctoral dissertation, University of Wisconsin, Madison.

Sills, B., & Henry, J. (1980). *The mother to mother baby care book.* New York: Avon.

Simenauer, J., & Carroll, D. (1982). *Singles: The new Americans.* New York: Simon & Schuster.

Smith, D. S. (1985). Wife employment and marital adjustment: A cumulation of results. *Family Relations, 34*, 483–490.

Smith, E. P., & Meyer, J. K. (1978). Attitudes and temperaments of nonorgasmic women. *Medical Aspects of Human Sexuality, 12*, 66–75.

Smith, G. T., Snyder, D. K., Trull, T. J., & Monsma, B. R. (1988). Predicting relationship satisfaction from couples' use of leisure time. *The American Journal of Family Therapy, 16*, 3–13.

Smith, P. K., & Daglish, L. (1977). Sex differences in parent and infant behavior in the home. *Child Development, 48*, 1250–1254.

Smith, R. E. (1988). *Smart House: The coming revolution in housing.* Columbia, MD: G. P. Publishing.

Sollie, D. L., & Fischer, J. L. (1985). Sex role orientation, intimacy of topic and target person differences in self-disclosure among women. *Sex Roles, 12*, 917–929.

Sollie, D. L., & Miller, B. C. (1980). The transition to parenthood as a critical time for building family strengths. In N. Stinnett, B. Chesser, J. DeFrain, & P. Knaub (Eds.), *Family strengths: Positive models for family life* (pp. 149–170). Lincoln, NE: University of Nebraska Press.

Spanier, G. B. (1976). Formal and informal sex education as determinants of premarital sexual behavior. *Archives of Sexual Behavior, 5*, 39–67.

Spanier, G. B. (1977). Sources of sex information and premarital sexual behavior. *Journal of Sex Research, 13*, 73–88.

Spanier, G. B., & Furstenberg, F. F. (1982). Remarriage after divorce: A longitudinal analysis of well-being. *Family Relations, 44*, 709–720.

Spanier, G. B., & Lewis, R. A. (1980). Marital quality: A review of the seventies. *Journal of Marriage and the Family, 42*, 96–110.

Spanier, G. B., Lewis, R. A., & Cole, C. L. (1975). Marital adjustment over the family life cycle: The issue of curvilinearity. *Journal of Marriage and the Family, 37*, 263–275.

Spanier, G. B., & Thompson, L. (1983). Relief and distress after marital separation. *Journal of Divorce, 7*, 31–49.

Spence, J. T., Deaux, K., & Helmreich, R. L. (1985). Sex roles in contemporary American society. In G. Lindzey & E. Aronson (Eds.), *Handbook of social psychology* (3rd ed.). New York: Random House.

Spitz, R. (1945). Hospitalism: Genesis of psychiatric conditions in early childhood. *Psychoanalytic Study of the Child, 1*, 53–74.

Split decisions: Divorce and consequences. (1982, February 8). *Time*, p. 66–67.

Sporakowski, M. J., & Hughston, G. A. (1978). Prescriptions for happy marriages: Adjustments and satisfactions of couples married 50 or more years. *The Family Coordinator, 27,* 321–327.

Sprenkle, D. H., & Cyrus, D. L. (1983). Abandonment: The sudden stress of divorce. In H. I. McCubbin & C. Figley (Eds.), *Stress and the family: Volume II. Coping with catastrophe* (pp. 53–75). New York: Brunner/Mazel.

Stack, C. B. (1974). *All our kin: Strategies for survival in a black community.* New York: Harper & Row.

Stack, C. B. (1980). Domestic networks: Those you can count on. In *Annual Editions: Anthropology 80/81* (pp. 117–123). Guilford, CT: Dushkin.

Staines, G. L., Pottick, K., & Fudge, D. A. (1986). Wives' employment and husbands' attitudes toward work and life. *Journal of Applied Psychology, 71,* 118–128.

Staples, R. (1981). *The world of black singles: Changing patterns of male/female relations.* Westport, CT: Greenwood.

Staples, R. (1985). Changes in black family structure: The conflict between family idealogy and structural conditions. *Journal of Marriage and the Family, 47,* 1005–1013.

Staples, R., & Mirande, A. (1980). Racial and cultural variations among American families: A decennial review of the literature on minority families. *Journal of Marriage and the Family, 42,* 887–903.

Stark, E. (1986, May). Friends through it all. *Psychology Today,* pp. 54–60.

Stark, E., & Flitcraft, A. (1981). *Therapeutic intervention as a situational determinant of the battering syndrome.* Paper presented at the National Conference for Family Violence Researchers, Durham, NH.

The state of working America. (1988, November). *American Family Newsletter,* pp. 10–11.

Stechler, G., & Halton, A. (1982). Prenatal influences on human development. In B. Wolman (Ed.), *Handbook of developmental psychology* (pp. 175–189). Englewood Cliffs, NJ: Prentice-Hall.

Stein, P. J. (Ed.). (1981). *Single life: Unmarried adults in social context.* New York: St. Martin's.

Stein, P. J. (1978). Lifestyles and life changes of the never married. *Marriage and Family Review, 1,* 3–11.

Stein, P. J., & Fingrutd, M. (1985). The single life has more potential for happiness than marriage and parenthood for both men and women. In H. Feldman & M. Feldman (Eds.), *Current controversies in marriage and family* (pp. 81–90). Beverly Hills, CA: Sage.

Steinbeck, J. (1961). *The winter of our discontent.* New York: Viking.

Steinmetz, S. K., & Straus, M. A. (Eds.). (1975). *Violence in the family.* New York: Dodd.

Stephen, T. D., & Harrison, T. M. (1985). Gender, sex-role identity, and communication style: A Q-sort analysis of behavioral differences. *Communication Research Reports, 2,* 53–61.

Stevenson, P., Lee, P., Stinnett, N., & DeFrain, J. (1983). Family commitment and marital need satisfaction. *Family Perspective, 16,* 157–164.

Stiff, J. B., Dillard, J. P., Somera, L., Kim, H., & Sleight, C. (1988). Empathy, communication, and prosocial behavior. *Communication Monographs, 55,* 198–212.

Stinnett, N. (1983). Strong families: A portrait. In D. Mace (Ed.), *Prevention in family services: Approaches to family wellness* (pp. 27–38). Beverly Hills, CA: Sage.

Stinnett, N. (1985). Six qualities that make families strong. In G. Rekers (Ed.), *Family building* (pp. 35–50). Ventura, CA: Regal.

Stinnett, N., Carter, L., & Montgomery, J. (1972). Older persons' perceptions of their marriages. *Journal of Marriage and the Family, 34,* 665–670.

Stinnett, N., & DeFrain, J. (1985). *Secrets of strong families.* Boston: Little, Brown.

Stinnett, N., & DeFrain, J. (1989). The healthy family: Is it possible? In M. Fine (Ed.), *The second handbook on parent education* (2nd ed.) (pp. 53–74). New York: Academic Press.

Stinnett, N., Kimmons, L., DeFrain, J., Lynn, D., & Fuenning, S. (1984). Personal wellness and family strength. *Wellness Perspectives, 1,* 25–31.

Stinnett, N., Knorr, B., DeFrain, J., & Rowe, G. (1981). How strong families cope with crisis. *Family Perspective, 15,* 159–166.

Stinnett, N., & Sauer, K. H. (1977). Relationship characteristics of strong families. *Family Perspective, 11,* 3–11.

Stinnett, N., Smith, R., Tucker, D., & Shell, D. (1985). Executive families: Strengths, stresses, and loneliness. *Wellness Perspectives, 1,* 21–28.

Straus, M. A., Gelles, R., & Steinmetz, S. K. (1980). *Behind closed doors: Violence in the American family.* New York: Doubleday.

Strauss, J. (1986). The study of American Indian families: Implications for applied research. *Family Perspective, 20,* 337–350.

Streib, G. F., Folts, E., & Hilker, M. A. (1984). *Old homes—new families: Shared living for the elderly.* New York: Columbia University Press.

Streissguth, A. P., Barr, H. M., & Martin, D. C. (1983). Maternal alcohol use and neonatal habituation assessed with the Brazelton scale. *Child Development, 54,* 1109–1118.

Stribling, C. R. (1987). *Growing up financially.* New York: Ballantine.

Strober, M. H. (1979). Strategies used by working and nonworking wives to reduce time pressures. *Journal of Consumer Research, 6,* 338–348.

Strong, B., & DeVault, C. (1986). *The marriage and family experience.* New York: West.

Strong, B., & DeVault, C. (1988). *The marriage and family experience* (3rd ed.). St. Paul, MN: West.

Strong, B., Wilson, S., Robbins, M., & Johns, T. (1981). *Human sexuality: Essentials.* St. Paul, MN: West.

Strube, M. J., & Barbour, L. S. (1983). The decision to leave an abusive relationship: Economic dependence and psychological commitment. *Journal of Marriage and the Family, 45,* 785–793.

Study says marriage lengthens cancer patients' survival period. (1987, December 7). *Tuscaloosa News,* p. 21A.

Summit, R., & Kryso, J. (1978). Sexual abuse of children: A clinical spectrum. *American Journal of Orthopsychiatry, 48,* 237–251.

Swensen, C. H., Eskew, R. W., & Kohlhepp., K. A. (1981). Stage of family life cycle, ego development, and the marriage relationship. *Journal of Marriage and the Family, 43,* 841–853.

Swihart, J. J. (1985). Teaching communication skills to families. In G. Rekers (Ed.), *Family building* (pp. 293–309). Ventura, CA: Regal Books.

Tanfer, K. (1987). Patterns of premarital cohabitation among never-married women in the United States. *Journal of Marriage and the Family, 49,* 483–497.

Tavris, C., & Jayarante, T. (1976, June). How happy is your marriage? What 75,000 wives say about their most intimate relationships. *Redbook,* pp. 90–92.

Tavris, C., & Wade, C. (1984). *The longest war: Sex differences in perspective.* San Diego, CA: Harcourt Brace Jovanovich.

Taylor, S. E., & Brown, J. D. (1988). Illusion and well-being: A social psychological perspective on mental health. *Psychological Bulletin, 103,* 193–210.

Tedeschi, J. T., Schlenker, B. R., & Bonoma, T. V. (1973). *Conflict, power and games.* Chicago: Aldine.

Teenage pregnancy: The problem that hasn't gone away. (1981). New York: Planned Parenthood Federation of America, The Alan Guttmacher Institute.

Telch, C. F., & Lindquist, C. V. (1984). Violent versus nonviolent couples: A comparison of patterns. *Psychotherapy, 21,* 242–248.

Tempest, R. (1986, August 17). Gandhi battling tradition to curb population growth. *Los Angeles Times,* Part I, pp. 1, 23, 24.

Thayer, S. (1986). Touch: Frontier of intimacy. *Journal of Nonverbal Behavior, 10,* 7–11.

Thayer, W. (1988, April). Home alarms like those the pros put in. *Business Week,* p. 112.

Thomas, P. L. (1981, April). How to stop fighting over housework. *Redbook.*

Thomas, S. P. (1982). After divorce: Personality factors related to the process of adjustment. *Journal of Divorce, 5,* 19–36.

Thompson, C. L., & Rudolph, L. B. (1983). *Counseling children.* Monterey, CA: Brooks/Cole.

Thorman, G. (1983). *Incestuous families.* Springfield, IL: Charles C. Thomas.

Tiedje, L. B., Wortman, C. B., Downey, G., Emmons, C., Biernat, M., & Lang, E. (1990). Women with multiple roles: Role-compatibility perceptions, satisfaction, and mental health. *Journal of Marriage and the Family, 52,* 63–72.

Toffler, A. (1970). *Future shock.* New York: Random.

Tognoli, J., & Keisner, R. (1972). Gain and loss of esteem as determinants of interpersonal attraction: A replication and extension. *Journal of Personality and Social Psychology, 33*, 201–204.

Troll, L. E., Miller, S. J., & Atchley, R. C. (1979). *Families in later life*. Belmont, CA: Wadsworth.

Trovato, F., & Lauris, G. (1989). Marital status and mortality in Canada 1951–1981. *Journal of Marriage and the Family, 51*, 907–922.

Trussell, J., Hatcher, R. A., Cates, W., Stewart, F. H., & Kost, K. (1990). Contraceptive failure in the United States: A critical review of the literature. *Studies in Family Planning, 21*, 51–54.

Trygstad, D. W., & Sanders, G. F. (1989). The significance of stepgrandparents. *International Journal of Aging and Human Development*, pp. 119–134.

United Nations. (1985). *Demographic yearbook*. New York: United Nations.

Updated estimates of the cost of raising a child. (1988). *Family Economics Review*, 36–37.

U.S. Bureau of the Census. (1981). *Population Reports*, Series P-25, no. 1017. Projections of the population of states by age, sex, and race: 1988–2010. Washington DC: U.S. Government Printing Office.

U.S. Bureau of the Census (1985a). Marital status and living arrangements, *Current Population Reports*, Series P-20, no. 410. Washington DC: U.S. Government Printing Office.

U.S. Bureau of the Census. (1985b). Money income of families—Aggregate mean, and per capita income by family characteristics. *Statistical abstract of the United States: 1985* (105th ed.). Washington, DC: U.S. Government Printing Office.

U.S. Bureau of the Census. (1985c). Money income of families—Median family income in current and constant (1983) dollars, by race and Spanish origin of householder: 1950 to 1983. *Statistical abstract of the United States: 1985* (105th ed.). Washington DC: U.S. Government Printing Office.

U.S. Bureau of the Census. (1986a). Money income of households, families and persons of the United States. *Current Population Reports*, Series P-6, no. 159. Washington, DC: U.S. Government Printing Office.

U.S. Bureau of the Census. (1986b). *Statistical abstract of the United States, 1987* (107th ed.). Washington DC: U.S. Government Printing Office.

U.S. Bureau of the Census. (1987a). Money income and poverty status of families and persons in the United States. *Current Population Reports*, Series P-60, no. 157. Washington DC: Government Printing Office.

U.S. Bureau of the Census. (1987b). *Statistical abstract of the United States: 1988* (108th ed.). Washington, DC: U.S. Government Printing Office.

U.S. Bureau of the Census. (1988). Household and family characteristics. *Current Population Reports*, Series P-20, no. 437. Washington DC: U.S. Government Printing Office.

U.S. Bureau of the Census. (1989a). Household and family characteristics: March 1988. *Current Population Reports*, Series P-20, no. 437. Washington DC: U.S. Government Printing Office.

U.S. Bureau of the Census. (1989b). *Statistical abstract of the United States, 1990* (110th ed.). Washington, DC: U.S. Government Printing Office.

U.S. Department of Commerce. (1985). Marital status and living arrangements: March 1984. *Current Population Reports*, Series P-20, no. 399. Washington, DC: U.S. Government Printing Office.

U.S. Department of Health and Human Services. (1985). *Condition of education, 1985 edition*. Washington, DC: U.S. Government Printing Office.

U.S. Department of Labor, Women's Bureau. (1982). *Employers and child care: Establishing services through the workplace*. Pamphlet no. 23. Washington, DC: U.S. Government Printing Office.

Uzzell, O. (1985). Family planning: The artificial control of gender. *Family Perspective, 19*, 279–283.

Valentine, D. P. (1982). The experience of pregnancy: A developmental process. *Family Relations, 31*, 243–248.

Vander Mey, B. J., & Neff, R. L. (1982). Adult-child incest: Review of research. *Adolescence, 17*, 717–735.

Vega, W. A., Patterson, T., Sallis, J., Nader, P., Atkins, C., & Abramson, I. (1986). Cohesion and adaptability in Mexican American and Anglo families. *Journal of Marriage and the Family, 48*, 857–867.

Veninga, R. L., & Spradley, J. P. (1981). *The work stress connection: How to cope with job burnout*. New York: Ballantine.

Verbrugge, L. (1979). Marital status and health. *Journal of Marriage and the Family, 41*, 267–285.

Verbrugge, L. M. (1985). An epidemiological profile of older women. In M. R. Haug, A. B. Ford, & M Sheafor (Eds.), *The physical and mental health of aged women* (pp. 41–64). New York: Springer.

Verny, T., & Kelly, J. (1982). The secret life of the unborn child. *Families*, 54–58.

Voydanoff, P., Donnelly, B. W., & Fine. M. A. (1988). Economic distress, social integration, and family satisfaction. *Journal of Family Issues, 9*, 545–564.

Vuchinich, S. (1987). Starting and stopping spontaneous family conflicts. *Journal of Marriage and the Family, 49*, 591–601.

Wahlroos, S. (1983). *Family communication*. New York: New American Library.

Waite, L. J., Haggstrom, G. W., & Kanouse, D. E. (1985). The consequences of parenthood for the marital stability of young adults. *American Sociological Review, 50*, 850–857.

Wallace, C. P. (1986, November 4). Arabs path to altar no walk in park. *Los Angeles Times*, pp. 1, 20.

Wallerstein, J. S., & Blakeslee, S. (1989). *Second chances*. New York: Ticknor & Fields.

Wallerstein, J. S., & Kelly, J. B. (1980). *Surviving the breakup*. New York: Basic.

Wallinga, C. R., & Sweaney, A. L. (1985). A sense of real accomplishment: Young children as productive family members. *Young Children, 40*(10), 3–8.

Wallinga, C. R., Sweaney, A. L., & Walters, J. (1987). The development of responsibility in young children: A 25-year view. *Early Childhood Research Quarterly, 2*, 119–131.

Walters, J. (1980). Widowhood: The clapping of one hand. In J. E. Montgomery (Ed.), *Handbook on aging* (pp. 59–67). Washington, DC: American Home Economics Association.

Walters, J. (1987). The wall of silence: Sexuality and the aged. *Advice for Adults with Aging Parents or a Dependent Spouse, 2*, 5–7.

Walters, J., & Walters, L. H. (1982, May). *The future of families*. Marshall University Distinguished Lecture Series, Huntington, WV.

Wampler, K. S., & Kingery, D. W. (1985, November). *Emphasizing the wife's career: Predictors and consequences*. Paper presented at the Theory Construction and Research Methodology Workshop, National Council on Family Relations, Dallas, TX.

Warner, C. T., & Olson, T. D. (1981). Another view of family conflict and family wholeness. *Family Relations, 30*, 493–503.

Warner, E. E. (1984). Resilient children. *Young Children, 40*(1), 68–72.

The Washington COFO memo. (1985, December 15). Malvern, PA: Coalition of Family Organzations.

Watkins, H. D., & Bradbard, M. R. (1982). Child maltreatment: An overview with suggestions for intervention and research. *Family Relations, 31*, 323–333.

Watson, M. A. (1981). Sexually open marriage: Three perspectives. *Alternative Lifestyles, 4*, 3–21.

We open up our marriage: An interview with David and Vera Mace. (1984). *Wellness Perspectives, 1*, 21–29.

Weingarten, H., & Leas, S. (1987). Levels of marital conflict model: A guide to assessment and intervention in troubled marriages. *American Journal of Orthopsychiatry, 57*, 407–417.

Weinstein, G. W. (1986). *Men, women, and money*. New York: New American Library.

Weiss, E. (1984). *The anger trap*. New York: Philosophical Library.

Weitzman, L. (1985). *The divorce revolution*. New York: Free Press.

West, D. J. (1981). Adult sexual interest in children: Implications for social control. In M. Cook & K. Howells (Eds.), *Adult sexual interest in children*. New York: Academic Press.

Wheeless, V. E., Zakahi, W. R., & Chan, M. B. (1988). A test of self-disclosure based on perceptions of a target's loneliness and gender orientation. *Communication Quarterly, 36*, 109–121.

Whipple, C. M., & Whittle, D. (1976). *The compatibility test*. Englewood Cliffs, NJ: Prentice-Hall.

Whitaker, C. (1980, September 5). *Characteristics of a self-actualizing family: A family that grows.* Workshop presentation, Minneapolis, MN.

White, K. L., & Bulloch, P. (1980). *Health of populations.* New York: Rockefeller.

White, L. K., & Booth, A. (1985). The transition to parenthood and marital quality. *Journal of Family Issues, 6*, 435–450.

White, P., Mascalo, A., Thomas, S., & Shoun, S. (1986). Husbands' and wives' perceptions of marital intimacy and wives' stresses in dual-career marriages. *Family Perspective, 20*, 27–35.

Whiteside, M. F. (1989). Family rituals as a key to kinship connections in remarried families. *Family Relations, 38*, 34–39.

Wilkie, J. R. (1981). The trend toward delayed parenthood. *Journal of Marriage and the Family, 43*, 583–591.

Williams, E. F. (1976). *Notes of a feminist therapist.* New York: Praeger.

Williams, F., & Berry, R. (1984). Intensity of family disagreement over finances and associated factors. *Journal of Consumer Studies and Home Economics, 8*, 33–53.

Williams, G. G. (1988). Gender, marriage, and psychological well-being. *Journal of Social Issues, 9*, 452–468.

Wilson, M. R., & Filsinger, E. E. (1986). Religiosity and marital adjustment: Multidimensional interrelationships. *Journal of Marriage and the Family, 48*, 147–151.

Winger, G. J., & Frasca, R. R. (1986). *Personal finance.* Columbus, OH: Charles E. Merrill.

Wiseman, J. P. (1981). The family and its researchers in the eighties: Retrenching, renewing and revitalizing. *Journal of Marriage and the Family, 43*, 263–266.

Wishon, P. M., & Eller, B. F. (1984). Understanding and helping sexually abused children. *Dimensions, 13*(1), 10–13, 30.

Wolfe, M. G., & Goldsmith, M. (1980). *Practical pregnancy: All that's different in life because you're pregnant.* New York: Warner.

Woman's Day. (1983, March). p. 8.

Wootan, G. (1985, January/February). An update on breast-feeding. *Mother Earth News, 91*, 84–85.

The world almanac and book of facts. (1987). New York: Pharos.

The world almanac and book of facts. (1990). New York: World Almanac.

Wynne, L., & Wynne, A. (1986). The quest for intimacy. *Journal of Marital and Family Therapy, 12*(4), 383–394.

Yankelovich, D. (1981). *New rules: Searching for fulfillment in a world turned upside down.* New York: Random.

Yllo, K., & Straus, M. A. (1981). Interpersonal violence among married and cohabiting couples. *Family Relations, 30*, 339–347.

Zill, N. (in press). *Happy, healthy, and insecure: A portrait of middle childhood in the United States.* New York: Cambridge University Press.

Zimmer, D. (1988). Does marital therapy enhance the effectiveness of treatment for sexual dysfunction? *Journal of Sex and Marital Therapy, 13*, 193–209.

Zollar, A. C., & Williams, J. S. (1987). The contribution of marriage to the life satisfaction of black adults. *Journal of Marriage and the Family, 49*, 87–92.

Zube, M. (1982). Changing behavior and outlook of aging men and women: Implications for marriage in the middle and later years. *Family Relations, 31*, 147–156.

NAME INDEX

SUBJECT INDEX